Russian Legal Theory

The International Library of Essays in Law and Legal Theory
Series Editor: Tom D. Campbell

Schools

Natural Law, Vols I & II *John Finnis*
Justice *Thomas Morawetz*
Law and Economics, Vols I & II *Jules Coleman and Jeffrey Lange*
Critical Legal Studies *James Boyle*
Marxian Legal Theory *Csaba Varga*
Legal Reasoning, Vols I & II *Aulis Aarnio and D. Neil MacCormick*
Legal Positivism *Mario Jori*
American Legal Theory *Robert Samuel Summers*
Postmodernism and Law *Dennis Patterson*
Law in History, Vols I & II *David Sugarman*
Law and Language *Fred Schauer*
Sociological Theories of Law *Kahei Rokumoto*
Rights *Carlos Nino*
Law and Psychology *Martin Lyon Levine*
Feminist Legal Theory, Vols I & II *Frances Olsen*
Law and Society *Roger Cotterrell*
Contemporary Criminological Theory *Francis T. Cullen and Velmer S. Burton Jr.*

Areas

Criminal Law *Thomas Morawetz*
Tort Law *Ernest J. Weinrib*
Contract Law, Vols I & II *Larry Alexander*
Anti-Discrimination Law *Christopher McCrudden*
Consumer Law *Iain Ramsay*
International Law *Martti Koskenniemi*
Property Law, Vols I & II *Elizabeth Mensch and Alan Freeman*
Constitutional Law *Mark V. Tushnet*
Procedure *D.J. Galligan*
Evidence and Proof *William Twining and Alex Stein*
Company Law *Sally Wheeler*
Privacy, Vols I & II *Raymond Wacks*
Lawyers' Ethics *David J. Luban*
Administrative Law *D.J. Galligan*
Child Law *Harry D. Krause*
Family Law, Vols I & II *Harry D. Krause*
Welfare Law *Peter Robson*
Medicine and the Law *Bernard M. Dickens*
Commercial Law *Ross Cranston*
Environmental Law *Michael C. Blumm*
Conflict of Laws *Richard Fentiman*
Law and Religion *Wojciech Sadurski*
Human Rights Law *Philip Alston*
European Community Law, Vols I & II *Francis Snyder*
Tax Law, Vols I & II *Patricia D. White*
Media Law *Eric Barendt*
Labour Law *David L. Gregory*
Alternative Dispute Resolution *Michael D.A. Freeman*

Legal Cultures

Comparative Legal Cultures *Csaba Varga*
Law and Anthropology *Peter Sack*
Hindu Law and Legal Theory *Ved Nanda*
Islamic Law and Legal Theory *Ian Edge*
Chinese Law and Legal Theory *Michael Palmer*
Russian Legal Theory *W. Butler*
Common Law *Michael Arnheim*
Japanese Law and Legal Theory *Koichiro Fujikura*
Law and Development *Anthony Carty*
Jewish Law and Legal Theory *Martin P. Golding*
Legal Education *Martin Lyon Levine*
Civil Law *Ralf Rogowski*
African Law and Legal Theory *Gordon Woodman and Akintunde Obilade*

Future Volume
Cumulative index

Russian Legal Theory

Edited by

W.E. Butler

University College London

NEW YORK UNIVERSITY PRESS
REFERENCE COLLECTION

Manufactured in Great Britain

First published in the U.S.A. in 1996 by
NEW YORK UNIVERSITY PRESS
Washington Square
New York NY 10003

Library of Congress Cataloging-in-Publication Data
Russian legal theory / edited by W.E. Butler.
p. cm. — (International library of essays in law and legal theory. Legal cultures ; 11)
Includes bibliographical references.
ISBN 0-8147-1183-9
1. Law—Russia (Federation)—Philosophy. 2. Jurisprudence—Russia (Federation). 3. Law—Philosophy. I. Butler, William Elliott, 1939– . II. Series.
KLB440.R87 1996
349.47'01—dc20
[344.7001] 95-22870
CIP

Contents

PART IV RUSSIA AND WORLD PUBLIC ORDER

Acknowledgements

The editor and publishers wish to thank the following for permission to use copyright material.

E.J. Brill, Leiden, for the essay: Paul Vinogradoff (1923), 'Historical Types of International Law', in *Bibliotheca Visserana*, pp. 3–70.

Columbia Law Review for the essay: Paul Vinogradoff (1924), 'Aims and Methods of Jurisprudence', *Columbia Law Review*, **XXIV**, pp. 1–7. This article originally appeared at 24 *Columbia Law Review* 1 (1924). Reprinted by permission.

Edinburgh University Press for the essay: Vladlen S. Vereshchetin and Rein A. Müllerson (1990), 'The Primacy of International Law in World Politics', in A. Carty and G. Danilenko (eds), *Perestroika and International Law*, pp. 6–14.

Harvard University Press for the essay: G.I. Tunkin (1974), 'The International Legal Ideas of the October Revolution and the Making of Contemporary International Law' and 'International Law in Relations Between the Countries of the World System of Socialism', in *Theory of International Law*, translated by William E. Butler, pp. 3–20, 427–47. Reprinted by permission of the publishers. Copyright © 1974 by William E. Butler.

Kluwer Academic Publishers for the essay: G.I. Tunkin (1990), 'On the Primacy of International Law in Politics', in W.E. Butler (ed.), *Perestroika and International Law*, pp. 5–12.

Simon & Schuster, Inc. for the essay: Andrei Y. Vyshinsky (1948), 'The Foundations of the Marxist-Leninist Theory of State and Law' and 'Soviet Socialist Public Law – Its Object and Its Methods', in Andrei Y. Vyshinsky (ed.), *The Law of the Soviet State*, translated from the Russian by Hugh W. Babb, pp. 5–38, 74–86. Copyright © 1948 by the American Council of Learned Societies.

I.B. Tauris & Company Ltd for the essays: W.E. Butler (1991), 'Perestroika and the Rule of Law', in W.E. Butler (ed.), *Perestroika and the Rule of Law: Anglo-American and Soviet Perspectives*, pp. 7–21; R.Z. Livshits (1991), 'Jus and Lex: Evolution of Views', in W.E. Butler (ed.), *Perestroika and the Rule of Law: Anglo-American and Soviet Perspectives*, pp. 22–36.

Every effort has been made to trace all the copyright holders but if any have been inadvertently overlooked the publishers will be pleased to make the necessary arrangement at the first opportunity.

Series Preface

The International Library of Law and Legal Theory is designed to provide important research materials in an accessible form. Each volume contains essays of central theoretical importance in its subject area. The series as a whole makes available an extensive range of valuable material which will be of considerable interest to those involved in the research, teaching and study of law.

The series has been divided into three sections. The Schools section is intended to represent the main distinctive approaches and topics of special concern to groups of scholars. The Areas section takes in the main branches of law with an emphasis on essays which present analytical and theoretical insights of broad application. The section on Legal Cultures makes available the distinctive legal theories of different legal traditions and takes up topics of general comparative and developmental concern.

I have been delighted and impressed by the way in which the editors of the individual volumes have set about the difficult task of selecting, ordering and presenting essays from the immense quantity of academic legal writing published in journals throughout the world. Editors were asked to pick out those essays from law, philosophy and social science journals which they consider to be fundamental for the understanding of law, as seen from the perspective of a particular approach or sphere of legal interest. This is not an easy task and many difficult decisions have had to be made in order to ensure that a representative sample of the best journal essays available takes account of the scope of each topic or school.

I should like to express my thanks to all the volume editors for their willing participation and scholarly judgement. The interest and enthusiasm which the project has generated is well illustrated by the fact that an original projection of 12 volumes drawn up in 1989 has now become a list of some 60 volumes. I must also acknowledge the vision, persistence and constant cheerfulness of John Irwin and the marvellous work done by Mrs Margaret O'Reilly and Sonia Hubbard.

TOM D. CAMPBELL
Series Editor
The Faculty of Law
The Australian National University

Towards an Introduction to Russian Legal Theory

This volume contains the single most extensive and representative selection of original works spanning ten centuries of Russian legal theory that has yet to be published in the English language. Yet it is thoroughly unrepresentative of Russian legal theory, most especially prior to the late 19th century – a reflection not on this volume but rather on the unexplored depths of Russian political and legal doctrines of the mediaeval era. This Introduction aims to broaden the contextual background of Russian legal theory and of the works published therein.

In the Russian perception, legal theory is not an arid subject to be divorced from the 'practical' aspects of legal study. One modern legal theorist has called his field 'the methodological laboratory of political theory ... with a view to forecasting the ways and means of the further development and perfection of contemporary historical knowledge on State and Law'.[1] The linkage between State and Law, and between politics and Law, is crucial in Russian thinking. The 'legal succession of ideological structures as a whole and of political-legal knowledge in particular, is not merely an immutable condition for their further development, but also for perfecting the process of State-legal construction'.[2] In other words, in terms of the development of law and legal institutions, the past is part of a direct continuum to policy decisions of the present.

To say, as we have above, that the depths of Russian legal doctrine remain unplumbed is itself part of the legacy of the recent and remote past. Russian legal theory was in its infancy before the revolutions of 1917, and the history of Russian legal theory even more so. Russian theorists looked principally to their contemporary European colleagues for inspiration as well as to the classics of European political and legal thought in Russian translation. The highly regarded five-volume work by B.N. Chicherin on political doctrines made no mention of Russian legal theory.[3] The Soviet Union had little use for political and legal doctrines of the Russian past, particularly those rooted in theological postulates, and consequently offered the most superficial of surveys in compulsory subjects in law school. The considerable attention given to so-called 'revolutionary-democratic' Russian thinkers, while deserved, was unbalanced by other ideological constraints which prejudiced objectivity. A separate subject, ignored in both East and West, is the contribution of the Russian emigré community to legal and political theory in the 20th century. Russian international legal theory likewise was indebted to Western thinking and only recently has found its proper voice.[4]

Legal Doctrines of the XIth to XIVth Centuries

Russian legal and political thought is presumed to have originated with the Ancient Russian state in the 10th century, although no original contemporaneous sources have survived. The development of Kievan Rus civilization by the 11th century, most notably during the reign of Iaroslav Mudryi (the Wise) (1019–54), enables certain inferences to be drawn. It is to Iaroslav's wisdom and energy that the compilation of the code of laws known as the 'Russkaia Pravda' is attributed, whether it be an original codification or a consolidation of positive enactments and customary law. He too is credited with the introduction of canon law documents which incorporated rules of Russian law together with Byzantine tenets.

The emergence of the formal trappings of the Grand Princedom of Kievan Rus was accompanied by a manuscript culture which included translations into Church Slavonic of texts by Aristotle, Plato, Plutarch, Homer, Zenon, Epicurus, Herodotus, Demosthenes and others, together with legal texts from Byzantium and southern Slavdom. These contributed in turn to the tradition of Russian chronicles that treated, inter alia, issues of law and politics and accounts of voyages by Russian travellers who described laws of the lands they visited. In the course of time these sources addressed the origin of Kievan Rus and the ruling dynasty, the unity and sovereignty of the Grand Prince and his officialdom, possible forms of limitation on the absolute power of the Grand Prince (consultative councils and advisers), legality and the settlement of disputes. A legal terminology came into being, and concepts such as law (jus [pravo] and lex [zakon]), truth and justice were discussed.

Ilarion. Assuming that the texts of the documents and chronicles which have survived from the Kievan era or which are attributed to that era are contemporary and genuine – assumptions which are not beyond dispute – the early works of Russian legal theory are several. Perhaps the earliest is the *Slovo o Zakone i Blagodati* [Sermon on Law and Grace], believed to have been written in the mid-11th century by Ilarion before he was elevated to the office of Metropolitan of Kievan Rus in 1051. Composed principally for theological instructional purposes and comprising a unique source of Ancient Russian vocabulary, grammar and literary style, the *Slovo* is treated by Russian historians as the 'earliest surviving political treatise of Ancient Rus'.[5]

The *Slovo* addressed three main issues: the relationship between Law and Grace, the significance of baptism for Kievan Rus, and the future development of the Kievan Rus state. Ilarion did not distinguish sharply between human and divine laws, nor offer any form of classification of legislation. Law amounted to the performance of an obligatory prescription, whether of divine origin or issued by the sovereign, and was contrasted with Truth, achieved as the result of the realization of man's free will and informed by the moral and aesthetic teachings of the New Testament. Modern Russian political theorists suggest[6] that the divine origins of Law do not preclude Law also being understood teleologically and juridically as external prescriptions regulating behaviour of the individual in society by way of prohibitions.

In Ilarion's perception, Law and Truth were not juxtaposed to one another. Truth was comprehended by man thanks to Law and not despite Law; Jesus Christ was sent to this world not to violate Law, but to perform or execute Law. This in turn led to a terminological issue which continues to bedevil contemporary discussions of legal theory (see Chapters 9 to 11 in this volume). The issue turned on his use of the Russian terms 'pravda [justice]' and 'zakon [lex]'. The term 'pravda' is associated above all with positive law codifications or systematizations – the Sudebnik, the Russkaia Pravda, the Pravda Iaroslavova, the Sborniki ulozhenii, and others – with the power to judge, to chastise, to pardon. But the word also was used in a broader legal and philosophical sense to embrace 'truth', 'virtue', 'justness' and the like, in which case these elements inform the content of Law. In a still larger sense, Ilarion uses 'pravda' to describe both the content and the moral motivation of Law as a 'legal formula' which 'means consideration of a case according to Law irrespective of the final result'.[7] This approach is believed to have influenced the Teachings of Vladimir Monomakh and later compositions of legislative material.

In declaring all Christian peoples to be equal, Ilarion disputed Byzantium's claim to hegemony. As for the nature of political society itself, Ilarion treated the essence of the State as divine since it represented a realization of Divine Will. The bearer of supreme power is in communion with and a descendant of the heavenly Kingdom. The origin of power is by way of inherited succession, and Ilarion sought to establish the legitimacy of rules contemporary to him by tracing their lineage back to the 'ancient Igor'. While supporting the concept of rule, whereby the Grand Prince was the sole and sovereign power within the lands subject to his rule, the Prince was not to be arbitrary; he was to rule on the basis of Law (which presumably meant Law in both its positive and moral senses), mercy, generosity towards his subjects, and concern for orphans, the ill, widows, the church and monasteries.

Justice, he wrote, must be administered according to Law and with mercy, thus setting out moral criteria with which a Christian ruler should comply when dispensing punishment. These ideas were accepted almost entirely by Vladimir Monomakh in his Teachings and later developed by Daniil Zatochnik (see below). Ilarion also posited the notion that a ruler was accountable to his subjects before God, an issue much discussed by later Russian writers.

Povest' vremennykh let. The tradition of Russian chronicles is customarily associated with the establishment of the metropolitan see in Kievan Rus. Of numerous manuscripts, the *Povest' vremennykh let* [Tales of Times Past] is attributed to Nestor, a monk who apparently spent the last years of his life in the Kievo-Pechersk Monastery composing his work on the origins of Kievan Rus, the origins and succession of the Kievan dynasty, the role and place of Kievan Rus in the international community, and the unity and sovereignty of State power. Although the so-called 'Norman' origins of Kievan Rus set out by Nestor are no longer accepted by the majority of Russian historians, the issues raised in the *Povest'* dominated Russian politico-legal history for centuries.

Works of Vladimir Monomakh. In or about 1113 the grandson of Iaroslav Mudryi, Vladimir Monomakh, came to the throne in Kievan Rus. To him are attributed three works: *Pouchenie detiam* [Teachings for Children], *Poslanie Olegu Chernigovskomu* [Message to Oleg Chernigovskii], and an autobiographical sketch known as *Otryvok* [Fragment]. These works touch upon the powers of the Grand Prince, relations between Church and State, and principles for administering justice. The *Pouchenie* gives considerable attention to organizing and exercising supreme power. He advises future princes to rule with the advice of a Council and not to permit unlawfulness or injustice in the land. To be just means to adjudicate according to Law. Monomakh proposed that the ruler should exercise judicial functions himself, not permitting a violation of the laws and dispensing mercy to his most defenceless subjects. Blood feud and capital punishment were rejected, including in inter-princely relations.

Monomakh elaborated Ilarion's notion of the ruler's accountability to his subjects. Military forces should not cause harm to peasant villagers and, wherever possible, internecine conflict should be avoided. The ruler and his princes should seek means to achieve accord and disputes should be settled peacefully. As for Church and State, Monomakh accorded the former an honourable but subordinate place.

Slovo o polku Igoreve. In the late 12th century the *Slovo o polku Igoreve* [Tale of the Field of Igorev] was composed by a secular writer possibly from Chernigov, perhaps even Prince Sviatoslav Chernigovskii or, if not, a senior official in the court of Ol'govicha. The occasion for the work was the death of Prince Igor in a legendary battle in 1185. The author chronicled the misfortunes and costs of military campaigns against neighbours and the ideal attributes of rulers. The historical ideal was Vladimir Monomakh. Power achieved by legal means, not by military conquest, was considered to be lawful, and emphasis was placed on the ruler's duty to be concerned for his subjects.

Daniil Zatochnik. Manuscripts attributed to Daniil Zatochnik of the late 12th or early 13th century (by which time Kievan Rus had broken up into countless warring princedoms and was on the eve of being subjugated by the Mongols and Tatars from the East) counselled centralization of power in the interests of defending Rus against invaders. Whether the manuscripts were by one author or two, the *Slovo* [Tale] or *Molenie* [Supplication] (titles vary from one manuscript to another) posits an idealized Grand Prince who is physically attractive and merciful and rules with strength, tempered by wisdom and justness. His State is a strong one, well-organized and orderly. His task in ruling is to select good and wise advisers, though not necessarily only the old and experienced, whose assistance and counsel he accepts. This account suggests that Daniil Zatochnik regarded Vladimir Monomakh as having represented the ideal form of power.

The Grand Prince must also have good military forces capable of defending his lands against outside enemies. But peace is to be generally desired, as is the peaceful settlement of disputes. Daniil advises the Grand Prince to recruit foreigners to his service for the benefit of the country. Strong warnings are given against internal threats to the Grand Prince in the form of the arrogation of power by boyars – a commentary on the fractionalization of Rus into warring princedoms under way at the time. These were themes continued and enlarged upon in the manuscript culture that emerged after the celebrated Battle of Kulikovo in 1380, when the Moscovy Grand Prince Dmitrii Ivanovich defeated the Mongol forces amassed against him.

Legal and Political Theory: 1500–1613

In the period 1500 to 1613, the forces of decentralization in Muscovy had been overtaken by those of centralization. The Mongol hordes, gradually defeated in Russia and called back by internal dissension at home, receded and the Grand Princes Ivan III (1462–1505) and Vasilii III (1505–33) succeeded in uniting the appanage princes and their lands under the rule of the Grand Prince of Muscovy. With the fall of Constantinople in 1453 and the marriage of Ivan III to Sophia-Zoe Paleologue, Princess of Byzantium, Moscovy laid claim to the two-headed eagle of the Eastern Roman Empire and to succession as the Defender of Orthodoxy, the Third Rome.

The principal themes of earlier works continued to be debated: the formation of a single sovereign political community, the type of monarchy which should emerge, the origins of the Russian State and the lineage of its princes, the organization of State administration, the relations of Church and State, and the administration of justice. The position of the Church itself – now a centre of wealth, land and power – began to be debated.

The Russian clergy came to be conditionally divided into those who favoured a reorganization of the Church under which it would renounce all its wealth and lands and refrain from any interference in the affairs of State, and those who preferred preserving the existing forms of church organization and its economic status.

Nil Sorskii (1433–1508). Idealizing the early Christian communities, Nil Sorskii organized his own Nilo-Sorskii Hermitage in the Vologda region. There he and his followers drew attention to those passages in the Gospels where Christ and his disciples renounced all worldly goods and counselled his fellow monks to follow that example. In relations between Church and State, Nil Sorskii departed from the Byzantine tradition, which encompassed a complex combination of the two, and suggested that each had its own domain of activity and therefore its own measures of dealing with problems confronting it.

These rather general propositions were elaborated by his friend and follower Vassian Patrikeev, who directly raised the question of depriving monasteries of their wealth and even of eliminating them in their current form. He favoured a sharp legislative delineation between the spheres of operation of State and Church and the principle of non-interference in one another's affairs.

Maksim Grek (d. 1556). The ideals of Nil Sorskii were most fully elaborated by a theologian of Serbo-Croatian origin who came to Russia in 1518 by invitation of Grand Prince Vasilii III to translate theological works from the Greek language into Russian. Maksim Grek had spent many years in Italy, where he had witnessed the movement and heard the teachings of Savonarola, then returned to a monastery on Mount Athos before accepting the invitation of the Grand Prince. His Russian years were not happy ones. He aroused opposition in senior circles of the Russian Orthodox Church; twice condemned by assemblies of the Church, he spent nearly 25 years in exile where he continued to write.

Drawing upon his years of learning at the University of Paris, he advocated broadly-based education in all disciplines and not merely the theological sciences. He developed Nil Sorskii's teaching on free will, laying the groundwork for natural law conceptions that were to follow. His political and legal views have been extensively investigated by Russian historians of political thought.[8]

Maksim Grek argued that a legitimate ruler could come to the throne either by way of succession-descent or by way of election by a representative assembly, citing the example of Alexander of Macedonia. The principal task of the ruler or the State was to ensure the peaceful and quiet life of his/its subjects and a stable internal order. The preferred form of power was one in which the ruler relied upon wise and conscientious advisers, councils and councillors, which in Russian conditions meant not merely the boyars but also other representatives of the nobility – an interpretation of Maksim Grek which remains controversial.[9]

The limitation of the ruler's power was to be achieved not only by advisers, but also by Law and accepted moral criteria. He interlinked jus, lex and legality in his concept of justice.

Injustice he equated with a violation of law, a crime against Law. Although his understanding of 'justice' is broad, it takes on juridical forms in a number of instances, most notably court proceedings in which punishment must be meted out on the basis of Law, without hypocrisy and with mercy. Maksim Grek is regarded as the first figure in Russian politico-legal literature to develop a detailed doctrine for limiting the actions of a ruler by positive Law, following Divine teachings and laws.

The quality of justice in Muscovy was remarked upon by virtually all writers of the period. Maksim Grek subjected the judicial system to scathing criticism, condemning the bribery of judges who 'steal estates and property from widows and orphans'. Such practices, he wrote, not only bring harm to subjects of the princedom, but also undermine the authority of the Tsar and the prestige of the State itself. He opposed the mediaeval practice of casting lots as inherently unjust, preferring in its stead witness testimony and oath.

Maskim Grek linked the application of the Law with the extending of mercy. The unlimited power of the ruler would be curtailed through Law by creating a just court system and eliminating extrajudicial and arbitrary decisions on the part of the ruler himself and his officials. He held that the Tsar had no right to appropriate what was privately owned by another nor to take the possessions of his servitors. One limit on his power was the right of private ownership protected by Law.

The duties of a ruler to his subjects were elaborated in a late work written about 1545: 'Message to Tsar Ivan Vasil'evich'. There he enumerated the duties of the Tsar: he must rule with justice and reason, respect his officials, reward the military, listen to the advice of his wise counsellors and the clergy, protect orphans and the indigent and, overall, order the life of his subjects on the basis of good laws.

Iosif Volotskii (1439–1515). The philosophical and jurisprudential protagonists of Nil Sorskii and Maksim Grek were those who identified with Iosif Volotskii. Volotskii's principal works were *Poslaniia k razlichnym litsam* [Messages to Various Persons] and a number of sermons directed against heretics, later collected under the title *Prosvetitel'* [The Enlightener]. His political orientation in Muscovy changed several times; initially an opponent of the Grand Prince because of a commitment to secularization, he came to successfully defend the monastery system for its good deeds – the building of monasteries and churches, provision for monks, assistance for the needy and the like.

He differed from Nil Sorskii and Maksim Grek in his doctrine of power, distinguishing between the concept of power as being Divine in origin from the actual fact of an individual person realizing power by acting as Head of State. While the ruler attempts to achieve Divine purposes, in so doing he relies upon ordinary mortals who inevitably err and cause harm to the realm. Consequently, the ruler and his princes are not guilty before God for all the misfortune and misadventure that occur. For the first time in Russian politico-legal literature this distinction made possible a discussion and critique of the merits and actions of the actual ruler, condemning those who proved to be bad rulers and against whom one might legitimately resist.

Iosif Volotskii also postulated the supremacy of spiritual over secular power. He adhered to the long-established Byzantine concept of a 'symphony' of powers – an alliance of power under which the secular authority was obliged to assist the church, to persecute enemies of the church and heretics, and not to appropriate church property; the church in turn was required to support the authority and lawfulness of the secular ruler, provided however that it retained its dominant role. Much attention was accorded by Iosif Volotskii to the issue of heresy. He undertook to prove that heresy was a crime both against religion and the church, and also against the State. As a political offence it should be persecuted (including investigation and punishment) by the State – a position which led Iosif Volotskii to come close to according primacy of place to the State. By drawing parallels between ordinary criminal behaviour and heresy, he was able to justify the trial and punishment, even the death penalty, of heretics in ordinary State courts.

The 'symphony' of powers concept led Iosif Volotskii to postulate a classification of laws which undertook to combine all the rules and norms by which man should be guided within a single system. Accordingly, he did not distinguish sharply between Divine Law and positive, manmade Law. Divine will, in his view, was both a source of power for the ruler and a source of all legislation, especially as formulated in assemblies and councils of the Russian Orthodox church. Free will had no place in his approach, and he drew no sharp distinction between Law and Morality.

After 1504 Iosif Volotskii and his followers became dominant in Muscovy and their ideas played an influential role in Russian legal and political thought throughout the 16th century.

Feodosii Kosoi. The ideas of Nil Sorskii and Maksim Grek were taken further by Feodosii Kosoi, who succeeded in transforming them into heresy. Direct writings by Kosoi do not survive; his teachings are known in substance through his contemporary and adversary, Zinovii Otenskii. Summoned to Moscow in 1553–54 to account for his heretical views, he escaped from confinement and fled to Lithuania where he married a widow of another faith.

Feodosii Kosoi regarded Jesus Christ as an ordinary man born according to the natural laws of nature just like all other people on Earth. This led Feodosii to elevate natural law, which he regarded as the embodiment of Divine Will and having supremacy over manmade laws. Man accordingly had natural rights which no State nor church could offend.

Kosoi adhered to a concept of the classification of laws contrary to that accepted by the Russian Church. Divine Law was the source of all legislation; he then distinguished between natural law as the basis of life for the entire organic world and positive ('civil') law as the aggregate of State prescriptions regulating the lives of individuals. Positive law must correspond to Divine and natural law. Positive laws which failed to do so contributed to the preservation of an unjust order, ensuring wealth and freedom for some at the expense of slavery and poverty for others.

Communion with God was achieved through simple forms of worship in ordinary dwelling houses in which icons and other religious artifacts were absent. God was present in the hearts of people; he read all their secret thoughts, hopes and expectations. In Kosoi's view, therefore, the church as an organization of spiritual power on earth was unnecessary, as was State power. Scholars disagree as to whether Kosoi believed in community property to the exclusion of private ownership; more modern readings of his postulates suggest that Kosoi favoured common ownership, a duty to work and just remuneration for one's labour. Many of Kosoi's ideas were analogous to those of the Reformation in Western Europe. Russian political theorists credit Kosoi with positing the first communal utopia based on both theory and the practical lessons of monastic life.[10]

Zinovii Otenskii. Believed to have been close to Maksim Grek until the latter's exile, Zinovii Otenskii was then sent to a monastery near Novgorod where he spent the rest of his days. It was Otenskii who disseminated the ideas of Feodosii Kosoi by refuting the latter's teachings, and it was in that refutation that Otenskii formulated his own views relevant to legal theory.[11] Critical of prevailing practices in the administration of justice and of State price and taxation policies, Zinovii also defended the monastery system against its detractors.

As regards legal concepts, however, Zinovii shared much with Maksim Grek. He developed the notion that, by their very nature, people cannot live in society without a ruler, without leaders. In defining the purpose of the State, Zinovii is close to Aristotle, sufficiently so that one suspects he was directly acquainted with early manuscript sources of Aristotelian texts. Drawing upon the Holy Trinity, Zinovii followed Maksim Grek in elaborating the concept of a representative monarchy. The Tsar is the supreme ruler, states Zinovii, but he must heed the advice of his counsellors in order to achieve the common good, security, peace and quiet of his subjects. A Tsar who does not comply with these strictures is labelled 'tyrant', by which is meant unlawfully using supreme power in the interests of those in authority to the detriment of those being ruled.

Following the classification of laws posited by Iosif Volotskii, Zinovii distinguishes among three categories of laws. The first consists of Divine Law contained in the teachings of God, the holy scriptures and the decisions of church assemblies. The second category consists of customary rules formed in each land on the basis of geographic and climatic factors. These rules are a direct expression of Divine Will. Positive legislation comprises the third category, which Zinovii subdivides into general laws issued by the Tsar and local laws. Both subcategories derive from the historical practices of the people and directly express commonly accepted moral principles. All must obey the Law, including the Tsar and his officials.

Zinovii identified the fulfilment of the Law by the Tsar as the embodiment of justice and offered a detailed and informed critique of the contemporary judicial system. He commented on red tape, the bribery of witnesses and judges, and the arbitrariness of judicial officials who punished or pardoned, not in accordance with law, but capriciously and willfully. His chief demand was for a just and expeditious court able to decide cases without delay. He also devoted considerable attention to an issue which preoccupied mediaeval Russian writers: mercy towards the guilty person. Zinovii argued that mercy had its place, but not before trial; it must not preclude the actual unmasking of an evil deed and punishment for committing it. He also opposed so-called 'amicable settlements' which court officials often imposed in order to avoid investigating and hearing cases or to extending this practice to inquisition trials which he felt were not inherently subject to amicable settlement.

Filofei. 'Moscow – the Third Rome' is a doctrine whose developed form is traditionally associated with Filofei, a follower of Iosif Volotskii. Though of uncertain social and educational background, he was undoubtedly of a pro-Muscovy orientation. His politico-legal views were formulated in a series of 'Messages' addressed to the Pskov Namestnik Mikhail Grigor'evich Misiur-Munekhin and to the Grand Princes of Muscovy, although precisely which remains in dispute amongst scholars.

Filofei set out a doctrine of supreme power which stressed the legality of the origin of the Grand Princes, their succession and their stature as God's representatives on Earth. The

Tsar must be concerned for his subjects; to be so, his kingdom must be in awe of God, symbolized by the sceptre in his hand and his crown of a laurel wreath. The image of the Tsar was dwelt upon at length. The Tsar was severe with all who broke the law, but showed justice to all of his subjects, being especially solicitous of the weak. His subjects were in turn subordinate to him without reservation.

Following many mediaeval thinkers, Filofei did not distinguish between morality and law [jus]. Accordingly, any immoral act was in his view unlawful whether it had a legal basis or not. His concept of justice also included moral principles.

The unification policies of Muscovy vis-à-vis its near neighbours convinced Filofei that the time had come for Russia to fulfil its historic mission, a mission that in his eyes was inseparable from that of Russian Orthodoxy. Russia was the sole remaining kingdom true to Orthodoxy and consequently its sole successor: 'two Romes have fallen, a third stands, and a fourth will not be'. This historic role of grandeur was confirmed by Russia's recent experience – fidelity to Orthodoxy, defeat of the Tatar-Mongols, successful defence of Russian frontiers and a promising diplomacy. The might and glory of Byzantium and Rome had passed to Muscovy, to the Russian State. Whether the doctrine of the Third Rome was an expansionist and aggressive one continues to be much discussed; comparisons are made with the Soviet era and more recently with renewed Russian interest in other Slavic peoples.

It followed that the centre of Orthodoxy could be nothing less than a sovereign State enjoying universal respect and being possessed of sufficient power to defend the faithful wherever they were situated. This was a strong impetus to those who supported a centralized Muscovite State and figured as a central tenet of Russian foreign policies for centuries thereafter, at least in words. 'There are sufficient grounds to assert that the political formula of Filofei was part of documents expressing the official ideology of the State and for a long time was a constituent part thereof.'[12]

Fedor Karpov. The emergence of Muscovy as a centralized grand dukedom gave rise to a manuscript literature commenting on changes in the form of rule and State structure. Fedor Karpov, publicist and diplomat, was amongst those who addressed these issues. Close to Maksim Grek and his followers, Karpov set out his views in a 'Message to the Metropolitan Daniil', ascribed to the 1530s. His political discourses and terminology have been studied extensively and variously construed. It is generally accepted that he favoured a representative form of rule under the Grand Prince and his senior officials and accepted the Aristotelian position that every city and kingdom required a Tsar plus his counsellors. As regards the categories of justness and law [jus], which he combined into one, Karpov required that all laws must be just, directing his attention to existing schemes of payment for labour. Earnings must be fair and wealth equitably distributed. Subjects unfairly paid, including those in military service, might cease to listen to their Tsar. Compliance with law [lex] was both the moral base of social life and the foundation of the well-being of the State. Illegality was the consequence of a decline in morality.

Karpov offered an original interpretation of 'groza', widely translated into English as 'terror' but having in fact a strong connotation of 'awe'. Many Russian political theorists held that the ruler should incorporate 'awe' as a vital component in the exercise of power. Karpov held that 'awe' was not an attribute of power, but rather an attribute of law [lex] itself. Order in a State created the necessary foundations for the element of 'awe' in law and thereby enabled the sovereign and his officials to rule effectively and protect their subjects against 'evil' people. Laws [lex] and the State were human creations. Karpov divided laws into three categories: natural, Divine (the Laws of Moses and those of Jesus Christ), and positive (State), the last being enacted on the basis of the former. He rejected justifications for any illegal actions, even if founded on such ethical categories as 'patience' and 'forgiveness'.

As a diplomat and public official, Karpov is credited with according overriding attention to the interests of the State and the status of its citizens. His theory of law and politics is regarded as being close to that of Niccolo Machiavelli, although there is no evidence that he was aware of Machiavelli's writings, or indeed of being a 'material link' in the process of forming an autonomous juridical doctrine in Russia based on natural law and human reason. Instead, that process was evidence of Muscovy moving to a new stage of 'cultural-historical development' closer to the thinkers of the Renaissance.[13]

Ivan Semenovich Peresvetov. The programme of State and legal reforms associated with the name of Peresvetov may or may not have originated with him, with a group of individuals or even (as some suspect) with Tsar Ivan IV himself. Whatever the case, the ideas associated with his name addressed a number of principally legal matters, including the creation of a system of unified legislation applied by a centralized judicial system. Without being enmeshed in the religious disputes of the day, his writings elaborated and substantially extended many of the ideas advanced by Maksim Grek.

The judicial reforms favoured by Peresvetov were directed above all towards eliminating the evils of localism. Judges should be appointed directly from the centre and be paid from the State treasury. Court costs and duties should accordingly be recovered by the State treasury and not by the judges who should rely only upon the law [lex] in administering justice. He would also have endowed judges with certain administrative and supervisory functions on behalf of the central authority. The great attention accorded in Peresvetov's writings to matters military was reflected in his proposal for a military court to be organized separately from the civil courts. The military court was to be local, expeditious, just and without cost to those who appeared before it.

In matters of administering justice, Peresvetov favoured severe punishments, including the frequent application of the death penalty, at least in principle, in order to create the right climate of obedience to law. He too introduced the concept of 'terror' or 'awe' to instil respect for law, having in mind a scheme of strict punishments which might be applied to miscreants. Within half a century following the publication of his writings, many of his proposed reforms were acted upon. With respect to legislation, the Tsarskii Sudebnik of 1550 was introduced.

Ivan the Terrible. Foreign impressions of the less salubrious side of Russian mediaeval and subsequent political-legal thought are invariably associated with the legacy of Ivan IV, known principally through two works attributed to him which may or may not be contemporary: his so-called 'epistles' and a correspondence with Prince A.D. Kurbskii (see below). The essence of those ideas reduced to absolute autocracy, terror and a police State. Following the tradition of Russian political thought in tracing the origins of the crown back to its historical roots, Ivan IV reputedly rejected the idea that the legitimacy of the ruler depended in part upon his personal and moral qualities. The bearer of ultimate power was accountable solely to God in the hereafter, not in any way to his subjects here on earth. As for representative rule, the Tsar's sole counsel was God himself and no one else. Similarly, he refused to combine spiritual and secular power with the Patrichariate, favouring a sharp delineation between the two and rejecting any limitation on secular power by the spiritual authorities.

In the Tsar's view, the supreme ruler also combined the role of lawgiver and judge. The type of punishment and precise penalty should be determined, not by the law, but by the Tsar himself. The scale of severe punishments applicable was entirely arbitrary and derived principally from examples of various honourable rulers rather than from legislative material. Punishment might extend not merely to wrongful deeds, but to evil and dangerous thoughts.

Ivan the 'Terrible' (or 'awesome') conferred new meaning to the word which has come down in history attached to his name. The term no longer implied concern about the safety of the realm against external enemies or good order for its own sake. 'Terror' or 'awe' was secured by the 'oprichnina' or special police created by the Tsar. 'Awe' came to be mixed with fear and the lawlessness associated with his arbitrariness. From the 'beginning of Russian literature until the end of the sixteenth century not a single political doctrine is to be found which understood the power of the Tsar to be as absolute so as to be decisively unlimited'[14] except for the doctrine of Ivan IV.

Andrei Mikhailovich Kurbskii. A major source for the political thinking of Ivan IV is correspondence which reputedly passed between the Tsar and Prince Kurbskii. In any event this exchange proved to be a vehicle by which juxtaposed politico-legal approaches, arising out of disagreements between the Tsar and senior officials in the late 1550s and early 1560s, could be expressed. Those disagreements led to the disgrace of the senior officials concerned, mass repressions and the flight into exile of Kurbskii himself.

In the writings attributed to him, Kurbskii criticizes the style of rule introduced by Ivan IV as tyrannical, comparing the Tsar with King Herod. Addressing matters of law and administration, he reiterated many of the criticisms levied against the courts by Maksim Grek, Otenskii and Peresvetov, extending their comments to embrace legislation. He analysed both the processes of creating legislation and applying it. Invoking the traditional Russian concepts of justness and law, Kurbskii asked whether a law [lex] adopted by the State should always be complied with, for instance if it failed to conform to those criteria which a good law should satisfy? His reply, based to some extent upon the actual application of law, was that law [jus] and justness must coincide for a law [lex] to be considered lawful.

As for legislation, Kurbskii believed that a law [lex] must contain prescriptions which can actually be complied with; he described illegality not only as failure to comply with a law, but also the adoption of cruel laws. The latter type of legislation Kurbskii labelled 'criminal'. In the view of V.S. Nersesiants, Kurbskii was the 'first in the history of political and legal thought to put the question that justness and justice, and also the natural rights of man (natural laws), are a source of rights and freedom of the individual not subject to the arbitrariness of the legislator'.[15]

Following Peresvetov, Kurbskii criticized the actual application of the law within and without the courts. The courts, he said, dispensed neither justice nor mercy. He singled out trials in absentia for special condemnation: a slandered individual had no opportunity to defend himself against his accusers – a fate experienced by those with whom Kurbskii was politically associated. The terrorist regime introduced by the oprichnina, Kurbskii argued, rendered judicial and representative organs useless. Accordingly, Kurbskii elaborated upon the theory posited by Iosif Volotskii concerning the right of a people to resist the ill-intentioned exercise of power.

Kurbskii favoured a limited monarchy, a monarch advised by representatives from various strata of the populace who took part in all the major decisions of state. A distinction was drawn between what might loosely be described as legislative powers, to be exercised by the Tsar together with a representative council, and administrative or executive powers, to be exercised by the Tsar together with councils of advisers chosen for their wisdom and experience.

Ivan Timofeev and the Time of Troubles. The end of the 16th century in Muscovy found the realm in disarray as the Rurik dynasty came to be succeeded by the Romanovs. A substantial politico-legal literature emerged addressing the issues of succession to the throne and the political organization of society, of which perhaps the most noted is a manuscript entitled 'Vremennik'. Discovered in 1834 and attributed to a senior official, Ivan Timofeev [Semenov], the 'Vremennik' is regarded as the most significant and influential example of such literature from that time.

Addressing principally political rather than legal issues, the manuscript interpreted the issue of succession traditionally, considering those tsars to be legitimate who succeeded either by way of inheritance or lawful election. Illegal tsars were those who seized or appropriated the throne, thereby offending human and Divine will; inevitably they would be subject to punishment for their misdeeds. A stern opponent of Boris Godunov, Timofeev regarded the False Dmitrii as being sent by God to punish Russia for allowing Boris Godunov to assume the throne.

Timofeev supported a limited monarchy, basically following the reasoning of Maksim Grek, F. Karpov, Z. Otenskii, Ivan Peresvetov and A. Kurbskii, but substantially elaborating the argumentation in favour of such a scheme. He advocated the formation of a Council of Cities of the Realm which would recognize and confirm the authority of the Tsar and help him in exercising his functions.

The formulations advanced by Timofeev led many later students of his manuscript to believe that he advocated more than a mere Council to assist the Tsar. Such a Council should express and reflect public opinion, thus laying the basis for resisting laws and acts of the Tsar that were considered to be unlawful or unjust. Given the tenor of the times, Timofeev strongly endorsed the thesis that subjects of an evil ruler not only had the right, but also the duty, to resist his reign.

Timofeev accepted the classifications of legislation advanced by Maksim Grek, Z. Otenskii and Kurbskii. He used the words 'natural law [lex]', distinguishing it from 'ustavnoi zakon [lex]' or positive law. Natural laws he sometimes called 'reasonable'; he would appear to have accepted the view of Kurbskii that natural law categories emanate from Divine will and express eternally just and reasonable principles. Positive law must conform to natural law. By 'ustavnoi zakon', Timofeev meant all positive legislation in force from the very earliest days of Kievan Rus. His concept of justice, however, went beyond the classical limits of law to embrace elements of faith and morality. Although an opponent of Boris Godunov, Timofeev praised his devotion to justice and the eradication of injustice.

Legal Theory and Romanov Absolutism: 1613–1800

The accession of the Romanovs to the Russian throne in 1613 led in the course of time to a decline in those Russian institutions which had contained elements of representative power – the assemblies (Zemskii sobor) giving way to the Boyar Duma and the Osviashchennyi sobor, both formed on a nonelective basis. By the mid-17th century the Romanovs were firmly in place and, under Tsar Aleksei Mikhailovich, a series of major reforms commenced that would produce deep divisions in Russian society and also new politico-legal theories. In 1649 a massive systematization and codification of Russian law, unparalleled in Russian history, was introduced in the form of the Sobornoe ulozhenie, immediately followed in 1650–51 by a similar systematization of canon law and, in 1654, by sweeping church reforms. The last led to schisms within the Russian Orthodox church, of which the group known as the Old Believers continued to adhere to liturgies and scriptural readings of the prereform era and to favour a different relationship between Church and State.

Simeon Polotskii. The consolidation of Romanov power led to politico-legal theories which justified various forms of absolute monarchy. Samuil Petrovskii Sitnianovich (1629–80), born at Polotsk and known by his monastic name of Simeon, is associated with the doctrine of the 'enlightened absolute monarch' in Russian politico-legal theory.

Simeon first extolled the person of the Tsar; comparing the Tsar with the Sun, he introduced into the Russian political language the formula 'Tsar-Sun'. He rejected comparisons between the Tsar as a human personage and his subjects. God and Tsar were virtually of equal greatness: 'The Tsar – a celestial citizen – is the Father of all'. In Simeon's view, the Tsar and the State were identical, and he accordingly gave much attention to the former's nurture and education. The Tsar must above all be an educated individual who acquires knowledge and wisdom from books and from wise people. Books about history were of special importance so that the ruler might master the historical experience of other countries and peoples and live by their example. Distinguishing between the Tsar and a tyrant, Simeon observed that to know the difference, one should read Aristotle.

An enlightened monarchy, Simeon taught, is one in which the State is based on laws: 'All punishments must be suffered under the law'. There should be no exception, neither for the Tsar himself, nor his son, nor any subjects. The courts must establish the truth and not be a source of retribution nor administer harsh sanctions. He urged the creation of a court before which all were equal, as well as a unified judicial system without red tape.

Iurii Krizhanich. Born in Croatia (1618–83), educated at Zagreb and then Vienna, and resident in Rome for nearly two decades, Iurii Krizhanich came into Russian service in 1659. Victim of a libellous denunciation in 1661, he was exiled to Tobolsk for 15 years. After two further years in Moscow, he left Russia forever in 1678. While in Tobolsk he devoted himself to composing reflections on government, the best known being his treatise on 'Politika'.

Krizhanich's European background and education and his command of Russian history and theology placed him in a special position amongst Russian politico-legal theorists. He criticized those Russian thinkers who endeavoured to trace Russian tsars back to the Caesars of Rome. Such kinship, he suggested, would be shameful rather than honourable. He also questioned the doctrine of Muscovy being the Third Rome, dismissing this view as merely one means of extolling Ivan the Terrible.

His treatise on politics ranged widely over many affairs of state. He accepted the divine origin of the ruler. All kings, he wrote, are placed by God and are themselves divine. The purpose of the State is to achieve the 'common good' for all members of society. Krizhanich considered the best form of rule to be a perfected absolute monarchy which must be secured against transformation into tyranny by certain guarantees. Amongst the guarantees which Krizhanich enumerated were the presence on the throne of a philosopher-king, compliance with good laws which were in accord with Divine and natural law, and the normative regulation of all estates and officials of society by which their rights and duties would be defined.

As an educated European, Krizhanich had been well schooled in the 'Digest' of Justinian, and his writings frequently contain propositions derived from that source. Those who draft Russian laws, he counsels, should have a thorough command of all laws and customs of the country and, when necessary, also study the laws of long-established States (including contemporary France) in order to draw upon their experience. All officials of State should strictly comply with the law in their activities. However, the philosopher-king he placed technically above the law; the King is himself the living law and not subject to other laws except Divine law – here his writings repeat virtually verbatim passages from the 'Digest' of Justinian.

Kirzhanich criticized the Russian laws of his day as being excessively cruel and harsh: 'By reason of such harsh laws all European nations with one voice call the Orthodox Kingdom tyrannical. ... And moreover they say such tyranny is greatest here.' Krizhanich put forward certain proposals to improve the judicial system. He recommended that a Boyar's Court be instituted to settle serious criminal cases by majority vote, and that lesser criminal and civil cases be referred to one judge (chosen from among the boyars) for settlement.

A.L. Ordin-Nashchokin. By the late 17th century Russian legislation began to manifest mercantile protectionism, usually accompanied by various projects and programmes for the economic transformation of Muscovy. One of the most able Russian diplomats, Afanasii Lavrent'evich Ordin-Nashchokin (1605–80), attempted to encourage entrepreneurship partly by means of legal reform.

Ordin-Nashchokin prepared the draft New Trade Statute (1667) which contained rules regulating foreign and domestic trade and gave Russian merchants the same legal status accorded to foreign merchants and others who were granted certain immunities. The Statute was partly based on foreign practice and experience. However, more than a century elapsed before the politico-legal underpinnings of his programme came to the forefront of the Russian agenda for reform.

I.T. Pososhkov. The trend towards absolute monarchy as a form of rule intensified under Peter the Great. In his legislation Peter proclaimed: 'His Majesty is an Autonomous Monarch Accountable to No One in the World'. The Senate and Synod declared Peter to be the Emperor of All the Russias, thereby transforming the Grand Dukedom of Muscovy into the Russian Empire. The Duma of Boyars was replaced by the Ruling Senate; the administrative departments (prikazy) became colleges operating under special Reglaments; the patriarchiate was abolished and a Synod created to administer the Church.

Among the most noted political theorists of the Petrine era was Ivan Tikhonovich Pososhkov (1652–1726) who flourished in a variety of entrepreneurial/industrial capacities and travelled widely throughout Russia. In 1724 he prepared his 'Book on Poverty and Wealth' addressed to the Emperor; here he set out his views on a number of matters which he believed should be the subject of urgent attention, amongst which was the system for the administration of justice. The book was not published at the time and may have led to the author's arrest and death in prison. Whether Peter the Great ever saw the manuscript or not is unknown. It was eventually rediscovered in 1842 and published, although even then not without difficulties with Russian censorship.

Pososhkin set himself the task of identifying why poverty and illegality were so widespread in Russia. The manuscript was largely devoted to issues of organizing industry and trade. Merchants, he advised, should be given the right of free trade, and internal commercial duties and taxes should be uniform throughout the realm. Pososhkov believed that the State should ensure that enterprises had a labour force, if necessary by assigning prisoners for this task. Merchants should in turn trade honourably, and in certain cases statutory prices should be introduced for goods. As regards serfdom, he recommended the enactment of a special law which would precisely define the extent of duties of peasants and the limits of tied labour. A progressive land tax was suggested as a source of revenue for the State which should not permit the use of land free of charge.

Considerable attention was given to the eradication of injustice. Pososhkov basically accepted the position of Peresvetov with respect to the relationship between justice and law [lex]. Illegality was injustice. He proposed a draft scheme for 'direct justice' to be effectuated by judge-bureaucrats of the State and paid from the State treasury. Judges should come from the lower classes since the nobility was too susceptible to bribery. For unjust activity, Pososhkov proposed severe penalties, including capital punishment.

Court proceedings should be transcribed in writing according to rules laid down in law, and any State revenues from trials should be paid directly into the State treasury. He also urged that judges should be informed at once about all detentions of suspects so that no one was unlawfully detained.

Pososhkov recommended codification on a large scale – to include all ancient and recent laws, to add whatever provisions were necessary, and to set out the entire body of legislation in precise detail. Both Russian and foreign legislation should be used as models, including Turkish examples. He recommended that a special commission be appointed to undertake codification; this would include two to three persons from each province of the Empire and from all social strata, including peasants and soldiers. The entire commission would sign the final draft and submit it to the Tsar for confirmation, ensuring democratic participation in the drafting but leaving the final decision for the Emperor.

V.N. Tatishchev. Known as an historian, diplomat and distinguished military officer, Vasilii Nikitich Tatishchev (1686–1750) was charged by Peter the Great in 1717 with compiling a geographic description of Russia and preparing a history of the country. This task he worked on episodically, eventually completing the work after 1745 when he fell into disgrace under the Empress Elizabeth. His views were based on natural law and a contractual theory of the origin of the State.

The State originated in a social contract amongst peoples who could not otherwise ensure their safety and security against outsiders or achieve the common good. Historically, he suggested, all known human communities first concluded contracts between spouses, then between parents and children, and ultimately between lords and servitors. As families became extended, entire societies emerged which required a head who became the monarch and to whom all were subordinate, just as children are subject to their father. The social contract thus represented a series of contracts. Serfdom was one such contract which could not be dissolved at the instance of one of the parties without the agreement of the other.

Tatishchev devoted considerable attention to the forms of State. He postulated that the various forms of rule reflected the size of territories and the degree of security required from foreign threat. Peoples who were few in number and not subject to attack could establish democratic forms of rule, whereas vulnerable and large States required a strong leader. The worst possible type of rule was tyranny, and the best monarchy. In his view the most effective monarchy would rely upon a two-chambered elective organ, the first a Senate of 21 representatives from the nobility and the second a consultative Council of 100 persons elected on a representative basis. While the monarch was the supreme legislator, the laws he issued had to correspond to natural law, justness and the general good. One individual alone could not perform the task of legislation; the monarch was a formal legislator who had to rely upon his departments and elected institutions to prepare draft laws. The task of the monarch was to sign the draft laws prepared.

Tatishchev urged the preparation of a new Ulozhenie to replace that of 1649. The new legislation should be written in precise accessible language comprehensible to all. Through codification, contradictions and inconsistencies in the law could be eliminated.

As regards court organization and procedure, Tatishchev advocated the professional training of judges, a view ultimately introduced in the 1864 judicial reforms.

M.M. Shcherbatov. Prince Shcherbatov (1733–90) wrote extensively on matters of law and law reform, having served in 1767 on the famous commission of deputies convoked by Empress Catherine II to discuss her famous Nakaz. He saw no real distinction between an absolute and an 'enlightened' monarch. A limited monarchy was essential, as was compliance with law in all domains of State activity.

Shcherbatov also adhered to the social contractual origins of the State. All people were originally equal in a state of nature before communities emerged. But differences in the abilities and power of people gradually led to the demise of such equality. Nature itself had provided for the possibility of inequality, and it was entirely natural that inequalities should pass from generation to generation. Much in Shcherbatov is reminiscent of Thomas Hobbes and John Locke, both of whose writings were familiar to him.

Shcherbatov distinguished among four forms of State power: monarchy, aristocracy, democracy and despotism. However, he argued that none of these had ever existed in a pure form. The type of rules and laws which developed in any particular State depended upon climate, size of territory, soil fertility and extent of population. Of all the existing political systems in his day, he preferred that based on separation of powers and the determination of competence of State organs by law. Amongst monarchies he considered the limited English form to be superior to the absolute version in Russia. Limited monarchy was traditional in Russia, he argued; Ivan the Terrible, Peter the Great and Catherine II were exceptions to the general rule of Muscovite grand princes, governing jointly with wise counsellors, boyars, elders and the clergy.

He suggested the creation of a government consisting of five departments: criminal cases, State revenues, trade, sea and land forces, and foreign affairs. All issues would be decided in each collegially. Judges would be elected to office; the court would consist of six judges and a chairman elected for one year by the court itself. While judges would be professional, Shcherbatov did not intend to separate the judiciary from the legislative branch of government. Local government would be established on representative principles, elected from the nobility and the merchants. The monarch was the executive head and directed the administration of the country within the limits of the law. He was accountable for violations of law up to and including those requiring imprisonment. Thirty years after a monarch's death, subjects would discuss his activities and decide the fate of his memory: posthumous honour, monuments or condemnation.

Shcherbatov gave considerable attention to legislative activity. He favoured placing legislative responsibility in the hands of a special commission consisting of competent individuals. He also advocated the compilation of 'books of laws' which should twice be submitted for discussion to the whole populace. Both ruler and ruled were required to comply with all laws.

Shcherbatov followed the natural law school in classifying laws. He divided all laws into Divine, natural and positive, averring that the last must conform to the first. On matters of court procedure, he supported reforms then actively under discussion by his European contemporaries: the openness and transparency of trials and the participation of defendants. He favoured the presumption of innocence and argued that a citizen should be arrested only with the authorization of empowered agencies and according to the procedure provided for by law. The gravity of punishment should be commensurate with the gravity of the crime. In principle he opposed severe sanctions, favouring the use of capital punishment only in exceptional situations.

S.E. Desnitskii.. The first Russian professor of law, Desnitskii (c. 1740–89) completed his studies at the Theological Seminary at the Troiste-Sergiev Monastery and then the Petersburg Theological Academy before being sent by Catherine II to read law at Glasgow University in Scotland in the company of Ivan Tret'iakov. There he came under the influence of Adam Smith and John Millar; upon returning to Moscow, he translated William Blackstone into Russian at the request of Catherine II. He also published a number of works in which he set out rather radical proposals for the legal transformation of Russia.[16]

Desnitskii did not accept the contractual theory of the origin of the State. He suggested that mankind had proceeded through historically succesive 'states': the first period consisted of hunting; the second, herding; the third, cultivation; and the fourth, commercial. Collective possession predominated in the first two stages, whereas full-fledged ownership arose in the third and fourth. Following John Locke, he stated that the right of private ownership originated in the expenditure of labour. The State was essential only in the fourth stage of societal development.

The purpose of the State was to achieve good for the greatest number of people. The best form of statehood was the consitutional monarchy founded on the separation of powers. The three principal powers were legislative, judicial and punitive. Legislative power would be exercised by the monarch together with a unicameral parliamentary organ called the Senate and consisting of 600–800 persons. Deputies from all social strata, including the intelligentsia, would be elected. Senators would be equal irrespective of social origin.

Desnitskii's ideas relating to the courts included a number of proposals of a constitutional character. He believed the judiciary should be entirely separate from the administration and recommended the jury system, open trials, direct and continuous trials, and allowing the accused to defend himself. At the lower levels of the court system, however, he compromised on these principles and allowed links between the courts and local government.

Punitive power was within the jurisdiction of the Emperor and local officials who would be responsible for combating crime, executing court judgments, prisons and the collection of land duties. He classified law into State (the person and the State), civil (parents, children, spouses), criminal (crimes against society and the State) and judicial (relations between persons). In terms of court proceedings, he favoured the introduction of democratic principles such as equality of all before the law, equal punishment for identical crimes, commensurate punishment according to the gravity of crimes, and greater emphasis on crimes against the individual and private ownership than on those against religion, the church and the State. The death penalty might be applied only for intentional homicide and treason, and execution methods should be less cruel than in his day.

Ia. P. Kozel'skii. A noted educator and translator of French enlightenment works, Kozel'skii (1729–95) produced a number of essays which touched upon legal matters. He too accepted the social contractual origins of the State, which was formed in order to achieve the general good of the people. Such a contract could be forcibly dissolved by the people if the ruler failed to fulfil his terms of the agreement. Of the various forms of rule, Kozel'skii favoured that of a republic, although he saw some merit in an enlightened absolute monarch.

Kozel'skii distinguished sharply between pravo [jus] and zakon [lex]. There were four types of jus: Divine, natural, international and civil (State). All laws [lex] issued by the State must conform to these types of jus, otherwise they were deemed to be unjust. On this reasoning Kozel'skii severely criticized the criminal law sanctions in contemporary Russia as failing to conform to natural law.

A.P. Radishchev. The efforts of Russian legal and political philosophers in the late 18th century to identify the most desirable form of law and government produced, in the case of Aleksandr Radishchev (1749–1802), a genuinely radical response. Born into a family of the nobility with large landholdings, he read law at Leipzig University and pursued a civil service career before turning to literary pursuits. His mission was to help put an end to serfdom and autocracy, understanding by the latter term the concentration of unlimited power in the hands of a monarch. In his works, autocracy was no longer a description of the sovereignty and independence of supreme power; it designated a form of rule which in time came to be accepted as characterizing that which existed in Russia.

In Radishchev's eyes, autocracy was a state of being contrary to human nature. All forms of monarchy, whether 'enlightened' or otherwise, were equally pernicious. An 'enlightened' monarch had never been and could not be. He also criticized the bureaucracy which surrounded the throne and in Russia was notable for being divorced from both the monarch and the people.

Radishchev proceeded from a theory of natural human rights and the contractual origin of the State. The natural sociability of people was the reason for creating States. Following J.J. Rousseau, he attributed the formation of States to the emergence of private ownership and the attendant inequalities among people. The social contract was a tacit one, concluded for the purpose of ensuring a prosperous life for all and defending the weak and oppressed.

Positive legislation enacted by a State must be based on natural law; if legislation is contrary to natural law, it is invalid – a point of departure used by Radishchev to reject serfdom. Contradictions such as this between natural law and positive legislation led Radishchev to the revolutionary proposition that an oppressed people had the right to rise up against the State if their natural rights were being flagrantly violated.

His social ideal was a society of free and equal owners of property. Land should be given to those who cultivate it. Social privileges should be abolished and the rights of the nobility made equal to those of all other strata of society. The Russian Table of Ranks should be eliminated, and the bureaucracy reduced and made accountable to a representative body. He favoured a Republic within Russia based on the model of the mediaeval city-states of Pskov and Novgorod.

Radishchev rejected the doctrine of the separation of powers on the principle that only the people are the true rulers. The State should secure for its people their sacred natural rights: freedom of thought, speech, action, self-defence when the law could not protect them, ownership, and to be judged by their equals. The administration of justice he recommended placing in the hands of zemskii courts elected by citizens of the Republic. The judicial system should be made up of church, civil, military and equity courts, and he urged the introduction of juries.

Legal and Political Theory: 1800–1850

M.M. Speranskii. Close to Jeremy Bentham and his circle, Mikhail Mikhailovich Speranskii (1772–1839) was associated throughout the first four decades of the 19th century with Russian law reform, being widely credited as the 'father' of the *Complete Collected Laws of the Russian Empire (1649–1825)* and the *Digest of Laws of the Russian Empire* (1832). His reforming zeal caused him to be exiled to Nizhnii Novgorod in 1812 and then to Perm', and later to be appointed as Governor in remote posts, returning to St Petersburg only in 1820.

Jurisprudentially, Speranskii was deeply influenced by his seminary training; he believed that God was the supreme legislator of the Universe. He considered the contractual conception of the State as a hypothesis – the contract, if such existed, being a realization of the will of God. In his perception, Russia had reached the stage of industrialism, which required constitutional limitations on supreme power and the granting of political and civil rights to all subjects (security of the individual, protection of ownership and guarantees of personal political rights). He believed that Russia was on the eve of major transformations, not by revolution as in the West, but by means of evolution based on 'proper laws' granted by the Emperor to the people. Reformation of the State, he counselled, occurs over decades and centuries, not in two or three years.

He devised various schemes for transforming the State into a constitutional monarchy based on law. He linked legality to the separation of powers, favouring the creation of a two-chamber Duma which would meet at regular intervals to discuss and adopt laws. As head of the executive branch, the monarch would participate in the activity of the Duma, but no new laws, taxes or duties could be introduced without its assent. The judicial system would include the jury system and be headed by a Senate. A Council would be formed to combine and coordinate the efforts of the three branches of State; chaired by the Tsar, it could initiate legislation but this would subsequently have to be adopted by the Duma.

His various writings on law reform generated opposition amongst the noble classes of Russia. In the first decade of the 19th century, so did the several edicts and laws which he authored introducing reforms into the bureaucracy and proposing to reduce the privileges granted to the upper classes. A number of his proposed reforms came to pass nearly a century later in the early 1900s.

N.M. Karamzin. Best known as a writer, publisher and historian, N.M. Karamzin (1766–1826) also had influential views as regards the form of rule and substance of legislation. These he developed in his monumental *History of the Russian State* and in his *Note on Ancient and Modern Russia in its Political and Civil Aspects*, composed in 1811 for Tsar Alexander I. In the latter work he investigated the forms of rule most suitable for Russia, condemning the reign of Ivan IV as a tyranny. He declared himself to be a 'republican' in spirit, albeit one who was content with a monarchy. His ideal was a strong monarch, though not necessarily one who gained the throne by succession. Such a monarch would base his activity upon law and nurture the moral and political enlightenment of his people.

Although he found much that was positive in the country's past, Karamzin believed a number of things required change in contemporary Russia. He criticized the system of taxation, the procedure for bureaucratic appointments, the excessive size of Russian military forces, and the lack of firm civil and State laws.

Karamzin differed from Speranskii chiefly by the ways in which he believed reforms should be implemented. Whereas Speranskii proposed the transformation of State institutions, Karamzin urged the appointment to office of properly qualified individuals. The greatness of Peter I, he suggested, lay not in his institutional reforms of the Russian State, but in his appointment to office of men who were wise, honourable and noteworthy. Local government, counselled Karamzin, could best be reformed by finding 50 intelligent and competent persons to perform the tasks entrusted to them.

The Decembrists. The reformist spirit evident in the reign of Tsar Alexander I contributed to the emergence of tiny oppositionist organizations created by like-minded individuals who outlined programmes for altering the absolute Russian monarchy and abolishing serfdom. These secret societies ultimately contributed to the so-called Decembrist uprising in December 1825 in St Petersburg, whose perpetrators were severely punished by exile or death.

A key figure was **Pavel Ivanovich Pestel'** (1793–1826), born in Moscow, educated at home and then in Germany; upon returning to Russia he became the first graduate of the Corps of Pages. Spurning a promising military career, he joined the secret societies and later became organizer and head of the Southern Society for which he composed a 'Russkaia Pravda' as a programme for action. He was executed in 1826 for his role in the December uprising.

In philosophical terms, Pestel' was a materialist and an atheist. He believed in the natural equality of all individuals and their mutual aspiration to satisfy their needs on the basis of a social organization through the division of labour. The State, he said, should exist to introduce legal order into society and to balance the mutual rights and duties of the government and the people. The task of government was to choose the best means of achieving general prosperity for each and every person. Pestel' divided laws into three types: spiritual, natural and civil. Spiritual laws are disclosed through the Holy Scripture; they link the spiritual and the natural worlds. Natural laws arise from the requirements of nature and natural needs; they are imprinted in our hearts. State or civil laws are decrees of the State whose aim is to secure general prosperity; consequently they must be issued in full accordance with spiritual and natural laws. Such conformity, he said, was an absolute condition of the validity of State laws.

Pestel' also believed that State laws must conform to social interests in the sense that the advantage of the whole must always prevail over the advantage of the particular. Consequently, civil laws should be so composed that the interests of an individual do not take precedence over the interests of the whole of society. Any action contrary to the general prosperity should be deemed criminal. Every just society must be based on the absolute authority of law and not the personal predelictions of the ruler.

Addressing the differences which exist in the basic laws of various countries and peoples, Pestel' argued that these arose principally from the variety of social and political institutes and institutions which had developed in each State or society, thus rejecting Montesquieu's view that such differences were caused by varying climates and geographic positions.

The Russian State, said Pestel', did not attempt to achieve social prosperity and therefore represented an abuse of power which ultimately would lead to the demise of the State itself. He suggested that the flouting in Russia of natural, spiritual and positive laws required 'changes to the existing State order and the introduction in its place of that which would be based only on precise and just laws and decrees …'. In these propositions lay the right of the people to overthrow a government which violated spiritual, natural and positive laws.

Pestel's 'Russkaia Pravda' contained a scheme for social and political transformations in Russia as well as the means for achieving these ends which were radical, in the true sense of the word. It proposed the abolition of serfdom and the division of land amongst the peasants free of charge on the premise that, according to natural law, land is the weal of all of the people. Each individual should hold a participatory share therein since land is the principal source of food for mankind. However, he recognized that private ownership existed and was so deeply imbedded in people's consciousness that eliminating ownership was impossible. Accordingly, Pestel's idea was not to eliminate land ownership, but to transform all Russians into landowners.

Politically, Pestel' described himself as a republican because he saw the greatest possibilities for Russian prosperity in that form of rule. State power would be divided between legislative and executive; all male citizens of 20 years or more would enjoy the right of suffrage except those in service. The legislative branch would be a single-chamber parliament elected for five years, with the annual election of one-fifth of its membership by rotation. No one had the power to dissolve parliament. Executive power would be lodged in five persons elected for a five-year term to a Derzhavnaia Duma; all ministries and governmental bodies would be subordinate to this executive organ. Supervisory power over the legislative and executive branches would be vested in an assembly, or sobor, consisting of

120 persons called boyars. Appointed for life, they would not take part in either legislative or executive affairs. Candidates would be nominated by the provinces. Each new law would be sent to the assembly, which would not consider it in substance, but carefully verify that all the necessary formalities had been complied with as a condition for the law entering into legal force.

The other supervisory functions of the assembly would be exercised through the appointment of one of its members to each ministry and to each region of the country. The sobor would appoint the supreme military command and could send for trial any official of any level who had abused his power.

Pestel' proposed that the Russian State operate under a Constitution which he called the 'State Testament'. Under his scheme, Russia would be divided into a federation composed of ten regions and three udels; each region in turn would consist of five provinces or national areas, each province of uezds, and each uezd of volosts. He proposed to transfer the capital of Russia to Nizhnii Novgorod which he regarded as the geographic centre of the country and the cradle of Russian freemen.

The best means to achieve these transformations in Russian life, Pestel' counselled, was a military-revolutionary coup with the immediate scrapping of the monarchy and the physical elimination of members of the Imperial family to prevent its restoration. The creation of a new order would require a provisional supreme ruler headed by a dictator for a period of 10 to 15 years. A constitutional order would come into being only when the previous order had ceased to exist and when memories of it had been erased from people's minds.

A second key figure in the Decembrist movement was **Nikita Mikhailovich Murav'ev** (1796–1843) who became head of the Northern Society. His intellectual development was shaped by the ideas of French Enlightenment, the Greek and Roman classics, and Russian writers and historians, of whom Karamzin was especially important. After the December uprising, he was sentenced to 25 years forced labour in Siberia.

Murav'ev composed three draft constitutions which contained the essence of his social and political programme. The third draft, written at the behest of the investigative authorities while in prison, was the most radical. He was well-grounded in the United States Constitution and the documents of Revolutionary France. Deeply religious, Murav'ev combined natural law doctrines with those of the New Testament and, from these positions, criticized absolute monarchy as being contrary to natural law. The Russian people, he wrote, are free and independent and may not belong to any person or family. The people are the source of power and have the exclusive right to make the basic provisions of political power for themselves.

The first step in transforming the State, said Murav'ev, should be the abolition of serfdom and slavery. He considered a constitutional monarchy based on the principle of separation of powers to be the best for Russia. Legislative power would be placed in a two-chamber parliament. All individuals who had attained their majority and who owned moveable or immoveable property, except those in private service, would have the right to vote. One chamber of parliament would be elected for six years, one-third of its membership being renewed every two years. Members of this chamber must be at least 30 years old and own property of a specified minimum value. The other chamber would consist of 450 members and be elected for a term of two years; this chamber presupposed the creation of a federated Russian State. Laws would be adopted by majority vote; any member of parliament or minister had the right to initiate legislation.

As head of the executive, the monarch could not change or repeal laws nor appropriate legislative functions. But he was endowed with extensive powers in Murav'ev's scheme, including being the commander-in-chief of the armed forces and representing Russia in negotiations with foreign powers. The monarch could convoke both chambers of parliament and change the time of their sessions, but not for longer than two months. All powers of the monarch would be supervised by the parliament, including even visits to other countries. His courtiers would enjoy no special rights or privileges and could not be elected or appointed to State offices. Women could not inherit the throne.

A Constitution would make provision for the competence of the chambers of the parliament and for local government on an elective basis. Murav'ev proposed a rather complex judicial system which would have reinstated courts of equity, originally introduced briefly under Catherine II. Amendments to the Constitution could only be introduced according to a special procedure including the election of a people's assembly whose principal responsibility was to draft and submit major laws and constitutional amendments. The monarch would be required to take an oath to comply with the Constitution.

Murav'ev did not accept Pestel's version of social transformation, which envisaged a temporary dictatorship, for he apprehended that this might lead to the creation of conditions which encouraged arbitrariness and illegality.

Slavophiles and Westernizers. In the 1830s and 1840s there emerged two orientations in social and political thought which dominated the next decades of Russian politico-legal discourse. The central theme of the dialogue was the historical fate of Russia, the place and role of Russians amongst other peoples, and the distinctiveness of Russia's political and legal development against the background of European and Oriental experience.

Law and legal institutions were a minor component of this dialogue, but of interest nonetheless. The Slavophiles urged the need to reassess certain elements of earlier Russian experience; those of legal interest included the peasant community, local self-government and the correlation of law and custom. The communities and customs of early Russia had given way to mercenary judges, vain boyars and power-worship amongst the clergy. The extent of power wielded by the State had led to the destruction of regional rights and the stifling of local self-rule and, under Peter the Great, to a Westernization of Russia which was completely alien.

The Westernizers responded that Russia should not be juxtaposed to Europe. Russia and Europe shared a belief in Christianity; the differences between them lay in the special types of Christianity, in their distinctive orientations towards Enlightenment, and in differences in private and personal life. A leading proponent of the Western position and one of the founders of the so-called 'State school' in interpreting Russian history was **Konstantin Dmitrievich Kavelin** (1818–85). According to his approach, the moving force in history was the struggle between the individual desiring freedom and the gradual changes of social forms from family to the State. Russia had traversed the same historical path as Europe in this regard, but more slowly; therefore, being behind, it had to borrow the achievements of civilization where appropriate. The reforms of Peter the Great placed Russia on the path of Europeanization with respect to freedom and administration on the basis of modern acts and laws.

The Golden Age: 1850–1900

As an historical benchmark, the year 1850 is purely arbitrary. The socio-legal reforms of 1861, linked with the emancipation of serfs and the judicial reforms of 1864, gave new stimulus to legal theory, new varieties of political programmes and new groupings amongst those writing on the subject. The latter may be roughly classified into reformers, radicals, liberals and conservatives.

The Reformers

The practicalities of land reform engaged the attention of legal theorists from the 1850s. Various drafts circulated in government, the minimal position being to grant peasants the right to acquire ownership of their house and immediately adjacent plot of land. Under this scheme peasants would only obtain the right of use over other lands, with attendant duties according to local circumstances and customs. Later drafts recognized that greater rights over land needed to be given; this was in response to a considerable public reaction that peasants should acquire land and freedom without obligatory duties to the landowner or to the State. The so-called Narodnik movement pressed this view, drawing upon earlier discussions of the role of the obshchina – or community – in Russian life and maintaining that, as the community was liberated from the dual yoke of serfdom and bureaucratism, so would it take on its own natural life.

These views were shared to some extent by **Aleksei Mikhailovich Unkovskii** (1828–1893/94), a reformer from the ranks of the nobility who initiated the most radical draft regarding the peasant question. His version, submitted to Tsar Alexander II as early as 1857 in the name of the nobility of Tver Province, recommended that peasants be accorded the right to acquire, immediately and compulsorily, both their personal plot and field allotment. Neither expectation was fully met by the reforms of 1861.

The Radicals

The 1860s also saw the emergence of new social movements advocating radical programmes and radical social actions. Some Russian historians have called this period the formation of revolutionary utopian socialism in Russia, a combining of utopian peasant socialism and a mass revolutionary movement amongst the intelligentsia. Leading representatives of this movement were **Alexander Herzen** (1812–70) and N.G. Chernyshevskii. Herzen placed great hopes in the revival of the Russian obshchina, a theme pursued in its legal aspects by **Nikolai Gavrilovich Chernyshevskii** (1828–89).

Chernyshevskii believed that the existence of a high level of civilization, as achieved in contemporary Europe, did not preclude the concept of obshchina possession of property as the highest form of relations between man and land. In his view, this form was much to be preferred to private ownership because it better secured the general prosperity by combining owner, master and worker into a single person. Contrasting intra-obshchina with governmental regulation, he concluded that the former was preferable due to the absence of interference from any central and outside administration, thereby enhancing the freedom of the individual. Intra-obshchina regulation was inherently more reasonable than governmental as it was built up over generations on the basis of legal customs and agreement. Although private ownership in Western Europe had its virtues, in his eyes it led to excessive individualism and competition, which in the end meant the strong triumphing over the weak and labour being the victim of capital. The way out was to create an alliance and brotherhood among people on the basis of everyone coalesing into a society with shared interests which used the forces of nature and science in common. In the domain of land ownership, this brotherhood was to be expressed in the transfer of land to obshchina use, whereas factories would become the company of all of their workers and also be transferred as obshchina weal. When he became convinced that the existing State apparatus could not be reformed, he advocated peasant revolution and the formation of a society and State free from bureaucratism; local representative government and self-rule; an independent and just court; limitation of imperial power, and administration on the basis of laws.

Also amongst the radicals, **Mikhail Aleksandrovich Bakunin** (1814–76) is associated with the ideas of collectivist anarchism, a species of ultra-revolutionary socialism. He cautioned against the uncritical acceptance of the Russian obshchina, criticizing it in Russian history for its humiliation of women, absolute denial of women's rights and honour, patriarchal absolutism and despotism, disrespect for the mir, and the lack not only of legal rights but even elementary justness in decisions of the mir. Bakunin's treatment of the rights of the individual or duties of State officials was natural-law based; he rejected State laws and regulation as having been formed under negativist influences and as being inherently despotic. So-called political legislation was inevitably hostile to freedom and contrary to the natural laws of nature. The greatest guarantee of freedom in Bakunin's view was control over State power.

Another noted anarchist was **Petr Alekseevich Kropotkin** (1842–1921) who sought to combine the doctrine of anarchism with his studies of the science of nature and society. He linked the historical development of the State with the emergence of land ownership and the aspiration of one class to concentrate such ownership in its own hands. The State, he said, was in essence a mutual insurance society composed of landowners, the military, judges and clerics, each seeking to maintain their respective power over the people and to exploit the poor. The organization of State power was accordingly closely linked with law and the system of justice. The court administered legalized revenge called justice.

The Liberals

The liberals favoured reforms of autocratic Russia and greater recognition of the worth of the individual. Respect for law was a central theme of liberal writings about legal subjects. Leading representatives of the liberal orientation included B.N. Chicherin and S.A. Muromtsev, as well as two individuals represented in this volume: N.M. Korkunov and M.M. Kovalevskii (Chapters 3 and 1 respectively).

Boris Nikolaevich Chicherin (1828–1904) wrote widely on the history of political and legal thought and the philosophy of law. In his view the State in history was an alliance of people linked by law in a single legal entity and administered with supreme power for the benefit of all. The aim of the State was not the good of the individual, but rather to ensure the safety of the person and to create a moral order, defining and defending civil rights and freedoms (but not natural rights). The domain of natural law, as contrasted with positive law, is truth and justness – the system of general legal norms arising from human reason and obligations which serves as a standard and guide for positive legislation. Justness is the standard by which the domain of the freedom of individual persons is demarcated and the requirements of laws established. The aim of socio-political development is to avoid the extremes of individualistic anarchism and mechanical statism, to know how to combine individual freedom harmoniously with the general law.

Law does not reduce, he said, to benefit or to interest; it is inextricably linked with freedom as an individualistic and a priori metaphysical principle. From this standpoint, law is the external freedom of the individual, determined by external lex. Lex determines – defines – freedom and its limits or boundaries as well as the relations arising from them. In part Chicherin was influenced by the Hegelian proposition that law is a development of the idea of freedom, but he was critical of its statist and anti-individualistic implications. Chicherin schematized freedom as external (law), internal (morality) and social. Freedom as subjective morality becomes objectified and is combined with law as a norm of freedom in social linkages – the family, civil society, church and State.

The essence of liberalism in Chicherin's perception was the individual as a free being who preserved that status even when becoming part of society. Thus, even when the individual voluntarily limited his freedom in the interests of the freedom of others and accepted civil duties and the authority of the State, he retained his human dignity and inherent right to develop his powers of reason. Freedom of conscience, freedom of thought – these are the Divine sources of spiritual power which impart true freedom to the individual.

S.A. Muromtsev contributed significantly to the study of law from a sociological perspective in Russia, directing attention to law as the existing legal order and justifying the creation of legal rules by judges. He hoped that judges would further the evolution in Russia of a more liberal regime. 'There is no reason to fear arbitrariness on the part of judges', he wrote. Indeed, there were many grounds for allowing them to participate in the law-creation process: their high level of education and orderly progression in the ranks of the judiciary; the very 'corporation of jurists' reflected in their methods of selection, openness of proceedings and stability of tenure in office; their adherence to law, custom and legal doctrine, and their social conscience, justness and morality.

Muromtsev's originality lay in his concept that law is not merely the aggregate of legal norms, but rather the aggregate of legal relations – the legal order. This perception contributed in Russian jurisprudence to a more profound understanding of law not merely as the will of the ruler (tsar, parliament), but to the entire complex of legal relations in Russian society. A strong proponent of constitutional reforms, he was elected chairman of the I State Duma. When he died his students placed a wreath on this grave inscribed: 'To the first Russian citizen – from future citizens'.

N.M. Korkunov, who is represented in this volume with a substantial contribution (Chapter 3), developed the ideas of Muromtsev and of Jhering. Society, said Korkunov, is an objective social order representing conflicting personal and social interests in the political, economic and religious domains. These conflicts are coped with by imposing certain limitations on each subject of legal relations. Law both demarcates the interests and acts as an instrument for ensuring order in the process of the emergence and settlement of conflicts of interests.

Korkunov was influential in his day for his sociological and philosophical approaches to the study of law which contrasted to the formalistic orientation of dogmatic jurisprudence dominating in the universities. The translation into English of his general theory of law established Korkunov in Western circles as the best-known Russian jurist of his generation.

M.M. Kovalevskii, also represented in this volume (Chapter 1), was a jurist of many parts: legal theorist, comparative lawyer, publicist, publisher and member of the State Duma. He spent considerable time in England where he came to know the work of Sir Henry Maine; he pursued and developed Maine's comparative legal thought, combining the study of law with an analysis of its interlinkages with State institutions. Through his studies of customary law, Kovalevskii also achieved a considerable reputation as an ethnographer.

The Conservatives

As a group, those legal theorists classified as 'conservatives' were noteworthy for their patriotic cultural-nationalism and their growing distrust of the relevance for Russia of European political and legal experience. This encompassed a distrust of representative rule, of the idea of equality, and of respect for the rights and freedom of man and citizen.

In a monumental work contrasting the cultural and political relations of Russia and Europe, **Nikolai Iakovlevich Danilevskii** (1822–85) developed a theory of the cultural-historical types of human civilization. Though not a jurist, his views and approach – sometimes described as a species of comparative Russian culturology – nonetheless influenced many Russian legal theorists. In particular he believed that the only possible special guarantees of political and civil rights were those which the supreme power in a society wished to grant to its people. He ridiculed the notion of a social Russian parliament although, unlike many other neoslavophiles, he did value freedom of speech as a natural right and not merely a privilege granted by the State.

Konstantin Nikolaevich Leont'ev (1831–91) was a strong proponent of the terror of power personified in the status of the Tsar as supreme ruler. Developing the ideas of Danilevskii, Leont'ev believed that the future of various cultures and historical types of society was capable of being predicted, provided that a sufficient time frame was allowed – at least a century or half-century. State organisms proceeded through cycles which Leont'ev calculated occurred every 1200 years.

Leont'ev rejected the egalitarian principles of liberalism which he equated with a species of anarchism. He believed that Russian statehood and law were derived partly from Byzantium and partly from Europe. The cycles of statehood led States to commence as aristocracies, develop into monarchies, and then decline and die as egalitarian and liberal democracies.

V.S. Solov'ev. Vladimir Sergeevich Solov'ev (1853–1900) does not fit neatly into any of the preceding categories but nonetheless made a unique contribution to Russian legal thought. A patriot and very much a Russian philosopher, he nonetheless cautioned against the 'extra-European' and 'anti-European' views then prevalent in Russian society as an 'empty pretension'. Among the ideas of Western Europe of which he approved was the rule-of-law State which he saw as a step towards a more perfected variant of community. He gave considerable attention to theocracy in his published writings, and in later years to social Christianity. In his understanding of law, Solov'ev endeavoured to identify the moral value of law and of legal institutes and principles. He defined law as the 'lowest limit or certain minimum of morality binding equally upon all'. Natural law was the formal idea of law rationally derived from the general principles of philosophy. For Solov'ev, natural law and positive law were merely two sides of the same coin. Natural law embodied the 'rational essence of law' while positive law personified the historical phenomenon of law whose realization depended upon the state of moral consciousness in a particular society and on other historical conditions. Positive law constantly adds to natural law.

Natural law is an algebraic formula which can be reduced to two essential factors: freedom and equality. Freedom is a necessary substratum, and equality the necessary element thereof. The aim of a normal society and law is the common good and not merely the collective good (the sum of individual purposes). By its nature, this common good links everyone and everything through joint and several actions to achieve the common aim. Law endeavours to effectuate justness, but this aspiration is merely a general trend – the 'logos' and idea of law. Positive law embodies and realizes, albeit not always fully, this common trend in specific forms.

Solov'ev's ideas about law in some measure influenced the legal views of Novgorodtsev, Trubetskoi, Bulgakov and Berdyaev, amongst others.

The Twilight Years: 1900–1917

Among the thinkers influential at the turn of the century was **G.V. Plekhanov**, sometimes styled the 'father of Russian Marxism'. Departing from the 'narodniki', Plekhanov believed that Russia had to pass through a full phase of capitalist development, not only in terms of production forces but also the appropriate superstructure, including a constitution and parliamentary rule. The 'great mission' of the working class was to complete the task commenced by Peter the Great – the Westernization of Russia. In August 1903 he advocated the slogan 'the Good of the Revolution is the Highest Law', a phrase which explicitly justified any means to that end, but he also advocated the existence (adapting the English expression) of a 'Long Parliament' and its rapid demise when necessary. Constitutional revolutionary law played a purely auxiliary role; the dictatorial power of the State was for him the highest law, not being circumscribed by constitutional requirements or prescriptions.

The mainstream of Russian legal philosophers was preoccupied with constitutionalism in the early years of the 20th century. **Sergei Aleksandrovich Kotliarevskii** (1873–1940) wrote a major treatise on the rule-of-law State (1915) in which he observed the following:

> ... the idea of the rule-of-law State came into the practice of modern civilised States, in aggregate those expectations which turn a member of a State union into the leaders thereof. A rule-of-law State became one of the political tasks. The crisis of legal consciousness, the loss of faith in the majesty of law and institutions, has been noted many times ... the conviction that the State must take on the face of a rule-of-law State remains unshakeable.

Kotliarevskii believed that the principal purpose of a rule-of-law State was to promulgate justness, which presupposes that lex must always be just. The first requirement or first principle of a rule-of-law State, wrote **A.S. Alekseev** (1851–1916),[17] is the inadmissability of changing its legal order without the participation of popular representation. The second requirement is the supremacy of jus (and not of lex): 'It is not lex which gives force to jus, but jus which gives force to lex, and the legislator must not create, but must find jus, worked out in the consciousness of society'.

Gabriel Feliksovich Shershenevich (1863–1912), a noted legal philosopher and specialist in civil law, combined professional legal dogmatism with philosophical positivism, arguing that the State is the source of law since it represents power. Power is linked with the will and knowledge of rulers to oblige others to adapt their behaviour accordingly. He supported the sociological contention that it is difficult to base the concept of the State on power or on a legal relationship, but it is possible to imagine the State as a combination of power and will. State power in this sense is based on the autonomous will of some (those who rule) who subordinate others to it (the ruled).

Bogdan Aleksandrovich Kistiakovskii (1868–1920) is credited with taking the initiative in posing the question of how a socialist rule-of-law State would act in order to overcome the imperfections of a bourgeois rule-of-law State. He criticized the Russian intelligentsia for neglecting law and for having an underdeveloped legal consciousness, especially those who linked their fate with revolutionary ideas and causes. He accused the Slavophiles of legal nihilism. The narodniki, he felt, exaggerated the so-called ethical preoccupation of the Russian people which inhibited the transition from custom to written legislation in the countryside. He himself favoured a Kantian definition of law, which in contemporary terms was the 'aggregate of norms establishing and delimiting the freedom of persons'. From a sociological point of view, he preferred to treat law as an aggregate of norms capable of creating a compromise among various demands.

Evgenii Nikolaevich Trubetskoi (1863–1920) defined law as 'external freedom granted and limited by a norm'. He criticized definitions of law based on concepts such as 'power', 'State' and 'coercion' because they failed to take into account that any State and any power must themselves be conditioned by 'law' [jus]; they overlooked the fact that varieties of law exist independently of whether they are recognized or not by a particular State, examples being canon law, international law and certain legal customs.

Trubetskoi sought to harmonize natural law and positive law; natural law was the moving principle in history. The very idea of natural law gave the individual the possibility to climb above his historical milieu and save him from being enslaved by that which had gone before.

Pavel Ivanovich Novgorodtsev (1866–1924) distinguished himself early as a legal historian and philosopher. He was a member of the Kadet political party and elected to the State Duma. After the Russian revolutions he emigrated to Prague where he formed the Russian Law Faculty with the assistance of the Czech government. Recognized as the leader of a school of 'reborn' natural law, his pupils included I.A. Il'in, B.P. Vysheslavtsev, N.N. Alekseev and A.S. Iashchenko.

Author of several noted works, most fundamental perhaps is his *Introduction to the Philosophy of Law* (1907–17), published over a decade in three parts. The first treated the need for a renaissance of natural law; the second investigated what he called the 'crisis' in the use of the ideals and values of the Enlightenment, including those of the rule-of-law State. In his last volume, on the 'social ideal', he analysed the ideals of socialism and anarchism. His own position was that there should be a break with the traditions of exclusive historicism and sociologism and a transition to a system of moral idealism: 'Natural law structures are an integral property of our spirit and evidence of its high calling. A society which has ceased to create ideal structures would be a dead society; each time these structures show a spirit is alive, that there is movement of moral feeling and consciousness.'

Russian Legal Theorists in Emigration. In the aftermath of the Russian revolutions, Russian legal theorists unsympathetic to Bolshevism found themselves in Kharbin (Manchuria), Prague, Berlin, Paris, London and various cities in Yugoslavia. A detailed study of early Soviet legal experience by a collective of Russian jurists, published in Prague in 1925, contained essays by **N.N. Alekseev** (1879–1964)[18] and **N.S. Timashev**. They observed that the constitution had played no role in establishing a dictatorship in Soviet Russia; a direct and multifarious political experiment was underway. The category of zakon [lex] was irrelevant because in practice the distinction between lex and subordinate enactments – the existence of a hierarchy of legal norms – was inoperative. Alekseev observed that power had been seized by the oppressed; thus naked power had not created Soviet Russia, but a force 'empowered' with the idea of a struggle for liberation. According to this logic the proletarian State possessed a right of limited coercion, which presupposed the elimination of all coercion – propositions which Alekseev based on his interpretation of natural law.

Other noted Russian legal theorists in emigration included **P.A. Sorokin** (1889–1968), who commenced his academic career at Petrograd University and then at Minnesota and Harvard. He had been the personal secretary of M.M. Kovalevskii and in 1919 offered the first course of lectures on sociology. After the Russian Revolution he became the personal secretary of A.F. Kerenskii. In 1922 he was exiled from Soviet Russia and took up his posts in Western institutions. In philosophical terms, **Petr Berngardovich Struve** (1870–1944) evolved from legal Marxism to State liberalism in the spirit of Kaverin and Chicherin; after the Russian revolutions he lived in Belgrade and Berlin.

P.G. Vinogradoff. Although contemporary Russian treatises on the history of legal thought categorize Sir Paul (Pavel Gavrilovich) Vinogradoff (1854–1925) as a Russian emigrant,[19] his experience was not typical and had nothing to do with the coming to power of the Bolsheviks in 1917. A fellow student at Oxford in the 1880s with Henry Maine and Frederick Pollock, he resigned his Chair at Moscow University in 1902 and accepted election to the Corpus Chair at Oxford University. He was elected Academician of the Imperial Academy of Sciences in 1914, and also of other Academies including that in Britain.

Vinogradoff came to historical and jurisprudential studies at a time when social history had become fashionable. He was the first Russian legal scholar to choose English history as a field of research, having also devoted considerable attention to mediaeval Lombardy. His interests later expanded into the history of jurisprudence which he viewed as the study of doctrines and institutional activity.

In his perception, legal history dealt with waves of doctrine and institutional activity which, across many centuries and State frontiers, pass from one historical formation into another. Archetypal examples of such cultural succession include the reception of Roman Law in mediaeval and modern Europe and the linkages between Roman codifications and their Oriental predecessors.

His perception of Law as a social phenomenon and part of social experience caused him to undertake a wide range of research across the humanities and social sciences. He gave considerable attention to the law of ownership, maintaining that how society structures its law of ownership determines how it establishes the status of the family, of women, of labour relationships, of crime and punishment and of State structure and organization.

Political theory he believed was a constituent part of jurisprudence, part of the 'literary development of State Law'. 'The various branches of State law and the sundry norms of civil, criminal and canon law stand together with State Law, covering it like a shield and dustwrapper.'[20] Although Vinogradoff enjoys a kinship with those legal theorists pre-occupied with 'law in action', his historical orientation, which he himself called a 'synthetic' approach, always led him to examine the origins and evolution of law; in this he also departed from the positivism of Jeremy Bentham and John Austin. The weakness of the analytical school, he counselled, was its preoccupation with abstract concepts and terms, so that it was in danger of losing sight of social realities. The 'world of concepts' could thus become an end in itself.

His late works were strongly interdisciplinary, exploring how other branches of the social sciences and humanities might profitably use legal facts in their researches. His studies were always comparative in spirit if not in substance, and he remains one of the greatest Russian progenitors of comparative law. In the early 1920s his attention turned to the history and typologies of legal systems and law, a line of enquiry interrupted by his death.

Soviet Legal Theory

In comparison with prerevolutionary Russian legal theory, we are relatively well endowed with excellent English-language translations of the principal contributions to Soviet legal theory, at least up to 1970. This volume contains key selections and bibliographic guidance to the rest. We do not dwell on the legal views of V.I. Lenin, himself a lawyer, nor of I.V. Stalin and other leaders of the Soviet State, although their writings and utterances did much to shape the ideological structures and constraints which guided or limited acceptable dialogue about the nature, essence and even future of law in the Soviet Union.

In one sense it is perfectly true to say that, in the Soviet period, the history of legal thought was a battleground in which various forms of Marxism-Leninism fought against what was perceived to be State and Law in their noncommunist sense, against a bourgeois worldview. Massive resources were dedicated to systematically replacing a history and ideology of law [jus] with one based on a proletarian, Bolshevist, Marxist-Leninist, communist ideology, and also with reinterpreting the historical past into one congenial with the nature of Soviet institutions and a postulated withering away of State and Law.

In the early years after the Russian revolutions, numerous discussions and dialogues addressed the fate of law under the new socio-political circumstances and alternative theories emerged. Law as an instrument of the dictatorship of the proletariat figured centrally in the writings of **D.I. Kurskii**, an early People's Commissar of Justice. Law under the dictatorship of the proletariat, he said, was an expression of the interests of the proletariat, leaving no place for recognizing and defending the rights and freedoms of the individual. He extolled the revolutionary people's courts as a new source of law-creation; their principal function being 'criminal repression', he asserted that the courts should be absolutely free and should be guided above all by their legal consciousness.

The new 'proletarian communist law' was based on the Soviets, on a free family and on the ownership of all the instruments of production by the proletarian State. With the transition to the New Economic Policy (1921–28), Kurskii asserted that Soviet Law had become a species of 'rule-of-law' State, although the interests of the State were always postulated to prevail over the competing personal rights of individual citizens.

P.I. Stuchka viewed law as a procedure for social relations. The basic principles for a new revolutionary Marxist law Stuchka reduced to three: the class character of any law; the revolutionary-dialectical method (as a substitute for formal legal logic); and material social relations as the basis for explaining and understanding the legal superstructure (instead of proceeding from a law and legal ideas).

In his role as a senior legal official, Stuchka was able to pursue his ideas in the drafting of legislation. Writing about the preparation of the 1919 'Guiding Principles of Criminal Law of the RSFSR', he said: 'When before us, in the collegium of the People's Commissariat of Justice, was the necessity to formulate our own, so to speak, "Soviet understanding of law", we rested on the following formula: "Law ... is a system (or procedure) of social relations corresponding to the interests of the ruling class and protected by the organized power thereof".'

The exchange concept of law is associated with E.B. Pashukanis whose principal work on legal theory is partly reproduced as Chapter 5 in this volume. He rejected the concept of 'proletarian law' because, in his perception, bourgeois law – the historically most developed type of law – could not be followed by another, postbourgeois law. He accordingly developed an 'anti-law' position and offered the 'commodity exchange theory' of law. Soviet critics accused Pashukanis of applying abstract characterizations of law which existed before and outside of socialism; these were not applicable to proletarian law. In the course of time Pashukanis was obliged to accept that a new postrevolutionary and postbourgeois 'Soviet Law' did in fact exist, though with very special and specific characteristics.

The psychological conception of class law is associated with **M.A. Reisner** who, even before the Russian revolutions, began to pursue these lines of enquiry under the influence of L. Knapp and L. Petrazhitskii. Law as a form of social consciousness was developed by **I.P. Razumovskii**. He offered the following general definition of law: 'The procedure of social relations, ultimately relations between classes, insofar as it is reflected in the social consciousness, is historically inevitably abstracted, differentiated for this consciousness from its material conditions and, objectified for it, receives further complex ideological development in systems of "norms"'. The withering away of bourgeois law Razumovskii described as the 'death of law as an ideology'.

From the late 1920s to the early 1930s there occurred in Soviet legal history what is known as the 'struggle on the legal front', culminating in 1938 with a conference devoted to the science of Soviet law and State, convoked by **A.Ia. Vyshinskii**. Soviet jurists of all orientations – influenced by the transition to a Planned Economy, the collectivization of agriculture, and campaigns against various forms of ideological 'deviations' – adjusted their jurisprudential positions. This led to an increased politicization of legal science and greater direct influence of the Communist Party on the substance of legal doctrine. An address by L. Kaganovich on 4 November 1929 to the Institute of Soviet Construction and Law of the Communist Academy signalled the unleashing of a campaign of Bolshevist criticism and self-criticism. Kaganovich accused communist legal theorists of being imprisoned by the 'old bourgeois legal methodology' which led to such doctrines as State agencies being subordinate to the commands of law: 'We have our laws. Our laws determined the functions and ambit of activity of individual agencies of State power. But our laws are determined by revolutionary expediency at each particular moment.'

This struggle on the legal front contributed to a polarization of the two principal positions in Soviet jurisprudence of the day: those of Pashukanis and Stuchka. Pashukanis subjected himself to self-criticism and began to recant in favour of considering law and policy (or politics) to be identical, interpreting law as one of the forms of policy or as a component of policy (or politics). Stuchka in turn acknowledged an excessive reliance in his early writings on the bourgeois sociological school of law. In 1931 the I All-Union Congress of Marxist specialists in the State and legal sciences attempted to form a single correct position and line. The Congress was dominated by adherents of Pashukanis, but in the end adopted an eclectic resolution in order that the various approaches could save face.

The adoption of a new Constitution for the USSR in 1936 – to mark the transition of the Soviet Union to a society building socialism – required a new concept of law. In that year Pashukanis advanced the concept of 'socialist law', abandoning his former characterization of all law as 'bourgeois': 'The Great Socialist October Revolution dealt a blow to capitalist private ownership and laid the principle of a new socialist system of law. Therein is that which is fundamental and principal for an understanding of Soviet law, its socialist essence as the law of a proletarian State.'

From 16–19 July 1938, 600 legal workers, teachers and practitioners assembled in Moscow to attend the I Conference on Questions of the Science of the Soviet State and Law. The aim of the conference, organized by **A.Ia. Vyshinskii**, was to lay down a single true Marxist-Leninist, Stalinist-Bolshevist general line in legal science and, on that basis, to reorientate all approaches and conceptions posited by jurists of earlier periods, most of which were rejected as 'hostile' or 'anti-Soviet'. In his initial theses submitted to the conference and in his oral address, Vyshinskii defined Law [jus] as 'the aggregate of rules of conduct established by State power as the power of the ruling class in society, and also customs and rules of community life sanctioned by State power, effectuated in a compulsory procedure with the assistance of the State apparatus for the purpose of protecting, consolidating, and developing social relations and procedure advantageous and suitable for the ruling class'.

In the final written text of Vyshinskii's address and in the theses approved by the conference, this definition was altered as follows. Law [jus] is 'the aggregate of rules of conduct expressing the will of the ruling class established in a legislative procedure, and also the customs and rules of community life sanctioned by State power, the application of which is ensured by the coercive power of the State for the purposes of the protection, consolidation and development of social relations and procedures advantageous and suitable for the ruling class'.

Together with this general definition of law, the conference also approved a definition of Soviet law: 'Soviet law is the aggregate of rules of conduct established in a legislative procedure by the power of the working people expressing their will, the application of which is ensured by the entire coercive power of the socialist State for the purpose of the defence, consolidation and development of relations and procedures advantageous and suitable for the working people, the full and final destruction of capitalism and its survivals in the economy, domestic life and consciousness of people, and the building of a communist society'.

This definition dominated Soviet legal thought throughout the remainder of the Stalin era and beyond. All principal doctrinal writings on law repeated it verbatim. The thaw of the mid-1950s was accompanied in legal circles by some embryonic criticism of the Vyshinskii position, and its monopoly as the official line was sundered forever. Now styled a 'narrow-normative' approach by its critics, it began to be supplanted by doctrines of law as a unity of legal norms and legal relations (S.F. Kechek'ian, A.A. Piontkovskii) or as a unity of legal norms, legal relations and legal consciousness (Ia.F. Mikolenko). The substance of these positions acknowledged the normativity of law as laid down in 1938, but attenuated such normativity by recognizing the importance of law-in-action.

Not until the 1970s, however, did Soviet jurists begin to publicly question the identification of pravo [jus] and zakon [lex] which underlay Vyshinskii's theses. To distinguish between the two in some measure meant a return to the thinking of those Russian jurists of the past and an involvement in the drafting and ratification of the 1976 covenants on human rights. The dialogue is one which has not been followed in detail by Western scholarship, but will repay study in due course, for in that dialogue lie, in part, the roots of perestroika and the eventual dissolution of the Soviet Union. The search for freedom, equality and rule-of-law [jus] in the post-Soviet era clearly has its roots in the jurisprudential legacy of Russia.

International Law

The evolution of prerevolutionary Russian views on the nature of the law of nations has been traced by V.E. Grabar.[21] In the Soviet era such dialogue as occurred with regard to the nature of public international law was largely a collateral discussion of the nature of law generally. Nevertheless, a dialogue did occur, and the principal views and approaches are set out in the selections which appear in the present volume.

Notes

1 See V.S. Nersesiants (1976), *Политические учения и соврeтенность*, p. 6.

2 See I.A. Isaev and N.M. Zolotukhin (1995), *История политических и правовых учений Rossii xi-xx вв.*, p. 3. Analogous views are expressed in the magisterial work of V.S. Nersesiants (ed.) (1995), *История политических и правовых учений*. Also see V.S. Nersesiants (ed.) (1995), *История политических и правовых учений XX в*. This Introduction draws upon these studies and others of the postsocialist era without further citation; collectively they are the most objective and thorough introductions to Russian legal theory to appear in the Russian language in nearly a century.

3 See B.N. Chicherin (1869–79), *Политические учения*.

4 V.E. Grabar (1990), *The History of International Law in Russia 1649–1917*, ed. and transl. W.E. Butler.

5 See V.S. Pokrovskii (1960), *История политических учений*, p. 134.

6 Zolotukhin, in Isaev and Zolotukhin, note 2 above, pp. 10–11.

7 Ibid, p. 12.

8 For his views on the law of nations, see Grabar, note 4 above, pp. 18–19.

9 For the view that Maksim Grek favoured boyar-aristocratic rule, see S.A. Pokrovskii (1971), "*Из истории русской политической тысли XVI в.*," *Труды Всесоюзного юридического зауоного института*, pp. 5–7. This view is challenged in N.A. Kazakova (1973), "*Максим Грек в советской исориографии*," *Вопросы истории*, no. 5, p. 155; id (1975), "*Максим Грек и идея сосдовно-прегставитепей монархии*," in *Общество и государство феодапьной России*, pp. 159–170.

10 See Zolotukhin, in Isaev and Zolotukhin, note 2 above, pp. 67–68.

11 Otenskii's views were published in *Истины показание к вопросившим о новом учений* (Kazan, 1865).

12 Ibid., p. 85.

13 See A.K. Leont'ev (1977), "*Государственной смрой право, и суд*", in *Очерки русской культуруы XVI в.*, p. 74.

14 See V. Val'denberg (1916), *Древнерусские учений о предепах царской впасти*, pp. 359–60.

15 See V.S. Nersesiants (1983), *Право и закон*, p. 196.

16 See A.H. Brown, "The Father of Russian Jurisprudence: The Legal Thought of S. E. Desnitskii," in W. E. Butler (ed.) (1977), *Russian Law: Historical and Political Perspectives*, pp. 117–42; I.S. Ross (1995), *The Life of Adam Smith*.

17 See V.A. Tomsinov (1996), "A.S. Alekseev (1851–1916)," in *Sudebnik*, I, 83–90.

18 See Tomsinov (1996), "N.N. Alekseev (1879–1964)," *Sudebnik*, I, 91–100.

19 See V.G. Grafskii, in V.S. Nersesiants (ed.) (1995), *История политических и правовых учений. XX в.*, pp. 27–30.

20 See P.G. Vinogradoff (1908), *История правоведения (Курс для историков и юристов)*, p. 10.

21 See note 4 above.

Part I
Imperial Heritage

[1]

LECTURE IV.

OLD RUSSIAN FOLKMOTES.

It is a common saying among the Russian Conservatives, who have lately been dignified in France by the name of "Nationalists," that the political aspirations of the Liberals are in manifest contradiction with the genius and with the historical past of the Russian people.

Sharing these ideas, the Russian Minister of Public Instruction Count Delianov, a few years ago ordered the Professors of Public Law and of Legal History to make their teaching conform to a programme in which Tzarism, the unlimited power of the Russian emperors, was declared to be a truly national institution.

Some of the professors who refused to comply with this order were called upon to resign, others were simply dismissed from their chairs. The question I am about to discuss in this and the following lecture is, whether this theory bears the test of history. Is it true that Russian autocracy is a thoroughly national institution, the roots of which are found in the remotest period of Russian history?

Is it the fact that no folkmotes and no representative institutions ever existed in the eastern part of Europe, and that the Byzantine principle of an unlimited monarchical power, having no other source but its divine right derived from God himself and being responsible to no one but Heaven, has been always recognised by my countrymen?

I shall begin by saying that, had such been the case, the historical development of Russia would form a monstrous anomaly to the general evolution of political institutions, at least among people of Aryan blood.

It is not before an Oxford audience that I need recall this well-established fact, that in earlier times the assembly of the people, the Folkmote, shared in the exercise of sovereign power side by side with the elected head of the nation, whatever may have been his title. Professor Freeman and Sir Henry Maine have left no possibility of doubt on this point; the first, when treating of the Greeks, Romans, and Germans; the second, in relation to the ancient Celtic population of Ireland. The barrier of language, of which Sir Henry Maine so often complained to me, prevented these two eminent scholars from completing their comparative study of early political organisation by a minute investigation of that of the mediæval Slavs; but recent researches, carried on both in Russia and in Poland, Bohemia and Servia, permit us to extend to Slavonic nations the general conclusions which have been arrived at by those English scholars, who have taken as their basis a careful study of Hellenic, German, and Celtic law.

Byzantine chronicles, which contain the earliest information on the social and political condition of the Slavs, are unanimous in the assertion that the Slavonic people knew nothing of a strongly centralised autocratic power. "From the remotest period," says Procopius, a writer of the sixth century, "the Slavs were known to live in democracies; they discussed their wants in popular assemblies or folkmotes" (chapter xiv. of his "Gothica seu Bellum Gothicum"). Another authority, the Byzantine Emperor Mauriquius, when speaking of the Slavs, writes as follows: "The Slavs like liberty; they cannot bear unlimited rulers, and are not easily brought to submission" ("Strategicum," chap. xi). The same language is used also by the Emperor Leo. "The Slavs," says he, "are a free people, strongly opposed to any subjection" ("Tactica seu de re militari," ch. xviii. 99).

Passing from these general statements to those which directly concern some definite Slavonic people, we will first of all quote the Latin Chronicles of Helmold and Dithmar of Merseburg, both of the eleventh century, in order to give an idea of the political organisation of the Northern Slavs dwelling on the south-eastern shore of the Baltic. Speaking of one of their earliest chiefs named Mistiwoi, Helmold says that he, the chief, once complained to the whole assembly of the Slavs of an injury he had received (Convocatis omnibus Slavis qui ad orientem habitant, intimavit eis illatam sibi contumeliam).

The Russian scholars who have made a special study of the history of those Slavonic tribes who were so early Germanised, give us a description of the proceedings and functions of their popular assemblies. The folkmote was convened in an open place. In Stettin the market-place was furnished for this purpose with a kind of stand from which the speakers addressed the multitude. The folkmotes were not periodical assemblies, but were convened as often as there was some question of State which needed public discussion.

It is well known that the privilege enjoyed in our days by the majority was quite unknown to the primitive folkmotes. In early times the decisions of the people were unanimous. This does not mean that it was always easy to arrive at a general agreement. Opinions were certainly as divided then as they are now. What is meant is only this—that, in case of difference of opinion, the minority was forced to acquiesce in that of the majority, unless it could succeed in persuading the majority that they were in the wrong. In the Chronicle of Dithmar of Merseburg the "unanimous vote" is distinctly stated to be a peculiarity of the primitive Slavonic folkmotes:

"Unanimi consilio," says this author, "ad placitum suimet necessaria discutientes in rebus efficiendis omnes concordant." In case some one refused to acquiesce in the common decision, he was beaten with rods. If any opposition to the vote of the majority arose after the assembly had been held, the dissentient lost all his property, which was either taken from him or destroyed by fire, unless he was ready to pay a certain amount of money, varying according to his rank. The unanimous vote is very often mentioned by contemporary chroniclers, who for this purpose employ the following expressions: "Remota controversia," or "quasi unus homo."* The matters discussed at these early Slavonic folkmotes were of a great variety: the election or the dethroning of a prince, decisions about going to war or making peace, are more than once mentioned by contemporary authors as the direct work of these assemblies.

If we turn our attention to the study of the earliest period in the history of Bohemian political institutions, we shall see the development of facts similar or quasi-similar to those just mentioned. The Bohemian folkmote, the "*snem*," as it was called, is known to Latin chroniclers under the names of *conventus*, *generale colloquium*, or *generalis curia*. Persons of different estates or orders constituted the assembly. The chronicles mention, as a rule, the presence of the *majores natu*, of the *proceres* and *comites*, as also that of the higher

---

* Herbord. ii. 15–30.

clergy, *in clero meliores;* but in addition we find at these meetings, at least as far back as the end of the eleventh century, the common people, the *populus, Bohemorum omnes, Bohemicae gentis magni et parvi, nobiles et ignobiles.* In the year 1055 the people are especially mentioned as taking part in the election of a duke, and in 1068 and 1069 as engaged in the nomination of a bishop. In 1130 the Duke Sobeslav convened an assembly of 3000 persons, *nobiles et ignobiles,* to judge those who had conspired against him. At a later period, after the beginning of the twelfth century, the common people disappear from these assemblies, and the *proceres* and *majores natu* remained alone with the high clergy to discuss the affairs of the State. But in the early days with which we are at present concerned the constitution of the Bohemian *snem* was not very unlike that of an ordinary folk-mote, to which all classes of society were equally summoned. Like the folkmotes of the Baltic Slavs, the Bohemian *generalis conventus* was not a periodical assembly. Like them also, its decisions were the result of a unanimous consent, a fact which is shown by the contemporary documents, when they state that this and that matter have been settled at the assembly "*communio consilio et voluntate pari*" (Cosmus of Prague, ii. 87), or even more explicitly, "de consensu omnium," "unanimiter."

The election first of the duke and later on of the king, the nomination of the bishop, the confirmation or rejection of the laws proposed by the king and his council, the judicial decision of certain exceptionally important cases, such were the regular functions of the Bohemian folkmote. You will have no difficulty in seeing that these functions are the same as those of the popular assemblies of the Baltic Slavs.

In Poland, the folkmotes, known under the name of *congregationes generales*, sometimes also under that of *conciones*, *colloquia*, or *consilia*, were in early days composed not only of the higher orders of society, but also of the common people. The Latin Chronicle of Gallus mentions an occasion on which king Boleslaus "imprimis majores et seniores civitatis, deinde totum populum in concionem advocavit." The meaning of this quotation leaves no doubt as to the popular character of these early Polish political assemblies. In no Slavonic state was this popular character so early lost as in Poland. As early as the beginning of the thirteenth century the higher nobility and clergy, the "milites" and the knights, begin to be the only constitutive parts of the Polish "general council."

The other feature of the primitive folkmote, the unanimous vote, was much better preserved by the Polish parliament. From the earliest times down to the fall of their political independence, the Poles remained faithful to this very incongruous system. The "*liberum veto*," the right of each member to make null and void by his single opposition the decisions of the entire assembly, became through the interference of foreign States one of the best means of keeping in check the political activity of the nation. By this veto, Russian, Austrian, and Prussian intrigues more than once prevented the passing of laws and measures, which might have preserved the independence of the country. That the *liberum veto* had its roots in the most remote period of Polish history may be shown by quotations like the following. According to the chronicle of Cromer, the Polish throne had been offered to the half mythical Cracus, "*una sententia*," *i.e.*, by the unanimous decision of the people, who had, as we know, no other means of manifesting their feeling than the folkmote. The same unanimous consent is mentioned by another chronicle on the occasion of an election which took place in 1194.

The legal power of the Polish general council was identical with that of the Bohemian *snem*. It elected the chief ruler of the land and entered into written covenants with him; it discussed questions of international policy, expressed its opinion on matters of taxation, gave its sanction to the legal enactments of the king, the so-called *statuta* and *constitutiones*, and from time to time it exercised judicial authority in certain exceptionally important civil cases. In a word, it possessed the same multiplicity of powers which we have noticed when studying the powers of the Bohemian folkmote.

Hitherto we have consulted only the history of the Northern and Western Slavs. Let us now turn to that of the Southern Slavs. The democratic element is less prominent in the constitution of the ancient Servian and Croatian folkmotes. At a very early period the high nobility and clergy took possession of the various powers of the popular assembly. But this does not mean that no documentary evidence has reached us concerning the part which the lower classes of society, at least in Croatia, were anciently called upon to play in the political organisation of the country. The old Croatian chronicle explicitly states that in the time of Svonomir, the first elected Croatian chief, the "*Ban*," the national assembly known in later times under the name of "*Sobor*," was composed not only of the higher orders (viteze, barune, vlasnike), but also of the common people (puk zemlie). The same common people is mentioned by the Latin chronicle as having had its share in the election of this first Ban, who was chosen "concordi totius cleri et populi electione." This happened in the second half of the eleventh century (1076). During the following centuries the nobility, and among them the higher class of nobles represented by seven Bans, alone had a direct influence on the nomination of the Croatian king. But the memory of old days, when the people chose their rulers, was still preserved down to the end of the fifteenth century, as may be seen from the following words of a charter issued in 1490 by King Vladislas the second : "Domini, prelati et barones, cæterique primores et universi incolœ regni, ad quos scilicet jus eligendi novum regem ex vetustissimâ regni ipsius libertate et consuetudine devolutum exstiterat . . . . oculos mentis ipsorum in nos conjecerunt."

The texts already quoted establish the fact that like other Slavonic assemblies, the Sobors of Croatia were ignorant of the rights of the majority and insisted on the necessity of a unanimous decision. Expressions like "concordi electione," "omnibus collaudantibus," and the complete absence of any information concerning decisions taken by a majority of voters, leave no doubt on this point. The same texts mention several of the functions which the Sobor was called upon to exercise, and first among these was the election of the political heads of the nation, who might be simple bans or kings. Questions of peace and war were also settled by this assembly.

But the chief occupation of the Sobor was of a legislative character. From time to time the chronicles state that "many good laws have been made" by this or that assembly, and Professor Bogisic has succeeded in tracing a whole list of the different statutes resulting from their deliberations.

The existence of these national councils did not prevent the people of different localities from meeting in some kind of provincial assemblies, and from exercising in them even legislative functions. An instance of this fact is presented by the island of Vinodol, the inhabitants of which in 1288 met in a kind of local folkmote—at which certain men were chosen to make a general codification of old laws, the memory of which was still preserved. In this way was formed the celebrated statute of Vinodol, one of the chief sources of information as to the early law of the Southern Slavs.

The Servian States-General, although much less democratic than the Croatian, merit our attention on account of the great influence which they exercised on the management of public affairs. It is true that the Servian Sobor is rather a council of the higher orders, a sort of Anglo-Saxon Witenagemote, than a folkmote or popular assembly. The third estate was not admitted to its meetings either as a body or by representation, and one of the paragraphs of the celebrated code of Stefan Douschan (fourteenth century) even strictly forbids the peasants to meet in political assemblies. But the lower nobility, who afterwards played such a prominent part in the destinies of the Polish nation, regularly sat in those meetings side by side with the king, his council, the superior officers of State, the patriarch, the ecclesiastical synod, and the members of the higher nobility. These orders taken together exercised pretty nearly all the functions of sovereignty. They made legal enactments, such as the code just mentioned, and they were the authors of the different amendments introduced into it in the course of time. They very often elected the king, and sometimes dethroned him. The archbishop and the provincial governors were also chosen by the Sobor, which likewise disposed of the public lands, and discussed the most important matters of civil and ecclesiastical government.

This rapid and rather superficial sketch of the early political institutions of the Slavs, may at least serve to show how considerable was the influence which the higher orders of society, and very often the common people, exercised in the management of the Slavonic State. My necessarily dry exposition of ancient chronicles and charters, cannot fail to recall the well-known passage in the "Germania" of Tacitus: "De minoribus principes consultant, de majoribus omnes." Like the old Germanic folkmote the Slavonic was a sort of supreme council, convened on certain exceptionally important occasions. During an interregnum all authority passed into its hands, and it was accordingly empowered to choose the future ruler of the land, and to declare under what conditions he was to be admitted to the exercise of the sovereign power. In the ordinary course of public affairs, the folkmote discussed important matters of civil, and in some countries even of ecclesiastical government. It pronounced on questions of war and peace, controlled the exercise of the legislative authority, and was sometimes even directly engaged in the making of new, and the codifying of ancient laws. Although its authority was less prominent in executive and judicial matters, yet it very often exercised the supreme right of dethroning a king, and of judging persons accused of high treason.

When we call to mind these facts, the idea of an early Russian autocracy, admitting of no control on the part of the governed, will certainly appear to us to be in direct contradiction not only of the general evolution of political institutions, but also of its usual form among Slavonic nations. We must refuse to accept an anomaly unless it is established on the authority of well-authenticated historical facts. But no such facts can be produced. The Russian chronicles, in which, from the want of other sources of information, we are obliged to seek for the chief elements of a general theory of ancient Russian political institutions, show us a state of things, which has nothing in common with absolute monarchy. On the first pages of the chronicle attributed to the monk Nestor, the Eastern Slavs are spoken of as possessing a sort of "gens" organisation; "each one living with his kindred, and these kindreds occupying distinct territorial districts." (Kojdo s svoim rodom i na svoich mestech, kojdo vladeiusche rodom svoim.) In the sentence just quoted, the chronicler describes the social organisation of the most enlightened tribe of the Eastern Slavs, the Polians, and immediately afterwards he speaks of three brothers and their sister, who exercised in common some sort of political authority over the tribe. According to this chronicler, the direct descendants of these brothers ruled over the Polians. It is also recorded of the Drevlians, another Slavonic tribe, that it had its own prince,

Mal, but the Polians and the Drevlians seem to have been the only tribes living under monarchical rule. The rest of the Slavonic tribes established in Russia are represented to us as having no princes, but as living divided into clans or "gentes," which were often at war one with another (vsta rod na rod), a state of things which at length induced them "to seek a foreign prince (kniaz) to command and judge them according to justice." The establishment of monarchical power thus appears to have been the direct result of a free decision on the part of the people. The chronicle speaks of the tribes, which sent for a foreign prince, as having previously assembled together (snidoschasia vkoupe, sobravschesia). This means that the decision to call in a foreign prince was the work of a folkmote. Such is the first mention we possess of a Russian popular assembly. The facts I have recorded happened in the second half of the ninth century, in the year 862. Alluding to them, the chronicle of Sousdal, under the year 1176, makes the following general statement. "The inhabitants of Novgorod, of Smolensk, of Kiev, and of Poloczk, and of all the principalities (volosti) of Russia, were from the beginning, and are still, in the habit of meeting at folkmotes as at a sort of council." The term employed to designate the folkmote is that of *veche* from the verb *veschat*, to announce, to declare. According to the sentence just quoted, the veche may be traced from the oldest period of our national existence. This is directly confirmed, in relation to the Polians, by the following statement: "In the years next following," says Nestor, speaking of the end of the ninth century, "they thought in common (sdoumavsche) and decided to pay to the Chasars a certain tax, the amount of which was one sword from every hearth." The Drevlians are also spoken of by the chronicle as having on one occasion "thought in common with their prince Mal," and decided to slaughter the son of Rurik, Igor. Now, this "thinking in common" of a whole tribe with its political head, can only mean that the prince consulted the folkmote, and with its help arrived at a definite decision.

A peculiar feature of the oldest Russian folkmotes, a feature which totally disappears by the end of the tenth century, is, that they are the assembly of a whole tribe, sometimes even of several tribes, and not of the inhabitants of one single urban district. The Chronicle of Nestor speaks of the Polians, the Drevlians, the Krivichs, the Sever, and such like people, as of persons coming together, consulting one another and "accomplishing certain acts in common." I have already said that these were separate tribes, each one subdivided into kindreds or "gentes" (rodi). Such being the case, the veche of the early days of Russian historical development, was a kind of tribal assembly very like those which Cæsar and Tacitus found among the ancient Germans.

With the beginning of the eleventh century, the Russian folkmote or veche acquired a new character, when the chief cities of Russia, the political centres of more or less independent states, obtained their separate assemblies. The chronicles mention on different occasions the veches of Belgorod, of Vladimir in Volhynia, of Berestie, of Riazan, Mourom, and Pronsk, of Smolensk, Poloczk and Koursk, of Rostov, Sousdal, Pereiaslavl and Vladimir on the Kliasm, besides those of Kiev, Novgorod, Pscov, and Viatka.

If we inquire into the internal constitution and functions of the veche, we shall have no difficulty in ascertaining that in both these points the Russian folkmotes did not essentially differ from those of other Slavonic nations.

The chronicles, when they speak of those summoned to these assemblies, briefly note the presence of all the citizens of a definite urban division. Expressions such as the following are also more than once met with in the course of the narrative : "the men of our land," "the whole land of Galich," and so on. Hence, it is evident that we have to deal with a thoroughly democratic assembly. But it does not follow that all the inhabitants of the city were summoned. The veche was not so much an assembly of the whole people as that of the heads of families, or rather of the natural chiefs of Slavonic house communities known to the earliest code of Russia, the Pravda of Jaroslav, under the name of "verv."

On several occasions the unknown authors of

Russian chronicles seem to imply that the men assembled at the folkmote made certain engagements, not only on their own behalf but also on that of their children. For instance, "the men of Kiev, in folkmote assembled," declare in 1147, that they will fight against the House of Oleg, one of the branches of the dynasty of Rurik, not by themselves alone, but also by their children. This declaration clearly shows that children did not appear at a Russian folkmote, but that their absence was solely caused by their personal dependence on the head of the undivided family. We may, therefore, infer that all those who were not free to dispose of themselves were excluded from the veche; and such was the case as regarded certain members of undivided households and those who had forfeited their liberty through war or debt. In a society based, like the old Russian, on the principle of blood relationship, undivided households must have been numerous, and the fact that the heads of these households were alone summoned naturally diminished the number of persons composing the veche. It may, therefore, be easily understood how a large square such as those on which the princely palaces of Novgorod or of Kiev were built, was quite able to contain an entire assembly, notwithstanding the fact that the citizens were not the only persons admitted to the meetings of the veche, for the suburbs and even the neighbouring townships had the right to have an equal share with them on the management of public affairs.

The chronicles very often mention the fact of the "black people," "the smerds," and the so-called "bad peasants" (terms designating the agricultural population of the country) being present at the veche. The urban district was as a rule very large, the lands owned by the citizens in some cases extending to hundreds and even thousands of miles outside the city wall. In order to preserve these widely scattered possessions, the city often built fortresses, which in case of war offered a refuge to the inhabitants of the surrounding country. In time of peace these fortified places answered another purpose; markets were regularly held in them and hence in course of time artisans and merchants were induced to choose them for their settled abode. The population increased day by day, the fortress became surrounded by suburbs, and a new city appeared where originally there had been nothing but a wooden fence with a moat or ditch around it. The inhabitants of this new city had generally the right to appear at the veches of the metropolis, but they usually preferred meeting at assemblies of their own. The roads being bad and not always safe, they did not see what was to be gained by a long journey, but chose rather to stay at home and hold their own folkmotes from time to time.

The chronicles of Sousdal seem to imply that the decisions of the local folkmotes did not, as a rule, differ from those of the metropolis. "What has been established by the oldest city, is maintained by its boroughs." Such are the words in which the chronicle expresses the mutual relations of the metropolis and the daughter towns. The real meaning of the sentence is not at all that of dutiful subjection on the part of the new town towards the mother city. The writer merely wishes to suggest the idea of a good understanding between the metropolis and the boroughs it has built. This good understanding was not always maintained, and on more than one occasion the borough came to a decision the reverse of that of the chief city. A similar disagreement occurred more than once between different quarters (konzi) of the same city. Such was often the case at Novgorod, divided as it was into five different administrative districts or wards, which more than once held their own separate folkmotes and opposed the decisions of the general assembly. Such a misunderstanding sometimes ended in open war, the minority refusing to submit to the decision of the majority.

This fact alone shows that the Russian veches admitted no other mode of settling public affairs than that of unanimous decision. It has been already shown that this mode was general amongst Slavonic peoples. A few quotations will prove its existence among the Eastern Slavs. Whenever the chronicler has occasion to speak of one of their decisions he employs such expressions as the following: "It was established by all the oldest and all the youngest men of the assembly that," &c.; "all were unanimous in the desire"; "all thought and spoke as one man," &c.

If unanimity could not be arrived at, the minority was forced to acquiesce in the decision of the greater number, unless it could persuade the members of the majority that they were wrong in their opinion. In both cases the veches passed whole days in debating the same subjects, the only interruptions being free fights in the street. At Novgorod. these fights took place on the bridge across the Volchov, and the stronger party sometimes threw their adversaries into the river beneath. A considerable minority very often succeeded in suspending the measure already voted by the veche, but if the minority was small, its will had soon to yield to open force.

The competence of the Russian folkmote was as wide as that of similar political assemblies among the Western and Southern Slavs. More than once it assumed the right of choosing the chief ruler of the land; but it was not an unrestricted right which they enjoyed, the choice being confined to members of the family of Rurik; for the Russians considered that outside Rurik's dynasty, no one had a right to exercise sovereign power. The folkmote was merely empowered to give its preference to some distinct line of the house of Rurik, for instance to that directly descending from Vladimir Monomach, from which the veche of Kiev elected its rulers. It was also free to pronounce in favour of a younger member of Rurik's family, notwithstanding the candidature of an older one. The choice made was often in open contradiction of the legal order of succession maintained by the dynasty of Rurik. This order was very similar to the Irish law of tanistry, according to which the Irish crown devolved upon the oldest representative of the reigning family. In practice it generally meant the succession of the deceased's next brother, not that of his eldest son. The strict application of this law of tanistry would have necessitated a constant change in the person of the ruler, not only in Kiev, which was for a long time considered the most important principality of Russia, and which was, therefore, the appanage of the chief representative of the dynasty, but also in the other Russian dukedoms, which were subdivided into a great number of secondary principalities. Open force had very often to decide which of the two systems, that of free election or that of legal succession, was to prevail.

Whatever was the issue of such a struggle the new ruler was only admitted to the exercise of sovereign power after having subscribed a sort of contract by which he took upon himself the obligation of preserving the rights of those over whom he was called to rule. These very curious documents, known under the name of "riad," have unfortunately been preserved in only one of the Russian principalities, that of Novgorod,—a fact which has induced many scholars to believe that this right of covenanting with the duke was limited to this Northern principality. Professor Sergievitch, the well-known Professor of Legal History in the University of St. Petersburg, was the first to prove by a considerable number of quotations from Russian chronicles, that covenants like that of Novgorod were known all over Russia. More than once mention is made of a prince securing the throne by a compromise with the men of Kiev (s liudmi Kieva outverdisia). These compacts or covenants between prince and people, so far as they are known to us by the few examples among the archives of Novgorod, were a kind of constitutional charter securing to the people the free exercise of their political rights, such as the right of the folkmote to discuss public affairs and to elect the ruler of the State. This latter right had been already guaranteed to Novgorod by a general assembly of Russian dukes held in 1196. We read in the text of the decisions come to by this princely congress; "All the dukes recognise the liberty of Novgorod to choose her ruler wherever she likes." Other constitutional restraints on princely power are—no declaration of war without "Novgorod's word"; no foreigner to be nominated to the post of provincial governor (volostel); no public official to be dismissed without legal cause, acknowledged to be such by the decision of a Court of law. Thus the principle according to which most English officials hold office "during good behaviour" was already recognised in Russian principalities in the middle of the thirteenth century. This efficient mode of securing the independence and dignity of public officials has been completely abolished in later days under the Tzars and Emperors, although once more in 1863 its necessity was admitted by the legal enactments of Alexander II. Unfortunately no attention is any longer paid to the promises given to this effect by the codes of civil and criminal procedure, and many a judge has been removed in recent times by a simple order of the Minister of Public Justice.

Returning to the constitutional guarantees secured by the new ruler to his future subjects, I must point out that those already mentioned seem to have been common to all the different principalities of Russia. The same cannot be said of the following two: first, the obligation to judge nobody without the assistance of a special officer, called the posadnik, and secondly, the right of the folkmote to choose this official, a right which first appeared in the beginning of the twelfth century. These exceptions once made, we have the right to say that the compacts entered into by the people of Novgorod with their future ruler, give us a fair idea of the relative strength of the prince and of the popular assembly all over Russia.

Our review of the agreement signed by the prince on his accession to the throne has already revealed to us some of the functions of the veche. Questions of war and peace were regularly decided by it. No war could be begun but with the consent of the people, because, in the absence of a regular army, the prince could levy no other force but that of the militia. Treaties of peace and alliance were also signed in the name of the prince and people, as may be seen from the following words used in the treaty of Igor with the Byzantine empire in 945; "This treaty has been concluded by the Grand Duke of Russia, by all the dukes whatsoever and by all the people of the Russian lands." Sometimes, it is true, the duke decided on going to war against the wish of his people, but in such a case he had to rely exclusively on his own military followers, his so-called "drougina," an institution very like the old German "comitatus" (Geleit). As long as the system of land donations remained unknown, and the duke had no other property to distribute among his followers but that taken in time of war, the drougina or comitatus was far from being numerous. Hence the duke was forced to ask the veche for assistance whenever he thought himself obliged to go to war. The veche either agreed to his demand and ordered the levy of military forces, or refused all help; in the latter case the duke had no other alternative but to abandon his project entirely, or to resign his throne. The control in matters of peace and war was maintained by the people so long as the duke had no other troops than the militia. But a kind of regular army had been created by the end of the thirteenth century, owing to the custom of rewarding military service by grants of land. The so-called "pomestnaia" system, which was similar to the Carlovingian system of "benefices," produced in Russia effects similar to those produced in France. The popular militia was superseded by a sort of feudal army, paid not in money but in land. In case of war the duke was not so much interested in having the acquiescence of the people as that of the "men of service," *slougilii liudi*, who constituted his military force, and corresponded somewhat to the knights in feudal England. This change, as we shall hereafter see, had a great influence on the future destiny of the Russian folkmote.

Another function of the folkmote, which appears to be peculiar to the Northern principalities, and especially to those of Novgorod and Pscov, is that of legislation. That the legislative functions of the veche were unknown in the Southern principalities of Russia may be seen from the fact, that no mention is made of them in the most ancient code of the country. The Pravda of Jaroslav in its different versions shows no trace of the interference of the people in matters of legislation; it is the exclusive work of the duke and his councillors. The few amendments introduced into this legal code during the first part of the twelfth century have also no other source but the express desire of the dukes and the decisions of their Doumas or Councils.

The exercise of legislative power by the veches of Novgorod and of Pscov, at least during the fourteenth and fifteenth centuries, is illustrated by two judicial charters, those of 1397 and of 1471, which, as is evident from their contents, were drawn up by the popular assembly. The charter of Pscov plainly states in one of its later versions (that of 1467), that whenever the posadnik, the supreme judge elected by the people, has to decide a case to which no existing law applies, he must consult the assembly of the people. The same veche had the right to annul every article of the judicial charter which no longer met with its approval. Mention of this right is made in the charter itself.

As to judicial powers, they remained unknown to the veche, at least in the Western and Southern principalities of Russia, which knew no other judges than the duke and the officers whom he appointed. I do not allude to those arbitrators to whom private persons frequently had recourse to settle their differences.

But in Novgorod, the fact of the election of the chief judge, the posadnik, by a popular vote, shows that the people were not indifferent to the exercise of judicial power. Appointed as he was by the folkmote, the posadnik could be judged by no other tribunal than the folkmote itself. Cases of high treason were also referred to the popular assembly just as they were in Poland and Bohemia.

What has been stated establishes beyond a doubt the great extent of the rights and privileges belonging to the folkmote in the Northern principalities of Russia. The same cannot be said of some Western principalities, such as those of Volhynia and Galicia.

The example of Poland, where the aristocracy was very powerful, induced the boyars of those two countries to make more than one attempt to concentrate in their own hands the chief rights of sovereignty. The large estates which they possessed and the considerable revenues, which the rich black soil of the country yearly secured to them, greatly favoured their oligarchical aspirations. In 1210, they seem to have attained their ends. The dynasty of Rurik had ceased to rule over the country, and a boyar, a member of the local aristocracy, had been raised to the throne. But his rule did not last long. His contemporaries, the other rulers, looked upon his elevation as illegal, and the King of Poland was the first to declare that a boyar had no right to occupy a throne. To oppose the oligarchy of the boyars Duke Daniel, in 1230, convened the popular assembly, the veche, and with the help afforded him by people, fought the army of the boyars and reduced them to obedience. This is, however, the only case in which the veche seems to have played any part in the political history of the country. The power of the nobles prevented any further development in that direction, and when the principality passed into the hands of the King of Poland, it was already under the yoke of the aristocracy.

Nevertheless, even under Polish rule, the memory of the old folkmotes was preserved by the country. Documents of the fifteenth and sixteenth centuries sometimes mention the existence of the veche as of a local assembly with very considerable executive and judicial rights.

Of all the principalities of Russia those of the North-East seem from the most remote times to have been unfavourable to the growth of popular assemblies. In those of Sousdal and of Riasan, the dukes early freed themselves from the necessity of election by the people by establishing primogeniture as the law of succession to the crown. The way in which the eldest son was admitted to succeed to the throne was by associating him, during his father's lifetime, in the exercise of sovereign powers. Vsevolod III. was the first prince who benefited by such a course. He secured the throne to his descendants and thus annulled one of the most important rights of the folkmote, that of choosing the ruler of the land. It is not to be wondered at, therefore, that from the middle of the thirteenth century no mention is made of the popular assemblies of Sousdal.

Up to this point we have tried to show that during the Middle Ages Russia was a loose federation of principalities, in which the people were wont to exercise, on a larger or smaller scale, legislative, executive, judicial, and even political power. By political power I mean the right of electing and dismissing the ruler, of declaring war and making peace. The people exercised their right side by side with the prince, the "knias," who gradually increased his own power to the prejudice of the power of the folkmote or veche. At the end of the fifteenth century Novgorod and Pscov alone maintained the primitive relations between the prince and the popular assembly, for they still kept the power of electing and dismissing the chief magistrate of the state, as well as the highest officials, the posadnik, and the "head of thousands." In the south-western part of Russia the popular assembly became, during the fifteenth and sixteenth centuries, a local administrative, financial, and judicial body, but it lost all political power. In the northern principalities, and especially in Vladimir and Moscow, the folkmotes totally ceased to exist. The growth first of Vladimir and then of Moscow was followed by the complete annihilation of the political rights of the people, and this seems to have been recognised by the writers of the day. Describing the proceedings by which the republic of Novgorod was subjected by the Tzar, Ivan the Third, the chronicle, known under the name of the Patriarch Nikon, says: "In the year 1478 the Tzar declared to the republic "that he wanted Novgorod to be in the exercise of the same power as that which he possessed at Moscow." The inhabitants agreed to comply with his wishes on certain terms, whereby his autocracy would be limited. The Tzar immediately sent the following reply: "I told you that I wanted in Novgorod a state similar to that of Moscow; and instead of that I hear you teaching me how I ought to organise my state in a way different from what it is at present." On hearing this, the citizens sent another embassy to ask what the Tzar meant by saying that he wanted in Novgorod a government like that of Moscow. He answered: "No popular assembly, veche; no elected magistrate; and the whole state in the power of the Tzar."* This answer left no doubt as to his autocratic intentions and their accomplishment in the Moscovite state.

Let us now inquire into the causes which produced this increase of monarchical power. The first seems to have been the great change which had been brought about in the relations between the prince and the popular assembly by the subjection of the prince to the power of the Khans. It is well known that the Tartars, after having established the centre of their European empire on the shores of the Volga, not far from where it joins the Caspian Sea, in the neighbourhood of the modern city of Astrachan, reduced the different principalities of Russia to the condition of vassal states. Leaving the government in the hands of the dynasty of Rurik they forced the Russian princes to receive investiture at the hands of their khans. In such a state of things the prince had no longer any need to trouble himself about his acceptation by the popular assembly of the principality that he intended to govern. In order to secure the throne to himself and his heirs, all that he had to do was to undertake a journey to the southern parts of the Volga and make his appearance at the court of his suzerain—the Khan. Here he had to

* "Complete Collection of Russian Chronicles," vi. 213.

lay out large sums of money in presents and bribes, until at last the Khan was induced to grant a charter, "jarlik," acknowledging the right of the claimant to occupy the throne of his ancestors. From the beginning of the fourteenth century the Moscovite princes had no longer to undertake the journey in person, as the khans had consented to forward the charter of confirmation direct to Moscow on condition that they first received large sums of money from the prince who claimed the throne. The succession was settled at each vacancy by an agreement between the suzerain and the vassal, and the popular assembly had no opportunity of interfering.

Foreign events, especially the rise of the Florentine Union and the capture of Constantinople by the Turks, also largely contributed to the increase of the Moscovite autocracy.

During the period which began with the acceptance of the tenets of the Greek Church by the Russian duke, Vladimir, at the end of the eleventh century, and which ended with the decision of the Byzantine Emperor to subscribe the act of union with the Roman Church, the Russian State as well as the Russian Church remained to a certain extent dependent on the Greek Patriarch and Emperor at Constantinople. In ecclesiastical matters this dependence was manifested in the direct nomination of the Russian Metropolitan by the Byzantine Patriarch, very often not without interference on the part of the Emperor. In secular matters it was rather theoretical than practical. The Russian clergy more than once advised the Grand Duke of Moscovy to recognise the "Tzar of the Greeks" as his lord paramount, and each time they repeated the popular theory that the Byzantine Emperor was the chief of the whole Christian world and therefore the sovereign lord of all Christian kings and potentates. This theory had been first brought forward by Byzantine writers, who actually declared that Constantine the Great had conferred the title of Tabularius on the ruler of Russia as a recompense for his allegiance to the Greek Empire. Up to the end of the fourteenth century the title of "Tzar" was exclusively applied in Russia to the Emperor of Constantinople, and no Russian prince was allowed to dignify himself with it. The Russian clergy, in offering public prayer for the health of the Emperor at Constantinople, spoke of him as of "the Emperor of the Romans and Ruler of the Universe."*

The attitude of Basileus III., Grand Duke of Russia, during the time of the Florentine Union, his bold opposition to the Patriarch Photius and to any compromise with the Romish Church, led the Russian clergy to look upon him and his heirs as the champions of orthodoxy in religion. While the Duke of Moscovy was considered the sole protector of the Greek Church, the Emperor at Constantinople had become, in the eyes of the Russians, a schismatic.

* Compare Diakonov, "The Supreme Power of the Moscovite Tzars," Petersburg, 1889.

It was in order to free Moscovy from all dependence on a schismatic Emperor that the account of the conversion of the Eastern Slavs to Christianity was altered. The apostle St. Andrew, who, according to Armenian and Georgian traditions had been the first to preach the Gospel in the Caucasus, was officially declared to have been the St. John the Baptist of the Russians ; Constantinople, being thus deprived of the honour of being the birthplace of Russian Christianity, was accordingly dispossessed of any right to exercise ecclesiastical supremacy over the Russian Church.

The fall of Constantinople, which closely followed the Florentine Union, settled the question of the ecclesiastical autonomy of Russia, and contributed at the same time to strengthen the power of the Moscovite Duke. The Greek Church had lost her secular head in the person of the last Emperor of Constantinople, and the Slavonic principalities of the Balkan Peninsula, as well as the subjugated Greeks, naturally turned their eyes towards the most powerful of the Orthodox rulers. This was the Grand Duke of Moscovy, whose firm allegiance to the ancient creed, and uncompromising attitude towards the Florentine Union, contrasted favourably with the attitude of the last Emperors towards the Popes of Rome. People were led to acknowledge that the fall of Constantinople was a well-deserved punishment on a schismatic ruler, and they were also induced to believe that the conquest of that city by the Turks ought to be the occasion for the transfer of civil supremacy over the Greek Church from Constantinople to Moscovy, from the Emperor to the Grand Duke.

These ideas grew in strength when the last Emperor's sister, Sophia Palæologus, became by marriage the wife and mother of Moscovite princes. A report was spread that the Imperial title had been transferred to the Grand Duke Ivan by no less a person than his wife's brother, the legal heir of the Byzantine Empire. The Grand Duke was anointed with great solemnity, and received the title of "Tzar," a title which, as we have seen, had hitherto been exclusively given to the Greek Emperors. An offer which the German Emperor made through his special envoy, Herbertstein, to grant the title of "king" to the Moscovite Grand Duke on condition of his recognising his dependence upon the Holy Roman Empire, was solemnly rejected; and in order to confirm the new theory of the complete autonomy of the Russian tzardom, a genealogy was invented, showing the direct descent of the house of Rurik from Augustus and his supposed brother Pruss, the mythical founder of Prussia. One fact, however, stood in the way of a universal recognition of these new pretensions to complete autonomy; that was the continued dependence of the Moscovite rulers on the khans of the Tartars. But this was put an end to by Ivan III., who was consequently the first to adorn himself with the title of "Autocrat" (Samoderjez), which to this day continues to be the title of the Russian Tzars.

As Greek monks, and among them the well-known Maxime, began to settle in Russia, Byzantine ideas about the derivation of monarchical power from God, which were already entertained by some of our monkish writers, were rapidly spread among the people. It is not without good reason that the celebrated antagonist of Ivan the Terrible, Prince Kourbsky, accuses the monks of having been the chief source of the servile theory, according to which "the Tzar, in order to preserve his independence, ought to have no counsellors more intelligent than himself." This theory was accepted with avidity by such tyrants as Ivan the Cruel, who refers to it more than once in his correspondence with the Polish king, Stephen Bathory. The fact that this prince was surrounded by a sort of parliament, the Polish Seim, was declared by the Russian Tzar to be a manifest proof of his political inferiority. "Autocracy (samoderjavsto)," according to Ivan's idea, "was impossible with an elective council; the autocrat must do everything by himself; he has to give orders to his subjects, and these last must obey like serfs, and that according to the command of God."

These ideas, which had been expressed centuries before by monkish writers, who had found them set forth in Byzantine treatises, were far from being those of the generality of Russian statesmen and thinkers. When Prince Kourbsky advised the tyrant Ivan to seek good and useful counsel, not only among the members of his *douma*, a sort of *curia regis*—but also among the representatives of the people—*vsenarodnich chelovok*—he gave utterance to an old political desire. Another contemporary writer, the unknown author of *The Sermon of the Saints of Walaam*, gives way to the same feeling in the following terms: "The clergy ought to advise the Tzar to keep a constant general council, composed of persons coming from all the cities and districts of his dominions. Such a council must be kept, and their advice taken day by day on every question which may occur."

Two different institutions were meant by those who advised the Czar to rule by the advice of his councillors. One was as old as the monarchy itself, and belonged to those old customs, which, according to contemporary writers, had been scrupulously maintained by former potentates. I refer to the Council of the Boyars—the Douma. The other institution, the history of which will form the principal subject of our next lecture, was, on the contrary, quite recent—the States-General of Moscovy, the Zemskii Sobor.

I will conclude what I have to say on the political organisation of Russia during that intermediate period which lasted from the fall of the ancient folkmotes to the convocation of the States-General by a description of the first-named council, the Douma.*

* This subject has been very ably discussed by Professor Kluchevsky.

The study of the internal constitution of the Douma is indispensable for the comprehension of the part which the higher nobility were called upon to play in the management of the Moscovite State. It will show that the power of the Moscovite princes, absolute as it was, was yet to a certain extent limited by the power of the nobility. Up to the middle of the sixteenth century the Boyars were the only persons admitted to the exercise of executive, military, and judicial authority. Under the name of voevods we find them at the head of provinces, commanding their military forces and managing their administrative interests. As members of the Douma, they had to advise the Tzar on all kinds of political, executive, military, and financial questions. No law was promulgated until after previous deliberation on it by the Douma. The same Douma furnished the chief rulers of the State during the minority of the Tzar, and it was in this way that the power of the Boyars made itself felt among the lower classes of the population, who soon came to look upon them as the chief cause of their misery.

The composition of the Moscovite council was at the beginning very like that which we find in France under the early Capetian kings. The *curia regis* was chiefly formed from among the high court officials, such as the majordome, the marshal, the constable, the chancellor or cancellarius, the camerer or camerarius, etc. The same may be said of the Moscovite Douma of the fourteenth century, as well as of the privy council of each and every of the principalities into which mediæval Russia was divided anterior to the centralising growth of the Moscovite power. The business transacted at the court of a Russian prince being distributed among different departments, the heads of these departments were summoned to sit in the council and received the name of boyars. Money being scarce, the boyars were paid for their services by the donation of crown lands, and this mode of payment being known under the name of "pout," the surname of the boyars was "poutevii boyari." Most of the boyars summoned to sit in the Douma were exempted from military service, and especially from the duty of opposing the enemy at the head of their own retainers, not so much in the open country as in their own castles. Hence the origin of another surname "wedennii boiari" which distinguished the most powerful members of the Russian mediæval nobility. If we inquire into the origin of those admitted to the princely council, we shall see that they belonged to the same class as that which furnished officers to the army and the chiefs of the central and provincial administration. This class is precisely that known to the Anglo-Saxons as Thanes, and to the Merovingian kings under the title of Antrustions. The peculiarity of mediæval Russia consisted in this, that, being divided into a great number of principalities, it left to the knightly class the liberty of freely choosing the prince whom they would like to follow. The Russian knightly class, corresponding to the "ministeriels" of feudal Germany, the so-called "slougili liudi" or "men of service," were authorised by custom to remain in the service of any prince as long as they pleased, and to change from one prince to another according to their own pleasure. Before attaching himself to any prince the "man of service" signed a sort of contract with the political head of the country in which he intended to settle. On taking service, a charter was delivered to the knight in which his duties and rights were precisely stated, and the prince had no right to infringe these conditions. In case of bad treatment, the knight found no difficulty in leaving the prince whom he was serving and in entering into similar relations with some other of the numerous petty potentates, who ruled over mediæval Russia. This right of freely passing from the service of one prince to that of another was clearly recognised by the following sentence in a treaty signed by the prince of Tver with the Grand Duke of Lithuania, Kasimir, as late as the middle of the fifteenth century, 1449; "Our boyars and men of service may freely withdraw from one of us to the other." This document is probably the last recognition of the liberty of removal once enjoyed by the knightly class.

The increasing power of the Grand Duke of Moscovy could not tolerate this survival of federal autonomy. This prince did not object to the liberty of removal as long as it served his own purposes by increasing the number of persons seeking service in the Moscovite army and Moscovite civil service, but as soon as the tyranny of some of the Grand Dukes caused their own knights to withdraw to Poland and Lithuania, severe measures were taken to put a stop to this movement of emigration. The Grand Duke began to confiscate the grants of land ("*pomestie*") of the departing knights, and every time he could lay hands on one of these seceders he was sure to throw him into prison, very often together with his wife and children. The clergy, always on the side of the secular power, more than once likened the behaviour of a seceding knight to the conduct of Judas, and declared it to be not only treason against the State but also a sin in the eyes of God.

Keeping in mind the facts just mentioned, we shall have no difficulty in explaining the concourse of knights and men of the sword in the grand duchy of Moscovy. The territorial extension of the duchy had necessitated the abolition of a great number of small principalities, and persons formerly belonging to the ruling dynasties and united by ties of blood to the Tzar, were anxious to enter his service. In this manner the knightly class began to number in its ranks a whole group of princely families who were the descendants of those potentates whose dominions had been conquered and annexed by Moscow. Before long the number of persons desirous of taking service under the Grand Duke totally excluded the possibility of personal and separate conventions, such as those which settled the mutual rights and duties of prince and knight in the other principalities of Russia. These personal agreements were superseded by a general enactment, which declared that the man of service occupied a higher or lower rank in the political hierarchy according, first, to the dignity of the family to which he belonged, and, secondly, to the number of years his family had been engaged in the Moscovite service.

It was generally acknowledged that a princely family—that is, a family that had once belonged to the number of ruling dynasties, ought to have precedence over all others among untitled nobles. Whoever could show among his ancestors persons in a high official post had the right to refuse any inferior situation, especially in those cases in which a person of a comparatively new family was to be set over him as his superior. This order of precedence was more than once set aside in consequence of the low condition to which this or that wealthy family had been reduced by the loss of its estates. A Russian noble in a miserable state of poverty was as little entitled to occupy a high official position, as was a penniless English duke, or earl, to take his seat in the House of Lords in the fifteenth century, in the reign of Edward IV.

The rules of precedence, constituting what our ancestors of the fifteenth and sixteenth centuries called "*mestnichestvo*," were scrupulously observed both in the army and in the civil service. They also found expression in the constitution of the Council or Douma. The titled nobility, the princely families, as a rule, occupied the highest rank in the hierarchy of the councillors, the rank of "*doumn iboyars*," or boyars of the Council.

A certain number of the old Moscovite nobility were allowed to retain their original rank, but the rest of the nobles were by degrees lowered to that of persons whose only distinction was to be "the children of ancient boyars." The documents of the time speak of them in precisely these terms, calling them "*boiarski dieti*," children of the boyars.

The second rank among the members of the Douma was occupied by those known under the name of "*ocolnichii*," or persons living immediately about the Duke. This rank in the Douma belonged, as a rule, to members of the old Moscovite nobility, as well as to some of the smaller princely families. The Duke had the right to confer on his "*ocolnichy*" the higher title of boyar as a recompense for his services. The rest of the knightly class were either entirely unconnected with the Council or were simply summoned to be present at some of its sittings. They were known under the general name of "noblemen belonging to the Douma," "*dumnii dvoriani*," and formed the third rank of Councillors.

The fourth or lowest rank in the Council was composed of those members of the knightly class who condescended to hold second-rate posts in the different executive bodies of the duchy, such as the Foreign Office ("*Posolsky prikaz*"). or the board presiding over temporary or life grants of land (*Pomestni prikaz*). These second-rate bureaucrats, known under the name of secretaries, *diaki*, were regularly admitted to the sittings of the Council, where they formed the lowest but by no means the least influential order.

From what has been said it will be seen that autocratic power in Russia had to deal with certain counterpoises and moderating influences in the political constitution of the country even after the fall of the ancient folkmotes. These checks and restraints had their roots in the old political rights exercised by the chiefs of the almost independent principalities which constituted the unorganised federacy of Russian states. Whilst submitting to the power of the Moscovite prince, these once independent chiefs insisted on the recognition of their privilege to be next after the Tzar, the principal ruler of the country. The so-called *mestnichestvo* was, therefore, a sort of unwritten constitution, recognising in each of the members of the higher nobility his distinct right to a place in the machinery of the State. The lower classes alone had no part in the conduct of public affairs. An end was put to this anomalous situation by the convocation of the States-General. The origin of these States-General, or Sobors, and their further development, will form the subject of our next lecture.

[2]

LECTURE II

RUSSIA

THE Russian law[1] possesses some interesting peculiarities for the universal history of law. It is the only Slavonic law which shows a continual development

[1] I shall draw the attention of the reader only to the books which include the whole Russian history of law and to the writers, important for some greater parts of it. Two professors, one of Petersburg, Sergejevitch, another of Kiev, Vladimirski-Budanov, have treated the whole history. Both of them acknowledge the existence of the natural laws which rule social life, but their points of view are different. Prof. Sergejevitch in *Lekcii i izsledovanija po istorii russkago prava* ('Lectures and Studies on the History of the Russian Law), 1889, 1890, seems to take for granted that the social life not only happens by laws, but also that the course of social events is more or less the same everywhere, viz. even that the history of the Russian law repeats partially the history of law in the West; therefore Sergejevitch likes to elucidate the Russian events by a comparison with the German, French, or English legal history. Prof. Vladimirski-Budanov in *Obzor istorii russkago prava* ('A Sketch of the History of the Russian Law'), 1900, on the contrary, supposes the existence of legal ideas proper to the Slavs, and therefore expounds the Russian events by a comparison with the history of the other Slavonic nations. This difference of views proceeds, I think, from a different extent of knowledge. Mr. Sergejevitch is a profound connoisseur of the history of the Western law; on the contrary, Mr. Vladimirski-Budanov has made independent studies in the history of the Polish and Croatian law. And so the two writers often complete one another: the national

during more than a thousand years, and two states were formed on the territory of the Russian tribes principally from the Russian ethnographical elements in the fourteenth century, Moscow and Lithuania. Whilst the first grew under Byzantine influence, the second lived under the dominion of Western ideas. The law of Moscow evolved itself little by little from the old

traits of the Russian law are explained by other Slavonic laws in Budanov's work, and features common to the other laws, and proceeding from universal human nature, are made clear by Sergejevitch. Besides, Prof. Vladimirski-Budanov has published *A Chrestomathy of the History of the Russian Law*, where the most important monuments are printed according to all scientific needs (three volumes, including the juridical monuments from the tenth century to the year 1649, many editions). Prof. Samokvasov, of Moscow, as an archaeologist, is worthy of note, but his lectures, published in 1896, are destined more for students than for the public. Prof. Leontovitch, of Warsaw, has great importance as an investigator of the history of the Lithuanian law, and is now preparing a publication of his whole course of lectures. Prof. Latkin, of Petersburg, principally treats the history of the eighteenth and nineteenth centuries, *Uchebnik istorii russkago prava perioda imperii* ('A Manual of the History of the Russian Law of the Period of the Empire'), 1899. Prof. Zagoskin, of Kazan, after some important studies on the history of the Moscow period, has published a very full bibliography of the history of Russian law (*Naouka istorii russkago prava*, Kazan, 1891), and laid in the year 1899 the foundation to a monumental history of the Russian law in twelve volumes: *Istorija prava russkago naroda* ('The History of the Law of the Russian Nation'), vol. i, Kazan. Finally, the English public has a very good history of Russia, written by Prof. Morfill (*Russia*, by W. R. Morfill, London, 2nd ed., 1891); the author has laid great stress on the evolution of Russian society, and described it with a wonderful understanding of the Russian relations even in points most difficult to conceive for a foreigner. In the following pages I shall not cite the editions of the monuments; they can be very easily found in Budanov's *Chrestomathy*, with a survey of the whole literature and many important elucidations.

Russian elements and became in time the law of the Russian Empire. The Lithuanian law preserved the old Russian character longer, but came from the sixteenth century under the predominant influence of Polish legal ideas, and died out with the Polish state; it has also been much less studied. Thus we have the interesting fact of the same nationality being subject to two different influences.

I shall have the honour to explain to you the sources of Russian law in three periods, the first from the tenth to the fifteenth centuries, the second from the fifteenth to the eighteenth centuries, and the third from the eighteenth century up to the present time.

We have said that the first period of every Slavonic state reveals a struggle between heathen ideas and imported ones. There is a time during which diverse tribes grow together into one nationality. This process of coalescence was extremely troubled in the Balkan peninsula; on the contrary, it was rendered much easier in Russia by the absence of mountains and by one dynasty, which felt itself strong enough to subject all tribes and to exterminate all their princes. We do not encounter a mighty aristocracy; society is levelled. But, on the other hand, the extent of the country and the sparseness of the population, which was lost between forests and swamps, hindered extremely the spread of foreign views. This sufficiently explains the fact that the princes of the dynasty of Rurik were very much like the heathen tribal princes. Indeed, society differentiated very little and took a large part in government, although the annalists—Greeks by learning, not by blood—spoke of the princes as of aristocrats. Thus Russia after an epoch of unification presented a crowd of independent states from the middle of the eleventh century. Even the invasion of the Mongols did not produce a great change; it showed only to the people the necessity of unity, and began to accustom them to subject themselves to the will of one monarch, namely to the khan of the Mongols.

The long duration of the just-mentioned struggle between the old and new ideas produced, as we know, a great uncertainty of social rules. The autonomy of the individual, that is the right of every man to settle his relations according to his agreements with his fellow men, was the basis of the whole of the social life. Just as a private person regulated his business after negotiations with the person concerned, so a prince determined his activity either alone, or with the consent of his people, when the latter were interested therein. Therefore the political treaties with Byzantium, with the cities of the Hanseatic league, conventions of princes with one another and with the people were the oldest and most frequent monuments of legal rules, whilst the private agreements, which are to our great sorrow almost totally lost, took the same place in private life. Such agreements (*mir*, *rjad*, *dokontschanie*, *celovanie*) stand evidently on the ground of the customary law, but notwithstanding this they formulate it more sharply, and even at times change it. The rules of common law very often gradually grew from treaties; for instance, we find the same settlements and even the same words in the mutual conventions of princes from the eleventh to the sixteenth centuries; so the relations of princes to the communes of Novgorod and Pskov became from conventional regulations—regulations of the common law. This transformation must have been greatly facilitated by the primitive similarity of their not complex relations.

The Russian prince of the first period had, according to the old customs, an almost independent sphere of activity. He regulated certain administrative affairs, for instance, the quantity of the tribute, the succession to the throne, and decided law suits. He could, in his last character as judge, appoint other judges in his place, could give them indications how to judge and try criminals; finally, he could give some general rules for jurisdiction. Some remnants of this twofold activity remain to this day. The enactments regarding the clergy and the church of St. Vladimir, of Jaroslav, of Vsevolod and Svjatoslav of Novgorod, of Rostislav of Smolensk, beginning with the tenth century till the year 1150, exist even now, although the authenticity of the first two is very doubtful. Many more enactments have come down to us that belong to the civil judgements of the prince. The annals and so-called Russkaya Pravda transmitted to us a considerable number of such decisions. All these germs of the statute law had legal force only during the life of the prince, their author; this explains the frequent petitions for their confirmation made to his successor. The usual name of these diverse enactments was *ustav*; besides, they were called also *urok*, *sudnaja gramota*, *sudebnik*, *ulozhenie*.

Only when it was necessary to change the usual order of life, the prince felt the need to consult his retinue or the oldest among the people, and to ask the consent of the whole population. These relations began to alter in course of time; where the princely authority prevailed, the prince acted more independently; where the assembly of the people (as in Novgorod and Pskov) became more influential, it took the legislative power into its hands. Besides, the legislative power could in those times never be regarded as a separate power. The customary law was considered as regulating all relations, and the enactments of princes and assemblies contained almost exclusively sharper definitions of the customary law. It could not be otherwise, as the art of reading was little known and the schools of law did not exist.

The uncertainty of the law in the first period provoked great private activity, which gave vent to several juridical works, existing now in a great many MSS. and known under the name of Russkaya Pravda. The last results of scientific investigations on them are the following. We can distinguish three collections: the Pravda of Jaroslav, the Pravda of the sons of Jaroslav, and the enlarged Pravda.

The Pravda of Jaroslav was composed not later than during the life of that prince; not all the enactments of Jaroslav found place therein; they were arranged in systematic, but not chronological order. One article on assassination is followed by eight articles on wounds; mutilations and personal offences by six articles on transgressions against property and by two additional ones.

The Pravda of the sons of Jaroslav was evidently looked upon as a supplement of the just-named Pravda; it is an incomplete collection of their enactments, arranged in chronological order; the laws changed and amended are preserved with later ones amending them.

The enlarged Pravda consists of two parts; one probably of the time of Vladimir Monomakh, and the other a supplement. The first half is a systematic code of the laws of Jaroslav, his sons, and later enactments; the second contains later additions of the twelfth and perhaps of the thirteenth centuries, which were inserted as complete statutes, for instance on inheritance, on slaves. This enlarged Pravda has a more scientific character; we find in it the enactments of diverse times contracted into one, the homogeneous enactments generalized, the casual form of laws abolished. The contents of the enlarged Pravda were finally fixed not later than in the middle of the thirteenth century, it being included in the so-called Kormchaja (a collection of the ecclesiastical laws), written about 1284.

The main source of Russkaya Pravda is the enactments of the princes; the kernel, round which the whole began to arrange itself, is the laws of Jaroslav. The decisions of legal suits may be looked upon as a separate source, although they are principally founded on the customary law. Finally, even the Byzantine influence can be already felt. The ancient theory that Russkaya Pravda is based on old Scandinavian and German customs is now completely exploded.

Thus the Russkaya Pravda is a series of private collections of princely enactments, customary law as well as parts from Byzantine sources.

Quite another character have two very important legal monuments of the legislative activity of the assembly of the people, namely, the Charters of Pskov and Novgorod (Pskovskaja sudnaja gramota and Novgorodskaja sudnaja gramota), as instructions for judges. The former has been preserved entire until now. It is uncertain when it received its present form, as known to us, because its date is erroneous. It says itself that it was made 'by the whole community of Pskov on the assembly of the people after the benediction of the priests of all the five councils in 6905 (1397).' As the fifth council of the clergy took place in 1462, the mistake as to the time is quite evident. These contrary testimonies point probably to a difference of time between its component parts; at least we can clearly distinguish three chronological strata (1–76, 77–108, 109 to the end), every one of them beginning with laws on the organization of justice. Thus the period of its origin probably continued during the hundred years commencing 1397. The sources of the Charter of Pskov are indicated in the heading, namely, the charters of two grand-dukes, Alexander and Constantine, and the old legal customs (*poshliny*). The charter contains the law proceedings, criminal law, and private law. It was exclusively extracted from the customs and manners of the time (even in the princely enactments), so that it distinguished itself from the customary law only by its written form and by an oath of adherence by the people. Finally, this charter is interesting also as attempting for the first time to settle the legislative power; after art. 108 the chief chosen magistrate (*posadnik*) of the city has the right to be the first in making a proposal, and the assembly of the people decides upon the fate of his motion.

We have only the beginning of the Charter of Novgorod; it was probably promulgated about the middle of the fifteenth century, 'by all the five parts of the city, by the people of the Lord Great Novgorod assembled in the court of Jaroslav'; it was in 1471 only copied in the name of the Grand-Duke Ivan III after the taking of the city. The remnants contain the law proceedings and the law of evidence. This charter does not indicate its sources; we can infer from its contents that its foundation is the old customs (*po starine*), which had partially already taken a written form, namely, in the statutes of the people and in the treaties with the princes.

Thus these two charters contain only the customs, which were deposited little by little during hundreds of years; we cannot discover in them any traces of the reforming spirit of the Moscow law. On the contrary, the old republics wished to preserve as long as possible the legal traditions of ancient times. Therein lies the importance of these two monuments; they show us the Slavonic law as yet almost unaltered by foreign influences. So we have during the first period three legal monuments, of which the first refers to the customs of South-Western Russia and the two last to Northern Russia.

If we take a final glance at this period we find therein a great variety of political formations, which were certainly reflected in the diversity of customary law. Indeed, the princely power with some democratic spirit came greatly to prevail in North-Eastern Russia; the aristocracy began to have a great importance in the South-West; finally, the assembly of the people with some aristocratic spirit took in its hand the reins of state in the North-West. Thus the primordial Aryan unity of prince, senate, and assembly of the people began to differentiate according to the different local influences.

Second Period.

The first signs of modifications appear at the end of the thirteenth and the beginning of the fourteenth centuries. They were called forth by great changes in the surroundings, which determined their tendency. Formerly the Russian princes had a pre-eminence over the different non-Slavonic tribes; now they were encircled on the east and south by the Mongols, before whom all Europe trembled: formerly feeble, semi-barbarian Lithuanian and Finnish nations lived on the western confines, among whom the Russian culture spread itself rapidly; now began the formation of a powerful state, Lithuania, which looked with contempt upon the feeble Russian principalities; finally, this mighty state subjected itself more and more to Western influences and to the Roman Catholic religion. If we looked into the heart of a Russian of the fourteenth century, we should find almost despair. There was, however, one enormous force which held up the Russian people: that was their faith. They believed with all the power of their hearts that they alone had the true Christian faith, and that the promise of Christ, that Christianity would endure for ever, could not be false. Here lies the real cause of the extremely close union of the State and the Church, which is felt in Russia even at this moment, and constitutes it 'Holy Russia' in the eyes of the Russian people. This is the cause of the complete devotion of the clergy to the chief of the State; this explains also that a nation, eager for liberty and little disciplined, willingly took upon itself the enormous burdens imposed by the State. So the instinct of self-preservation identified itself with the religious sentiment and created a force so vast that before it, as history teaches, retired the wild energy of the Mongols and united Lithuania and Poland.

All these peculiarities of the Moscow state were

intensified by the fall of Byzantium. This fact produced an enormous impression on the whole of Europe, but it was particularly felt in Moscow. This state from this moment not only began to look upon itself as the heir of Byzantium, as the third Rome, which will never fall, but was also presumed to be so by other Orthodox peoples. Evidently this tended to raise the self-esteem of the Moscow state and strengthen its aggressive and defensive forces. This explains why Lithuanian nobles, notwithstanding the great privileges granted them by the Polish kings, at times took the part of the Russians during the wars between the two states, and why the Russian armies always found support among the Orthodox populations not of Slavonic blood during the wars with Turkey.

Such conceptions, so powerfully impressed on the minds of the people, must of necessity transform society. The grand-dukes, as representatives of the state, being indispensable for sustaining faith and self-preservation, became autocratic, the continual wars with Mussulmans and Latins rendering a strong government absolutely necessary. The freedom of the classes to settle their rights and obligations by contract is replaced by the claim of the State, that every member of society must serve the State in the most convenient manner; while some defended it on the fields of battle, others brought to it their manual labour and furnished revenues to the state treasury. At the beginning (in the fifteenth and sixteenth centuries) these classes were almost equal; in the archives we sometimes find requests of the lower nobility (*deti boyarskie, dvorjane*) for permission to remain as peasants in their village, because it is too oppressive for a poor *dvorjanin* to serve in the army.

But this petition is never granted ; the State places the different social groups under severe control. Thus in Moscow classes appeared as a consequence of the diversity of the obligations to the State. These diverse social groups are called in Moscow 'chini'; they must agree with each other, and all of them with the tsar, on the question of how the interest of the State may be best promoted. Thus we see that the parliaments in Moscow were a necessary consequence of the political ideal, which inspired all Russian society, from the tzar to his humblest subject. The will of the tsar gave juridical force to the acts of government, but these acts were the results of a most profound knowledge of the real conditions of the State, which could only be obtained from the *chini.* The great difference between these Moscow parliaments and the parliaments of Western Europe was, that in the first the idea of obligations prevails, while in the second the idea of rights soon began to prevail. Therefore powerful social classes alone took part in the Western parliaments, whilst the humblest citizen was called to them in Moscow; he also belonged to a certain group who bore certain burdens of the State, occupying himself specially with a certain kind of labour; therefore good counsel could be expected even from him as to his special interests. Thus the separation of the legislative power began. These enormous changes must evidently show themselves also in the sources of the law.

The second period is very rich in monuments of the activity of grand-dukes and tsars which establish social rules (*ukaznaja dejatelnost*). This activity is produced by a conscious desire of the chief of the State and of the highest class (*bojare*) to found a single great state without breaking with the old social forms of life. As was said, great modifications, long ago prepared, in the mental tendencies of the masses took place at the end of the thirteenth and the beginning of the fourteenth centuries; the educational activity of the Church accustomed the people to the idea of one great state with one central power; the subjugation by the Mongols tended to raise the conviction that only one strong power could break the humiliating yoke. The necessity of preserving the old order of life was prescribed by the want of culture, which formerly shone from Byzantium and now was arrested by the hordes of the Mongols; there was no source from which new ideals for the structure of a single state could be drawn. The Moscow Government wished in two ways to fulfil this difficult problem—to build something new on an old basis and by old means; namely, by a multitude of separate enactments, given for an uncertain time and for a limited district, and by legal codes which were designed for the whole of the realm.

The enactments are extremely numerous and multiform. The Government used for such charters various names; almost every one contained privileges, and was most probably given on the petition of the people; therefore the great difficulty, even impossibility, of finding firm principles for grouping. Excluding enactments on a single case, we meet so-called *ustavnyja gramoty*, by which the government of a larger or smaller district was carried on; these are adjustments of general legal rules to the local conditions, and usually founded on ducal grants. Their contents change in course of time as the administration changes. *Ustavnyja gramoty* of the fourteenth and fifteenth centuries are limited to the definition of the power of princely functionaries over the inhabitants; these charters have principally in view the lower classes, they suffering most from local authorities. The most ancient and important ones are the charters given to the communes of Dvina (1397) and Beloozero (1488). So-called *gubnyja gramoty*, a new kind of *ustavnyja gramoty*, began in the thirties of the sixteenth century and continued to the end of the period; the central power decided to organize self-government in the provinces, namely, to leave to the inhabitants the prosecution and punishment of highwaymen. These charters are addressed to all classes of people; they establish the necessary offices and contain much criminal law. Self-government was introduced to a much greater extent by Ivan the Terrible, and this called forth from 1552 a new kind of charters (*ustavnyja zemskija gramoty*). They contain legal rules on the whole of the private and administrative law, which the chosen authorities needed, because self-government included the whole of the administration of the provinces; the most important charters are *Vazhskaja gramota* (1552) and *Dvinskaja gramota* (1556).

It is not difficult to perceive that this activity was a natural continuation of the efforts of former grand-dukes; for instance, the way they settled the position of the Church. As a consequence of the independent political life of some provinces we find therein the same variety of local customs; that was the first attempt at establishing the administration of provinces newly annexed. The Moscow Government, however, very probably even then introduced modifications for the sake of greater administrative unity, thereby much lightening the administration.

This activity must have created on the one hand the need for general principles for administration; it facilitated greatly on the other hand their appearance by the accumulation of multiform experiences. If the administrative questions differed almost in every province, the activity of the Government was the same almost everywhere, namely, the organization of justice and law proceedings, the level of mental development differing nowhere. In this manner the first code (*Sudebnik*) appeared in 1497, in which 'the grand-duke determined how the lords (*bojare* and *okolnitchie*), must judge.' The code was projected by the *djak Gusev* (secretary of the state) and afterwards sanctioned by the grand-duke, his children, and lords. The sources of the code are principally the above-named provincial charters, from which the rules about the central courts are taken, those concerning the provincial courts being copied word for word; the so-called Russkaya Pravda and the Mosaic legislation gave materials for the code only to a very insignificant degree. Tsar Ivan III established also without doubt some legal rules. The author knew also the Charter of Pskov, as is evident from some articles on private law, but the corresponding paragraphs are sometimes greatly altered. As the code contained additional and not material law, the customary law found almost no place therein. The grouping of the articles is as follows: central law-courts with the criminal law (1–36), provincial law-courts of the ducal governors (37–44), mostly private law (46–68). A code with such poor and exclusive contents evidently could not take the place of the customary law. Its insufficiency was the cause of Ivan's son completing his father's code; this latter work is not preserved.

The first tsar, Ivan the Terrible, was penetrated with the Byzantine idea and therefore aimed at great reforms. His idea was to exterminate the high nobility, to raise the lower classes, to give them a large part of self-government, to abolish the ancient freedom of nobles to take leave of their prince and to pass over to other princes, for instance to that of Lithuania. For that reason he convoked in 1548 the first great council of the realm. So these great assemblies began to appear, which took a large part in the future legislative activity of the State and the Church.

Ivan the Terrible in 1550 promulgated with his brothers and lords a Book of Law (*Sudebnik tsarskij*), and in the following year gave it to the council, consisting of clergy, his brothers, princes, and warriors, to be revised and sanctioned. The original of the code ought to be signed by the members of the council and conserved in the treasury of the state. The sources of it are the former codes and the legislative activity from 1497 to 1550. As we do not know the second code, it is quite impossible to separate the results of this activity in the two codes. We can only presume that the laws, which limit the arbitrary power of the nobles and confirm the self-government of the lower classes, belong to Ivan the Terrible. The contents of this code are also very insufficient; it consists generally of articles on organization of courts and on law proceedings; hardly any private law is included therein; notwithstanding this, it is already laid down as necessary that all cases be submitted to the effect of statute law.

The same council of 1551, named 'of the Hundred Chapters,' was occupied with the reforms in the organization of the Church and clergy. The decisions of this council exist up to the present time under the name, *Book of the Hundred Chapters*, and are very interesting, although they had only transient legal force. They give a vivid picture of all society, ecclesiastical and civil, in Moscow, on account of the close union of the State and Church. The abuses and superstitions appear with great clearness[1].

The last great legislative act of the first tsar was the criminal code, promulgated about 1555. Therein is regulated the activity of the office of investigation, judging and punishment of robbers. This code was completed by the later tsars. This office did not operate during the civil wars after the extinction of the dynasty of Rurik, and only in 1617 a new criminal code (*ustavnaja kniga razboinago prikaza*) was worked out on the basis of the former laws. As this office continued its activity, new enactments were given on various doubtful questions (1624–31), and these were inserted in the code.

The above-mentioned injunction of the code of the first tsar, that all new cases ought to be determined by the tsar with all his lords, caused the insertion of all such decisions, although given sometimes orally, by every office into its copy of the code. In this manner appeared a considerable number of codes in which the inserted part was different. The diversity of the sphere of activity of different offices caused the supplements of offices, particularly important, to grow into great collections of laws. All this regulating activity of the Government, however, could not satisfy all wants; therefore extracts were made from the beginning of the

[1] The enactments of this council were published in Kazan in 1862 by the Ecclesiastical Academy, and in Petersburg in 1863.

seventeenth century from the third edition of the Lithuanian code and were incorporated in the codes of diverse offices. These supplements had a subsidiary force and were practically used. This reception was much facilitated by the close relations between Moscow and Poland in the seventeenth century.

A plan of Tsar Feodor's code was only discovered a year ago. The public has not yet become acquainted with its composition, contents, and sources.

This development of the legislative activity since the year 1550 had many weak points; the laws were often unknown to different offices, therefore the demand on them embarrassed and delayed the exercise of justice. There was even the possibility of laws being lost or destroyed, e. g. the fire of 1626 destroyed all the laws concerning the domains of the crown, which were given to the serving classes for their use. This uncertainty of the legal bases of society produced arbitrariness and vexations on both sides, and called forth revolts in Moscow, Pskov, and Novgorod. Therefore the tsar, lords, and clergy decided in 1648 to bring all the laws into mutual agreement, to add to them new enactments, to unite them into one code, and to summon a council of the realm for their examination and sanction. The plan of a new code was worked out by a commission of five persons, was analysed in detail by the assembly, of which traces remained in the code itself, and in 1649 approved and printed; the name itself, 'Code made in Council' (*sobornoje ulozhenie*), points also to the importance of society taking part in the codification at this time. The sources of this code are as follows: (1) The former codes and the above-named regulations of diverse offices (*ukaznyja knigi*). (2) The Byzantine laws, the Ecloga, Justinian's novellae, the rules of Basil the Great, and principally the Prochiron. These Byzantine sources were taken from the collections of the canonical law (*kormtchija knigi*). The extracts are, however, not very large, and were not in accordance with other laws proceeding from native sources; some cruelties of the criminal law can be explained by these extracts. (3) A very abundant source is the Lithuanian Statute of 1588. All the constitutional law and some supplements to the criminal law, besides some paragraphs in other chapters, are taken from it. The cruelty of the Lithuanian criminal law is softened. The manner of borrowing varies; some articles are copied word for word; sometimes only the system and the order of the subject discussed are the same; often the case is taken from the statute, but the decision is independent. New articles probably are few and not composed by the commission, but by the deliberative council. The *Ulozhenie* consists of twenty-five chapters, which contain 967 paragraphs. The system arose probably under the influence of the Lithuanian Statute. It seems to be as follows: (1) the constitutional law (chaps. i–ix), (2) organization of justice and the law proceedings with law of contracts (x–xv), (3) property (xvi–xx), (4) criminal law (xxi, xxii), (5) supplementary part (xxiii–xxv). The *Ulozhenie* is essentially a combination of rules already obligatory in Moscow; it is national notwithstanding its partially foreign sources, because it adjusts all the foreign elements to the Moscow standard, and therefore it distinguishes itself from the laws of the latter period. The incorporation of the foreign law was manifestly produced by the necessity for creating new rules and by the impossibility of drawing them from the customary law, which could not give any point of support on account of the relaxation of society and of the appearance of quite new social relations. The derivations from Byzantium and Lithuania, where the West-European influence was so strong, already point to Moscow being halfway between the East and the West.

The insufficiency of the *Ulozhenie* and the need of changes in the course of time produced a new supplementary legislation, so called new regulating articles (*novoukaznyja statii*). They relate to the criminal law and the law of property. The statute on robberies and assassinations (*novoukaznyja statii o razbojnnyh i ubijstvennyh delah*, 1669) contains a whole criminal code, which substantially was the completion of the *Ulozhenie*; its principal source was the Byzantine legislation; the cruelty of punishments of the *Ulozhenie*, however, was especially softened. A whole series of laws regulates different kinds of law of property.

Novoukaznyja statii stood still on the ground of the Moscow law; but *ustavnaja gramota* of 1645 and *novotorgovyi ustav* of 1667 appeared already under reformatory tendencies, produced by the West-European influences. Thus the Moscow period passes little by little into the Russian law of the empire.

I have endeavoured to unveil to you the spirit of Moscow society, to point out to you the necessity of building something new on an old basis and by old means on account of want of new ideals; finally, I described this same activity in its twofold form, by singular enactments and by codes. Now we shall take a glance at the customary law and its relation to the regulating activity of the tsar.

The importance of the customary law remained the

same in the second period, that is, it was looked upon by the grand-dukes and tsars, and by the people, as the principal basis of the whole social structure. Therefrom, however, it cannot be concluded that the legal rules of the customary law were exactly formulated; on the contrary, the grand-dukes, leaning upon their autocratical power, felt their power little limited by the customary law, and endeavoured to create completely new customary rules by their administrative action, in which also they perfectly succeeded. The importance of the customary law was, however, evident, and the princes and tsars did not consider themselves as called upon to establish rules for ever obligatory for everybody; but they aimed at finding points of support for their administrative and legislative action in the customs and manners. If customary rules grew little by little from their singular administrative enactments, they looked upon the latter as upon eternal rules. The highest powers in Moscow also could not prevent the rise of pernicious usages, for instance the necessity of recurring to the pedigrees of families in appointing officers of the crown. We find the first signs of a change in the relations of the customary law to the statute law under the reign of the first tsar. We meet in his code an article that 'in future all cases ought to be judged after this code' (97); the next article added to this says that cases not decided in the code must be determined, not by the customary law, but by the enactments of the legislative power (98). The cause of such enactments is revealed in the *Book of the Hundred Chapters.* The tsar said therein that 'the manners and customs were unstable in ancient times, nobody took care of the traditional rules, therefore affairs suffered'; but the statute law aims at rules uniform for ever. Although this specially refers to the sphere of the Church, it can also be ascribed to the civil sphere on account of the multitude and importance of the civil elements in the Council of the Hundred Chapters. It is evident that the weak point of the customary law was remarked, and its removal was aimed at. Notwithstanding this, Ivan IV did not think for an instant of setting aside the customary law; on the contrary, he calls the benediction of the ecclesiastical council on 'the improvement of the code after the ancient usages and manners' (*po starine*); all the contents of his code, even his whole legislative, politic, and administrative action, seem to him a realization of the oldest customary law and not at all as an act of his arbitrary will. The weakness of the statute law in comparison with the customary law is explained partly by the incompleteness, uncertainty, and insecurity of the former. A great many relations were left undecided by codes, and what were regulated were often not thought obligatory. For instance, the *Ulozhenie* forbade every complaint of children against their parents, and menaced them with punishment by the knout. Notwithstanding this, the State received complaints of children against their parents for unprofitable change of landed property by parents, and even nullified such contracts. Generally the petitions against a definite law were accepted, collected, and laid before the highest power, which often preserved them and changed the laws according to the wishes of the petitioners by new and contrary enactments. Such unusual phenomena were the consequences of the origin of laws in Moscow. The Government is induced by petitions of the interested persons to pass a law; as not all interested, however, are of the same opinion, the highest power receives immediately after the promulgation of the law petitions of contrary tenor. The acceptance of such petitions seemed to the Government to be required by justice. The great number of such petitions incites the Government to examine the affair once more, and so a completely contrary result is often attained, which is authorized as a new law. In a word, this instability of the laws was a consequence of the ignorance of the Government how to collect the petitions of all the persons concerned and to settle the relative strength of the parties.

From this comes during the whole Moscow period the conviction of the governing and governed classes, that the power of passing obligatory rules lies with the people; this power appears in manners and customs, and arises from the interests of all concerned. The enactments of the highest power receive only then their full obligatory force if they convince the people, otherwise they can be easily changed. The highest authority was, after the idea of that time, destined by God to judge society and to regulate its relations, but this judging and regulating action could only be worked by decisions, obligatory for a limited time. At the beginning of the period, as in former times, the enactments of the grand-dukes were looked upon as obligatory only during their lives; the new representative of the highest power confirmed them again after the death of his predecessor. Thus the firm basis of social order was still the customary law. In a word, the regulating action of the tsar was considered not as a true legislative power, but rather as *ius edicendi* of the Roman magistrate. The true statutes must be published by the tsar only after approval by the whole of the people.

The first signs of political literature appear at the time of Ivan IV in the remarkable correspondence of Prince Kurbski with the tsar [1]. The former is a passionate defender of the old Russian life, with its liberty to regulate by contracts even the relations of the serving classes with the State, with its weak princely powers and with its large self-government. We find further signs of this literature in the work of Kotoshikhin, his descriptions of the administration under the Tsar Alexis being interwoven with sarcastic observations [2]. The first dawn of the Slavophile idea appears in the works of Krizhanich, written in Siberia [3]. Finally, the schism in the Russian Church, produced by the revision of the liturgical books, called forth also a great literary movement. But I cannot call your attention to this literature, not only on account of want of time, but also because it is not yet studied from political and social points of view.

Passing on now to Lithuania, we assist at the formation of a Lithuanian state on the basis of rules much resembling Western feudalism. But the influence of Russian culture, language, and orthodoxy was strongly felt through the thirteenth and fourteenth centuries, and

[1] N. G. Ustrjalov, *Skazanija knjaza Kurbskago*, Petersb., 1868, 3rd ed.

[2] His work is published by the Archaeological Commission under the name *O Rossii v tsarstvovanii Alekseja Michajlovitcha*, Petersb., 1884, 3rd ed.

[3] Two of his works, 'About Business' (*o promysle*) and 'Conversations about Power' (*razgovory o vladatelstvu*), were published by Bezsonov in Moscow in the years 1859 and 1860.

this greatly facilitated the concentration of the weak Russian principalities in the west and south-west round this Lithuanian kernel. This, however, was stopped by the elevation of the Lithuanian grand-duke to the throne of Poland. Poland in Slavonic history was a passionate admirer of Western ideas; her mission, as it seemed to her, was the spreading of these ideas as far as possible. But the clergy, orthodox and heathen, in Lithuania were opposed to all this, and the close union of all social classes did not facilitate the foreign influences. As new Western ideas could not be assimilated by the whole mass of the people, political reason dictated the necessity of propagating Roman Catholicism and disintegrating society in order to make at least one class accessible to Western culture. So the first privilege appeared in 1387, which gave to the noble warriors of the Roman Catholic Church in Lithuania all the rights of Polish chivalry. These rights were by degrees applied to all the nobility, Lithuanian and Russian, Roman Catholic and Orthodox, of several provinces, and were confirmed in 1457 to the whole nobility and chivalry of Lithuania. Finally, the great privilege of 1492 founded the political omnipotence of the aristocracy in Lithuania; this magna charta of the Lithuanian nobility not only confirmed the former liberties of the nobility in the safeguarding of nobles in all matters relating to their persons and their property, it not only confirmed the largest self-government, but also consolidated the preponderance of the aristocracy in all the course of political life. It can be said that the Lithuanian principality became from this year an aristocratic Republic, the grand-duke—a pure president of an aristocratical council—only an executive organ of its decisions. We need not stop to consider the long series of privileges given to the different classes of the people (*zemskie privilei*) and to distinct provinces (*oblastnye privilei*), because their characteristic is always the same, namely, the ever greater endowment of the nobility with the rights which it had acquired in Poland. Certainly we find in these charters also testimonies of old customs and manners, but this does not form their principal contents. Care for other social classes can be observed only where the Russian influence prevailed. The great difference between Moscow and Lithuania is evident in the charters of the two states; whilst the Moscow charters regulate the relations of all classes, establish the different obligations of classes to the Government and look upon all of them as equal, because, while some defended the State on the field of battle, others brought to it their manual labour, Lithuania cares only for the nobles, and looks upon the other classes only from the point of view of the nobility.

Privileges of towns in the municipal law of German origin follow the endowments to the nobility and single the inhabitants of cities out from the old unity of population in a district. Thus the differentiation of society into the clergy, nobility, citizens, and peasants, little by little, arises under Western influences.

This tendency to dismember society in order to make its component parts more accessible to foreign influences was very soon noticed by the people and led to great conservatism. The people defended eagerly their old manners and customs, because they dreaded to lose with them their nationality and religion. That is the reason why the regulating activity of the grand-dukes, inasmuch as it did not concern the constitutional and the administrative law, had only established the old customs and manners. These were determined in law-courts by the testimony of old men, who knew from memory the most ancient customary law. Therefore Lithuanian law, except for the above-named tendency to dismember society, is nearer to old Russian law of Russkaya Pravda and the two charters of Pskov and Novgorod than the Moscow law, in which the idea prevailed of building something new. Therefore also the almost independent life of different provinces was preserved much longer. The highest authority in Lithuania aims at instilling new ideas into society in order to make it more like Poland, and society protests against this and wishes with all its power to retain the old way of life; society in Moscow at the same time is too feeble to protest in the face of the united powers of the Church and the State, and little by little transforms its own manners and usages.

This conservatism of the Lithuanian law is evident in manifold legal monuments in the Code of Casimir of 1468, giving an instruction for judges, but principally in the first Lithuanian Statute of 1529 and the second of 1566. These two statutes, if we exclude the rights of the nobility, are a true picture of the customary law of old Russia as it has been evolved in the course of time. Thus they are very near to the so-called Russkaya Pravda, chiefly because they appeared on the same territory. And all who loved the old Slavonic liberty, looked to Lithuania; while, on the contrary, all who were attracted by Orthodoxy and by the brilliant idea of putting a stone in the building of the third Rome, which should never fall, sped to Moscow. At all events the two statutes are very important monuments of the Russian law, drawn from the pure customary law and from the above-named charters; the customary law gave material for all kinds of law except constitutional, which is taken from the charters. This tendency of the first statute was so perfectly well known to the leading men that they inserted in it an article that an event, which happened under laws preceding the statute, should be judged by this statute. They did not find in this enactment the impossible rule that a code can have legal force before its publication; the logical consequence being that the statute gave a more determined form to the customary law, which has reigned and will continue to do so. Besides all this the Lithuanian Statutes were distinguished from Moscow legislation by a better system, by definition of rules and by less casuistry, because the Roman law and science of law of that time are felt therein. It is a great pity that they are little studied; the attention of students was drawn to them comparatively recently. Polish influence is greater in the second statute, and so the Lithuanian law loses itself in the history of Polish law; meanwhile Western ideas began to prevail in the Moscow law to the end of the seventeenth century. Now we turn to the third period of Russian law[1].

[1] The three statutes of the Lithuanian principality of 1529, 1566, and 1588, are published in *Vremennik obstchestva istorii i drevnostej rossijskih*, 1854, bk. 18 (St. of 1529), bk. 19 (St. of 1588), and 1855, bk. 23 (St. of 1566). A Polish edition with Latin letters appeared in Posen, 1841, Dzialyński, *Zbiór praw litewskich od roku* 1389 *do roku* 1529. A short but very instructive survey of the history of the sources of Lithuanian law was published by Prof. Leontovitch, Warsaw, 1894, *Istochniki russko-litovskago prava*.

Third Period.

The need of foreign elements, as soldiers, architects, painters, was felt in Moscow from the middle of the sixteenth century. Certainly Western ideas came with these immigrants; close relations with Lithuania, the invasion of the Poles, the wars with Poland, ending with the incorporation of large tracts of land from Poland, tended more and more to enforce Western ideas which were to be ingrafted on the Moscow stock. We have described the Moscow society, as pervaded by a vivid consciousness of the necessity for a mighty state with a strong monarchical authority, as very religious, as extremely illiterate, as possessing equal rights because equally serving the State by its labour, as warriors, or labourers given to warriors in order to maintain them, as traders, paying to the State treasury and selling also the goods of the Crown. Quite other views began now to operate on such a society. In the West feudal society fell to pieces in the seventeenth century and the idea appeared that a mighty king is necessary, as a representative of the cultivated classes of society, fit to rule the people according to the mandates of reason (*absolutisme éclairé*). Convictions considerably different came from Poland and Lithuania; there it was said that the ruling by the cultivated class almost alone is much better than a powerful king who can abuse his power. Polish society, however, was also fully persuaded that light can shine only from the cultivated class, which must be rich and independent enough to preserve and develop knowledge, sciences, good customs. And now we shall see in Russia a curious struggle between the spirit of equality, worked out by a long series of centuries and spread among the masses of the people and the wishes of the minorities, sometimes even upheld by the Government, to persuade the people that only the nobility is destined for independent life; that only the nobility, and not the whole of the people, is the support of the throne. These Western ideas of the seventeenth and eighteenth centuries began to prevail in Russia and made possible the enormous influence of foreign law; and up to the middle of the nineteenth century the Government turned its attention almost exclusively to the nobility, evolved from the higher serving classes of the Moscow period. The great reforms of Alexander II, and principally the emancipation of the serfs, certainly drew out the whole mass of the people, but we find in the last twenty years again a return to the nobility. This is also due to foreign influence. We see in all Europe and even in America an apprehension of the powerful spread of the democratic spirit; the wealthy classes are afraid that the masses would not have intelligence, time, and knowledge enough to take care of themselves, that their emancipation comes too early, some even think it altogether impossible; and this state of opinion is evident in Russia in recent years.

These great changes in the ideas of leading men must tend to a change in the legislative power. The participation of society becomes weaker and weaker. Plans of new laws are made by commissions of bureaucrats and are transformed into laws by the Emperor's signature; therefore they are sometimes almost the will of the Emperor, and for that reason uncertain, multiform, and contradictory. This state of the law could certainly not strengthen the sense of justice and consideration for the law. An improvement begins with the nineteenth century, when the council of the State is established for examining the proposals of new laws. Finally the necessity is more and more felt to hear the wishes and opinions of specialists and of the people concerned. Almost every great change in the legal order from the time of Alexander II is made after hearing deputies of the persons concerned, but always nominated by the Government itself, and never by vote.

We can very well understand this ignoring of society in the eighteenth century. Not only the mass of the people, but even the clergy was averse to the above-mentioned transformations, and all dissenters were the avowed foes of Western influence. The reforms found support only in some circles of the nobility. Only in the second half of the eighteenth century was this last class entirely permeated by the new spirit after it was freed from obligatory service under Peter III (1762) and received great privileges with some self-government from Catherine II in 1785. Besides, the scientific conceptions of the natural school of law, omnipotent in the eighteenth century through the whole of Europe, excited the craving for radical reforms. This school upheld the statute as the only source of law, and the statute ought to express the will of the legislator, who must draw the substance of the law from the nature of relations in accordance with reason.

Turning now to the sources themselves, we find a very good sample of this tendency in Peter's military code of 1716 (*voinskij ustav*). It contains the organization of the army, the military criminal law, and law proceedings; the last two parts were applied also to civil persons and regulated the criminal practice during almost the whole of the eighteenth century. The first two parts of the code are translations word for word of Gustavus Adolphus' military laws of 1621–32, of the edition of 1683, of some laws of the Emperor Leopold I, of King Christian of Danemark and of French ordinances and regulations; the sources of the third part are unknown. This code was even published in Russian and German. This transplantation of Western laws, mostly Swedish and German, sometimes even word for word, continued until the middle of the eighteenth century. The influence is great enough even afterwards, but the national peculiarities are considered and the laws are never translated after the time of Elizabeth and especially of Catherine II; the samples of laws are taken mostly from France, but some from England and Germany. Finally, the wish to express in statute law national principles after the time of Nicholas I is evident, but this could only be attained after the emancipation of the serfs and the greater economical independence and mental culture of the masses.

The enormous multitude of laws, often contradictory, made it most desirable to establish all social life on firm basis. So commissions were appointed for making one general code, which continued to sit almost without intermission from 1700–1832, and by which the opinions of leading circles were expressed with great clearness. From 1700–19 Peter I wished to found the code upon a historical foundation and principally upon the *Ulozhenie*, and the commission worked with this object; he decided in the year 1719 to translate foreign laws, principally Swedish ones, word for word, and Catherine I added to this commission two persons from the clergy, as well as members from the civil, military, and merchant classes. This participation of society was augmented in 1728, when five persons (afterwards only two) were sent to Moscow from the nobility of every province. Special commissions were appointed for the codifications of the laws of Livonia and Little Russia in the same year. Not all these legislative attempts were successful; only the commissions under Elizabeth[1], Peter III, and Catherine II worked out proposals for the law proceedings and criminal code; the latter seemed to be important, but was not sanctioned, and is only lately published.

The most important commission was, however, under Catherine II in 1767–8; it was composed almost exclusively of members of society, of deputies elected by the nobility, town inhabitants, cossacks, peasants, dissenters, and of the delegates of some offices of the State, the total number amounting to 564 members. It received from the Empress the celebrated instruction, which had no legal force, but which is often quoted in later laws. This instruction consists of twenty-two chapters with 655 articles, and is drawn partially from Montesquieu's *Esprit des lois* and Beccaria; it has a scientific character and is permeated by humanitarian principles. Such a numerous commission could evidently not compose a project, but only examine a proposal already written. Notwithstanding this failure, the wishes expressed by different classes of the nation had a great influence on the organization

[1] The plans of the criminal code of 1755 and of 1766 were published in Petersburg in 1882, *Projekty ugolovnago Ulozhenia* 1754–66. The plan of the third part (private law) of the new code was published in Petersb., 1893, by Prof. Latkin, *Projekt novago Ulozhenia.*

of society and administration of very important laws of Catherine II [1].

We see in the commissions under Alexander I for the first time an open struggle between the reforming faction, at the head of which stood Speranski, who worked out in 1809 a proposal for a code of private laws after the Code Napoleon, and the national conservative faction, which wished only a clear formulation of rules already existing. As the commissions under Alexander I had also done nothing, Nicholas I, in 1826, transferred the whole work to Speranski, who had come to power again. The latter tended now more to the national faction, and therefore published firstly a collection of all the laws from the *Ulozhenie* up to the day of the ascension to the throne of Nicholas I, in chronological order, under the title, *A Complete Collection of Laws*, in 1830. This collection ought not to have ended with this edition of the code, but to have been continued; it does not answer to its title, because it contains much which is not law, while many real laws are wanting.

Speranski, relying upon this enormous material, chose legal rules which, not being abolished, are still obligatory, and brought them all into systematical order. Later search shows, however, that he had taken much from the code of Napoleon in his codification of

[1] Prof. Lappo-Danilevski has published, in the *Journal of the Ministry of National Education* in 1895, an article 'Upon the Collection and Code of Laws of the Russian Empire' made under Catherine II. The classical work upon all the legal commissions of the eighteenth century is written by Prof. Latkin, *Zakonodatelnyja kommissii v Rossii v XVIII st.*, Petersb., 1887.

the private laws[1]. His system was founded on the idea that two unions exist in every state, a State union and a civil union. Both of these unions call for laws of two kinds, laws which determine the essence of the State union or of the civil union, and laws which only guard the unions already constituted. Thus this *Code of Laws of the Russian Empire*, containing with few exceptions all the laws of Russia in fifteen volumes, was edited in 1832. After this first edition followed two complete ones in 1842 and 1857; besides which a great number of new editions of different volumes and even different statutes exist.

The great reforms of Alexander II produced considerable legislative activity. The emancipation of the serfs and the necessity to determine their future position gave the first impulse to reforms, which embraced the administration of justice, organization of self-government in provinces, cities, and universities. His successors satisfied themselves with some modifications of the bases laid by Alexander II; in course of time, however, two commissions were appointed, one for the code of criminal law and the other for the code of private law.

It is quite evident that the relation of the Government to the customary law must change in the third period. Indeed, the tsar declares, in two laws upon economical relations, as early as the second half of the seventeenth century, that he will abolish the abuses which have penetrated into the usages, and that he will reform the commercial law after the examples of the neighbouring states. The Government entered

[1] M. Vinaver, 'Upon the Sources of the tenth volume of the Code of Laws,' *Journal of the Ministry of Justice*, 1897, bk. vi.

finally on the path of reform from the eightieth year of the seventeenth century, and Peter the Great published a law as early as 1722, that every case must be decided according to a statute law. A new tendency began only in 1861, when twenty millions of serfs received legal qualifications. These people lived for hundreds of years after their old customs and usages outside the rules of the statute law. Therefore the Government established law-courts for the people, which judge after customs and manners; even magistrates of the crown could use the customary law in cases which were not determined by the statute law. All this, with the influence of the German historical school, which saw in customs and manners a source of law, drew the attention of the learned to the customary law, and now this branch of legal literature is unusually rich in Russia.

Finally, turning to the literature, we see that the reforming activity of Peter the Great evoked a great literary movement, Pososhkov[1] being one of the most eminent economical writers[2]. But afterwards we find no legal literature until the second half of the eighteenth century, when the universities were opened.

[1] Pososhkov's work 'Upon Poverty and Wealth' (*O skudosti i bogatstve*) is edited by M. P. Pogodin, Moscow, 1842.

[2] The time of Peter the Great is very rich in political literature. The reference and analysis of this literature can be found in the work of Miljukov, *Gosudarstvennoe hozjajstro Rossii v pervoj tshetverti XVIII st. i reformy Petra Velikago* ('The Economy of the State in Russia in the First Quarter of the Eighteenth Century, and the Reforms of Peter the Great'), Petersb., 1891, and in the book of Pavlov-Silvanski, *Projekty reform v zapiskah sovremennikov Petra Velikago* ('The Projects of the Reforms in the Writings of Contemporaries of Peter the Great'), Petersb., 1897.

The first teacher of law, Desnitskij, a pupil of the University of Glasgow, brought from England, where he was sent in order to study the law by the Moscow University, a vivid sense of the importance of a knowledge of the obligatory legal rules and their investigation from the historical, economical, and even comparative points of view. He laid the foundation, too, for a more practical direction of legal studies than his fellow teachers, who, under French and German influence, tended to the abstract construction of the natural school of law. But this tendency of legal studies soon disappeared, and the abstract investigation of legal rules, under the influence of France and principally Germany, commenced to prevail more and more. The nineteenth century produced an enormous legal, political, and social literature, but it seems to me a little too theoretical, too alienated from the real conditions of life. This is caused partially by the influence of German literature, which, in spite of its craving after system and in spite of its philosophical depth and solidity, is too abstract and too far from the needs of practice. This theoretical tendency of the Russian juridical literature is strengthened still more by the fact that it is almost exclusively written by professors of the universities, alien to all kinds of business, and not by judges, barristers, solicitors, and so on.

[3]

BOOK II

LAW FROM THE OBJECTIVE AND THE SUBJECTIVE POINTS OF VIEW

CHAPTER I

LAW OBJECTIVELY CONSIDERED

THON. Rechtsnorm und subjektives Recht.
BIERLING. Zur Kritik der Juristischen Grundbegriffen. B. II., 1883.
THOEL. Einleitung in das Deutsche Privatrecht.
BINDING. Die Normen und ihre Uebertretungen. B. II., 1872.

Section 22. *The Objective and the Subjective Points of View in Law*

In regulating human activity, legal rules give to men's relations with each other a special character. From relations of fact they transform them into relations of law. Every man regulates his own activity according to legal rules. His relations with his fellows are not determined in each case of conflicting interest, according to the facts which present themselves, but according to the delimitation of those interests by law. Men's mutual relations controlled by legal rules are made up of rights and obligations which correspond to and depend upon each other. In delimiting the interests in conflict the legal rule sets, first, the limits within which a given interest may be realized. This is the right. Second, it sets at the same time corresponding limits excluding other contemporary interests. This is the obligation. The relation thus established between right and obligation is a juridical one.

In this way law comprehends at the same time rules and relations. These legal rules and legal relations are two quite distinct, if inseparable sides of law, the objective and the subjective sides.

Legal relations are called law (right) in the subjective sense because the right and the obligation alike pertain to the "subject," their bearer.[1] Without him they could not exist. Rights and obligations must necessarily pertain to some one. On the other hand, legal rules do not necessarily imply any one's presence. They have a general and abstract character, and are not designed for any particular person (subject). This law is in a sense objective.

As we are proceeding now to examine the distinctive characteristics of legal rules and relations, we will commence with objective law, which from its abstract character submits itself more readily to analysis. We must observe meanwhile that objective law did not precede subjective right; quite the contrary. Historical development begins with the particular, not with the general. So, at the beginning, rights (subjective law) first spring up. Then come the general rules which regulate these rights.

Before the appearance of a single general themis, there was a belief in a plurality of such deities, applying themselves to the determination of individual cases. The primitive judge did not apply pre-existing general rules of law to particular cases, but for each new case affirmed a new law, and only by the method of successive and gradual generalization of the particular decisions in time reached general rules, rules not yet presenting at first a high degree of generality, but comparatively narrow casuistical rules.

Of whatever sort they are, general legal rules once accepted, necessarily control subjective rights. The formula for determining every such right takes the form of a syllogism. The legal rule serves as major premise, the different interests controlled by it as the minor one, and the statement of rights and obligations which results forms the conclusion.

[1] "*Pravo*" (law) in Russian, like *droit* in French and *jus* in Latin, and *Recht* in German, has the double meaning of "law" and "right."

Section 23. *Juridical Norms. Orders*

SAVIGNY. System. 81. §25.
THOEL. Einleitung, §34–39.
THON. Rechtsnorm und subjektives Recht, §345.
BIERLING. Zur Kritik der Grundbegriffe II, 307.
ZITELMANN. Irrthum und Rechtsgeschäft, 1879. s. 200–229.

Juridical norms, as in general all others, are requirements to do something, and in this sense, orders. Being orders, they are not permissions, enunciations, or indications. They always command. They indicate what is to be done and in what way it is necessary to proceed for the accomplishment of an act in order to avoid a clash of interests.

It is by no means necessary to conclude from this, as is sometimes done, that all juridical norms are the work of a conscious will or of the authority of some man. The rule as to what is to be done contains, certainly, a command, but it is not an order emanating from an individual will. Thus, we know that technical rules are not the work of any man, but the natural consequences of the existence of certain natural laws, just as moral rules, to the extent that they are not divinely revealed, are not established by any one's will, but result from a moral sentiment. This is equally the case with juridical laws. To the degree that they present themselves at first under the form of customs, they are not acts of any ordaining will.

Zitelmann, who contests the imperative character of legal rules, as dispositions established by volition, is clearly right on this point, but he goes too far when he affirms that these legal rules, even in their content, are not commands, but only judgments, as to relations of cause and effect between juridical facts. He himself acknowledges, however, that a legal rule is a hypothetic judgment as to what is to be done; but every judgment of this sort constitutes in itself naturally a command. Moreover, the relation of juridical acts, determined by juridical norms, is not one of fact and necessity. Such a relation will only be recognized by those men who consider it as obligatory.

Legal rules do not carry permission, definition, nor enumeration. Sometimes the articles of a law take such a form as to lead to the belief that there are other than ordaining rules and such as to produce a belief in the existence of rules which authorize or which define. This opinion has had followers even amongst Roman jurists, as Modestinus, who distinguished four categories of law. *Legis virtus*, said he, *est imperare, vetare, permittere, punire.* But even then his definition was questioned and Cicero, for example, admitted the existence only of ordaining and prohibiting laws. *Legem esse æternam* (De legibus, II, c. 4).

Modestinus' classification is evidently wrong. We cannot, indeed, put *imperare, vetare, permittere* and *punire* in the same rank. Penal laws which indicate punishment do not in truth contain the order for punishing the criminals. That belongs to the tribunal. For a long time, however, Modestinus' definition prevailed. Savigny gave it a decisive blow and showed the impossibility of setting in a separate group the rules for punishment. On the contrary, a good many jurists have always admitted the existence of rules which authorize, and even of those which define, as was done by Thöl.

It is in the meanwhile difficult to recognize, in the form of these different rules, anything which modifies them essentially. If in a legislative act we find an article exhibiting the form of a definition, nevertheless, in its actual application this act is nothing but a command.

So, if law gives the definition of a contract or a crime, there is here only an order for connecting with human actions constituting a contract or a crime, the juridical consequences of such contract or crime.

It is important to observe here that the juridical rule is not expressed by a single article but in several. One defines, the others indicate the juridical consequences connected with the acts previously defined.

Sometimes it happens that the legislator employs the descriptive form instead of the imperative one. Instead, for example, of saying that some person ought to do this, he says that the person does do it. So, for example, article 47 of the Fundamental Laws declares that "The government of the Russian Empire rests upon the solid basis of laws." This means undoubtedly that it ought to be so. Otherwise the legislator would appear to go so far as to deny the possibility, even, of failure of compliance with his rule. When the law describes the personnel and the organization of institutions and state services, it says that these subdivisions of the administration have at their head certain persons, that they possess a certain organization. This means, in fact, that there ought to be such persons and that such an organization is fixed by law. The replacing of the imperative form by the descriptive is explained either simply by greater convenience of expression, or by a briefer turn of phrase; sometimes, also, by the desire of impressing upon the disposition created by law a more absolute character. The imperative form, in fact, would appear to suppose the possibility of a reality not corresponding to that required. The descriptive form, on the contrary, which sets forth that which ought to be, as already existing, excludes even the idea of a reality different from that indicated in the legal formula.

The existence of rules carrying a permission is warmly disputed. The partisans of this category of rules assert the existence of articles of this nature in all legislation. They add some considerations of a more general theoretic character. In all legislation we meet, in fact, quite frequently with articles having the character of permission which may be divided into four distinct groups. The first group of articles of this kind is explained historically. They are those which indicate the suppression of a prohibitive rule formerly existing. The suppression of a prohibition is naturally a permission, but we must observe that it institutes no new rule, only suppresses an older one.

Then there are some articles in which the authorization is the consequence of the terms of the formula. They serve in general as an introduction to distinct prohibitions, limiting the scope of these latter by certain permissions.

After an article like this, "All the world is authorized to, or may," follows a series of articles enumerating the exceptions to this general permission. Evidently the juridical rule is contained in the special prohibition and not in the general authorization. If we suppose the authorization suppressed, there would be no change in the legal rule; only its form would require some modification. To say that an act is permitted except in some particular case or to say that in that case it is forbidden, is absolutely the same thing.

The character of the articles which compose the third group is more disputable. In the laws which organize the public service of a state we meet frequently with articles providing that "there can be taken such a measure or such other one."[1] In reality these articles are not rules carrying permissions. Legislation in organizing a public service, that of justice for example,

[1] The character of these provisions raises the more doubt because they are generally intercalated between others which contain unquestionable commands.

imposes upon it usually the absolute duty of doing some certain act if certain facts are presented. The tribunal cannot set aside such a rule. It is not permitted to inquire whether the application of this rule in the given circumstances is indispensable or even useful. Sometimes, on the contrary, the law leaves to the tribunal itself the duty of ascertaining according to the circumstances the necessity for applying the measure. Does this mean that the tribunal can according to its liking apply it or not? By no means, for if the necessity or utility of the measure is recognized, the tribunal is bound to apply it.

Such a law, then, is not an authorization to the tribunal; on the contrary, it imposes a double duty, the estimating of the need of the measure, and the applying of it, if such need is recognized.

If the law says that in certain cases the police may call the army to assistance, this means merely that if the police recognize the utility of such a measure, its duty is to employ it.

The fourth group is made up of rules by which alternative obligations are created, when no direct command is given, but the choice is left of doing some one of several given acts.

Here, then, it is a matter of course that the alternative order keeps its character of a command and the alternative rules are distinctly imperative ones. The permission consists wholly in the fact that choice between the performing of several obligations is authorized. The juridical force of these rules consists not in the permitting of a choice, but in forbidding the making of a choice outside of the established alternative.

So all the examples given of rules asserted to carry permissions are without force. It remains still to examine one proof furnished to support the existence of these rules of permission. It is of a more general character than those just examined. Some have gone so far as to deny the general rule that that which is not forbidden is permitted. They have set forth that not to forbid is not the same thing as to permit. The absence of prohibition does not give a right to perform the unforbidden action. Permission given by law to perform an act establishes, on the other hand, a right.

To answer this it is necessary to establish first clearly the meaning of the maxim, "Everything not forbidden is permitted." If we consider permission as equivalent to the creation of a right, man has a right to do every permitted act and undoubtedly what is not forbidden cannot on that account be considered as permitted. In making no prohibition, no right was created, because a right, as we shall see later, supposes always a corresponding obligation, and merely from the fact that the law does not forbid an act, we should not conclude that any obligation is imposed by such fact. The law does not forbid anybody to look at the setting sun, but this does not mean that I am compelled to place my house so as not to interfere with another's view of the west. Permission to one does not mean obligation upon another. A permitted act can become a right only when everything is forbidden which might interfere with that permitted action, because it is only on this condition that any corresponding obligation arises. So a right can find birth only in a prohibition and not in a mere permission.[1]

We conclude, then, that all legal rules are commands, but commands may take various forms. Every limitation upon the realization of interests which are in conflict may be of two kinds. We can reduce them either to the prohibition of acts which prevent the performance of some act, or to the requirement of the per-

[1] A legal right, then, is not merely capacity to do an act, but capacity aided by law through establishing an obligation.—*Translator.*

formance of the acts necessary to the realization of such interests. So one may say that the command in a legal rule may be either positive or negative, an order properly so called, or a prohibition. It is true that every command may be expressed under the form of a prohibition and every prohibition under the form of a command. To direct the performance of an action is the same thing as to forbid its non-accomplishment. This does not destroy, however, the importance of the distinction between positive and negative rules, between commands and prohibitions.

This difference is manifested especially in the obligations which each creates. Orders produce obligations to do, positive obligations; prohibitions engender obligations to abstain, or negative ones. From this distinction among obligations depends, as we have already seen, the coercive effectuation of commands, and all prohibitive rules admit of coercive realization. Rules which contain the injunction to perform a positive act are susceptible of coercive realization only when they create no personal obligation.

Section 24. *Elements of the Legal Norm*

TSITOVICH. Course in Civil Law. I. p. 45.
BINDING. Normen. I. p. 74.

Juridical norms are not simply commands, they are at the same time conditional commands. The limits given for the realization of an act are variable, and the rules arising from the realization of this act vary according as this or that interest, more or less important, opposes such realization.

So the explanation of a legal norm depends upon the presence of certain facts. There are no absolute juridical norms. Even the rule absolute from the moral point of view, like the provision against attacking a human life, is not absolute as a legal norm. The greater number of human interests ought, it is true, to yield to the interest of preserving life, but not all. In the case of lawful defense, war, and in the application of penal laws, to kill is permitted by law. Legal rules, then, are conditional rules. Each one consists naturally in the definition of the conditions for applying the rule and in the exposition of the rule itself. The first of these two elements is styled hypothesis or supposition, and the second, disposition or order. Such a legal rule can be expressed in the following fashion: "If . . . then . . ." Example: "If the deceased has several sons, then his goods shall be divided into equal parts." "If any one commits a theft, then he is punishable by imprisonment."

Each article of the law does not always necessarily contain these two elements. The rule may be set out in several articles. One article may contain the hypothesis and another the disposition. So it happens that the law may not contain an express declaration of its conditionality. Instead of: "If . . . then . . ." we can use another formula, "He who does this or that is punishable by . . ."; or, better, "In such case the goods which . . . shall return to . . ."

But all these formulas come finally to, "If . . . then . . ." That is the fundamental formula to which the others can be reduced, while the other formulas cannot be applied in every case. Thus, the laws which regulate the descent of estates cannot be expressed by the formula, "He who shall do such act shall have the right . . ." The command being the form common to all juridical norms, the hypothesis and disposition are their universal elements.

These two elements may take different forms. The hypothesis can in effect be expressed under a general and abstract form, or under a concrete, casuistical, one.

The circumstances on which the application of the norm depends may be the result of general principles and the hypothesis will be under an abstract form, or on the other hand, they may have their origin in individual instances and the hypothesis will take a casuistical form.

The thought in all primitive peoples assumes the concrete form. Their legal rules, consequently, are clothed at first in concrete forms applied to each particular case and it is only little by little, in generalizing themselves, that these concrete forms become abstract and general definitions.

The casuistical form is defective, for it causes a multiplicity of rules and does not adapt itself to the generality of legal definitions.

With casuistical rules each case demands for itself a separate rule and meanwhile, as the diversity of possible cases is infinite, the casuistical rules, however great their number, cannot always include every case which life presents.

The abstract form, on the contrary, has great advantages. In a single definition all the homogeneous cases are indicated and combined. It requires, then, only a quite moderate number of rules, which at the same time are fully comprehensive.

It presents, however, some inconveniences. In the first place, the abstract form, because of its too general character, leads to a certain vagueness in the application. There is no embarrassment as to the casuistical rule in knowing whether or not it is to be applied to a given case. With the abstract form it is not always so, and a large field is sometimes opened for contradictory interpretations.

Besides the differences which we have just indicated among the hypotheses, sometimes casuistical and sometimes abstract, there are others which arise from different degrees of definiteness in the hypotheses. These hypotheses may be, indeed, absolutely determined or undetermined or may be relatively determined.

A hypothesis is said to be absolutely determined when the facts on which it depends are distinctly indicated in its own form, when we indicate, for example, that every contract involving an amount greater than five rubles must be upon stamped paper.

There is an absolutely indeterminate hypothesis when the rule comprises no mention of the facts on which its application depends, but places upon each agent of authority the necessity of stating them. For example, if the law permits "in case of necessity" the taking of such or such a measure. Here the hypothesis is absolutely indeterminate.

When will the condition arise? On what terms? The law does not say; in this last case the agent charged with accomplishing the rule has a power which is called discretionary. He can act, taking for a guide certain considerations, but he is only bound by the formal restrictions of the law.

Lastly, we say that the hypothesis is relatively determined when the application of the law is subjected to certain conditions; for example, if certain measures are prescribed only in case of an epidemic, and in such case not absolutely, but only under condition that these measures shall be recognized as necessary by competent authority. The rule may then, under this hypothesis, not be applied at all, and if an epidemic supervenes, it will be applied only if it is recognized as necessary.

Rules with the hypothesis relatively or absolutely undetermined are found often in administrative law and also in procedure. The courts have, in fact, a quite extensive discretionary power.

The necessity for the application of these rules depends on circumstances so varied that it is unavoidable to give to administrations and courts of justice some discretionary power.

Concrete restrictions, unchangeable at law, must be replaced by definitions which are elastic, so to speak, adapting themselves readily to the multiplicity and variability of facts. These definitions are given by judges and administrators.

The distinction between casuistical and abstract forms is not applicable to the disposition. This latter contains, in fact, a rule, a command, and contains nothing else.

We distinguish several kinds of "dispositions" according to the degree of determination of the commands which they contain.

Like the hypothesis, the disposition may be absolutely determined, absolutely indeterminate, or relatively determined.

In the disposition absolutely determined, the command is a categorical rule. No discretion or latitude is given to him who executes it. Such, for example, are dispositions of the kind which indicate the date when a bill of exchange is outlawed, or those which indicate the eldest son as the successor to a throne. These are categorical commands, leaving no option to the one charged with their execution.

Dispositions of an indeterminate form are, on the contrary, those which leave to the one who is to apply them a discretion to moderate their application or even not apply them at all. For examples we will cite the texts which authorize the police to take some measure deemed necessary in case of a riot for the re-establishment of order, or again, in case of epidemic, all the useful measures for arresting the spread of contagion. All the dispositions of the criminal code are indeterminate. Criminal laws, in fact, are applied by tribunals which have the right to choose between laws.

We observe in all our examples that the exact and immediate application of the rule is confided to some organ of government, or of the police, or of the court. These agencies are bound to fulfill this function and at need can be constrained to do so. There are rules also which require some given individual to enforce them. Ranged in this class should be the rule which requires that goods of a defunct shall belong to a devisee indicated in the will of the deceased, or that which in a contract leaves to parties the privilege of arranging details. Doubtless there are fixed limits to the rights of the devisee or parties to the contract, but there is, none the less, a large share in the application of the rule confided to them.

Experience has shown that parties to a contract do not employ very freely the authority which the law gives them of arranging their mutual relations, and the law usually fixes some general rules which operate by the side of those which the contracting persons establish for themselves. If these last do not indicate in the contract all the details of its application, it will be necessary to refer to those which the law has established. These rules, which apply only in cases where the interested persons have fixed none themselves, might be called dispositive rules and the others which apply in every case, prescriptive rules. Rennenkampf has recently proposed the name "ordinative" instead of dispositive, and "imperative" instead of prescriptive, respectively, for such rules; but his names have not prevailed.

The relatively determinate disposition may have two forms. It can fix merely the extreme limits within which the competent authority, or the persons interested, may choose. For instance, when the maximum or the minimum of a reparation is fixed, or the maximum of delay in a contract of hiring, leaving to the parties the right of stipulating for a shorter one. It can also take an alternative form, limiting itself to indicating several measures between which choice must be made in applying the rule. For example, the court has often the choice between requiring a reparation to be made or the imprisonment of the guilty party. The trial judge may have a discretion to order an imprisonment or to satisfy himself with a reprimand.

Individuals themselves have quite frequently to apply dispositions of this kind. The victim of a crime, for example, can institute proceedings for damages before a civil tribunal or a prosecution before the criminal jurisdiction, just as, also, one who has to complain of a violation of a contract with the treasury can take his demands before the administrative, or before the judicial, tribunals.

All which has just been said as to juridical norms and the elements which compose them is absolutely general. The hypothesis and the disposition are indispensable elements in every legal norm. They are, of course, in every penal law; but they take then some particular names because of the special situation occupied by penal laws in the general system. Each penal law is composed of two parts; in the first are indicated the acts, the facts which constitute the crime or delict, and in the second are the punishments.

All the formulas for penal laws can be reduced to this one: "If any one commits such or such an action, he shall suffer such or such a penalty."

In our modern legislation we do not usually indicate that all forbidden action is to be punished. This is understood. It is the natural conclusion resulting from the penalty incurred by the doer of the act.

Also, in a penal law the first part contains, besides the indication of the facts constituting the offense, the disposition of another rule which forbids the criminal action, and this is why criminalists reserve this word "disposition" for that first part, while they denominate as "sanction" the second part of the penal rule. The penalty constitutes the sanction for the observance of the legal rule, since it can be incurred only as that law is violated.

Section 25. *The Matter of Juridical Norms*

Because of the great diversity of interests at play and also of the numerous juridical principles by which they are controlled, the matter of legal rules is extremely varied. The detailed knowledge of them is nothing less than that of all branches of positive law, of law studied in its historical evolution and in comparative legislation. We shall limit ourselves here to some general rules and to the summary indication of the fundamental categories into which all the matter of juridical norms may be reduced. Such a generalization is possible, because all human interests, despite their great diversity, are on the whole subjected to identical conditions.

To reach a proposed end, man employs forces. Thanks to these, he produces changes in the conditions of his existence, of his individual well-being. The forces which man employs for the satisfaction of his needs and pleasures are limited. Meanwhile, the man cannot attain his ends without a certain exhaustion of these forces. The struggle between individuals thus appears to us as a struggle for the possession of those forces which alone can assure to individuals the realization of their projects. Legal rules have precisely for their end the regulation of the human struggle for the control of these forces.

Laws, in fact, enjoin upon the man, first, not to employ for the realization of his interests other forces than those which the law recognizes as good; second, the performing only of acts leaving possible for other men the utilization of forces corresponding in their limits with those assigned by law.

Legal rules, then, have for their end the avoiding of

the shock of the collision of individual interests; they are established with a view to order.

As the relations between the different interests under consideration are not the same, the content of legal rules, while keeping certain general traits, varies also. We can bring into three groups these different conflicts of interest: first, the conflict of interests absolutely equal belonging to different persons; second, the conflict of equivalent but unequal interests; and third, the conflict of interests which are not equivalent.

The first group presents some interests offering this peculiarity, that it is quite difficult to assign to them an exact limit. Since the two interests in view are absolutely equal, there is no reason to prefer one to the other. Their realization, therefore, should be admitted in an exactly equal degree. If, on the other hand, the realization of only one of them is possible, then the choice between the two is left absolutely to chance. We find frequent application of this rule. Thus we accord the use of a thing to the party who first takes possession, according to the rule, *Qui, prior tempore, potior est jure.* In the same way in case of danger incurred by two persons, if the safety of one can be obtained only by the destruction of the other, the issue is left to brute force as between the two. Sometimes the law is used to decide between the interests in conflict.

The unequal but equivalent interests may be compatible or may not. Compatible interests are delimited as in the case we have just examined, by applying the rule of perfect equality.

We must observe always a difference. If in the case of absolutely equal interests we were to apply perfect equality, it would be arithmetical equality. In the case we are now concerned with, however, it is proportional, geometric equality which is required. The forces are distributed between the interests which ought to be delimited in a fashion proportional to the quantity which is necessary for their realization as regards each other.

In the case of incompatible equivalent interests the choice can be left merely to chance. These interests being different, it is easy, as a matter of fact, to find reasons for a choice between them. It will be, for example, the interest of the majority or that of the minority, or the one will be older than the other and already recognized by usage, and will be preferred for this reason.

This difference between the interests may arise, either from the subjects, that is, the bearers of the interests, or from their matter, of what sort they are. The organization of society into classes is an application of this difference of interests, as to the subject. It happens also that general interests are naturally preferred to individual ones. Interests of the state, for example, are estimated higher than those of a province, or of a commune, and these latter are given consideration before those of an individual. Even in this last case it may happen that the interests of one should be preferred to those of another. Thus, in the case of violation of a law, the interests of the just are preferred to those of the wrongdoer. When it is necessary to choose between the interests of the mother and those of an unborn infant, the mother's are preferred. The mother exists already; the infant has only a problematic existence. It is plain that the importance attached to a certain interest depends upon the moral ideas dominant in society.

Let us observe besides, that in the application of legal norms, general interests, even for a particular case which concerns only a conflict between individuals, are taken into consideration merely for the reason that, as we have alreadv seen, laws are established with a view to order. Peace being a very important general interest, it is in the interest of peace for the most part that the interests in play will be regulated. Hobbes was not wrong in considering as a fundamental law the Roman rule, "*Pax quærenda est,*" and Herbart gave as the origin of all law the necessity of settling conflict. However it is obtained, peace is always an advantage. It procures an economy of force which in its absence would be absorbed in the conflict. It permits the regarding of the future with confidence, while on the other hand, the issue of a struggle is always uncertain.

So, in view of the great advantages which peace offers, when we are controlling the interests under consideration, whatever they may be, we give preference to the adjustment which contributes most to the establishment of peace. For this reason law in general is disposed to preserve interests already existing and applies the rule "*Beati possidentes.*" For this reason, too, effective possession if it lasts long enough, assures to the possessor property in the object and turns into a right in him. Property can be acquired even by unlawful possession, provided it be old enough.

Besides this very general interest, which precedes the others and which peace offers in regulating the interests at play, there are others which, without having so general a value, are also applied, as the interest of individual liberty which plays such a great rôle in modern law. Because of it, modern law gives preference to the solutions best compatible with individual liberty. It is needless to say that other collective interests are set in play by the conflicts between individuals. Their greater or less importance affects the solution adopted by the legislator.

Section 26. *The Sanction of Legal Rules*

Legal rules as orders addressed to the conscious wills of men are not always observed; so they have need of special guaranties for their enforcement.

It is necessary to constrain the man to the observance of legal rules; without such constraint the rules would remain a dead letter. These means of constraint are "sanctions." In what do these sanctions consist? Each violation of a legal rule gives birth to a new clash of contradictory interests. On the one side we find the interest of him who is injured by the violation of law. He wants compensation. On the other side is found the interest of the wrongdoer, the author of the harm. Frequently, too, he can invoke some rights for his defence.

We can say that the general consequence of violation of any legal norm is the birth of a new rule created to regulate the interests brought into presence as a result of the violation of law. Let us examine how these interests are regulated.

Law is violated generally because it interferes with us in the accomplishment of some act, because it prevents the realization of some of our interests.

The first means for producing observance of legal rules is to prevent the actions which violate those rules from attaining their end. Such acts are to be recognized as void. For example, the sale of immovable goods by a secret act is considered as void, without value to any one. Property sold in this manner is considered as unsold. The purchaser gets no rights of property. The law requires every sale of this kind to be made before a notary. The object is thus attained, and if by private act the sale cannot take place, there is no motive for individuals to proceed in that fashion.

The laws which have as their sanction the inefficacy of acts which violate them are called perfect, for they come the nearest to a law of nature. This inefficacy may have two forms. The acts may be absolutely null at law, or they may be only voidable, that is, such as may be annulled. They are absolutely null when that is the result decreed as a consequence of non-observance of the law. Such, for instance, is the result of a sale of real property by a private act, although the parties were agreed as to the intention to transfer the property. It is, on the other hand, only voidable, when rescission can be demanded by one of the parties interested in the contract. Thus a contract produced by duress can be annulled only on the application of the party subjected to the violence.

It is necessary to distinguish farther, absolute from relative nullities. The act violating the law and considered as totally non-existent is stricken with absolute nullity, as for example, the sale of real estate by a private act. When the act is only relatively void, it is because some clauses of the contract may be upheld. A bill of exchange, for example, given by a married woman without her husband's consent is void as a bill of exchange. It has, however, a certain value. It is that of an ordinary obligation.

Sometimes a void act has already produced its result. It will not suffice then to proclaim or demand the nullity of the act. The annulment of the act must be followed by one which re-establishes the violated right. Such a re-establishment of the violated right may be accomplished by the agents of authority and may consist either, first, in the cessation, if necessary by force, of an unlawful condition, the expulsion, for example, of a renter from a house which does not belong to him; or it may consist, second, in the accomplishment of a violated obligation and this at the expense of the one who has violated it, as the repairing of a pavement of a torn-up street.

There are also some cases where the act which violates a right contains in itself the realization of the object with which the wrong was done,—robbery for example; some cases where the right violated cannot be re-established,—murder for example. To acknowledge the crime is not sufficient in such a case to repair the injury done, so law has established other sanctions. These acts, which violate law, bring with them consequences indicated in the law, as in the laws which the Romans called *leges plus quam perfectæ*. These consequences may be of two kinds, civil damages for the benefit of the injured, and punishments set up by public authority in the general interest.

We might say that to a certain extent every violation of law works an irreparable injury.

This harm is from one point of view that offense which every injured person experiences and from another point of view is the violation of the law itself, all whose prescriptions are meant to be scrupulously followed. These harms are of so great a variety that it is impossible to classify them. They depend usually upon the conditions under which they are wrought.

We know only that private damages are the oldest. As to penalties denounced for the general interest, we may say that they depart farther and farther from private damages in the degree that governmental authority is augmented; and in our modern law the sphere of application of these punishments is not fixed by any general principle, but by different considerations which are set forth in the penal code.

These consequences attached by the law to the

criminal act which it punishes do not render unnecessary the re-establishment, so far as possible, of the violated right. Thus in the case of forgery, besides the penalty to which the guilty one is subjected, the writing is void. So in a case of robbery, besides the punishment involved of the robber, he is required to restore the stolen things. It may happen meanwhile that the re-establishment of a violated right may bring on forbidden consequences to those absolutely strangers to the doing of the acts. The annulment of a marriage, for example, may bring upon children the consequence of becoming illegitimate. So the nullity of a marriage results only from a very grave violation of law. Any less important act may bring about the punishment of the parties, but leaves the marriage valid.

It is the same when a contract has not been made upon stamped paper. The wrongdoers pay a penalty. The validity of the contract as to third parties remains.

Such laws, whose violation brings penalties upon those who violate them while preserving the legal force of the act, are called "*leges minus quam perfectæ*."

Besides these laws, classed so by the sanction which they carry, the existence must be recognized of a whole category of laws which offer no sanction, the consequences for whose violation have not been fixed. These laws deserve some attention. They are for the most part laws fixing the rights of the organs of authority.

The organization of a service charged with the execution of the laws is considered by itself, as a preventive measure against action contrary to the law, and for this reason it is in public law that the *leges imperfectæ* are the most numerous.

But the organization of a service is always weakened by such imperfection, since the agents who have it to do are men. If a certain liberty, however, is not given them in the performance of their task, such an organization will become stiff and dead. It will by no means satisfy the numerous requirements of the development of life and movement of society. If you make an organization more vital, more mobile, better applicable to concrete conditions, to the necessities of the times, you give necessarily to individual tendencies the possibility of manifesting themselves. The organizations employed for the development of the state consequently explain, but without justifying them, the *leges imperfectæ*. The vice of such a system commences to show itself.

We must consider as inapplicable the theories of the constitutional school which boasted above all of the organization of its governmental machine.

There is general agreement today in recognizing the necessity of attributing a sanction to the rules of public law. The prosecutions which can be instituted in our day against acts of administration have transformed a good part of them from imperfect laws into *leges perfectæ*.

There are, however, some laws which necessarily will remain always without sanction. These will be the ones which establish the supreme power. This supreme power, which is not subjected here below to any authority, which is controlled only by its own moral dignity, can in fact possess only in itself the guaranty for the accomplishment of all the duties which devolve upon it.

CHAPTER II

THE SUBJECTIVE RIGHT

SAVIGNY. System d. heut. röm. Rechts B. I.
IHERING. Geist. d. röm. Rechts. B. III.
IHERING. Zweck im Recht B. I. s. 72.
MUELLER. Die Elemente des Rechts und der Rechtsbildung, 1878.
BIERLING. Zur Kritik der juristischen Grundbegriffe. Jh. II. 53, 47–148.
REGELSBERGER. Pandekten I, 1893, §§57–82; 195–233.

Section 27. *Legal Relations*

NEUNER. Wesen und Arten der Privatrechtsverhältnisse, 1886.
PLOSZ. Beiträge zur Theorie des Klagerechts, 1880. §§65–76.
PUNTSCHART. Die moderne Theorie des Privatrechts und ihre grundbegriffischen Mängel, 1893.
MOUROMTZEV. Fundamental Definitions and Divisions in Law, 1879, pp. 53–122.

Since legal relations are also social relations, but governed by a legal rule, it is necessary in order to explain them satisfactorily to treat first of the relations in general.

Every relation supposes a "lien," a dependence, and a capacity of influence by means of this "lien." Where there is no dependence there is no relation. If between several trigonometrical quantities, for instance, it is said that there exists a given relation, this means that they depend one upon the other and that changes in one of them provoke corresponding changes in the others. So, then, if between given phenomena there exists a causal relation, this means that the consequences depend upon the cause and that the presence of the cause produces that of the consequence. On the other hand, if between several things there is no dependence, we assume that there is no relation between them.

So, human relations consist in some sort of a dependence, in the power which certain individuals have over others.

Men's mutual dependence is caused by several conditions which may be placed in three groups: physiological, economical, moral.

The physiological distinctions of sex and age introduce mutual dependence among men. Because of their sexual inclinations, human individuals experience the necessity of uniting. The child from its birth requires the care of the parents and these last become old and require in their turn the aid of their children. We might add to this the influence of the laws of heredity, which are also physiological laws. By their means men of a common origin present strong physiological and moral resemblances and form natural groups according to race, independently of their wills. To this group also, must be added the propagation of maladies among men by contagion or by heredity. From the point of view of their health men are thus dependent upon one another.

In the same way man's necessity for protecting himself against external forces of nature, which is the basis of economical activity, brings also mutual dependence. The forces of one isolated man are too weak for the struggle with the elements around him. Men find themselves compelled to mutual aid in two ways; there is simple collaboration in regard to a labor performed by united forces, and the complex collaboration which we call the division of labor. In this latter each man does something special and each for all and all for each.

The moral life of man increases still more the mutual dependence of one upon another, since the necessity of exchanging thoughts is one of the very strongest, and mankind support isolation only with great difficulty. The mutual dependence of men from the moral point of view, indeed, is so much stronger that in the psychical development of man the social factor plays, perhaps, the chief rôle. Our turn of mind is not, for the most part, our own work, but the product of the social life to which we belong. It is necessary only to recall the important rôle played in the development of mind by language, which by its essence is necessarily a product of the social life, common to all, and cannot be an attribute of any single person. The dependence of men with regard to each other, springing from society, increases in direct proportion to the development of social life, and even the physiological conditions of such dependence act with greater and greater force. Thanks to the development of social culture the time during which the man lives under relations of dependence on his parents grows longer and longer. The bonds which unite the spouses become stronger since their relations with each other include those necessary for education of their descendants. To the influence of heredity is added that of education which gives the child traits of character not possessed by his ancestry.

The increasing density of population, and the lack of space, introduces among men a dependence in increasing degree which we might call hygienic. The force, and action, and economic demands of these dependences increase unceasingly. On the one side economic necessities augment, and on the other the division of labor grows. Social development is inseparably bound up with the development of man's moral faculties. It increases these latter, augments their moral interests in extending the moral solidarity of ever enlarging groups. Because, also, of these conditions human life is made up of many different relations among men. These relations have doubtless an artificial character, but men are combined by their means, and through them exercise influence over one another.

Men, so far as they aid themselves by legal rules, transform their social relations into legal ones, social dependence into a legal obligation, and the power of influence which they have over each other into rights. The legal rules fixing human interests delimit necessarily the realization of those interests and impose upon each man some obligation of guaranteeing the realization of others' interests. So the law adds to the existing bases of mutual dependence a new one, a legal base. If my relations with other men are fixed by law, the realization of my interests depends not only upon social conditions, but also upon my legal rights and my legal duties. At the same time, conformably to these obligations there is created for others a possibility of influencing me in a particular way under the form of legal claims.

Legal relations suppose, then, a dependence under the form of rights and duties, and suppose also a legal claim, that is to say, an enforceable right, which is the consequence of this dependence.

Among Roman jurists these relations, established by law, were designated by the expression *juris vinculum*. The characteristic peculiarity of these legal relations consisted for them precisely in the dependence upon objective law. The active side of the legal relation, that is to say, the legal claim occupied their attention so little that the conception of a subjective right in the sense of a capacity had not even taken birth.[1]

The jurists of western Europe, on the other hand, and in the very beginning, the glossators, attributed a particular value to the active side of the relation, to the assertion of the legal claim. They do not assign the origin

[1] Bekker. Pandekten. I. 1886, p. 46.

of the legal claim to the legal relation, but, on the contrary, consider the relation as a consequence of the assertion of the claim.

The explanation of the difference between the schools is readily accounted for by the "subjectivism" peculiar to the Germanic peoples in opposition to the "objectivism" of antiquity, and also by this second reason that Christianity developed the rôle of the will with peculiar force.

The law, as it is concerned in western Europe, does not consider its subjective side as an element of legal rules, but as a free and individual will, recognized and protected by law.

Since in law this individual will is recognized, there results the altogether natural consequence, that the duty of other men is not to encroach upon the domain of this will, and thus are established the relations between two wills.

The logical development of this conception leads naturally to the complete negation of legal relation and to its replacing by the simple conception of subjective right in the sense of a legal assertion as Brinz exhibits it.[1] But the exclusive importance given to the legal claim is not compatible with the real character of legal phenomena. In public law especially, it is impossible to consider the legal claim as the formative principle, the fundamental base of the manifestation of law.

The obligations in public law are indicated in an extremely clear fashion. The subjects of such obligations are always exactly determined, while, on the contrary, rights are scarcely more than the consequences of these obligations and it is an indeterminate body of persons who enjoy them. Nearly all constitutional law reduces itself to the study of the duties of the organs of authority, and the rights which are given them are so many

[1] Brinz. Archiv. f. civil. Praxis. Bd. LXX. s. 379.

conditions, guaranteeing their assurance of the possibility of accomplishing their duties. Judges, for example, are bound to render justice and it is with this view only, that of accomplishing this function, that they are accorded certain rights.

So, too, all the relations of private law cannot be explained as consequences of the legal pretensions of the owner of some right. The relations of passive action of right, as Ihering defines it, cannot be thus explained. We find such action only where there is an obligation without a corresponding assertion of claim. Such are the obligations which the law imposes for the protection of the interests of unborn children. Such are the duties of a debtor with regard to an unknown creditor, a debt whose proprietor is anonymous or unknown, and such the duties of the owner of a servient tenement where the dominant one is *res nullius*.

These different examples show clearly that the obligation can exist without there being a corresponding right in any definite person to assert it, and that it is, consequently, impossible to derive all legal relations from the assertion of right.

A legal claim, on the contrary, cannot exist without a corresponding duty. If nobody is bound to yield to my assertion of a legal right, if it is not obligatory upon anybody, it has no legal validity. This is why in legal relations as generally in all others, it is the passive side, the obligation, which has most importance. This importance is recognized today even by the civilists. It is thus that Puntschart thought it necessary to replace the conception of juridical relation by the conception of juridical dependence (*Rechtsverband*), translating by this term the Roman expression *juris vinculum*.

This new conception is scarcely practical. The juridical connection is a term recognized by all, and which offers this advantage, that it embraces the idea of the realization in the active rôle and at the same time in the passive one, of the action, as well as of the dependence.

Every relation is defined by circumstances of fact as well as by legal rules. There is no relation completely and exclusively determined merely by the law. Rights and obligations exclusively fixed by the law do not exist. The relations, for example, of husband and wife, lessor and lessee, master and servant, are governed by the law and also by the social situation, by their practicability, the character of the parties, their mutual dispositions, their moral and religious convictions, etc. It is by the diversity of these social conditions that the individual and peculiar physiognomy of each concrete and peculiar relation is created, but the juridical form of all these identical relations, all marriages, for example, all contracts for leasing, remains absolutely the same because the same legal rule is applied to all. Since it is precisely the juridical form of relations which concerns a jurist, we comprehend readily how important it is for the juridical critic to distinguish this legal form from the variety of facts.

So the jurists have imagined the conception of legal relations which should be completely and exclusively determined by legal rules. In these relations there is only one legal form common to all the identical ones. These relations are called juridical institutions. They are a legal abstraction from the concrete, actual matter, and if this legal form is common to all the relations of a certain kind, it serves as the common type for all the relations of that sort.

The different interests which make up our social life are so closely bound up that the legal relations, which have the struggle between these interests for a base, are not isolated, but on the contrary form an inseparable whole. This combination of legal relations forms what we call the juridical state. It is the same with legal institutions considered as the common type of legal relations. They form a whole which we will call the juridical order.

Every legal relation, as we have seen, is composed of a right and a duty. Neither can exist separately. They are necessarily attributes of some subject. So the indispensable element in every legal relation is the subject. This element is not always single. The right is the possibility of realizing an interest and the realization of my interests supposes necessarily the use of some sort of means. Every right requires, then, necessarily to be exercised on an object whose use leads to the realization of the sought-for interest; so every legal relation supposes a subject of right, a subject of obligation, and object. It is by the examination of these elements that we reach the determination of legal relations.

This examination, meanwhile, is not all. Legal relations do not stand immovable; they change, they evolve without ceasing. It is then necessary, besides studying their form, to regard also their conditions and changes.

Section 28. *The Subject of Juridical Relations*

KIERULT. Theories des Civilrechts B. I. s. 82.
ROEDER. Naturrecht B. I. §52 und ff.
TRENDELENBURG. Naturrecht. §§85–88.
LASSON. Naturrecht. §46.
BEKKER. Iherings Jahrbücher für Dogmatik. B. XII. Rechtssubjekten.
WALLASCHEK. Studien zur Rechtsphilosophie, 1889. ss. 144–181.

Juridical rules, being rules for the delimitation of human interests, are applicable only to relations between men. Moral rules are absolute duties. They do not depend upon the interest which other persons may have in their accomplishment. There can, therefore, be moral duties towards oneself and these duties have for each man an obligatory force. Law, on the other hand, having for its end the delimitation of interests in conflict, presupposes a relation between these interests and therefore between persons.

We cannot in this matter subscribe to the opinion of Dernburg,[1] Regelsberger, Mouromtzev and some others who recognize the existence of juridical relations with regard to things. The relation of the proprietor of a thing with that thing is not distinguishable from the relation of that thing towards one who has no right over it. The proprietor, just like one who has no ownership but uses it, employs the object according to fixed technical rules and according to personal taste. The only difference between the one and the other is in relation to other persons. When a relation is established with respect to the thing by another person, then a legal claim would appear. Legal relations exist then, not between an

[1] Dernburg, Pandekten, I. §22.

individual and a thing, but only between several individuals on account of the use of a thing.

Legal relations, it is readily seen, are possible, then, only between individuals. Only individuals can be subjects of juridical relations. They alone are capable of them. This faculty of being subjects of legal relations we shall call "capacity."

Law in its modern conception recognizes in fact the existence of legal capacity only in man. It was not always so. Primitive man, assimilating natural phenomena to human acts, considered them as the manifestations of some conscious will. Legal rules were not limited to their action upon human relations, and were recognized as to things and animals, giving them rights and duties. Even in the middle ages animals were brought to judgment and punished; but at present only men are recognized as accountable for their acts.

The punishments inflicted upon those who mistreat animals do not contradict this principle. It is not in the animal's interest that the punishment has been fixed, but with a view to protecting the sentiment of humanity in those who would be offended at the purposeless torture of an animal. The proof of this is that if the harm to the animal has some reasonable object, whether in the interest of science, or to supply the table, there is no punishment.

A quite recent German opinion, specially advanced by Bekker, maintains, however, that animals can also be subjects of legal relations. If, for example, someone leaves by will certain goods under this condition, that they shall serve after his death for the maintenance of his dog or his horse, these animals become proprietors of the goods and are subjects of certain rights.

Some years later, however, in the Pandects, Bekker recognized that it is better to restrict the conception of subject of a right to persons alone. Such a limitation is necessary not only in the interest of convenience, but also in that of truth.

We can in truth assign goods to any use we please, but as a matter of fact these goods are assured of their destination only so long as there is a man interested in some way in its accomplishment, whether by esteem for the memory of the deceased or for some other cause; so, after the disappearance of the interested person, the interests of the dog or horse are no longer guaranteed. Then, even in this case the interests of the animals do not constitute by themselves directly the basis of the legal relation, but only in a conditional, indirect fashion, and to the degree in which they serve some human advantage or interest. The real subject of the legal relation even here is one or more persons interested in the accomplishment of the devise made for the animal's profit.

As much, also must be said as to what concerns supernatural beings and physical forces. The repression of religious crimes does not have for its purpose the interest of the divinity, for the divinity has no need of such protection, but only the religious sentiment of the believers. The goods of which the church is the proprietary assure the satisfaction of religious needs, those of the ministers of the cult, and consequently of men.

We come thus to another question. To recognize only men as subjects of legal relations, does not this contradict the conception of the legal personality of moral persons? This conception is based, we know, upon the fact that certain rights and certain duties exist for the advantage, not of individuals, but of a class of individuals,—corporations, for example, or establishments. We distinguish, for example, the goods and the duties of the actionaries from those of the society which they serve, those of individuals from those of the state, those of the administration of a hospital and of the sick who are found there, from those of the hospital itself considered as a public establishment.

As Savigny, who is an authority in this whole matter, urges, such juridical persons are not genuine subjects of legal relations but are only a fiction. Brinz goes farther yet and rejects absolutely the whole idea of fiction; this whole conception of legal persons is, as he says, entirely unnecessary.

The writers, on the other hand, like Beseler, Gierke, Dernburg, Regelsberger, defend the existence of legal persons, and recognize them as real subjects of legal relations and not as pure fictions. Regelsberger formulates thus his opinion: The object of the laws, says he, is the guaranteeing of human interests, but a good many of these interests cannot be realized in whole or in part except by the combined powers of several individuals. This is why there exist other subjects of legal relations than individuals. There are these moral juridical persons. While possessing no corporal individuality, they are real subjects of rights; they constitute social organisms. Their vivifying element comes from man, but in so far as they are members of the organism and act conformably to its purpose these men give birth to a particular force (*verbandsleben*), and to a collective will distinct from their individual wills. In the view, then, of the defenders of the real existence of moral juridical persons as distinct subjects of right, the purpose is always the same; it is some human interest, but an interest common to a whole group of individuals. The force of this moral person is the product of the activity of all the members or representatives of this group; its will is that of the individuals who compose it. All the juridical relations of a moral person can, then, be reduced to relations of individuals, but these relations are very complex, greatly mingled, and it is for this reason that they are considered for the advantage of legal analysis as the relations of a single subject artificially constructed, and this subject is the moral person.

It is in this way that Ihering explains his conception of a juridical moral person. The conception of juridical person is for him only a particular process in the juridical construction of the actual relations of physical persons.

Here, also, are some men who are the real bearers of interests delimited by law, but these interests are common to the whole group of individuals whose composition can be varied without changing its identity; so the legal rules, instead of delimiting separately the identical interests of a throng of individuals, consider these identical interests as a single one and the group itself as a single subject of legal relations, as a single juridical person.

It is only a special process for reaching a simplification of the mutual relations of men. It would be very difficult, for example, to determine the relation existing between the person who buys something of a stock company and each stockholder of the society, or again, the relation which exists between every holder of a state's obligation and each citizen of the state. It is much simpler to consider the relation only between the purchaser and the society, or between the citizen and the state.

Our conception of legal personality might be compared to that of the parentheses in algebra. Just as in algebra we place within the parentheses the quantities united by signs plus and minus to simplify the calculation, so in law we place together all the identical interests of a certain group of persons by the conception of juridical personality, and determine afterwards the relations between the group and each member.

It is, as we have seen, only men who can be subjects of legal relations. This does not mean that all would always be "capable."

The history of modern law, on the other hand, offers us a good many examples to support this idea. For a long time slaves were considered only as things, goods, which could not be subjects of legal relations, and were without any juridical capacity. In modern civilized states slavery has been abolished under all its forms, but in the barbarous states like those in central Africa it still exists.

Modern law, then, recognizes all men as "capable" but each one does not possess equal capacity for all rights. This capacity can be more or less extended. All the incapacitated can be brought, however, into four different categories: those who are smitten with natural restrictions, or with social restrictions, those which have their source in incompatibility with certain legal relations, and finally, those which result from penal restrictions.

By natural restrictions we mean restrictions which have for cause age, sex, race. It is thus that in a general way women are recognized as incapable of exercising political rights. Individuals under sixteen years of age cannot serve as administrators. Deaf-mutes cannot be members of a jury.

Social restrictions depend upon social situations, as the inequality between classes, between professions, and between religions. Members of religious bodies, for example, cannot own land. Innkeepers are sometimes denied the right of being electors in the towns. The Jews are not allowed to live outside the territory assigned to them.

The restrictions which have their source in certain incompatibilities with legal relations arise from the fact that the possession of certain rights precludes others. A married person cannot marry again so long as the preceding marriage is not dissolved. High functionaries in the state cannot at the same time hold private employments.

Finally there is, we have said, a class of penal restrictions. These are the consequences of an arrest or a judgment. They are an integral part of the penalty involved upon one condemned.

Capacity means that the person can have certain rights, but does not necessarily mean that the person actually possesses them. To have ability to acquire a right, and to exercise it, are not the same thing. If one is capable of possessing an ownership of real property, this does not mean that everybody has it. Capacity and possession are two quite different things.

Certain rights require, besides capacity, the presence of particular facts, certain events, as, for example, the death of a testator, or certain acts, an acquisition, for example, by which the connection between the person and the right is created.

The appropriation of rights by their subject is called the acquisition of right, and the rights are rights acquired. There are rights which have an exclusive character and which cannot be exercised at the same time by several persons, and as an example of such rights we cite the right of property, but if the right is not exclusive and may belong at the same time to an indefinite number of persons, the presence of the conditions necessary for capacity suffices for their possession; for example, the electoral right.

Capacity commences at birth, to end only at death. It is only living persons who have it. The child born dead cannot be the subject of legal relations. It is considered by the law as if it had never existed. However, certain rights exist for the advantage of the infant not yet born, but under the condition that it shall be born alive, and thus certain duties are imposed upon persons who have, so to say, charge of the birth and life of the infant. They cannot, for example, during pregnancy divide the father's estate if he is already dead.

Man is recognized as capable of rights from the instant of his birth; from the complete detachment of his body from that of his mother. This capacity lasts until his death, that is to say, until the final disappearance of the last signs of life, the beat of the heart and the respiration.

A prolonged absence, if the dwelling place is unknown, is equivalent to death and brings to the absent a loss of capacity. Some legislative enactments, that of the Baltic, for example, recognize as dead one who in his absence has attained the average age of mankind,—that is to say, seventy years of age. Other legislators, Russian for example, recognize as dead one who has been absent a certain length of time independently of his age.

With death, capacity completely disappears. A dead body has no rights. If the law has proclaimed penalties against the desecrater of tombs, it is with a view to the protection of those persons whom such conduct would offend owing to their relations to the deceased.

Section 29. *Rights and Duties*

IHERING. Geist des röm. Rechts. B. III.
THON. Rechtsnorm und subjektives Recht, 1878, 223 und ff.
BIERLING. Kritik der jurist. Begriffe, II. 49, ff.
BEKKER. System, I. s. 46.
SCHUPPE. Der begriff des subjektiven Rechts, 1888.
ZENTHOEFER. Das subjektives Recht, 1891.
SCHLOSSMANN. Der Vertrag, 1876. ss. 213, ff.

The explanation of the conception of right in the subjective sense, of right-power, is the most difficult and controverted question in the study of legal relations.

The influence of legal rules over the conditions for realization of our interests is so varied and these different forms of influence interpenetrate so closely that it is very difficult to proceed to a special examination of each of them and to separate with clearness the "right-power" from other consequences which the legal rule draws with it into the sphere of the realization of our interests.

Legal rules first of all forbid the use of certain means for realizing human interests and so make a distinction between what is permitted by the law and what is forbidden by it.

The prohibition limits the possibility of actual realization of an interest, restricts it. Permission, on the other hand, brings no change in the conditions of the realization of an interest. What is not forbidden may within the limits of possibility be done. Where the law does not forbid the doing of a thing, only the lack of material means serves to prevent its accomplishment under this permission.

It is permitted to all the world to ride in a carriage, but he only can do it who has the necessary means. The legal rule here neither creates nor guarantees the possibility, but authorizes it as it in fact exists.

The influence of legal rules over the conditions for the realization of human interests is not limited solely to negative action. It is shown also under a positive form, and may have as a result an extension of the actual possibility.

In forbidding the employment of certain means for the realization of human interests, it enlarges by this very fact the possibility of the realization of other interests. The other interest may reach its realization not only within the limits of actual possibility but its owner can demand also that the prohibition in the law be observed and the obligation imposed, of not doing some particular act, obeyed. In this case the legal rule adds a new force and increases the favored person's power for the realization of his interests. It is this direct and positive influence of legal rules, this influence which confers an enlarged possibility of realization, which we call "subjective right" or "right-power." In other terms, this right is a possibility of the realization of an interest to which corresponds a legal obligation.

By this fact, that the law creates a corresponding obligation, it is distinguished from a simple permission. When one has a right to anything, all is permitted to him, but he has no right over all which is permitted, but only over the things guaranteed by the creation of a corresponding obligation. These rights can exist only between individuals and not in our relations to the phenomena of the outer world.

We must distinguish, then, the simple permission to do something which is only an absence of restrictions, from the right created by the increased possibility of accomplishment resulting from the extension of a corresponding capacity.

The influence of the legal rule can also take another form, a form which holds the mean at the same time between the simple absence of interdiction and the creation of a new right. Human interests are, in general, so closely bound together that any change produced in the conditions for the realization of one of them brings always some consequences for other interests which are bound up with it more or less complexly.

So the creation by a legal rule of a duty to guarantee the realization of any interest brings always consequences as to the realization of other connected interests. So, for example, the creation of a higher tariff upon imports brings advantages, not only to the producers of the commodity in the interior of the country, but also to smugglers. The obligation on the proprietor's part, as the result of a contract with his tenant, to maintain a stairway to the rented story, and cover it with a carpet, gives to the tenants on the lower stories the possibility of using each.

But neither the smuggler nor the tenant have rights because of the advantages which they draw from the existing legal obligation. They can make use of it only under the circumstances of fact which the contract points out. If the circumstances change and they can no longer use these advantages, they have no right to ask of anybody the re-establishment of the former state of things, so as to use the carpet or to draw greater profits from smuggling. The person, on the other hand, who has a right, if circumstances intervene which interfere with its exercise, can demand its restoration and this by virtue of a legal rule.

We should, then, distinguish right from mere power, as a possibility to which directly corresponds a legal obligation, as distinguished from the possibility which we have of using accidental consequences of others' rights for the realization of our interests. The action of legal rules here exhibited is called by Ihering reflex action of law. The obligation corresponding to a right can be imposed upon all those whose situation would lead to resistance to its use. In this case the subject of the obligation is not determined by his personal character, but by an objective character, from the opposition which arises as a result of the use of the given thing.

The rights to which such an obligation, which is common to all, corresponds are called rights over things. They are called also rights against all, or again, real rights. Opposed to them are rights against persons. The obligation corresponding to these last rests only upon a determinate individual or individuals. It is only by connection with this obligation that rights as against persons can be realized.

The right of property might serve as an example of the "real right" (*in rem*). The owner of the thing can require of everybody that he do not stand in the way of the owner's right of property. As an example of rights against persons, *in personam* may be cited in hiring for service.

Every right supposes, necessarily, a corresponding obligation. If the obligation does not exist, there will be only a permission and not a "right." But an obligation may sometimes exist without a corresponding right. This happens when the interest which constitutes the subject-matter of the corresponding right arises subsequently to it or is temporarily suspended. Thus the obligation not to assail the right of an unborn child corresponds to no right, since the fœtus is not yet a subject of right. The obligation is here created in expectation and by way of protection of the life of the infant to be born.

In the same way when a bill of exchange is lost and is temporarily out of possession of anybody, the obligation of the acceptor has not for the time being any corresponding right. The obligation meanwhile does not disappear on this account, because the instrument may be found by some person and this person acquire the rights given by the bill of exchange. The action in such a case Ihering calls passive action of law.

We have defined subjective right (right-power, *droit-pouvoir*, *pravomochia*) as the possibility of the realization of an interest to which corresponds directly an obligation. The definition assumes the formal and material point of view of legal right. On the external and formal side this right is a claim (*Rechtsanspruch*) of an individual for the performance of the obligation by the one subject to it. On the internal and material side it is the possibility of the realization of an interest, and as this realization supposes always the use of some natural forces the "matter" of the legal right is, in general, the use of such forces. Their use supposes only the presence of needs. The assertion of a claim supposes necessarily a conscious will. Our will can be set in movement not only to satisfy our personal needs, but also those of others.

Man can act in the interest of another, but the use he makes of goods is inseparable from the need which he has of them. The claim which he has for the performance of an obligation, guaranteeing the satisfaction of his needs, can be realized by other persons. This clearly happens when the subject who has the need has no conscious will or not enough. To guarantee the realization of his interests it is, then, necessary that there be the will of another person who directs him. Guardians act thus for the demented and for minors.

The same effect is reproduced with a view to convenience when a regulation of interests common to a whole group of individuals is attempted. Instead of all the wills acting together in the common interest, one of these wills acts for the whole, and so arises what we call the legal person. Meanwhile, even when such a distinction is under consideration as that between the subjects of a will, serving a given interest, and that interest itself, one ought to separate the bearer of the interest, the beneficiary, from the bearer of the will, the director. When the will acts for the advantage of another there results, not a right, but an obligation. He for whose advantage the right exists which produces a legal rule is not always the bearer of the right. Sometimes, owing to the reflex action of law, he enjoys the advantage of a right which he could not have independently. He would become the subject of a right only if the possibility of the use of it is guaranteed to him by a corresponding title, even if that title is realized by another's voluntary action.[1]

Most jurists, on the contrary, in defining the notion of the subject of a right, attach importance only to the right, or to the claim, or rather, to its employment, and they reach in this way some radically false consequences.

It is thus that we must explain Bekker's paradoxical doctrine, System I, s. 56. According to him, the owner of the right over given goods is the party whose bills, drawn against them, are guaranteed by these goods; as if it were possible to decide what bills are secured by the goods if one does not know to whom the goods belong.

[1] It is in this precise way that Bernatzik, Kritische Studien über Begriff für juristischen Person (Archiv für öff. R. B. V., 1890. s. 223) defines the subject of a right. "Rechtssubjekt ist der Träger eines jeden menschlichen Zweckes, den die herrschende Rechtsordnung als Selbstzweck dadurch anerkennt, dass sie dem zu seiner Realisirung erfordlichen Willen rechtliche Kraft verleiht."

The "matter," the content, of the right over things, we have said, is the employment of those things by the bearer of the right. Such is the general definition of the matter of a right, but the usage of the right may be extremely various. It may be, first, a simple use with no necessity of excluding others from the use of the same object nor the possibility of varying the means of such usage. This use consists in the right to employ a thing in common with other persons and conformably to its predetermined organization. Such a usage is a fundamental element of the matter of an obligation in this sense, that it is absolutely indispensable to the exercise of any right; but, it is the most restricted form of a right. The use which each of us makes of public roads is an example of such a right.

There is for every right not only a fundamental element like this usage, but a natural element which depends upon the very nature of our needs and not upon the complexity of social relations. Simple usage serves for the immediate satisfaction of human needs, so only physical persons can make use of things. Legal persons cannot of themselves, and without an intermediary, make use of objects.

A second fundamental element of the matter of a right is possession. It consists in the possibility of excluding other persons from the usage of the object over which we have rights. For example, the lessor of an immovable thing cannot only use that thing to satisfy his needs, but he has, besides, the right of excluding all other persons from its use, even when he is not employing it.

From its nature, then, possession is a condition which facilitates and guarantees the use of goods, but possession has at the same time a more independent scope. It augments use, enlarges, so to speak, its natural limits. Man has the use of goods which he employs to satisfy personal wants. Possession gives him the added possibility of exploiting for his own profit the needs of others. If a man has the right by possession to prevent others from making use of the object, he has also the right to authorize its usage under certain conditions, notably under the form of compensation. We see appear thus the advantage of acquiring in this way possession of things of which we have no immediate need, but from which we may draw in the meanwhile a profit by letting them to others.

The third element in the content of a right is that of disposing of the object, the *jus disponendi*. Ihering defines it as the right of changing or modifying the manner of using the object. Neither usage nor possession quite embraces this power of disposition of the object. The possessor of an object ought to keep unchanged its original organization and purpose. The lessor of a house, for example, can neither remodel nor destroy it.

The right of disposing of an object is made up of three different elements. It includes, first, the right of modifying the usage without destroying the object and without turning it over to another person. This is the *jus abutendi*. It includes also the right to transmit the object to another person, the *jus alienandi*, for this is one way of using the object. Finally, the third element is the right of destroying the object, of annihilating it. This is the *jus disponendi de substantia*. This third element exists only if the right of usage is applied to things.

Section 30. *The Objects of Rights*

REGELSBERGER. Pandekten I. s. 357.
BEKKER. System. I. s. 81.
KIERULF. Théorie, I. s. 129.
IHERING. Zweck im Recht, I. s. 70.
GOLMSTEIN. The Principle of Identity, p. 49.

Since the "matter" of a right is the use of something and there can be no such use if there is no object to which it applies, every right has, therefore, an object. Every actual right is over some particular thing. Some, as Bekker for example, admit, however, the existence of rights without objects. This comes from their taking into consideration only a particular element of right, the legal claim or title, but the "matter" of the right is always the use guaranteed by this legal title, a use which necessarily supposes an object. The object of a right may be anything which serves as a means for the realization of interests delimited by law. All our interests are realized by the aid of some force, and so it may be said in a general way that forces are the objects of right.

The employment of the forces which serve as means for the realization of our interests exhibits itself most frequently in the way of acts. For this reason some jurists have considered acts as the sole objects of right. It is, however, a conception which we cannot admit, for, if we examine it closely, it results in some consequences impossible to sustain.

Take the case, first, where rights belong to persons who cannot legally perform any act, for example an infant or a demented person. In such case it is another person, a guardian, who does for them the acts necessary for the preservation of their estates. Consequently in recognizing acts as the sole object of right it would become necessary to admit that the object of certain rights, rights of property for example, may vary according to their subject. If the holder of a right of property carrying with it a certain obligation is a person of full capacity, the object of the right corresponding to this obligation is certainly the personal action of the owner, but if he is not a person of full capacity, the object of this same right is no longer his personal action, but only that of another, his guardian for example.

We see that there are two altogether different objects in the same right. If we do not consider the acts of the guardian as the object of the right, then this right, as long as it relates to one without legal capacity, is without an object, for an infant at the breast can of himself do nothing in the way of acts necessary for realizing the use of the goods belonging to him.

The forces which are the objects of rights are exceedingly various, both in their own nature and according to the persons who are the subjects of such right. In the legal point of view the distinction of the nature of the forces has no importance, but the connection between the forces and the bearer of the right has some effect over the character even of the right. The objects of the right are classified according to this connection.

We distinguish four categories of objects: first, the personal forces of the subject; second, the forces of nature; third, the powers of some other person; fourth, the forces of society.

Each of these objects has a different connection with the subject of the right. Personal forces are the inalienable property of the bearer of the right. They are created at the time of his birth, and their division among men is the work of nature herself. The law does not give to man the use of these forces, but limits and protects them. The powers of other men are not created for our use and bestowed upon us by nature herself, for our profit, but to obtain their use we must employ the means set at our disposal by the law. These forces, being intimately connected with human personality, this very connection makes necessary a limitation of each one's rights over their object, for if the right was unlimited by hypothesis, it might result in a right not only over another man's power, but over his very person.

Man can make use of nature's forces so far as they are exhibited in things. These things are not equally distributed among men by nature; they possess no direct connection with the human person. This is why legal rules not only fix the usage of these things, but also fix the principles of their distribution amongst men. These rights over things are the most complete and absolute of all rights.

The forces of society belong to no individual, but to society as a whole and present this characteristic peculiarity, that each individual as a member of society is subject necessarily to the action of its forces.

The use of personal powers, physical and moral, is the prime necessary condition for the realization of our interests, but this usage may at the very start have for consequence the preventing of the realization of the interests of another. It is necessary, then, to apply certain restrictions to the use of these personal powers, and, as this usage is manifested always by some act of the man, these restrictions cannot be other than restrictions upon the liberty of human actions.

In the second place, the activity of other men may also cause hindrances to the use of our own personal powers. There is need, then, of guaranteeing by legal rules the use of personal power, in imposing upon others a corresponding obligation.

According to a rule common to all juridical restrictions, it is only those actions which bring about an external realization of our thoughts and our desires, which produce changes in the external environment, that are subjected to such restrictions, for only such actions can bring about any hindrance to the realization of other men's interests. An action amounting only to a manifestation of thought without tending towards its realization would not be subjected to such a restriction. The simple manifestation of the intention to commit a crime is not punishable, excepting always the case where the form of manifestation is itself an assault upon the interests of others. Thus, it is forbidden to express an opinion as to another having an offensive form. It is forbidden, also, to show under the form of menace a desire to do that which the law forbids. The manifestation of ideas by the press or the public tribune is subjected to special regulation, since in these particular cases the manifestation takes a very general scope.

The reader cannot know in advance what is the question treated in a pamphlet or a newspaper article, and after reading it he cannot rid himself of the impression which such reading has produced. It is the same with what has taken place in the casual passer's hearing of a public discourse.

The conception of liberty of thought is in a general way a relatively recent one. In the ancient law, on the contrary, even the simple manifestation of the thought was sought to be controlled. In former times it was believed there was possibility of doing harm by the simple thought, by the evil eye, as they said, or at least by words to which were attributed some of the force of acts designed to put them into execution.

The employment of our own personal forces is, then, guaranteed. This guarantee has for its purpose the protecting of our life, our health, that of body as well as that of mind. It happens often that individual powers do not suffice for the realization of an interest and that the collaboration of a number of individuals is necessary, and thus arise rights over the forces of other men. The modern idea of right does not, however, admit the existence of rights over the very person of a man. It admits only the existence of rights to his services, and even these rights have very frequently no absolute character.

If he who is employed to do an act, to perform some particular service, refuses to do it, he may not be constrained. These rights have a special character. The employee is permitted either to perform the act or to indemnify by a sum of money his employer. Only the right of the state over the services due from its citizens has an absolute character, such as the obligation to military service.

As to different parts of the human body, distinction must be made between those which are separated from it and those not so. Thus, the hair once cut, a tooth once extracted, may be compared to any other object because this hair or this tooth have no force, no means of action by themselves, once they are separated from the man's body.

On the other hand, the parts which are not detached cannot be subject to legal rights of others, can be subjected to no power of another, for no rights can be held over the human body or its members. We cannot acquire a right of property in another's hair not yet cut off, or in another's teeth still undetached. No right can be acquired to the use of the body of another individual, of a monster, a dwarf or a giant for example, with a view of exhibition. Rights can be acquired only over the action of the man, the promise to use his body or some parts of it, but if he refuses this usage, he cannot be constrained to it; he can only be required to find an indemnity for damages resulting from his refusal.

Besides these individual powers, the general human ones, the powers of nature serve also as means for the realization of human interests. The action of natural forces appears always in some form of physical phenomena and man can utilize this action for the realization of his interests only if he possesses the matter showing these phenomena. The different parts of matter are things; it is these things and not the natural forces which are the direct objects of right.

All things cannot be objects of right, but those only can fill this rôle which are subject to human influence. For this reason the stars, the firmament, cannot be objects of right. There are some things which can be objects of right only in connection with particular persons. There are others whose use by all is authorized by nature, like air, running water, the high sea. These are *res communes omnium*.

Certain things which by their nature are capable of becoming objects of private possession are, however, not left by positive legislation in the domain of private things. These are public things, the *res publicæ quæ extra commercium sunt*, for example, roads and highways. Physically, they are susceptible to private ownership, but such a situation is regarded as incompatible with their design. Among these public things we should distinguish those which are outside of the private domain only accidentally. These are such as belong to nobody, *res nullius quæ extra patrimonium nostrum sunt*.

In the same thing may appear the action of not merely one, but of several forces. The law may permit to a man the use of all the powers in a given thing, or only of a part of its manifestations. In the first case, as is readily seen, the power of the person over the thing is at its fullest extent. It is the complete right of property, its *dominium*.

The owner may employ all the powers of a thing which belongs to him, at least so far as these powers have not been excluded from the permitted use of the thing. On the contrary, a person who has only the right of enjoyment, who has not over the thing the right of property, can use the thing only within the limits which this right of usage confers upon him. The same thing, therefore, may be at the same time susceptible of a right of ownership and of other less complete rights than this, right of usage, rights of enjoyment, *jura in re aliena*.

To the distinctions between the different physical properties of things it is necessary to add the different legal properties of those things. In legal language, for example, a great difference is established between movable goods and immovable goods.

Immovable goods are the soil and everything which is completely adherent to it, as trees and houses. All others are movable goods. Here is a distinction which has serious consequences in acts of division, for example, in rules of inheritance and in the guarantees furnished by law.

The thing, being a portion of matter, is in its turn divided into portions. This notion of portions of matter has only a very relative force. The part can be considered at the same time as dependent upon the whole object, or as itself forming a distinct whole. One readily acquires an idea of things composed of parts and forming a whole, *universitas rerum*, which, formed out of many things, serves, however, only for the realization of a single interest. Legally, this whole is considered as one single thing, as in the case of shops and stores and their merchandise, flocks, etc. The connection of these different things with each other is sometimes a relation of subordination, and it results that one thing is an attribute of another; the door, for example, may be considered as an attribute of the house. We call attributes certain things without which the principal thing could not answer its purpose, the design for which it was organized; as for example, a carriage deprived of its wheels. The attributes are always subject to the same disposition as the principal object.

The final category of objects of right which we have enumerated is that formed by the forces of society. We must distinguish them from the powers of the individual. In reality this force of society is not, as one might suppose, the sum of the forces of each of the members who compose it; it is a much greater force than that. The explanation is found in the organization of the society, which unites the individual forces in the habit of each one's submitting himself to the requirements of the social life and in the moral authority which every society has with regard to its own members.

The relations between men have multiple forms. The smaller society is subject to the greater and the weaker of two powers can be very often regarded as a force dependent upon the greater.

Finally, all human associations are reducible to one, to the greater society *par excellence*, to humanity. Humanity embraces all societies and absorbs them into itself. But all societies have not an evident external influence. Only those which are organized possess this. The force of those societies which act directly upon each of their members can be the object of right. The most important of these societies are the church, the state, and the family.

Section 31. *Juridical Facts*

IHERING. Geist, III. §53.
ZITELMANN. Irrthum und Rechtsgeschäft. s. 200 ff.
THON. Rechtsnorm und subjektives Recht. ss. 71 ff. ss. 325 ff.

Juridical relations are not unchangeable. They arise, evolve, and disappear. On what do these different changes depend?

Every legal relation supposes necessarily a right and an obligation resulting from the application of legal rules. We have already seen that this application depends upon certain facts fixed generally by the hypothesis under consideration.

Legal relations, then, depend upon these "juridical facts." Generally, indeed, the application of a legal rule gives birth to several of them and not to one. To acquire, for example, a right to property by possession there is necessary, first, the intention of holding the thing by proprietary title; second, a given duration of such possession; third, an uninterrupted possession; and fourth, an uncontested possession. It is only when these four conditions combine that possession gives birth to a right of property.

A combination of all the circumstances necessary for the application of a legal rule may be called the "content of the suppositions of fact," in German, *Thatbestand*. The different conditions which form the suppositions of fact may pertain either to external facts or to the mind and will of an individual. In the last supposition they can exist only so far as they are relations between human actions, for it is only in such actions that the human will is manifest.

It is necessary, then, to distinguish between the "objective" and the "subjective" content of suppositions of fact. So, for a will to be valid there are necessary besides certain conditions of outward form, writing, presence of a certain number of witnesses, etc., certain subjective conditions on the part of the testator, sound mind, sufficient memory, freedom, etc. The combination of conditions of form, external conditions, constitutes the objective side of the testament. The moral conditions of the validity of the testament form, on the other hand, its subjective side.

The application of the legal rule may depend merely upon objective conditions. This happens when the juridical facts are not human actions. An inheritance, for example, is declared open by the simple fact of the death of the former holder, and is opened for the advantage of all the heirs by the simple fact of their existence. There is no subjective condition. The law does not interfere with regard to facts which embrace only subjective conditions. Indeed, the law has only to do with ideas which have already received their application. These alone have legal importance. We easily recognize, then, in every application of law two elements,—the subjective one, which is the thought, and the objective one, which is the external manifestation of that thought.

Here, then, is a primary distinction to be made among juridical facts; facts which are exclusively objective, and actions which are essentially at the same time objective and subjective.

There is commonly a harmony between juridical facts and the law. It may happen, however, that certain of these facts are opposed to it, and we have, then, facts which are legal and others which are illegal. Hence, a new distinction between legal facts conformable to law, and others opposed to it.

To look a little closer at the distinctions to be made

between facts and acts and between legal and illegal facts we may class them in four categories: first, legal facts; second, legal acts; third, illegal facts; and fourth, illegal acts. Such a classification presents, however, some inconveniences.

It is the truth that certain of the legal acts are juridically considered as facts because their objective side is of little importance. These acts, whether conscious or not, have always an absolutely identical legal weight; for example, the destruction of a thing does away with all right over it; whether this destruction was voluntary or not, the result is always the same.

So, actions whose legal consequences are not affected by their subjective side ought to be classed with facts and are most commonly called so, juridical facts properly so called. Illegal acts alone form a distinct group, whose juridical importance depends specially upon the intention with which they are performed. It is necessary, moreover, to observe that illegal acts have juridical importance only so far as they give rise to a durable illegal situation, a situation requiring the re-establishment of a violated right. For the rest, usually instead of saying illegal facts we say illegal condition, and more commonly designate illegal acts under the name of violations of right.

We distinguish, then, four categories among juridical facts: first, juridical facts, properly so called; second, juridical acts; third, illegal states or conditions; fourth, violations of right. Juridical facts, properly so called, comprise all those which embrace nothing contrary to legal rules, nothing anti-legal, and whose accomplishment does not bring with it any creation of new rights or, rather, any change or extinction of rights or obligations already existing. Rights and obligations never have importance except as they serve to delimit the contending interests; it is only facts bringing forward new interests which will be determined by new laws. So, on the birth within the state's territory of a man whose father was a citizen of that state, it is presumed that the individual takes the nationality of the country of his birth.

The fact of not using a right for a long while generally indicates that an interest formerly in existence exists no longer, and that in disappearing it has taken with it the right. All extinctive prescriptions are established upon this idea.

In other cases, the juridical fact constitutes the cause which puts an end to the existence of an interest or modifies it. Thus, a person's death deprives him of all interest and all right. All interests in the meanwhile are not bound up thus closely with specific facts. We can even say that more frequently interests do not present through facts specific indications of the birth, the modification, or the extinction of a right. In these cases the hypothesis of the rule does not contain its index, and the application of the rule is subordinated to the presence of certain interests. The work of adaptation of the rule to the interest is performed by those of whom duty or their own personal interest requires it. The interests, which call most frequently for the performance of a juridical act, usually exhibit themselves in the specific act, especially when it has for its purpose the maintenance of the existence of the interest. These interests are difficult to recognize in fortuitous acts and in those compelled by overwhelming force. Consequently, the application of rules delimiting interests depends either upon external signs, which reveal themselves readily, or upon special acts having its purpose; that is to say, upon acts performed with a view to bring about their application.

These juridical acts are of two kinds. If their accomplishment is left to private persons with an object simply personal, they are contracts; in the Roman law, *negotia juris;* if, on the contrary, their accomplishment depends upon functionaries charged with this care by their duty or their functions, they are orders, decrees, *Verfügungen*. Both may be unilateral or bilateral. The first are those which contain the manifestation of the will of but one of the parties to the agreement; the second, those which contain the manifestation of the will of two or of several parties.

A unilateral contract relates only to the rights of the executing parties because it is those rights alone which such a contract can regulate. We cite as examples of this category of contracts the testament and the contracting of ourself for service. The unilateral order of administration acting as authority can affect the rights of individuals, can restrain or even suppress them.

A bilateral contract is one having for its base an agreement of independent persons one with the other and not connected by any bond of subordination. The bilateral order, on the contrary, has not the same character. Of the two wills forming it the one is the master and the other the subject. The two wills are brought into connection, the one in order to demand, to solicit, the other to authorize, agree and ratify.

The performance of every contract, just as of every order, requires certain relative conditions; some as to the subject who shall perform the contract or the order, others as to the form which the contract or order should assume. The capacity of forming a contract we call capacity to contract. Minors, the insane, those who have lost their civil rights, do not possess this contractual capacity.

It is necessary also to indicate certain acts for which there exist special restrictions and which require a special capacity, the act if performed by an incapable individual being void.

Capacity to give authority to orders or decrees constitutes competency. General competency is impossible, and the order performed outside of its assigned limits, determined by the rules of administration, has no more validity than the contract of an incapable.

For some juridical actions special forms have been established. Sometimes these forms are not closely obligatory and serve only to give greater force to the contract or to establish the proof for the future of its due execution. These forms are established not only with a view to proof, *corroboration*, but sometimes such forms are necessary attributes of the act itself. Without them the act has no juridical value. It is considered as void and as never having existed. These are necessary forms to the act itself, *corpus negotii*.

The written form of a bill of exchange may serve as an example for forms of the first category. A loan of money may exist without written proof; if the debtor acknowledges his duty there is no need of any writing. As example of form which makes an integral part of the act itself, that required for a purchase or sale of real property may be cited. This sale or purchase must be evidenced by writing, without which it is not recognized as valid even when nobody contests its existence. With regard to the orders of government or administration this distinction applies also. Some forms are imposed only with a view to convenience and their omission may bring disciplinary penalties, but the order be none the less valid. Other formalities, on the contrary, are absolutely necessary that the order may be valid and obligatory upon the citizens.

By juridical representation certain acts can be performed by one person instead of another. The representative performs the act in the name of his principal and under the condition that all the juridical consequences of the act shall belong to the party represented. Juridical representation may be forced or voluntary. The representation is said to be forced when it is on behalf of persons who cannot themselves do legal acts, who, as we have already stated, have no contractual capacity. It is said to be voluntary when a perfectly capable person instead of doing an act himself charges some other person with doing it in his place.

The illegal situation and the violation of right have this in common, that both are in opposition to the legal rule. They present always an important difference as follows: The requirements of legal rules address themselves to the deliberate will of man. Law cannot in fact control the actions, the unconscious forces of nature, so only man's will can violate a right. Nothing which is the work of other forces can amount to a violation of right.

The unconscious forces of nature may meanwhile cause a condition of things in open opposition to the requirements of a legal rule. The wind, for example, may displace an object and carry it over into another's domain. We can class with these cases, those where the man acts unconsciously,—in an attack of insanity, for example. In all these cases there is no violation of right; there is only an illegal condition. The illegal condition requires always the re-establishment of a disturbed right, the restoration of a condition which existed before and which conforms to the requirements of the legal rule. This right exists always for the advantage of the one whose right has been disturbed.

The violation of right brings, besides, other consequences. It is a great danger indeed for a legal rule that by non-compliance its authority is seriously assailed and with it that of law in general. Hence, the necessity of the sanction to avoid the recurrence of wrongful acts.

A conscious violation of law supposes always fault on the part of the author of the wrong and requires an indemnity. Finally, the author of the wrong may exhibit a condition of mind which requires to be corrected.

Punishment inflicted on the author of the wrong serves to realize three ends,—to prevent the wrong; to furnish indemnity by the delinquent to the injured party; to correct the delinquent. But all violations of law are not punishable. Only those violations which involve features of a general interest ought to be punished; the others, those which comprise only an assault upon rights of individuals, upon rights of private interest, require only an indemnity to repair the damage caused.

Violations of law which result in punishment are called crimes. To constitute a crime there must be a conscious, intended act violating the law, and one ought to distinguish between premeditated crime, which is one having for its purpose the violation of a right, and the infraction committed by imprudence, which ought, however, to be punished also because it results in consequences contrary to law.

CHAPTER III

PUBLIC AND PRIVATE LAW

Section 32. *Classification of Rights According to their Matter*

SAVIGNY. System I. s. 23.
STAHL. Die Philosophie des Rechts, II. s. 300.
AHRENS. Encyclopädie. s. 117.

Juridical relations are extremely various. The detailed study of their groups constitutes the very science of law.

The general study of law cannot do without a profound examination of the fundamental peculiarities of each group of special rights, and for this purpose a general classification of juridical relations is necessary. A fundamental division universally recognized is that into public and private law.[1] There are numerous discussions, however, as to the exact point of distinction between them. The Romans placed it in the character of the interests protected by law; the ensemble, the totality, of public interests protected, constituted public law, and that of private interests formed private law. "*Publicum jus est* [*Inst. Ulpian. II.* §2, *De Justitia et Jure,*] *quod ad statum rei Romanæ spectat, privatum, quod ad singulorum utilitatem pertinet, sunt enim quædam publice utilia quædam privatim.*"

Down to our times this definition has found partisans. Bruns (Holzendorff's Encyclopädie 3 Auf. s. 340) and Neuner (Privatrechtsverhältnisse, s. 1) have adopted it.

[1] By the side of public and private law are recognized ecclesiastical (Walter), international (Warnkönig), and social (Mohl, Rösler) law.

It has been resisted, however, for a long time by a good many jurists. This Roman definition does not define anything at all. It does not delimit or determine in any way the different regions of law. Interests cannot be opposed to one another as being public or private. They can exist nowhere except in the man, and every general interest is nothing but a combination of individual interests. We can say in a certain sense that the whole law is created for the protection of the interests of individuals, that is to say, private interests. Moreover, legal protection is only extended to those interests of individuals which have a more or less general scope, which relate, for example, to a whole group of individuals, as physicians, or to a person whose interest, like that of a monarch, by reason of his important position, is of a general order. In this sense we might say that the law protects only general interests.

We can distinguish again between public interests, and divide them in their turn; but, without insisting upon the altogether relative character which such a distinction presents, it may be said that it does not correspond with any actually existing. It cannot be established, as a rule, that public law is concerned with more general interests and private law with those which are less so.

Faults committed in the course of a campaign by a furnisher of supplies, faults which may lead to a famine in a whole army corps and bring about its defeat, have a much more general interest than the election of a member of some municipal council; and, meanwhile, in the first case, the market for supplies is under the control of the civil law, and in the second, the nomination and election of the functionary under that of public law. So again, the organization of a ministry presents an interest incomparably less important and less general than the regulation of the conveyance of real estate or of hiring for service, and yet in the first case we are in the domain of public law and in the second that of private law. The insufficiency of Ulpian's definition, its lack of precision, has induced many attempts to reach a more precise one.

We will examine first the classification proposed by Savigny. His system, accepted by Stahl, might be called the teleological system. It is a definition borrowed partly from that of Ulpian, but distinguished from it radically, however, by certain points.

Ulpian defined the law according to the interests which it regulated. Savigny and Stahl, on the other hand, distinguish legal relations according to their purpose. In public law, according to Savigny, the state is the purpose, the individual holds only a secondary place. The contrary is the fact in the civil law. The individual is the end, and the state only a means.

Stahl says almost the same: "Certain legal relations have as their end the satisfaction of individual needs; others seek to establish a combination of men under a single authority and to cause them to live in that unity."

This distinction between legal relations according to their purpose has been quite recently developed by Ihering in his work Das Zweck im Recht (Bd. I, 1877? s. 452). He indicates its real meaning, and distinguishes the relations by their purpose into three classes, according as the beneficiary in view is the individual, society, or the state.

But this distinction is not for Ihering a fundamental one in law, and he shows that each juridical institution may have as its beneficiary the individual, the society, or the state. For example, property can be private, social or public. This distinction, then, cannot be a fundamental one in a legal system. We seek, in fact, a classification of institutions, and not a classification of forms which the same institution may take in succession.

Savigny and Stahl have tried in their classification to group together two schemes of classification, up to that time distinct, the one established according to the interest regulated by the law, and the other according to the position of the subject, regarded sometimes as an independent individual, sometimes as a member of a social organization. Ahrens has equally tried the same combination of these different processes of classification, and opposes the immediate purpose to the final one. The final end of all law is the human personality, but the human personality can be at the same time the immediate end of a juridical relation, and this immediate end is a relation of private law. If it is, on the other hand, society or the state which is the immediate object of the legal relation, we find ourselves then in the presence of a relation of public law.

So, then, the purpose, the final function of public and private legal relations, is the same. It is only the means employed for the accomplishment of this purpose, for its realization, which is varied. In private law this purpose is realized by the individual determination; in public, by the collective act of the entire society.

Ahrens' classification is insufficient. His theory, like Stahl's as well as Savigny's, does not explain how it happens that the state is so frequently the subject of relations of a purely civil and private character.

When the state buys, sells, exchanges, or hires, it is itself the object and not the means (Savigny); the furnishing of boots for the army does not have for its end, evidently, the satisfaction of an individual (Stahl); and the end sought is not attained by individual volition, but by the activity of the entire state, which pays the expense of furnishing them (Ahrens).

Finally, Ahrens seems to forget that juridical protection, whatever be the interest which it concerns, supposes the collaboration of the whole society and not the mere determination of an individual.

These unfortunate attempts to adapt the definition left us by the Romans have urged several modern jurists, especially Russians, to wholly abandon the Roman conception. Some have sought the basis for the distinction between public and private law in the distinction of interests according as they have or do not have a patrimonial character. Others have seen especially in private law a right of disposition. The partisans of the first opinion are Mayer, Oumov, and especially Kaveline; the second opinion has been maintained by Zitovich.

Kaveline [1] thinks that the distinction ordinarily made between public law and private law rests upon no theoretical foundation. Private law comprehends some parts totally different from each other, and this can be explained only because it is transmitted to us thus combined by the Romans. The one of these different parts presenting a certain degree of unity, having some rules from pretty much the same source, has been combined under the name of civil law, that is, the *jus civile* of the Romans, a term which they gave to their whole law.

In our day, in Russia particularly, there is no reason to keep this group intact and apply to it the same name as in the ancient classification, since today civil relations are no longer determined by the Roman law. Instead of this classification, with its at present purely historic importance, Kaveline proposes a classification which he thinks more rational and at the same time more simple. His classification has for its base the distinction which he establishes between patrimonial rights and all other rights. The modern civil law, says

[1] "What the Civil Law?" 1864. "What is Private Law's Place in the System of Law in General?" (Journal of Civil and Penal Law, 1880.)

he, is the mass of laws affecting our patrimony. It is necessary to exclude from it all the legal relations which have no patrimonial character, as for example, the family relations.

The civil law thus understood according to Kaveline ought to embrace the totality of relations affecting any title to the patrimony. A good many legal relations which are classed nowadays in the public law ought, he thinks, to be put into the private law, as for example the laws as to taxes, penalties, and the privileges and compensations of functionaries.

Such a classification has in its favor an apparent simplicity and clearness. A careful examination shows us, however, that it is scarcely admissible. It is not possible to conclude with Kaveline that the modern conception of law is due simply to chance, that it rests upon no rational basis. Even if it were true, as Kaveline affirms, that the civil law in its actual condition offers only an agglomeration of parts of law more or less distinct, combined together by the Roman law, this agglomeration, we are convinced, is not the work of chance.

It is because these different laws continued always to answer to the requirements of social life that they have been preserved, and it is only that which is indispensable in all legislation which has been transmitted to us by the Roman law.

The private civil law is precisely that part of it which exhibits the greatest unity. It is in the civil law that the least trace is left of the vanished years and the numerous differences between races. This suffices to require us to make of the rules which constitute it, and of the relations which it governs, a group apart, a distinct category. Moreover, as Mouromtzev has already shown, it is wrong to pretend that the actual civil law is identical with that which we have received from the Romans.

Moreover, it is only starting with the XVI century that the bringing together of the *jus privatum* and the *jus gentium* has been attempted.

There are institutions, the bill of exchange, for example, which were quite unknown to the Roman law. It is not, then, precisely correct to say that it is merely because it is derived from a common source that the civil and private law has been classified as it actually is.

We should observe, besides, that the simplicity and clearness in Kaveline's classification are only apparent. In reality to separate patrimonial rights from rights which are not so, is no easy thing. All rights, personal ones as well as others, have an economic scope and touch in some sort material interests affecting our patrimony. Kaveline places in the private civil law some relations, considered till that time as relations of public law; for example, the penalties inflicted by law. But who does not see that other penalties, for example that of deportation, might also have an economic effect bearing upon our patrimony and sometimes do have this, as their chief scope?

Even if we classify in the private civil law some relations like those existing between the state and its functionaries [1] from the point of view of their powers, or those between the state and the citizens [2] from the point of view of the military system, and of taxes, there is no reason for not also placing in the private civil law some relations which are incontestably relations of public law; for example, the rights resulting from the organization of the government, and from the organization of political representation as established in the country.

Do not these relations offer an economic side at the point of view, for example, of indemnities to which deputies and senators are entitled, or if the function of

[1] Rights over Goods, p. 326.
[2] *Ibidem*, p. 228.

these representatives of the people is gratuitous, at the point of view of the expenses which are caused necessarily in the performance of their duty?

If we connect with private civil law the different relations which control the sustenance of the poor, it is necessary to place there also the combination of dispositions with regard to gratuitous primary instructions, and so on. We shall come by this method easily to place in private civil law all the social relations.

The classification of Kaveline, besides, lacks precision in not defining the "material value" of patrimonial right, which is the juridical relation which serves as the basis of this whole classification. What does he mean by it? He gives evidently to these words the meaning which the economists attribute to them, but these latter employ the words in two essentially different meanings, value in use, and value in exchange.

To the idea of value in use one attaches the whole idea of the importance of that which serves in one fashion or another for the satisfaction of man's needs. Wagner, for example, considers the political organization as susceptible of being measured by its economic value. Evidently a classification based upon value in use cannot be applied to legal relations. Every right, in so far as it serves as a means for the realization of human interests, can be considered as having value in this sense.

The conception of value in exchange is more limited. To define it, savants themselves appeal to the idea of law. Everything which may be the object of a private right has value in exchange. When slavery existed, man himself had such value. When offices and employments were subjects of commerce under the system of selling offices, these charges and employments had also their value in exchange. If land by any chance became incapable of private ownership, on that day it would no longer have value in exchange. The distinction between public and private law cannot, then, rest upon the conception of value in exchange since this value depends upon that very distinction.

Kaveline's system offers serious inconveniences for the study of law. It leads necessarily to arbitrary distinctions. It results in separations between those things which constitute naturally part of the same branch of law. It is in this way that he goes on to separate the recovery of a ruler's taxes from the imposition of them; to treat in two different parts of the law the privileges assigned to functionaries, and the theory as to the legal situation of such functionaries in the state. It is impossible, meanwhile, to give a clear explanation of this theory without speaking of the privileges of functionaries and their rights and duties.

Finally, let us observe that in his definition Kaveline gives us no idea of what the public law is, out of what materials he composes it, or what are its relations with private law.

Zitovich [1] thinks also to find the fundamental distinction between public and private law in the economic nature of these rights, but he reaches this result by a quite different route from that followed by Kaveline. According to him private, or civil law, is the ensemble of institutions, of rules of positive right, which fix the distribution of economic wealth at a given time or among a given people, or, more briefly, the civil law is the law of distribution (*Verkehrsrecht*). It must be observed that his definition does not exclude from the civil law thus understood the relations of family rights. These relations, he says, are in reality rights of distribution. They indicate in a precise fashion the causes which lead to the distribution of wealth, the principal of these causes being inheritance. Finally, the individual who very often

[1] Course in Russian Civil Law, I. 1878. pp. 4–7.

is at the same time the author and the subject of the division is regarded under different aspects. His situation as a member of a family may have a great importance. Finally, the subdivision, here under consideration, is not exactly an economic distribution; it is a distribution which has at its base the moral unity, the internal solidarity, of each family.

We may, once for all, observe that what Zitovich says in speaking of the family applies equally to the state. The relations of the state with the citizens give rise, also, to distribution. The state allots privileges, distributes gratifications, makes loans, pays debts. In all these operations the individual appears as the author and the subject of distribution, and it is of importance for the law to consider him under this relation and observe what his situation is, not now as a member of a family, but as a member of the state. The distinctions between classes have had great importance in this point of view.

All the wealth which the state accumulates by means of taxes which are imposed upon the nation, and also by means of revenues derived from domainal goods,—all this wealth is not distributed according to the laws of economic distribution, but rather according to political reasons In a general way we can say that the organization of the state has as extensive an influence over the distribution of wealth as has that of the family.

Reasoning in this fashion, Zitovich ought to come to the conclusion that all juridical relations, being relations of distribution, should be placed in the private law. Public law, for him, also, results necessarily in the deplacement of wealth in the economic order, and then can we assert that there is in the civil law nothing but relations of distribution? Evidently not. Family rights, for example, comprehend quite a different thing and contain dispositions which do not all affect the patrimony. On the contrary, in the public law certain branches, like financial legislation, deal exclusively with relations of economic distribution.

We see, then, that all the attempts to establish distinctions between private and public law have remained unfruitful. The distinctions among interests which constitute the matter of juridical relations do not suffice as a basis for the classification of those juridical relations

Since juridical norms determine, not the interests themselves, but only the different limits which exist between them, the forms which they affect, let us seek, then, to distinguish the juridical relations, not in accordance with those interests which are the same in all the phenomena of social life, but in accordance with the manner in which those interests are delimited, according to their form.

This impossibility, which we have just recognized, of finding in the matter of juridical relations the basis for a distinction between public and private law is further confirmed by the examples furnished by the history of law, by the different forms in which relations absolutely identical, so far as their matter is concerned, have been clothed.

In the middle ages, for example, certain powers, certain prerogatives of public power, were only accessory rights attached to the possession of the soil.

Section 33. *Formal Classifications*

KANT. Metaphysische Anfangsgründe der Rechtslehre, 1797. s. 161 ff.

PUCHTA. Vorlesungen über das heutige röm. Recht. I. s. 75 ff.

JELLINEK. System der öffentlichen subjektiven Rechten, 1892. ss. 40–65.

THON. Rechtsnorm und subjektives Recht. ss. 108–146.

MOUROMTZEV. Definition and fundamental divisions of law, pp. 185–217.

The insufficiency of classifications founded upon the matter and content of the juridical relations has led savants to seek a classification of public rights and private rights from external signs, from the forms of juridical relations. Several formal classifications have been tried. We may group them under two categories. Some think to find the basis of a distinction between public rights and private rights in the different situations in which the subjects of juridical relations find themselves; the objects, for example, which rights give to a man are given him either as a member of society or as a human individual. Others recognize a distinction in the character of the protections which the law gives to defend injured individuals and look to see if these protections are granted on the initiative of the individual injured or on the intervention of public authority.

The first of these two conceptions owes its origin to the influence asserted by the school of natural law, the school of the state of nature, which is conceived as having preceded the formation of society.

Law at its origin by the formation of society is exclusively private law. This law continues to exist when the society is formed, but it is then surrounded and completed by institutions which have for their end the organization of the state and of its organs and of its functions. This additional law is public law. The relations it has with private law are those of support and protection.

All public law has been created to serve as a support for the sanction of private law. This is an opinion adopted by Kant, amongst others, to serve as a distinction between public and private rights.

This classification, due to the theory of the natural state, has had meanwhile the same fate as the theory from which it came. This theory lost its favor some time ago, and nobody today defends it. The classification, however, to which it gave birth, is still admitted by a good many authors and has even been somewhat expanded.

It is to the historical school, which was one of reaction against the school of natural law, that we owe the author who has best defended this classification. Puchta in his works appears as its determined partisan. Puchta distinguishes rights according to whether the man holds them as an individual or as a member of an organized society. In the first division are the rights of property and rights of family; in the second, public and ecclesiastical rights. The rights of property and rights of family constitute private rights, hence his division of rights into three great classes, private rights, public rights, and ecclesiastical rights.

We observe at once an incoherence in this classification. In fact, if it has for its basis the distinction of rights which belong to a man according as he appears as an individual or as a member of a society, it is necessary to oppose the right of property to all other rights. But Puchta combines rights of property with rights of family.

Other writers have brought modifications of Puchta's

theory and have corrected his definition to this extent, that they have divided all law into two categories only, public and private. Public rights, they have said, include only rights which necessarily presuppose the existence of an organized society among men and which cannot exist without such a society. Private rights are those which suppose only a simple coherence of men. Rights of family in this new theory will be considered as private rights, since they can exist outside of society and independently of the state.

While this theory seems more logical and more complete, it presents, nevertheless, a grave defect. It has for a basis this idea, that men can live without being organized in society and that one can admit among these men, living outside of all society, the existence of rights. This is an altogether false conception. We are more and more convinced that right exists only in society; no society, no right. There are, it is true, a good many degrees in the organization of a society, but even a crowd assembled by chance is not without some bonds of connection, without some relations between the individuals who make it up.

Let us look at some of the developments of this last theory. The relations of private right, marriage, exchange, gifts, say the partisans of this doctrine, are possible even where there is no state and no organized society. They can exist even amongst a band of brigands, amongst individuals gathered together by accident in a desert.

But the relations of a public character, for example election to parliament, are possible only in an organized state. It is easy, however, to use these very examples to refute this theory.

Without doubt we can elect a member of parliament only where there is a parliament. That is very true, but we can also form certain agreements, perform certain acts of exchange only where there are notaries and by consequence, an organized society.

Moreover, even a crowd assembled by chance can hold discussions over their common affairs and give directions in the general interest. Let us suppose a ship which suffers wreck and over which the captain does not exercise, as he might do, his right of commanding the passengers; these latter may discuss together their present situation and take necessary measures for the common safety. Among them the more energetic will speedily become dominant. Doubtless it might be said that there is here nothing organized, that there can be no question of a vote, of a right to vote, but nevertheless the vote exists in the throng under such circumstances. The sexual union itself will be only a fact, nothing else; the exchange or the gift also will be only facts and not the result of the exercise of a right. The thing may be transmitted, but no right, for there is none.

Another defect resulting from a classification so extended is that it results logically in introducing into the public law the relations between members of any association, any society, that of the stockholders in an incorporated company, for example, or even the relations of the family group.

The partisans of the system go so far without recoiling from the overthrow which they are giving to the current conception which rules as to the matter.

Bahr, for example (Rechtstaat, 1865), would divide all law into private law (*Privatrecht*) and the law of societies (*Genossenschaftsrecht*). The first includes the relations of men considered as members of an organism, state, society, church. Public law thus considered is only a subdivision of the law of associations.

Gierke holds equally to this same opinion; but such a classification does not answer at all to the historic grouping of the relations men hold to each other.

Jellinek, under a form a little different, accepts this distinction of rights into public and private rights. He distinguishes rights into two categories,—there are bearers of rights who can exercise choice and others who can only hold (*dürfen und können*). The law, said he, can only recognize as permitted those relations which existed before it, and independently of it, to which it brings no new element, unless it be that individuals who previously had power to act can now act legally (*dürfen*). The consequences of the recognition of this power to act appear very clearly when it is attempted to study the effects of legal prohibitions. Every prohibition can be reduced to this formula,—you may not, you cannot legally (*du darfst nicht*). In every case the prohibition does not render an act impossible to do, it merely declares the doing of it illegal. The prohibition can always be violated. But the action of the law is not limited merely to permissions and prohibitions. The law can add to the individual's capacity a new element. It can give to acts and contracts a juridical force which brings with it some new consequences quite different from those attached by nature to the same act or contract. It has, then, that which is called juridical force (*rechtliches Können*).

These two elements, power and force, are so closely connected that the first never exists without the second. What I may do legally is only the sum of my power over actual facts, recognized and assented to by the law; but juridical force may exist meanwhile without such "power"; in the case, for example, where the law does not merely protect the natural capacity of the person, but gives to him a new capacity.

Jellinek's distinction between public and private law has its foundation exactly in this correlation of juridical power and juridical force. In private law the first element, the power, exists always; in public law one requires always the presence of the second, the state's force, and public rights are all based on a force resulting from the law. They are no part of the natural liberty regulated by law, but constitute an enlargement of this natural liberty.

This distinction is purely artificial, and if examined closely loses all its value. *Dürfen und können, pouvoir et puissance,* "power and force," are not essential elements of the matter of subjective right. Such a distinction between these two elements depends not upon the matter of the right, but upon consequences brought on by the violation of a right. If the violation of a legal rule results only in a liability on the part of him who violates the law (*lex minus quam perfecta*), it may result that one cannot violate this law, but he finds that he has had the force to do so. If such a violation brings about the legal nullity of the act forbidden by the law (*lex perfecta*), the power to perform such act does not exist. If, finally, the violation of the rule brings at the same time a liability upon the doer of the act and the legal nullity of the act (*lex plus quam perfecta*) there is neither power nor force to violate such a rule.

On the other side, it is necessary to observe that the element of "*Dürfen,*" of permission, is not at all a stranger to public law.

The individual who does not possess the needed legal capacity not only has not "*Können,*" ability, to accept a given function, but neither has he "*Dürfen,*" permission, since the usurpation of this function is a punishable act.

A classification having for a base the distinction of consequences which the violation of the law involves, has been proposed by Thon. If the violation of law brings to him who has suffered by its violation the right of an indemnity, the right in this case is a private one; if, on the contrary, this violation brings about the intervention of public authority, then it is a public right.

More briefly, private rights are those which are specially protected by the initiative of the person who has suffered damage; public rights are those protected by society, the state, independently of the intervention of the injured individual. This classification of Thon has found a good many partisans amongst Russian jurists, among others Mouromtzev, Gambaroff and Duvernoi. It is, however, not very accurate.

First, the distinction between public and private rights would appear only when they are violated, but even when they are not violated, we distinguish quite clearly between public rights and private ones. Thus all the world, for example, knows that one can transfer family rights, while public rights are not subject to alienation.

Then, it is not precise to claim that private rights are the only ones protected by private initiative. There are also crimes or offenses pursued only upon the complaint of the one who has been the victim. When there is a system of administrative justice the right of pursuit is left to private persons the more frequently even if the public rights have suffered some injury as to their protection by the administration.

Finally, and this is the most important point, the right of pursuit given to individuals who have suffered injury and the action of authority are not two pursuits which exclude each other. They can very readily take place simultaneously as the consequence of a single act violating some single right. Let us take as examples the case of robbery and assassination. There is a criminal proceeding instituted, but there is also a civil pursuit on the part of the victims or the successors. These two prosecutions to be sure, are quite distinct, but they cannot serve to establish a criterion, a mark of distinction between public and private rights. Otherwise, we would be compelled to admit that the same right can be at the same time a public and a private one.

Section 34. *The Distinction Between Public Rights and Private Rights*

All the theories which we have just examined have furnished no satisfactory explanation of the distinction between public and private law. They give, however, some characteristic indications of this distinction. They have shown us that it is necessary to avoid seeking the basis of this distinction in the different interests in view of which public and private rights are created. The basis of the whole distinction should be sought in the form with which juridical relations clothe themselves. Such a distinction ought by no means to have as its principal foundation merely the subject of the right or the consequences which the violation of the right brings. This distinction ought to be more general and ought to be applicable even when there has been no violation of the right.

All rights being appendant to human beings regarded as members of society, it is necessary to seek the explanation of the distinction between public and private right in the diversity which the legal forms of all the relations established among men present.

The right, as we have seen, is in general the power to make use of something. This faculty can be guaranteed to an individual under a double form. The simplest form is that of dividing the object into several parts, and each of these parts being assigned to an owner. Thus, we establish the difference between *tuum* and *meum*. The whole conception of private property is founded on such a division. It is again this same principle of division which serves as a basis of the institution of the family, excluding the intervention of outside persons, the law having assigned the family a proper sphere of action.

This distribution is often taken for the fundamental idea in law because all questions of law are connected with property. Some consider the idea of communism as the negation of all rights because it excludes this division, together with the idea of property.

However, the simplest form of distribution is not the only one, nor the oldest, nor the most perfect for assuring the use of an object. By the side of this form which depends entirely upon the distinction between *tuum* and *meum*, there is another form, that of the adaptation of the object to the joint realization of certain interests.

The insufficiency of the first form of which we have just spoken, that of division, appears readily. There are objects which it is impossible to divide; for example, the different parts of a navigable river, of a public highway, cannot be apportioned. If one should proceed with the attempt, he would destroy at a stroke the public utility of these objects. Other objects, although divisible, require an adaptation, some sort of a change, for the realization of the interests concerned. With money, for example, it is not sufficient merely to divide up the gold and silver among individuals; it is necessary to give it a form, to coin it, to preserve the gold and silver from counterfeiting and deceit.

Consequently alongside the distinction of *tuum* and *meum* there must exist another form of delimitation of interests, another mode of distribution and division. This second form we will call "adaptation," and we will distinguish it thus from the first, from "distribution." The portions of land, highways, for example, left for the use of all, the money whose coinage guarantees the value of the metal employed, are "adaptations." Each of these forms, taken alone, is insufficient. Even if private property is not recognized, private possession has need to be protected. We can imagine the state of things in which there would be no such protection. Suppose, for example, the soil, the other objects which we use here, to be for the use of the whole world and without individual appropriation. It would be necessary, none the less, to establish some security for that portion of the soil, for that object, which we are employing at the very moment when we are serving ourselves with it.

If there were no right of property to be protected, there would be at least a temporary possession which would require to be guaranteed.

This right to the possession of an object, the same as ownership of an object, supposes a preliminary distribution of objects, placing them at the disposition of individuals. This is the division, as we have seen, between *tuum* and *meum; meum* is not only what I have acquired by lawful means, but what I find really in my own possession.

So these two forms of the guarantee of legal possibility are equally necessary. They cannot be replaced, the one by the other. Always and everywhere their coexistence is indispensable. So, and very advantageously, they can be regarded as the basis of all classification of legal phenomena. But the grouping which has its principal foundation in the distribution of objects among individuals, or in their adaptation to common needs, does it correspond to public rights on the one side, and to private rights on the other, as their historic development has exhibited them? I think the answer should be in the affirmative.

We can explain all the differences between public rights and private rights by the distinction between distribution and adaptation as above explained.

The most remarkable differences existing between public and private rights are those which connect themselves with the acquisition of rights and their loss, with their content and with the relations between rights and obligations.

Private rights are acquired as a result of special circumstances having a distinctly individual character and connecting directly or indirectly with some particular individual. And this individual character of the acquisition is strengthened constantly by the special bond which arises between the thing assigned and the person receiving it. Also, in private right we distinguish, always vigorously, between capacity and possession, between possibility of acquiring a right and actually getting it. All those who have capacity may in general possess a thing, but it is only those who have received the right of possessing a thing who have really a control over it.

When an object adapted only to common usage is under consideration, it cannot be in the same way. An act of acquisition, of individual appropriation, even temporary, cannot intervene, since it is a group of persons whose interests are served by the object. It suffices to be one of the group in order to have over this thing a right of use. Here the capacity and right come together. This is what happens in the exercise of all public rights. All those who satisfy the required conditions for electoral capacity have the right to vote. For the exercise of this right there is no need of any special individual qualification.

It is quite otherwise with the private right. If, for example, I am capable of participating in the issuance of a bill of exchange, this does not by any means require that I shall be the owner of the rights and obligations resulting from a bill of exchange.

The loss of a public right results from a loss of capacity, independently of the will of the bearer of the right. Private rights, on the contrary, can be lost without any change whatever in the juridical capacity of the person and by the mere fact of his will. He can renounce a right, can alienate it, can grant it to another to be exercised in his place. We see here, further, an application of our distinction between the distribution and the adaptation of the object.

The right possessed by the member of any society to the collective use of an object is lost when this member ceases to be a part of the society. He cannot grant the usage of his right to another individual who does not belong to this society. Alienation is not applicable to public rights. It could not have as a result any transfer of the right, the other members of the group having already a right to the use of the thing.

As to the object over which a right extends, if as a result of distribution it is assigned to a particular person, its adaptation, if any, is made by the owner and according to his will. He makes the object conform to the purpose which he proposes and in the way he wishes. A sovereign power of disposition belongs to him, for his own personal interest. Such is the matter of all private rights. They are absolute rights, including at once use and disposition.

In the public right, on the contrary, the power of disposition does not exist. This power takes the form of an obligation. The administration of the railroads, for example, has the right to control their iron roads, but this is at the same time only an obligation. The administration cannot use this power for alienation. It will make use of the iron roads not in its own interest, but in the interest of all.

It is the same with common roads and highways. It is impossible to give to each of those who use them the right of disposition, and those who have them in charge have equally no right of disposing of them except in the general interest.

From this distinction between distribut on and adaptation result, also, the differences which exist in the correlation between right and obligation, differences which we recognize in the public and private right. When the object belongs to an individual, the personality of the bearer of the right is always exactly determined. On the contrary, when the object is adapted to a collective usage, it is society considered as a whole which possesses it. The determination is here general, and persons who form the society are not specific individuals. On the other hand, the subject of the obligation is exactly determined.

All the peculiarities of public and private law, we see by the foregoing, are explained, then, in a satisfactory manner by the distinctions between distribution and adaptation.

We can by the same criterion furnish the explanation for the existence of private rights in the state for its own profit.

If the power given by the state is attributed to it with a view to the adaptation of a thing to the general use, we find ourselves in the presence of a public right. Such is the right of the state over its means of communication. If, on the contrary, the object which the state possesses has been given that it may serve itself with it in order to get therefrom the necessary means for the adaptation of other objects, this is a private right. Such is the right which the state possesses over its own goods. The revenues from such property serve for the maintenance of this or that grand division of administration.

It remains still to explain the numerous classifications which we have examined above. We shall do so by further use of the distinctions established between "distribution" and "adaptation." The preceding classifications derive their foundation from a secondary point, from one of the accessory consequences of the leading idea which we have just set forth.

Let us observe first of all that if we divide an object amongst several individuals, the will of each of these individuals plays a preponderant rôle in the application of the thing to some given use. How or in what fashion shall each one employ the object? This will depend upon the bearer of the right. The answer is altogether different if the object is applied to the collective use of all. In this case the manner in which each one shall use the thing, and the adaptation to be made of it for the common interest of all, is according to a rule fixed by the legislature. Here the liberty of disposing of the object no longer exists. Each person, who has a right of use over the object, finds himself bound by exact limits, can modify neither the object nor its value, because an identical right exists for the advantage of every other member of the society.

For this reason, the first form of these two actions of law, the distribution, results in consequences presenting a more individual character; the second, on the other hand, in consequences of a more social character.

The predominance of patrimonial rights among private rights, the facility with which these rights are transformed into a value which is the price of the object, can also very easily be explained upon our theory. When we proceed to a distribution of certain objects among individuals it happens frequently that the object assigned to an individual does not correspond to any need he has. Exchange is the only means to be employed in such a case.

The facility with which a thing can be exchanged or alienated has, then, a great importance. It is a quality of things of a general order which has even more value than the other. This capacity which things possess of being exchanged makes them applicable to all needs without exception, and, if the capacity of exchange is expressed always by price, it is evident that all efforts tend everywhere to transform the right over an object into a right over its price.

In the individual distribution of objects, private law leaves to each the necessity of determining what means he shall employ for the satisfaction of his own wants and for the production of other values. Public law, on the other hand, adapts the object to a given public use and regulates at the same time the use of the object and the means of its production. Private law in economic matters does not attempt to regulate either the employment or the production of wealth, but merely its distribution. It is this which permits Zitovich to define civil law as a law of distribution.

The assigning of an object does not take place without an individualization of the thing as well as of him who has a right over it. The application of an object to a common use combines several individuals together and brings about their association by this community of use. Hence the notion that private rights belong to man, considered individually, and public rights to man, considered as a member of an organized society.

The right to dispose of the thing of which one is the owner makes him the one upon whom depends the protection accorded to this object. If the object is applied to a common usage, on the contrary, this protection will depend no longer upon the will of any individual.

In this secondary consequence of the distinction between rights over things accorded to a collectivity of individua s and those granted to an individual, Thon and his disciples have sought to find the sole basis of the distinction between public and private law.

BOOK IV

POSITIVE LAW

CHAPTER I

THE SOURCES OF POSITIVE LAW

Section 49. *Positive Law*

The permanent connection between men leads us to make our conception of law objective. Legal rules primitively elaborated by the subjective consciousness find an objective expression under the conditions of social life in customs, which are a result of juridical practice, and in legislation, the instrument of governmental power. All these external forms of law do not depend for existence merely on the subjective consciousness. Customs, judicial practice, legislation, present themselves as something objective. The very changes which occur in customs and in law and which go to make up the phenomena of social life, are not caused according to the laws of mental phenomena, but according to the special laws of social life. However, the subjective conception of rights is not destroyed by customs, by judicial practice, nor by legislation. This conception goes on developing as a necessary manifestation of the individual's psychic life and as it is more mobile and not so subject to laws of its own, it can hardly fail to develop differences from the law which is expressed in objective forms.

Hence a division of law into two parts: the legal rules on the one side expressed under the forms of customs and of legislation constituting the positive law, and the law, "right," on the other side, under its subjective form which develops freely. This division exists not only in law but throughout the whole domain of human activity under the influence of the conditions of social life. Doubtless, in spite of the subjective conditions of human activity, despite all individual qualities, knowledge, and experience, the social and intellectual life go on developing more and more. They have grown unceasingly by the labor of former generations and may be considered as the capital of human activity. But all this culture thus obtained cannot destroy the individual factor and is at the same time a guarantee of the development of the race. A fruitful activity is impossible for any one unless it is conformed to this social culture which has been slowly elaborated, but the creative factor remains always the individual. This social culture is, like capital, the fruit of labor, and powerless to produce new values unless new labor comes to its aid. So, the development of human life depends upon subjective conditions.

Positive law is only one element of this social culture, and, as each social stage is only a heritage from past generations, it results that it can neither destroy nor replace that subjective conception of law and right which springs from the immediate needs of the present life and upon which depends the further development of the positive law itself.

To imagine a juridical life which should be absolutely determined by positive law alone, without any participation of the subjective conception, is something as impossible as to imagine a religion without any religious sentiment, morals without conscience or feeling of moral duty, or a nation without the individual's productive activity.

Positive law depends necessarily upon the subjective conception of right, but, at the same time, as it consists in a heritage from the past it can never be in perfect correlation with the subjective conception of the present generation. In positive law there is always an element, already grown old, which does not answer to modern needs or to modern conceptions of justice. This is why positive law has sometimes been regarded as an hereditary malady of human society.[1]

In all cases the subjection of human relations to the rules of positive law is something vexatious and troubles somewhat the free development of social life. Some such considerations as to positive law are mingled, however, with others much more favorable.

First of all positive law offers the same advantages as are possessed by society. In using the positive law to regulate our mutual relations we are using something which has been modified and elaborated by a whole course of generations. The individual's subjective conception cannot embrace the infinitely varied and multiplied relations of the law. I might elaborate, myself, voluntarily, a number of cases in which my interests would conflict with those of my fellows, but these cases, relatively few, might easily fail to fit some circumstances of which I had not dreamed. Positive law, being a product of the experience of many centuries, is always much more complete than any possible conception of subjective right.

The idea of doing without positive law, constructed by successive generations, might be held at a time when it was believed that there was a natural law, a system of legal rules created by nature herself. This eternal and absolute law must appear as more complete than the gradually developed positive law. But if we no longer recognize the existence of natural law, we can no longer set up against positive law any but a subjective conception of right and law, a conception itself gradually devel-

[1] "Es erben sich Gesetz und Rechte
Wie eine ewige Krankheit fort." — *Goethe*

oped under the influence of multiplied conditions and which cannot possibly replace positive law.

If positive law is more complete, it is also more general. Juridical norms regulate our interests, all the interests of men. This is why they ought to be known by all. To be sure, since the subjective conceptions of law also spring up, as a result of social conditions, it, too, presents a certain generality; but this generality is altogether conventional and limited by numberless individual peculiarities and a great diversity of human consciences. So, the generality of the subjective conception of law is limited to a very small circle of individuals. Society, on the other hand, grows unceasingly, and a constantly increasing number of men must be taken into the circle of legal relations, and this is why legal rules must be known of all men and be recognized as obligatory by everybody. Only positive law can answer such a requirement.

Positive law itself, also, is very diverse and much varied. It, too, depends upon conditions of time and place, but this dependence is expressed by external signs. For this reason positive law is distinguished by great precision.

The changes which take place in the subjective conception of law arise in an intangible way, which very often shows no outward indication. On the contrary, changes in custom, in judicial practice, or in legislation are manifested by facts which are external and easily recognizable.

It is, then, only the positive law which can furnish these principles which are assumed to be known to all within the sphere of its action. It is on this principle that the doctrine rests, that no one may claim not to know the law, and no man's ignorance of it shall do away with his responsibility. *Error juris semper nocet.*

Section 50. *Foundation of the Positive Law's Action*

The foundation for the law's action rests in general among the vital conditions of society. With this thought one can say that law acts upon humanity as the sole and indispensable agency for establishing some kind of harmony among the constantly clashing individual interests, not permitting the overthrow of society, nor sacrificing to social order the independence of individual people and their freedom. Starting from another point of view as to the very essence of law we would reach an altogether different statement of it. Thus Stahl says: "*Gottes Ordnung ist der Grund des Ansehens des Rechts.*" According to Kant the foundation for the obligation of obedience to law is the latter's accordance with reason; according to Bentham it is in the possibility of betterment, the advantage of the greatest number of people.

Just now we shall not enter upon this question. In speaking of the foundation for the action of legal norms, I have in view the question of why in a given government, a given society, there acts inevitably some given system of positive law, with all its peculiarities and differences from other systems, acting with it in the relations of time and space.

The need of some juridical order is universal in human societies which have attained a certain degree of development. As a matter of fact, this immutable law shows itself under very various forms because in each society it is not merely law in general which has effect, but a system of legal rules fashioned for that very society. Law, in furnishing order to the social life, subjects the state to the conditions of time and space.

It is for this reason, in order that it may always answer

its purpose and not become a dead letter that the law must always assume a form adequate to its epoch and environment. Subject to this reservation, laws act in an independent fashion, whether or not they harmonize with divine precepts or with the results of reason. The rules of positive law act with the same independence. All this leads to the question as to the foundation for this relative independent action of each system of positive law.

Law is not something which, like natural and physical forces, exists independently of human action and may be opposed to this latter. It is, on the contrary, an order established by men and for themselves. It does not matter, so far as concerns this, whether the man acts according to the law of causation or acts freely. Whichever it be, law established in accordance with the principle of causation, or by uncaused voluntary action, it is always the work of man. It is also a rule for the mutual relations of men to each other. It is a social order. This is why the need of law and the possibility, even of its creation, is out of the question apart from society. Law can exist only as there exists union among men. Law, therefore, is nothing foreign imposed upon men from without. It is a product of human consciousness and for it to exist there must be association, a social life, among men. Law, born with the society, is created by that society as the rule governing the relations of the associated. In each society it acts as if created to bring about the union of all the members.

So the foundation for the action of positive law consists in the fact that it is made by the society itself, and in each society has no force except in so far as it is the work of that society.

It sometimes seems that there are exceptions to such a rule. It sometimes happens that there is found in a society a law which originated outside, in some neighboring society. In this case it is important to distinguish between the law of the country itself and that which comes from the neighbor. We have in mind at this moment, not any distinction in the material, but only a distinction according to the form, according to the basis, for the action of the law. Consequently, if the legislator takes his material in part from foreign laws and in part from native ones and local customs and makes of the whole one common law, no distinction from our present point of view will be left between the national and the foreign law. But it may happen that a foreign law as a whole has effect over a country. Ought such a case to be considered as an exception to the principle that the positive law is to be considered as always the product of the society where it is applied? In the German Empire of the XIII and XIV centuries Roman law, without being fused with German law, has weight of its own and a power independent of local law.

It might seem at first sight that such a fact would completely destroy our thesis that law acts only in the society in which it was made. To settle this question, however, it is not enough to show the force of Roman law in Germany in those centuries. The route by which it got there must be examined.

The *corpus juris civilis* is a legislative compilation. Three compilations, all three the work of legislative power, have gone to make it up and give it all the force it has. But, carried into Germany, it became a customary law. By consequence of such custom, by connecting with such a basis of action, it renewed itself completely. In Germany the *corpus juris civilis* acted not as the will of the emperor of Rome but as German custom. Consequently, in fact, while certainly derived from a foreign source, this law so far as it was German positive law, manifests itself as the work of the German nation. This is why in Germany Roman law is recognized as acting only within the limits of the usage which applies it, absolutely as German customary law. Its appropriation was based on the work of the glossators, but they did not interpret all parts of the *corpus juris civilis*, and the parts they laid aside were never applied in Germany.

This appropriation of Roman law offers for Russia a practical interest since, thanks to it, Roman law acts still as a subsidiary law in the Baltic provinces which were once under Livonian rule, a fief of the Holy Roman Empire. Roman law has left its mark on nearly every state in Europe. In France it never ceased to act in the southern part, and later the lawmakers brought it into the northern provinces also. Even in England and Russia, which are among the states most distinguished by a special legal development, Roman law has had great influence, at least upon the practice of special tribunals. Thus in England, aside from the church, which according to one jurist's expression, *vivit lege Romana*, Roman law has found application in the admiralty jurisdiction. It has, in fact, formed the basis of international customs, known under the name of Rules d'Oléron, which is mostly made up of rules from Roman law.

In Russia, Roman and Byzantine law were frequently placed under contribution by the church tribunals, and it is truly to be said that the ecclesiastical jurisdiction was formerly quite extended. Roman law received among us the form of a canonical law and its influence has been very great over the development of all law and especially that of the family.

Greco-Roman modifications of the *jus civile* have penetrated even into the Caucasus and into Georgia. The second part of the Georgian code, that of Bachtang V, who lived at the end of the VII century, contains some laws of Leon the Wise, of Constantine, and of other

Byzantine emperors, relating to the administration of justice. Georgian law is distinguished by large borrowings. Besides those indicated there are many from the Pentateuch and from Armenian legislation. Since Georgia's subjection to Russia it is the code of the Council of 1649 and the military code of Peter the Great which is in force.

Foreign law may be adopted by legislative act. Thus, for example, the French code was adopted in Poland, Belgium and Italy, etc. Such an example is found too in the mediæval history of the cities on the Baltic. Thus, the city of Rega took from its founder, Bishop Albert I, the law which was in force in Visbi, a town distinguished for its mixed population so that every nation had a street in it. The city of Revel is of interest juridically. The Danish King Erik V in 1228 bestowed upon it the legislation then in force in Lubeck. According to the ideas of that day the Lubeck magistrate was the highest court for Revel. So the Revel magistrate in cases of doubt betook himself with his question to Lubeck and got there a determination. Lubeck law prevailed in Revel not merely as it was when adopted, but with later additions and changes. At the same time similar relations prevailed between Revel and Narva.

In southwest Russia prevailed in the same way the law of Magdeburg which had been bestowed by the kings of Poland and was continued in force by the Moscow Czars.

In all the preceding examples foreign law prevailed without change of form, controlling unchanged the foreign society by its adoption, but special action in that society introduced it, the will of the local government. Consequently this borrowed law, none the less on that account, presents itself as taking its force from the act of that same society in which it is in force.

Section 51. *The Sources of Law*

PUCHTA. Gewohnheitsrecht, I. ss. 143–148. Vorlesungen I.
SAVIGNY. System, I. ss. 6–57.
MUELLER. Die Elemente der Rechtsbildung. ss. 427–443.
AUSTIN. Lectures, II, pp. 526 ff.
ADICKES. Zur Lehre von Rechtsquellen, 1872.
REGELSBERGER. Pandekten, I. Sec. 82 ff.

We have already said that the correlation of the positive law with the subjective law, the sense of right, is not complete, that this was to be regretted, but it must, however, be recognized that the positive law offsets this by its precision and the ease of knowing it.

In considering the origin of law we showed that it had been first established as a determinate order of the mutual relations which men have with each other. Each individual expects his neighbor to observe the same conduct under the same circumstances, and if it happens that this expectation is not realized, then he will require of the one responsible for the injurious act compensation for any wrong which he suffers. Under such conditions each of us asks the same question, how to distinguish the general rules of law, which are obligatory upon all, from those rules which have only a subjective force.

It is highly important for each of us to determine beforehand with all possible precision what are the rules which govern us, and what are the rights they give us, and the obligations they charge us with. An exact reply can be made only as to rules which have become objective. To do this they must assume some specific form. This is why the theory of the forms which make up the objective character of a law has such importance for the jurist.

These objective forms of legal norms which serve to indicate the obligatory character of the rule are called "sources of law." To understand the doctrine of the sources of law, it is very important not to confuse the technical meaning of the phrase with that ordinarily given to it. We must distinguish, in fact, the meaning here given to the expression "sources of law" from that of mere means of knowledge, *fontes ex quibus notitia juris hauritur*. Sources means also historic monuments, and the word is used in this sense in the historic sciences. These notions can be applied in part to the very matter now under consideration, but never by more than an altogether superficial analogy, due to accident. If, for example, we have the authentic text of an enactment, we may say that we have the source of the law in the technical sense of the word and that we have at the same time its source in the meaning that we have the means of knowing it. But if such a text is not to be had, if we have the law only in the same indirect way as we do, for example, the twelve tables, or the law of Voconia, or others, such original laws are still sources of law without being any longer in any sense sources of knowledge of the law. In the same way if we learn of some rural custom in Ephimenko's or Pachmann's collections, these collections are the source of our knowledge of it, but the custom itself is the source of the law or of any effect upon law thereby produced.

These different conceptions have been often confused, especially in antiquity. So among the Romans it is, thanks to a confusion of these two notions of source, that there arose a distinction into written and unwritten law. (*Jus scriptum* and *jus non scriptum.*) This distinction was rigorously applied and the written law included, besides legislation, the prætor's edicts and the *responsa prudentium*. It was required that the law be at its origin written down (*inscriptum quod ab initio litteris mandatum est*). From this it resulted that a custom written down after its establishment, remained, notwithstanding, unwritten law, and the jurists established a new distinction between a law created by written enactment or establishment, and one already existing which is then set down in writing. Despite the slight importance of such a distinction it was sedulously preserved, and was even developed by later jurists. Thibaut puts this distinction at the head of his classification of sources of law, and Glück developed it very far. He accepts like a good many others the distinction between the *jus scriptum sensu grammatico* and the *jus scriptum sensu juridico*, which latter includes only law consciously established by means of written language.

A later confusion is that which has arisen between the source of law considered as the mark which distinguishes it as obligatory, and the source considered as the matter from which the content of legal rules is drawn. Such a confusion grew out of the fact that before the time of the historical school it was thought that law was the legislator's creation pure and simple.

The will of the legislator was then recognized as the sole cause of legal rules. The command, laid down by sovereign power, to observe a given rule was according to the opinion of that time the sole authority for saying that the rule was obligatory. We, on the other hand, are able to recognize that legislation is one force for creating rights, but that it is only one of the forms under which right, the work of conscience, law, is expressed.

The legislator does not create the law arbitrarily. He has no power to make rules which are not prepared for by the march of social advance. Legislation passed in any other way remains a dead letter and totally unapplied. The question of the sources of law thus put is totally different from that which we are seeking now to examine. For this, it would not be important to know whether or not a rule is obligatory upon all, but merely to know what factors participate in its establishment.

If we understand the question in this last fashion we may admit with Adickes that the general source of law is subjective reason, or, better said, the subjective consciousness. All the other factors affect the formation of law only through our consciousness. Divine orders, the nature of things, reason, conformity to an end, moral duty, all this can induce the formation of legal rules, only on one condition, which is that all these motives are admitted by the human consciousness. The general consciousness is only the sum of individual ones, and this is why it can be said that the subjective consciousness is like a hearth where concentrates the action of all the creating factors of law. But this subjective consciousness cannot be admitted as the source of law in the technical sense, because the subjective consciousness of a norm is not the index of its obligation over us and is not the form of its objectivity.

In the practical meaning of the term only custom, judicial practice, and legislation can be recognized as sources of law. It cannot be admitted that the nature of things is a source of law, for such nature is very differently understood among men. The conception recognized by enacted and established law, customs, and judicial practice, is the only one obligatory for all the world. It is necessary to say this much as to the conception of justice which is held by all, but in such different fashions, and which receives objective precision only on condition of being expressed through the sources of positive law above indicated.

Finally, and for the same reasons, we must place in this category of false sources, the science of law. The numerous controversies, which the question as to what are to be considered sources of law, has given birth, come most of all from wrong notions as to the action and function of the sources of law.

Before the appearance of the historical school, when positive law was still considered as a voluntary human institution, it was believed that legislation, expression of the creative will of law, was the sole force in setting up positive law. Therefore legislation was then recognized as the sole source of it because there was no other creating force to produce it.

The historical school taught a diametrically opposed theory. The force creating law is for them the genius of the people which embraced all positive law even before it was externally expressed by the "sources," which were then considered as only sources of our knowledge of the law, living in the genius of the people. In this way these authors considerably enlarged the notion of the sources of law by adding to it the science of law, which certainly serves as a source of our knowledge of law, but which cannot furnish the quality that makes these rules obligatory. The definition which we have accepted of sources of law, the recognition of what they are as necessary juridical forms for setting up objective law and serving at the same time as the mark of the obligatory character of the rules, this definition holds the mean between the two other definitions we have discussed.

Therefore the source of law has importance only as a test of the obligatory character for us of the given rule. Legislation or custom are not forces which create law, but merely forms by which we decide that a law is obligatory. Any rule may have its effect, but one which is not expressed through legislation, custom or judicial usage is of slight effect and supposes for its complete on the enactment, custom, or judicial acceptance. Its action has little precision because it lacks the external index of an obligatory character. It is impossible to show in advance what its action will be or to indicate to what particular cases it will apply. Its application to each case must be shown. On the contrary, a rule expressed in the general sources of law can be precisely limited in advance. In such precision there may be a distinction of more or less, but this is nonessential. Only the action of legislation can be exactly delimited. It is only of it that we can say in a general way, accurately in advance, to what cases in both space and time it will apply. The same precision cannot be reached as to customs and judicial usage. The precise moment when the action of a rule of custom or judicial usage will commence cannot be foretold. Custom is established little by little, and it is hardly possible to fix the exact boundary between the established custom and the one only forming. Judicial usage presents a form a little better ascertained, notably so as regards decisions of a given time; but the existence of a rule in a decree or judgment supposes that it was previously recognized as obligatory, for the judgment always rests on anterior facts.

To this peculiarity of precise action which legal rules have, another should be added. They are presumed to be known to all. No one may claim not to know the law; it is presumed always that each individual can easily take knowledge of rules contained in any of these sources. If he does not know, his ignorance is his own fault. There is no need to prove to the tribunal the rules of positive law. It knows them. *Jura novit curia.* Only facts are proved. Laws are not.

This doctrine that the laws are known is not justified by facts as to all kinds of rules. It may easily happen that the judge does not know the common law or local legislation. The common law is precisely one in which jurists have taken no part. It is established without them and independently of their activity. It is not the jurists who are familiar with the common law, but those who create and follow this law derived from custom. This law presents the peculiarity of changing with locality and with classes of individuals. So the parties can more easily than the judge, who is placed outside the *milieu* of these customs, bring together the proofs of the actual existence of this law. In the same way the judge cannot know the law of all foreign states. The conscientious study of the law of only one country takes up a good deal of time. It is to be added that the cases for the application of the laws of foreign countries are rare. So, for customary law and for foreign law the principle of *jura novit curia* is not rigorously applied.

As for customary law its application was, according to some jurists, a question of fact, always to be proved by the party in order to warrant its application. Without this the judge would not apply it even if he knew it. In such procedure the judge knew only what was produced during the hearing. *Non refert quod notum sit judici, si notum non sit in forma judicii.* This was Hofacker's and Wenning-Ingenheim's opinion. It was the logical result of the conception then held of the natural law as the mechanical theory held it. If the action of a rule of customary law depended solely upon a simple definite observation of a given custom, certainly the existence of such a custom is only a question of fact, as is admitted today in cases of trade usages. These latter are distinguished from juridical customs in that they carry in themselves no *opinio necessitas.* They are the result of simple observation of a given fashion of acting, and are only questions of fact and not of law.

The customary rule thus considered as a mere fact depending upon circumstances, harmonizing badly with certain rules of procedure, several authors, Thibaut (1722–1840) and Hönner (1746–1827), the celebrated opponents of Savigny as to codification, introduced a modification of this idea and demanded that a thoroughly notorious custom be regarded as a law. If accepted by only a small number of persons it might be regarded as a question of fact. Such a distinction is, nevertheless, entirely abstract. How, indeed, can this transformation of a question of law into a question of fact be explained according to the greater or less notoriety of the custom?

Puchta and Savigny produced a more accurate conception. They recognized that the existence of norms of customary law is always absolutely a question of law, that customary law is, like all others, always supposed to be known to the tribunal *ex officio*, and that it is only in case of actual impossibility for the court to know the custom that it is permitted to expect a party to set up the custom and prove its existence. But if they claim a custom known to the judge there is evidently no need of requiring proofs as to the existence of such a custom.

The same rules are applied to foreign law. The question of its application is absolutely one of law. And since it is impossible for the judge to know the law of the whole universe when the question is one of applying a foreign law the proofs of it ought to be brought by the parties claiming under it.

Section 52. *Customary (Common) Law*

GLUECK. Ausführliche Erlauterung der Pandektem nach Hellfeld, ein Commentar, 2 Ausg. B. I., 1797. s. 442, n. ff.

KLOETZER. Versuch eines Beitrags zur Revision der Theorie vom Gewohnheitsrecht, 1813.

PUCHTA. Das Gewohnheitsrecht, 2 B., 1828, 1837.

BOEHLAU. Mecklenburgisches Landrecht. B. I., 1871. s. 315.

ADICKES. Zur Lehre von Rechtsquellen, 1872.

SERGEIEVICH. Essay upon the Study of Customary Law. In the Observer, St. Petersburg, 1882. Nos. 1 and 2.

SCHUPPE. Gewohnheitsrecht, 1890.

Customary law is the primitive form of positive law. None the less, the recognition of custom as an independent source of law was scarcely established before the second quarter of the nineteenth century. Up to that time legislation was thought to be the sole independent source of law. However, few went so far as to wholly deny the obligatory force of custom. Of those who did so the most celebrated in the eighteenth century were Thomasius and Grolman. They admitted custom only as a reason for affirming the existence of a contract or of legislation compatible with it. Most writers recognized the existence of customary law-making without attributing to it any independent force. In democratic states, where the legislative power belonged to the people, customary law was deemed merely a special form of such popular legislation. The obligatory force of the law and of such custom was thought to be the same. In both cases it was the people's will, in one case directly expressed and in the other by facts leading to an *a posteriori* conclusion of its existence (*facta concludentia*). This exception gave birth to the notion of a silently established law, *lex tacita*, and it was this idea that under republican *régimes* replaced customary law. Such an explanation could not be admitted for monarchical states, especially for autocratic ones such as most European states were in the XVIII century. In those states legislative power did not in fact belong to the people. So, to explain the obligatory force of customary law recourse was had to the idea that the legislator gave to custom its obligatory character. It was held that the custom became obligatory as a result of the legislator's assent (*consensus imperantis*). There was dispute as to whether this consent applied to all the customs in general (*consensus generalis*) or only to all those which were specially for some particular cases (*consensus specialis*). Some required a special consent for all customs without distinction. Others like Hufeland, Thibaut, and Glück required such a consent only for those which derogated from legislation. Others like Heffner, Baltzen and Kestner, admitted as sufficient in all cases a general consent. Special consent was supposed to be given silently by the very fact that the custom could be applied. It was thought, on the other hand, that general consent came directly from the *corpus juris civilis*.

The weakness of all these theories is evident. They are all based upon absolutely arbitrary fictions, and all turn in the same vicious circle. The doctrine of the identity of the will of the people as expressed both in the customs and the legislation of democratic states is wholly fictitious. In the most favorable cases the national assembly includes only one generation. Custom, on the other hand, is slowly formed, and is the work of many generations. Only will expressed in determinate forms can create legislation. Customary law is built up outside of all forms. It furnishes form to the formless.

The famous sanction of custom supposed to be given

by the legislator is also clearly a fiction, for it is not legislation which precedes customs in the historic sequence, but quite the contrary. Customs appeared long before legislation. It is therefore impossible to maintain that legislation serves as the basis of customs. The precise contrary is the truth. Sovereign power at the beginning rested entirely upon custom. As to the general consent which some authors think to find in the *corpus juris civilis*, it is sufficient to recall that the *corpus* itself cannot be considered in our time as having anywhere legislative force. Accepted in practice, but having behind it no executive force except some text of legislative enactment, it must be considered itself as merely customary law for modern nations.

The historical school, and especially among the authors of that school, Puchta, gave the finishing stroke to all these theories. His Das Gewohnheitsrecht remains to this day the best study of the subject. In it Puchta established the new theory. He not only recognized for customary law a wholly independent significance, independent of any harmony with the legislative will, but that it is an antecedent condition for legislation. The foundation of customary law, said he, is the natural generality of the conviction of the nation's purpose. This immediate national conviction finds expression in customs, and its realization in laws is therefore by the establishment at the beginning of customary law.

Manners and customs form the primitive law of peoples, just as some kind of a system is the primitive law of jurists, and verbal expression of the legislator. If customary law stands in such strict and necessary connection with the natural conception of the nation, and is the immediate result of the latter's activity in the legal direction, can it be asked, then, whether custom has independent force as law, or why it has? Customary law, if this is the case, acts for the same reason as all law does, the reason which produces this conviction of nationality and that there are such things as peoples. If the existence of a unified people is in fact recognized, some activity must be attributed to the genius of that people, and consequently some conception of moral and legal freedom be formed, and since customary law is nothing but this conviction in its immediate and concrete form, the existence of customary law is inseparably bound up with the people's existence.

There is still less need of direct proof that the force of customary law does not come from connection with the other sources of law; for the establishment of law immediately through legislatures and the activity of jurists, presupposes an immediately established law through custom giving them authority. For if there were no nation and no immediate consciousness of nationality there would be no state and no jurists, and by consequence no juristic or enacted law; so, the very essence of these forms of law affirms the force of previously established customary law, and there can be no doubt as to this point.

So Puchta attributed to customary law an absolutely independent capacity, but only so far as related to the customs of an entire people. Customs of this kind are always relatively rare. Local customs, on the contrary, are quite numerous. This observation was made by Unterholzer in his critique of Puchta's theory, and by Muhlenbruch. Savigny, also, thought to correct Puchta's doctrine by recognizing the unity of the people as a necessary common basis for the formation of the custom and a ground for its force as law; but that just as legislative power can promulgate laws at the same time for the whole state and for special localities in it, in the same way the people's immediate consciousness of law may take the form of customs for distinct localities, as well as for distinct classes, which are considered as organic parts of the nation.

Savigny in formulating this theory started with this idea, recognized by the historic school, that the unity of a people is not a result of historic evolution but something innate and which existed from the beginning. This, however, is not what history teaches us. As Sergeievich has shown, it is not general customs which are found at the origin of nations, but rather special ones, and only little by little do they become general. And again, as is admitted elsewhere, Savigny's theory does not explain the formation of certain customs, as in ecclesiastical law, and certain international customs which cannot in any way be admitted as customs taking their origin spontaneously from the general unity of the people.

For all these reasons the doctrine of the historical school ought to be regarded as insufficient. In very recent times the birth of a new conception is to be observed, one which considers that customs are obligatory simply by the fact of their long standing. This is notably Adickes' opinion. According to him, the very long existence of a custom compels us to recognize its obligatory character. This is explained first of all by the fact that for a legal judgment the existence of *some* definite rules is generally the most important point and it matters relatively little just what the rules are. Besides this, it is necessary to consider that in most cases customs are conformed to some end, since they are the work of individual interests. Finally, time has, in general, the quality of giving a special stability in man's eyes.

This opinion, however, cannot be accepted. In seeking to escape the too exclusive result of the historic doctrine, Adickes has fallen into the opposite extreme. The historic school believed that the creation of obligatory customs was only possible as a result of the unity of a people. Adickes did not regard the fact that the custom, considered altogether as law and not as habitude, is not simply a manner of conduct long observed but it is only such a particular manner as is observed in a given human society as obligatory.

The existence of unvarying habits among the men with whom we are in relation presents this advantage, their fixedness compels us to accept them as they are, even if this causes some trouble. But a mere individual habitude is not a custom, and its duration cannot be considered as the index of the obligatory character of a rule. Custom, as we have already shown, is one of the forms of consciousness of a law which has become objective. A man in expressing himself uses the forms of grammar and rules of style elaborated by a people's common life, and at the same time his language becomes not merely the expression of his own ideas but, also, a part of the popular language and a vehicle for expressing the ideas of that people. In the same way a man expressing his ideas as to law uses forms elaborated by the common life in society; these forms are taken up and become the expression of the collective consciousness of law, that is to say, they are transformed into juridical customs. When I act conformably to custom, because it is custom, my consciousness of law is thereby expressed in a manner which conforms to the consciousness of law on the part of others who, themselves also, observe the same custom. If it were otherwise there would be no custom. For this reason the custom exhibits a juridical norm which is accepted not by me alone, but by all who are members of the same society with me. In other words, not because the practice is ancient is it obligatory, but because it is common in that character to all the society.

Some analogous discussions have arisen, also, as to the

origin of customs. Customary law forms little by little through the very life of society and outside of fixed forms, and for this reason controversies about it are so numerous. We cannot directly observe the formation of custom. We can determine its origin only by more or less complex considerations. Till Puchta's time the mechanical theory of the formation of customs prevailed. This theory explained the origin simply by the observance of the same rule in several identical cases. At that time any other explanation was difficult, as we recall that the obligatory character of the custom was supposed to be due to the legislator's recognition of it. The juridical character of the custom was considered in this theory as coming from above, from the legislator's will; but the legislator can give obligatory force to a set of uniform rules drawn up at hazard and which have nothing to do with customs.

This explanation fell of itself with the recognition in customs of an independent capacity as laws. It was necessary to find in the custom itself and in the conditions of its formation the basis of its obligatory character. Instead of the mechanical theory, Puchta set up a spiritualistic one of the origin of customary law, absolutely opposed to the old conception. He affirms that the observance of a rule does not make of it a customary law. Its observance is only the material expression which shows us its existence. The rule existed before it was followed, and was already regarded as an obligatory norm. The juridical custom is distinguished from the simple habit in that it is an external and conscious expression of the rule which existed already in the national consciousness of legal rules. Simple habits are those created by a chance uniformity unconsciously introduced into the conduct of individuals in identical cases. Savigny early showed that Puchta's theory could not be admitted without some reserves. There are, said Savigny, some customs whose formation cannot be explained by the conscious application of an already formed juridical conception.

Such, for example, are the terms to be used in making a formal contract, and the number of witnesses necessary. The juridical idea can only indicate that it is desirable to have the terms and the number of witnesses appropriately fixed, but cannot itself precisely determine either. It is evident that no legal principle can determine just how many witnesses should be present at a given act. For this reason Savigny thought that, besides customs born of the conscious application in private cases of a rule existing already in the popular consciousness, there were other juridical customs, established, notwithstanding their obligatory character, by the fortuitous and unconscious observance merely as habits of some particular fashions of acting.

It is easily understood that Savigny's correction of Puchta's theory does not correct, while it shows clearly the impossibility of explaining the origin of juridical customs by this theory. The theory in reality explains nothing. It considers the juridical norm as the external expression of a norm already existing in the consciousness of the people, but does not explain how any such popular conscience is formed or exists. Has it more reality than the legislator's assent?

If the general explanation of the origin of law before given in this book, is accepted, that of customary law is very simple. In setting forth our conception of the origin of law, it was not possible to lay aside customary law which is its primitive form. We were compelled to recognize that the commencement and the continuance for a time of the custom resulted unconsciously, and that it became "juridical" only when to its observance was added the consciousness of its obligatory character. The consciousness of its obligatory character would appear as a consequence of the tendency we have to believe that identical conditions always produce identical acts. As ndividuals, people so believe each time, in advance of observation, of the order already established, and whenever this order is violated, it produces reaction. If this opinion is accepted, the explanation of the origin of all customs is easy. They are inevitable.

The history of the theories as to the marks of the existence of a juridical custom is equally interesting. The glossators required only two conditions, a long enough time, and reasonableness. Then the number of conditions became greater. Barthol counted three, *longum tempus*, *tacitus consensus populi*, *frequentia actuum*. Their successors indicate, besides, *quod consuetudo sit introducta non erronea sed cum ratione et quod sit jus non scriptum*. The number of required conditions went on always increasing, and at the commencement of this century they counted eight, *rationabilitas*, *consuetudinis*, *diuturnitas temporis*, *consuetudo contradicto judicio firmata*, *pluritas actuum*, *uniformitas actuum*, *continuitas actuum*, *actus publici*, *actus consuetudinis introductivi*, *opinio necessitatis*.

The modern *jurisconsulti*, like Böhlau for example, require, as formerly Placentin, only two conditions,—first, the custom must express a juridical conviction; second, it must be old enough. The controverted question is to know what is the connection between custom and law. Can or cannot the custom abrogate the law? Has it that force which is called derogatory?

No law, no rule, being able to claim eternal existence, the possibility must be recognized of applying derogations by future rules, legislative or customary. But there is sometimes in legislation a prohibition against applying customary law either general or outside of the cases indicated. Can such a prohibition take away the derogatory power of customary law? Such prohibitions make very difficult, to be sure, the development of customs derogatory to the law. Tribunals as well as interested parties can by supporting themselves with such a prohibition very easily prevent the application of customs. But if the custom developed all the same despite the prohibition, it could not be denied obligatory force.

It goes without saying that the formation of such a custom is admissible only where the violated law is in the general opinion unreasonable and unjust and with the condition that such opinion is absolutely shared by everybody, by the tribunals, as well as the persons interested. On these conditions surely no one can doubt the obligatory force of a custom which abrogates an unjust law recognized as such by everybody.

Section 53. *Judicial Usage*

IHERING. Unsere Aufgabe. Gesammelte Aufsätze I, 1881. ss. 1–46.
MOUROMTZEV. The Courts and the Civil Law. Juridical Messenger (Russian), 1880. pp. 337–393.
MAINE's Ancient Law. pp. 25–34.
UNGER. System des Oesterreichischen allgemeinen Privatrechts. 3 Aufl., 1878. B. II. s. 151–257.
BUELOW. Gesetz Richteramt. 1895.
FRANKEN. Vom Juristenrecht. 1889.

Judicial usage offers a good many resemblances to custom. Just as in customs, in judicial usage legal rules are not expressed under any general form but only under a form applicable to special and distinct cases. It, too, supposes that the rule before being expressed in judicial conclusions was obligatory. It, no more than custom, fixes the period of the rule's action and it is not surprising that for all these reasons a good many authors, perhaps a majority in our time, have considered judicial usage as a special form of customary law.[1]

There are serious objections, however, to such a conclusion. Judicial usage and precedent occupies an intermediate place between custom and legislation. It presents points in common with each. Like legislation, judicial usage is consciously shaped. While, primitively, custom would appear as simple habit, wholly unconscious of legal relation and entirely outside of all regulation, judicial usage and decision is, like legislation, the result of a conscious effort towards the ap-

[1] Wächter, "Pandekten," I. 1880. s. 112. Stobbe, "Handbuch des deutschen Rechts," I. 1871. s. 146. Malichev, "Course in Russian Civil Law," I. 1878. p. 85. Lüders, "Das Gewohnheitsrecht." Böhlau, "Mecklenburgisches Landrecht," I. 1871. s. 320.

plication of a legal rule. The custom, too, does not become a "legal" one, a law, until to the observance of the rules which it prescribes is added the consciousness of its utility; but the matter of the custom is furnished always by habit. It is formed unconsciously. The legal consciousness which transforms a simple habit into a juridical custom finds a material ready made. On the contrary, the judgments of courts which make up judicial usage are absolutely conscious acts. The matter of each judgment is elaborated consciously and precisely in order to regulate the relations of the parties by law.

Another difference between judicial usage and custom is that, like legislation, judicial usage is not created by society or by some distinct class, but by an institution. This is why, differing in this respect from custom, judicial usage has, like legislation, a recognized authentic legal form. There are recorded authentic orders and judgments. Let us observe, too, that like legislation, judicial precedents ordinarily appear in a written form, while custom, in the beginning at least knows nothing of writings.

There are, then, between customs and judicial usage such differences that it is impossible to class them together and regard judicial usage as a special form of custom. But in refusing to identify them are we not compelled to deny the existence of judicial usage as an independent source of law? Is not the sole mission of the tribunal to declare and apply existing law? Charged with determining special cases, ought it not to limit itself merely to applying the legislation in force when the action was brought before it? To recognize judicial practice as an independent source of law, is this not entirely the same thing as to recognize a right in the tribunal to judge, not according to law or custom, but according to its own will, and to establish thus the uncontrolled arbitrament of the judges instead of a general obligatory rule?

If there is no doubt that the tribunal ought not to decide at its own pleasure but according to law or custom, we cannot on that account deny all creative value to judicial usage and precedents. The government in constitutional states is itself limited to the terms prescribed in the legislation put out by the two legislative houses. However, its acts, decretals, orders, rules of procedure, are an independent source of law. In the same way in many states the two houses have their power limited by constitutions which they have no right to change, and meanwhile the ordinary laws are recognized as a source of law. We see the same phenomena develop in connection with judicial practice. Just as ordinary laws or administrative rules have of necessity a creative capacity, the tribunals themselves are not strangers to the creative genius. The tribunal which decides practical cases, problems which require very often extremely varied and diverse legal conceptions, applies necessarily the legislation in force. Otherwise it could never find the directing thread in the casuistical labyrinth.

But, in fact, legislation is not formed *en bloc*. It is formed gradually, and its parts have been shaped under the influence of diverging, even of opposing ideas. The same thing to a certain extent is true of the different parts of the same legislative act, since all laws are results of compromise between the extremely divergent tendencies which control government or parliament. A legislative act is very rarely the complete expression of a single idea. If logical unity is to be found in it, it is the tribunal's part to develop that unity. This is certainly a creative activity. Legislative institutions have their field, a comprehension in which propositions vary greatly. The same thing which under one conception might be a general rule, might very well under another view be regarded as only a stringently limited exception. Independently of this, in all legislation we find contradictions. They can be dealt with in various ways, and the choice made by judicial usage among the methods has also a certain creative force.

To bring legislative institutions into a logical whole, to avoid the contradictions which they present and complete their *lacunæ*, the tribunal uses general principles of law and supports itself by scientific reasoning. This has led a good many writers, particularly among the ancients, to regard legal science as an independent source of law. But in this branch of law contradictions were numerous, and it became necessary to set up a more general rule that the judge must base his decision upon the combined voices of the most general opinion (*communis opinio doctorum*).

But how find out this opinion? What is the common opinion of all the learned? For this purpose there were several rules of an essential mechanical character. The *communis opinio doctorum* was that which was held by seven savants, or better yet, that which Barthol and the Glosses, that is to say, the *glossa ordinaria*, admitted. If this means gave no result, then the opinion of the oldest savants was to be admitted. A jurist then, had more authority the older he was. Such rules adopted in the middle ages could not remain in force. Most authors, perceiving how impossible it was to replace them with other rules for getting an infallible means for choosing between contradictory scientific opinions, have very logically concluded that science was not an independent source of law.

The historical school, however, found this to be an extreme opinion. The naïve rules of the middle ages, based upon the assent of a greater or less number of jurists, must assuredly be set aside. It was not necessary, however to conclude from this that science in general could not be regarded as a source of law.

The representatives of the historical school have not found any rule for choosing between such contradictory opinions. If there is no possibility of a correct choice, the rules established by science alone have no direct application. Consequently, science cannot be recognized as a source of law in the technical sense in which customs, judicial usage and legislation are; that is to say, as an absolute index to the obligatory character of a rule. It is only judicial application which furnishes the mark of an obligatory norm. In other words, it is not theory, but the practice that embodies a given theory, which is an independent source of law.

In recognizing judicial practice as an independent source of law we must observe that it is not necessary to conclude that a decision once rendered binds the tribunal forever. If every law can be replaced by a new one, surely judicial usage on its side cannot be condemned to perpetual rigidity. But on the other hand, the rigidity which judicial practice has and the precision of its rules have certainly a great value.

One of the first conditions of justice is that the laws be applied equally for all, but such a thing would be impossible without a durable and steady, uniform system of administering justice. For this reason the tribunal is always ready to apply again a principle previously accepted. It requires very important reasons to produce a change in the jurisprudence which a given tribunal has recognized, and it ought to be admitted on principle that a rule once established should be followed in later judgments of the same tribunal.

Section 54. *Legislation*

SAVIGNY. System I. ss. 16–20.
ZACHARIAE. Vierzig Bücher vom Staate. B. IV. s. 1.
BOEHLAU. Mecklenburgisches Landrecht. B. V. s. 283.
JELLINEK. Gesetz und Verordnung. 1887.
SELIGMANN. Der Begriff des Gesetzes. 1886.
HAENEL. Gesetz im formallen und Materialen Sinne. 1888.
KORKUNOV. Executive Orders and Legislation. 1894. pp. 227–228.

The expression of legal rules in customs and judicial determinations has always a casuistical and indefinite character. Legal customs as well as judicial precedents are gradually formed to the extent that there is call for the application of legal rules to special and definite cases. Legal rules cannot therefore find in these forms an expression which is at the same time precise and general. These are defects that become more and more strongly felt as the developments of social life become more complex and varied. Governmental power, designed to uphold and protect law, cannot accept such forms as legal rules. To the degree that it becomes strong enough and firmly enough established, it proceeds to replace these indefinite principles of customary law and judicial precedents by more precise and fixed rules of legislation.

At first this is done only as regard rules that especially concern the government and its organs which are charged with applying them. The relations of individuals with each other, those having to do with property, those of the family, such are the things which customary law controls the longest. But gradually as legislation goes on little by little increasing in scope, it comes to subject to itself all the branches of the law, and thus becomes the general form in which the law clothes itself, and custom and judicial precedent become only subordinate principles of law, secondary and almost exceptional.

Legislation, in the large sense of the word, is every legal rule established by direct action of governmental organs. It is defined often as the will of the organs of governmental power, or of the state. Such a definition is too broad. The organs of the state's power may express their will without any intention of giving to the emitted rule the force of an obligatory norm for all the citizens. Such, for example, are the words which terminate the manifesto announcing the enfranchisement of the peasant. "Make the sign of the cross, believing people, and call down upon you the blessings of God upon your free labor, with the prosperity of your house and your happiness among your fellows."

On the other hand, the definition of legislation as a direct expression of will cannot be accepted because it is too narrow. Even if the legislative act contains only one general rule, it cannot be said that all its special consequences are equally contained and expressed in the law. Even if it interdicts such and such actions in carefully determined cases, the same actions are authorized in all other cases. The law acts, then, not only within the directly prescribed limits, but also within the limits of that which is the natural consequence of the orders put forth, that is, in many cases, beyond any human foresight or any human will.

Very many writers have thought it worth while to put back into the definition of legislation, the idea that it is promulgated only after a procedure instituted precisely for that purpose. This is entirely superfluous. If the required procedure necessary to make what will be recognized as an obligatory rule is not followed, there will be no law, but only a personal command of the person or persons emitting it as representatives of governmental power. If such representative has not observed the required forms, he cannot be recognized as acting in the name of the state. The definition we have given of legislation as a rule established by governmental organs, supposes as already established regular forms for acts in the name of the state. In this definition we have said nothing about publication, which has been by many writers recognized as an essential attribute of legislation. But, in truth, history shows us many examples of unpublished laws. Among ourselves today the fundamental laws provide a category of legislation which remains secret.

As to the question of what is the basis of the obligatory character of legislation, there is no firmly settled theory recognized by the whole world. The representatives of the natural law school have recognized as such basis an implied agreement among men. Every citizen, they say, ought to obey the law because he holds a part in such a contract. Certain ones, like Hobbes and Grotius, add, also, that such an agreement might operate to confer upon some given person or institution the right to make laws.

This opinion in the second half of the eighteenth century was replaced by another according to which each distinct legislative act was regarded as the expression of the general will. Rousseau and Kant and their successors shared this opinion. This theory supposes that every agreement is obligatory in itself and that there is no need of proving this obligatory character, since it is *a priori* evident.

In reality, we often see facts wholly the other way. All agreements are not obligatory, but only those which conform to the law's requirements. By consequence, it is precisely the law which furnishes the basis of their obligation. In all cases to attribute to the law's obligatory character such a foundation as contract, is a pure fiction, and quite often we see laws which do not at all have the approbation of society.

The historical school considered as the basis of the law's obligatory force the legal consciousness of the people. But this, too, is a fiction, as much so as that which made the obligation rest on contract. We cannot deny the existence of a conception of law, common to the nation, but it is impossible to affirm that all laws express only this conception which the people have as to law. Legislation may not agree with this conception, and may even contradict it.

In states whose population comprises different races not yet united by political life, such a contradiction between legislation and the notion of law, prevailing among some of the populations in the state, are even necessary. For all legislation independently of its matter has obligatory force.

A basis for the obligatory character of legislation remains, then, to be sought. Legislation is set up by the organs of power who can on the one side constrain individuals by force to submission, and who have on the other hand an authority in the eyes of the public which often suffices to make their rules observed.

Legislation is established for the most part by those organs of governmental power which have under their direction the organs charged with practically applying it. The same state has usually several sets of organs, and we can thus distinguish legislation into groups according to the organ which produces it.

The most important juridical rules are confided to a special legislative institution, which concerns itself only with legislation and the care of the administration. The less important rules are the work of the executive power properly so called. We shall divide, then, into two groups the rules established by these two branches of authority: legislation (*zakon*, *lex*, *loi*, *Gesetz*) and rules or orders (*ukazi*, *décrets*, *Verordnungen*). Since the directions of the executive power must be carried out in conformity with legislation, and such execution is subordinated to the legislative body, executive rules and orders are subject to enacted law. The order is only valid as long as it does not contradict law.

This formal distinction of legislation and "orders" according to the different powers which establish them, is found at the bottom of the matter out of which they are made. The most important legal rules, those which relate to the most important interests of the citizens, should have their assent, or at least that of their representatives. The details may be arranged by the executive or its departments more competent for such technical questions.

This distinction, however, between laws and orders cannot be formulated in a precise manner, since it is impossible to find any external measure, any absolute outside mark for distinguishing the more important from the less so. So, everywhere in constitutional states, it has been established in practice that an executive order cannot nullify a legislative act. By consequence, all matters already held by the legislative remain within its exclusive competency, at least so far as it does not authorize the executive to regulate such matter by orders.

For all those questions, on the other hand, which have not been regulated by legislation, it is the executive's duty to provide as need arises, by orders. This general rule establishing the relations between legislation and executive orders, suffers, however, one exception. In case of extreme necessity, when the safety of the state is endangered, it is impossible to employ the legislative method. In such a case the executive can take measures and make orders contrary to law, but the ministers are responsible to the houses of the legislature. Legislation and executive orders can each in their turn be divided according to the organs producing them. In a good many states legislation, properly so called, the rules made by organs other than those of the executive, are subdivided into ordinary laws and constitutional provisions which are elaborated either by special organs or by a special procedure. Executive orders are also distinguished according as they are made by the chief executive or by inferior organs of administration, departmental or municipal.

Since this distinction between laws and executive orders is a distinction resting purely upon form, in opposing them to each other, we are advancing a conception resting purely on form. Legislation in the formal sense is merely acts of a legislative body, and this definition can, in a way, be opposed to the one already given of legislation as legal rules established by an organ of governmental power whether under the form of a legislative act or an executive order. The conception with which we are now dealing of legislation relates purely to the form it takes on. The executive orders, so far as they contain legal rules, can be considered as legislation in the only important sense of the word.

The preparation of laws is divided in constitutional states into several parts clearly distinct. For example, in all states where legislation is the work of the executive and legislature combined, there are distinguished: 1st, the initiative; 2d, the discussion; 3d, the sanction; 4th, the promulgation; 5th, the publication of the law. The initiative is the power to propose a law for discussion before the legislature. It can be organized in four ways: 1st, the government alone can have it, as in France under the second empire; 2d, parliament alone, as in the United States at the present time; 3d, the government and the legislature, as in most constitutional states; and 4th, the whole people, as in Switzerland today.

The discussion of the law is the chief function of the national representation. Wherever there is popular representation in the legislature, it performs this function. But the right may have two forms essentially different. It may be simply a right to accept or reject the projected law without right to offer any amendment or modification. Such a situation necessarily supposes that the initiative belongs only to the government.

In modern states a broader right is established which consists not only in accepting or rejecting the project, but also in proposing amendments to it. If parliament is composed of two chambers as happens in most modern states, each of these two chambers has equally the right of discussing projects of law and these projects of law can be sanctioned by the chief executive only after they are passed by the houses, or by one of them.

The sanction or confirmation of projects of law belongs always to the chief executive. The right of sanctioning supposes the right of rejecting, that is, of the veto, which may be absolute or suspensive. An absolute veto is an absolute right existing in some monarchical states of stopping all projects of law after they have been adopted in the legislature. The suspensive veto only checks the project for the time being, but if the chambers insist, the project may become a law under certain conditions in spite of the chief executive. This form of veto is found in republics and in some monarchical states, Norway for example.

The law accepted by the chambers and sanctioned by the chief executive may then be executed by promulgating, and is finally published that everybody may have knowledge of it.

In most constitutional states, as we have said, legislation in the narrow sense of the word is divided into ordinary laws and constitutional provisions. These last are those which establish the fundamental principles of the organization of the government and by consequence are more complete than the others. In some states the right to make constitutional provisions belongs to the same institutions as the right of passing ordinary legislation. The provisions as to their discussion, however, call for more complicated forms, designed to insure maturity of consideration. Such is the case in Prussia and in France. In other states the power of establishing constitutional provisions, which may be called the constituent power, is separated from the ordinary legislative power, and is regarded as the special privilege of the whole people and not of their representatives. In Switzerland, for example, this is the means in use for making a constitutional provision.

Legislation is distinguished, essentially, from the other sources of law, in that it is not an act of application of a rule, like custom, or judicial usage, but an act which lays down a rule.

Therefore the action of legislation is precisely determinate not only as to relations of place, but also in relations of time. Legislation acts only from the moment when it is promulgated and all projects of legislation prior to that are not law. It can also be arranged to have force only during a given time. In any case the action of the law ceases when it is abrogated, or replaced by a new law, or by custom.

The moment when legislation has the force of law is ordinarily that of its publication. The publication of a law is by means of its insertion in a paper specially designed for such service, but the law may not be known on the very day when its text is published in the journal; it requires a certain time for the journal to reach all the towns and villages of the state, and become generally known. So it is reasonable to require, as is done in Germany, that legislation be not enforced until a certain number of days after the publication. If the term is long enough, it ought to be the same for the whole state and all its cities. This gives the advantage of having the law in force on the same date throughout the state. In Germany the time fixed is fourteen days for the mother country and four months for the colonies.

The action of legislation ceases, either by the expiration of its term, if the law was made for a fixed term, or because of a new law abrogating the preceding one. The promulgation of a new enactment abrogates the old one only as to those parts which were actually designed to be replaced. The other rules, set up by the old law and which are not replaced by the new, keep their full force. They can no longer, however, be considered as constitutional provisions. At least, this is so in France.

Legislation is made up of a succession of dispositions, one after the other, at the requirement and according to the degree of needs. Such a diversity presents very grave inconveniences which make the study of legislation more and more difficult, but these inconveniences are further aggravated by the fact that special dispositions arising at quite different epochs are often the expression of totally opposite principles, according to the epoch in which they arose and according to the interest controlling the government's action. As a result there are grave contradictions in the several parts.

A systematic re-enactment of legislation, a complete revision of different laws in order to form a systematic whole, is an extremely practical and necessary thing. Such unification can be obtained in two different ways,—either by incorporation or, better, by codification.[1] Incorporation is a means of codifying law, but merely for those in force, without change of form, so that at bottom they are not modified. It is the unification of the legislation in force. It produces, therefore, only an

[1] Zhinuliak. "As to codification and its influence on legislation and the science of law." Legal Messenger (Russian), 1876.

apparent unification. It does not remove the numerous contradictions which the existing laws previously contained.

Codification does not limit itself to a mere change in the forms of law. It permits the obtaining of a systematic unification from the very bottom of the law, and for this reason the codifier is not limited to working upon actually existing legislation. He can draw from customary law, from judicial decisions, from foreign law, or from the science of law. The code is not simply ancient legislation under a new form, it is new law in the most complete sense of the word.

[4]

COLUMBIA LAW REVIEW

VOL. XXIV JANUARY, 1924 NO. 1

AIMS AND METHODS OF JURISPRUDENCE*

One of the pioneers of Western Jurisprudence, Azo of Bologna,—whom our own Bracton followed as Dante followed Vergil—spoke in glowing terms of the glory and power of the teachers of Roman law. He says at the beginning of his *Summa on the Institutes*,[1] "to speak truly (the doctrine of Justinian) has conferred the dignity of princes of the world on professors of law by making them sit in the hall of the emperors to judge as masters nations and tribes, plaintiffs and defendants." In striking contrast with this statement Hobbes has set forth with his usual vigor a radical view of the development of English law. In the *Dialogue between a Philosopher and a Student of English law* the former explains to his companion that "it is not wisdom, but authority that makes a law . . . that the law hath been found by grave and learned men, meaning the professors of the law, is manifestly untrue; for all the laws of England have been made by the kings of England, consulting with the nobility and commons in parliament, of which not one of twenty was a learned lawyer."

The exaggeration of these opposing views is evident, and English Common Law by its very existence affords a refutation in fact of these absolute statements: it is neither an aggregate of measures passed tentatively by more or less ignorant legislators, nor the direct product of theoretical thought; it rests indeed upon the doctrines of learned men, but its doctors are in the first place "learned judges." Their learning is, however, derived not only from the consideration of particular cases, but also from general principles. The literary influence of prominent writers like Blackstone, Bentham, Maine, Maitland, Dicey, Langdell, Ames, has stretched far beyond their lecture rooms and contributed powerfully to shape actual law.

Now, in any study of law you may aim at one of three things. If you are preparing for current practice you must of course make yourself acquainted with legal rules and procedure. If you want to obtain an insight into the

* This paper served as a text for the first of the Carpentier Lectures delivered at Columbia University, November, 1923.

[1] English works (Molesworth ed. 1840) vol. 8, p. 5.

principles underlying legal rules and suggesting rational decisions, you will turn to the study of dogmatic jurisprudence, sometimes called analytical on account of its method. If you enquire into the causes which have determined legislation or influenced decisions and into the tendencies striving to alter existing rules, you are led to examine law as a subject of social science. It is with these two latter approaches to legal studies that I propose to deal, but in treating of them, I will try as much as possible to illustrate abstract propositions by reference to the actual practice of law.

Laws are rules; claims are supported by arguments; decisions are conclusions; rules, arguments, and conclusions are bound to conform to the requirements of logic. They must be systematically coördinated and carried to their consequences. We need not dwell on the many occasions when single judgments are pronounced on the strength of proper analysis and with due attention to logical safeguards. The whole body of legal doctrines can be considered and is often considered as a more or less closely woven tissue of propositions and deductions. The ideas which constitute this tissue are not presented to society ready-made; they are gradually unfolded by processes of collective thought: sometimes particular points get generalized and subjected to principles: at other times inferences are drawn from general propositions. These processes constitute the *dialectics* of law. Let us illustrate the bearing of this method on the study of jurisprudence by an example drawn from the history of the doctrine of Toleration.

One of the consequences of the Reformation was the growth of the law as to superstitious uses and practices. Practices of this kind were suggested, among other things, by the belief that prayers for the dead are efficacious means of obtaining God's mercy and the remission of sins of the deceased; hence, numerous bequests and donations had been made for the purpose of ensuring the celebration of masses by priests in chantries, chapels and churches for the benefit of the souls of departed members of the Church. The Chantries Act of I Ed. VI (1547) decreed the confiscation of property bequeathed or granted for such purposes. There followed a string of decisions and textbook statements which interpreted the Act as a general prohibition of bequests for superstitious uses. Such prohibitions were enforced in connection with the view that the creed of the established church of England should be the one confession recognised and protected by the State, a doctrine formulated for instance in a law of 23 Eliz. (1581). The first inroad into the general acceptance of this doctrine was made by the Toleration Act of 1 and 2 Will. & Mary (1689), passed after the uprising against James II. It removed certain disabilities of Protestant dissenters. The bearing of this admission on the dialectical development of the law was emphasized in a remarkable manner by Lord Mansfield in his judgment in *Harrison* v. *Evans* (1767). He said: "Dissenters, within the description of the Toleration Act, are restored to a legal consideration and capacity; and one hundred *consequences will from thence follow which are not mentioned* in the Act. For instance, previous to the Toleration Act, it was unlawful to devise any legacy for the support of dissenting congregations or for the benefit of dissenting ministers . . . and such a devise was absolutely void, being left to what the law called superstitious purposes. But will it be said in any Court in England that such a devise is not a good and valid one now? *And yet there is nothing said of this in the Toleration Act.*" Lord Mansfield's *dictum* was referred to by Lord Buckmaster in his judgment in *Bourne* v. *Keane*.[2]

It took a hundred years for English legislators and judges to recognize that Roman Catholics were substantially in the same situation as the Dissenters and that religious toleration ought to be extended to them. This was done to some extent by the Act of 31 Geo. III (1791) with the express reservation that all previous restrictions concerning the holding and disposal of property should remain in force. The Acts of 9 Geo. IV, c. 7 (1829) and 2 & 3 Will. IV (1832) and of 23 & 24 Vict. c. 134 (1860) brought further relief in respect of the celebration of masses, the endowment of schools and other charitable institutions. And yet the prohibition of bequests for superstitious uses was reaffirmed and applied in a number of cases, the leading authority being Lord Cottenham's judgment in *West* v. *Shuttleworth*.[3] The principle of freedom of opinion on religious questions was, however, gaining ground, and the facilities conceded to Jews and to agnostics could not in fairness be denied to the Roman Catholics. The inevitable conclusion was reached in the decision of the House of Lords in *Bourne* v. *Keane*.[4]

We are not concerned with the technicalities of interpretation and construction of which Lord Birkenhead and his colleagues availed themselves in order to justify the change of attitude as regards a certain class of bequests. Apart from such subleties of case law process there is a significant recognition of the material force of a principle once admitted in certain points and pressing to be extended to other points.

We have thus before us an instance of a juridical process which could be described in terms of growth, as if we were dealing with the life of an independent organism, say of a plant. But such a comparison does not imply that the doctrine in question is a thing existing and moving by its own force: we have the means to disclose at any given moment the movements of opinion and the personal factors which account for the various links in the argument. Lord Ellesmere, Lord Mansfield, Lord Cottenham, Lord Parker, Lord Birkenhead, and others have taken up the various parts and formulated certain positions, objections, and conclusions. But the controversy as a whole may be described as the *unfolding of an idea*, and this possibility opens the way for one of the characteristic methods of jurisprudence—*its dialectical*

---

[2] (1919) A. C. 815, 866–7.
[3] (1835) 2 Myl. & K. 684.
[4] (1919) A. C. 815.

approach. It avails itself of the logical and analytical bent of juridical thinking and can be applied to all the principal doctrines of a given legal system. Sometimes its application may result, however, in the discovery of heterogeneous elements and insoluble contradictions: this calls necessarily for a different set of considerations which the purely dialectical method cannot supply.

Legal rules and judicial decisions are not mere scholastic exercises: their object is to provide conditions for the transaction of business, guarantees of social order, remedies for the redress of grievances, standards of compensation for wrongs and losses. In all these respects lawgivers and judges have to consider not only logical deductions, but public utility and private claims. In other words the course of law is shaped not only by the unfolding of ideas, but by the conflicts of interests. As an example of legislation inspired by the conflict of social forces, let me refer to the Trade Disputes Act of 1906 by which the funds of trade unions were exempted from liability to execution in cases when wrongs had been committed by agents of the trade unions. The Act was passed in direct opposition to the dogmatic principles prevailing at the time as to liability for torts and the responsibility of principals for tortious acts of their agents. The dialectical side of the problem had been fully considered and settled by the judgment of the Court of Appeals in the *Taff Vale Case.* Parliament, however, passed the Trades Disputes Act as a measure necessary to allow organized labor to exert its action as a counterpoise to the power of capital wielded by the employers. This legislative action constituted an exemption from ordinary rules of liability for the benefit of a particular class and this was fully recognized by its promoters. The Act corresponded to certain social tendencies of modern jurisprudence, but produced a break in the dogmatic consistency of the Common Law system. The contrast between the dogmatic and political arguments of the contending parties is well illustrated by a comparison between the speeches of F. E. Smith, at that time member for the Walton division of Liverpool, and Sir Henry Campbell Bannerman, the Prime Minister. Mr. F. E. Smith said among other things: "Since the Judicature Act and the order of 1883 a representative action had become possible on the common law side. The law was therefore clear that a trade union could be properly sued in representative action, and their funds made liable for any damages in which they might be cast. No body of men in this country to-day was able to establish a claim of immunity such as was put forward by honorable Gentlemen below the gangway. . . . The Attorney-General admitted that 'you are proposing class privileges.' That was what the Government was going to do if it left the question to the House. They were going to create a privilege for the proletariat. They were going to remove from the unions and particularly from the agents the sense of responsibility. He would much rather give the vote which the Labour Members were going to give, because they honestly believed in the principle that underlay the Bill, than the vote which would be given by the members of the Treasury Bench, for a measure which the Chancellor of the Exchequer had said was wrong."

Now let us attend to The Prime Minister (Sir H. Campbell-Bannerman, Stirling Burghs): . . . the great object was, and still is, to place the two rival powers of capital and labour on an equality, so that the fight between them, so far as fight was necessary, should be at least a fair one. The great mass of opinion in the country recognize fully now the beneficent nature of the trade union organization and recognize also the great services that those organizations have done in the prevention of conflict and the promotion of harmony between labour and capital. This new departure in legislation may serve as an example of a juridical process determined by forces acting outside the domain of pure reasoning.

The corresponding approach in legal study has been described as the interpretation of legal history in terms of engineering.[5] This expression seems to be altogether inappropriate in so far as it suggests comparison with processes of mechanical fabrication. Now social arrangements are not pieces of mechanism, the materials with which law deals are not lifeless things, nor are juridical problems solved by mere calculation. Statesmen, social groups and nations, when they are striving passionately for some great change of law, do act sometimes as if the desired solutions could be achieved by sudden feats of legislative engineering, but the consequences of purely mechanical cures are dangerous and sometimes disastrous; in any case they entail strong reaction and refitting. The point is that social life, as well as individual life, is an organic process and not a mechanical contrivance. Granted that surgical, if not engineering, operations may be occasionally necessary, a surgeon has to reckon with the antecedents of the patient, with his strength and with the effect of the operation on the sources of life in heart and brain, on circulation and respiration. Law as well as hygiene and medicine must seek directions in the study of life.

This is where the need of a historical jurisprudence asserts itself. History in the wide sense is nothing else but the social experience of mankind. The life of mankind is orientated toward the future, but its roots are in the past and stretch sometimes very deep into the past. On the other hand it is long since historical jurisprudence has passed the stage of clinging to tradition and turning away from problems. To name only one of its leaders, Ihering, may be sufficient in order to lay stress on the orientation of historical systems and doctrines towards social purposes and ideals. Therefore if discussions about the aims and methods of law are not to be an aggregate of casual remarks and outbursts of approval and disapproval, they must be fitted into the framework of historical experience

[5] Roscoe Pound (1923) *Interpretations of Legal History*, chap. VII.

The historical examination of any single factor of legal activity is bound to rely largely in the comparative study of similar processes in different countries and at different epochs. Now a comparative study of any kind starts from some grouping of the material into classes according to some common and outstanding features. As a result the heterogeneous mass of data is coordinated according to *types* in connection with some selected factor. Montesquieu's famous work on the *Spirit of Laws* coordinates juridical data in connection with political types. In the nineteenth century it was usual to conduct studies in comparative law on the lines of economic evolution: the legal arrangements of hunting and fishing tribes, of nomads, of agriculturists were contrasted with those of industrialism in its beginnings and of capitalistic societies on a grand scale.

Another classification of juridical types starts from the variety of social organization in which economic, political and cultural factors coöperate to produce characteristic social groups: the tribe, the city, the theocratic state, sovereign states on a territorial basis, contractual relations between individuals, unions of men striving for autonomy on the ground of common work. On the present occasion, we must be content, as it were, with a cut through the historical texture of jurisprudence at one characteristic epoch and I am choosing the twentieth century for that purpose. Let us take stock of some striking features of this historical stage, which constitute a kind of framework for its law. I have already mentioned the fact that legal arrangements may be coördinated on the basis of various forms of social activity—economics, culture, religion, morals, science, art, literature, political and social intercourse, etc. In all respects, our age is evidently an epoch of transition, of struggle between conflicting principles in which neither one side nor the other has obtained complete victory. A certain amount of struggle and change may be noticed, of course, in all periods of human history, because change is the index of life. But in some cases the historian is able to point out some guiding principles clearly predominant in the process of organic development. If we look at our time with a view not of advocating one or the other party-creed, but of noticing the relative strength and position of various parties, we must, I think, come to the conclusion that we live in a state of enhanced fermentation, of critical conflicts. In economics, labor is struggling with capital, because the part played by each one of them in the material production of goods has to be readjusted in connection with the spread of class consciousness and with altered standards of welfare. In religion, the confessional forms of Christianity are losing their hold on European civilization, and, though there is an evident demand for a religious revival which would lend a spiritual meaning (λόγος) to the mystery of human existence, there is no new gospel in sight which would satisfy the inquiring mind as well as give rest to the weary. No wonder the moral standards of the age appear shaken and doubtful as regards the most fundamental rules of conduct. The constitution of the family, the relations between the sexes, the defence of the country, the allegiance to law, all these points are challenged daily and the challenges are delivered not only by the impatient and the treacherous. I am mentioning these familiar facts merely in order to bring home to you the perplexities and contradictions of the modern legal situation. In important respects the conflict may be described as one between individualistic and collectivistic ideals and the results achieved may be tabulated from the point of view of their polar conceptions. A great master, Dicey, has attempted to trace some of them in his brilliant work on *Law and Public Opinion*. A scientific study of this kind reveals some doctrines in an evident state of dissolution; while as to others it seems possible to set up certain definite conclusions. Reaching a conclusion in theory means defining the conditions of a reasonable decision of the problem. In practice the decisions arrived at are often anything but reasonable and we see daily great nations floundering in the morass because they have embarked on suicidal policies. What a social study based on historical jurisprudence may attempt is a diagnosis of the juridical life of a given society and some indication as to the proper direction of efforts in the legislative and the judicial domain.

PAUL VINOGRADOFF

OXFORD UNIVERSITY

Part II
The Soviet Legacy

[5]
The General Theory of Law and Marxism

INTRODUCTION
The Tasks of the General Theory of Law

The general theory of law may be defined as the development of the basic, i.e. the most abstract juridic concepts. The latter include, for example, such definitions as "legal norm", "legal relation", "subject of law" etc. Because of their abstract nature, these concepts are equally applicable to any branch of law; their logical and systematic meaning remains the same irrespective of the specific content to which they are applied. No one would deny, for example, that the concepts of a subject of civil law and a subject of international law are subordinate to the more general concept of a subject of law as such and that, therefore, this category may be defined and developed independently of its specific concrete content. On the other hand, if we remain within the limits of any one branch of law, then we may say that these basic legal categories do not depend on the specific content of legal norms, in the sense that they retain their significance whatever the changes in the specific material content.[1]

We therefore conclude that developed juridic thought, whatever the material to which it is applied, cannot do without a certain number of highly abstract and general definitions.

Nor may our Soviet jurisprudence do without them if it is to remain jurisprudence, i.e. if it is to answer to its immediate practical tasks. The basic, i.e. formal, legal concepts continue to be in our codes and in the commentaries corresponding to them. The method of legal thought also remains in operation with its specific approaches.

But does this prove that the scientific theory of law must be occupied with the analysis of these abstractions? A rather widespread view assigns a purely artificial and technical significance to the basic and most general legal concepts. Dogmatic jurisprudence, we are informed, uses these designations for the purpose of convenience and only for convenience. They have no other theoretico-cognitive significance. However, the fact that dogmatic jurisprudence is a practical, and in a certain sense a technical discipline, still does not provide grounds for the conclusion that its concepts may not enter into the structure of the corresponding theoretical discipline.[2] Political economy itself began its development with practical questions primarily of monetary circulation—it originally intended to show "the methods by which governments and nations acquire wealth". Nevertheless, in these technical suggestions we already find the bases of those concepts which, in deeper and in enriched form, entered the structure of a theoretical discipline—political economy.

Is jurisprudence able to develop into a general theory of law without thereby transforming itself either into psychology or into sociology? Is it possible to analyse the basic definitions of the legal form in the way that political economy analyses the basic and most general definitions of the form of a commodity or of value? These are questions whose solution depends on the possibility of considering a general theory of law as an independent theoretical discipline.

Sociological and psychological theories (sic) of law are distinguished by the fact that they simply ignore this problem. From the very beginning, they operate with concepts of an extra-juridical nature, and if they also examine legal definitions, then it is only for the purpose of declaring them "fictions", "ideological fantasies", "projections" and so on. Upon first sight this naturalist or nihilist approach undoubtedly commands a certain sympathy, and particularly so if one contrasts it with the ideological theories of law which are saturated thoughout with teleology and moralizing. After lofty phrases on "the eternal idea of law" or "the absolute significance of the individual", the reader seeking a materialist explanation of law turns with great interest to theories which treat law as the result of a struggle of interests, as a phenomenon of state coercion, or even as a process played out in the real human psyche. Many Marxist comrades have thought it sufficient to introduce the element of class struggle into these theories, to obtain a truly materialist Marxist theory of law. As a result, however, we obtain a history of economic forms with a more or less weak legal colouring, or a history of institutions, but by no means a general theory of law.[3] Moreover, on the one hand bourgeois jurists, Gumplowicz for example, in trying to present more or less materialist views, consider themselves obliged, so to speak, *ex professio*, to ponder the arsenal of basic legal concepts even if only to declare them artificial and conventional constructs. Marxist authors, on the other hand, as individuals with no responsibilities to jurisprudence, simply and silently have usually avoided formal definitions of the general theory of law, devoting all their attention to the concrete content of legal norms and the historical development of legal institutions.[4]

In refusing to analyse basic legal concepts, however, we obtain only a theory which explains the development of legal regulation by the material needs of society and, consequently, the correspondence of legal norms to the material interests of given social classes; but legal regulation itself, despite the wealth of historical content which we embed in it as a concept, remains unanalysed as a form. Instead of seeing the completeness of its internal parts and relationships, we will be forced to use poor and approximately observed characterizations of law—so approximate that the borders between the legal and other spheres are entirely erased.[5]

Such an approach can hardly be considered correct. The history of the economy may be described entirely without the finer points and details, say, of the theory of rent or wages. But what could we say about a history of economic forms in which the basic categories of economic theory—value, capital, profit, rent etc.—were diffused in a vague and undifferentiated concept of economy? We are not even speaking of how the attempt to present such history as a theory of political economy would be received. However, in the area of the Marxist theory of law, this is in fact the situation. It is of course possible to console oneself with the fact that even the jurists themselves are still seeking, and cannot find, definitions for their concept of law. However, if most of the textbooks on the general theory of law usually begin with a certain formula, well-defined and externally exact, in fact even this formula gives us merely a confused, approximate and undifferentiated concept of law in general. It may be affirmed as axiomatic that we understand law least of all from these definitions and that, on the contrary, the relevant scholar will allow us a better understanding of the form of law the less attention he devotes to its definition.

The cause of this is entirely clear: such a complex concept as law cannot be exhausted by defining it according to the rules of the school of logic *per genus et differentia specifica*.

Unfortunately, even those few Marxists who have dealt with the theory of law have not avoided the temptations of scholastic wisdom. Renner, for example, grounds his definition of law in the concept of an imperative addressed by society (as a person) to the individual.[6] This simple construct seems entirely sufficient for him to investigate the past, present and future of legal institutions.

The basic flaw in formulae of this type is their inability to embrace the concept of law in its actual movement, revealing the plenitude of its internal parts and relationships. Instead of displaying the concept of law in its most final and exact form, and thereby showing the significance of this concept for a specific historical period, they present us with purely verbal general propositions about "external authoritarian regulation"—which apply equally well to all periods and stages of development of human societies. A complete analogy to this is provided by those attempts to give a definition of the concept of economy (in political economy) which would include all historical periods. If economic theory consisted in such fruitless scholastic generalizations, it would hardly deserve the title of a science.

Marx, as is well known, begins his research with the analysis of commodities and value, and not with opinions about economy in general. This is because economy, as a particular sphere of relations, is differentiated with the appearance of exchange. So long as the relationships of exchange-value are absent, economic activity may only with difficulty be separated from the remaining totality of life functions with which it constitutes a single synthetic whole. A purely natural economy may not be the object of political economy as an independent science. Only commodity–capitalist relationships comprise, for the first time, the object of political economy as a distinct theoretical discipline which uses its own specific concepts.[7]

Our observations here may be transferred to the general theory of law. The basic juridic abstractions, which are produced by the development of juridic thought, and which are the closest definitions of the legal form, in general reflect specific and very complex social relationships. The attempt to find a definition of law which would correspond not only with these complex relationships, but also with "human nature" or "human relationships" in general, must inevitably lead to scholastic and purely verbal formulae.

When we have to move from these inanimate formulae to the analysis of the legal form—as we meet it in reality—we inevitably encounter a series of difficulties. These difficulties are only overcome by strategies which are obviously contrived. For example, having been given a general definition of law, we are usually taught that in fact there are two types of law: subjective and objective, *ius agendi* and *norma agendi*. Moreover, the possibility of such a dichotomy is not at all anticipated in the definition itself; it therefore becomes necessary either to deny one of the species, declaring it to be a fiction, a fantasy etc. or to establish a purely external link between the general concept of law and its two species. However, this duality in the nature of law—its dissolution into a norm and a power—has a significance no less essential than the dichotomy of a commodity into exchange-value and use-value.

Law as a form cannot be understood outside of its immediate definitions. It exists only in antitheses: objective law/subjective law, public law/private law etc. These basic limitations must, however, be attached mechanically to the basic formula if the latter is constructed with the intention of it embracing all periods and stages of social development, including those which did not even know such contrasts.

Only bourgeois-capitalist society creates all the conditions necessary for the legal element in social relationships to achieve its full realization. If one leaves aside the culture of primitive peoples—where law can only with difficulty be segregated from the general mass of social phenomena of the normative order—then even in medieval Europe, legal forms were distinguished by their extreme underdevelopment. The aforementioned contrasts were combined into a single undifferentiated whole. There was no distinction between law as an objective norm and law as a power. A norm of a general nature was not distinguished from its specific applications; correspondingly, judicial and legislative activities were merged. The contrast between public and private law was entirely hidden both in the organization of the Mark and the organization of feudal power. There was no contradiction, so characteristic of the bourgeois period, between man as a private person and man as a member of a political union. A long process of development was necessary in order for the boundaries of the legal form to crystallize with full distinctiveness. The main arena of this was the city.

The dialectical development of basic juridic concepts therefore gives us not only the form of law, in its most overt and elemental nature, but also reflects the real historical process of development. This is nothing other than the process of the development of bourgeois society.

Objections may be raised that the general theory of law, as we understand it, is a discipline which deals only with formal and contrived definitions and artificial concepts. No one doubts that political economy studies something which really exists, although Marx warned that such objects as value, capital, profit, rent etc. "cannot be discovered with the aid of a microscope and chemical analysis". The theory of law operates with abstractions which are no less "artificial"; the methods of research in the natural sciences cannot discover a "legal relation" or a "subject of law"; but very real social forces are hidden behind these abstractions.

From the perspective of a man living in a natural economic environment, the economics of value relationships would appear just as artificial a distortion of simple and natural objects as juridic reasoning appears to the good judgement of the "average" man.

To think that the basic concepts which express the meaning of the legal form are the product of arbitrary thought processes. is to fall into the same mistake which Marx noted among the teachers of the eighteenth century. As the latter, in Marx's words, were unable to account for the origin and development of the puzzling forms assumed by social relationships, so they sought to denude them of their strange appearance by ascribing them to a conventional origin.

It is impossible to deny that a significant proportion of juridic concepts in fact have a very transient and artificial nature. Such, for example, are most of the concepts of public law. We shall try to explain the causes of this phenomenon below. But now we shall confine ourselves to the observation that the form of value, under conditions of a developed commodity economy, becomes universal; it assumes, along with its original expressions, a series of derivative and ephemeral expressions which emerge as the selling price of objects which are not products of labour (land), and which are completely unrelated to the process of production (e.g. military secrets bought from a spy). This does not prevent value, as an economic category, from being understood from the perspective of the socially necessary labour expenditures required for the production of one product or another. Likewise, the universality of the legal form must not prevent us from searching for the relationships which constitute its real foundation. We will show that those relations which are defined as public law are *not* this foundation.

Another objection to our conception of the tasks of the general theory of law consists in the argument that the abstractions which lie at the basis of the analysis are recognized as essential only to bourgeois law. Proletarian law, we are told, must find other generalizing concepts for itself, and indeed this search should constitute the task of the Marxist theory of law.

At first sight this appears as a serious objection; yet it rests on a misunderstanding. To demand its own new generalizing concepts for proletarian law appears to be a revolutionary direction *par excellence*. But this is to proclaim the immortality of the legal form since it tries to wrench this form away from those definite historical conditions which enable its full fruition, and to declare it capable of constant renewal. The withering away of the categories (but not the injunctions) of bourgeois law does not signify their replacement by new categories of proletarian law. Similarly, the withering away of the categories of value, capital, profit etc. during the transition to socialism, will not mean the appearance of new proletarian categories of value, capital, rent etc.

The withering away of the categories of bourgeois law will under these conditions signify the withering away of law in general, i.e. the gradual disappearance of the juridic element in human relationships.

As Marx pointed out in *The Critique of the Gotha Programme*, the transitional period is characterized by the fact that human relationships will for a time involuntarily be limited by the "narrow horizon of bourgeois law". It is interesting to analyse what, in Marx's opinion, constitutes this narrow horizon of bourgeois law. Marx assumes a social order in which the means of production belong to all society, and in which the producers do not exchange their products. He thus takes a stage which is higher than the New Economic Policy in which we live. The market relationship has already been completely replaced by an organizational relationship and, in accordance with this, "the labour expended in products is not reflected in the form of value essential to those products, since here, in contrast to capitalist society, individual labour no longer exists in an indirect way but directly as a component part of collective labour".[8] But even with the elimination of the market and market exchange, the new communist society, in Marx's words, must for some time bear "in every respect, economically, morally and intellectually, the clear imprint of the old society from whose womb it appeared". This is reflected in the principle of distribution, whereby "the individual producer receives (after deductions have been made) from society exactly what he contributes to it". Marx stresses that despite the radical changes in content and form, "the same principle prevails as that which regulates the exchange of commodities: a definite amount of labour in one form is exchanged for the same amount of labour in another form". To the extent that the social relationships of the individual producer continue to preserve the form of equivalent exchange, so too they continue to preserve the form of law. "By its very nature, law is merely the application of an equal scale." But this ignores inherent differences in individual ability, and therefore "by its content this law, like every law, is a law of inequality". Marx says nothing about the necessity of state power which would forcefully ensure the fulfilment of these norms of "unequal" law preserving its "bourgeois limitations", but this is necessarily understood.[9] Once the form of the equivalent relationship exists, this means that the form of law exists, that the form of public, i.e. state authority exists, which therefore remains for a period even when classes no longer exist. The complete withering away of state and law will be accomplished, in Marx's opinion, only when "labour has ceased to be a means of life and has become life's prime want", when the productive forces have expanded with the all-round development of the individual, when everyone labours voluntarily in accordance with his own abilities, or, as Lenin says, "when the individual does not calculate with the heartlessness of a Shylock whether he has worked half an hour longer than anyone else", in a word, *when the form of equivalent relations will be finally overcome.*

Marx therefore envisioned the transition to developed communism, not as a transition to new forms of law, but as the withering away of the legal form in general, as the liberation from this inheritance of the bourgeois age which the bourgeoisie was itself condemned to endure.

At the same time Marx indicates that the basic condition for the existence of the legal form is found in the economy, in the matrix of labour expenditures according to the principle of equivalent exchange, i.e. he revealed the innermost connection between the form of law and the form of commodities. Depending on the condition of its productive forces, a society which is compelled to preserve equivalent exchange between labour expenditure and compensation in a form even remotely resembling the exchange of commodity values, *will be compelled* also to preserve the form of law. Only proceeding on this basis is it possible to understand why a whole series of other social relationships assume a legal form. But therefore to conclude that courts or laws will always remain, or that even under maximum economic prosperity certain crimes against the person etc. will not disappear, is on the contrary to identify secondary and derivative elements as the main and basic. Indeed, even advanced bourgeois criminology has theoretically concluded that the struggle against crime may be seen as a medical-pedagogical task for whose solution the jurist—with his "categories of crime", codes, concepts of guilt, "full or diminished responsibility", with his fine distinctions between participation, abetting and inciting etc.—is perfectly unnecessary. And if this theoretical belief has not yet led to the elimination of criminal codes and judges, then this is because transcending the form of law is related not only to advancing beyond the horizons of bourgeois society, but also to the radical liberation from all remnants of the past.

In criticizing bourgeois jurisprudence, scientific socialism must model itself on the criticism of bourgeois political economy furnished by Marx. For this it must first repair to enemy territory. In other words it must not discard those generalizations and abstractions which were developed by bourgeois jurists who proceeded from the needs of their time and class, but must put them at the basis of its analysis to reveal their true significance, that is, the historical formation of the legal form.

Every ideology disappears with the social relations which produced it. But this final disappearance is preceded by a moment when an ideology, under the blows of criticism levelled at it, loses its ability to mask and surround the social relations from which it arose.

The exposé of the roots of an ideology is a true sign of its imminent end. As Lassalle says, "the dawn of a new age always consists in the consciousness of what the previous reality actually was."[10]

CHAPTER I

Methods of Constructing the Concrete in the Abstract Sciences

Every generalizing science, in studying its subject matter, turns to one and the same reality. One observation, for example the observation of the movement of heavenly bodies across the meridian, may provide conclusions for both astronomy and pyschology. And one fact, ground rent for example, may be the object of political economy or law. The difference between various sciences depends, therefore, essentially on their respective methodological and ontological approaches. Every science has its particular method, and by this method it seeks to reproduce reality. Moreover, each science constructs a concrete reality with all its wealth of forms, relations and dependencies, as the result of the combination of the most simple elements and abstractions. Psychology seeks to reduce consciousness to its simplest elements. Chemistry solves the same task with respect to substances. When in fact we cannot reduce reality into simpler elements, abstractions come to our aid. The role of abstractions is extremely important in the social sciences. The greater or lesser the perfection of abstraction is determined by the maturity of a given social science. Marx brilliantly explains this with the example of economic science.

It would seem entirely natural, says Marx, to begin research with the concrete totality, with the population living and producing in specific geographical conditions; but this population is but an empty abstraction without the classes which constitute it; in their turn, the latter are nothing without the conditions of their existence, conditions which are wages, profit and rent. The analysis of these assumes the simplest categories of price, value and, finally, commodities. Proceeding from these simplest definitions, the political economist reconstructs the concrete totality not as a chaotic, diffused whole, but as a unity replete with internal dependencies and relationships. Marx adds, moreover, that the historical development of science regressed; the seventeenth-century economists began with the concrete—with the nation, state and population—in order to arrive at rent, profit, wages, price and value. However, that which was historically inevitable is by no means methodologically correct.[11]

These observations are most applicable to the general theory of law. In this case, too, the concrete totality of society, population and the state, must be the result and the final stage of our conclusions, but not their starting point. For in moving from the simple to the more complex, from a process in pure form to its more concrete forms, we can follow a methodologically well-defined—and therefore more correct—path, than when we hesitantly move with only the diffused and undissected form of the concrete whole before us.

The second methodological observation, which must be made here, concerns one peculiarity of the social sciences. More correctly, it concerns their concepts. If we take some natural science concepts, for example the concept of energy, then we may of course establish precisely the chronological moment when it appeared. However, this date is significant only for the history of science and culture. In natural science research, as such, the application of this concept is not associated with temporal limits. The law of the transformation of energy was in effect before the appearance of Man and will continue after the cessation of all life on earth. It is extra-temporal; it is an eternal law. It is possible to ask when was the law of the transformation of energy discovered, but it is futile to concern oneself with the question of establishing the moment when these relations were reflected in that law.

Let us now turn to the social sciences, or only to political economy, and take one of its basic concepts, such as value. The real history of value is at once glaringly obvious—historically, both in the concept as a component of our thought, and also of the history of the concept as it constitutes part of the history of economic theory. The development of social relationships, therefore, gradually transforms this concept into historical reality. We know exactly what material relationships were necessary in order for the "ideal", "imaginary" quality of the object to assume "real" and therefore decisive significance. In comparison with the natural qualities which transform the product of labour from a natural phenomenon into a social phenomenon, we thus know the real historical substratum of our cognitive abstractions. At the same time we are convinced that the limits within which the application of this abstraction makes sense, correspond with the limits of the real development of history and are determined by it. Another example, adduced by Marx, shows this most clearly. Labour, as the simplest relationship of man to nature, is encountered at all stages of development, but as an economic abstraction it appears relatively late (compare the succession of schools: mercantilist, physiocrat, classical). But the development of the concept corresponded to the real development of economic relationships, obfuscating the distinction between different types of human labour and substituting labour in general for it. So, conceptual development corresponds to the real dialectic of the historical process.[12] Let us take another example, external to political economy—the state. Here we can observe both how the concept of the state gradually obtains definitional rigour and finality, developing the full scope of its definitions, and also how in reality the state develops and how it is "abstracted" from patrimony and feudalism, and how it is converted into a self-sufficient force which "penetrates all social interstices".

Thus even law, most generally defined, exists as a form not just in the minds and theories of learned jurists. It parallels a real history which unfolds itself not as a system of thought, but as a special system of social relationships. People enter these relationships not because they have consciously chosen to do so, but because the conditions of production necessitate it. Man is transformed into a legal subject in the same way that a natural product is transformed into a commodity with its mysterious quality of value.

This is a natural necessity which is confined to the framework of bourgeois conditions of existence. Therefore, natural law doctrine consciously or unconsciously lies at the basis of bourgeois theories of law. The natural law school was not only the clearest expression of bourgeois ideology in the period when the bourgeoisie, acting as a revolutionary class, formulated its demands openly and consistently; it also provided a model for the most profound and distinct understanding of the legal form. It is no accident that the flourishing influence of the doctrine of natural law closely coincided with the appearance of the great classical writings of bourgeois political economy. Both schools set themselves the task of formulating, in the most general and therefore in the most abstract form, the basic conditions of existence of bourgeois society. Bourgeois society appeared to them as the natural condition of existence of all societies.

Rather than dwelling in more detail on the changing schools of legal philosophy, we may note some evolutionary parallels between legal and economic thought. Thus, their historical direction may in both cases be regarded as a phenomenon of the feudal aristocracy, and partly also of the petit bourgeois reaction. When their revolutionary ardour was finally dissipated in the second half of the nineteenth century, the bourgeoisie ceased to be attracted by the purity and clarity of classical doctrines. Bourgeois society now sought stability and strong authority. The central focus of legal theory became not the analysis of the legal form, but the problem of justifying the coercive power of legal rules. A unique blend of historicism and legal positivism was created which led to the denial of all law other than law emanating from the state.

The psychological school of law may be categorized alongside the psychological school of political economy. Both try to transfer the object of analysis to the realm of the subjective conditions of consciousness ("evaluations", "imperative-attributive emotion"), failing to see that the corresponding abstract categories express social relationships in the regularity of their logical structure—social relationships which are hidden from individuals and which extend beyond the limits of their consciousness.

Finally, the extreme formalism of the normative school (Kelsen) undoubtedly expresses the most recent general decadence of bourgeois scientific thought. This is accomplished by its exhaustion in the fruitless subtleties of method and formal logic, and the tendency to divorce itself from reality. In economic theory a similar position is occupied by representatives of the mathematical school.

The legal relationship is, in Marx's phrase, an abstract and one-sided relationship; but in this it appears not as the result of the product of the mind of a conscious subject, but as the product of social development.

"In any historical and social science, and also in the development of economic categories, it is always necessary to remember that in reality, and therefore in the mind, the subject is already given—here, bourgeois society. Categories therefore express only the forms of being and the characteristics of existence—often only of individual aspects of this specific society, this subject."[13]

What Marx says here about economic categories is fully applicable to legal categories. The latter, in their false universality, in fact express particular aspects of a specific historical subject—of bourgeois commodity production.

In the same *Introduction*, which we have repeatedly cited, we find still another profound methodological observation by Marx. This concerns the possibility of clarifying the meaning of preceding formations in terms of the analysis of subsequent and more developed formations. Marx explains that only having understood rent can we understand tribute, the tithe and the feudal corvée. The more developed form explains the previous stages in which it existed only embryonically. Evolution, as it were, reveals those intimations which were hidden in the distant past.

> Bourgeois society is the most developed and perfected historical organization of production. The categories which reflect its relationships and its organizations, simultaneously enable comprehension of the structure of the production relationships of all obsolete social forms—from whose fragments and elements this society is erected, partly continuing to bear its legacy, which it has not succeeded in overcoming, and partly articulating that which formally was there only by implication.[14]

Applying the above mentioned methodological consideration to the theory of law, we must begin with the analysis of the legal form in its most abstract and simple aspect, moving gradually by way of complexity to the historically concrete. In so doing we must not forget that the dialectical development of concepts corresponds to the dialectical development of the historical process itself. Historical evolution produces not only successive changes in the content of norms and legal institutions, but also the development of the legal form itself. The legal form appeared at a certain cultural level in a long embryonic stage, internally unstructured and barely distinguishable from neighbouring spheres, e.g. mores, religion. Then, gradually developing, it achieves maximum maturity, differentiation and precision. This higher stage of development corresponds to specific economic and social relationships. At the same time this stage is characterized by the appearance of a system of general concepts theoretically reflecting the legal system as a distinct whole.

Accordingly, we can achieve a clear and exhaustive definition only if we base our analysis on the fully developed legal form of law which interprets its antecedent forms as its embryos.

Only then can we perceive law, not as a characteristic of abstract human society, but as an historical category which responds to specific social *environs* and which is constructed on the contradictions of private interests.

CHAPTER II

Ideology and Law

In the recent polemic between Comrade Stuchka and Professor Reisner, an important role was played by the question of the ideological nature of law.* Relying upon a handsome collection of citations, Reisner tried to show that Marx and Engels considered law as one of the "ideological forms", and that the same view was held by many other Marxist theorists. Of course it is not necessary to dispute these statements and citations. Likewise, it is impossible to deny the fact that law is experienced by people pyschologically, in particular in the form of general principles of rules or norms. However, the task is by no means to recognize or deny the existence of legal ideology (or psychology), but rather to show that legal categories have no other significance than the ideological. Only in the latter case do we recognize Reisner's conclusion as "necessary", namely, "that a Marxist may study law only as one of the subtypes of the general type ideology". In this little word "only" lies the whole essence of the matter. We will explain this with an example from political economy. The categories of commodity, value and exchange-value are undoubtedly ideologically produced distortions, mystifying (in Marx's expression) forms of ideas, in which exchange society imagines a labour bond between individual producers. The ideological nature of these forms is proved by the fact that if one goes to other economic structures, the categories (of commodity, value etc.) lose all significance. Therefore, with complete justification we may speak of a commodity ideology, or as Marx called it, a

* This debate is found in M. A. Reisner's critical review of P. I. Stuchka's *The Revolutionary Role of Law and State* (1921); Stuchka's reply appeared in *Vestnik sotsialisticheskoi akademii*, no. 3, 1923 [eds.].

"commodity fetishism" and categorize it in the list of psychological phenomena. This by no means signifies that the categories of political economy have *exclusively* psychological significance, that they relate *only* to experiences, impressions and other subjective processes. We know very well that, for instance, the category of commodity, despite its clear ideological nature, reflects an objective social relationship. We know that whatever degree this relationship has developed, its greater or lesser universality, are material factors subject to inquiry as such, and that it exists not merely in the form of ideological–psychological processes. Thus, the general concepts of political economy are not only an element of ideology, but they are also a type of abstraction, from which we may scientifically, i.e. theoretically, construct objective economic reality. In Marx's words: "These are socially significant, and thus objective, forms of thought within the limits of the productive relationships of a specific, historically determined, social form of production—commodity production."[15]

We must, therefore, demonstrate both that general juridic concepts may enter and actually do enter into the structure of ideological processes and ideological systems—this is not subject to any dispute—and that in them, in these concepts, it is possible to discover social reality which has, in a certain way, become mystified. In other words, we must determine whether or not legal categories are such objective forms of thought (objective for an historically specific society) which correspond to objective social relationships. Consequently, our question is: *is it possible to understand law as a social relationship in the same sense in which Marx termed capital a social relationship?*

Such a statement of the question pre-empts reference to the ideological nature of law, and all our consideration is transferred to an entirely different level.

Recognition of the ideological nature of concepts by no means frees us from the work of searching for objectively existing reality, i.e. in the reality of the external world, and not simply in consciousness. In the opposite case we would be compelled to erase any boundary between the world beyond the grave—which also exists in the conceptions of some people—and, say, the state. Professor Reisner, incidentally, does just this. Relying on the well-known quotation from Engels concerning the state as the "primary ideological force", dominating people, Reisner quickly equates the state with state ideology. "The psychological nature of the phenomena of authority is so obvious, and state authority itself—existing *only in the psyche of people* (our italics, E. P.)—is so deprived of material features, that it would seem no one considers state authority in any way other than as an idea. It is real only to the extent that people make it a principle of their action."[16] This means that finances, the military, and administration, are all entirely "deprived of material features", that all this exists "only in the psyche of the people". And what can be done, in the words of Professor Reisner himself, with that "huge" mass of the population which lives "outside state consciousness"? It must obviously be excluded. These masses have no significance for "the real" existing state.

And what about the state from the perspective of economic unity? Or customs or the boundaries of custom, are these also ideological and psychological processes? Many such questions can be posed, but all with the same meaning. The state is an ideological form, but simultaneously it is a form of social existence. The ideological nature of a concept does not eliminate the reality and materiality which the concept reflects.

The formal completeness of the concepts of state, territory, population and authority, reflect not only a specific ideology but also the objective fact of the formation of a real sphere of domination, bound to one centre, and, accordingly, even more important, they reflect the creation of real administrative, financial and military organizations with corresponding human and material apparatuses. The state is nothing without methods of communication, without the possibility of giving orders and decrees, of moving armed forces etc. Does Professor Reisner think that the Roman military roads, or modern methods of communications, relate to phenomena of the human psyche? Or does he suppose that these material elements must be entirely ignored as a factor in the formation of the state? Then of course nothing else will remain for us but to equate the reality of the state with the reality of "literature, philosophy, and other spiritual productions of man". It is regrettable that the practice of political struggle, of the struggle for authority, radically contradicts this psychological concept of the state, for at each step we are confronted by objective and material factors.

However, one cannot but note that an inevitable result of the psychological perspective (on which Professor Reisner depends) is subjectivism and solipsism. "As the creation of as many psychologies as there are individuals, and of as many different types as there are groups and social classes, state authority will appear inherently different in the consciousness and conduct of a cabinet minister and that of a peasant who has not yet contemplated the idea of a state; in the psyche of a political activist and in the principles of an anarchist—in one word in the consciousness of people with very different social positions, professional activity, upbringing etc."[17] From this it is clearly obvious that if we remain on a psychological level we quite simply lose every basis to speak of the state as some objective unity. Only by considering the state as a real organization of class authority, i.e. taking into account all (including not only psychological but material) elements, and the latter first of all, do we obtain firm ground under our feet, i.e. we may study the state itself as it is in reality, and not just the innumerable and varied subjective forms in which it is reflected and experienced.

But if abstract definitions of the legal form indicate not simply certain psychological or ideological processes, but if they are concepts which express the very essence of an objective social relation, then in what sense do we say that law regulates social relationships? Do we not want to say by this that social relationships therefore regulate themselves? Or when we say that a social relationship assumes a legal form, then does this not imply a simple tautology: law adopts the form of law?[18]

At first glance this objection is most convincing, and would seem to leave no other alternative than to recognize law as ideology and only ideology. However, let us try to disentangle these difficulties. In order to lighten our task let us again resort to comparison. Marxist political economy teaches, of course, that capital is a social relationship. It may not as Marx says, be discovered under a microscope, but nevertheless it by no means is exhausted by experiences, ideologies and other subjective processes which occur in the human psyche. It is an objective social relationship. Further, when we observe, for example, in the sphere of small-scale production, the gradual transition from working for a customer to labouring for a monopolist, we postulate that the corresponding relations have assumed a capitalist form. Does this mean that we have fallen into a tautology?

By no means; we have merely said that the social relation which is called capital began to colour or gave its form to another social relation. Thus we may consider all that occurred purely objectively, as a material process, entirely eliminating the psychology or ideology of its participants. Cannot this be done in exactly the same way with law? Being itself a social relationship, it is capable to a greater or a lesser extent, of colouring or giving its form to other social relationships. Of course, we may never approach a problem from this perspective if we are guided by a confused impression of law as a form in general—similar to the way in which vulgar political economy cannot glean the essence of capitalist relationships by beginning with the concept of capital as "accumulated labour in general".

Thus, we can escape from this apparent contradiction, if by way of analysis of the basic definitions of law, we succeed in showing that it is a mystified form of some *specific* social relationship. In this case it will not be meaningless to say that this relationship in one or another instance gives its form to another social relationship, or even to the totality of social relationships.

The situation is no different with the second apparent tautology: law regulates social relationships. For if we exclude a certain anthropomorphism inherent in this formula, then it is reduced to the following proposition: under certain conditions the *regulation* of social relationships *assumes a legal character*. Such a formulation is undoubtedly more correct and, most importantly, more historical. We may not deny that collective life exists even among animals, nor that life there is regulated in one way of another. But it never occurs to us to affirm that the relationships of bees or ants is regulated by *law*. If we turn to primitive tribes, then although we may observe the origins of law, nevertheless a significant part of the relationships are regulated by a means external to law, e.g. by the prescriptions of religion. Finally, even in bourgeois society such things as the organization of postal and railroad services, military affairs etc. may be assigned entirely to legal regulation only upon a very superficial view which allows itself to be deceived by the external form of laws, charters and decrees. A railroad schedule regulates the movement of trains in a very different sense than, say, the law on the liability of railroads regulates the relationship of the latter with freight shippers. Regulation of the first type is primarily technical; the second primarily legal. The same relationship exists between the mobilization plan and the law on compulsory military service, between the instructions on the investigation of criminals and the Code of Criminal Procedure.

We will return to the difference between legal and technical norms later. For the moment we merely note that the regulation of social relationships assumes a legal nature correlative with the development of the specific and basic legal relationship.

The regulation of norms, or the creation of norms for social relationships are in principle homogeneous and thoroughly legal only upon a very superficial or purely formal view of the matter. Actually, there is an obvious difference in this regard between the various fields of human relationships. Gumplowicz sharply distinguishes between private law and state norms, and only agreed to recognize the former as the domain of jurisprudence. In fact the most consolidated nucleus of legal obscurity (if it is permissible to use such a phrase) lies precisely in this area of the relations of private law. It is here that the legal subject, "persona", finds a fully adequate embodiment in the concrete individuality of the subject engaged in egoistic economic activity, as an owner and bearer of private interests. It is in private law that legal thought moves most freely and confidently; its constructs assume the most finished and structured form. It is here that the classical shades of Aulus Agerius and Numerius Negidius—those personages of the Roman procedural formula—constantly soar above the jurists, and it is from them that the latter draw their inspiration. In private law the *a priori* assumptions of legal thought are clothed in the flesh and blood of two disputing parties, defending "their own rights", with *vindicta* in their hands. Here, the jurist's role as a theorist is directly merged with his practical social function. The dogma of private law is nothing more than an endless chain of arguments *pro* and *contra* imaginary claims and potential suits. Behind each paragraph of this systematic guide stands an unseen abstract client ready to use the relevant propositions as advice. The scholarly legal arguments on the significance of a mistake, or on the distribution of the burden of proof, do not differ from the same disputes before a judge. The difference here is no greater than that between knightly tournaments and feudal wars. The first, as is well known, were conducted sometimes with even greater fierceness, and demanded no less expenditure of energy and sacrifice, than real skirmishes. Only the replacement of individual enterprise with planned social production and distribution will end this unproductive expenditure of the forces of the human mind.

The basic assumption of legal regulation is thus the opposition of private interests. At the same time the latter is the logical premise of the legal form and the real cause of the development of the legal superstructure. The conduct of people may be regulated by the most complex rules but the legal element in this regulation begins where the individualization and opposition of interests begins. "Controversy", says Gumplowicz, "is the basic element of everything legal". Unity of purpose is, on the contrary, the premise of technical regulation. Therefore the legal norms concerning the liability of railroads presume private claims, private individualized interests; the technical norms of railroad movement suppose a single purpose, e.g. the achievement of maximum freight capacity. Let us take another example: the curing of a sick person presupposes a series of rules both for the sick person himself and for the medical personnel; but to the extent that these rules are established from the perspective of a single purpose, the restoration of the patient's health, they are of a technical nature. The application of these rules may be accompanied by coercion with respect to the patient. But so long as this coercion is considered from the perspective of the same single purpose (both for the rulers and the ruled), it remains solely a technically expedient act. Within these limits the content of the rules is established by medical science and is altered with its progress. There is nothing here for the lawyer to do. His role begins where we leave the basis of unity of purpose and move to the consideration of the perspective of individualized and antagonistic subjects, each of whom is the bearer of his own private interest. The physician and the patient are now transformed into subjects of rights and duties, and the rules which connect them are legal rules. At the same time, coercion is now considered not just from the perspective of expediency, but from the perspective of formal, i.e. legal, permissibility.

It is not difficult to see that the possibility of taking a legal perspective derives from the fact that the most diverse relationships in commodity-producing societies are organized on the model of relationships of commercial circulation, and inscribed in the form of law. Likewise, it is natural for bourgeois jurists to deduce the universality of the legal form from the external and absolute qualities of human nature, or from the fact that the orders of the authorities may extend to any subject. It is not necessary to provide any particular proof of this. An article in Volume Ten obliged a husband "to love his wife as his very own body". However, even the most daring jurists would hardly try to construct a corresponding legal relationship involving the possibility of libidinization etc.

On the contrary, however artificial and unreal a specific juridic construct may seem, nevertheless, so long as it remains within the bounds of private law, and primarily property law, it has a firm basis. Otherwise, it would have been impossible to explain the fact that the basic lines of thought of Roman jurists retained their significance up to the present time as the *ratio scripta* of every type of commodity-producing society.

We have to a certain extent now anticipated the answer to the question posed at the outset: where shall we look for that unique social relationship whose inevitable expression is the form of law? We will try to show in more detail that this relationship is the relationship of possessors of commodities.[19] The usual analysis, which we find in any philosophy of law, identifies the legal relationship as a will relationship, as a voluntary relationship between people in general. The reasoning here proceeds from the "existing results of the process of development", from the "ongoing forms of thought", but it ignores their historical origin; whereas in reality, in proportion to the development of a commodity economy, the natural premises of exchange become the natural premises of every form of human relationship and stamp their imprint upon them; in the heads of philosophers, on the contrary, the circulation of commodities is represented as merely a partial instance of a general form which for them assumes an eternal nature.[20]

Comrade Stuchka, from our point of view, correctly identified the problem of law as a problem of a social relationship. But instead of beginning to search for the specific social objectivity of the relationship, he returned to the usual and formal definition—although a definition now influenced by class characteristics. In the general formula given by Stuchka, law figures not as a *specific* social relationship but, as with *all* relationships *in general, as a system of relations which corresponds to the interests of the ruling class and which protects it with organized force*. Accordingly, within these class boundaries, law as a relationship is indistinguishable from social relations in general, and Comrade Stuchka is therefore not in a position to answer Professor Reisner's venomous question: how do social relationships become legal institutions, or how is law converted into itself?

Stuchka's definition, perhaps because it emerged from the depths of the People's Commissariat of Justice, was tuned to the needs of the practising lawyer. It shows the empirical limit which history always places upon legal logic, but it does not reveal the deep roots of this logic itself. This definition reveals the class content included in legal forms, but it does not explain to us why this content adopts such a form.

For the bourgeois philosophy of law, which considers relationships as an eternal and natural form of all human relationships, such a question does not arise in general. For Marxist theory, which tries to penetrate the secrets of social forms and to reduce "all social relationships to man himself", this task must occupy the first place.

CHAPTER III

Relationship and the Norm

As the wealth of capitalist society assumes the form of an enormous accumulation of commodities, society presents itself as an endless chain of legal relationships.

The exchange of commodities assumes an atomized economy. A connection is maintained between private and isolated economies from transaction to transaction. The legal relationship between subjects is only the other side of the relation between the products of labour which have become commodities. The legal relationship is the primary cell of the legal tissue through which law accomplishes its only real movement. In contrast, law as a totality of norms is no more than a lifeless abstraction.

Nonetheless, the standard view posits objective law or a norm as the base of the legal relationship both logically and in reality. According to this conception, a legal relationship is *generated* by an objective norm:

> The norm of the right to demand repayment of a debt does not exist because creditors usually demand repayment, but on the contrary creditors demand repayment because the norm

exists; law is not established inductively from observed instances, but by deduction from a rule established by someone.[21]

The expression, "the norm *generates* the legal relationship", can be understood both in the real and logical sense.

Let us turn to the first of these. Above all it should be noted that the totality of norms, written and unwritten, belongs *per se* more to the sphere of literary creativity, a situation acknowledged frequently among the jurists themselves.

This aggregate of norms obtains real significance only because of those relationships which are conceived of as having arisen and, in fact, have arisen according to these rules. Even the most consistent advocate of the pure normative method, Hans Kelsen, had to recognize that somehow a slice of real life, i.e. of the actual conduct of people, had to be harmonized with the ideal normative order. In this sense, to consider the statutes of tsarist Russia as law currently in effect is possible only in an insane asylum. The formal juridical method, which is concerned only with norms which are "considered as law", can assert its independence only within very narrow limits, only so long as the tension between fact and norm does not exceed a definite limit. In material reality a relationship has primacy over a norm. If not a single debtor repaid a debt, then the corresponding rule would have to be regarded as actually non-existent and if we wanted nevertheless to affirm its existence we would have to fetishize this norm in some way. Indeed a great many theories of law are concerned with such fetishism, justifying the preoccupation on very slender methodological grounds.

Law as an objective social phenomenon cannot be exhausted by a norm or a rule, whether written or unwritten. A norm as such, i.e. in its logical content, either is directly derived from existing relationships already or, if it is published as statutory law, then it presents itself only as a symptom by which one may assess, with some degree of probability, the likely emergence of the corresponding relationships in the near future. It is not sufficient to know the normative content of law in order to confirm its objective existence. It is necessary to know if this normative content is realized in practice, that is in social relationships. A common source of confusion is the dogmatic jurist's method of thought according to which the concept of operative law and operative norm does not conform to what the sociologist or historian understands as objectively substantive law.

When a dogmatic jurist decides the question of whether a given norm of law is operative or not, he usually does not have in mind the question of the presence or absence of a particular objective social phenomenon. Instead, he is concerned only with the presence or absence of a logical connection between the given normative provision and a more general normative premise.[22]

Thus, the norm is the only thing that exists for the dogmatic jurist who, confined to the narrow framework of his purely technical task, may serenely equate law and norm. In the case of customary law he must turn to reality regardless. But when statutory law is the jurist's only normative assumption (expressed in his technical language, the source of law), then the jurist's conclusions, and his dogma about "operative" law, are by no means obligatory for the historian who wants to study the law actually existing. Scientific, i.e. theoretical, study can deal only with facts. If certain relationships are actually formed this means that the corresponding law has been created. If a statute or decree was merely published, but the corresponding relationships did not in fact arise, this means there was an attempt to create law but the attempt failed.[23]

It is possible moreover to modify this thesis and make its cornerstone the objective social regulatory forces or, as jurists express it, the objective legal order, instead of norms.[24] But even in this new formulation, the thesis can be subjected to further criticism. If social regulatory forces are understood to be the same relationships in their regularity and constancy, then we have a simple tautology. If instead they are understood as a special, consciously organized order ensuring and guaranteeing the given relationships, then the logical error will be entirely clear. It is impossible to say that the relationship between creditor and debtor is *generated* by a coercive order which exists in a given state for recovering debts. This objectively existing order *ensures*, but certainly *does not generate* the relationship. This is not mere scholasticism—that is best shown by the fact that we can conceive of, as well as find, a tremendous variety of historical examples of the ideal functioning of this externally coercive and regulatory social apparatus, and consequently the most diverse degrees in which relationships are guaranteed. Moreover these relationships themselves do not undergo any structural changes. We can imagine so extreme a situation as when—except for the two parties entering the relationship—no other third force exists capable of establishing a norm and guaranteeing its observance (for instance some contract between the Varangians and the Greeks): the relationship remains even here. But one merely needs to imagine the disappearance of a party, i.e. of the subject as the bearer of a distinct autonomous interest, and the very possibility of a relationship also disappears.

In this respect one may argue that if one departs from the objective norm, then the very concepts of legal relationship and legal subject are in abeyance, lacking definition. In general, this objection reveals the very practical and empirical spirit of modern jurisprudence. It knows but one truth; that any lawsuit is lost if the party cannot rely on an appropriate paragraph of some statute. However, the belief that a legal subject and a legal relationship do not exist and are not definable external to an objective norm, are just as theoretically mistaken as the belief that value does not exist and is not definable outside the framework of supply and demand (because empirically it is reflected precisely in price fluctuations).

The prevalent style of legal thought which initially posits the norm as the authoritatively established rule or conduct, is distinguished by that same incisive empiricism which—also seen in economic theories—goes hand in hand with extreme and lifeless formalism.

Supply and demand can exist for any objects including those which are by no means the product of labour. The conclusion can be drawn from this that value may be defined without any reference to the socially necessary labour time required for the production of a specific commodity. The empirical fact of an individualized value serves as the basis for a formal-logical theory of marginal utility.

Similarly, norms issued by the state may deal with the most varied objects that have very different qualities. From this the inference can be made that the essence of law is exhausted by the form of command or order which proceeds from higher authority, and that the very substance of social relationships contains no elements which could generate the legal form. The empirical fact that relationships protected by the state are better secured is placed at the foundation of the formal-logical theory of legal positivism.

Our question, expressed in the Marxist terms of historical materialism, is reduced to the problem of the relationship between the legal and political superstructures. If a norm is recognized as the dominant element in all relationships then, before seeking the legal superstructure, we must assume the presence of a norm-establishing authority, i.e. in other words a political organization. Thus we would have to conclude that the legal superstructure derives from the political superstructure.

However, Marx himself emphasizes the fact that the basic and most deeply set stratum of the legal superstructure—property relationships—is so closely contiguous with the base that they are "the same relationships of production expressed in legal language". The state, i.e. the organization of political class domination, develops from definite relationships of production and property. Production relationships, logically expressed, comprise what Marx, following Hegel, called civil society. The political superstructure, and in particular the state apparatus, is a secondary, derivative element.

The way in which Marx envisioned the relationship between civil society and the state is apparent from the following quotation:

> The egoistic individual of bourgeois society may in his insular imagination, in his lifeless abstraction, depict himself as an atom, i.e. a coherent and self-sufficient being, without needs or embellishments. The harsh reality is that our sensory perceptions are not concerned with his fantasies. His feelings compel him to believe in the reality of the external world and also of other individuals; every day he is reminded that the external world is not empty, but that it is the external world which fills his stomach. Each of his natural activities, each of his qualities, and each incentive to live becomes a requirement, a need which transforms his egoism into a hunger for the objects and people of the external world. But since the need of one individual has no inherent meaning for another egoistic individual (who has the means for satisfying this need), and since accordingly the need is not directly linked with its satisfaction, then each individual is compelled to make this bond in order to become in his turn the intermediary between another's need and the object of that need. Thus, natural necessity is the characteristic of the human condition. However alien they may seem to one another, the members of civil society are united through self-interest. *Civil, not political life, this is the real bond.* It is not the state that binds the atoms of civil society, but the fact that they are atoms only in imagination and transcendental fantasy. In reality they are very unlike atoms—they are not divine egoists, but egoistic human beings. *Only political superstition forces us to believe that civil society is the creation of the state; on the contrary, the state is the creation of civil society.*[25]

Marx returns to the same question in another article, "Moralising Criticism and Critical Morality", where, in a polemic with the representative of true socialism, Heinzen, he writes:

> If in general the bourgeoisie politically, i.e. with the help of state power, "supports unjust property relationships" [Marx puts Heinzen's words in quotation marks here], then *it does not create them*. "Unjust property relationships" aided by the modern division of labour, the modern forms of exchange, competition, concentration, etc., do not *flow from the political domination of the bourgeois class*, but, on the contrary, the political domination of the bourgeois class derives from these modern relationships of production—which bourgeois economists proclaim as inevitable and eternal laws.

Thus, the path from production relationships to legal or property relationships is shorter than imagined by so-called positivist jurisprudence, which cannot function without an intermediate link—state power and its norms. Man as a social producer is the assumption from which economic theory proceeds. The general theory of law must proceed from this same basic assumption. Thus, for instance, the economic relationship of exchange must be present for the legal relationship of the contract of purchase and sale to arise. In its real movement, the economic relationship becomes the source of the legal relationship, which first emerges at the moment of a controversy. A dispute, a conflict of interest, elicits the form of law, the legal superstructure. In a dispute, i.e. in a lawsuit, the parties engaged in economic activity already appear as parties, i.e. as participants in the legal superstructure; the court in its most primitive form—this is the legal superstructure *par excellence*. Through the judicial process the legal is abstracted from the economic, and appears as an independent element. Law historically emerged from controversy, i.e. from a claim, and only thereafter did it overlap with the earlier (purely economic or factual) relationship. From the very beginning it thus assumed a dual nature—economic and legal. Dogmatic jurisprudence ignores this sequence and at once begins with the end result—with abstract norms through which the state, so to speak, juridicizes its actions and infuses all social spaces. The basic defining element (from the simplistic perspective of relationships of purchase and sale, credit, loans etc.) is not the actual material economic content of these relationships but the imperative directed to the individual in the name of the state. This point of departure is useless to the legal practitioner both for the study and explanation of the concrete legal structure, and particularly for the analysis of the legal form in its most general definitions. State power injects clarity and stability into the legal structure but it does not create its preconditions which are rooted in the material relationships of production.

Gumplowicz, in his *Rechtsstaat und Sozialismus*, of course comes to the directly opposite conclusion proclaiming the primacy of the state, i.e. of political domination. Turning to the history of Roman law, he thinks that he has succeeded in proving that "all private law was once public law". In his opinion this was because all the most important institutes of Roman civil law, for example, emerged as privileges of the ruling class, as public law advantages in the hands of the victorious group for the purpose of consolidating its power.

It cannot be denied that this theory is convincing, to the extent that it emphasizes the element of class struggle and ends the idyllic view of the emergence of private property and power. But Gumplowicz makes two major errors. First, he gives coercion such a constructive role, and loses sight of the fact that every social order, including those which were formed on the basis of conquest, is determined by the specific conditions of the social forces of production. Second, in speaking of the state he erases any difference between primitive relations of domination and "public power" in the modern, i.e. bourgeois sense of the word. He therefore infers that private law is generated by public law. But from the fact that the most important institutes of the ancient Roman *ius civile* (ownership, the family, the procedure for inheritance) were created by the ruling class to support their domination, it is also possible to draw the diametrically opposed conclusion—that "all public law was once private law". This will be just as true, or rather just as false, because the antithesis between private and public law corresponds to much more developed relationships and loses its meaning and application in the primitive era. If the institutes of the *ius civile* really were a mixture of features of public law and private law (using modern terminology), then they equally included religious and, in a broad sense, ritualistic elements. Consequently, at this level of development the purely legal element was inseparable from its reflection in the general conceptual system.

The development of law as a system was evoked not by the requirements of the state, but by the necessary conditions for commercial relations between those tribes which were not under a single sphere of authority. This is recognized, incidentally, by Gumplowicz himself. Commercial relations with foreign tribes, with nomads, and plebeians, and in general with those not participant in the union of public law (in Gumplowicz's terminology), ushered in the *ius gentium*, which was the prototype of the legal superstructure in its pure form. In contrast to the *ius civile*, with its undeviating and ponderous forms, the *ius gentium* discards all that is not connected with the goal—with the natural basis of the economic relation. Public law embodies the nature of this relationship and therefore appears as "natural" law; it strives to reduce this relationship to the minimal number of assumptions, and therefore develops easily into a logically structured system. Gumplowicz undoubtedly is right when he equates legal logic with the logic of the civilian, but he is mistaken in thinking that the system of private law could have developed, so to speak, in a derivative fashion from public power. His train of thought is approximately as follows: because private disputes did not directly or materially touch upon the interests of authority, then the latter gave the corpus of jurists full freedom to refine their mental abilities in this sphere. In the field of public law, conversely, reality resisted the jurists' efforts, because authority tolerates no interference in its own affairs and does not recognize the omnipotence of juridic logic.

It is most obvious that the logic of juridic concepts corresponds with the logic of the social relationship of commodity production, and that the history of the system of private law should be sought in these relationships and not in the dispensation of the authorities. On the contrary, the logical relationships of domination and subordination are only partially included in the system of juridic concepts. Therefore, the juridic concept of the state may never become a theory but will always appear as an ideological distortion of the facts.

Wherever the first layer of the legal superstructure exists, we find that the legal relationship is generated directly by the existing material production relationships of people.

From this it follows that for the analysis of the legal relationship, in its simplest form, there is no need to proceed from the concept of a norm as an external authoritative command. It is sufficient to take as a basis a legal relationship "the content of which originates in the economic relation itself" (Marx), and to study the "legal" form of this juridic relationship as one of its partial aspects.

The question of whether a norm should be considered a prerequisite of a legal relationship in historical reality, led us to the problem of the relationship between the legal and political superstructures. On logical and systematic grounds, the problem seems to be the relation between objective and subjective law.

In his text on constitutional law, Duguit called attention to the fact that the word "droit" signified "things which are undoubtedly deeply intermingled, but which are extremely different from one another". Here, he means law in the objective and subjective senses. In fact we come here to one of the darkest and most disputed areas of the general theory of law. Before us is some sort of strange dual concept; although both aspects are located at different levels, they nevertheless undoubtedly condition each other. Law is simultaneously a form of external authoritative regulation and a form of subjective private autonomy. The basic and essential characteristic of the former is unconditional obligation and external coercion, while freedom is ensured and recognized within definite boundaries. Law appears both as the basis of social organization and as the means for individuals "to be disassociated, yet integrated in society". On the one hand, law completely merges with external authority, and on the other it completely opposes every external authority not recognized by it. The duality of law as the synonym of official state power, and as the slogan of revolutionary struggle, is the arena for unlimited controversy and the most impossible confusion.

Consciousness of this deep and hidden contradiction produced mighty efforts somehow to eliminate this troublesome conceptual dichotomy. For this purpose no small number of attempts were made to adopt one of the "meanings" at the sacrifice of the other. Thus, for instance, the same Duguit, who in his treatise declares the expressions–objective and subjective law—"successful, clear, and exact", in another of his works refines the proof that subjective law is "simply a misunderstanding, a *metaphysical conception untenable* in an era of realism and positivism such as ours".

The opposite trend, whose German representative is Bierling, and among us the psychologists headed by Petrazhitsky, are inclined to declare objective law "a fantasy", deprived of real significance "an emotional projection", a product of the objectification of internal, i.e. psychological, processes etc.

Discarding for now the psychological school and trends related to it, let us consider the view whereby law should be understood exclusively as an objective norm. Proceeding from this concept we have, on the one hand, an authoritative prescription of the necessary (or the norm), and on the other the subjective obligation corresponding to, and generated by it.

Dualism is apparently uprooted, but this is merely a temporary victory, because as soon as we move to the practical application of this formula, immediate attempts are made by circuitous and indirect routes to introduce those contours necessary for the conceptual creation of subjective law. We now return to the same dichotomy, with the only difference that one part of it, subjective law, is artificially depicted as some species of ghost; no combination of imperatives and obligations can provide us with subjective law, in the independent and real sense in which any proprietor of bourgeois society embodies it. In fact, it suffices to exemplify property alone to be convinced of this. If the attempt to reduce the *law* of property to *prohibitions* directed to third parties is no more than a logical confusion, an ugly and inverted concept, then the depiction of the bourgeois law of property as a social obligation is also a mystification.[26]

Every owner and everyone around him, understands clearly that the *right belonging to him* as an owner has only this in common with an obligation: they are polar opposites. Subjective law has primacy for it is ultimately based on a material interest which exists independently of external, i.e. conscious, regulation of social life.

The subject as the bearer and addressee of all possible demands, and the chain of subjects bound by demands addressed to one another, is the basic juridic fabric corresponding to the economic fabric, i.e. to the social relations of production which depend on the division of labour and exchange.

Social organization, including the instruments of coercion, is the concrete totality to which we must turn, having previously understood the legal relationship in its pure and simplest form. Thus, obligation as the result of an imperative or order, is now the actualizing and complicating element in the consideration of the legal form. In its most abstract and simple form, a legal obligation must be considered as an expression and correlation of a subjective legal claim. In the analysis of a legal relationship we clearly see that an obligation does not exhaust the logical content of the legal form. It is not even an independent element of it. An obligation always appears as an expression or correlation of an appropriate legal right. The obligation of one party is what is owed to and therefore what belongs to another. What appears as a right for the creditor appears as an obligation for the debtor. The category of legal right becomes logically complete only when it includes a bearer and an owner of rights, whose rights are neither more nor less than the obligations of others to him.

Thus, the legal relationship not only gives us law in its real movement, but also reveals the most characteristic peculiarities of law as a logical category. Conversely, the norm itself, as a prescription of what is required, constitutes the elements of morality, aesthetics and technology as much as of law.

The legal order is distinguished from every other social order in that it comprises isolated, private subjects. A norm of law acquires its *differentia specifica*, distinguishing it from the general mass of regulatory rules—moral, aesthetic, utilitarian etc.—because it presupposes a person endowed with a right and actively asserting it.

The attempt to make the notion of external regulation the basic logical element in law leads to the equation of law with the authoritatively established social order. This current of legal thought truly reflects the spirit of that period when large-scale capitalist monopolies and imperialist policy replaced the Manchester School and free competition.

It is not difficult to show that the idea of unconditional obedience to an external norm-establishing authority has nothing in common with the legal form. It is sufficient to take examples which have been marked out with extreme rigour and which are therefore clearest examples of such a structure. One example could be the military unit, where the majority of persons are subordinated in their movements to general orders whose single, active and autonomous origin is the will of the commander. Another example is the Jesuit order. Here, all members blindly and uncomplainingly fulfil the will of the leader. It is sufficient to think of these examples to conclude that the more consistently the basis of authoritarian regulation is applied, thereby excluding any suggestion of a separate and autonomous will, the less will be the opportunity for the application of the category of law. This is particularly sharply felt in the field of so-called public law. Here, legal philosophy faces the greatest difficulties. At the same time as civil law, operating at the primary legal level, broadly and confidently uses the concept of subjective rights, the application of this concept in the theory of public law steadily creates misunderstanding and contradictions. The system of civil law is therefore characterized by simplicity, clarity and completeness, while the theories of public law are replete with constructs that are rigid, artificial and grotesquely one-sided. The legal form, with its aspect of subjective legal authority, is born in a society consisting of atomized bearers of private, egoistic interest. When all economic life is constructed on the principle of accord between independent wills, then every social function, in one or another explicit way, assumes a legal nature, i.e. becomes not merely a social function but also the legal right of the person who fulfils this function. However, since private interests cannot inherently achieve such full development and overwhelming significance in the political organization as they can in the economy of bourgeois society, therefore even subjective public rights act as something ephemeral, deprived of real roots, and are constantly in doubt. At the same time the state is not a legal superstructure—it can merely be *imagined* as such.

Legal theory cannot equate "the rights of parliament", "the rights of executive authority" etc., for example, with the creditor's right to repayment of a debt. This would be to place a distinct private interest where bourgeois ideology presumes the authority of a general impersonal state interest. But at the same time every jurist knows that he cannot invest these rights with any other basic content without the legal form escaping him. Public law can exist only as the reflection of the form of private law in the sphere of political organization, or else it ceases to be law. Attempts to depict a social function as it really is, i.e. simply a social function, and a norm merely as an organizing rule, mean the extinction of the legal form. However, the real premise for the transcendence of the legal form and legal ideology is that social condition in which the very conflict between individual social interests has become superfluous.

A characteristic feature of bourgeois society is the fact that general interests are alienated from private ones, and are opposed to them. But in this opposition they unwillingly adopt the form of private interests, i.e. the form of law. Thus, as should be expected, the legal elements of state organization are primarily those which harmonize with the system of antagonistic, isolated, private interests.

Thus, the very concept of public law may be developed only in that process in which, figuratively, it constantly diverges from private law, trying to define itself as the latter's antithesis, and then turns to it as if it were its centre of attraction.

The attempt to proceed in the reverse direction, i.e. to find the basic definitions of private law (which are nothing other than the definitions of law in general) by using a norm as the conceptual platform, can produce nothing except lifeless formal concepts, fraught with internal contradiction. Law as a function ceases to be law, and power without the private interests supporting it becomes elusive and abstract, easily becoming its antithesis, i.e. an obligation (every public right is at the same time an obligation). Just as the legal "right" of the creditor to receive repayment is elementary, clear and "natural", so the legal "right" of parliament to approve the budget is tenuous and problematic. If, in civil law, scholastic arguments are conducted on the level of what Jhering called legal symptomatics, then the very basis of jurisprudence is placed in jeopardy. This is the source of methodological distortion and hesitation. It is this which threatens to turn jurisprudence into a hybrid of sociology and psychology.

CHAPTER IV

Commodity and the Subject

Every legal relation is a relationship between subjects. A subject is the atom of legal theory, the simplest and irreducible element. And with it we begin our analysis.

At the same time as idealist theories of law start with some general idea and develop the concept of the subject, i.e. in a purely speculative way, dogmatic jurisprudence uses this concept in a formal manner. For it, the subject is nothing more than "a means for the legal qualification of phenomena from the perspective of their suitability or unsuitability for participation in legal relations". It therefore does not ask itself why man turned from an animal environment into a legal subject, since it proceeds from the legal relation as an antecedent form.

Marx's theory, on the contrary, considers every social form as historical, and therefore sets its task as the explanation of those historical, material conditions which make one category or another real. The material premises of legal relationships, or the relationships of legal subjects, are explained by Marx himself in the first volume of *Capital*. It is true that he did this obliquely, and in the form of the most general allusions. However, these allusions provide much more for the understanding of the legal element in the relationships between people than the multi-volume treatises on the general theory of law. For Marx the analysis of the form of the subject flows directly from the analysis of the form of commodities.

Capitalist society is above all a society of commodity owners. This means that in the process of production the social relationships of people assume an objectified form in the products of labour and are related to each other as values. Commodities are objects whose concrete multiplicity of useful qualities becomes merely a simple physical covering of the abstract quality of value, and which appears as the ability to be exchanged for other commodities in a definite ratio. This quality appears as something inherent in the objects themselves, by force of a type of natural law which acts behind people's backs entirely independent of their will.

But if a commodity acquires value independently of the will of the subject producing it, then the realization of value in the process of exchange assumes a conscious volitional act on the part of the owner of the commodity. Or, as Marx says, "commodities cannot send themselves to a market and exchange themselves with one another. Accordingly, we must turn to their custodian, to the commodity owner. Commodities are objects and therefore defenceless before man. If they do not go of their own will, he will use force, i.e., appropriate them".[27]

Thus, in the process of production, the social relationships of people realized in the products of labour and assuming the form of an elemental law, require for their realization a particular relationship of people as managers of products, and subjects "whose will rules objects".

Therefore, simultaneously with the product of labour assuming the quality of a commodity and becoming the bearer of value, man assumes the quality of a legal subject and becomes the bearer of a legal right. "A person whose will is declared decisive is the subject of a legal right."[28]

Simultaneously, social life is reduced on the one hand to the totality of elemental objectified relationships in which people appear to us as objects (such are all economic relations: the level of prices, surplus value, profit etc.) and, on the other hand, those relationships which define man only by reference to an object, i.e. as a subject, or in legal relationships. These two basic forms are different in principle, but at the same time are very closely connected and mutually dependent. The social, productive relationship appears simultaneously in two incongruous forms: as the value of a commodity and as the ability of man to be the subject of rights.

In the same way that the natural multiplicity of the useful qualities of a product is in a commodity a simple mask of its value, while the concrete species of human labour are dissolved into abstract human labour as the creator of value—so the concrete multiplicity of man's relationship to an object appears as the abstract will of the owner, while all the concrete peculiarities, which distinguish one representative of the species *Homo sapiens* from another, are dissolved into the abstraction of man in general as a legal subject.

If economically an object dominates man, since as a commodity it embodies in itself a social relationship not under the authority of man, then man legally dominates the object because as its possessor and owner he himself becomes merely the embodiment of the abstract, the impersonal subject of rights, the pure product of social relationships. Expressing this in the words of Marx, we say:

> In order that these objects may relate to one another as commodities, their guardians must relate to one another, as persons whose will resides in those objects; and must behave in such a way that each does not appropriate the commodity of the other, and part with his own, except by means of an act

> done by mutual consent. They must, therefore, mutually recognize in each other the rights of private proprietors.[29]

Having fallen into servile dependence upon economic relations surreptitiously created in the form of the laws of value, the economic subject—as if in compensation—receives a rare gift in his capacity as a legal subject: a legally presumed will, making him absolutely free and equal among other owners of commodities. "All must be free and no one may violate the freedom of another . . . each person possesses his own body as a free instrument of his own will."[30] This is the axiom from which the theory of natural law proceeds. And this idea of separation, the inherent proximity of human individuality, this "natural condition", from which "the infinite contradiction of freedom" flows, entirely corresponds to the method of commodity production in which the producers are formally independent of one another and are bound by nothing other then the artificially created legal order, by this very legal condition or, speaking in the words of the same author, "the joint existence of many free beings, where all must be free and the freedom of one must not prevent the freedom of another". This is nothing other than an ideologized philosophical abstraction transferred to heavenly heights, freed from its crude empiricism; independent producers meet in this market because, as another philosopher teaches us, "in the market transaction both parties do that which they want and do not claim greater freedom than they themselves grant the others".

The increasing division of labour, the expanding social relationships and the development of exchange deriving therefrom, make exchange-value an economic category, i.e. the embodiment of social production relationships which stand above the individual. For this it is necessary that separate and random acts of exchange turn into a broad systematic circulation of commodities. At this stage of development, value is torn from arbitrary assessment, loses its character as a phenomenon of the individual psyche and assumes an objective economic significance. Similarly, real conditions are necessary for man to be transformed from a zoological being into an abstract and impersonal subject of law, into a juridic person. These real conditions consist in the condensation of social relations and the growing power of social, i.e. class organization, which achieves its maximum intensity in the "well organized" bourgeois state. Here, the ability to be a subject of rights is finally torn from the living concrete personality, ceases to be a function of its active conscious will, and becomes a purely social quality. Legal capacity is abstracted from the ability to have rights. The legal subject receives his *alter ego* in the form of a representative while he himself assumes the significance of a mathematical point, a centre in which a certain sum of rights is concentrated.

Accordingly, bourgeois capitalist property ceases to be a weak, unstable and purely factual possession, which at any moment may be disputed and must be defended *vi et armis*. It turns into an absolute, immovable right which follows the object everywhere that chance carried it and which from the time that bourgeois civilization affirmed its authority over the whole globe, is protected in its every corner by laws, police, courts.[31]

At this stage of development the so-called will theory of subjective rights begins to seem incongruent with reality. It is now preferable to define a right in the subjective sense as "the sum of benefits which the general will recognizes as belonging to a specific person". Moreover, this latter does not require a person to have the ability to will and to act. Of course, Dernburg's definition is better suited to that view of the modern jurist which must deal with the legal capacity and rights of idiots, infants, juridic persons etc. In its extreme conclusions the will theory was equated with the exclusion of these categories from the subjects of rights. Dernburg is certainly nearer the truth in understanding the subject of rights as a purely social phenomenon. But on the other hand it is very clear to us why the element of will played such an essential role in the construction of the concept of the subject. Dernburg himself sees this in part when he affirms that:

> rights in the subjective sense existed long before a conscious state order was created; they were based upon the personality of the individual man and upon the respect which he could win and compel with respect to himself and his property. Only gradually, by abstraction from the concept of existing subjective rights, was the concept of the legal order formed. The view that rights, in the subjective sense, are merely the result of objective law is ahistorical and untrue.[32]

"To win and to compel" is obviously possible only for someone who enjoys both the will and also a significant amount of power. On the other hand, Dernburg forgets that the concept of the subject arose and developed from its contrast with an object or thing. A commodity is an object; a man is a subject who disposes of the commodity in acts of acquisition and alienation. It is in the exchange transaction that the subject first appears in the full totality of its definitions. A formally and perfected concept of the subject, which would simply be left with legal capacity, further diverts us from the living real historical sense of this legal category. This is why it is difficult for jurists completely to surrender the active, volitional element in the concepts of the subject and subjective legal right.

The sphere of domination, which has assumed the form of a subjective right, is a social phenomenon which is attributed to the individual on the same basis as which value, also a social phenomenon, is attributed to an object, to a product of labour. Commodity fetishism is complemented by legal fetishism.

Thus, at a certain stage of development, the relationships between people in the process of production assume a doubly perplexing form. On the one hand, they appear as a relation of objects-commodities, and on the other as will relationships of individuals independent and equal to one another—legal subjects. Along with the mystical quality of value something appears no less perplexing—a legal right. Simultaneously a single whole relationship assumes two basic abstract aspects—economic and legal.

In the development of legal categories, the ability to execute exchange transactions is only one of the concrete phenomena of the general quality of the capacity to have legal rights and to conduct transactions. However, it is historically mainly the exchange transaction which furnished the idea of a subject as the abstract bearer of all possible legal claims. Only in the conditions of a commodity economy is the abstract form of a right created, i.e. the capacity to have a right in general is separated from specific legal claims. Only the constant transfer of rights taking place in the market creates the idea of their immobile bearer. The person receiving an obligation in the market undertakes an obligation himself at the same time. The position of a creditor is transferred to that of a debtor. Thus, the possibility is created of abstracting from the concrete differences between these subjects of legal rights, and of putting them under one generic concept.[33]

Similar to the way in which the exchange transactions of developed commodity production were preceded by random exchange acts and such forms of exchange as mutual gifts, the legal subject with the sphere of legal domination expanding around him was morphologically preceded by the armed individual or, more often, group of people, clan, horde, tribe, capable in a dispute or a battle of defending that which was the condition of their existence. This close morphological tie clearly unites the court with the duel, and the parties and the proceedings with the parties in armed struggle. With the growth of social regulatory forces, the subject proportionally loses his material tangibility. His personal energy is replaced by social power, i.e. class power, organization, which finds its highest expression in the state. This impersonal and abstract subject corresponds, as his expression, to the impersonal abstract state authority which acts in ideal equilibrium and continuity in space and time.

But before enjoying the services of the state mechanism, the subject relies upon the organic continuity of relationships. Similar to the way in which the regular repetition of acts of exchange constitutes value, as a general category raised above subjective evaluations and random exchange ratios, likewise a regular repetition of one and the same relationship—custom—gives a new meaning to the subjective sphere of domination, justifying its existence by an external norm.

Custom or tradition, as a higher basis than the individual for legal claims, corresponds to the feudal system with its limitations and stagnation. Tradition or custom is in essence something included in notoriously rather narrow geographic boundaries. Therefore, every right is thought of merely as an attribute of a specific concrete subject or of a group of subjects. In the feudal world, "each right was a privilege" (Marx). Each city, each estate, each guild lived according to its law which followed a man wherever he was. The idea of a formal legal status, common to all citizens, general for all people, was absent in this period. Corresponding to this in the economic field were self-sufficient closed economies, prohibitions of import and export etc.

"The content of individuality was not one and the same. The estate, property position, profession, belief, age, sex and physical strength led to deep inequality in legal capacity."[34] Equality between subjects was assumed only for closed relationships in a definite narrow sphere; thus, members of one and the same estate were equal to one another in the sphere of estate rights, members of one and the same guild were equal in the sphere of guild rights etc. At this stage the legal subject, as the general abstract bearer of all conceivable claims to rights, appears only in the role of the possessor of specific privileges.

At this stage "legal consciousness sees that the same or equal rights were attributed to individual persons or collectives, but it does not conclude that these persons and collectives were one and the same in their attribute of having rights."[35]

To the extent that in the Middle Ages the abstract concept of a legal subject was absent, so also the idea of an objective norm, directed to an imprecise and broad circle of persons, was mixed and merged in the establishment of concrete privileges and "liberties". As late as the thirteenth century we find traces of some clear impressions of the difference between objective law and subjective legal rights or powers. In certificates of privileges and dues, which were given to cities by emperors and princes, the mixture of these two concepts is encountered at each step. The usual form of establishing some general rules or norms was the recognition of a definite territorial unit, or of the population in a collective sense as having specific legal qualities. Such a character was borne by even the famous formula *Stadtluft macht frei*. The abolition of judicial battles was conducted in the same form; along with these decrees, and as something entirely of the same type were included the rights of city dwellers, for instance in the use of the prince's or emperor's forest.

The same mixture of objective and subjective elements was at first observed in municipal law itself. Municipal statutes were in part provisions with a general character and in part a list of individual rights or privileges which were enjoyed by some group of citizens.

Only with the full development of bourgeois relationships did law obtain an abstract character. Each man became a man in general, all labour was equated with socially useful labour in general, every subject became an abstract legal subject. Simultaneously, the norm also assumed the logically perfected form of the abstract general law.

Thus, the legal subject is the abstract commodity owner elevated to the heavens. His will—will understood in a legal sense—has its real basis in the wish to alienate in acquisition and to acquire in alienation. For this desire to be realized it is necessary that the desires of commodity owners be directed to one another. Legally, this relationship is expressed as a contract or an agreement of independent wills. Therefore, contract is one of the central concepts of law. In haughty language, it becomes a component part in the idea of law. In the logical system of legal concepts the contract is only one of the forms of transaction in general, i.e. one of the methods of concrete expression of the will with whose aid the subject acts upon the legal sphere around him. Historically and in reality, on the contrary, the concept of transaction grew from contract. Outside contract, the very concepts of subject and will exist only as lifeless abstractions in the legal sense. In contract these concepts obtain their full movement, and simultaneously the legal form, in its simplest purest aspect, receives its material basis in the act of exchange. The act of exchange thus concentrates, in its focus, all the essential elements of political economy and law. In exchange, in Marx's words, "a volitional or legal relation is produced by economic relationships themselves". Once it has arisen, the idea of contract strives to assume universal significance. Before possessors of commodities "recognized" each other as owners, they were of course already such but in a different, organic and extra-juridical sense. "Mutual recognition" signifies nothing other than an attempt to interpret, with the help of the abstract formula of contract, those organic forms of appropriation which depend on labour, conquest etc., which a society of commodity producers finds ready at its inception. By itself, the relationship of man to an object is deprived of all legal significance. This is felt by jurists when they try to make sense of the institution of private property as a relation between subjects, i.e. between people. But they construe this purely formally and negatively, as a universal prohibition which excludes everyone except the owner from the use and disposition of the object; this conception, while suitable for the practical purposes of dogmatic jurisprudence, is most unsuitable for theoretical analysis. In its abstract prohibitions the concept of property loses all actual meaning, and renounces its own pre-legal history.

But if the organic, "natural" relation of a man to an object, i.e. its appropriation, genetically constitutes the starting point of development, then the transformation of this relationship into a legal one took place under the influence of those requirements which were invoked by the circulation of boons, i.e. primarily purchases and sales. Hauriou calls attention to the fact that even maritime exchange and caravan exchange did not initially create a requirement for the guarantee of property. The distance which separated those engaging in exchange gave a better guarantee against any claims whatsoever. The formation of a stable market invoked the necessity of regulating the question of the right to dispose of commodities, and accordingly, of the right of ownership.[36] The title of ownership in ancient Roman law, *mancipatio per aes et libram*, shows that it was born simultaneously with the phenomenon of internal exchange. Likewise, transfer by inheritance began to be fixed as a title of ownership only from the times when civil transactions showed an interest in this transmission.[37]

In exchange, speaking in Marx's words, "one commodity possessor only by the will of another . . . may acquire for himself another's commodities, alienating them as his own". It is precisely this thought which representatives of the natural law school also strive to express, trying to base property on some initial contract. They were right, of course, not in the sense that such a contract ever occurred historically, but in that natural or organic forms of appropriation obtain a legal character and begin to display their legal "intelligence" in mutual acts of appropriation and alienation. Here it is necessary to look for explanations of the contradiction between feudal and bourgeois property. The greatest shortcoming of feudal property in the eyes of the bourgeois world, lies not in its origin (conquest, force) but in its immobility, in the fact that it is incapable of becoming an object of mutual guarantees, moving from one hand to another in acts of alienation and appropriation. Feudal or estate property violates the basic principle of bourgeois society—"the equal possibility of obtaining inequality". Hauriou, one of the keenest bourgeois jurists, correctly emphasizes mutuality as the most effective guarantee of property, and thus achievable with the least amount of external compulsion. Thus mutuality, insured by the laws of the market, assumes its own nature as an "eternal" institution. In contrast to this, a purely political guarantee, given by the apparatus of state compulsion, is simply for the defence of the specific proprietary group, i.e. it is an element which has no principled significance. Class struggle frequently led in history to a new distribution of property, to the expropriation of money lenders and owners of latifundia. But these upheavals, however unpleasant they were for the classes and groups that suffered, did not disturb the basic foundations of private property—the economic fact of economic transactions by exchange. Those people who rose up against property, on the next day had to affirm it, meeting in the market place as independent producers. This is the path of all non-proletarian revolutions. Such is the logical conclusion from the ideal of anarchists who, discarding the external signs of bourgeois law—state compulsion and statutes—maintain its internal essence: free contract between independent producers.[38]

Thus, only the development of the market initially makes possible and necessary the transformation of man, who appropriates objects by means of labour (or theft), into a legal owner.

Karner offers another conception of property. According to his definition:

> *de jure* property is nothing other than that the power of person A over object N, the simple relation of the individual to an object of nature, which involves *no other individual* (our italics, E. P.) and no other object; an object is a private object, the individual a private person; the right a private right. This is the way the matter is in fact in the period of simple commodity production.[39]

This whole citation is one broad misunderstanding. Karner reproduces here his favourite Robinson Crusoe world. But how meaningfully can the two Robinson Crusoes, neither of whom knows of the existence of the other, imagine *legally* their relationship to objects when that relationship is fully exhausted by the *factual* relation? This right of an isolated man deserves to be placed next to the famous value "of a glass of water in the desert". Both exchange-value and the law of property are generated by one and the same phenomenon: the circulation of products which have become commodities. Property in the legal sense appeared not because people decided to assign this legal quality, but because they could exchange commodities only having donned the personality of an owner. "Unlimited authority over a thing" is merely a reflection of the unlimited circulation of commodities.

Karner states "an owner decides to cultivate a legal relationship of property by way of alienation".[40] Does Karner not think that "the legal" begins from this "cultivation", and until its acquisition does not go beyond the bounds of the natural or organic?

Karner agrees that "purchase, sale, loan and rental existed earlier but with a minimal objective and subjective sphere of action". Yet these legal forms of the circulation of economic boons existed so much earlier that we find a clear formulation of the relationships of rental, loan and deposit before the very formula of property was developed. This alone already provides the key to the proper understanding of the legal nature of property.

On the contrary, it seems to Karner that people were independent owners before they pledged, bought and sold objects. These relationships seem to him merely "auxiliary and secondary institutions filling the gaps of petit bourgeois property". In other words, he proceeds from the idea of entirely isolated individuals who (it is unclear for what purpose) decided to create a "general will", and in the name of this general will to order each one to refrain from infringements upon an object belonging to another. Then considering that the owner could not be treated as a universalist, either in terms of his labour power or as a consumer, these isolated Robinson Crusoes decide to supplement ownership with the institutions of purchase and sale, loans, rental etc. This artificial scheme puts the true development of objects and concepts on its head.

The bond between a man and an object which he produced or won himself, or which figuratively (as arms, or decoration) constitutes part of his personality, undoubtedly emerges historically as one of the elements in the development of the institution of private property. It represents its initial crude and limited form. Private property obtains its perfected and universal character only with the transformation to a commodity or, rather, to a commodity–capitalist economy. It becomes indifferent to the object and severs all connection with any organic union of people (kinship-group, family, commune). It appears in the most general meaning as "an external sphere of freedom" (Hegel), i.e. as the practical realization of the abstract ability to be the subject of rights.

In this purely legal form, property has logically little in common with the organic or everyday principle of private appropriation, either as a result of personal efforts or as a condition of personal consumption and use. To the extent that the bond between man and the product of his labour, or, for instance, between man and a parcel of land which he has cultivated with his personal labour, is in itself something elementary, accessible to the most primitive thinking;[41] to that extent the relationship of the owner to property is abstract, formal, artificial and rational from the time when all economic reality began to be reduced to the sphere of the market. If, morphologically, these two institutions—private appropriation, as the condition of unimpeded personal use, and private appropriation as the condition of subsequent alienation and acts of exchange—have a direct connection with one another, nevertheless logically these are two separate categories, and the word property which covers them both introduces more confusion than clarity. Capitalist ownership of land does not assume any organic connection between the land and its owner; on the contrary, it is possible only on the condition of full freedom of transfer of land from hand to hand, and freedom of transactions with land.

Capitalist property is essentially the freedom to transform capital from one form to another, and to move it from one sphere to another to receive the maximum unearned income. This freedom to dispose capitalist property is impossible with the presence of individuals deprived of property, i.e. of proletarians. The legal form of property does not contradict the fact of expropriation of property from a significant number of citizens. For the quality of being a subject of rights is a purely formal quality. It qualifies all persons as equally worthy of property, but by no means makes them property owners The dialectic of capitalist property is marvellously depicted in Marx's *Capital*, both where it penetrates the "immobile" forms of law, and where it disrupts them by direct coercion (the period of primitive accumulation). In this sense Karner's study provides very little new in comparison with the first volume of *Capital*. When Karner tries to be independent he introduces confusion. We already noted this with respect to his attempts to abstract property from the element which legally constitutes it, i.e. from exchange. This purely formal concept entails another mistake. Having considered the transfer from petit bourgeois property to capitalist property, Karner states: "The institution of property achieved broad development, experienced full transformation, without having changed its legal nature", and in the same place he concludes "the social function of legal institutions changes but their legal nature does not change".[42] It may be asked: what institution does Karner have in mind? If he is discussing the abstract formula of Roman law then of course nothing in it can change. But this formula regulated small-scale ownership only in the period of the development of bourgeois-capitalist relationships. If we turn to guild crafts or to peasant economy in the age of the attachment of peasants to land, then we find a whole series of norms limiting the right to property. Of course it may be objected that all these limitations have a public law character and do not affect the institution of property as such. But even in this instance the whole situation is that a certain abstract formula is equivalent to itself. On the other hand the feudal guilds, i.e. organic forms of property, had already revealed their functions—the extraction of another's unpaid labour.[43] We can therefore come to a conclusion opposite to Karner, that "norms change and their social function remains unchanged".

In proportion to the development of the capitalist mode of production the owner is gradually freed from technical production functions, but at the same time he loses the totality of legal domination over capital. In a stock corporation the individual capitalist is merely the bearer of title to a certain share of the unearned income. His economic and legal activity, as owner, is limited exclusively to the sphere of non-productive consumption. The basic mass of capital becomes a fully impersonal class force. To the extent that they participate in market circulation, which supposes the autonomy of its separate parts, these parts appear as the property of legal persons. In fact the comparatively small circle of the largest capitalists can dispose of it acting through their hired representatives or agents. The legally distinct form of private property does not now reflect the actual position of objects, for with the assistance of methods of participation and control actual domination goes far beyond purely legal bounds. Here we come to the moment when capitalist society is already sufficiently mature to transform into its antithesis. The necessary political prerequisite for this is the class revolution of the proletariat.

However, as experience has shown, planned and organized production and distribution may not replace market circulation, and the market bond between individual economies on the day after the revolution. If this were possible, then the legal form of property would at that moment be historically finally exhausted. It would have completed the cycle of its development having returned to the starting point, to objects of direct individual use, i.e. have become again an elementary living relationship. And with it the form of law in general would be condemned to death.[44] Until the task of the construction of a single planned economy is realized, so long as the market bond between individual enterprises and groups of enterprises remains, the form of law will also remain in force this long. We are not now speaking of the fact that the form of private property remains almost unchanged in the transitional period in the context of the means and instruments of production of the small-scale peasantry and crafts economy. But in the relationships of large nationalized industry, the application of the principle of economic accountability signifies the formation of autonomous units whose connection with other economies is established through the market.

To the extent that state enterprises are subordinated to the conditions of circulation, so the bond between them is shaped not in the form of technical subordination, but in the form of exchange. Thus, a purely legal, i.e. judicial procedure, for regulating relationships becomes possible and necessary; however, along with this there has been preserved, and with the passage of time undoubtedly will be strengthened, direct, i.e. administrative–technical management by the procedure of subordination to the general economic plan. Thus, on the one hand we have economic life flowing into natural categories, and the social bonds between production units represented in its rational, unmasked (non-commodity) form—to this corresponds the method of direct, i.e. technical-content instructions in the form of programmes, production and distribution plans etc., specific instructions constantly changing depending upon the change in conditions. On the other hand, we have the bond between economic units expressed in the form of the value of circulating commodities, and therefore in the legal form of exchange. To this, in its turn, corresponds the creation of more or less firm and constant formal boundaries and the rules of the legal relationships between autonomous subjects (civil and possibly also commercial codes), and of agencies implementing this commerce in practice by means of decisions of disputes (courts, arbitration commissions etc.). It is obvious that the first tendency does not include any possibility for the legal art to flourish. Its gradual victory will mean the gradual withering away of the legal form in general. It is possible, of course, to object that the production programme, for example, is also a public legal norm since it proceeds from state authority, enjoys coercive force, creates rights and duties etc. Of course, until the time when the new society will be built from the elements of the old, i.e. by people who understand social relationships only as "a means for their private purposes", even the simple technically rational instructions will adopt the form of a power alienated from man and standing above him. Political man will still be, expressed in Marx's words, "an abstract artificial man". But the more radically the former relationships, and the earlier psychology in this sphere of production, are outgrown, the faster the hour of that final emancipation will strike, which Marx discusses in his article "On the Jewish Question".

> Only when the real individual man will perceive in himself the abstract citizen, and as individual man shall become a universal being in his empirical life, in his individual work, in his individual relations, then when man recognizes and organizes his *forces propres* (personal efforts) as social forces, and therefore, when he no longer separates social forces in the form of political force from himself, only then will human emancipation be completed.[45]

Such are the perspectives of the unbounded future. With respect to our transitional period, the following should be noted. If, in the age of domination of impersonal finance capital, the real opposition of the interests of individual capitalist groups (disposing of their own and other's capital) continue to be preserved, nevertheless proletarian state capitalism eliminates the real opposition of interests with nationalized industry and preserves the separation of autonomy of individual economic organizations (similar to private business) *only as a method*. Thus, those *quasi*-private economic relationships which are formed between state and industry and the small labour economy, and also between individual enterprises and combinations of enterprises within state industry itself, are placed in strict bounds, which at any specific moment are defined by the successes achieved in the sphere of planned construction. Therefore during our transitional period the form of law as such does not conceal those unlimited possibilities which were opened up for it by bourgeois capitalist society at the dawn of its birth. On the contrary, it temporarily binds us to its narrow horizons. It exists only so as finally to exhaust itself.

The task of Marxist theory consists in verifying this general conclusion, and researching it in concrete historical material. Development may not proceed equally in various areas of social life. Therefore, painstaking work of observation, comparison and analysis is necessary. But only then, when we study the tempo and forms of outmoded value relationships in economics and, together with it, the withering away of private law elements and the legal superstructure, and finally the gradual expulsion of the legal superstructure itself, only then can we say to ourselves that we have explained at least one aspect of the process of creating the classless culture of the future.

CHAPTER V

Law and the State

Legal relations by their "nature" do not assume a condition of peace just as exchange initially did not exclude armed robbery, but went hand in hand with it. Law and violence—apparently opposed concepts—in fact are connected with one another in the closest manner. This is true not only for the ancient ages of Roman law, but also for the later eras. Modern international law includes a very solid dose of self-help, repression, reprisals, war etc.). Even within the limits of the "developed" bourgeois state the realization of a right is conducted in the opinion of such a capable jurist as Hauriou, by each citizen "at his responsibility and risk". Marx expressed himself even more sharply: "club law is nevertheless law". In this there is nothing paradoxical because law, like exchange, is a method of relating atomized social elements. The degree of this separation may historically be more or less, but it is never equal to zero. Thus, for instance, the enterprises belonging to the Soviet state in fact fulfil one general task; but working by the methods of the market they each have their own distinct interest, oppose one another as buyers and sellers, act at their responsibility and risk, and therefore necessarily must be in a *legal relationship*. The final victory of the planned economy will place them exclusively in a technical-expediency relationship with one another which will destroy their "legal personality". Accordingly, if the legal relationship is depicted to us as an organized and ordered relationship—thus equating law with the legal order—then in so doing it is forgotten that in fact the legal order is merely a tendency and a final result (and moreover far from perfected), but never the starting point and assumption of a legal relationship. The very condition of peace which appears universal and homogeneous to abstract legal thinking was far from this at the initial stages of legal development. Ancient German law knew various degrees of peace: peace under the roof of a house, peace within the boundaries of a fence, and the limits of a settlement etc. A greater or lesser degree of pacification found its expression in a greater or lesser harshness of punishment provided for the violation of peace.

A condition of peace becomes necessary where exchange assumes the nature of a regular phenomenon. In those cases when there were too few prerequisites for the preservation of peace, the parties engaging in exchange preferred not to meet with one another but to view the commodities in each other's absence. But, in general, exchange requires that not only commodities but also people meet. In the age of clan life, every outsider was considered as an enemy and was as defenceless as a wild beast. Only the custom of hospitality made possible relationships with other tribes. In feudal Europe the Church tried to limit the uninterrupted private wars, by proclaiming a so-called peace of god (for specific times). At the same time fairs and local markets began to enjoy special privileges in this respect. Tradesmen going to the market received special safe passage, their property was guaranteed from arbitrary appropriation; at the same time the performance of contracts was safeguarded by special judges. Thus, a special *ius mercatorum* or *ius fori* was created which then lay at the basis of city law.

Initially, the markets and fairs constituted a part of feudal holdings and were simply profitable, productive items. The gift of the peace of a fair somewhere had the purpose of filling the treasury of some feudal owner and accordingly was intended to effect the private interest of the latter. However, because feudal authority acted as the guarantor of the peace necessary for exchange transactions, it took on a new trait previously uncharacteristic of it, that of a *public nature*. The authority of a feudal or patriarch type knows borders between the private and the public. The public laws of the feudal lord, with respect to the villain were at the same time his rights as a private owner. On the contrary, his private rights could be interpreted upon desire as political, i.e. public rights. Thus, the *ius civile* of ancient

Rome was interpreted by many, for instance Gumplowicz, as public law since its basic source belonged to a clan organization. In fact, in this case we encounter a legal form being born which still had not developed the internally opposed and correlated definitions of private and public. Authority therefore, bearing the traces of patriarchal or feudal relationships, is characterized at the same time by the predomination of the technical element over the legal. The legal, i.e. rational interpretation of the phenomenon of authority, becomes possible only with the development of exchange and the money economy. These economic forms bring with them an antagonism which with time takes on the nature of something eternal and natural and becomes the basis of every legal teaching about authority.

The "modern" state (in the bourgeois sense) is born at that moment when the group or class organization of authority includes in its bounds a sufficiently broad market relationship. Thus in Rome exchange with foreigners, travellers and others required the recognition of civil legal capacity for persons not belonging to the kin-group union. This already supposed the differentiation between public and private law.

Factual exercise of authority obtains a clear legal nature of public authority when along with it, and independent of it, appear relationships connected with exchange acts, i.e. private relationships *par excellence*. Acting as a guarantor of these relationships, authority becomes social, public authority, authority pursuing the impersonal interest or order.

The state as an organization of class domination, and as an organization for the conduct of external wars, does not require legal interpretation and in essence does not allow it. This is where so-called *raison d'état* (the principle of naked expediency) rules. On the contrary, authority as the guarantor of market exchange not only may be expressed in terms of law, but itself appears as law and only law, and is merged entirely with the abstract objective norm. Therefore, every juridic theory of the state which wishes to embrace all the functions of the latter, necessarily appears inadequate. It may be a true reflection of all facts of state life, but gives only an ideological, i.e. distorted reflection of reality.

Class domination, both in its organized and unorganized form, is much broader than the area which can be designated as the official authority of state power. The domination of the bourgeoisie is expressed in the dependence of the government upon the banks and capitalist groupings, in the dependence of each individual worker upon his employer, and in the fact that the staff of the state apparatus is personally connected with the ruling class. All these facts, and the number of them may be multiplied without limit, do not have any official legal expression. But in a mysterious manner they correspond in their significance with the facts which find their official legal expression, and represent themselves as the subordination of the same workers to the laws of the bourgeois state, to the orders and decrees of its agencies, to the verdicts of its courts etc. Along with the direct and indirect class denomination, there grows an indirect reflected denomination in the form of official state authority as a special force separated from society. With this the problem of the state arises, which presents no fewer difficulties for analysis than the problem of commodities.

Engels considers the state as an expression of the fact that society is hopelessly enmeshed in class contradictions; "so that these opposed classes with antagonistic economic interests", he says, "did not devour one another and society in hopeless struggle, for this a power became necessary, a power seemingly standing above society, a power which moderated the conflict, and held it within the limits of 'order'. And this power arising from society but placing itself above it, and more and more alienating itself from it, is the state."[46] In this explanation there is one passage which is not entirely clear, and it is revealed later when Engels speaks of the fact that state power naturally evolves in the hands of the strongest class, "which, with the help of the state, becomes the politically dominant class". This phrase provides a reason for thinking that state power is generated not as class power, but as something standing above classes and saving society from dissolution, and that only after its emergence does state power become the object of usurpation. Of course, such an understanding would contradict the historical facts; we know that political apparatuses were created everywhere by the forces of the ruling class, and were the work of that class. We think that Engels himself also proposed such an interpretation, but however that may be his formula has remained unclear. The state arises because otherwise the classes would have mutually exterminated themselves in an intensified struggle, and thus society itself would have perished. Accordingly, the state arises when none of the struggling classes can seize decisive victory. This means one of two things: either the state strengthens this relationship—then it is the force above classes, and this we cannot recognize—or it is a result of the victory of one class, but in this case the necessity for a state disappears from society since, with the decisive victory of a class, equilibrium is established and society is saved. Behind all these controversies one basic question is hidden: why does the dominance of a class not become that which it is, i.e. the actual subordination of one part of the population to another, but instead assumes the form of official state authority? Or, what is the same, why is the apparatus of state coercion created not as a private apparatus of the ruling class, but distinct from the latter in the form of an impersonal apparatus of public power distinct from society?[47] We cannot limit ourselves to a reference to the fact that for the ruling class it is *expedient* to employ an ideological mask and hide its class domination behind the screen of the state. Although this reference is entirely indisputable, nevertheless it does not explain why this ideology may be created, and, accordingly why a ruling class may use it. The conscious use of ideological forms is not the same as their origin, which usually does not depend upon the will of people. But if we wish to explain the roots of some ideology we must search out those actual relationships which it expresses. Here, incidently, we strike upon the fundamental difference between the theological and legal interpretation of state authority. To the extent that in the first instance—the deification of authority—we are dealing with unbridled fetishism and, accordingly, with corresponding impressions and concepts, we do not succeed in revealing anything other than the ideological duplication of reality, i.e. of those actual relationships of authority and subordination. To such an extent the legal conception is merely a biased conception, and its abstractions express one of the aspects of actually existing society, i.e. of commodity-producing society.

Opinion holds that the basis of the competition dominant in the bourgeois-capitalist world does not provide the possibility of connecting political power with the individual enterprise in the way that under feudalism this power was connected with large landholdings. "The freedom of competition, the freedom of private property, 'equality' in the market and the guarantee of existence for one class, create a new form of state power—democracy, which places in power the class as a collective."[48] Although it is most true that "equality" in the market creates a specific form of authority, however, this connection between these phenomena is not entirely how Comrade Podvolotsky sees it. First, authority may be unconnected with an individual enterprise but nevertheless remain the private affair of capitalist organizations. Associations of industrialists, with their war coffers, blacklists, boycotts and strike-breaking patrols, are undoubtedly agencies of authority existing along with the public, i.e. state authority. Second, authority within the enterprise remains the private affair of each individual capitalist. The establishment of the rules of internal order is an act of private legislation, i.e. a true piece of feudalism, however bourgeois jurists may have tried to clothe it in modern dress. Introducing the fiction of the so-called contract of adhesion (*contrat d'adhésion*) for the extraordinary authorization which the capitalist owner receives, reportedly, from the agencies of public authority for the "successful fulfilment of the functions of the enterprise necessary and expedient from this social point of view".

However, the analogy with feudal relationships is not unconditionally exact here, for as Marx indicates:

> the authority which the capitalist enjoys as the personification of capital in the direct process of production, and the social function with which he is invested as manager and master of production, are essentially different from the authority which emerges on the basis of slave, serf, etc. production. On the basis of capitalist production the mass of direct producers is confronted by the social nature of their production in the form of the strictest regulating authority, as the social mechanism of their labour process developed in a complete hierarchy; however, the bearers of this authority use it only as personification of the conditions of labour, in contrast to labour itself, and not as political or theocratic masters as happened in earlier forms of production.[49]

Thus, under the capitalist means of production, relationships of subordination and authority may exist unalienated from the concrete form in which they appear as the domination of the conditions of production over the producers. But the very fact that they do not act in masked form, as under slavery and serfdom, makes them elusive for the jurists.

The state apparatus actually realizes itself as an impersonal "general will", as "the authority of law" etc., to the extent that society appears as a market. In the market each seller and buyer is, as we saw, a legal subject *par excellence*. For the categories of value and exchange-value to appear on the stage, the prerequisite is the autonomous will of those engaging in exchange. Exchange-value would cease to be exchange-value, and a commodity would cease to be a commodity, if the exchange ratio is determined by an authority situated above the inherent laws of the market. Coercion, as the command of one person directed to another and supported by force, contradicts the basic assumption of exchange between commodity owners. Therefore, in a society of commodity owners the function of coercion may not appear as a social function, because it is neither abstract nor impersonal. Subordination to the person as such, to man as a concrete individual, signifies for commodity-producing society subordination to arbitrary power, because it corresponds to the subordination of one commodity owner by another. Even coercion, therefore, cannot appear here in its unmasked form as an act of expediency. It must appear as coercion proceeding from some abstract general person, as coercion exercised not in the interest of the individual from whom it proceeds—for each person in commodity society is an egoist—but in the interest of all the participants in legal transactions. The authority of one person over another is exercised as the authority of law itself, i.e. as the authority of an objective impartial norm.

Bourgeois thought, for which the framework of commodity production is the eternal and natural framework of all societies, therefore declares abstract state authority to be an attribute of every society.

This was more naïvely expressed by the theorists of natural law, who, basing their teaching on authority in the idea of intercourse between independent and equal personalities, proposed that it proceeds from the principles of social intercourse as such. In fact, they merely developed the different ways in which the idea of authority bound independent commodity owners to each other. This explains the basic features of the doctrine which appears clearly in Grotius. In the market the primary factors are commodity owners participating in exchange. The system of domination is something derivative, secondary, something imposed externally on the existing commodity owners. Therefore, the theorists of natural law consider authority not as a phenomenon which has arisen historically and which is connected with the forces active in a given society, but as abstract and rational. In the exchange between commodity owners the necessity for authoritative coercion arises when the peace has been broken, or when a contract has not been performed voluntarily. Natural law doctrine therefore reduces the functions of authority to the maintenance of the peace, and declares the exclusive purpose of a state to be an instrument of the law. Finally, in the market place a man is a commodity owner by the will of other men, and all are commodity owners by their common will. The theory of natural law thus derives the state from the contract between individual and isolated personalities. This is the skeleton of the doctrine which admits many concrete variations, depending on the historical situation, political sympathies and dialectical abilities of one author or another. This theory admits republican and monarchical tendencies and diverse degrees of democratism and revolutionism.

In general and in its entirety, however, this theory was the revolutionary banner under which the bourgeoisie conducted its revolutionary battle with feudal society. And this determined the fate of the theory. From the time when the bourgeoisie became the ruling class the revolutionary past of natural law began to be troublesome for it, and as quickly as possible the ruling theories hastened to relegate the past to the archives of history. It goes without saying that the theory of natural law cannot stand the least historical or sociological criticism, for it gives an entirely inadequate picture of reality. But the main curiosity consists in the fact that the juridic theory of the state, which took its place in the name of positivism, distorts reality to no less a degree. It is forced to do this for every *juridic* theory of the state must necessarily proceed from the state as an independent force distinct from society. This is in what its *juridic* nature consists.

Therefore, although in fact the activity of the state organization occurs in the form of orders and decrees proceeding from individual persons, the juridic theory presumes in the first place that the state, not persons, gives orders and, second, that its orders are subordinates to general norms of law which also express the will of the state.

On this point natural law doctrine does not differ by one iota in its fiction than any of the most positivist of the juridic theories of the state. For the doctrine of natural law the basic argument was that along with all the types of real dependency of one man upon another (this doctrine was exempt from such dependence), there was still one further type of dependence upon the impersonal general will, namely, the will of the state.

But it is just this construction which constitutes the basis of the juridic theory of the state as a person. The natural law elements in the juridic theories of the state lie much deeper than it seemed to the critics of natural law doctrine. They are rooted in the very concept of *public* authority, i.e. of authority placed above *all* and addressed to *all*. Adjusting itself to this concept, the juridic theory inevitably loses its connection with reality. The difference between the doctrine of natural law and the most recent legal positivism is merely that the former much more clearly felt the logical bond between abstract state authority and the abstract subject. It took these mystified relationships of a commodity-producing society, in their necessary context, and therefore produced a model of the classical clarity of constructs. On the contrary, so-called legal positivism does not even take account of its own logical premises.

The *Rechtsstaat* is a mirage, but a very useful mirage for the bourgeoisie because it replaces the disappearing religious ideology. It hides from the masses the fact of the rule of the bourgeoisie. The ideology of the *Rechtsstaat* is also more useful than religious ideology because, not reflecting the totality of objective reality, it nevertheless depends on it. Authority as "the general will", as "the authority of law", is realized in bourgeois society to the extent that the latter is a market. From this point of view even a police statute may appear to us as embodying Kant's ideas on a freedom which is limited by the freedom of another.

Free and equal commodity owners meeting in the market are free and equal only in the abstract relationship between buyer and seller. In actual life they are tied to each other by many relationships of dependence. These are the shopkeepers and the large wholesaler, the peasant and the estate owner, the ruined debtor and his creditor, the proletarian and the capitalist. These countless relations of real dependence constitute the true basis of state organization. However, for the juridic theory of the state it is as if they do not exist. Further, the life of the state is based upon the struggle between various political forces, i.e. of classes, parties and all possible groupings; here are hidden the real mainsprings of the state machinery; for juridic theory they are equally inaccessible. Of course, a jurist may show a greater or lesser flexibility in his adaptation to the facts, for example by taking into account written law in addition to those unwritten rules which have been formed in state practice, but this does not change his fundamental position in relation to reality. There is an inevitable divergence between legal proof and that proof which constitutes the goal of historical and social research. It is not merely that the dynamics of social life overturn the rigid legal form, and that therefore the jurist is condemned to be somewhat late in his analysis; even limiting himself to the very day of a fact, the jurist communicates his analysis differently than the sociologist. For the jurist, remaining a jurist, proceeds from the concept of the state as an independent force distinct from all other individual and social forces. From the historical and political points of view the decisions of an influential class, or party organization, have the same and sometimes even greater significance than the decisions of parliament or some other state institution. From the legal point of view, facts of the first type are seemingly non-existent. Conversely, in any decree of parliament, once the legal point of view is abandoned, it is possible to see not an act of the state, but a decision adopted by a particular group, a clique of persons moved by the same individual egoistic or class motives as any other collective. The extreme normativist Kelsen concludes from this that the state in general exists only as an imaginary object—a closed system of norms or obligations. But of course, such barrenness in the subject of the theory of state law must deter practising lawyers. For if not by intelligence, then by instinct, they feel the undoubted practical significance of their concepts in this sinful world and not merely in the kingdom of pure logic. The "state" of jurists, despite all this "ideologizing", relates to some objective reality much as the most fantastic dream nevertheless depends on reality.

This reality is pre-eminently the state apparatus itself, with its material and personal elements. Before creating completed theories, the bourgeoisie began to construct the state in practice. In Western Europe this process began in city communes. At a time when the feudal world knew no difference between the assets of the feudal lord and the assets of the political union, the public city treasury first appeared in cities, originally as a sporadic and then as a permanent institution; "the spirit of statism" received, so to speak, its material foundation.

The appearance of state forms makes possible the appearance of people who live off these forms, officials and bureaucrats. In the feudal age the functions of administration and the court were fulfilled by the servants of the feudal lord. In the city communes they appeared for the first time in public offices; in the full sense of the word, the public nature of authority found its material embodiment. The absolute monarchy had merely to adopt the public form which had taken shape in the cities and to realize it within a broader territory. All further improvements to the bourgeois state—which proceeded both by revolutionary explosions and by peaceful adaptation to monarchic-feudal elements—can be summed up in one principle: neither of two persons exchanging in the market may appear as an authoritative regulator of the exchange relationship; for this, some third person is required who embodies the mutual guarantee which the commodity owners as owners give to one another, and who is accordingly the personified rule of exchange between commodity owners.

The bourgeoisie put this juridic concept of the state at the basis of its theory, and attempted to realize it in practice. It certainly did the latter, guided by this elementary principle.[50]

For the sake of theoretical purity the bourgeoisie never forgot the other side of the matter, namely that class society is not only a market where independent commodity owners meet, but also an arena of intensified class war in which the state apparatus is one of the most powerful weapons. And in this arena the relationships formed are far from being in the spirit of the Kantian definition of law as the limitation of the freedom of the individual and the minimum limit necessary for common life. Here Gumplowicz is profoundly right when he asserts that "law of this type never existed, for the amount of freedom is determined only by the amount of authority of another, the norm of common existence is dictated not by the possibility of common existence but by the possibility of authority". The state as an element of force in internal and external policy—this is the correction which the bourgeoisie had to make in its theory and practice of the *Rechtsstaat*. The more unstable the authority of the bourgeoisie became, the more compromising its corrections became, the more the *Rechtsstaat* turned into an incorporeal shadow, until finally the extreme intensification of the class struggle forced the bourgeoisie completely to discard the mask of the

Rechtsstaat and to reveal the essence of authority as the organized force of one class against another.

CHAPTER VI

Law and Morality

People must relate to each other as independent and equal personalities in order for the products of human labour to be related to each other as values.

If one person is under the domination of another, i.e. is a slave, his labour ceases to be the creator and substance of value. The labour power of a slave, like the labour power of a domestic animal, merely transforms a definite part of the cost of its production, and reproduction, into a product.

On this basis Tugan-Baranovsky concludes that political economy can be understood by starting from the guiding ethical idea of absolute value and, therefore, of equivalence between human personalities. Marx, of course, arrives at the opposite conclusion, in that he connects the ethical idea of the equal value of human personalities with the form of a commodity, i.e. he derives it from the practical equivalence of all forms of human labour.

In fact, man as a moral subject, i.e. as an equal personality, is nothing more than a prerequisite of exchange according to the law of value. Man as the subject of rights is such a prerequisite, i.e. as a property owner. Finally, both these definitions are closely connected with a third—man as an egoistic economic subject.

All three definitions are not reducible to each other, and are even contradictory as it were. They reflect the totality of conditions necessary for the realization of the value relationship, i.e. a relationship in which the bonds between people in the labour process appear as the material nature of the products being exchanged.

If one abstracts these definitions from the real social relationships which they reflect, and attempts to develop them as independent categories, i.e. by pure reason, then as a result one obtains a tangle of contradictions and propositions which are mutually exclusive. But in the real relationship of exchange these contradictions are dialectically united in a totality.

The party to the exchange must be an egoist, i.e. be guided by naked economic calculation, otherwise the value relationship cannot appear as a socially necessary relationship. The exchanging party must be the bearer of a right, i.e. have the possibility of making an autonomous decision, for *his will* must "be embedded in objects". Finally, the exchanging party must embody the basic principle of the equality of all human personalities, because in exchange all types of labour are equalized and are reduced to abstract human labour.

Thus, these three elements (or, as it was earlier preferable to term them, three bases): egoism, freedom and the supreme value of the personality, are inextricably bound up with each other, appearing as a totality to be the rational expression of one and the same social relationship. The egoistic subject, the subject of a right and the moral personality are the three basic masks under which man appears in commodity production. The key to the understanding of legal and moral structures is provided by the economics of value relationships, not only in the sense of their real content but also in the sense of their form itself. The idea of the principle of value and the equality of the human personality has a long history: through Stoic philosophy it entered into the use of Roman jurists and into the teaching of the Christian Church, and then into the doctrine of natural law. But whatever clothed this idea one could discover nothing in it other than an expression of the fact that the different concrete types of socially useful labour were reduced to labour in general, insofar as the products of labour began to be exchanged as commodities. In all other relationships, social inequality (sexual, class etc.) is so conspicuous in history that one must wonder not at the abundance of arguments against the doctrine of the natural law of social equality, but that until Marx no one posed the question of the historical origins of this prejudice against natural law. If in the course of centuries human thought returned with such emphasis to the thesis of social equality, and developed it in a thousand ways, then it is clear that some objective relationship must be hidden behind this thesis. There is no doubt that the concept of the moral or equal personality is an ideological formation, and as such does not adequately describe reality. The egoistic, economic subject is no less an ideological distortion of reality. Nevertheless, both these definitions are adequate for only one specific social relationship, and reflect it only abstractly and therefore one-sidedly. We have already had occasion to declare that the concept or word "ideology" must not restrain us from further analysis. To be satisfied with the fact that one man is equal to another is the offspring of an ideology intended to oversimplify the problem. "Down" and "up" are nothing more than concepts expressing our "earthly" ideology. However, the earth's gravity is their factual basis. When man understood the real reason which made him distinguish "down from up"—i.e. the force of gravity directed toward the centre of the earth—then he reached the limits of these definitions, and their inadequacy as applied to all cosmic reality. Thus, the discovery that these concepts were ideological was another aspect of the process of discovering that they were true.

If moral personality is nothing other than the subject of commodity production, then moral law must reveal itself as the rule of exchange between commodity owners. This inevitably produces a duality. On the one hand, this law must have a social character and, as such, stand above the individual personality. On the other hand, the commodity owner is inherently the bearer of freedom (freedom to appropriate and alienate), therefore the rule governing exchange between commodity owners must be stated in the spirit of each of them, and each must internalize this law. The Kantian categorical imperative synthesizes these contradictory requirements. It is above the individual because it has nothing in common with any natural desires—fear, sympathy, pity, feeling of solidarity etc. In Kant's terms, it does not frighten, does not convince, does not flatter. It is generally external to all empirical, i.e. purely human motives. At the same time it seems to be independent of all external pressures in the direct and crude sense of the word. It acts exclusively by virtue of realizing its universality. Kantian ethics are the typical ethics of a commodity-producing society, but at the same time they are a pure and perfected form of ethics in general. Kant gave a logically complete tenor to the form which atomized bourgeois society tried to embody in practice, liberating personality from the organic ties of the patriarchal and feudal periods.

The basic concepts of morality are meaningless if we abstract them from commodity production and try to apply them to some other social structure. The categorical imperative is not a social instinct. The basic purpose of the imperative is to act where no natural or organic supra-individual motivation is possible. When individuals have close emotional ties which erase the boundary of the I, then the phenomenon of moral obligation may not occur. To understand this latter category it is necessary to proceed not from the organic connection which exists, for instance, between the cow and the calf, or between the tribe and each of its members, but from the condition of alienation. Moral existence is a necessary supplement to juridic life—both are methods of exchange between commodity producers. All the pathos of the Kantian categorical imperatives is reduced to the fact that man "freely", i.e. by voluntary persuasion, acts under the coercion of law. The very examples which Kant adduces for the illustration of his thoughts are typical. They are reduced entirely to the manifestation of bourgeois respectability. Heroism and exploits have no place within the Kantian categorical imperative. Personal sacrifice is not required because one demands no sacrifice from others. "Mindless" acts of penance and oblivion, in the name of fulfilling one's historical calling, or one's social functions, actions in which the most intense social instinct appear, lie outside ethics in the strict sense of the word.

Schopenhauer, and Vladimir Solov'ev after him, define law as an ethical minimum. It would be more accurate to define ethics as a certain social minimum. Intensified social enthusiasm is external to ethics and is inherited by modern man from the earlier periods of organic, and particularly tribal, existence.

Nevertheless, for a commodity-producing society, ethical reason is the highest possible achievement, and a higher cultural good of which one must speak only in the most exalted tone. It is necessary to remember Kant's well-known words:

> two things fill the spirit with ever new and increasing amazement and satisfaction the more often and deeply we think of them: the starry sky above my head and the moral law within me.[51]

And moreover, when discussion turns to examples of the "voluntary" fulfilment of moral duty, upon the stage appears just the same immutable alms or a refusal to lie when it would have been possible to lie with impunity. Uniquely, ethical reason universally triumphs over powerful and irrational social instincts. It breaks with all the organic and inherently narrow limits (kin-group, tribe, nation) and strives for universality. In this sense it reflects definite social material achievements, and transforms exchange into world exchange. "There is no Hellas, no Judaea"—this reflected the historical reality of the peoples united under the power of Rome. On the other hand, Kautsky apparently correctly notes that the rule "consider another as an end in himself", makes sense only when in practice one man may be subjected to another. Moral pathos is indissolubly bound to, and nurtured by, the immorality of social practice. Ethical doctrines pretended to change and correct the world when in fact they were but a distorted reflection of one aspect of it: namely, that in which human relationships were subordinated to the law of value. It must not be forgotten that moral personality is but one of the hypostatic forms of a triad. Man as an end in himself is only another aspect of the egoistic economic subject. An act which is the unique and real embodiment of the ethical principle in itself includes the latter's negation. The large-scale capitalist *bona fide* ruins the small capitalist, without for a moment encroaching upon the absolute value of his personality. The personality of a proletarian is "in principle equal" to the personality of a capitalist; this finds its expression in the fact of the "free" contract of employment. But for the proletarian this very "material freedom" means the possibility of quietly dying of starvation.

This ambiguity of the ethical form is not accidental, nor is it some external defect caused by the specific inadequacies of capitalism. On the contrary, this is an essential characteristic of the ethical form itself. To eliminate the ambiguity of the ethical form would mean to effect the transition to a planned social economy, and this would mean to realize a system in which people can think and construct their relationships using simple and clear concepts such as harm and benefit. To eliminate the ambiguity of the ethical form in the most essential area (in the area of material social existence) means to destroy this form altogether.

Pure utilitarianism, striving to disperse the metaphysical haze which surrounds ethical doctrines, leads to conceptualizing good and evil from the perspective of harm and benefit. Thereby, of course, it simply destroys ethics, or rather tries to destroy and transcend them. The transcendence of ethical fetishism in fact may be achieved only simultaneously with the transcendence of commodity and legal fetishism. People who are guided in their actions by clear and simple concepts of harm and benefit will require that their social relationships be expressed either in terms of value or of law. Until this level of historical development is attained by mankind, i.e. until the legacy of the capitalist period is transcended, theoretical effort can merely proclaim this pending liberation but not implement it in practice. We must remember Marx's words on commodity fetishism:

> The most recent scientific discovery that the products of labour, to the extent that they contain value, are merely a material reflection of the labour expended in their production, and that this constitutes a period in the historical development of mankind, by no means eliminates the material objectivity of the social nature of labour.

But it is objected that the class morality of the proletariat is already liberated from all fetishes. The morally necessary is that which is beneficial to the class. In such a form, morality includes nothing absolute because what is useful today may not be so tomorrow. It also includes nothing mystical or supernatural because the utilitarian principle is simple and rational.

There is no doubt that proletarian morality (or more accurately, that of its advanced strata) loses its particularly fetishist character, being liberated from religious elements. But morality, even entirely devoid of the mixture of religious elements, nevertheless remains moral, i.e. it is a form of social relationship in which not everything is yet reduced to man himself. If the conscious link to a class is in fact so powerful that the borders of the "I" are, so to speak, erased, and the advantage of the class actually merges with personal advantage, then there is no sense in speaking of the fulfilment of moral duty. In general, the phenomenon of morality is then absent. When such a merger has not occurred, then inevitably the abstract relationship of moral duty arises with all its attendant consequences. The rule: "act for the greatest advantage of one's class" sounds identical to Kant's formula: "act so that your conduct may serve the principle of universal legislation". The difference is that in the first case we introduce a concrete limitation, and erect class boundaries on ethical logic.[52] But within these boundaries it remains in full force. The class content of ethics by itself does not eliminate its forms. We have in mind not only the logical form, but also the form of the real phenomenon. Embedded in the proletariat (in the class collectivity) we observe formally the same methods of realizing the moral duty, which are comprised of two opposing elements. On the one hand, the collective does not fail to use all possible means of putting pressure upon its fellow members to motivate them in their moral duty. On the other hand, the same collective qualifies conduct as moral only in the absence of externally motivating pressure. Therefore to study morality means, to a certain degree, to study falsehood. Morality, like law and state, is a form of bourgeois society. If the proletariat is compelled to use them, this by no means signifies the possibility of the further development of those forms in the direction of filling them with a socialist content. They are incapable of retaining this content, and must wither away in the course of their realization. Nevertheless, until the end of the present transitional period, the proletariat necessarily must use these forms inherited from bourgeois society in its class interest, and then exhaust them. For this, it must above all have a very clear understanding, free from ideology, of the historical origin of these forms. The proletariat must critically and soberly relate not only to the bourgeois state and to bourgeois morality, but even to its own state and to its own proletarian morality, i.e. it must recognize the historical necessity of their existence as well as of their disappearance.

In his criticism of Proudhon, Marx among other things notes that the abstract concept of justice is by no means an absolute and eternal criterion by which we might construct an ideal, i.e. a just exchange relationship. This would signify the attempt to measure an object by its own reflection. But the very concept of justice is drawn from the exchange relationship, and expresses nothing outside of it. Essentially speaking, the very concept of justice does not include anything new in comparison with the concept of social equality which we analysed above. Therefore, it is ridiculous to see any independent and absolute criteria in the idea of justice. It is true that in its artful usage it provides greater possibilities for interpreting inequality as equality, and therefore is particularly useful for obscuring the equivocal ethical form. On the other hand, justice is the step by which ethics descend to law. Moral conduct must be "free"; justice must be compelled. Compulsory moral conduct tends to deny its own existence; justice is openly "applied" to man; it allows external realization and an active egoistic interest in demanding justice. Here are found the main points of contiguity and divergence between the ethical and the legal forms.

Exchange, i.e. the circulation of commodities, assumes that the exchanging parties recognize one another as property owners. This recognition, assuming the form of inner conviction or the categorical imperative, represents the conceivable maximum which a society of commodity producers may achieve. But besides this maximum there exists a certain minimum through which the circulation of commodities can nevertheless flow without hindrance. For the realization of this minimum, it is sufficient that the commodity owners conduct themselves *as if* they recognized each other as property owners. Moral conduct is opposed to legal conduct which is characterized as such irrespective of the motives which produce it. Whether a debt is repaid because "in any event I will be forced to pay it", or because the debtor considers it his moral obligation to do so, makes no difference from the juridic perspective. It is obvious that the idea of external coercion, both in its idea and organization, constitutes an essential aspect of the legal form. When no coercive mechanism has been organized, and it is not found within the jurisdiction of a special apparatus which stands above the parties, it appears in the form of so-called "inter-dependence". The principle of inter-dependence, under the conditions of balance of power, represents the single, and it can be said, the most unstable basis of international law.

On the other hand, a legal claim as distinct from a moral claim appears not in the form of an "inner voice", but as an external demand proceeding from a concrete subject who, as a rule, is at the same time the bearer of a corresponding material interest. Therefore, the fulfilment of a legal obligation takes on an external and almost material form of *satisfaction of demand* and is finally divorced from all subjective elements on the part of the obligee. The very concept of legal obligation therefore becomes most problematic. If we are fully consistent, it is necessary to say, as Binder does, that an obligation which corresponds to a right has nothing in common with "duty" (*Pflicht*), but exists juridically only as responsibility (*Haftung*); "obliged" means no more than "answers with his property (or in criminal law also with his person) by means of the judicial process and the compulsory execution of the verdict". Binder's conclusions are paradoxical for the majority of jurists, and are expressed in the short formula: *Das Recht verpflichtet rechtlich zu nichts* (law legally does not impose any duty). In fact this represents only the consequence of following the conceptual dichotomy already established by Kant. But it is precisely this clarity in the demarcation of the moral and legal spheres, which provides the source of the most insoluble contradictions for the bourgeois philosophy of law. If legal obligation has nothing in common with an "inner" moral duty, then subordination to law cannot be distinguished from subordination to force *per se*. If, on the other hand, one accepts that an essential characteristic of law is the element of obligation, of even the weakest subjective kind, then the meaning of law as a socially necessary minimum slowly loses its meaning. Bourgeois philosophy of law exhausts itself in this basic contradiction, in this endless struggle with its own assumptions.

Moreover, it is interesting that one and the same contradiction essentially appears in two different forms, depending on whether one speaks of the relationship between law and morality or the relationship between the state and law. In the former case, when the independence of law was affirmed with respect to morality, law is merged with the state because of the increased emphasis upon the element of external authoritative coercion. In the latter case, when law is contrasted with the state, the element of obligation (in the sense of the German *sollen*, not *müssen*)—actual domination—inevitably appears on the scene, and we have before us, so to speak, a united front of morality and law.

Here, as always, the contradiction of the system reflects the contradiction of real life, i.e. that social environment which created within itself the forms of morality and law. The contradiction between the individual and the social, between the part and the whole can never be reconciled by the bourgeois philosophy of law. This contradiction constitutes the conscious basis of bourgeois society as a society of commodity producers. This is embodied in the real relationships of human subjects who can regard their own private struggles as social struggles only in the incongruous and mystifying form of the value of commodities.

CHAPTER VII

Law and Violation of Law

Russkaya Pravda—that most ancient historical monument of the Kievan period of our history—consists of 43 articles (the so-called academic register). Only two articles do not relate to violations of criminal or civil law. The remaining articles either determine a sanction, or else contain the procedural rules applicable when a law has been violated. Accordingly, deviation from a norm always constitutes their premise. The same picture is presented by the so-called barbarian laws of German tribes. For example, in the Salic Law only 65 of 408 articles do not have a punitive nature. The oldest monument of Roman law—the laws of the Twelve Tables—begins with rules defining the procedure for initiating litigation: "*Si in ius vocat, ni it, antestamino. Igitur im capito*". (If a man is called to court and he does not go, this should be attested, and he should be taken there.)

According to the observation of the well-known legal historian Maine, "it is necessary to recognize as a rule that the more ancient the code, the fuller and more detailed will be its statement of the criminal section".[53]

Non-observance of a norm, or violation of it, the disruption of normal intercourse and ensuing conflict: this is the starting point of the most important content of ancient legislation. Conversely, what is normal is not fixed in the beginning as such—it merely exists. The requirement that the scope and content of mutual rights and obligations be fixed and exactly established, appears when calm and peaceful existence is violated. From this perspective Bentham is right when he asserts that a statute creates rights as it creates crimes. Historically, the legal relationship assumes its specific character pre-eminently in the facts of violations of law. The concept of theft was defined earlier than the concept of private property. The relationships attending a loan were fixed when the borrower did not want to repay it: "if one tries to recover a debt and the debtor refuses etc." (*Russkaya Pravda*, Academic Register, Art. 14). The original significance of the word *pactum* was not that of contract, but *pax*, peace, i.e. an amicable conclusion to hostility, "peaceful" (*Vertrag*) supposes the end of "unpeaceful" (*Unvertraglichkeit*).

Thus, if private law directly reflects the most general conditions of existence of the legal form as such, then criminal law is the sphere where the legal relationship achieves its maximum intensity. Here, above all and most clearly the legal element is isolated from everyday life and obtains full independence. The transformation of the actions of the concrete person into the action of a party, i.e. into a legal subject, takes place particularly clearly in the judicial process. In order to emphasize the difference between everyday activities and expressions of will on the one hand, and juridic expressions of will on the other, ancient law used special ceremonial formulae and rituals. The drama of the judicial process noticeably created a separate juridic life contiguous with the real world.

Of all types of law it is criminal law that has the ability, by its own direct and crude manner, to assume a separate personality. This law has always, therefore, attracted the most ardent and practical interest, and punishments for its violation are usually closely associated with each other—thus, criminal law, so to speak, assumes the role of the representative of law in general. It is the part which replaces the whole.

The origin of criminal law is historically linked with the custom of the blood feud. It is certain that these phenomena are genetically close to one another but a feud becomes *fully a feud* only when fines and punishment follow it, i.e. even these later stages of development, as is often observed in the history of mankind, explain the intimations included in the preceding forms. If one approaches the same phenomena from the opposite direction, we see nothing but a struggle for existence, i.e. a truly biological fact. For the theorists of criminal law viewing the later period, blood feud corresponds with *ius talionis*, i.e. with the basis of equal retribution, under which the avenging of an insult by the insulted (or by his tribe) eliminated the possibility of further feuding. In fact, as Kovalevsky correctly points out, the most ancient blood feuds did not have this nature. Internecine wars are transmitted from generation to generation. An insult, although committed in retribution, itself becomes the basis for a new feud. The insulted and his relatives become insultors—and so on from one generation to another, sometimes until the entire struggling kin-groups are liquidated.[54]

Feud begins to be regulated by custom and is turned into retribution by the Talic rule "an eye for an eye and a tooth for a tooth". Only then does a system of composition or a monetary fine begin to be established alongside it. The notion of equivalence, this first purely juridic idea, always has its source in the form of a commodity. A crime may be considered as a particular aspect of exchange, in which the exchange (contractual relationship) is established *post factum*, that is, after the intentional act of one of the parties. The ratio between the crime and the punishment is reduced to an exchange ratio. Therefore Aristotle, in discussing equivalent exchange as a type of justice, divides it into two aspects: equivalence in voluntary and in involuntary actions. Economic relationships such as purchase and sale, loan etc. are classified as voluntary actions; these include various types of crime invoking punishment as an equivalent. The definition of crime as a contract concluded against one's will, also belongs to Aristotle. Punishment emerges as an equivalent mediating the harm done to the victim.

This notion was adopted, as is well known, by Hugo Grotius. However naïve these constructs may seem at first glance, they latently contain much more sensitivity to the form of law than do the eclectic theories of modern jurists.

In the example of blood feud and punishment we can observe, with extraordinary clarity, the imperceptible stages through which the organic or biological is connected with the legal. This merger is intensified by the fact that man is not capable of renouncing that to which he is accustomed, i.e. the legal (or ethical) interpretation of this phenomenon of animal life. He involuntarily finds in the actions of animals that which is placed in them, factually speaking, by later development, i.e. by the historical development of man.

In fact the act of self-defence is one of the most natural phenomena of animal life. It makes no difference whether we encounter it as the individual reaction of a particular animal or as a collective exercise in self-defence. According to the testimony of scholars who observe the life of bees, if a bee tries to penetrate a strange hive to steal honey, then the bees protecting the entrance at once attack it and begin to sacrifice it; if it actually penetrates the hive then they kill it immediately. There are similar cases in the animal world when the reaction is separated by a certain interval of time from the circumstance which instigated it. The animal does not respond to the attack immediately, but puts it off to a more suitable time. Self-defence here becomes a feud in the true sense of the word. Since for modern man feud is inseparably tied to the idea of equal retribution, it is not surprising that Ferri, for example, is ready to recognize the presence of the "juridic instinct" among animals.[55]

In fact the juridic idea, i.e. the idea of an equivalent, becomes fully clarified and objectified only at that stage of economic development when it becomes the standard form of equivalent exchange, i.e. not in the world of animals but in human society. For this it is by no means necessary that feud was entirely forced out by blood money.

And even when blood money is refused as something shameful—and such a view was dominant for a long time among primitive peoples—the realization of a personal feud was recognized as a sacred obligation. The very act of feud assumed a new form which it did not have when there was not yet an alternative. Specifically, it now included an image of the only adequate method: retribution. The refusal of blood-money in monetary form emphasized that blood-money was the only equivalent for blood spilled earlier. The feud is transformed from a purely biological phenomenon into a legal institution to the extent that it is linked with the form of equivalent exchange, with exchange-value.

The criminal law of antiquity emphasizes this bond with particular clarity and immediacy, because damage to property and personal injury are directly equated with a naïvety that later eras abandoned in shame. From the perspective of ancient Roman law there was nothing surprising in the fact that an insolvent debtor paid with parts of his body (*in partes secare*), and one guilty of mutilation answered with his property. The idea of equivalent exchange appears here in all its starkness—uncomplicated and not obscured by any related circumstances. Accordingly, criminal procedure also assumes the character of a commercial transaction. "We must", says Jhering, "imagine a market in which too much money is asked by one side and too little is offered by the other, until a bargain is reached. An expression of this was *pacere*, and for the price agreement itself—*pactum*." "The duty of an intermediary selected by both parties", adds Jhering, "finds its beginning here. In ancient Scandinavian law an intermediary determined the amount to be paid for reconciliation (*arbiter* in the original Roman sense)."[56]

With regard to so-called public punishments, there is no doubt that they were originally introduced mainly for fiscal reasons, and that they served as a means of filling the treasury of the representatives of authority. "The state", says Henry Maine, "has not taken a fine from the defendant for the harm which he is supposed to have done to the state, but has commanded for itself only a certain share of the compensation made to the plaintiff in the form of just retribution for the loss of his time and peace."[57] From Russian history we know that "just retribution for loss of time" was so eagerly collected by princes that, according to chronicled testimony, "the Russian land was impoverished by fines and sales". Moreover, this phenomenon of judicial theft was observed not only in ancient Russia, but also in the empire of Charlemagne. In the eyes of the ancient Russian princes, judicial revenues were no different from other patronage bestowed on their servants etc. It was possible to buy one's way out of a prince's court by paying a certain sum (the barbarian *wer* or fine of *Russkaya Pravda*).

However, in addition to public punishment as a source of income, punishment appeared rather early as a method of ensuring discipline and as a major safeguard of the authority of priestly and military power. It is well known that in ancient Rome the majority of serious crimes were at the same time crimes against the gods. For instance, one of the most important violations, for the landowner, was the wilful moving of boundary markers. From ancient times this was considered a religious crime, and the head of the guilty party was condemned to the gods. The priestly caste, acting as the guardians of order, pursued not some ideal but a most essential material interest, because the property of the guilty party was confiscated for its use. On the other hand, the punishment which the priestly organization inflicted on those who tried to appropriate its incomes—in the form of deviations from established ceremonies and gifts, attempts to introduce new religious teachings etc.—bore the same public character.

The influence of the priestly organization (i.e. the Church) on criminal law was felt in the fact that although punishment preserved its nature of equivalence or *retribution*, this retribution was neither directly linked with harm to the injured party nor based upon the latter's claim. Indeed, punishment attained a higher abstract meaning as godly punishment. The Church thus tried to combine the material element of compensation or harm with the ideological motive of expiation and cleansing (*expiatio*). It thus tried to construct a more appropriate mechanism for maintaining social discipline (i.e. class domination) than that provided by a criminal law based on private vengeance. Indicative of this were the solicitations of the Byzantine clergy with respect to the introduction of capital punishment in Kievan Russia.

The same goal of maintaining discipline determines the nature of the punitive activity of a military commander. The latter renders justice and reprisal, both over subjugated peoples and over his own troops who had planned a mutiny, treason, or who were simply disobedient. The notorious story about Ludwig—who with his own hands decapitated a disobedient soldier—shows the primitive nature of this reprisal in the formative period of the German barbarian states. In earlier times the task of maintaining military discipline had been conduced by a popular assembly; with the consolidation and expansion of monarchical authority this function naturally adhered to the monarchs and was naturally identified with the protection of their own privileges. As far as general criminal offences were concerned, the kings of the German tribes (and also the princes of Kievan Russia) for a long time showed only a fiscal interest toward them.

This state of affairs changed with the development and consolidation of class and estate boundaries. A spiritual and temporal hierarchy valued the protection of its privileges, in the struggle with the lower and oppressed classes of the population, as its first priority. The decomposition of the natural economy and the concomitant increase in the exploitation of the peasantry, the development of commerce and the organization of a class state, gave different tasks to criminal justice. In this period criminal justice became less a method of raising income for the authorities and more a method of merciless and harsh reprisal against "evil people", i.e. primarily against peasants who had fled from unbearable exploitation by landlords and the landlords' state, and against the pauperized population, vagrants, mendicants etc. The police and the investigative apparatus had to play the main role. Punishment became a method of physical elimination or of instilling terror. This was the era of ordeals, corporal punishment and cruel methods of capital punishment.

Gradually, therefore, that complex amalgam was prepared which now constitutes modern criminal law. We can easily discern the composition of its historical strata. In essence (that is, from a purely sociological point of view) bourgeois society supports its class state by its system of criminal law and thereby holds the exploited class in obedience. In this respect, its judges and its private "voluntary" organizations of strike-breakers pursue one and the same goal.

The criminal jurisdiction of the bourgeois state is organized class terror. This differs only in degree from the so-called extraordinary measures applied at times of civil war. Spencer indicated the full analogy and even the identity between the defensive reaction directed against external attacks (war), and the reaction directed against violators of the internal order (legal or judicial defence).[58] Measures of the first type (i.e. criminal punishment) are applied primarily against *déclassé* social elements, and measures of the second type primarily against active proponents of a new class rebelling against authority. This fact does not change the essence of the matter, nor does the greater or lesser correctness and complexity of the procedure applied. An understanding of the true meaning of the punitive activity of the class state is possible only by perceiving its antagonistic nature. So-called theories of criminal law which derive the principle of punitive policy from the interest of society as a whole are occupied with the conscious or unconscious distortion of reality. "Society as a whole" exists only in the imagination of these jurists. In fact, we are faced with classes with contradictory, conflicting interests. Every historical system of punitive policy bears the imprint of the class interest of that class which realized it. The feudal lord executed disobedient peasants and city dwellers who rose against his power. The unified cities hanged the robber-knights and destroyed their castles. In the Middle Ages, a man was considered a lawbreaker if he wanted to engage in a trade without joining a guild; the capitalist bourgeoisie, which had barely succeeded in emerging, declared that the desire of workers to join unions was criminal.

Thus, class interest places the imprint of historical concreteness on each given system of punitive policy. Only the full disappearance of classes enables the construction of a system of punitive policy in which every element of antagonism will be excluded. But the question remains of whether a punitive system is still necessary in these conditions.

If by its content and nature authoritative punitive activity is a weapon for the maintenance of class domination, then in its form it acts as an element of the legal superstructure, and is included in the legal system as one of its branches. We showed above that the naked struggle for existence adopts a legal form through the introduction of the principle of equivalence. The act of self-defence ceases to be merely an act of self-defence, and becomes a form of exchange, a type of intercourse which takes its place alongside "normal" commercial exchange. Crime and punishment become such (i.e. assume their legal nature) on the basis of the redemption transaction. As long as this form exists, so too will the class struggle be conducted through law. Conversely, the very term criminal will lose all meaning to the extent that the element of the relation of equivalence disappears from it.[59]

Considering the nature of bourgeois society as a society of commodity owners, we would have to suppose *a priori* that its criminal law was the most juridic in the sense we established above. However, we at once encounter certain difficulties here. The first difficulty is the fact that modern criminal law does not proceed primarily from the harm done to the victim but from the violation of the norm established by the state. Once the victim and his claim recedes to the background then, it is asked, where is the form of equivalence? But in the first place, no matter how far the victim recedes to the background he nevertheless does not disappear, but continues to constitute the setting in which the criminal law action is played out. The abstraction of a violated public interest rests on the fully real figure of the victim, who participates in the process—personally or through representatives—and who gives this process a living significance. Moreover, even when the concrete victim in fact does not exist, when "merely a statute" is assailed, this abstraction implies its real embodiment in the person of the public prosecutor. This division, in which a state authority appears both in the role of a party (the prosecutor) and in the role of a judge, shows that as a legal form the criminal process is indivisible from the figure of the victim demanding "retribution". It is therefore indistinguishable from the more general form of agreement. The prosecutor, as is expected of a "party", asks a "high price", i.e. a strict punishment; the criminal seeks leniency, a "discount", the judge decrees "according to justice". Discard this form of agreement, and you will deprive the criminal process of its "juridic spirit". Imagine for a minute that the court is actually occupied only with the consideration of how to change the conditions of life of a given person—in order to influence him in the sense of correction, or in order to protect society from him—and the very meaning of the term punishment evaporates. This does not mean that every criminal court and punitive procedure is entirely deprived of the simple and comprehensible elements mentioned above. But we wish to show that there is a peculiarity in this procedure which is not covered by the clear and simple considerations of social purpose. This is an element that is irrational, mystifying and incoherent, and it is the specifically legal element.

Further difficulty lies in the following fact. Ancient criminal law knew only the concept of harm. Crime and guilt, occupying such an eminent place in modern criminal law, were absent at this stage of development. Conscious, careless and accidental actions were evaluated exclusively by their consequences. The customs of the Salic Franks and the modern Ossetians stand at the same stage of development in this respect. The latter made no distinction between death resulting from a blow with a knife, and death proceeding from the fact that a rock was knocked off a hill kicked by the hoof of another's bull.

From this, as we see, it does not follow that the concept of responsibility was in itself alien to ancient law. It was merely determined by another method. In modern criminal law—in accordance with the radical individualism of bourgeois society—we have the concept of strict personal responsibility. But ancient law was penetrated by the principle of collective responsibility: children were punished for the sins of their parents, and the kin-group answered for each of its members. Bourgeois society dissolves all earlier primitive and organic ties between individuals. It proclaims as its basis: every man for himself, and it implements this most consistently in all areas, including criminal law. In the second place, modern criminal law introduced the psychological element into the concept of responsibility and thus gave it a greater flexibility. It divided it into degrees: responsibility for a result which was foreseen (intent), and responsibility for a result which was unforeseen but which could have been foreseeable (negligence). Finally it constructed the concept of non-imputability, i.e. the complete absence of responsibility. However, this new element, the degree of guilt, by no means excludes the principle of equivalent exchange, but derives from it and creates a new basis for its application. What does this division signify other than a clarification of the conditions of the bourgeois judicial transaction! The gradation of liability is the basis for the gradation of punishment—a new, if you wish, ideal or psychological element, which is combined with the material element (the injury) and the objective element (the act)—in order to provide a joint basis for determining the ratio of punishment. Responsibility is heaviest for an action committed with intent and accordingly, *ceteris paribus*, entails a heavier punishment; if an action is committed negligently the responsibility is less heavy: *ceteris paribus*, the punishment is reduced; finally, if responsibility is absent (criminal intent is non-imputable), there is no punishment. If we replace punishment with *Behandlung* ("method of influence"), i.e. a legally neutral, medical-pedagogical concept, we reach very different results. This is so because primarily we will be interested *not in the proportionality*, but in the *correspondence* of the measures taken to the goals which are placed before it, i.e. to the goals of protecting society from the criminal etc. From this point of view the relationship may appear as the opposite; that is, in the case of the least responsibility the most intensive and long-lasting measures of influence may seem necessary.

The idea of responsibility is necessary if punishment is to appear as a method of payment. The criminal answers for the crime with his freedom, and he answers with an amount of his freedom which is *proportional* to the gravity of what he has done. This idea of responsibility is unnecessary when punishment is liberated from the character of equivalence; and when no remnant of this remains, punishment ceases to be punishment in the legal sense of the word.

The juridic idea of responsibility is not scientific because it leads directly to the contradictions of indeterminism. From the viewpoint of the causal chain which leads to an event, there is not the slightest basis for preferring one link to the others. The actions of a man who is psycologically abnormal (irresponsible) are just as conditioned by a series of causes, i.e. inheritance, conditions of life, environment etc., as are the actions of a normal (responsible) man. It is interesting to note that punishment applied as a pedagogical measure (i.e. outside the legal idea of equivalence) is entirely unconnected with considerations of imputability, freedom of choice etc., and does not require these ideas. The expediency of punishment in pedagogy—we speak here of course of expediency in the most general sense, independent of the selection of forms, leniency, strictness of punishment etc.—is determined exclusively by the presence of the sufficiently developed ability to understand the connection between one's action and its unpleasant consequences, and the retention of this connection in one's mind. Even persons whom the criminal law does not hold responsible for their actions—children of a very young age, and the psychologically abnormal—are considered responsible in this sense, i.e. they are subject to influence in a definite direction.

Punishment proportionate to guilt chiefly represents the same form as revenge related to damage. Above all, it is characterized by the numerical, mathematical expression for "severity" of the sentence: the number of days, months etc., of deprivation of freedom, the amount of monetary fine, deprivation of various rights.

Deprivation of freedom—for a definite term previously indicated in the judgement of a court—is the specific form in which modern, that is, bourgeois capitalist criminal law, realizes the basis of equivalent retribution. This method is deeply, but unconsciously connected with the concept of the abstract man and of abstract human labour time. It is not accidental that this form of punishment grew strong and eventually seemed natural and expected, in the nineteenth century, i.e. when bourgeois society was fully developed and had consolidated all its particular features. Prisons and dungeons, of course, existed even in ancient times and in the Middle Ages, alongside other means of physical coercion. But at that time prisoners were usually confined until their death or until the payment of a ransom.

A necessary condition for the appearance of the notion that payment for a crime should be by a previously determined amount of abstract freedom, was that all concrete forms of social wealth had to be reduced to the simplest and most abstract form—to human labour time. Here we undoubtedly observe yet another case affirming the mutual protection of the various aspects of culture. Industrial capitalism, the Declaration of the Rights of Man and the Citizen, Ricardo's political economy, and the system of terms of incarceration in prison—these are phenomena of the same historical period.

Equivalence of punishment—in its crude and overtly material form as the causing of physical harm or the exacting of monetary compensation—specifically because of this crudeness preserves a simple meaning accessible to everyone. But it loses this meaning in its abstract form of the deprivation of freedom for a definite term, although we continue to speak of a measure of punishment *proportional* to the gravity of the act.

Therefore, it is natural for many criminal law theorists (primarily those who consider themselves the most advanced) to attempt to remove this element of equivalence because it has clearly become inconvenient, and to concentrate attention on the rational goals of punishment. The mistake of these progressive criminologists is that in criticizing so-called absolute theories of punishment, they suppose that they are confronted only by false views and confused thoughts which can be dissolved simply by theoretical criticism. In fact, the inconvenient form of equivalence does not derive from the confusion of individual criminologists, but from the material relationships of commodity production, and it is nurtured by them. The contradiction between the rational goal of the protection of society—or the re-education of the criminal—and the principle of the equivalence of punishment, exists not in books and theories but in life itself, in judicial practice, in the social structure itself. Similarly, the contradiction between the fact of the bond of social labour as such, and the inconvenient form of expression of this fact in the value of commodities, exists not in theory, and not in books, but in social practice itself.

Sufficient proof of this is found in various elements. If, in social life, punishment was considered as an *objective*, then the keenest interest would be aroused in the implementation of punishment and, above all, by its result. However, who would deny that the centre of gravity of criminal procedure—for the overwhelming majority—is the court room and the moment of pronouncing the verdict and sentence?

The interest which is shown towards enduring methods of influencing the criminal is utterly negligible in comparison with the interest which is aroused in the effective moment of pronouncing the verdict and sentence, and in the determination of the "measure of punishment". Questions of prison reform are a live issue only for a small group of specialists; broadly, the correspondence of the sentence to the gravity of the act occupies the centre of attention. If, according to common sentiment, the equivalence is properly determined by the court, then the matter will be concluded here, and the subsequent fate of the criminal is of no interest. "A study of the execution of punishment," complains Krohne, one of the leading specialists in this area, "is the sore point of the science of criminal law." In other words it is relatively neglected. "And moreover", he continues, "if you have better laws, better judges, and better sentences, and the civil servants carrying out these sentences are worthless, then you may freely throw laws into the rubbish bin and burn your sentences."[60] But the authority of the principle of retributive equivalence is not only discovered in the distribution of social interest. It appears no less clearly in judicial practice itself. In fact, what other bases are there for those sentences which Aschaffenburg cites in his book *Crimes and the Struggle against Them?* Here are just two examples of a long series: a recidivist, convicted 22 times for forgery, theft, extortion etc., was sentenced for the 23rd time to 24 days in prison for slandering an official. Another, who had in all spent 13 years in prison and the penitentiary (*Zuchthaus*), having been convicted 16 times for extortion, theft etc., was sentenced (the 17th time) for extortion to 4 months in prison.[61] In these instances one obviously does not discuss the protective or corrective function of punishment. Here the formal principle of equivalence triumphs: for equal guilt—an equal measure of punishment. And in fact what else could the judge do? He could not hope to correct a confirmed recidivist by 3 weeks' detention, but he also could not isolate the prisoner for life because of the mere slander of a civil servant. Nothing is left to him but to have the criminal pay in small change (a certain number of weeks of deprivation of freedom) for a minor crime. For the rest, bourgeois jurisprudence ensures that the transaction with the criminal is in accordance with all rules of the art, i.e. that each may be convinced, and may verify that the payment is justly set (public judicial proceedings), that the criminal may bargain freely (adversary process), and that in so doing he may use the services of an experienced judicial expert (admission of the defence) etc. Briefly, the state conducts its relationship to the criminal within the framework of a *bona fide* commercial transaction in which there are, ostensibly, guarantees of criminal procedure.

The criminal must know beforehand why he owes something and *what* is expected of him: *nullum crimen, nulla poene sine lege*. What does this mean? Does it require that each potential criminal be exactly informed of the methods of correction which will be applied to him? No, the matter is much cruder and simpler—he must know how much freedom he will forgo as a result of the judicial transaction. He must know beforehand those conditions under which payment will be demanded of him. Here lies the meaning of criminal codes and criminal procedure codes.

One must not imagine that in the beginning false theories of retribution held sway in criminal law, and then later the correct point of view of social defence triumphed. It is wrong to consider development as having taken place only on the level of ideas. In fact, both before and after the appearance of the sociological and anthropological trends in criminology, punitive policy included a social or, rather, a class element of defence. However, along with this it included, and still includes, elements which do not derive from this *technical* goal and therefore do not permit the punitive procedure itself to be expressed *wholly and with nothing remaining* as a rational, non-mystifying form of socio-technical rules. These elements—whose origins must be sought not in punitive policy itself but much deeper—give real meaning to the legal abstractions of crime and punishment, and ensure their full practical significance regardless of all the forces of theoretical criticism.

We remember Van Hamel's exclamation at the Hamburg congress of criminologists in 1905: the main obstacle for modern criminology are the three concepts "guilt, crime and punishment"; "when we free ourselves from them", he added, "all will be better." We may now reply that the forms of bourgeois consciousness will not be eliminated merely by ideological criticism, because they constitute a unity with those material relationships which they reflect. The transcendence of these relationships in practice—i.e. the revolutionary struggle of the proletariat and the realization of socialism—this is the only way to dispel those mirages which have become reality.

To proclaim that fault and guilt are prejudiced concepts in practice suffices for the transition to a punitive policy which would render them unnecessary. Until the time when the commodity form, and the derivative legal form, cease to place their imprint upon society, the essentially incoherent (from the non-judicial perspective) notion that the severity of each crime can be weighed on a scale and expressed in months or years of imprisonment, will continue to preserve its force and its real significance in judicial practice.

It is possible, of course, to refrain from expressing this notion in such a shockingly crude formulation. But this by no means signifies that therefore we are finally free from its influence in practice. What is the general part of every criminal code (including even ours) with its concepts of abetting, participation, contempt, preparation etc., if it is not a means to define guilt more exactly? What is the distinction between intent and negligence if not a distinction of a degree of guilt? What meaning has the concept of irresponsibility if the concept of guilt does not exist? Finally, why is the special part of the code needed if the matter is merely about measures of social (class) defence?

In fact the consistent execution of the principle of social defence would not require the fixing of individual *sets of elements of crime* (with which *measures of punishment* are largely linked and defined by statute or by the courts). It would require however, a clear description of *symptoms* characterizing a socially dangerous condition and the development of those *methods* which must necessarily be applied in each given case for social defence.

The matter is obviously not only that, as some persons think, a measure of social defence is connected in its application with subjective moments (form and degree of social danger), while punishment rests on an objective moment, i.e. the concrete set of elements of a crime established by the special part of the code. The importance lies in the character of this association. It is difficult to separate punishment from an objective basis, because it cannot discard the form of equivalence without losing its basic character. However, only the concrete structure of a crime provides something like a measurable amount, and accordingly something like an equivalent. One can make a man *pay* for an action, but it is senseless to make him pay for the fact that society has recognized him (i.e. the given subject) to be dangerous. Therefore, punishment presupposes an exactly fixed set of elements in a crime. A measure of social defence has no need for this. Payment by coercion is legal coercion directed towards a subject placed in the formal framework of a trial, a sentence and its execution. Coercion, as a measure of defence, is an act of pure expediency and as such may be regulated by technical rules. These rules may be more or less complex depending upon whether the purpose is the mechanical elimination of a dangerous member of society, or his correction; but in any event these rules reflect clearly and simply the objective which society has set itself. Conversely, this social objective appears in masked form in the legal forms determining punishment for certain crimes. A person subjected to coercion is placed in the position of a debtor paying a debt. This is reflected in the term "serving a sentence". A criminal who has served his sentence returns to his starting point, to an isolated social existence, to the "freedom" to undertake obligations and commit crimes.

Criminal law, like law in general, is a form of the relationships between egoistic and isolated subjects, bearing autonomous private interests as commodity owners. The concepts of crime and punishment—as is clear from the aforesaid—are the necessary definitions of the legal form. Liberation from them will only occur when the general withering away of the legal superstructure begins. And to the extent that in fact, and not merely in declarations, we begin to transcend these concepts and to do without them—this will be the best symptom of the fact that for us, finally, the narrow horizons of bourgeois law are disappearing.

Notes

Abbreviations

LCW	*V. I. Lenin: Collected Works* (1960–70), Foreign Languages Publishing House, Moscow, 45 volumes.
MESW	*K. Marx and F. Engels: Selected Works* (1970), Progress Publishers, Moscow, 3 volumes.
Sochinenii	*Vladimir Il'ich Lenin, Sobranie Sochinenii* (1920–1926), Moscow, 20 volumes in 26 books.

The complete footnotes to the *General Theory* have been translated in J. Hazard (ed.), *Soviet Legal Philosophy* (1951), Harvard University Press, Cambridge, translated by H. Babb, pp. 111–225 [eds.].

1. Of course these most general and simplest juridic concepts are the result of the logical treatment of the norms of positive law. They represent the latest and highest product of conscious creativity in comparison with the randomly formed legal relationships and the norms which express them.
2. One may agree with Karner [the pseudonym used by Karl Renner—*eds.*] that the science of law begins where jurisprudence ends. But it does not follow from this that the science of law must simply discard those basic abstractions which reflect the basic essence of the legal form.
3. Even Comrade Stuchka's *The Revolutionary Role of Law and State* (1921, Moscow), which deals with a series of problems of the general theory of law, does not treat these concepts systematically. His discussion accentuates the class content of the historical development of legal regulation in comparison with the logical and dialectical development of the form itself.
4. It should be noted that in discussing juridic concepts Marxist authors commonly and primarily refer to the concrete content of legal regula-

tion inherent in a specific period, i.e. that which people at a specific stage of development consider to be law. However, it is undoubtedly true that Marxist theory must study not only the material content of legal regulation in various historical periods, but that it must also provide a materialist interpretation of legal regulation *per se* as a definite historical form.

5. An example of how richness of historical exposition can co-exist with the most incomplete outline of the legal form is found in M. Pokrovsky, *Essays on the History of Russian Culture* (1923), Moscow, 2nd edition, vol. 1, p. 16.
6. Law is also defined as coercive norms issued by state authority in Bukharin's *Historical Materialism* . . . . All these definitions stress the connection between the concrete content of legal regulation and economics. At the same time, however, they attempt to exhaust the legal form by defining it as state-organized coercion. In essence, this goes no deeper than the crude empirical applications of the most pragmatic or dogmatic jurisprudence—whose defeat must constitute the task of Marxism.
7. "Political economy begins with *commodities*, begins from the moment when products are exchanged for one another—whether by individuals or by primitive communities." F. Engels, "Review of Marx's *Contribution to the Critique of Political Economy*" (1859), *MESW*, vol. 1, p. 514.
8. K. Marx, *Critique of the Gotha Programme* (1875), *MESW*, vol. 3, p. 19.
9. Lenin concludes in *State and Revolution*: "With respect to the distribution of products for *consumption*, bourgeois law of course inevitably presupposes a *bourgeois state*, because bourgeois law is nothing without a *coercive* apparatus capable of *enforcing* adherence to the norms of law. It follows that for a certain time bourgeois law is effective under communism, but that so also is the bourgeois state without the bourgeoisie!" V. I. Lenin, *State and Revolution* (1917), *LCW*, vol. 25, p. 471.
10. F. Lassalle, *The System of Acquired Rights* (1861), Leipzig.
11. See K. Marx, *Introduction to the Critique of Political Economy* (1857), in *The Grundrisse* (1973), translation and foreword by M. Nicolaus, Random House, New York, p. 100.
12. *ibid*. pp. 104–105.
13. *ibid*. p. 106.
14. *ibid*. p. 105.
15. K. Marx, *Capital* (1867), International Publishers, New York, 1967, vol. 1, p. 76.
16. M. Reisner, *The State* (1911), Moscow, 2nd edition, vol. 1, p. xxxv.
17. *ibid*.
18. See the review of Stuchka's *The Revolutionary Role of Law and State* (1921), by Professor Reisner, *Herald of the Socialist Academy*, no. 1, p. 176.
19. cf. V. V. Adoratsky, *On the State* (1923), Moscow, p. 41: "The tremendous influence of legal ideology on the entire system of thinking of law-abiding members of bourgeois society is explained by the

significant role of ideology in the life of this society . . . . A person living in bourgeois society is constantly regarded as a subject of rights and obligations. Every day he effects an endless number of legal actions involving the most diverse legal consequences. No society has such a need, therefore, of the idea of law (in its practical, everyday use), nor develops this idea in such detail, nor transforms it into such an essential instrument of daily exchange, as does bourgeois society."

20. K. Marx, *Capital* (1867), *op. cit.* vol. 1, p. 81.
21. G. Shershenevich, *The General Theory of Law* (1910), Moscow, p. 274.
22. The Russian language, incidentally, derives the designations "law in effect" and "law in force" from the same root. In German, the logical distinction is facilitated by the use of two very different verbs: *wirken* (in the sense of in effect, or being realized) and *gelten* (in the sense of being significant, i.e. logically related to a more general normative proposition).
23. The point of view expressed here by no means signifies a denial of class will as a factor of development, an abjugation of planned interference in the course of social development, "economism", fatalism and other terrible things. A revolutionary political action may accomplish a great deal; it can realize for tomorrow that which does not exist today, but it can not cause that which did not in fact exist in the past. On the other hand, if we affirm that the intention to construct a building—and even the plan of the building—is still not the actual building, then it does not follow from this that neither the intention nor the plan are essential for the construction of the building. But when the matter has gone no further than the plan we cannot affirm that the building has been constructed.
24. However, it is necessary to declare that social-regulatory activity can operate without previously fixed norms. The fact of so-called judicial lawmaking convinces us of this. Its significance is particularly clear in those periods when the centralized enactment of laws was generally unknown. For the ancient German judges, therefore, the concept of a norm given externally was entirely alien. Collections of rules of every type were, for the *Schöffengericht*, not binding laws, but were a heuristic device by which they formed their own opinion. See J. Stintzing, *Geschichte der Deutschen Rechtswissenschaft* (1880), vol. I, p. 39.
25. K. Marx and F. Engels, *The Holy Family, or a Critique of Critical Criticism* (1844), in *Marx and Engels Collected Works* (1975), Progress Publishers, Moscow, vol. 4, pp. 120–121.
26. In his commentary on the Civil Code of the RSFSR, Goikhbarg stresses that advanced bougeois jurists still refuse to consider private property as arbitrary subjective law, but that they see it both as rights accruing to the individual and as positive obligations with respect to the whole. In particular, Goikhbarg relies upon Duguit. Duguit affirms that an owner of capital must be defended by the law only because and to the extent that he fulfils a socially useful function in providing a correct application for his capital. . . .

Duguit's statement—that an owner will be protected only when he fulfils a social obligation—is meaningless in such a general form. For the bourgeois state it is hypocritical; for the proletarian state it is a concealment of the facts. For if the proletarian state could directly assign to each owner his social function, it would have done so, taking from the owner the right to dispose of his property. And once it cannot do this *economically*, this means it is compelled to protect private interests as such, and that it can only set certain quantitative limits to them. It would be illusory to affirm that every X who has accumulated a certain quantity of money is protected by our laws and courts simply because he provided, or will provide, a socially useful application for money accumulated. But Comrade Goikhbarg forgets about capitalist property in this, its most abstract (i.e. monetary) form, and he argues as if capital only exists in the concrete material form of productive capital. The anti-social aspects of private property may be paralysed only *de facto*, i.e. by the development of a socialist planned economy at the expense of the market. But no formula, even though derived from the most advanced Western jurists, can transform all transactions concluded on the basis of our Civil Code into socially useful ones, and every owner into a person fulfilling social functions. Such a verbal transcendence of the private economy and private law will only obscure the conditions for their real transcendence.

27. K. Marx, *Capital* (1867), *op. cit.* vol. 1, p. 84.
28. Man is a commodity (i.e. a slave) only when he adopts the role of a distributor of commodities—of objects—and when in becoming a fellow participant in exchange he attains the effective status of a subject. On the rights of slaves to conduct transactions under Roman law, see I. A. Pokrovsky, *History of Roman Law* (1915), Petrograd, vol. 2, p. 294. Conversely, when a free man (i.e. a proletarian) seeks a market for the sale of his labour power in modern society, he is treated as an object and falls under the law on emigration with the same prohibitions, quotas etc., as other commodities transported across the state border.
29. K. Marx, *Capital* (1867), *op. cit.* vol. 1, p. 84.
30. J. Fichte, *Rechtslehre* (1812), Leipzig, p. 10.
31. The development of the law of war is nothing other than the gradual consolidation of the principle of the inviolability of bourgeois property. Until the era of the French Revolution the population was robbed without hindrance or restriction, both by its own soldiers and by the enemy. Benjamin Franklin first proclaimed (1785) as a political principle that in future wars "peasants, craftsmen and merchants must peacefully continue their occupations under the protection of both warring parties". Rousseau, in his *Social Contract*, asserts the rule that war is conducted between states but not between people. The legislation of Covenant strictly punished thefts by, soldiers both in their own and in an enemy's country. Only at the Hague, in 1899, were the principles of the French Revolution elevated to the rank of international

law. Moreover, justice requires that it be noted that Napoleon, in declaring a continental blockade, felt a certain embarrassment and considered it necessary, in his address to the Senate, to justify this measure "affecting the interests of private people because of a dispute between states" and "recalling the barbarity of olden times"; in the last world war the bourgeois states, without any embarrassment, violated the property rights of the citizens of the warring countries.

32. H. Dernburg, *Pandekten* (1906), Moscow, vol. 1, p. 39.
33. In Germany this occurred only when Roman law was received, which is proved, *inter alia*, by the absence of a German word for the expression of the concepts of "person" (*persona*) and "subject of rights". See O. Gierke, *Geschichte des deutschen Körperschaftsbegriffs* (1873), Berlin, p. 30.
34. *ibid.* p. 35.
35. *ibid.* p. 34.
36. M. Hauriou, *Principes du droit public* (1910), Paris, p. 286.
37. *ibid.* p. 287.
38. For example, Proudhon declares: "I want a contract and no laws. For me to be free we must reconstruct the whole social order on the basis of mutual contract." However, he adds later: "The norms by which the contract must be fulfilled will not depend exclusively on justice, but also on the common will of people who participate in life together, a will which must compel the fulfilment of the contract even with coercion." See P. J. Proudhon, *Idées générales de la Révolution* (1851), Paris, X, pp. 138, 293.
39. K. Renner, *The Institutions of Private Law and their Social Functions* (1949), Routledge and Kegan Paul, London, pp. 266–267.
40. *ibid.* p. 268.
41. The defenders of private property therefore eagerly appeal to this elementary relationship because they know that its ideological power exceeds many times its economic significance for modern society.
42. K. Renner (1949), *op. cit.* p. 252.
43. Property under simple commodity production, which Karner contrasts with the capitalist form of property, is just as pure an abstraction as simple commodity production itself. The transformation of even part of the products into commodities, and the appearance of money, constitute a sufficient condition for the appearance of usurer's capital—in Marx's expression, that "antediluvian form of capital"—which, together with its twin (mercantile capital), "long precedes the capitalist mode of production and can be observed in various socio-economic formations". See K. Marx, *Capital* (1867), *op. cit.* vol. 3, *op. cit.*
44. The intensification of the transcendence of the legal form would be reduced to the gradual transition from the equivalent method of distribution—definite quantities of products for definite quantities of labour—to the realization of the formula of developed communism: "from each according to his abilities, to each according to his needs".

45. K. Marx, "On the Jewish Question" (1843), in *Karl Marx: Early Writings* (1975), introduced by L. Colletti, Penguin and New Left Review, p. 234.
46. F. Engels, *The Origin of the Family, Private Property and the State* (1884), MESW, vol. 3, p. 327.
47. In our time of intensified revolutionary struggle we can observe how the official apparatus of the bourgeois state recedes into the background in comparison with the "voluntary guards" of the fascists and their ilk. This once more shows that when social equilibrium is disrupted it then "seeks salvation", not by creation of "an authority standing above classes", but by the maximum pressure of the forces of the struggling classes.
48. I. Podvolotsky, *The Marxist Theory of Law* (1923), Moscow, p. 33.
49. K. Marx, *Capital* (1867), *op. cit.* vol. 3, p. 881.
50. The English bourgeoisie, which earlier than others won for itself the domination of world markets, and which felt invulnerable because of its insular position, could go further than others in the practice of the *Rechtsstaat.* The most consistent actions based on law in the mutual relationships between authority and the isolated subject, and the most effective guarantee that the bearers of authority did not transgress their role as the personification of an objective norm, was the subordination of state agencies to the jurisdiction of an independent (not of the bourgeoisie, of course) court. The Anglo-Saxon system is, in its own way, the apotheosis of bourgeois democracy. But, so to speak, if worse comes to worse in other historical conditions, the bourgeoisie will make peace with a system which could be baptised as a system of "separation of property from the state", or a system of Caesarism. In this case the ruling clique, by its unlimited despotic arbitrariness (having two directions: internal, against the proletariat, and external, expressed in an imperialist policy), creates the background for the "free self-determination of the individual" in civil exchange.
51. I. Kant, *Kritik der practischen Vernunft* (1914), German edition, p. 96.
52. It goes without saying that in a society torn by class struggle, classless ethics may exist only in the imagination, but by no means in practice. A worker, having decided to take part in a strike—despite those deprivations with which this participation is associated for him—may formulate this decision as a moral duty to subordinate his personal interests to the general interests. But it is clear that this concept of general interests may not also include the interests of the capitalist *against* whom the struggle is waged.
53. H. Maine, *Ancient Law* (1873), Russian edition translated by N. Belozersky, p. 288.
54. cf. M. Kovalevsky, *Modern Custom and Ancient Law* (1886), Petersburg and Moscow, pp. 37–38.
55. E. Ferri, *Criminal Sociology* (1900), Russian edition translated and with a preface by Dril', vol. 2, p. 37.

56. R. Jhering, *The Spirit of Roman Law* (1875), Russian edition, vol. 1, p. 118.
57. H. Maine, *Ancient Law* (1873), *op. cit.* p. 269.
58. H. Spencer, *Principles of Sociology* (1883), Russian edition, p. 659.
59. Thus, criminal law is a constituent part of the legal superstructure to the extent that it embodies one of the varieties of that basic form to which modern society is subordinated: the form of equivalent exchange with all the consequences which derive from it. The realization of this relationship in criminal law is one of the aspects of the *Rechtsstaat* as an ideal form of relationship between independent and equal commodity producers who meet in the market. But since social relationships are not limited to the abstract relationships between abstract commodity owners, the criminal court is therefore not only the embodiment of the abstract legal form, but it is also a weapon of direct class struggle. The sharper and more intense this struggle, the more difficult it is for a class to realize its domination through the legal form. In this case, the "impartial" court—with its guarantees—is replaced by an organization of direct class violence, and its actions are guided only by considerations of political expediency.
60. Quoted from G. Aschaffenburg, *Das Verbrechen und seine Bekämpfung* (1905), Heidelberg, p. 200.
61. *ibid.* pp. 205–206.

[6]

SEC. 2: THE FOUNDATIONS OF THE MARXIST-LENINIST THEORY OF STATE AND LAW

The nature of the state is the most important question in the science of public law. The theory of the state is the basis not only of the science of state law but also of law in general, inasmuch as a scientific understanding of law is impossible without a correct understanding of the state. Law and state cannot be studied separately and apart from each other. Law draws its force, and obtains its content, from the state.

"Law is nothing without a mechanism capable of *compelling* the observance of legal norms." [1]

This fundamental precept of the Marxist-Leninist theory defines the relationship between law and state. We shall later discuss this precept in greater detail when we describe in their entirety the bases of the Marxist-Leninist theory of law and state.

This theory illustrates to the last detail all the falseness and pseudoscience of the various bourgeois "theories" of the state, which pervert the nature of the state to gratify the exploiters in order to perpetuate capitalist exploitation.

It reveals the artificiality and the unscientific character of bourgeois theories of law. Those theories portray their subject perversely and falsely.

[1] Lenin (Russian ed.), Vol. XXI, p. 438.

They disguise the class-exploiting character of bourgeois law. By phrases about "the general welfare" and "social" and "popular" interests, they strive to conceal the fact that bourgeois law, that subtle and poisoned instrument which defends the interests of the exploiters, is oppressive and hostile to the people.

Opposed to bourgeois theories of law and state, which are utterly arbitrary and developed in complete abstraction with no truly scientific content, stands the authentic Marxist-Leninist theory—the only scientific theory—of law and the state. Starting from its general methodology of dialectic materialism, the Marxist-Leninist theory presents a strictly scientific explanation of the origin and development of law and state.

Marx wrote as early as 1844:

> My investigations have brought me to the conclusion that neither legal relationships, nor the forms of state, can be understood by themselves alone or by the so-called universal development of the human soul. On the contrary, they have their roots in the material conditions of life, the totality whereof Hegel (following the example of the English and the French in the eighteenth century) united under the name "civil society." The anatomy of civil society, however, must be sought in political economy, the study of which I began in Paris and continued in Brussels (where I moved following M. Guizot's order for my expulsion from Paris). The general conclusion to which I had come (and which served thereafter as the guiding thread in all my further investigations) may be briefly formulated thus: In the social production of their lives people enter into definite and necessary relationships which are independent of their will—production relationships, which correspond to the definite degree to which their material productive powers have developed. The totality of these production relationships constitutes the economic structure of society, the real basis upon which is built the juridical and political superstructure and to which definite forms of social consciousness correspond. The means of production of material life condition the social, political and spiritual processes of life in general.[2]

Here is a complete understanding of the fundamental laws of motion governing social development. Those laws similarly disclose the secret of the origin and the nature of law and state; and this revelation is one of the most important and original characteristics of Marxist-Leninist theory—its greatest strength.

Marxism-Leninism is forceful and vital in that in its practical activity it rests "specifically on the needs of society's material life to develop and is never separated from society's real life." [3]

Only by an analysis of the material conditions of human society can one

[2] Marx and Engels (Russian ed.), Vol. XII, Pt. 1, p. 6.

[3] *History of the All-Union Communist Party (of Bolsheviks): A Short Course* (Russian ed., 1938), p. 111.

understand the true nature of the law and state produced by "civil society," that is, by the totality of production relationships of society and of the social-economic relationships conditioned by it.

Criticizing Hegel's philosophy of law, with its idealistic interpretation of the relationship between society and the state, Marx wrote:

> The family and civil society turn *themselves* into the state. They are the moving element. But according to Hegel they are *created by* an actual idea. Their unification into the state is not the result of their own development but is predetermined by the development of the idea. Family and civil society are the spheres wherein this idea is finite. Their existence is conditioned by another's spirit, not by their own spirit. They are not self-defining but are definitions introduced by a third element. For this reason they are also defined as "finite," as the particular *finiteness* of the "actual idea." The object of their existence is not this existence itself. The idea separates these premises from itself so as, "passing through their ideal nature, to be for itself an eternal, actual spirit;" that is to say, a political sovereign cannot exist without the natural basis of family and the artificial basis of civil society. These are conditions indispensable to the state. But in Hegel the condition is itself conditioned, that which defines is itself defined, and that which produces is the product of its product.[4]

Having disposed of Hegel's views of state and law, and disclosing their complete indefensibility, Marx and Engels laid firm and accurate foundations for a scientific world outlook which explains all the most complicated questions of sociology, history, and law. We know from Engels how Marx arrived at this new world outlook. He wrote:

> Criticism of the debates in the Rhineland Landtag compelled Marx to the study of questions of material interests. He arrived at original views anticipated neither by jurisprudence nor by philosophy. Starting from Hegel's legal philosophy, Marx came to the conclusion that not the state (portrayed by Hegel as the "crown of the whole building") but rather civil society (which Hegel so disdained) was the sphere in which the key to an understanding of the process of man's historical development must be sought.[5]

What are the characteristics of that "civil society" which Hegel so disdained? According to Marx, in his *Holy Family:*

> *Natural necessity, qualities of the nature of man* (however estranged they may seem), *interest*—these are what bind the members of civil society to each other. The *real* bond between them is not *political* life but *civil* life. Moreover, it is not the *state* which unites the *atoms* of civil society, but precisely the fact that they are *atoms* (only as it seems in the *heaven* of their imagination, whereas in *reality* they are beings differing most markedly from atoms) and the fact that they

[4] Marx and Engels (Russian ed.), Vol. I, p. 539.
[5] *Ibid.*, Vol. XIII, Pt. 1, p. 317.

are not *divine egoists* but *egoistic people*. In our time it is sheer *political prejudice* to continue to imagine that the state unites civil life. The reverse is the fact: civil life unites the state.[6]

Studying the history of the development of human society, Marx and Engels came to conclusions which decisively changed and correctly evaluated all the views previously prevalent in science. This was particularly true of jurisprudence. Jurisprudence had floundered about, utterly impotent in a vicious circle of contradictions, which had actively influenced all bourgeois theories of law—even those of such authoritative and powerful thinkers of the bourgeois world as Kant and Hegel.

Marxism revealed the indefensibility of bourgeois scientific methodology, which was completely incapable of disclosing and formulating the basic laws of social development. Marxism revealed the pseudoscientific character of divers trends in the field of legal science. It put an end, once and for all, to the conceptions of formal jurisprudence and abstract idealism which had so completely muddled the idea of law and the state.

Marxism explained all the hitherto inexplicable questions and problems, and brought into a strictly scientific and logical system the solution to these questions, which were thus raised to the level of truly scientific theory. Marx and Engels showed that the state was the result of a definite plane of development of society's productive forces, that the state was founded on the ruins of the tribal regime, and that it experienced in its turn a series of cataclysms associated with the division of labor, the rise of classes, the appearance of private property in land, money, mortgages, and so forth.[7]

[6] *Ibid.*, Vol. III, p. 149.

[7] Engels, *The Origin of Family, Private Property and the State.* Concerning the social revolution in the tribal regime, Engels wrote: "The tribal regime was helpless against new elements which developed independently. It was postulated upon members of one *gens* or tribe living together in a single territory settled exclusively by them. This ceased long ago. Everywhere races and tribes were intermingled. Everywhere slaves, clients (*Schutzverwandte*), and foreigners lived among free citizens. Localized settlement came only at the end of the intermediate stage of barbarism and was occasionally destroyed by the mobility and change of abode consequent upon trade activity, occupational change, and the alienation of property in land. Members of tribal organizations could no longer meet to solve their common affairs—although there was perfunctory observance as to matters of small moment, such as religious festivals. Side by side with those demands and interests for whose disposition tribal organizations were summoned and adapted, there came (as a result of the revolution in conditions of production activity and the consequent changes in the social structure) new demands and interests not merely alien, but in every respect opposed, to the ancient tribal order. The interests of artisan groups which sprang up with the division of labor, and special demands of city as opposed to village, demanded new organs. And since each of these groups included people of different races, associations and tribes, and even foreigners, such organs had to come into being outside the tribal organization—side by side with it, and at the same time contrary to it. In every tribal organization in turn this conflict of interest found expression. It was sharpest where—within one and the same *gens* and one and the same tribe—rich and poor, usurers and debtors were united. There was the further addition of a mass of new population alien to the tribal groups, and capable (as in Rome) of becom-

The tribal form of society knew no antitheses within itself. But as Engels has said:

> Here a society arose, doomed by all its economic conditions of life to split into free and slave, exploiting wealth and exploited poverty, and not only unable to reconcile these contrasts but bound to make them constantly sharper. Such a society could exist only in constant, open struggle between these classes, or under the domination of a third power which (supposedly standing above the contesting classes) puts down their open conflicts and (which is most important) permits class struggle only in the economic field, in its so-called legal form. The tribal form of society became obsolete. It was destroyed by the division of labor and the consequent division of society into classes. Its place was taken by the state.[8]

The whole course of the development of the state—as a force brought about by the very development of society and in no sense attached thereto from without—is here shown in its entirety and with marvelous clarity.

> The state is the product of society in a certain stage of development. It is an acknowledgment that this society is inextricably involved in conflict with itself; that it has split into irreconcilable contradictions and is impotent to rid itself of those contradictions. And force became necessary in order that these contradictions, these classes with conflicting economic interests, might not devour each other and society in a fruitless struggle—force standing manifestly above society, force which would moderate the conflict, hold it within the bounds of "order." And this force, issuing out of society, but putting itself above society and ever more and more alienating itself from society, is the state.[9]

In the state, subjects settle throughout the territorial divisions, the state's social authority is established, exacting taxes, and consisting "not only of an armed population but also of material accessories, prisons and every sort of compulsory institution unknown to tribal society." [10] This authority is negligible where class contradictions are still not obvious (or not so obvious). Where they are sufficiently sharp and serious, however, the significance of authority and the part that it plays become stronger, and its influence grows in proportion. Authority here subordinates all persons to its influence. Its legal base is in statutes, by virtue of which those exercising the authority become particularly sacred and inviolable. Supreme power is here embodied

ing a force in the land. Moreover, this new population was too numerous to be included gradually in *gentes* and tribes related by blood. Opposed to this mass stood tribal groups—closed and privileged corporations. The natural democracy of primordial times became a hateful aristocracy. Finally, the tribal regime grew out of—and was only adapted to—a society which had known no antithesis within itself. It had no means of constraint other than social opinion." Marx and Engels (Russian ed.), Vol. XVI, pp. 143–144.

[8] Marx and Engels (Russian ed.), Vol. XVI, Pt. 1, p. 144.

[9] *Ibid.*, p. 145.

[10] *Ibid.*, p. 146.

in the coercive force of this authority which rests on the might of the class whose interest it serves.

The whole history of mankind proves that the state had its origin in class contradictions and conflicts created by the development of tribal society, in the need to "curb class opposition." It was precisely this fact that made the state the organ of the authority of the strongest—economically dominant—class which, with the support of the state, thus becomes the most powerful class politically as well. This in turn provides it with new means to crush and to exploit the oppressed class.

Such is the exploiter state of every sort—the ancient state, preeminently a slaveholders' state to crush the slaves and keep them in check; the feudal state, the organ of nobles and landholders to hold the peasant serfs in check; and the bourgeois state of our own time, the instrument whereby capital exploits hired labor.[11] "The state is an organization of the class of 'haves' to defend itself from the class of the 'have-nots.'"[12] "Political power, in the exact sense of the words, is organized force of one class to repress another."[13]

Marxism-Leninism gives a scientific explanation of the rise and development of the state, indicating its beginning and its end.

> The state did not always exist. There were societies which got along without a state and without any conception of state or state authority. At a certain stage of economic development, necessarily connected with the split of society into classes, and by reason thereof, the state became a necessity. We are now fast approaching the stage in the development of production where the existence of these classes has not merely ceased to be a necessity but has become a direct impediment to production. The future disappearance of classes is just as inevitable as was their rise. With their disappearance, the state will inevitably disappear as well. Society, organizing production in a new way, on the basis of the free and equal association of producers, will relegate the whole state machine to what will then be its proper place—a museum of antiquities, with the distaff and bronze axe.[14]

Bourgeois political scientists strive, each in his own fashion, to prove that the state existed from the beginning. They assert that it stands above life and history, as it were—an eternal category of some sort. This assertion is utterly arbitrary, however. There was a period when there was no state—the time when there were no classes in society and therefore no division of it into exploiters and exploited.

Lenin says in his lecture "On the State":

> Before the first form of man's exploitation by man, the first form of division

[11] *Ibid.*, p. 147.
[12] *Ibid.*
[13] Marx and Engels, *Communist Manifesto* (Russian ed., 1938), p. 52.
[14] *Ibid.*, Vol. XVI, p. 149.

into classes—slave-owners and slaves—there was the patriarchal (sometimes called the "clan") family ("clan" in the sense of "generation" or "gens" when people lived by races, by generations). Traces of these primordial times remained sufficiently well defined in the way of life of many primordial peoples. Take at random any work on primeval culture, and you always come up against more or less definite descriptions, indications, and reminiscences of how there was a time more or less like the primeval communism when there was no division of society into slave-owners and slaves. Then there was no state, no special apparatus, for the systematic application of violence and for subjecting people to it. Such apparatus is called the state.[15]

The state was always, and still is, an apparatus of constraint—of violence—with whose aid the dominant classes ensured the obedience of their "subjects." "The state is a machine to sustain the domination of one class over another." [16]

Under capitalism, as under feudalism and in ancient society, the state protects private property as the basis of exploitation and the interests of those who as exploiters hold private property. It serves to preserve and confirm the class interests of exploiters, dominant in that society. This is the part it plays, irrespective of forms of political organization.

The form of state domination may vary: capital manifests its force in one way where there is one form of domination and in another way where there is a different form. Power remains essentially in the hands of capital, however, whether a right is based on some qualification or otherwise, and whether or not the state is a democratic republic. Actually, the more democratic it is, the more crude and cynical is this domination by capitalism.[17]

Lenin pointed to the United States of America to illustrate this utterly cynical domination by capital:

Nowhere else is the power of capital—of a handful of millionaires—over all society manifested so crudely, with such open venality, as in America. Once capital exists, it dominates all society. Nor does any democratic republic, nor any right to vote, change the essence of the matter.[18]

Of course, the fact that the power of capital is dominant in modern bourgeois states in divers political forms does not exclude the necessity that the relation of the proletariat vary as does the form of bourgeois political domination.

Bourgeois-democratic republics and the regime of parliamentary representation, broader suffrage and more limited suffrage, fascist regime or bour-

[15] Lenin (Russian ed.), Vol. XXIV, p. 365.
[16] *Ibid.*, p. 369.
[17] *Ibid.*, p. 375.
[18] *Ibid.*

geois-democratic regime—these are not matters of indifference to the proletariat, which must differentiate in building its policy with reference to bourgeois states.

Under capitalism the proletariat is extremely interested in bourgeois-democratic "freedoms," and "civil rights," which ease the process of organizing its ranks and guiding its allies. "Without parliamentarianism, without the elective right, this development of the working class would be impossible." [19] The proletariat is interested in the movement of bourgeois society forward, not backward. Fascism drags this society backward from bourgeois democracy to the feudal state of lawlessness and to medievalism, perpetuating the slavery of the toiling class and dooming it to extinction and to eternal bondage.

The interests of the working class and of all toilers thus demand a decisive battle with the "totalitarian" state of fascism, and with fascism in its entirety. This does not derogate, however, from the significance of characterizing *every type* of bourgeois state—even the most "democratic"—as a machine to crush and to repress the toilers, as a bludgeon in the hands of the exploiters as against the exploited.

Marxism-Leninism rendered an enormous scientific service in defining and explaining scientifically the social nature of the state as an instrument of the socially dominant class, thus putting an end to the clerical-bourgeois notion of the state, and to the fiction that by nature it is superior to class and expresses and preserves the interests and the culture of all mankind alike.

> The machinery called the state, before which people pause in superstitious reverence, giving credence to old tales to the effect that it expresses the will of all the people—this machinery the proletariat casts out with the words: "This is a bourgeois lie!" [20]

Marxism-Leninism thus draws a sharp line between the bourgeois and the proletarian viewpoint of the state—between bourgeois and proletarian theories concerning the state—and finally discloses as myth the proposition that the state is neutral and is above all classes.

Despite the idealistic and mechanistic notion concerning the state held by bourgeois and pseudo-Marxian politicians and political scientists, Marxism-Leninism showed conclusively the historical development of the state as emerging and disappearing at a certain stage of economic development.

Marxism plucked from the state the flowers of idealistic romanticism and showed its true nature as the instrument of the dominant classes, as a means of suppressing and enslaving the laboring masses—where exploiters are dominant; as the means and instrument of emancipation from suppression,

[19] *Ibid.*

[20] *Ibid.*, p. 377.

beggary, and enslavement by the exploiters—where the toilers are dominant.

The Marxist-Leninist doctrine of the state is not limited solely to an investigation of the nature of the origin and disappearance of the state, of its nature and characteristics. It also exhaustively elaborates and illuminates a series of other and most important questions connected with the state on the one hand, and problems and interests of the proletarian battle for emancipation on the other. Typical of such questions are those concerning the state of the period of transition from capitalism to communism, concerning the proletarian state as a state form of proletarian dictatorship, concerning the state and democracy in general, concerning the Soviet state and socialist democracy in particular, concerning the forms and methods of reinforcing the proletarian state, concerning communism and the state, and, finally, concerning the state's disappearance or "withering away" in the highest phase of communism, complete and fully developed.

Marxism-Leninism gives a clear definition (the only scientific definition) of the essence of law. It teaches that legal relationships (and, consequently, law itself) are rooted in the material conditions of life, and that law is merely the will of the dominant class, elevated into a statute. It starts from the proposition that political, legal, philosophical, religious, and literary development is defined by—and is a superstructure over—economics.

Law is one of the superstructures above the totality of production relationships forming society's economic structure.

Marx wrote in a letter to Annenkov:

> Take a definite stage of development of production, exchange and consumption and you get a definite social order, a definite organization of the family, of social orders, and of classes—in a word, a definite civil society. Take a definite civil society and you get definite political relationships, the official expression of civil society.[21]

Elsewhere (in *The German Ideology*) Marx says:

> If, like Hobbes and others, we admit that force is the basis of law, then law, statutes, and so forth are merely a symptom, an expression of *other* relationships on which the authority of the state rests. In the material life of individuals (by no means dependent simply on their "will"), in their mode of production and the form of their community (these mutually condition each other), is to be found the real basis of the state, and this continues to be so (absolutely independently of the "*will*" of the individuals) in all states wherein division of labor and private property are still necessary. These actual relationships are in no way created by the authority of the state. On the contrary, they are themselves the force which creates state authority. Aside from the fact that the individuals domi-

[21] Marx, *Selected Works* (Russian ed., 1934), Vol. I, pp. 286–287.

nant in these relationships must constitute their force in the form of the *state*, they must give their will (conditioned by the definite relationships given) universal expression in the form of the state's will, in the form of a statute—an expression whose content is always given by the relationships of this class, as is proved particularly clearly by private (that is, civil) law and criminal law.[22]

Marx says further that a statute is "the expression of this will." But the existence of neither statute nor state depends upon this will.

In his *Critique of Hegel's Philosophy of State Law*, Marx brilliantly analyzes Hegel's understanding of law and reveals the indefensibility of Hegel's idealism.[23]

With extraordinary profundity, Marx reveals (in *The German Ideology*) the indefensibility of the idealistic notion that law and the state are generated by the "will" of the people. Here we read these notable words:

> So long as productive forces are still insufficiently developed to make competition superfluous, and so long as competition would accordingly be produced thereby again and again—the hitherto subordinate classes would be wishing for the impossible if they had the "will" to abolish competition, and with it state and law.[24]

Law and legislation—and crime also—are generated by the condition of production forces and not arbitrarily.

> The origin of crime—the struggle of the isolated individual against dominant relationships—like the origin of law, is not purely arbitrary. On the contrary, crime is rooted in the same conditions as is the governing power existing at the time.[25]

Marx satirizes the "visionaries" who see in law and legislation the dominance of some "independent," "general" will, and who

> can perceive in crime a simple violation of law and legislation. In reality the state does not owe its existence to any dominant will, but on the contrary, growing out of the material way of life of individuals it has likewise the form of the dominant will. If that will loses its dominance, this means that not only the will, but also the material being and life of the individuals, have changed, and for this reason alone their will is changed also.[26]

State and law emerge from the material form of life of people and have only the form of the dominant will. In other words, they represent an expression of that will. Marx further unmasks the specific illusion of jurists and politicians who imagine, on the contrary, that legislation depends on

[22] Marx and Engels (Russian ed.), Vol. IV, p. 311.
[23] *Ibid.*, Vol. I, pp. 535–649.
[24] *Ibid.*, Vol. IV, p. 311.
[25] *Ibid.*, p. 312.
[26] *Ibid.*

the whim of people. Philosophers, says Marx, could conceive of a peculiar development and dominance of pure thought, by reason of which "political and civil history is ideologically dissolved in the history of the dominance of successive statutes."

In the history of the development of the courts Marx points out the close association between juridical relationships and the development of production forces and production relationships.

> How close is the connection between juridical relationships and the development of these material forces arising out of the division of labor, is evident from the example of the historical development of the power of the courts and from complaints of feudal seigneurs against the development of the law (e.g. Monteille, fifteenth century). It was precisely in the transitional epoch between the dominance of the aristocracy and the dominance of the bourgeoisie, when the interests of both were clashing, when trade relationships between European races were growing and international relationships began accordingly to take on a *bourgeois* character, that the power of the courts began to increase. It attains the highest point under the dominance of the bourgeoisie, when this broadly developed division of labor becomes absolutely necessary. What those in bondage to the division of labor, the judges, or—most particularly—the professors of law, conceive therein is a matter of the utmost indifference.[27]

From the foregoing it is clear that Marx never confused juridical relationships either with the "material forces" arising out of the division of labor or with production relationships.

In *The German Ideology* he again emphasizes that law depends on, and is generated by, production relationships. He says in so many words: "Production relationships of individuals must likewise be expressed as legal and political relationships." [28]

Notwithstanding the extraordinary clarity of Marx's exposition of this question, we have several miscellaneous theories professing to be Marxism, yet representing a crude perversion thereof. Such anti-Marxist theories include that of Stuchka, who defined law as a system (or order) of social relationships and thus reduced it to economics. In his article, "Notes on the Class Theory of Law," he asserted that "Marx speaks of relationships of production" [29] or, "in juridical terms, relationships of property," [30] and claimed that the juridical and legal relationships are also production relationships. He either used an incorrect translation of the passage from the preface to Marx's *Critique of Political Economy*, however, or himself translated it incorrectly from the German. The expression of Marx which he translated "or, in juridical terms," should be translated, "or—which appears to be merely a juridical expression thereof." The difference is

[27] *Ibid.*, p. 326.
[28] *Ibid.*, p. 348.
[29] Marx, *Zur Kritik der politischen Oekonomie* (Russian ed., 1934), p. 5.
[30] *Sovetskoye Pravo* (*Soviet Law*) (1922), No. 3, p. 10.

obvious and eliminates any possibility of interpreting the famous instructions of Marx and Engels to mean that legal relationships are also, as it were, productive relationships, or a system of productive relationships. Confused in his analysis thereof, however, Stuchka tried to put the responsibility for his own confusion off upon Marx himself who had been brought up, as it were, on Roman law and on ideas of law for thirty years and was familiar with the terminology of Roman law. Stuchka went so far as to assume as an obvious matter that "now" Marx would speak another language. Complete confusion in defining the idea of law prevails also in bourgeois juridical science.

Because its representatives are not objective, and because of their class interest, bourgeois legal science is in no position to afford a correct and genuinely scientific explanation of the question. Furthermore, it is characteristic that, notwithstanding a great many utterly dissimilar and mutually exclusive theories, the bourgeois science of state law discloses with extraordinary clarity the ideological unity therein expressed. While each of the basic schools of bourgeois law refutes the other and attributes really scientific significance to itself alone, in reality all of them are unanimous in their obdurate yearning to veil the true essence of the bourgeois state as an instrument of class domination by a minority, to suppress and crush the people.

The contradictions distorting the science of bourgeois state law attest to the extraordinary weakness of the scientific propositions from which it starts, the fallibility of the fundamental sources and of the very bases of the scientific methodology of these schools.[31] Let us follow this into the ideas of individual representatives of bourgeois legal science. George Jellinek (1851–1911) was one of the most eminent of these representatives in the nineteenth century. Starting from his methodological ideas of principle, he deduces the very basis of the state, and knowledge of its purpose, from the general welfare. He defines the state as the expression of the inner unity of the nation. He speaks of the state as governed by the general will.

We have agreed that the tasks of the state are to preserve itself, to ensure the safety and development of its might, to organize and protect the law, and to cooperate with cultural interests. The guiding idea in this definition of purposes is the knowledge that *planned organization of safeguarding solidary national interests* (in so far as they require central guidance and can be satisfied by external means) can originate only in the most powerful of social factors, which is the state.[32]

[31] Even representatives of bourgeois legal science are forced to admit this. The "contemporary science of public law actually appears unstable in its foundations and in need of radical revision" according to Novgorodtsev in his preface to the Russian translation of Duguit, *Constitutional Law; A General Theory of the State*.

[32] George Jellinek, *A General Theory of the State* (St. Petersburg, 1908), pp. 170, 191–192. (Italics supplied by the compilers.)

The task of the state, therefore, according to Jellinek, is to be "guardian of the solidary national interests." (By "solidary national interests" he means the individual and national interests of mankind in general.) So he concludes that the state is

the dominant union of the people endowed with legal personality, satisfying (by means of planned and centralizing activity, operating with the aid of external means) the individual, national and solidary interests of mankind in general, in the direction of the progressive development of society.

This definition of state cannot withstand criticism.

Of course the bourgeois state, of which Jellinek is speaking, guarantees certain interests. But where is the proof that these are "solidary" and "national"? That the state and its activity exist specifically for the sake of satisfying these interests? Not only is this proposition not supported—it is categorically refuted—by history. It is without logical proof. Such an assertion is an abstraction and a fiction contradicting the facts of history.

Jellinek's definition of the state is extremely gratifying to the bourgeoisie, with its interest in glossing over class antagonisms and in propagandizing the view that the modern bourgeois state is to be regarded as the means of satisfying national needs and interests, an institution which preserves the rights of the people and guarantees to the people the development of their spiritual powers and the satisfaction of their cultural and material interests.

Jellinek clothes the state with legal form so as to give it the utmost authority in the eyes of the masses. The modern state, according to him, is a *Rechtsstaat*—a state bound and limited by statutes promulgated by itself. In defining the interrelation of law and state, he starts from the idea that law is a psychological phenomenon, existing only in our psyche, and calls it a certain part of the content of our consciousness. On the other hand, he proceeds to reason that law represents the totality of rules of human conduct, distinguished from rules of morality, from the imperatives of religion, morals, and the like, in that the purpose of law is to defend and to preserve human welfare and human interest. The legal norms are those issuing out of acknowledged external authority, and guaranteed, by external means at the state's disposal, to be obligatory. The entire legal order is, in his view, built on the conviction ("the average typical conviction of the people") that we are bound to follow these norms.[33] Such "conviction" of the people is construed by him as force not formed under the pressure of higher measures of a compulsive character, but influenced by another type of motivation which excludes constraint. The essential sign of the idea of law is thus not con-

[33] *Ibid.*, p. 244.

straint but *guarantee* (one of whose manifestations is constraint). Legal norms are less coercive than *guaranteed.*[34]

All this construing of "law" as a "guarantee" serves very well to suggest the idea that the people's subordination to their oppressors is voluntary, that inner morality approves this law, that the people morally excuse the violence inflicted upon them with the aid of the state and screened under the form of law.

Passing to the problem of law and the state, and seeking to answer the question whether or not the state is subordinate to the legal order, Jellinek starts from the fiction of a "general will"—making no distinction between the will of those who are dominant and that of those who are subject.

> The will of the state is the human will. The question is thus reduced to the establishment of the presence of norms binding upon the human will representing the state. The existence of such norms must be considered as proved as soon as their being and operation are confirmed both by those in power and by those subject to power.[35]

Jellinek's own theory is basically merely an eccentric modernization of the old theory of so-called natural law, although he also declares his dissent from the theories of that law.

He objects to the principle that the state is not bound by law:

> It follows from this theory that what is law for the subject (whether a private person, or an organ of the state) is not law for the state itself. In other words, if we look from the heights of the state at the lowlands of the law, we find only an empty place.[36]

He holds that the state is bound by law. The activity of the state is regulated by stable legal norms, binding upon state organs and upon the state itself. That even the state must be bound by legal norms is "a necessary condition of uninterrupted cultural development inasmuch as it alone also creates that social confidence without which mutual relationships between men would be possible only in the most elementary, rudimentary forms." [37]

The law is binding on the will of the state. The state creates all law, but finds in law its own self-limitation—a voluntary self-limitation, however, and therefore not prejudicial to its power, its sovereignty.

> In the act of creating law—however this law arose—the state takes upon itself, with reference to its subjects, the obligation to apply and to effectuate this law.[38]

[34] *Ibid.*, p. 246. (Italics supplied by the compilers.)
[35] *Ibid.*, p. 247.
[36] *Ibid.*, p. 269.
[37] *Ibid.*, p. 270.
[38] *Ibid.*

Legal literature has already noted that this theory of the self-limitation of the state is clearly artificial and without scientific significance. It does not start from real facts but from assumptions, assumptions which have no place in actual practice. Of course, law and statutes, as one of the forms of expressing law, are binding even upon the state—or rather, upon state organs, institutions, and officials.

It is impossible to conceive the state as a definite organization of social order, social relationships, without acknowledging the obligatory character and the universality of statutes promulgated by it. To say that they are binding upon organs of state authority is not an expression of the "self-limitation" of any will. It is an expression of this will itself. The core of the question, however, does not relate to this but to the very essence of the state will. According to Jellinek, the essence—the content—of this will is "solidary" interests "of the people." But this is not so. As regards its subjects, the state is not bound in any manner whatever. It is not obligated—it rather *obligates* its subjects. State statutes are the form wherein the class dominant in a given society obligates all other classes to definite conduct—to the precise conduct advantageous and pleasing to that dominant class.

We may mention Hauriou and Duguit as representing the modern bourgeois science of public law.

Hauriou starts from the proposition that the state is possible only where the nation has become civil society, i.e., where political power has been separated from private property and has acquired the features of public power. He maintains, accordingly, that the feudal state is not a state at all in the true sense of the word; only the modern bourgeois state, supposedly representing the entire nation, is such a state. "The state is the juridical personification of a given nation, consequent upon the political, economic, and juridical centralization of the nation's elements to the end of realizing civil life." [39]

On this theory, the state is formed to the end of making civil life and civil society real and effective. The civil order or regime of "civil freedom" is *"a regime of freedom and equality, established by a political organism* [the state] *in order that the automatism of economic society might be able to function within the state."* [40] What is this "automatism" of economic society? Apparently it is the famous *laissez faire, laissez passer*—"everyone who minds his own business is, almost inadvertently, minding society's business."

Hauriou's later exposition of the question reveals him as a bourgeois-reactionary, straining to prove that the highest realization of civil life is

[39] Hauriou, *The Foundations of Public Law* (Russian ed.), p. 294.
[40] *Ibid.*, p. 365.

manifested in the "middle class," as distinguished from "the rich" and "the poor."

In the spirit of narrow-minded, petty-bourgeois, sickly sentimentality, he outlines a seductive perspective of solving the "social question," by invoking the "common property" of employers and workers and at the same time preserving the "open bourgeoisie." Into the "open bourgeoisie" will pour the best of the working class (in proportion as it arrives at capitalist possession of land, money or enterprise), but there will always be reestablished therewith a class of toilers in the proper sense of the word.

The extraordinary banality of his ratiocinations regarding the essence of the state and the perspectives of its development is adequately shown by the tirade:

> The Roman state became a state of patricians and plebs, and it is entirely possible that the bourgeois state will, after an indeterminate time—after revolutions, debates, and accords—become a bourgeois-workers' state. . . . If we allow the civil order (the bourgeois state) to finish its business, it . . . will (at extremely low prices) provide all the objects necessary for life and actually furnish each normal individual with a minimum of property—be it only property in the form of an official position—which will make him—practically, and not merely theoretically—a free man.[41]

Enough has been said to demonstrate the pitiful pass to which even prominent representatives of bourgeois science are brought when their purpose is to vindicate—at whatever cost—the bourgeois state, and to justify its parasitic and exploiting character.

The same may be said of Duguit (1859–1928), who, in his time, notoriously influenced even a number of Soviet jurists who portrayed his theory as if it were a socialist theory of law and sought to reconcile it with Marxism.

Duguit criticizes the juridical conception of the state, categorically objecting to the theory (of Ihering, Laband, and Jellinek) that the state is the sole source of law. He seeks an explanation of the state which would neither put it above the law nor make law dependent upon, or a derivative of, the state.

> Human reason feels a strong need so to define the basis of law—understood as a social norm—that this norm be binding, not only upon individuals, but upon the state as well—however the state be understood, and irrespective of the fact that for us the modern state is above all the creator of norms (sanctioning obedience thereto by the material force at its disposal).[42]

He considers that his concept of law also solves the question of the state: the purpose of the state is to effectuate law.

[41] *Ibid.*, pp. 402, 408–409.
[42] L. Duguit, *Constitutional Law* (Moscow, 1908), p. 5.

The state is founded on force, but this force is lawful only when applied in conformity with law. We do not say (as Ihering does) that law is the policy of force. We assert that political power is force given over to serve the law.[43]

Duguit sees the principle of "social solidarity" as the basis of state and law alike, asserting that people are united by bonds of a social solidarity which embraces all members of the human race and is the source of law itself.

He sees the basis of legal form in the social obligations resting on each man, in his social role. Freedom is the right of man, but it is a right which man can realize only in proportion as he dedicates his activity to the realization of social solidarity. The very law of property is justified by the "social mission" supposedly resting upon the owner. A juridical act is a manifestation of will which conforms in purpose with social solidarity.

He rejects the idea that the state is a person, and looks at it from the point of view of factual possession of power, defining it in its most general sense as "every sort of human society wherein there is political differentiation between rulers and governed—in a word, political power."[44] He is particularly emphatic that the word "state" serves to designate specifically those societies where political differentiation has attained a certain degree of development and where, for that reason, political power presents definite and characteristic features.

He acknowledges that political power is a fact—a fact completely independent of the legality, or otherwise, of the power—and that this fact is a product of social evolution. He expressly declines to furnish philosophical justification of political power or to study all the details in the evolution of society in this direction. He confines himself to the task of merely showing the chief stage, and defining the most active factors, in the formation of society.

He defines the most important of these factors in a singularly inept manner. Some individuals, more powerful than others, make their will binding on the latter. They thus acquire definite political power with reference to those others. This political power, being factual, seeks no justification in the law. From the moment the conception of law is created in society, the idea emerges that the orders of this power are legitimate only in so far as they are in accord with the law; and that the application—by this political power—of material force is likewise legitimate only in so far as its purpose is to guarantee the sanction of the law.

Thus Duguit solves the question of the purpose of the state or of political power. This purpose is the realization of law. All the state does is done in

[43] *Ibid.*, p. 56.
[44] *Ibid.*, p. 25.

the interest of guaranteeing the law. The acts of the state must themselves be classified according to the action they exert in the world of the law—as an expression of the legislative, the judicial, or the administrative function of the state. At the same time, Duguit sees the state as possessing public power in the sense of a subjective right—the right to promulgate orders and forcibly to compel obedience to them—and also as a *Rechtsstaat*, as bound by law, as resting on a regime of legitimacy. The state is bound by statute, its legislative power is bound by objective law which is higher than the state and precedent thereto, or, more accurately, representative thereof.

The explanation of why the state is thus bound by the law is based neither on natural rights of individuals nor on the self-limitation of the state (Jellinek), but on the idea of social solidarity,[45] which is supposed to be the one foundation and the sole content of law and of legislation.

It is not difficult to show that this theory is indefensible. One need only point out that the very idea at the foundation of Duguit's entire conception of the state—"the more powerful individuals"—is utterly indefinite and devoid of scientific content. He was obviously in no position to explain the source of this "greater power" of some in relation to others. Unsuccessfully seeking to discover such source in the religious, economic, moral, or property advantages enjoyed by some in relation to others, he reveals his helplessness still more, being driven to confine himself to such lamentations as this: "The rulers always were, and are, and will be, those who are in fact the most powerful." [46] This explains nothing, for it does not explain the fundamental question—why some, rather than others, possess power.

His assertion that the aim of political power is the realization of law is completely arbitrary and devoid of historical content. His basic postulate—"social solidarity"—is itself artificial and metaphysical. But he begins from precisely this principle, considering that "solidarity is the life element of society of every sort." [47]

This "social solidarity" takes us back once again to the "general will" long cited by bourgeois philosophers and jurists in their efforts to conceal and gloss over the class and exploiting character of the bourgeois state. They strive to prove "solidarity" between bourgeoisie and proletariat—actually rather to subordinate the interests of the proletariat to the interests of the bourgeoisie.

The best possible refutation of these fables of "social solidarity" is the

[45] Conventional translations of Duguit into English designate the essence of his theory by the term "social contract." The Russian text, however, employs the term "social solidarity."—Tr.

[46] L. Duguit, *Constitutional Law* (Moscow, 1908), p. 49.

[47] "To say that the state must guarantee its existence is to say that it must cooperate with social solidarity—and consequently with law, which is generated by that solidarity." *Ibid.*, p. 57.

annals of the state-political life of any capitalistic country taken at random. Fair illustrations refuting them may be found in an analysis of bourgeois statutes. Characterizing English legislation, Engels said:

> Manifestly all legislation is directed to the protection of those who have as against those who have not. Statutes are necessary only because there are have-nots. . . . Hostility to the proletariat so regularly forms the basis of a statute that judges very readily acquire this sense—especially the inferior judges, who belong to bourgeois society themselves, and are the judges with whom the proletariat comes chiefly into contact.
>
> When a rich man is summoned—or rather invited—into court, the judge expresses regret that the rich man had to inconvenience himself and tries in every way to turn the matter to the rich man's advantage; and if he must, despite everything, condemn him, he again expresses his infinite regret, and so on. But if some one of the poor has to stand before that judge, he nearly always has to spend the preceding night in jail with a mass of others like himself; he is looked upon as guilty from the very beginning. He is shouted at, and all his efforts to justify himself are met by a contemptuous, "Oh! we know these excuses." . . . On the one hand these Dogberries [inferior judges] interpret the laws only in the strictest sense therein contained. On the other, they are themselves bourgeois, and see the chief foundation of every kind of true order in the interests of that class above all else. And the police are the same as these judges. No matter what the bourgeois has done, the police are always civil to him and keep strictly to the statutes. To the proletariat they behave coarsely and cruelly. Poverty itself casts suspicion of every sort of crime upon the proletariat, at the same time depriving it of lawful means of defense against arbitrary authorities. Consequently the statute does not defend the proletariat—the police, without the slightest hesitation, burst into a proletarian's house, arrest him and deal with him at will.[48]

Such are "equality" and social solidarity in England—one of the most "democratic" of the bourgeois countries. At the time of the 1926 coal strike in this same England, the famous Habeas Corpus Act was temporarily shelved so as not to hamper the police in dealing with the strikers in their own way. A quantity of similar examples could be cited from the practice of any of the capitalist countries. All this refutes, with sufficient eloquence, the professorial babbling of the law as the expression of "social solidarity" and of the state as the savior of this sacred altar of universal well-being.

The idea of "social solidarity," which is fundamental to Duguit's entire juridical conception of the state, contradicts the fact of the class division of society, and of the class struggle which destroys that solidarity. Duguit does violence to facts and falsifies history. He declares war on the German school of juridical formalism, only that he may set off against it juridical normativism. He takes a certain objective norm, standing above positive law, and

[48] Marx and Engels (Russian ed.), Vol. III, pp. 558–559.

binding upon both subjects and rulers (the state) alike, as the key to the solution of all questions of the modern building of state law. He operates with ideas and formulae which lead to error as to their actual content. Objecting to individualism and defending social solidarity, he describes the juridical norm as itself a means to compel the force at the disposal of the rulers to react to the service of social solidarity—he portrays the state as force put to the service of law.

This latter circumstance led the social reformists to see Duguit as representative of the new "social"—and all but "socialist"—trend, whereas in his teaching he asserts the principles of bourgeois law—completely defends the interests of capitalism.

Gumplowicz (1839–1909) claimed a still more socialist character for his doctrine. He warred against juridical formalism more decisively than did Duguit and flirted violently with "socialist" phraseology, although he did not in fact advance a single step over his bourgeois predecessors and contemporaries in solving the problems of state law.

He opposed the prevailing individualist theories of such political scientists as Laband, Gierke, and also the theory of law and state of which we spoke above. He sharply criticized the bourgeois science of state law as tendentious, concerned only to justify a given state order in conformity with the individual viewpoints of the authors and without taking the trouble to know its actual nature. The extent of the material to be studied in no way defined the difficulty of the scientific problem in this field, according to Gumplowicz. On the contrary,

> the difficulty of its task lies in the deceptiveness of this material. Nowhere, for some reason or other, has there been so much concealed and obscured as in state affairs. Nowhere is so much done for appearance as in public and in international law. Nowhere has there been so much lying, so much said and written with frank intent to deceive, as in this field. Nowhere is so much done on behalf of convention. Nowhere are so many deliberate comedies played out, as here.[49]

All explanations of the essence of the state given by the bourgeois science of law—from Welker, Robert von Mohl, Ahrens, Bluntschli, and Gerber to Hegel and Kant—are completely unsatisfactory to Gumplowicz. He defines correlation between state and law in these words: "Law is conceivable only in a state. It exists and falls with the state." [50]

He asserts further that the state did not arise on the basis of law, that law is not its cradle. Nor did it emerge by peaceful development out of the idea of law or in any other peaceful manner. The state arose through violence, which thus becomes the midwife of this new social phenomenon,

[49] Gumplowicz, *General Theory of the State* (Russian ed.), p. 16.
[50] *Ibid.*, p. 28.

and not out of the family nor by way of the family's development. "No, the state emerges only from various human groups, from various tribes, and consists of them alone. The victors formed the ruling class—the vanquished and the enslaved, the class of workers and servants."[51] He finds in tribes the fundamental bases—the actual cornerstones—of the state. The state was created from tribes. They and they alone preceded the state. With the foundation of the state is created a bond between such tribes as join the state life. These state unions turn the tribes into a nation. . . . The chief sign of a nation is a single state authority, under the principle whereof the nation stands and to which it is subordinated.

The state will—not to be confused with national will—also corresponds to this state power. This state will, according to Gumplowicz and to the satisfaction of the "racists," is the will of the predominant tribes with sufficient means and enough force at its disposal to make itself in reality the dominant will. In the process of state development, he continues, tribes turn into castes or classes and devote themselves to certain occupations, which are handed down by inheritance. These classes are welded together by the force of the state—an organization of domination.

> Consequently, domination—the government—takes this multiplicity in its grasp and forms a unity. The relationship of the elements dominant in the state toward those who are subject is expressed in the form of state organization. This form changes precisely as that relationship of domination changes and balances.[52]

Gumplowicz criticizes what has been done by such German jurists as Von Mohl, Stahl, and Lorenz von Stein, as well as the constitutional monarchy developed by Bluntschli—contrasting with it his own "modern *Kulturstaat*." This *Kulturstaat*, incidentally, is notable, in his opinion, as resting on culture and contributing to the further development of culture.

> The modern *Kulturstaat* is above all a state; and, as such, it is (like all states) always and everywhere an organization of domination, destined to support a certain legal order. Many years of development have resulted in remarkable mitigation of the forms of this domination. It now emerges in less severe shape. Old forms of slavery and servile dependency have disappeared, and "free" forms have appeared in their place. Their most important condition is that coercive domination is here realized on the basis of law, and not arbitrarily.[53]

There is, of course, no difference between the so-called *Kulturstaat*, so treated, and the so-called *Rechtsstaat*: law and statute operate in each alike as the supposed "court of last resort" of all social and state relationships.

Gumplowicz sees the essential sign of this *Kulturstaat* in the fact that

[51] *Ibid.*, pp. 120–121.
[52] *Ibid.*, p. 209.
[53] *Ibid.*, p. 248.

state activity is itself nothing more than the exaction of taxes and the conduct of wars (in the interests of the ruling dynasty), and that this activity supposedly aims at "promoting the national welfare in every way and thereafter affords active support to the aspiration to all higher, ideal, human purposes." [54]

Gumplowicz depicts state officials themselves as bearers of culture—as warriors for culture and progress—acting in the name, and in the spirit, of the law. With their cooperation legislation likewise works toward culture, ceaselessly and ever more strenuously, wherefore, he says, the field of law becomes ever wider and richer in the modern *Kulturstaat* and public law develops to dimensions literally unprecedented. The "cultured" character of this modern state finds expression in the attraction of the middle and the working classes, to participate—side by side with the privileged class of nobles—in social and state affairs. Freedom of speech guarantees the influence of the educated classes upon social opinion, upon the election of national representatives, and thus upon the participation of the democratic strata of the population in legislation and in all state government. The *Kulturstaat* is concerned with the population, with the national economy, with the "ideal side of national life," with the sciences and the arts—in a word, contributes to the successful solution of all problems "common to humanity in general"—problems connected with neither more nor less than "the social forms of the future." Such is Gumplowicz's portrayal of this famous "modern *Kulturstaat*." His teaching as to this *Kulturstaat* was, in its turn, caught up by social reformism and—in a particularly monstrous form—by fascism.

In reality there never was—and there can never be—any such *Kulturstaat* in the history of exploiter-societies. Not a single one of the qualities so sentimentally described by Gumplowicz was, or could be, possessed by the modern bourgeois state—qualities of this sort are in direct and sharp contradiction to the true "class" and "exploiter" nature of that state.

The best refutation of the juridical and cultural illusions of Gumplowicz and his reformist followers is to consider any of the modern "bourgeois" states. At each step they afford an infinite number of examples of an inhuman, bestial relationship to the exploited masses of the people, of complete and utter unconcern for their needs and interests, of total aversion from dealing with the problems of mankind in general—those problems which have never appeared on the agenda of any bourgeois (and, in general, exploiting) state. This is sharply manifest in the activity of fascist states, which have in fact reached a stage of plain cannibalism.

The modern bourgeois state is an imperialist state, which, every day

[54] *Ibid.*, p. 248.

and every hour, sacrifices culture and the interests of cultural construction to its rapacious policy of wars and aggressions, fire and the sword. How can one possibly speak of the culture of the "modern" bourgeois state unless he chooses to close his eyes to the grievous barbarism created by it in every corner of the earth where the power of capital and of exploitation holds sway?

Gumplowicz was in no position to understand the actual nature of the state, the sources of its origin, the laws of its development. Even criticizing the theories of a formal-juridical trend, and attempting to contrast with it a new "scientific" teaching in the field of public law, he was utterly helpless in solving the fundamental problems of the science of public law. One of the causes of this impotence is his failure to understand the connection of state and law, on the one hand, with the class organization of society on the other; his failure to understand the organic connection between law, state, and politics; his failure to understand that the activity of law and the activity of the state cannot be understood and correctly appraised in isolation from politics—which is the expression, and the struggle for existence, of the class interests prevailing in a given society.

His understanding of the actual problems of scientific investigation is perverted and utterly incorrect. He makes it a necessary condition

> of truly scientific and impartial investigation of political science to keep as far as possible from politics of every sort. . . . The political scientist must know how to draw the line between his science and politics. . . . It is for him to investigate the laws of political development in isolation from party life. Let . . . politicians and publicists quarrel among themselves as to *what conduct is proper*—study of the state is not occupied with such questions.

The attempts to explain the state from the viewpoint of juridical relationship are of significant interest. The chief representatives of this trend are the Germans: Loening and Affolter, and the (prerevolutionary) Russians: Korkunov, Lazarevsky, and others.

Criticizing the "will" theory of the state, Korkunov concludes that it begins with the explanation of the state from the fiction of a juristic person, whereas in reality "state domination is neither a fiction, nor a methodological mode, but the totality of real phenomena. . . ." Hence Korkunov considers that the scientific explanation of the idea of state power must relate to the establishment of domination as a particular group of the real phenomena of social life, rather than of a fiction of juridical construction. He correctly notes that all the phenomena of state life cannot possibly be reduced to the manifestation of any single will. He deems the very idea of a "single will" artificial—a juridical fiction. This is true, if we have in mind the will of all society. Korkunov—and others holding this theory—

believe that the idea of power does not coincide with the idea of will. Domination presupposes no dominant will. "Domination requires only the consciousness of dependence, not the reality thereof. If this is so, power is force conditioned by the subject's consciousness of dependence." [55] Thus reducing the whole matter to the "subject's" consciousness, this theory avoids answering the basic question: where and wherein must we see the forces of state power operating imperatively upon the consciousness of "subject" people? Unity of language, of customs, of culture (of which Korkunov speaks as though they were sources of the consciousness and of the bond of people with the state), ties of kinship, patriotism—these explain nothing here, since each of them requires to be itself explained.

"The state is a social union of free people with a peaceful order established by constraint by turning over the exclusive right of constraint to organs of the state alone." [56] The basic element of the state is, in his definition, independent coercive domination. "State power is force, conditioned by consciousness of dependence upon the state as a social union wherein peaceful order is established by constraint." [57]

Admitting that coercive state activity is the fundamental sign of state community, Korkunov emphasizes that another most important sign of state domination is domination over free people only.

It is pertinent to note that this is an obvious excuse for depriving of civil and political rights all who, by reason of the domination of exploiters, do not enjoy individual freedom. Korkunov frankly declares:

> He who is not free, but subject to the private power of another, is thereby excluded from participation in state life. Only the free participate immediately in state community—only those for whom state power is not overshadowed by the power of private persons over them.[58]

Basic to Korkunov's theory of state is his definition of power, not as "will," but as force conditioned by consciousness of dependence upon the state. He holds that the state's unity is based on the unity, not of its (imaginary) will, but of incitement to subordination to state domination. But he further reasons that such unity is no longer unity of personality but unity of relationship—hence the definition of the state as a single juridical relationship. Examining the state from this point of view, Korkunov proves that the interests making up its content are limited by the adaptation of the object to joint enjoyment by separate individuals.

This proposition of Korkunov amplifies the other proposition that state

[55] H. M. Korkunov, *Russian Public Law* (St. Petersburg, 1908), p. 10.
[56] *Ibid.*, p. 27.
[57] *Ibid.*, p. 37.
[58] *Ibid.*, p. 38.

power, in order to remain such, must be an object of common enjoyment by all those who constitute the state. "If the state itself is a juridical relationship, *its subjects are all those who participate in the state community*, from the monarch down to the lowest member." [59]

Korkunov "does not see" the difference in the position occupied in the state by the monarch and that occupied by the "lowest subject." Nor does he see the class nature of the state, which guarantees domination over their subjects to various monarchs and to the social forces supporting them. His formula is a typical abstract juridical formula. It conceals the true class character of the state wherein the actual subject, who bears state power, is not "all those who participate in the state community" but only certain social classes which make use of the machinery of state for their own class interests.

Korkunov himself sees the artificiality of his thesis, and is in no position to deny that, even in bourgeois-democratic states, the extent of the rights of those participating in this state community varies so widely as to afford no basis for maintaining that any broad democratic group of the population participates therein with equal rights. Accordingly, he is compelled, with reference to certain separate groups of the population (of the degree of whose rights he is speaking), to reduce rights to obligations—which, of course, destroys the basis of his entire theoretic structure.

To eliminate the absurdities inherent in this construction, he has to resort to a new juridical construction—"orders in the interest of another," so-called. This he understands as the actualization of obligations resting upon organs of state power, whereas he construes the state domination itself not as unilateral domination—not as issuing from opposition of rulers and subjects—but as starting from the distribution of domination among all who participate in the state community. To be sure, he himself admits that some people attain in addition a predominance of power and others an obligation to obey; but he holds that this does not exclude the possibility of speaking of the state as a juridical relationship and of the inhabitants as the subject thereof. The rights comprising the content of the juridical relationship of state domination he reduces to the right to influence the realization of coercive power to this or that extent.

> Thus from the legal point of view the state seems a juridical relationship of independent, compulsive domination, whose subject is the entire population of states, whose object is the compulsive power itself, and whose content is made up of rights to participate in domination and obligations to obey.[60]

Asserting that the state is "a real juridical relationship between ruler

[59] *Ibid.*, pp. 45–46.
[60] *Ibid.*, p. 48.

and subject," Korkunov and other advocates of this theory see this as a customary legal relationship resting on the principle that each side has equal rights—that the rights and obligations appertaining to each side are of equal range. This theory thus perverts the essence of relationships (which actually have place in the state) between rulers and subjects as relationships under which the dominant are not juridically—and are still less factually—equal with those whom they dominate. This alone is sufficient to refute completely the theory of the state as a juridical relationship and to demonstrate that it is a theory completely devoid of all scientific foundation and significance.

Even in its own time (the 1890's) Korkunov's theory, which regarded the state as a juridical relationship, provoked in legal literature a whole series of very substantial objections.[61] Korkunov characterized it as a theory of subjective realism, deducing the cause of subjection to state domination, neither from the individual will of the subjects nor from any metaphysical will having power over people, but from their own subjective (albeit "perfectly real") consciousness of their dependence upon the state.

To show the utter indefensibility of construing the state as a juridical relationship is a simple matter. It is enough to point out that, in reducing the cause of subjection to the subjects' consciousness of their dependence upon the state, Korkunov did not explain how this consciousness is defined and has therefore defined one unknown by another unknown. If the state were really founded upon the consciousness of individual people of their dependence upon the state, state unity would be utterly impossible. Consciousness is extraordinarily individual and diverse. It is defined by people's social position—by the place they occupy in production relationships, by their class position. Therefore consciousness (ideology) has of necessity a profoundly class character and so differs sharply in one class from the consciousness (the ideology) of another class. The theory of the state as a juridical relationship (it is still differently formulated as "community of domination") is vitiated by inner contradictions, insoluble if we remain within the field of so-called subjective realism. Critics of the theory point out, not without cause, that in the last resort it is a repetition, with certain modifications, of Montesquieu's theory of the separation of powers.

In the last resort the theory of the state as a legal relationship, beginning from the thesis that the entire population actualizes state domination, clearly contradicts historical facts. It has not the slightest confirmation in the slave-owning state, the feudal state or the capitalist state; in each of them the state power is actualized, not by the population, but only by an

[61] Profs. M. A. Dyakonov, A. S. Alexeyev, L. Z. Slonimsky, M. B. Gorenberg, V. V. Ivanovsky, and others.

insignificant minority which has concentrated in its hands economic domination over the majority, over the people.

The fundamental defect in the reasoning of Korkunov and other representatives of the "juridical relationship" school is the same as that of bourgeois scholars in general; they strive to deduce the idea of state and law out of themselves, to solve this problem with the aid of divers juridical constructions, of formal and abstract juridical thinking, or the formal structures of juridical logic. Meanwhile, the actual nature of state and law may be understood and defined from an analysis, not of juridical relationships *per se*, but of the relationships of social production, of which juridical relationships are only an expression. Attempts to cope with this problem—while keeping strictly within the sphere of juridical logic—are doomed to complete failure. Contemporary bourgeois science, however, is in no condition to emerge from the vicious circle of juridical scholasticism. Over it still hangs the weight of the prejudices of the trend of juridical formalism so characteristic of bourgeois jurisprudence in its entirety—irrespective of the differences between separate juridical schools, rivalling each other in subtlety and casuistry of juridical analysis.

Recent bourgeois juridical theorists modernize the ideas of Kant (1724–1804), who also erected his theory of law on the idea of the supremacy of human reason. According to him, the guiding principle of human activity is the demand of pure reason. The moral law or the categorical imperative is raised above all else. It prevails likewise in the field of law. Law itself is morality contemplated from the external side. Hence the fundamental requirement of legal rules: to act in conformity with the demand of the moral law, so that individual freedom be in consonance with the freedom of all other persons. The province of law is the province of external human relations. Therein operates private law (the law of tangible property, the law of persons, the law of marriage, and so forth) coercive in character, and defended in its totality by the common will which Kant defines as the state. But law of every sort has, according to Kant, the task of guaranteeing the actualization of law in general, and of the idea of justice.

The error of this reasoning is manifest: there never was, and there cannot be, any "idea" either of justice or of a "general" law endowed with a content independent of class. Hence to define law as the expression of any universal "idea," or of any abstract legal principle characteristic of law of every sort—law "in general"—is possible only if one is distracted from real social relationships, historically formed. Kant's "idea" of justice and "general law" or "law in general" is just as elusive as his *Ding an sich*.[62]

It is not difficult to perceive that Kant's basic legal ideas coincide with

[62] Lenin, *Materialism and Empirio-Criticism*, Vol. XIII, p. 82 *ff*.

those of Rousseau and the encyclopaedists, who started from the same abstract propositions as Kant—in particular, from the idea of the general will of the people. To Kant, law is the external expression of morality—merely a peculiar way of expressing morality.

A most important trend of bourgeois legal science formed under the immediate influence of Kant was *normativism,* which most sharply expressed Kant's fundamental idea, the separation of the juridical form from its social content. The most eminent representatives of normativism are Krabbe and Hans Kelsen.

The essence of normativism is in the complete dissociation of the juridical norm from social content—in asserting the supremacy of the juridical norm. Krabbe starts by admitting that "law is self-sufficient," and that "for law the principle of autonomy, and not of heteronomy, is operative."[63]

Consequently, the true and supreme criterion of law is found in law as such, not in phenomena lying outside it (economics, production relationships). Norms established by legislation are legal norms because the legal order acknowledges the legislator as an organ of law. The coercive force of this legal order is due to the conformity of its norms with the people's legal convictions. Legal norms are thus portrayed as expressing the legal convictions of the people and as such they are the supreme regulator of social and state life.

In clarification of the meaning of objective law Kelsen finds and construes the proper regularity of law. The state itself, from his point of view, is "the unity of the internal sense of legal propositions"—merely the personification of objective legal order, and properly to be understood "as a norm or order," as an idea identical with law or legal order. From the juridical point of view state and law are one and the same. Legal norms are absolute as ethical principles. Kelsen makes no distinction whatever between public and private law. He identifies the state with the legal order. He directly asserts that

the state is a legal order, but not every sort of legal order can be called a state. The legal order can be called a state only in case it establishes certain organs functioning on the basis of division of labor to settle and to execute the rules whereby it is formed. The legal order is called the state when it has attained a certain degree of centralization. The theory of three sorts of state power, or state functions, has as its object different stages of creating state order; state organs are understood only as organs of creating and actualizing law (*Rechtserzeugung*

[63] *Heteronomy* signifies dependence upon an external norm; in contrast, *autonomy* signifies dependence on a rule which the actor establishes for himself, G. F. Shershenevich, *General Theory of Law* (1911), p. 301.

und Rechtsvollziehung), and the state form is nothing but methods of creating legal order, figuratively called manifestation of the will of the state.[64]

Thus, normativism does not see the material content of social relationships, does not admit of the class structure of society—the struggle of social classes—and does not acknowledge the state as an organ of domination and repression. It excludes all this as metajuridical—lying outside juridical categories and normative ideas.

Normativism shows completely and logically the vacuity of neo-Kantian methodology which struggles only to disguise—by juridical norms and legal formulae—the class antagonisms destroying bourgeois society and the capitalist order. It is precisely for this reason that normativism became one of the havens of refuge for the spirit of reaction and for the trend of bourgeois juridical thought which expressed it.

By the examples of the chief bourgeois scholars of various tendencies we have shown that the theory of the state, created and developed by bourgeois science, was helpless to answer the fundamental questions of political science; that various attempts to do so ended inevitably in utter failure, and were essentially no more than attempts to rehabilitate the exploiter state because of hypocrisy and class interest—or from ignorance of what is described as representing and preserving the general welfare and general interests, the rights and interests of the people.

We observe the same picture of bankrupt bourgeois science in the field of legal theory also. Here, too, has accumulated a pile of scholastic rubbish, perverting the idea of law, its nature, its role in social history, its historic fate.

Even the works of outstanding scholars of the bourgeois world, who have left to later generations the best models of their investigation in the field of law (the school of natural law, Hegel, and the historic school of law), were likewise unable to lead bourgeois jurisprudence out of the labyrinth of contradictions, provisos, abstractions, fictions, and schemes. Kant had every reason to say of bourgeois science: "Jurists still seek a definition of the idea of their law." Gumplowicz noted that Kant's observation is valid even now.

> Even at the present time jurists are seeking a definition of law, but they will not soon find it, for they have wandered into a false path and are in dreadful error, thinking to find their way from law to state, which they see as produced by law.[65]

And bourgeois legal science, pursuing this false path and moving along

[64] Hans Kelsen, *Reine Rechtslehre*, pp. 116–117.
[65] Gumplowicz, *General Theory of the State* (St. Petersburg, 1910), p. 355.

it, is in truth unable to cope with problems of truly scientific investigation. Suffice it to say, that so outstanding a representative of bourgeois philosophy (and especially of the philosophy and history of law) as Auguste Comte finds a way out of this position by the forthright denial of law itself—denial of its right to exist. He asserts that "human rights," advanced by metaphysics against theocracy, played only a negative part.

The word "law" must in the same measure be eliminated from our present political language as must the word "cause" from our present philosophical diction. Of these two ideas of metaphysical theology, the former is just as immoral and archaic as the other is irrational and sophistical. . . . In the positive state, which acknowledges no divine principle, the idea of law irrevocably disappears. Each is obligated before all others, but no one has rights as such. . . . In other words, no one possesses any right other than the right always to perform his duty.[66]

To the question: "What is subjective law?" Duguit replies: "This is an idea of purely metaphysical order. . . . The eternal quarrels as to the actual nature of subjective law are the best proof of all the artificiality and instability comprised in that idea."[67]

Karner, clearly disclosing his ignorance as to the most important question of the origin of law, puts the question as to the part played by law in society thus: "How does society create its law? How does law create its society?" He found nothing more intelligent to say of legal science than to cite Kant: "A purely empirical theory of law is a head—like the wooden head in the fable of Phaedrus—which may be beautiful but is, unfortunately, devoid of brains." Karner adds: "The science of law therefore begins exactly where jurisprudence ends."[68]

Shershenevich, having analyzed various legal systems, comes to this conclusion: "There is no hope of discovering the desired trait, applicable to law of every sort, and capable of serving to distinguish law from other manifestations of society."[69] Completely without hope of discovering the material content of law, he concludes that it is necessary to pass from the material side of law to its formal side.

Bergbohm, Gierke, Maier, Gumplowicz, Jellinek, Ihering, Anton Menger, Krabbe, Duguit, Petrazhitsky, Kelsen, Karner, and others define law, each in his own way, but none of them is able to take a single step forward or beyond the pitiful idealistic conception which flutters in the clutches of abstractions—"spirit," "idea," "will," "general will," "private will," "social

[66] Auguste Comte, *Système de politique positive*, Vol. I, p. 361.

[67] L. Duguit, *General Reorganizations of Civil Law* (State Publishing House, 1919), p. 13.

[68] Karner, *The Social Functions of Law* (Moscow, 1923), p. 11.

[69] G. F. Shershenevich, *General Theory of Law* (Moscow, 1910), p. 280.

solidarity," "social function," and so forth. All the impotence of bourgeois legal thought is expressed with particular clarity in the utter inability of bourgeois legal scholars in the matter of explaining the very origin of law.

Characteristic in this regard is the doctrine of Stammler, who, as he says, set out in defining the idea of law not from *a priori* judgments and notions, but from experience. He contemplates law as one side of social life, another side of which is economics. "The legal order and the economic order are absolutely one and the same. The material for every sort of social regulation is joint human activity directed at the satisfaction of needs"; and he explains that by "joint activity" is to be understood "social economy"—"all social life."[70] He sees law itself as coercive regulation (of the social life of people) subordinated to the idea of the human community. The superficiality of his definition of law is obvious.

Von Ihering, one of the most outstanding representatives of bourgeois legal science, also acknowledged legal compulsion to be a fundamental and most important sign of law. Von Ihering set forth his basic views on this question in a treatise which is, perhaps, the most famous of all the juridical works of the nineteenth century (*Der Zweck im Recht*). He starts by admitting that the basic source of law is human interest, protected by law as a special form of constraint. "A legal proposition without legal constraint is an inner contradiction—fire which does not burn, light which does not illuminate."[71] He regards law as one of the provisos guaranteeing the vital conditions of society. He starts from the idea of the self-limitation of state authority, assuming that it is specifically in law that the state, guided by the interests of all society, puts limits on its activity.

It goes without saying that this conception is no less artificial than that of Jellinek, who started from the abstract idea of "social solidarity" as the source of legal and state life. Ihering's theory undoubtedly answered burning questions of the contemporary bourgeoisie and served to justify the bourgeois state and law, concealing their true exploiter-nature.

In the juridical literature of prerevolutionary Russia the same absolutely unscientific views prevailed as in the bourgeois theory of western Europe. It is enough to point to such outstanding jurists of old Russia as Chicherin, Gradovsky, Korkunov, and Petrazhitsky.

Instead of setting out a concrete definition of law, Korkunov obliterates the boundary between law and morality and talks of delimitation of interests as the fundamental task of law. Understanding law as the delimitation of interests, he was clearly bound to remove public law, criminal law, and civil law beyond its boundaries.

[70] R. Stammler, *Wirtschaft und Recht* (St. Petersburg, 1907), pp. 170, 208.
[71] Ihering, *Der Zweck im Recht*, Vol. I, p. 322.

Petrazhitsky considers the nature of law incognizable. Its nature, he says, drives jurists upon a false road and permits no knowledge of itself. . . . Nevertheless, he stubbornly seeks the key to cognition of the law and finds it in . . . psychology. According to him, law is a psychological experience, consciousness, emotions. "We shall understand law, in the sense of a special class of real phenomena—as those ethical experiences whose emotions have an attributive character." [72] His law is "intuitive law" and "there are as many intuitive laws as there are individuals." [73]

It would hardly be necessary to spend time on this theory if there were not connected with it, in legal history of the postrevolutionary period, an entire group of crude perversions and antiscientific acrobatics by pseudo-Marxist jurists, whose idealistic, psychological, and other "theories" and "theorists" of every kind threatened to submerge Soviet juridical literature.

In this connection it is impossible not to mention Professor Reisner.[74] In his words on law he perverts Marxism in the most blatant way, unceremoniously substituting Machism for it. Not Marx, Engels, and Lenin, but Mach, Avenarius, and Bogdanov [75] are Reisner's actual teachers, although he elaborately strives to conceal this fact, giving out his own eclectic concoction as true Marxism.

Reisner considers that his merit in the field of legal theory is to have "revised" Petrazhitsky's theory of intuitive law, "in the sense of putting it on a Marxian basis," by reason of which intuitive law "was transformed into the most genuine *class law*."

However, this perversion of intuitive, idealistic law into "class" law of the proletariat, of which Reisner speaks, really took place only in Reisner's own imagination. In historic fact, such a "metamorphosis" as idealism resting on a Marxist foundation has never occurred without—as happened in Reisner's case—that foundation itself being completely perverted.

Because of this radically mistaken (and diametrically anti-Marxist-Leninist) view of the essence of law, Reisner could tolerate the assertion that the foundation of our legal order, with all its special characteristics and class principles, was the application by the proletariat—victorious in 1917—of "intuitive law."

For Reisner there are no real legal phenomena in the sense of phenomena serving as intermediary links with social relationships. For him, the

[72] Prof. L. I. Petrazhitsky, *Theory of Law and the State in Connection with the Theory of Morality* (St. Petersburg, 1909), Vol. I, p. 85.

[73] *Ibid.* (1910 ed.), Vol. II, p. 480.

[74] M. Reisner, *Law: Our Law, Foreign Law, Common Law* (State Publishing House, 1925).

[75] Cf. Lenin, *Materialism and Empirio-Criticism*, Vol. II.

source of law is not production relationships, but the psyche, sensation, emotions, and ideas. He holds that law is a function of the psyche, and understandable only out of itself and of the human psyche as its basis. We are involuntarily reminded of the words of Marx:

> Society does not rest on law. That is a phantasy of jurists. On the contrary, law—in contrast to the arbitrariness of the separate individuum—must rest on society, must be an expression of society's general interests and needs, as they emerge from a given material means of production.[76]

Reisner arrives at the assertion that the highest criterion of law is justice—understood as a self-sufficient, *a priori* category (of a universal character which allows justice to be made the starting point for absolute, categorical judgments).[77] Starting from these vicious theoretical propositions (a repetition of the crudely idealistic and antiscientific "truths" of Mach, Avenarius, Bogdanov, and Freud) Reisner construes his "class law" as the law of different classes, a compounding of ideological fragments of diverse class ideas, a "parti-colored fabric, created on the basis of the legal demands and views of the most diverse social classes." [78] He flatly objects to the Marxist understanding of law as the law of the *dominant class,* showing that side by side with the law of the dominant class there exists the law of the dependent and suppressed class. To positive state law he opposes the law of these other classes.

The reactionary character of Reisner's legal theory is particularly clear from his crudely anti-Marxist-Leninist understanding of Soviet law. Completely incapable (because of the viciousness of his initial viewpoint) to explain the correlation of the law of the Soviet state with that of the proletarian dictatorship, he seeks in defining law, a "social side" which would put some distinction between law and state constraint, between law and authority. Finding no such distinction, he doubts the necessity of law where there is a "firmly realized class interest."

> Why legal regulation, once we have a firmly realized class interest and proper technical means to actualize it? . . . We remain as before in complete perplexity: thus we do not know *whether or not law is necessary to us, in what degree it is necessary to us,* and *whether or not we can put up with painting over the proletarian dictatorship and the class interests, for some reason, into enigmatic shapes and forms of law.*[79]

Such reasoning can be explained only by a completely perverted idea

[76] Marx and Engels (Russian ed.), Vol. VII, p. 254.

[77] M. Reisner, *Law: Our Law, Foreign Law, Common Law* (State Publishing House), p. 244.

[78] *Ibid.*, p. 184.

[79] *Ibid.*, pp. 33–34.

of law as "enigmatic shapes and forms of law." In fact law is no "enigmatic shape" but a living reality, expressing the essence of social relationships between classes on the basis of the dominance, domination, repression, and subjection, by the dominant classes, of other classes who are subordinate to this dominance.

It is precisely their failure to understand this basic phenomenon—this basic social fact—which explains the exceedingly crude perversions of the Marxist-Leninist doctrine of law and state and, in particular, of Soviet law and the Soviet state, in Reisner, Stuchka, and a group of other pseudo-Marxists who have spared no effort to litter our juridical literature with pseudoscientific rubbish.

SEC. 6: SOVIET SOCIALIST PUBLIC LAW—ITS OBJECT AND ITS METHODS

Soviet socialist public law is one of the most important branches of Soviet socialist law, which we have previously defined as the totality of the rules of conduct, established in the form of legislation by the authoritative power of the toilers and expressing their will—the application of said rules being guaranteed by the entire coercive force of the socialist state to the end (*a*) of defending, securing, and developing relationships and orders advantageous and agreeable to the toilers, and (*b*) of annihilating, completely and finally, capitalism and its survivals in the economy, manner of life, and consciousness of people, with the aim of building communist society.

The specific mark of Soviet law, distinguishing it, radically and in principle, from the law of all other societies and epochs, is that it serves, in the true and actual sense of the word, the people—society—which for the first time in history comes into its own. In the USSR for the first time in history the people—the toiling national masses themselves—are the masters of their fate, themselves ruling their state with no exploiters, no landlords, no capitalists.

Here the socialist system of economy and socialist property in the means and instruments of production hold sway. They were confirmed as a result of the liquidation of the capitalistic system of ownership, of the abrogation of private property in the instruments and means of production, and of the annihilation of the exploitation of man by man. Here the land and its natural deposits, waters, forests, mills, factories, coal and ore mines, transport (by railroad, water, and air), banks, post, telegraph and telephones, big state-organized agricultural enterprises (sovkhozes, machine tractor stations, and the like), as well as municipal enterprises and the bulk of the dwelling houses in cities and industrial localities—all these are state property—the property of the entire nation.

The economic basis of the USSR—defended and preserved by our Soviet socialist law—is the socialist system of economy, socialist property in instruments and means of production. The political basis of the USSR—likewise preserved and defended by Soviet socialist law—is the Soviets of Workers' Deputies, which have grown and become strong as a result of the overthrow of the power of landlords and capitalists and in consequence of the conquest of the proletarian dictatorship.

These two circumstances, of world-wide historical significance, are, in themselves, sufficient to enable us to see the socialist content of Soviet law. Only traitors and those who betray the interests of socialism (like Pashukanis, Krylenko, and other apostates of our country) could deny the socialist nature of Soviet law, asserting that our law is a mere replica or adaptation of bourgeois law. Soviet law protects the interests of the toiling masses, who have been emancipated from exploitation and the weight of capitalism. It directs all its might at crushing and annihilating exploiters and the very possibility of exploitation.

The Soviet state, and Soviet law from the first days of its emergence defend the interests of labor against capital, the interests of popular masses—the overwhelming majority of the people—against a handful of exploiters and parasitic elements of the old society. Only in a socialist state of workers and peasants are the interests and rights of man defended at the same time, inasmuch as individual well-being rests on the social wealth—the property of the people.

For the first time in human history there is eliminated the conflict between social interest and personal interest, society and the state, and between society and the state (on the one hand) and individuality and individual interests (on the other). In 1922 Lenin wrote to Kursky of the relation of Soviet law to the capitalist elements in economy:

> We acknowledge nothing as "private." For us *everything* in the province of economics is in the domain of *public law* and not of private law. We admit only the capitalism of the state. . . . Hence our task is to broaden the application of intrusion by the state into the relationships of "private law," to broaden the right of the state to abrogate "private" contracts, to apply not Corpus Juris Romani but our own *revolutionary legal consciousness* to "civil legal relationships," to show systematically, stubbornly, and insistently in a series of model processes *how* it is necessary to act with intelligence and with energy.[1]

On the same question Lenin wrote to Molotov:

> We should acknowledge the chief task of the commission as being: completely to guarantee the interests of the proletarian state from the viewpoint of the possibility of controlling (subsequent control) all private enterprises without exception and abrogating all contracts and private agreements—as contradictory alike to the letter of the law and to the interests of the toiling mass of workers and peasants. Not slavish imitation of bourgeois civil law, but a series of limitations thereof in the spirit of our laws without embarrassment of economic or trading work.[2]

These words of the great Lenin emphasized the characteristic feature of Soviet law which was established to defend the interests of workers and peasants—to defend the Soviet state.

The content of Soviet law is made up, not of the Corpus Juris Romani —the gospel of capitalist society which rests on private property—but of revolutionary legal consciousness which defends the interests of the people —of millions of toiling masses. Soviet law is the law of the socialist state of workers and peasants, born in the fire of the October Revolution which cast down the authority of the bourgeoisie and confirmed the authority of workers and peasants. Soviet socialist law preserves and defends the interests of the Soviet state and of socialism, and the interests and rights of the toiling people.

We live in socialist society. "The social organization which we have created may be called a Soviet, socialist organization—not yet completely built, but at root a socialist organization of society," as Stalin told Roy Howard. We still cannot proclaim the principle: "From each according to his capacities and to each according to his needs," but we can already say

[1] Lenin (Russian ed.), Vol. XXIX, p. 419.
[2] *Bolshevik* (1937), No. 2, p. 62.

(as does Article 12 of the Stalin Constitution) that labor in the USSR is a duty, and a matter of honor, for each citizen capable thereof, according to the principle: "He who does not work does not eat," and "From each according to his ability, to each according to his work." There is not the slightest doubt that each further success of socialism will see ever increasing obliteration of class boundaries, and that we shall build communism and be able completely to put into practice the communist principle "From each according to his ability, to each according to his needs." Already we embody in reality that whereof the best and noblest human minds have dreamed—Thomas More or Morelli, Saint-Simon, Fourier, Robert Owen.

Being socialist law, Soviet law expresses the victory and the triumph of socialist principles in all spheres of our life. Expressing the essence of new socialist relationships in the USSR, it grows and develops together with the whole country, with each year and each five-year period ever more completely and logically expressing in its institutes and its juridical formulae the principles of the socialism which is celebrating its triumph and preparing the transition to the highest phase of its development—to communism. It expresses the complete and final victory of socialist production and social relationships which found their embodiment in world history in the fundamental law of the USSR—the great Stalin Constitution.

The Stalin Constitution is the greatest act of Soviet socialist law which has consolidated the sum total of twenty years of triumphant development of the Soviet state and of twenty years of struggle for socialism waged by the proletariat and all those who toil in our land. It is the fundamental source of Soviet socialist law. Upon its basis must and can be worked out a system of Soviet socialist law, not hitherto worked out although all the necessary conditions were present.

The systematization of law presupposes the presence of a single, general guiding principle—unvarying for all legal institutes and branches of law. In Soviet law such a single and general principle is that of socialism—the principle of a socialist economic and social system resting on socialist property, annihilation of exploitation and social inequality, distribution in proportion to labor, a guarantee to each member of society of the complete and the manifold development of all his (spiritual and physical) creative forces, and true human freedom and personal independence. This is the principle of socialism! From the viewpoint of this principle Soviet statutes and entire branches of Soviet law can and must be brought into mutual interconnection, and the unity of the principles with which they are permeated can and must be shown. A general, legal idea—expressing the essence and the historical characteristics of the epoch of victorious socialism—can and must make them one.

The systematization of Soviet socialist law was decisively rejected by the people's enemies, who perverted socialist law and denied its creative role—predicting its "withering away" and "evaporation." It will, on the contrary, still further reinforce our law, for it will help each branch of law to take fresh stock of its weapons, to separate those that are of primary importance and to establish connections and transitions as between the different branches of law.

At present the science of Soviet socialist law lacks the necessary congruity and unity. Hitherto, for example, the development of public law, administrative law, and civil law among us has been parallel and almost without correlation and congruity of any sort. On the other hand, a series of problems (such as that developing contemporary kolkhozes) still await solution in each of these branches of law—often obtaining no proper answer from any one of them.

Soviet law is unitary because it expresses identical social relationships, serves identically the same purposes and problems, and employs identical methods in solving them. This is why, in speaking of Soviet public law, we must start by defining this idea from the Marxist-Leninist understanding of law in general and of Soviet law in particular. Soviet socialist state law is a branch of Soviet socialist law. It is distinguished by the same qualities and characteristics as is Soviet law in its entirety. Understanding of the essence and content of Soviet public law is possible only if we start from the Marxist-Leninist understanding of law in general.

In bourgeois science there is no unanimity of understanding of the content of public law. We have already seen how contradictory, and—above all else—how unscientific (and therefore fruitless) were the attempts of divers bourgeois scholars (and entire scientific schools and trends) to define the content of state and of law. This impotence of bourgeois legal science—and indeed of the rest of the bourgeois social sciences—is due to the vice and the ineptitude of the method ordinarily employed by bourgeois scholars. They invoke the aid of the theory of dogmatic jurisprudence to unriddle the secrets of social phenomena—a theory no more fit for this purpose than was the medieval theory of phlogiston [3] for the cognition of natural phenomena.

The formal-juridical method of investigation and cognition only conditions the manipulation of abstract ideas and notions instead of studying the phenomena concealed under the veil of such ideas and notions. It is a

[3] Phlogiston: a particular species of "imponderable fluid," by whose hypothetical existence chemists—down to the time of Lavoisier (1743–1794)—explained heat phenomena, and especially burning.

purely ideological method—a method which contemplates legal phenomena as self-contained entities, with their beginning and end originating within themselves and regardless of what exists in reality and in life outside of them. Hence the fallacy of its conclusions and the falsity of its judgments. It was no mere chance that Marx characterized the juridical method as "*juristisch—also falsch.*" It is a method of ignoring the actual world of phenomena. It strives to know these phenomena by purely speculative analysis of them, not by disclosing the material causes which generated them.

Hence the fetichism of bourgeois law and bourgeois legal ideas, which also—in their systematized and generalized form—make up the content of the science of bourgeois law. Hence the arbitrariness of diverse "doctrines" and "theories" created by innumerable scholars of all sorts as applicable to their political tastes and to the demands of their capitalist masters.[4]

The juridical method of investigation is abstract and departs from the concrete peculiarities of the phenomenon under investigation. The more subtle distinctions of individuality depart from the view of judge and jurist, as Jellinek, for example, says:

> They are satisfied with Gaius and Titius,[5] plaintiff and defendant, representing something general, analogous to tone in acoustics or to colors in optics. In actual life, however, all agreements and delicts are individualized. Here the ancient rule is operative: *Si duo faciunt idem non est idem.* In the great majority of cases, all purchases and sales effected in the market are lumped by the jurist under one and the same category.[6]

A jurist employing the juridical method is not interested in the economic position of the various owners or in the diverse economic conditions of the agreements they make—the latter is the affair of economists, statisticians, sociologists, and so on. The juridical art of abstraction from "collateral" phenomena lying outside the legal field reigns here. Hence juridical thinking, one-sided and devoid of content, is replete with abstractions and alien to concreteness.

Herein is the reason why it is impossible to use the so-called dogmatic-

[4] Jellinek's observation on this score regarding the absence, in bourgeois legal science, of reasoned methodology is characteristic. "In the literature on the doctrine of the state, there prevails in this regard the greatest confusion . . . right down to the present time, inconceivable fabrication in the sphere of state doctrine—if only presented with due aplomb—has attracted attention in literature and has been seriously considered. Assertions took the place of facts and convictions the place of proof. Vagueness passed for profundity, and arbitrary philosophizing for the highest knowledge. Chiefly for this reason, in the history of the literature of the doctrine of state there formed very recently so noticeable a gap that in the course of the last decades not a single systematic work has merited the slightest attention" (Jellinek, *General Theory of the State*, pp. 19–20).

[5] These are the conventional names of plaintiff and defendant in Roman law.

[6] Jellinek, *General Theory of the State*, p. 24.

juridical method for scientific investigation.[7] Even outstanding bourgeois jurists fail, however, to see the viciousness of the method they so widely employ, for which reason in large measure their scientific theories appear similarly vicious. The unsatisfactory character of such theories may be exemplified in any bourgeois conception of public law. Bourgeois science ordinarily defines the idea and content of public law by merely pointing at the aggregate norms defining the state organization.[8]

Such is the prevailing idea of the task and content of public law in bourgeois science, which elaborately avoids broadening the object of the science of public law (and of public law itself) to the point of contact with the "material substratum" of the state which serves as the foundation of each and every relationship, idea, and phenomenon of public law. The matter goes even further. A number of learned jurists hold that the tasks of the science of public law are limited to the study of a juridical nature of the so-called contemporary state alone.

> The historian of law studies legal phenomena in their gradual development over prolongation of many centuries. He needs a definition that would help him distinguish the state from other cognate phenomena when he encounters diverse social unions in diverse epochs and among diverse peoples. . . . With such a purpose in view, he will give a definition studiously isolated from all the characteristics of the legal order of these diverse states—from that which is especially studied by legal dogma. . . . The dogma of public law of our time needs, therefore, not a definition which would embrace states of all times and all nations, but one which would serve as the starting point for an explanation of the juridical order of the contemporary legal state.[9]

The science of public law cannot, however, be limited to a narrowly juridical sphere of investigation—to a study of the state, solely and exclu-

[7] To avoid misunderstandings it should be emphasized that denial of the juridical method of investigation does not mean refusal to investigate an object from its juridical side (that is to say, from the point of view of what legal relationships are connected with a phenomenon).

[8] See, e.g., Yelistratov: "The aggregate of norms defining state organization will constitute public law. . . . The science of public law studies the norms which define state organization. . . ." (*Public Law*, pp. 54–55).

Korf: "The Science of Public Law is the name given to the discipline dedicated to study of the legal structure of the state" (*Russian Public Law* [1915], Pt. 1, p. 3).

By legal structure of the state is here understood the totality of the "legal phenomena which define the state organization of a given nation, the details of its state life, the essence and structure of the given state authority, its functioning, and so forth." Korf, however, considers it inevitable for the science of jurisprudence to utilize the data of political science; "otherwise it appears without foundation, unreal, utopian, and without life." (*Op. cit.*, pp. 2–3).

"The task of the science of public law consists in examining the juridical principles which define the state's organization" (Korkunov, *Russian Public Law* [1908], Vol. I, p. 1).

[9] A. S. Alekseyev, *Russian Thought* (1894), Bk. XI, p. 59.

sively as a legal institute, a complex of certain juridical relationships. Science should start from actual social relationships. The nature of law and state cannot be understood by studying them isolatedly. The same is true if one seeks to understand and to portray how law and state arose, and how—and in accordance with what formulae—they developed. They may be understood and explained only on the basis of an analysis of social relationships, a study of the development of the latter (founded upon the production and distribution of material things in society), and a study of the history of the development of society and of the classes into which society split when private property in the form of instruments and means of production emerged.

The jurist, of course, is interested in the juridical nature of law and the state but has not the power to know that nature if he remains entirely within the limits of legal relationships and legal norms. Scientific cognition of the juridical nature of the state is possible only upon one condition: complete rejection of the formal juridical method of cognition, and unconditional transition to the method of dialectic materialism, which contemplates ideologies and other species of superstructure in connection with the production relationships upon which they are based. It contemplates state and law in connection with the life and development of all society, of all sides of its being—and above all that of its economic production.

The state as a form of organizing social relationships on the basis of dominance and subordination is to be explained only in the light of a study of its economic basis—of knowing the laws of historical development of society as the development of classes and class struggle. To separate the science of public law from the science of the economic development of society, away from sociology, history, and philosophy, is to leave a dead form, a dry skeleton affording no idea whatever of the entire organism—of the very essence of state and law. Juridical abstractions, illusions, and fictions flourish luxuriantly in this soil, giving off, like *ignes fatui,* their deceptive and lifeless glitter.

Bourgeois science of public law, following its vicious juridical methodology, portrays the object of public law incorrectly, limiting it as a rule to questions merely of state organization. From its point of view, of course, it is easy to understand the ignoring of questions of social organization and of the economic and political life and history of society and of the corresponding sciences. We categorically deny that these questions can be ignored. Only on the basis of the organic connection of legal science with these sciences can the study of problems of public law be fruitful and truly scientific. Only upon this condition can a solution of the questions attracting the attention of the science of public law be attained. Here, of course, method plays a decisive part. The only scientific method of cognition is the method of dialectic materialism.

In the *Eighteenth Brumaire of Louis Bonaparte* (1852), Marx wrote:

> Above the various forms of property, above the social conditions of existence, towers an entire superstructure of diverse and unique feelings, illusions, ideas, and world-views. The entire class creates and forms all this on the basis of its material conditions and the corresponding social relationships.[10]

Dialectic materialism was the key to cognition of society and of the essence of law and the state. From them it plucked the illusory flowers of idealist romanticism and showed them in their living shape and true light. Employing the method of dialectic materialism, Marxism-Leninism showed how, out of social life of one tenor, another develops because production forces have grown and production relationships have changed. The essence of the dialectic method is that it "requires that phenomena be contemplated, not only from the viewpoint of their being mutually connected and conditioned, but also from that of their moving, changing, developing—from the viewpoint of their emergence and their dying out."[11]

Marxism-Leninism scientifically illuminated all human history, all aspects of life of human society. It opened up and explained the history of the development of social relationships. It showed their true meaning and real essence. It revealed the perspective of the development and formulated the laws defining the trend and content of social relationships. Marxism answered all the most complicated—and hitherto seemingly inscrutable—questions of the history of philosophy, political economy, law and morality.

What was social science before Marx? "Pre-Marxian sociology" and historiography at *best* presented a desultory assemblage of crude facts and a portrayal of separate sides of the historic process. Marxism pointed the way to all-embracing, omnifarious study of the process of the emergence, development, and decay of social-economic formations. It contemplates the *totality* of all contradictory tendencies and reduces them to precisely defined conditions of the life and production of the various *classes* of society. It eliminates subjectivism and arbitrariness in choosing or interpreting separate "master" ideas. It exposes, without exception, the roots of all ideas and all different tendencies in the condition of material production forces. It is the people who create their own history. But how are their motives—and specifically the motives of the masses of people—defined? How are the collisions of contradictory ideas and aspirations evoked? What is the nature

[10] Marx and Engels (Russian ed., 1935), Vol. II, p. 273.

[11] *History of the All-Union Communist Party (of Bolsheviks): A Short Course* (1938), p. 101.

of the sum total of all these conflicts in the aggregate of human societies? What is the nature of the objective conditions of production of material life which create the basis of all the historic activity of people? What kind of law governs the development of these conditions? Marx directed his attention to all these questions, and pointed the way to the scientific study of history as one process, conforming in all of its diversification and contradiction to established principles.[12]

Marx and Engels turned socialism from a utopia into a science. They placed in the hands of the proletariat, struggling for emancipation, a new instrument which it had never seen before—scientific theory. Thus armed, the proletariat acquired the forces to conquer the old world and to build a new one—a new socialist society.

Marxism played a gigantic part in the development of all branches of knowledge, inasmuch as it provided a stable scientific foundation and an immensely powerful scientific method for cognition of phenomena—and, in particular, of social phenomena. It put an end to the mystification of social relationships and to the idealization of these. It showed that they result from a definite condition of productive forces, a definite state of economic development.

> The economic order of society of each given epoch represents the real basis whose qualities explain in the last analysis the entire superstructure formed by the sum total of the legal and political institutions—and likewise of the religious, philosophical and other views—of each given historical period. Hegel freed the understanding of history from metaphysics. He made history dialectic, but his own view of history was essentially idealist. Now idealism has been driven out of its last refuge—the field of history. Now the understanding of history has become materialist. Now a road has been found to explain human self-consciousness by the conditions of human existence whereas the old explanation was that human self-consciousness explained these conditions.[13]

Juridical ideas are the form of this human self-consciousness. In themselves they are powerless to explain anything, precisely as we are powerless to explain the ideas themselves if we remain locked within a circle of juridical concepts.

Public law is concerned with legal questions—with juridical relationships, phenomena, and concepts—which, however, it can explain only if it abandons "legal" ground and passes to that of actual social relationships. Starting from what has been already expounded, we must define the object of public law with notably greater breadth, and differently as to methodological principle, than does bourgeois science. We see the object of public law in the

[12] Lenin (Russian ed.), Vol. XVIII, p. 13.
[13] Marx and Engels (Russian ed.), Vol. XIV, p. 26.

study of the legal norms and institutes which reflect, confirm, and develop the social and state order of a given society, the system of social and state institutions, the principles of their interrelations, the extent of their rights and obligations, the methods of their activity, and likewise also the study of various sorts of public-law institutes which define rights and obligations of citizens both in their relationship to society and the state and in their relationship to each other.

Soviet public socialist law studies the socialist order—social and state—of the USSR, its emergence and development, and the system of Soviet state institutions and organs, their powers, obligations and problems (and methods of solving them). It studies the rights of citizens of the USSR—preserved by Soviet legislation—and the obligations to country, society, and state laid upon citizens by the Soviet state.

State territory is not merely an expanded basis for "realizing the power of the state" [14]—it is the material expression of supremacy, independence, and inviolability of the people who inhabit that territory. Territorial supremacy is an organic part of state supremacy, defended with all the might of state and social forces and means, with all the might of moral—political and state—unity of the population.

The idea of inviolability of Soviet state territory as the basis of the supremacy of the Soviet state has been most excellently expressed by Stalin: "We do not wish for a single inch of foreign land. But of our own land we will give not one single inch to anyone." [15]

Soviet public law is concerned also with the idea of state authority. It contemplates *authority* in the state as the organization of the domination, of the guidance of the population with the aid of methods (characteristic of the state) of repressing and educating the subject classes of society in the spirit of protection of the interests of the dominant class.

Contemplating such qualities of state authority as sovereignty, or such forms of state domination as federation and autonomy, Soviet public law is mindful first of all of the relationships of class domination. These are apparent from an analysis of the aggregate of social relationships, namely as relationships of domination.

In place of the formal-juridical analysis of such categories as territory, authority, and population, Soviet public law employs dialectic materialism to explain them, thereby disclosing all the content of the object in its entirety, showing the dynamics of its development and its particular qualities, and explaining the actual substance of its outward forms and filling these in with material substance.

[14] G. Jellinek, *A General Theory of the State* (Russian ed., 1908), p. 289.
[15] Stalin, *Questions of Leninism* (10th ed.), p. 361.

In contrast to the methodology of bourgeois science, which rends an object into two unconnected parts—form and substance—dialectic materialism insists that form and substance are one and contemplates phenomena from the standpoint of that unity. Marx presented a model for analyzing phenomena from the point of view of unity of form and substance in a brilliant article dedicated to the question of substantive and procedural law.

> If procedure represents nothing but empty form, then such formal triviality is of no independent value. From this point of view, Chinese law would become French law if squeezed into the form of French procedure. *Substantive law*, however, has its *necessary procedural forms inherent in it*, and as Chinese law must have a walking stick and mediaeval criminal law with its Draconian content required torture, so public, free procedure must necessarily have a substance which is public by nature and dictated by freedom—not by private interest. Procedure and law are just as closely connected with each other as, for example, the forms of plants and animals are with animal flesh and blood. *One* spirit must animate procedure and laws, since procedure is only *the form of the life of the law* and consequently a manifestation of its inward life.
>
> The pirates of Tidong break the legs and hands of their captives so that they cannot escape. To guarantee themselves against timber thieves the Landtag not only broke the law's hands and feet, but even pierced its heart. In its application of our procedure to certain categories of crime we definitely see no merit whatever. On the contrary we must pay proper tribute to the openness and logic with which unfree form has been given to unfree substance. If private interest which does not endure the light of publicity is factually brought into our law, then it is necessary to give it accordingly such secret procedure as not to arouse and nourish, at least, any sort of dangerous and illusory self-gratification. We consider it the obligation of all Rhine citizens (and especially jurists) to devote their chief attention at the present moment *to the substance of law*, so that there should not be left among us in the last resort an empty mask. Form has no value if it is not the form of a substance.[16]

Soviet public law cannot, therefore, limit its study merely to the formal side of the object under investigation. It seeks to know phenomena from the point of view of their inward content as well as of their outward form.

The object of the science of Soviet socialist law is the material substratum of state relationships as well as juridical form—not only the juridical nature of the state, but also its social-economic nature as the foundation and determinant of the juridical properties and peculiarities of institutes of public law.

Public law may be understood both in a broad and in a narrow sense. In the broad sense it embraces criminal law, administrative law, procedural law, and the foundations of civil law and international law. Criminal law is

[16] Marx and Engels (Russian ed.), Vol. I, pp. 257–258.

part of public law in the broad sense, since it defines the conditions of civic responsibility in the criminal court and the order of application of punishment. Administrative law is part of public law, since it regularizes the relationships of government, defines the organization of government, the system of administrative organs—their powers and their responsibility, and the forms of their activity. Procedural law cannot be separated from public law; it studies the organization of justice, the forms of organization of court organs and organs of the prosecuting magistrates, the procedural order of the activity of state organs, the conditions and order of holding one to responsibility or freeing him from it.[17]

It is harder to establish the connection of public law with civil law. In part of the law of domestic relations and of inheritance, this connection and kinship are beyond question. But even in other parts—in the field of the law of property and of the law of obligations—it is impossible to deny the connection. Thus the law of personal property in the USSR can be neither deduced nor understood nor explained save in connection with the Constitution.

The right to labor—the basis of Soviet labor law—is an object of public law in the broad sense of the word. The same should be said also of international law, which is most closely related to the legal activity of the state.

Thus in essence all branches of law may be included within the orbit of public law if by the latter term is understood the study of all sides of development and activity of the state as manifested in various legal forms.

Public law in the narrow sense, however, limits the range of its study to those questions of which we have previously spoken in establishing the object of the science of public law.

The present course of Soviet socialist public law has also defined its object from the viewpoint of the foregoing definition of our science, having put at the basis of all its exposition—as the proposition wherein it originates—the unshakable principles of the greatest act of victorious socialism: the great Stalin Constitution.

[17] In the history of law this connection of procedural law with public law is brilliantly clear, e.g., from the fact that the fundamental act of the English Constitution is nothing but a simple procedural statute defining the conditions of the arrest of citizens if they are held to criminal responsibility.

[7]

THE ESSENCE OF LAW

§ 1. The Legal Superstructure and Law Proper

Our job in the first chapter was to investigate the social sources of law and to describe its connections with the economy, state, and forms of social consciousness. In that respect all legal actuality is conceived as the whole specific form of social relations. When we were considering the external connections of legal phenomena there was no point or opportunity to single out the separate elements of the legal superstructure, including what should properly be considered law. When we are bringing out law's dependence on the relations of production, of course, we are usually brought up against legal relations and the rights and duties of subjects. The relationship of legal actuality and the state brings legislative norms to the fore. In connection with the ideological aspect of law our attention is turned mainly to sense of justice. A multilevel approach to law is necessary and useful, but in itself it does not as yet answer what law is and what is its essence. It only prepares us to tackle this radical problem of legal science, and creates the necessary premises for doing so.

If law is primarily the legal expression of relations of production, then a scientific, materialist theory of law should begin with the stating of ownership as the simplest legal relation; but ownership proves, on the historical plane, to be an undeveloped form of property. In the same way, the elementary legal connections and relations (of the individual, family, clan, community) of the period of the establishment of class formations were not a legal right or developed legal actuality. The development of property relations based on forced alienation and appropriation of another's materialised, embodied labour, entailed formation of the law of exploiter societies, which converted the fact of possession of property, of appropriation into a measure or yardstick of men's activity, in conformity with which other social relations are also built up. The rudiments of the legal reinforcement of the prevailing mode of production were converted from a realm of actual property relations (*jus rerum*), in which there was as yet no law properly speaking, into the actual existence of law and converted into a whole legal superstructure on the economic basis. The faster economically dominant individuals became conscious of their general class interests and organised their strength in the form of a state, and their will as state will, lending it universality in the form of a law, the more intensively did this process of legal phenomena's acquiring qualitative definiteness and relative independence proceed. The formation of a legal superstructure meant the appearance of a new kind of mental appropriation of social being.

There are always great difficulties connected with understanding's penetration into the essence of any subject of study. When it is a matter of law, analysis of its essence comes up against a specific complication, which is that it has hitherto been a moot question in jurisprudence as to what legal phenomena should be classed as law proper. It is not a simple question to answer. The essence of law, however, must of course be correlated only with its direct manifestation and not with the whole legal superstructure. Legal actuality and the legal superstructure consist of a whole aggregate of legal phenomena (sense of right or justice and recognition of law, legal rules, legal relations, rights and duties, legal order, and so on). But the term 'legal phenomenon' commonly used, which is applied to any component of the legal superstructure, is not identical with the phenomenon of law. The concept 'phenomenon of law' is related to the equally rigorous philosophical concept of 'the essence of law'. Phenomenon or appearance and essence form law proper in their contradictory unity. Consequently we must define at the very start the round of legal actuality relating to law proper and then penetrate from its appearance to the basis, to the essence of the subject-matter we are concerned with. In all probability law proper must be considered, as a first approximation, those components of legal actuality that serve as the original, generally binding yardsticks of social activity which make it possible to assess the legitimacy of conduct, to decide who is right in a dispute (i.e. on whose side the truth lies), to punish him who is guilty of a breach of law and order justly, to make the social opportunities granted by the law enjoyable without let or hindrance, and to require performance of the corresponding duties. There is no doubt that legal norms are this yardstick. The recognition of general rules of conduct as law is of fundamental significance, but can general rules be taken as absolute when it is known that they are often the result, on the genetic plane, of the generalising of already constituted personalised decisions that register the subject's actual right? And when, functionally, no one general rule can become a specifically legal regulator of conduct without being embodied in a right (or corresponding duty) or in an individualised yardstick?

The following picture of the formation and realisation of law and of the legal mediation of social relations can be drawn. The objective needs of a given mode of production find expression in the general class interests of the individuals who are dominant under this mode of production, in accordance with which their sense of justice is moulded and a single state will is developed that is expressed in generally binding legal enactments (laws) enforced by the state. General legal rules affect men's conduct and the activity of organisations by granting the subjects of social relations corresponding rights and the legal duties following from them, and by forming concrete legal relations in a whole series of cases. The juristic facts that entail the rise (alteration, or suppression) of legal relations also include acts applying the rules of law in which the rights and duties of the subjects of the legal relations are fixed. By exercising their rights and performing their duties the subjects of law in practice perform in social life what has been established by legal rules as possible (proper) conduct. Under a regime of legality (the rule of law) and the corresponding degree of consciousness of law, and of legal standards, realisation of the law leads to the existence of a certain legal order in a country without which the normal life of class society, and above all normal functioning of the prevailing mode of production, are impossible. Subsequent development of the productive forces and relations of production gives rise to new objective needs that in the final count cause changes in legislation; then a new cycle of law-formation and application and enforcement of the law begins, and so on and so forth.

The picture sketched above reflects only one way of law-formation, albeit the main one, in the modern world. Another process of the shaping of legal actuality, linked with judicial law-making and common law, had a significant place in history. This path still exists today, especially in countries where the Anglo-American legal system operates. We can thus speak of two lines (or forms) of the genesis of law; let us dwell on this point in more detail.

We have already remarked in another connection that law, in the early epochs of the formation of class society, was the actual relations themselves, which were enforced by barbarous means of direct force. In such cases the establishing of rights (and duties), and of concrete legal relations preceded the formation of general rules of law expressed in statutes and enforced by a professional law-enforcement apparatus (courts), differentiated on the basis of division of labour. Subsequently, however, there were also historical epochs when, during the forming of a new socio-economic stage of development, state protection of the social relations actually built up preceded the formation of new norms of law.

It would be wrong to suppose that any substitution of legal norms by sense of justice, and concrete sanctioning of the rights of the parties to social relations by judicial practice, has a reactionary character and is arbitrary. In the revolutionary periods of the establishment of new social formations, when an all-embracing new system of law (legislation) has not yet been built up, the sense of justice and judicial acts based on it that recognise rights (duties) of one kind or another and concrete legal relations may to some extent precede the formation of general rules of law, sometimes blazing the trail to new legislation and promoting social progress and the consolidation of a new type of legal order.

When a class-antagonistic formation, on the other hand, is stagnating (as for example in the epoch of imperialism), opposing of the sense of justice of the moribund classes and social groupings that are trying to retain political power and economic domination to the existing legal system has a reactionary significance. It is just as reactionary in such conditions, too, to counterpose judicial practice and outmoded legal customs, and the actual relations arbitrarily defended by the state's bureaucratic apparatus, to legislation. This happens sporadically when the class struggle becomes sharper in any period of the life of class-antagonistic formations, but takes on a systematic character in the historical decline of any of these formations, when the sovereign authority can no longer rely completely on legal, juristic means of suppressing the masses of the working people, which leads to the dissolution of the given type of legality and legal order.

In addition to the extreme processes of the counterposing of the juridical practice of judicial bodies to the law (general norms) one must bear in mind the other circumstance mentioned above. One must never forget about the second line of law-making, which has by no means a destructive influence on the legal system built up (on the law) but can, on the contrary, actively help fill gaps in the operative system of general legal rules. This also happens, in fact, when judicial practice is rejected in principle as a source of law, but is most intensive in countries where legal precedent, above all judicial precedent, is officially recognised.

The law-making power of judicial bodies is often used by ruling classes to break and circumvent laws adopted by the sovereign bodies, but in these cases it is a matter of the extreme process of the counterposing of judicial activity to statute law already described. In other circumstances judicial precedent can be a legally binding source of law supplementing the norm-making activity of the organs of government and administration, a phenomenon not rare in the history of class society.

It is quite clear that precedent law is evidence that rights (duties) are formed, if not prior to, then in any case simultaneously with, the forming of the general legal rule that follows from uniform judicial practice and is linked with the generalisation of personalised verdicts in concrete cases. Since judicial practice was a very common source of law in slave-owning and feudal society, and has remained a quite important source in bourgeois society (especially in the Anglo-American systems of law), the fact of the simultaneous formation of rights and the law cannot in itself be disregarded as concerns the mechanism of law-making and of law-enforcement in general. Even with effective legislative activity by the state and non-recognition in principle of judicial law-making, judicial practice encounters a certain need to fill gaps in the law, and is a real stimulus to the perfecting of legal regulation.

Law-making may thus proceed as follows. The objective needs of the prevailing mode of production lead to the constant formation of actual relations such as need consolidation in a certain form, define their subjects' claims, and are upheld and initially enforced by concrete verdicts. This upholding of claims and defence of the actual relations underlying them signify the formation of rights (duties and individual concrete legal relations) simultaneously with the formation of a general legal rule, the law, in the course of uniform judicial practice. This judicial (or administrative) practice is often subsequently generalised at the level of legislative reinforcement. Here the spontaneous formation of actual relations anticipates their general class recognition in a general norm of law, and proceeds from a case decision. In the past the law-making process described here was very common, and it has not disappeared even now, although it proves in principle to be simply supplementary in regard to direct norm-creation. Scholars interpreting the law of ancient society often confuse customary or unwritten law and judicial precedents with later codifications, so creating an impression of quite developed norm-creating activity by the state in the past. Hammurabi's Code of the eighteenth century B. C., for instance, was probably nothing but a codification of customary law, much like the much later Salic Law and Russian Law (*Russkaya Pravda*). The Russian law-books and collections of laws and edicts of 1497 and 1550 were already a systematisation of comparatively developed Russian feudal law, when the princely courts enforced not only customary norms but also the few acts of the sovereign. Only constitutional and political, and administrative relations, it should be noted, have been regulated legally since ancient times mainly by the sovereign's normative legal acts, witness the reforms of Servius Tullius in 594 B.C., the thirteenth century Magna Charta, the 1679 Act of the English Parliament, and the Bill of Rights of 1689. In the nineteenth century the position changed sharply on the Continent—witness not only the French Constitution of 1791 and all subsequent French Constitutions, but also the French *Code civil* (Code Napoléon) of 1804, the 1863-5 Civil Code of Saxony, the German Civil Code of 1900, the State Book (collection of laws in force) of the Russian Empire, which became effective in 1835. This practice also largely predetermined European scholars' theoretical conceptions of law (except in Great Britain, where the Common Law clearly took precedent over statute law right into the twentieth century). Judicial precedent, incidentally, continues to exist in all bourgeois countries; it is particularly common in England, the United States, Canada, and Australia.

The more legislation lags behind the dynamics of social relations and society's new needs, the broader judicial law-making is, which most clearly witnesses to the fact that general legal rules are genetically linked with actually formed relations and generalised verdicts in concrete cases. It is also shown, incidentally, by the facts (less and less often met in our time) of the state's sanctioning of customs that reflect actually existing relations. In this case we are far from giving a positive evaluation of precedent and common law, even when it does not develop in opposition to legislation (or other of the state's normative juristic acts), because both the one and the other exclude the active, creative role of legal regulation, juridically reinforcing only what has already formed in social relations. It is not, however, a matter of evaluation, which, incidentally, cannot be the same for all the facts and depends on definite historical conditions, but of the point that the law-making process noted above really exists and on the whole is a necessary condition, in spite of all its deficiencies, of spontaneous maintenance of legal systems at the level of the prevailing mode of production's objective needs. This process presumes the simultaneous formation both of the law and of rights. When it has a supplementary character, it does not undermine the authority of the general norms of law and the prestige of statute, and by its nature fills the gaps in a country's legal system. Only in the historical periods of the establishment of new socio-economic formations or, on the contrary, of the decline and decay of old formations can this line of law-making lose its supplementary character and reflect the formation of law of a new type or the breakdown of the old legal form.

Ideas that right inevitably comes after the law are thus unsatisfactory from the angle of the whole history of the development of legal form and do not allow for the law-giving process described above either in its extreme expression of the sharpening of class contradictions in periods of the revolutionary transformations, or in its expression in quieter conditions of the social basis's spontaneous effect on legal systems, when the process has a supplementary character but nevertheless invariably operates with greater or less force.

Has the picture of law-giving and law-enforcement painted at the beginning of our exposition of this theme, which postulates the establishment of right on the basis of the law, been abolished by what we have said? In no way. That is confirmed, above all, by the practice of socialism, which creates the premises for effective, scientifically grounded law-giving by the state authorities, capable of reflecting the people's urgent objective needs and will in the highest degree. A true general picture of the functioning legal superstructure is obtained when the one scheme of law-making is superimposed on the other. At closer quarters, however, it is clear that legal regulation cannot be enforced without embodying the general legal norms in rights (duties). Here we come up against yet another law, breach of which disrupts the process of realising general norms, undermines law and order, breaks the link between juridical laws and both social activity and social relations. Without rights the law does not work. That being so, at which there is no doubt, it turns out that reduction of law proper simply to a system of legal norms is only a consequence of sorts of an absolutising of them that does not reflect their dialectical unity with the system of rights of the subjects of social activity.

It is true not only that right, and the measure (or yardstick) of the conduct of a definite party to social relations, are defined and given shape as legal right only through being fixed in the norms of law (general yardsticks) but also that these legal norms can perform specifically legal regulation only by being embodied in rights (duties).

It is not out of place here to note that the dialectical unity of the law and right reflects, *inter alia,* the capacity of juristic action not simply to rely on state enforcement and the sovereign's binding orders but also to involve all legally empowered persons in ensuring legal order, since their enjoyment of their rights always depends on a corresponding performance of duties (by other persons or by themselves). On that plane right is largely the constitutive, activising factor in the performance of duties. This nicety of legal regulation is vital; without it it is difficult to understand the peculiarity of law. Politically it is clear that the broader the social basis of state power (sovereign authority), the more actively the machinery will operate in which rights prove to be primarily a personalised right to require obligatory conduct. Narrowness of the social base, a gulf between the state and the population, and the reactionary role of the ruling class lead, as regards the authority/subordinate relationship, to all rights being concentrated in the hands of a tiny group of officials, while almost only duties remain for the public, performance of which is required by the sovereign's authorised agents. However that may be, the inadequacy of the law alone to regulate social relations consists in particular in general orders of obligatory conduct not yet being reinforced, before the origin of rights, by the right of the persons concerned to require the appropriate conduct from obligees. We shall have to touch on this point in more detail later.

To what has already been said we would add, meanwhile, that right is not only a personalised yardstick of conduct but also in a certain respect a generally acceptable measure of conduct, recognised and therefore guaranteed by the state, and that the deepest roots of a right, as of a juridical law, go down into the objective needs of the prevailing mode of production and exchange. The sovereign cannot, in general, and on the whole, simply by the will

6*

of the persons wielding power, endow its citizens with rights and liberties or arbitrarily deprive them of vitally important rights. And if that happens under the rule of the haves, the source of rights ultimately proves to be economic necessity, which somehow or other makes itself felt. The state, by means of statutes and courts, legally reinforces the measure of guaranteed liberty, and the claims on it, of individuals, social groups, classes, and the people, in conformity with the interests of those who are dominant in the given relations, and therefore reflects the need of relations of production of this type.

Everything we have drawn attention to witnesses that right is not a 'side effect' of the law, both because it can arise simultaneously with the latter and also because legislative regulation of social relations is inconceivable without rights. These are by no means weak arguments in favour of the point that one must consider both the law and right in their unity to be law proper.

Jurisprudence was long unable to answer the point about the relationship of the law and right. In the struggle against feudal despotism the ideologists of the once revolutionary bourgeoisie advanced the idea of the natural rights of man, which (other things apart) exalted right by raising it not only above positive legislation but also above the sovereign authority itself. Later, however, having attained power, the bourgeoisie brought statute law, objective law, to the fore. In the epoch of imperialism, as we are aware, not only is the prestige of bourgeois law declining but right is being more and more often declared an artificial juristic construct supplementing duties.

We can clearly trace the course of the class struggle during the establishment, consolidation, and decay of capitalism in the changes in attitude of theory and practice to right and its relationship with statute law and duties. One can affirm, on the whole, that in the past either right or the law was often treated in an absolute sense, and that in any case their relationship was identified with the link between legal norms and legal relationships, treating the latter as the sole field both of legal duties and of legal powers and rights.

The socialist theory of law is able to bring out the real

dialectic of the interaction of legal norms and the rights of the subjects of social relations, and also their social, class content, but many problems still remain contentious.

In the description of the dialectical connection between the law and right in Soviet jurisprudence, the work of Piontkovsky has played a considerable role[1]; he resolutely, though rather one-sidedly, opposed reducing law to legal norms alone, considering it necessary to include legal relations in the concept and definition of law. Certain other theorists of socialist law, by identifying a multi-angle approach to the study of legal phenomena with the problem of the essence of law proper, have gone much further, suggesting that law is legal relations, legal norms, and sense of justice.[2] It is conceivable that, from the methodological aspect, the reason for the desire to unite norms and relations in one concept of law lies in a mistaken formalising of legal relations interpreted as the connection of rights and duties emptied of its proper social, active content, and also the incorrect idea that there are no duties and rights apart from legal relations, and that right is only an element of legal relations.

In recent years, however, quite rigorous proof has been adduced that the direct content of legal relations is the activity of their subjects and that right extends beyond the content of legal relations. It appears that recognition of the law and right as law does not necessarily entail inferring that law proper includes juridical social relations. Logic, moreover, does not permit the joining of a description of law at the attributive and institutional level into a single definition of law. Each of these levels has its own definition: only the substantive level, which presupposes formulation of law's essence, can provide a synthesised definition, but for that the whole basis of law must be

[1] See, for example: A. A. Piontkovsky, A Contribution to the Interrelationship of Law and Right, *Sovetskoe gosudarstvo i pravo*, 1958, 5. For further details see: B. L. Nazarov, *Sotsialisticheskoe pravo v sisteme sotsial'nykh svyazei* (Socialist Law in The System of Social Relations), Legal Literature Press, Moscow, 1974.

[2] See: Ya. F. Mikolenko, Law and Its Forms, *Sovetskoe gosudarstvo i pravo*, 1965, 7; Imre Szabó, *A jogelmélet Alapjai* (Budapest, 1971 (cited from the Russian translation *Osnovy teorii prava* (Fundamentals of the Theory of Law), Progress, Moscow, 1974).

found, i.e. its essence, which we shall deal with in the next section.

In recent years Soviet general theory and the particular legal disciplines have paid much attention to studying the content of legal relations as a variety of social relations connected with the interaction of their subjects. Khalfina, for example, is painstakingly investigating the real conduct of the parties to legal relations. [1] Unfortunately subjects' rights and duties continue to be interpreted in her work as the content of (direct) legal relations, so that their traditional formalisation is not wholly eliminated, and right is not thought of out of the context of legal relations. Then there remains, too, the old alternative—that if one does not consider legal relations as law, one has to consider only certain general norms to be such, or the law as it exists (objective law). In that case, however, there is ultimately a certain absolutising of general legal enactments, which is just as unacceptable as evidence of the priority of right, a priority that does not in fact exist. Only the reinforcement of subjects' rights in general legal norms signifies the full recognition of right. Without the law there are no established legal duties and legal powers and rights! At the same time, given the full significance of the norms of law in legal regulation, we must not lose sight of the fact that the general rules can only be realised through appropriate rights and duties. One has to repeat that because of the special significance of the actual possibility of exercising the rights granted, and of ensuring precise performance of duties, for the condition of legality and legal order. The very best juridical law has very little social value if it cannot find realisation in social relations.

One conclusion from this is that it is impossible to counterpose the law and right either in theory or in practice; their correspondence is natural and guarantees normal functioning of the legal form of social relations.

In conclusion a few remarks are called for apropos of the regulative role of sense of justice and of law-enforcement acts.

[1] See: R. O. Khalfina. *Obshchee uchenie o pravootnoshenii* (The General Doctrine of Legal Relations), Legal Literature Press, Moscow, 1974.

There are no grounds for doubting the regulative significance of sense of justice (social and individual). But as distinct from law proper no forms of legal consciousness can independently acquire the properties of a generally acceptable yardstick of conduct backed by the state. Even when the sense of justice of a revolutionary class just come to power proves in practice to be the source of law for a certain period, because of the absence or incompleteness of new legislation, it (sense of justice) is considered a generally acceptable, specifically legal regulator and yardstick of conduct only insofar as it finds embodiment in right and in the law that is taking shape in court (administrative) practice as a result of uniform decision of concrete cases. We know of cases when the works of certain eminent jurists of their day were sources of law, but their propositions were considered generally acceptable norms only insofar as they were reproduced in court practice creating law alongside legislation. On the whole a sense of justice is a *sine qua non* of law-making and of the application and enforcement of law. In that sense the law and right, and their realisation, are always directly dependent on it. The character and standard of the sense of justice both of the public and of the officials of the state machine, like their legal standards, essentially affect the rule of law and the state of law and order in a country.

Acts applying the law play an exceptionally important role in the realising of general legal norms, about which we shall speak in the section on law-enforcement. But can these norms be considered law in the proper sense of the term? One must postulate that they cannot. This negative answer does not apply solely to judicial (administrative) acts based on already existing general rules; there are no grounds for considering even verdicts that become official sources of law through the effect of precedent as law proper—they are only a form of its expression. Law proper cannot be reduced to its sources. This point is not just a legal nicety, it has fundamental significance. It follows from it that even in countries where legal precedent is developed, the individual act of a court in a concrete case cannot be considered law. Law is essentially contained only in the appropriate uniform judicial practice. The English lawyer, consequently, who says that law is what the court decides is not right, although judicial practice is a source of law in England. The law and right are not contained in any one judicial act but are only formed by many such acts.

§ 2. The Essence, Content, and Form of Law

Having established that by law we understand not the whole legal superstructure but only the law and right, we can pass on to study of the essence of these phenomena, and to bringing out their basis, by which philosophers understand the most profound moment of essence. A principled approach to understanding the essence of things and appearances has been formulated by Marxism-Leninism. It consists above all in the statement that appearances and their essence never coincide, although essence is always manifested in one way or another, and can therefore be ascertained.[1] Lenin wrote that

> human thought goes endlessly deeper from appearance to essence, from essence of the first order, as it were, to essence of the second order, and so on *without end*.
> Dialectics in the proper sense is the study of contradiction *in the very essence of objects:* not only are appearances transitory, mobile, fluid, demarcated only by conventional boundaries, but the *essence* of things is so as well.[2]

At the same time he stressed that '*law* and *essence* are concepts of the same kind (of the same order)'[3], and that appearance or semblance lies on the surface, vanishes more often, 'does not hold so "tightly", does not "sit so firmly" as "Essence"'[4].

So one must draw attention to the fact that essences (a) are of different levels; (b) include contradictions; (c)

[1] See: Karl Marx. *Capital*, Vol. III (Progress Publishers, Moscow, 1974), pp 312-313, 817-818; V. I. Lenin. Conspectus of Hegel's Book 'Lectures on the History of Philosophy'. *Collected Works*, Vol. 38, p 251.

[2] V. I. Lenin. *Op. cit.*, pp 251-252.

[3] V. I. Lenin. Conspectus of Hegel's Book 'The Science of Logic'. *Collected Works*, Vol. 38, p 152.

[4] *Ibid.*, p 130.

are most stable and constitute the basis of appearances and objects, but are still developing and fluid. How then does cognition occur? Initially there is simply the possibility of discovering the basis (or moment of the essence) only in its outward manifestations, i.e. in the law and rights. At this stage of knowledge the basis is formal, limited, and tautological. Properly speaking, we reached that stage when we established that not all legal form should be considered law but only the law and rights (objective and subjective law). Philosophically this statement is tautological and still far from disclosing the deep essence. The next stage is clarification of the real connections of law with the phenomena (appearances) that determine it. The real foundations of law are the various social factors of a political, moral, and economic nature that were described in Chapter One, in their connection with law. Each of the real foundations lends the possibility of formulating a certain definition of law. Taking into consideration law's conditioning by the economy, for instance, we can say that it is the legal expression of the relations of production (the attributive level of the apprehension of phenomena). The interaction of law and the state provides grounds for an institutional approach to legal form and calls for the definition of law as a system of legal norms upheld by organised coercion on the part of the state machinery. There can be other definitions as well. It is necessary, just the same, however, to find the full basis (essence) of law: only then do we get a chance to understand it at substantive level, and to provide a definition that includes a formula of its essence and its outward manifestation. The set of real foundations leads to a single (full) one that contains them in abstracted (sublated) form and explains all the most important qualities of law as such. This is achieved by means of the basic idea that expresses what is most essential in the nature of legal form. The main idea of Marxism consists in recognising the materially determined, class-willed nature of law. The formula of the essence of law, i.e. the complete basis of legal appearance, is to be found in the *Manifesto of the Communsit Party*.[1] The

[1] See: Karl Marx, Frederick Engels, *Collected Works*, Vol. 6 (Progress Publishers, Moscow, 1976), p 501.

essence of law is that it is the materially, economically determined will of the ruling classes (the dominant will) made into a law for all.

The making of the dominant will into a law for all signifies that it appears as a measure of conduct (activity) binding on all, as the supreme, indisputable yardstick of legitimate human acts, protected by the state.

The making of the dominant will into a law for all counterposes this will to arbitrariness and chance, makes the legal order independent of the desire of individuals, even of those belonging to the ruling class. Just as there are no grounds for confusing the scientific concept of the dictatorship of a class with the dictatorial political regime of an individual ruler (or elite), so one cannot assume that the making of any arbitrary direction of a dictator into a state law converts the same into law. Law is always the expression of the will of the classes (or of the people in developed socialist society) that are dominant under a given system of relations of production and therefore reflect the objective needs of the prevailing mode of production in one way or another. It is a matter of the dominant or prevailing will, and not of the will of one person or a tiny group of persons, who do not allow for the materially determined interests of the class, or of the whole nation (in developed socialist society), since such an individual or group will is in fact inherently arbitrary. Any one separate normative act may sanction arbitrariness, but it cannot become law.

The making of the dominant will into a law for all is the essence of law of the first order. It is decisive for understanding the specific properties of law itself: we shall therefore use it from now on wherever necessary, including attempts to define the concept of law and to describe its manifestations in the law and rights. We shall also have to demonstrate that this conception of the essence of law is quite relevant not only to law as a system of rules binding on all but also to right. It is important, first, however, to clarify why the making of the will of dominant classes into a law for all can be considered only the essence of law of the first order. The point is that the making of the will of the dominant classes into a law for all calls above all for its study, and for discovery of its genetic basis. Having brought out the contradictions inherent in essence of the first order, we will have the possibility to discover their basis and thus to pass on to a deeper understanding of law, to its essence of the second order, which already goes beyond the context of law itself. Marx and Engels, having stressed that the will-content of law is determined by the material conditions of the life of the dominant class, showed the way to deepen scientific understanding of law.

Spiridonov has made an interesting analysis of the essence of law on the historical plane,[1] but we must make the following point apropos of his and similar efforts. In going outside the framework of legal form, we must not forget that this form has its own direct content that cannot be ignored or reduced to the factual relations of property and exchange, which are simply the genetic basis of the law and right but are not the law itself of civilised society. In adopting the method of ascending from the abstract to the concrete in these investigations, we must remember Marx's caution that

> the method of rising from the abstract to the concrete is only the way in which thought appropriates the concrete, reproduces it as the concrete in the mind. But this is by no means the process by which the concrete itself comes into being.[2]

This remark was directed at the time, of course, against Hegel's method and put it back 'on its feet'.

What is the contradiction inherent in the essence of law of the first order, disclosure of which can bring out the deeper basis of law lying in the sphere of material relations? It is this, that the will of the individuals dominant in given relations of production is constituted as the generally binding yardstick of conduct for the whole population of a country, a yardstick that is represented through the state as both the expression of the will and the interest of all society. In other words, the needs and interests of a minority take the form of social needs and

[1] See: L. I. Spiridonov. *Sotsial'noe razvitie i pravo* (Social Development and Law), Leningrad Univ. Press, Leningrad, 1973.

[2] Karl Marx. *Grundrisse der Kritik der politischen Ökonomie (Rohentwurf) 1857-1858*, p 22.

interests. That is why the legal integument conceals not only the contradiction between the dominant and oppressed classes but also the contradiction, unavoidable with private property in the means of production and social division of labour, between the individual's interest and society's. The contradiction inherent in the essence of law of the first order has an antagonistic character in all formations associated with private property, and can therefore only be resolved in principle in a revolutionary way, but is partially overcome within the context of any one formation by the state coercion on which the dominant individuals' will relies. Only after the socialist revolution and the abolition of private ownership of the means of production and of exploiting classes are the conditions created for the antagonistic character of the contradiction in the essence of law to disappear; the contradiction itself, however, continues to exist in altered form since there is not yet full coincidence of the will of all the people and that of each individual, and the boundary line between public and personal interest and the difference between social and private needs are preserved and property inequality remains. The contradiction inherent in the essence of law will be fully and finally overcome in the higher phase of communism, but then the need for state maintenance of a yardstick of conduct applicable to all, too, will disappear, i.e. the need for legal form itself will pass.

Having laid bare the contradictory character of the very essence of law, we penetrate into the social content of the law and right, and come up against the claims of individuals, classes, and the people, and the interests and needs underlying them, that in one way or another express the objective needs of the prevailing mode of production, distribution, and exchange. In relation to them, will in law, measures applicable to all, state support, moral values, and social consciousness represent only a formal moment.

Legal, political, ethical, and ideological forms have material relations as their basis. The essence of law of the second order is the claims of individuals and classes to legal and political recognition of their interests, which are dictated by many circumstances but primarily by the objective needs of the production and exchange existing under social division of labour and economic inequality (the inability, at a given level of development of the productive forces, to provide for everyone according to his normal needs). Claims for the satisfaction of definite vital needs are converted into law only in certain conditions, one of which is invariably their correspondence to the needs of the ruling classes and of the mode of production with which they are associated. Those claims are also recognised in law that are dictated by the need to preserve the form itself of men's community, to maintain the social organisation and discipline without which no mode of production can exist. Law, like the state, performs functions linked with men's common affairs and control over deviant conduct, and with preventing asocial symptoms. Finally, claims that to some extent reflect the interests of the class opponents of the dominant social forces, to whom the latter make certain concessions during the class struggle in order to maintain their economic and political domination, may find sanction in law (in both the law and rights).

Understanding can penetrate deeper into law's essence of the third order from its essence of the second order. To do so it is necessary to disclose the contradictory nature of law's essence, but now essence of the second order, i.e. of claims. The contradiction in claims would seem to consist in its being impossible to satisfy the needs of every member of society, and of its being still a matter of the actual relations of production and exchange as such.

Marx's propositions about law in *Capital* evidently largely relate to analysis at the level of law's essence of the second order, and especially of the third order. They can in no way be couterposed to the statements of the founders of Marxism about the class-will character of law; they rather supplement, develop, and deepen them.

It is in the sphere of the relations of production, in particular in the realm of the exchange of commodities, that the economic basis of law is constantly reproduced, and it is there that its most important properties and qualities are generated. Marx analysed capitalist relations of production, establishing the objective significance of the relations of commodity-owners, whose rights are formally equal and ensure them the freedom of possession and disposal of things without which there are no commodity relations. Legal relations here are only the juridical form reinforcing actual relations due to the given mode of production. Subjects' rights (liberty, equality) are presented as man's 'natural rights', as the individual's juridically sanctioned 'natural' claims, which in fact do not follow from the natural character of man but are linked with his social nature and with social relations. The vital claims of individuals and classes prove to be due to actual relations that in one way or another must be defended by organised coercion. Marxism demonstrated that claims to ownership of the means of production under capitalism include a contradiction between the owning and the non-owning classes rooted in the bourgeois mode of production, distribution, exchange, and consumption. This mode of production is based on private property and exploitation, on constantly reconstituted economic relations that are of general significance for this society independently of whether they have yet been reinforced by legal form. The general significance and stability of material relations are rooted in their correspondence to the level of development of the productive forces achieved and the character of the social division of labour.

Actual economic relations thus underlie the very basis of legal form, relations characterised by the autonomy and formal equality of the parties, which require legal recognition and consolidation. These relations have a property (material) content and a volitional expression. Their volitional expression is the prototype of legal relations that have matured but whose formation has yet to be completed by consolidation in law as a result of official recognition by the state. It is important that the content of future legal connections and relations is already given and that their form is fixed (scale of rights and duties, and the equal, autonomous position of the parties). The actual economic relations will certainly be recognised by the ruling class and begin to be consolidated in an individual and then a general order, in legislative legal norms by the state's will, which ultimately depends on the actual relations, in one way or another reproduces an actually constituted model of future legal relations, and is itself, in the last resort, determined by the development of the productive forces and relations of exchange.[1]

Actual property relations in their material content and volitional mediation, which objectively need a legal form of consolidation, and which bear its important future properties within themselves, constitute law's basis (essence) of the third order. Marx could therefore speak of property relations being the juridical expression of relations of production (a statement we have already cited and analysed in Chapter One). Property relations are the basis of all the principles of law and, of course, lie outside its direct content. One cannot reduce law to property relations but it is impossible to ignore them when analysing legal form.

At the early stages of law's development, possession and property relations, defended and consolidated by barbaric violence and direct coercion, became law; Marx and Engels stressed this in *The German Ideology*. But the whole point is that this was only the embryo of law, law in its most elementary state; it was law that had not developed to its essence of the first order.

Here we must draw attention to the fact that the knowledge of law obtained as a transition from its essence of the first order to its essence of the second, and then of the third, order is contrary in direction to its real genesis and development. But it is the appearance of developed legal form under capitalism that has also made it possible to understand its essence fully in at least the three orders noted above. Because we have taken the actual relation of owners as the basis, the cellule, of legal actuality, we cannot stop at that; it is important to show in what way the claims of the persons involved in exchange of the results of production are manifested in a specific juridical form that embraces not only property relations in its development but also many other social relations, including the political relations of ruler and ruled, reinforcing state power in the hands of the economically dominant classes.

[1] See: Frederick Engels. Ludwig Feuerbach and the End of Classical German Philosophy. In: Karl Marx and Frederick Engels. *Selected Works*, Vol. 3, pp 369-370.

The starting point of the investigation is knowledge of law's essence of the first order, which includes the essence of the second and third order in sublated form.

In recognising actual relations defended by organised coercion as law we are speaking about undeveloped juridical form. By artificially projecting undeveloped juridical form onto modern legal reality we may crudely distort law's actual properties. It is impermissible to ignore law's essence of the first order in legal science because that would remove the point of the specific nature of law, i.e. the main object of its theoretical quest. But does jurisprudence need to concern itself with analysing law's essence of the second and third order? Should it, perhaps, be left to philosophy and political economy to concern themselves with this matter? No, a deep analysis of the essence of law is not fruitless; apart from the fact that it brings out the significance of the economy, needs, interests, and claims in the shaping of law, which is hackneyed for Marxist jurists in general, it is not difficult to notice that this approach makes it possible to demonstrate that abstract legal form (legislation, general legal rules) only fixes, supports, and promotes the development of factual relations that always exist in individual, concrete form. As regards actual economic relations, state policy, legislation, and legal rules are genetically secondary and derivative in character.

Law is not generated by the state's coercive power or by political compulsion, and does not have its source in juridical law. On the contrary, juridical law itself, and politics, are engendered by civil society, i.e. primarily by the aggregate of the prevailing relations of production and the needs of production and exchange.

The moulding of the law is genetically linked with the claims of the subjects of economic relations. From the methodological aspect, therefore, it is quite explicable that elements of voluntarism in the understanding of law usually entail *inter alia* lack of attention to rights, because they reduce law to state legislation, which was repeatedly opposed by the founders of Marxism. Disclosure of law's essence of the second and third order confirms the correctness of the statement that law proper embraces the rights of the subjects of social relations as well as the law.

Is such an understanding of law compatible, however, with its essence of the first order? The answer to that is of immense significance, because only law's essence of the first order directly predetermines its specific character and is associated with the peculiarities of juridical form, i.e. with its general significance, normativity and protection by the state, and class-will nature. The answer is the more important the less convincing from the purely outward aspect the statement seems that the making of the will of the ruling classes into a law for all can be the basis (main moment of the essence) of right as the effective right of the subject of social relations connected with his own claims, his will and interest, and his freedom of action. Here we come up against the fact that the ordinary conception is illusory.

Yes, the making of the will of the ruling classes (the dominant will) into a law for all is the basis of right as well as of the law. Doubts about the truth of that would probably be dissipated if it were remembered that law's essence of the first order does not yet affect the subject's activity and lies on the surface of the legal guarantee of freedom of action and of the claims of the parties to actual relations recognised by the state.

The making of the will of the ruling classes into a law for all (law's essence of the first order; we shall not henceforth state each time which order of essence it is) is expressed differently, of course, in the law and in right, but if each phenomenon or appearance is not identical with the essence, then definite manifestations of one and the same essence are not identical with one another.

In the law the dominant will, which has been made into a law for all, is manifested in generally acceptable, binding norms of a general character, upheld by the state, and relations in the appropriate conditions. In the second case will is manifested in generally acceptable and binding rules of a personalised character, upheld by the state, which are a yardstick of the conduct of the concrete subjects of typical relations in the approprite conditions. In the second case the yardstick is strictly linked with the subject but is also applicable to all and must be taken into account, and is upheld and protected. In both cases of the manifestation of will in law it is a matter of a generally binding measure of men's activity, but the yardstick and the character of its general binding nature are different. The general binding nature of the law is that everyone must observe its norms. The general binding nature of right consists in the legal obligation of a concrete authorised person to refrain from exceeding the limit of permissible conduct and to take the limits of the granted right into account. Both the law and right contain a yardstick or measure of conduct (but not the conduct itself); and both the one and the other are normative, but in the first there is a general rule while in the second the rule has been individualised and is a normativity of a particular quality. The law contains norms of possible and due conduct of an abstract character, while there is an individualised norm of possible conduct in a right that presumes the right of the empowered person to require performance of an obligation. In the general norm the expression of the will of the ruling classes is abstracted from the will of the subjects who will carry it out, and it is therefore only the objective aspect of the manifestation of the essence of law. In right the essence of law is represented by the subjective aspect of its manifestation; in it the dominant will is associated with an individual will and expressed as a measure of expression of the will of those who will carry it out by their actions and demands on obligees. The essence of law is such that it can only be represented in the law, which fixes the dominance of will abstractly and in general form. The will of the ruling classes is effective only when it finds embodiment in the rights of subjects who have the opportunity to make obligees obey the legal rules.

It is thus possible to discover a measure of conduct, a generally applicable yardstick of activity, a formal definiteness, normativity, general obligatoriness, state protection, and the will of the ruling classes both in the law and in right. In other words one can discover the essence of law proper, i.e. the will of the ruling classes made into a law for all (i.e. represented as a yardstick of activity binding for all and upheld by the state), the content of which in the last analysis is predetermined by economics.

The law and right are correlative manifestations of the essence of law. The law without right loses its specially juridical, regulatory function, while right without the law loses, or rather does not acquire, specifically juridical, general significance. In the absence of one of these correlatives there is only a one-sided, and therefore defective, expression of the essence of law.

Can there be such an anomaly in practice? Yes, of course there can; the necessary and natural link between the law and right may prove to be broken for social reasons of one kind or another. If the breach is sufficiently stable and assumes an organic character, normal, effective legal regulation of certain relations misfires; a certain distortion of the very essence of a legal enactment is not even excluded, and it may cease to be an expression of the will of the ruling classes made into a law for all, though the legal norm or right fixed in an individual state act remains, purely formally. An obsolete legal rule that does not find embodiment in the rights and duties of the parties to social relations thus ceases to be law in the proper sense. A subject's definite claim recognised within his legal right in certain circumstances but not corroborated in the law also ceases to be law in the strict sense.

There can also be anomalies of another character. It is quite possible that the will of the dominant social groups determined by the objective needs of the given mode of production is not expressed in some normative act or another of a state body, but instead what only seems to be law objectifies the expression of the will of certain persons or other granted sovereign legal powers or in fact ruling the state but not thereby representing either the general class interests or the needs of the country's economic development. This is frequently met in reactionary, anti-democratic regimes, especially during the decline of class-antagonistic formations. Both progressive and reactionary law are known, of course, with various historical types of state, but the point here is that the statute sanctions despotism and does not reflect law of any kind.

The falsification of legal form is historically transitory and unstable, is an extraneous phenomenon, and cannot of course abrogate the fundamental conclusion about the essence of law. Understanding of the actual essence and foundation of law, on the contrary, is a theoretical weapon for combating any falsification of law in practice and in ideology.

The general conception of the essence of law as the will of the ruling class made into a law for all requires appropriate concretisation. History has known several stages in the development of class society, and several historical types of law can accordingly be distinguished, each conditioned by a definite type of dominant relations of production. There were the slavery, feudal, and bourgeois types of law, and finally there is the law of socialist society. Socialist law differs radically from the preceding types and serves the communist transformation of society. Compared with the others it is a very new, developing type of law. The Marxist typology of law is based on an objective classificatory criterion, namely the prevailing mode of production of class society. Within the limits of one and the same type of law the class characteristic of its essence remains unaltered. The concept of a historical type of law helps decide precisely what class's will is or should be made into a law for all and constitute the basis of operative law. The answer can only be found by analysing the relations of production and the objective patterns lying in the field of economics.

A historical type of law has its content and appropriate form; after all, its essence embraces only its permanent, fundamental content and the most important features of its inner form. The fullest picture of a historical type of law is therefore always associated with bringing out not only its essence (of the first, second, and third order) but also with clarifying its quite fluid direct content and its inner and external form. As we lack the space to go into a detailed description of the forms and content of each historical type of law, we shall limit ourselves simply to considerations of principle enabling us to say what the content and form of law is in general.

If economic development is considered the content of social life, then all legal actuality, including law proper, is one of the forms of this material content. In that connection Lenin wrote that relations of production are clothed in political and legal forms.[1] From that angle we may speak of the legal form of the economy.

The concept of legal (juridical) form must not be confused with that of the form of law as the structure and expression of its direct content. Philosophically the concept of the legal form of the economy (or of other actual relations) indicates that law as a kind of superstructure is conditioned by relations of production and the needs, interests, and claims that arise from them, and that it has a deep-lying basis in the material conditions of society's life, in which its essence of the second, third, and other orders is rooted. Isolation of law from its socio-economic content, be it the law or right, ultimately leads to an idealist conception of legal appearances, to voluntarism in theory and practice, and to subjectivism. It is important for law to be linked with its economic basis in 'double harness', i.e. by the two processes of transformation about which we spoke above. In addition to understanding law as the juridical form of the economy, we must take the direct ideological, intellectual content of this form into account, the basis of which is the ruling class's will made into a law for all. The general class will, and any other will, are both a formal moment as regards the material conditions of society's life, and their content is ultimately economically determined and expressed in law as a rule of conduct.

When speaking of the law we have general norms in mind, as already mentioned, while by right we mean a personalised measure of conduct. But in law a norm is a unity of its volitional content, which is correspondingly moulded by, and often called by, its juridical content. The dominant will is always formed, 'made into a law for all', as the direct content of law and therefore has general applicability, normativity, and state obligatoriness. We shall deal later with the outward form of law; here, however, let us draw attention to the point that its inner form (the structure of its content) is built up from a whole series of levels of the connections of the elements of its volitional content. At one level it may be a matter of the structure of

[1] See: V. I. Lenin. The Economic Content of Narodism and the Criticism of It in Mr. Struve's Book. *Collected Works*, Vol. 1, p 410.

each general legal rule or each right, and at another level of the structure of the law as a system of general rules and of the structure of right as a system of the rights of the parties to social relations. Finally, law proper may be considered a unified system consisting of the interconnected elements of both the law and right. The inner form of law lends it a certain self-binding force based on the links of its yardsticks of conduct. An obligation rooted in external links with economic, political, and moral needs, and in links with the state, is more real of course but without inner form law would cease to be law proper (the inner connection, form, is the law of appearance!). Without law's inner, specific structure, its correspondence with economics, politics, and morality, and its defence by the state, could not ensure its specific normativity, general applicability, and general binding character. If the law, say, cannot for some reason or other be embodied in rights of the subjects of social relations, state coercion cannot ensure normal regulation of social relations by means of a law. If there is no sanction in a rule of law it may operate by virtue of compliance with moral requirements, but as a juridical enactment it is meaningless. Any one act of the state may express the will of the ruling classes, but if it does not contain general norms it is not yet the law.

Each type of law has its own content in the sense of expressing the class-determined dominant will; the character of this will largely determines the character of its inner structured nature (inner form). The general significance, normativity, and binding character of each type of law are not identical although they are characteristic in one way or another of the law of any formation.

The class character of will in law does not change within the limits of one historical type but it is predetermined by the relations it governs.

The level of development of the economy, culture, and consciousness alters quite markedly within a formation: changes may also occur in the field of politics, in the forms of the state, and political regimes, all of which affect law's content (while preserving its single class direction), including how far it is democratic or anti-democratic. Every country has its peculiarities of historical development, customs, and national traditions. Natural and geographical conditions that affect the character of the economy, and population problems, are also significant. The character of will in law is also determined by the needs of preserving society as such, and by the settling of common affairs already mentioned. The common affairs are extremely varied; today they are above all matters of health protection and social services, nature conservancy, problems of energy resources, and much else. The problems posed by the scientific and industrial (technical) revolution, the need to develop international relations and cultural exchange, and the activity of the mass media, and so on, also have an effect.

The legal systems of countries belonging to one and the same socio-economic formation are thus similar in the main but not identical, and sometimes have considerable special features. It is important to note that these features do not lose the class nature of the dominant will expressed in law, the content of which is determined in general and on the whole by a single type of relations of production.

A revolutionary change of historical types of law means a changing of the class character of the essence of law and an injection of new content into it. That, however, does not exclude a certain continuity of individual legal institutes, means of legal regulation, and juristic techniques and culture, concepts and terms. Recognition of the will of the ruling classes made into a law for all as the essence of law does not deny the fact that the legal system of a country is always, in a certain sense, a universal expression of its material and spiritual culture. To the extent that the revolutionary succession of social formations presupposes social progress on the whole (in spite of individual zigzags and backslidings) the succession of types of law presupposes general progress of legal actuality, which is inconceivable without assimilating at the new level of everything positive that has been achieved in the past. Socialist law, for example, is the highest type of law not only because it reflects a higher type of relations of production and of constitutional and political relations, but also because it has to reflect incomparably higher moral ideals and values, and accumulate everything positive, progressive, and best that has been achieved during the historical perfecting of juridical form and legal culture.

Any exposition of the question of the historical types of law must always bear in mind that the succession of socio-economic formations entails an inevitable transformation of law's essence of all orders; the most important changes, however, occur in the economic basis. It is these shifts that entail changes in the content of the will of the dominant classes made into a law for all. Insofar as division of labour, differentiated ownership of the means of production, commodity relations are retained within each class and socio-economic formation, and the economic law of value operates, economic inequality among men will not be overcome and legal form will retain certain features of similarity, albeit formally.

In other words, as society develops and historical types of relations of production and state succeed one another, law's essence of each order undergoes changes, but not so great that law ceases to be law. Only the higher stage of communism is associated with such radical changes in the mode of production and distribution as will exclude the objective need for legally binding yardsticks of conduct protected by the state; the normative regulation of social relations will acquire a quite different basis, in which the very essence of juridical law in its present expression and understanding will disappear.

The main criterion of the typology of law for Marxists is its appurtenance to a definite socio-economic formation. At the same time it is useful to know, so as to understand the specific character of the law of the country concerned, to what form (or family) the legal system operative in it belongs and what is the corresponding way of legal thinking of judges, and what are the peculiarities of the public's legal standards. When contacts between countries and nations are being strengthened, gaps in knowledge of the special features of their legal systems are undesirable; they can be filled by studying the above-mentioned forms (families) of these systems.

§ 3. The Ceneral Definition of Law

Any definition, as has long been known, has the inherent drawback that it does not embrace all aspects and properties of the thing being investigated, which is always developing. One must also add that any phenomenon has a variety of real foundations and can therefore have different definitions. But a scientific definition also has advantages associated with the fact that it succinctly formulates the existing concept of a given phenomenon and reflects the corresponding degree of cognition of this phenomenon. That also applies to the definition of law.

The definition of law also has practical value. The political and legal activity of any state is based on a corresponding understanding of law and definitions developed in theory. On the other hand, the definitions of law themselves reflect the political and legal practice existing in any particular country and, like all the most important tenets of legal science, have a class character and are determined by concrete historical conditions.

The concept and definition of law have always been a central point in legal science. It does not follow, however, that science has solved it either long ago or truly. A satisfactory definition of law can only be formulated on the basis of quite full understanding of its essence, content, and form. Science has long been unable to cope with that because of its own epistemological and class limitations.

The bourgeoisie's fight against feudalism was waged under the banner of the ideas of natural law. Grotius considered a human act consonant with nature and justice as law, while Rousseau wrote that liberty was a consequence of human nature and that there was therefore a natural law that was dictated by man's nature and upheld men's liberty and equality as their inalienable right. [1] Natural law. its devotees declared, was immutable, independent, and unconditional, and the positive law created by the state should be built in accordance with it. The essence of law

[1] See: Jean Jacques Rousseau. *The Social Contract.* Translated by G. D. Cole (Dent & Sons, London, 1935).

was human justice, its source man's nature, and its goal a society based on the reign of reason.

It was a fine idea, but far from a scientific understanding of law, a progressive, democratic idea for its time, directed against feudal absolutism, tyranny, and lawlessness. The reign of reason proclaimed by the conception of natural law turned out to be the domination of bourgeois orders: equality was reduced to formal equality before the law, liberty to freedom of private entrepreneurial activity, while private property was declared sacrosanct and inviolable and the right to it men's most basic natural right. On coming to power the bourgeois class forgot about ideas of natural law, which lost their old significance and gave way to a clearly expressed legal positivism. And when ideas of natural law were subsequently revivified from time to time, they were no longer coloured by political trends of a revolutionary-democratic character and were mainly held by ideologists of a conservative hue.[1] The theory of resuscitated natural law is closely linked with theology and expresses a certain scepticism in regard to modern legal positivism and sociological jurisprudence, which lack ideals of any kind. On the whole, in any case when capitalism flourishes, a legal outlook is characteristic of the bourgeois class and its ideologists that reduces actual economic and political relations to their legal form, while this form is considered in turn the very foundation of society.[2] This outlook is linked with an idealist conception of law and legal positivism, which isolate law from actual social relations. The defects of legal positivism have not prevented it from advancing study of the specific character of the form of law but have blocked the road to understanding its essence.

Legal positivism responded to the needs of perfecting bourgeois legal regulation, helped consolidate legality and limit judges' discretion, and put forward the idea of a legal state in the sense of the self-limitation of power by law. In the twentieth century, however, it has lost its former

[1] See: Paul Roubier, *Théorie générale du droit* (Libraire du Recueil Sirey, Paris, 1945), p 144.

[2] See: Friedrich Engels, Juristen-Sozialismus, In: Marx/Engels, *Werke*, Vol. 21 (Dietz Verlag, Berlin, 1962), p 492.

position and has undergone an essential transformation. It continues to survive in the special branches of law and in the general theory of law was developed within the context of Kelsen's Pure Theory of Law, an exclusively normativistic conception. [1]

For Kelsen law is only legal norms lying in the field of the Ought which is not causally linked with existing relations and can be studied and generalised in isolation from them. All general and individual norms repose on a *Grundnorm* of some sort. Kelsen completes the formalisation not only of law but also of the state, which is deduced from law and is understood as legal order. But the Pure Theory did not succeed, and in his later work Kelsen clearly linked law with politics and ideology, although continuing to insist that only his theory was free of metajuridical accretions. [2]

Kelsen's theory of law has been strongly criticised even in bourgeois science for its exceptional formalism and attempt to create an 'algebra of law'.

Normativity, it goes without saying, is a most important feature of law and it is scientifically and practically important to clarify the properties of legal norms and their logical interconnection, but Kelsen made an absolute out of law's normativity, separated the whole system of rules from their real economic and political basis, and emasculated not only law's class content but also its ethical aspect (the Ought for him is not an element, a category of ethics, but a property of Kant's transcendental logic, an *a priori* form of the practical comprehension of social processes). It is precisely the Kelsenian conception of law that deserves to be labelled strictly normative.

The epoch of imperialism faced the bourgeois science of law with new tasks that could not be solved by a formal, dogmatic conception of law. Acceleration of social development and complication of social relations, growth of the

[1] See: Hans Kelsen. The Pure Theory of Law and Analytical Jurisprudence. *Harvard Law Review*, 1941, 55.

[2] See: Hans Kelsen. *The Communist Theory of Law* (Stevens & Sons, London, 1965); *What Is Justice? Justice, Law and Politics in the Mirror of Science* (Univ. of Cal. Press, Berkeley and Los Angeles, 1960).

workers' revolutionary movement, and rapidly changing and sharply contentious situations have replaced the comparatively smooth development of nineteenth century capitalism and have necessitated flexible adaptation of legal form to contemporary actuality, and sometimes, too, rejection of the principles of legality proclaimed earlier. By the middle of the twentieth century the main trend in the West's general theory of law had seemingly become sociological jurisprudence.

The intensive development of the various trends of sociological jurisprudence was linked with the complete discrediting of legal dogmatism, which had no desire to concern itself with the problems of enforcing law and paid no attention to the deepening gulf between legislation and actual relations. In that connection it must also be remembered that the conception of law as what the court decides found favourable soil in countries where the Anglo-American system of law operates. One must not lose sight, too, of the fact that sociology, a new field of social science, has made definite progress in this century.

Sociological jurisprudence, having begun by criticising legal positivism, very quickly discovered its own limitations when it denied the significance of analysing legal norms and legislation and considered law a juristic technique reposing not so much on statutes as on values reflecting the needs of the day. A purely pragmatic approach to law, empirical sociology, a lack of understanding of the patterns of social development, and the reduction of legal actuality to actual relations exclude a scientific understanding of law and its essence, and prepare the soil for theoretical justification of the arbitrariness and lawlessness of the imperialist epoch.

One of the most eminent representatives of sociological jurisprudence, Roscoe Pound, put forward the idea of the three aspects of law. [1] In its first aspect it functions as legal order (a regime upheld by the state's systematic application of force and compulsion); in its second aspect law

[1] See: Roscoe Pound. *Jurisprudence* (in 5 vols.) (West Publishing Co., St. Paul, 1959); *An Introduction to the Philosophy of Law* (Yale Univ. Press, New Haven, 1961).

is the process of the administration of justice and jurisdiction (on the basis of a statute and in addition to a law). Only in its third aspect does law function as an aggregate of normative materials, as book law. Pound stressed that he and his adherents were beginning to think more and more in concepts of legal order and process rather than in the concept of book law, i.e. a collection of formulated results. Law was not so much the result as the engineering or technique of obtaining it.

One must not exaggerate the importance of general rules and statutes or isolate law from social relations, but no less harm is also done by a nihilistic attitude to legislation and the specific character of legal form, which also deprives one of the chance to bring out the actual essence of law. US sociological jurisprudence has not, so far, had appreciable success and many scholars are inclined today to reject the extremes of both Kelsen's normativism and Pound's functionalism. However, by taking a stand of justifying capitalism and its legal actuality, they inevitably go to other extremes.

Modern bourgeois theory, which is experiencing an acute ideological and scientific crisis, is seeking a way out in what is called juridical sociology, and in a 'new' philosophy of law, but without results. Jurisprudence is more and more acquiring an apologetic character in the West.[1]

The rise of Marxism meant a radical turn in social science, including the science of law. Historical materialism laid the foundations for a consistently scientific approach to the legal form of social relations. Every definition of law arising from the Marxist-Leninist world outlook is based on a materialist conception of law and recognition of its class-will nature. In the works of Marx, Engels, and Lenin we find a multi-level approach to legal actuality, a very negative attitude to arbitrariness and lawlessness, and a critique of bourgeois legal order, and of those juristic conceptions that justify arbitrariness and lawlessness in bourgeois society. The founders of scientific communism

[1] For more details on the state of the modern bourgeois theory of law see: V. A. Tumanov. *Contemporary Bourgeois Legal Thought* (Progress Publishers, Moscow, 1974).

revealed the essence of law and brought out its role in class society.

The Marxist-Leninist general theory of law has made definite progress in understanding legal phenomena, by constantly generalising the practice of socialist reforms and on that basis concretising the most important tenets of the materialist doctrine of society, the state, legislation, and justice. It is distinguished by its implacability toward idealism and metaphysics, dogmatism and scholasticism, by an open class and party approach to legal actuality and by defence of the progressive ideals and principles of socialist humanism, and has served, and is still serving, the cause of revolutionary transformation of society on the principles of scientific communism.

That, however, does not mean that the path followed in particular by Soviet legal science was an easy one and, at any rate, without obstacles, complications, and mistakes, or that Soviet legal scholars never erred but grasped the truth 'in the final instance'. The positions of individual theorists have not stood the test of time and historical experience, but in general the movement of Soviet scientific legal thought has on the whole had a progressive, consistent character, and that is the main point.

The definitions of law developed by Soviet legal science clearly reflect the stages in the formation and development of the Soviet legal system, the tasks of legal practice, the level of understanding of socialist society, and the patterns of the development of its superstructure.

From the early days of the establishment of Soviet power, the building of the state and legal superstructure necessitated the development of a corresponding definition of law. In 1919 it was recorded in *Guiding Principles for the Criminal Law of the RSFSR* that 'law is the system (regime) of social relations corresponding to the interests of the ruling class and defended by its organised force' [1]. This definition was proposed by Stučka and was directed against the ideas of legal positivism and psychological conceptions of law common in prerevolutionary Russia. It also, in addition, reflected the comparatively undeveloped charac-

[1] SU RSFSR (Collected Statutes of the RSFSR), 1919, 66:Item 590.

ter of Soviet legislation and of the system of the law. The main point of Stučka's definition was its accent on a materialist, class conception of law. It was necessary, in his view, to see two aspects in law—social relations and legal rules, the latter reflecting material relations. The sociological aspect predominated in this approach to law, so that the primacy of social relations over legal norms was given prominence.[1] Pašukanis interpreted law in a rather different manner, defining it as a system of legal relations.[2] It cannot be denied that Pašukanis tried to stress the specific juridical character of the legal superstructure. While Stučka still recognised the role of law, Pašukanis considered that the aggregate of legal norms belonged rather to the field of literary art.[3] The general weakness of both their positions can be taken as their underestimation of law's active role in the building of socialism and their simplified presentation of the prospects for the withering away of law. In the main this provoked criticism of the definitions of law they proposed. Now, decades since the discussion of the end of the 1930s, one can say that both Stučka and Pašukanis did much to establish the Soviet general theory of law, but that they did not pay enough attention to law's essence of the first order in their conception of legal form; that was the epistemological weakness of their position. In the Soviet legal science of those days, it is important to note, there were already the rudiments of a multi-level approach to law, as is evidenced by the existence of other definitions of it, including Krylenko's, which described law as an expression of social relations in statutes and legal customs that had regulation of these relations in the ruling class's interests as its content, and that was protected by the state.[4] This definition stressed law's normativity and regulatory function.

[1] See: P. Stučka. *13 let bor'by za revolyutsionno-marksistskuyu teoriyu prava* (Thirteen Years of Struggle for a Revolutionary, Marxist Theory of Law), Gosyurizdat, Moscow, 1931.

[2] See: E. B. Pašukanis. *Obshchaya teoriya prava i marksizm* (The General Theory of Law and Marxism), Krasnaya pechat', Moscow, 1924.

[3] *Ibid.*, pp 43-44.

[4] See: N. V. Krylenko. *Besedy o prave i gosudarstve* (Talks on Law and the State), Krasnaya nov', Moscow, 1924, p 33.

Lukasheva correctly notes that

> the forming of a Soviet general theory of law, and its development in the early stages, was characterised by a variety of scientific trends of general theoretical research: sociological (Stučka, Pašukanis), psychological (Reisner), normative and juridical (Krylenko).[1]

Later, in the 1930s and 1940s, study of the normative side of law predominated in theoretical research.[2] The study of law as an aggregate of legal norms yielded positive results. Those definitions of law that stressed attention to its normativity were a certain reflection of this trend of inquiry. These definitions also included those that were formulated under the influence of Vyshinsky's mistaken position, which suffered (as regards theory) from elements of dogmatism and voluntarism and exaggeration of the significance of state coercion. But Vyshinsky's fundamental errors were overcome by the mid-fifties which helped resuscitate and activise legal studies in the subsequent period, and the formulation of more substantiated definitions of law in the objective sense.[3] These definitions did much good in training legal personnel and opened the way to further development of Soviet legal science. Defence and substantiation of the normativity of law was a necessary and important stage in the movement of general theoretical juristic conceptions in the Soviet Union. Without it there would probably have been no chance of developing multi-level research into the legal form of socialist social relations on a higher and firmer theoretical basis. Nevertheless, this writer considers the definitions of law common in Soviet

[1] E. A. Lukasheva. The General Theory of Law and Multi-Aspect Analysis of Legal Phenomena. *Sovetskoe gosudarstvo i pravo*, 1975, 4:29.

[2] *Ibid.*, p 30.

[3] See: N. G. Alexandrov (Ed.). *Osnovy teorii gosudarstva i prava* (Principles of the Theory of the State and Law), Gosyurizdat, Moscow, 1963; A. I. Denisov (Ed.). *Teoriya gosudarstva i prava* (The Theory of the State and Law), Moscow Univ. Press, Moscow, 1967; K. A. Mokichev (Ed.). *Teoriya gosudarstva i prava* (Legal Literature Press, Moscow, 1970); A. M. Vasiliev (Ed.). *Teoriya gosudarstva i prava* (Legal Literature Press, Moscow, 1977).

A feature of all the definitions of law in these works is their identification of law with the law, which, from this writer's point of view, is very contentious and corresponds simply to traditional legal thought.

legal studies that reduce it to an aggregate of general rules to be inadequate.

The law of developed socialist society has a high democratic, moral, humanist potential. Under consolidated socialism the task of more fully guaranteeing the interests of the people and of each human being is coming to the fore. Socialist legality at the same time presupposes observance of the laws of the all-people's socialist state by all citizens and firm defence of the rights of each member of society. On the international plane the workers' and progressive forces' political struggle for democracy and peace, and for vital human and civil rights, against imperialism, reaction, lawlessness, aggression, and neocolonialism is developing. Life is posing new tasks for legal studies and jurisprudence. Soviet legal science is endeavouring to deepen understanding of the essence of law and to bring out more fully its social value and the specific character of its regulative function, and to investigate more thoroughly not only the law but also rights, legal relations and legal order, the ethical foundations of legislation and the administration of justice, the role of legal form in social progress and man's development and in satisfying his material and spiritual needs, by employing the advances of the other social sciences in every way for the purpose. Analysis of legal form from many aspects is acquiring an increasingly firm position in the general theory of law, which cannot help being reflected in the development of scientific definitions of law. [1]

[1] A varied approach on many planes to the concept of law is characteristic of the chapters of the textbook on the general theory of the state and law written by S. N. Bratus and E. A. Lukasheva; a broad view of law was also noticeable in S. S. Alexeev's two volumes of lectures. See also: V. M. Chkhikvadze et al. (Eds.). *Marksistsko-leninskaya obshchaya teoriya gosudarstva i prava. Osnovniye instituty i ponyatiya* (The Marxist-Leninist General Theory of the State and Law. Basic Institutes and Concepts), Ch. 9, Legal Literature Press, Moscow, 1970; V. E. Guliev et al. (Eds.). *Marksistsko-leninskaya obshchaya teoriya gosudarstva i prava. Sotsialisticheskoe pravo* (The Marxist-Leninist General Theory of the State and Law. Socialist Law), Ch. 1, Legal Literature Press, Moscow, 1973; S. S. Alexeev. *Problemy teorii prava* (Problems of the Theory of Law) (in 2 vols.), Vol. 1, Ch. 1, Sverdlovsk Legal Institute Press, Sverdlovsk, 1972-3.

There is a tendency to approach law as a social phenomenon that arises from the economic structure and is not reducible to statute law, but which is opposed to arbitrariness.[1] At the All-Union Scientific Co-ordinating Conference in 1972 many legal theorists expressed a critical attitude toward the definition of law as a system of norms.[2] It is typical that the present trend toward a broad conception of law does not always go hand in hand with the inclusion of legal relations in the definition of law.

Is there, however, in fact an alternative of either recognising the normativity of law and reducing it to general legal rules or of refusing to recognise its normativity and conceiving it broadly? We do not think that life poses such a choice. Our position on this point boils down to the following.

(1) A phenomenon as complicated as law has many definitions. Lenin wrote that there can be many definitions, for objects have many aspects'.[3] The definition of law as a system of general rules is a true and useful one of the law, but it cannot be made an absolute and considered universal.

(2) A substantive definition is better able to reflect the conception of law and to integrate abstract and concrete law in one definition, and to show that its essence is directly manifested in the contradictory unity of general and personalised yardsticks of conduct of a generally applicable and binding character upheld by the state and supported by the prevailing morality.

(3) Law proper is both the law and right, the complete basis of which (essence of the first order) should be considered the materially determined will of the ruling classes made into a law for all.

[1] See: D. A. Kerimov (Ed.). *Voprosy filosofii prava. Tezisy dokladov* (Problems of the Philosophy of Law. Theses of Papers), Moscow, 1973.

[2] See: S. V. Polenina et al. (Eds.). *Aktual'niye problemy teorii sotsialisticheskogo gosudarstva i prava. Materialy konferentsii* (Current Problems of the Theory of the Socialist State and Law. Proceedings of a Conference), USSR Academy of Sciences, Institute of the State and Law, Moscow, 1974, pp 19-36, 129-136, 177-182.

[3] V. I. Lenin. Conspectus of Hegel's Book 'The Science of Logic'. *Collected Works*, Vol. 38, p 234.

(4) The law of these classes, objectified in general norms, is in fact their will made into a law for all to the extent that it is embodied in the actual rights of men (and organisations) who enjoy social wealth and goods and are capable of fulfilling legal obligations.

(5) In life, in its dynamic, and in its functional aspect, law is the application of an identical, generally binding yardstick of conduct guaranteed by state coercion to the effective parties to social relations. 'All law,' Lenin wrote, 'is an application of an *equal* measure to *different* people.'[1]

The definition of law that follows logically from these arguments should include a formula of its essence in unity with its direct manifestation in the law and right. Such a definition does not postulate its substitution for other definitions. It synthesises, supplements, and develops them. From this angle law is the materially determined, general class will (under socialism the will of all the people) made into a law for all and directly expressed not only in general, constitutionally binding enactments but also in the actual rights of the subjects of social relations consolidated by these acts, the character and content of the rights being objectively determined.

Introduction of the formula of the essence of law into the concept of law determines the philosophical level of the definition (obviously the expression made into a law for all' is used here in the broad sense). The definition also stresses the indissoluble nature of the link between the law and right, stresses normativity as an indispensable property of any law, and quite distinctly opposes law to arbitrariness. It is also of no little importance that the definition proposed is applicable in any country and any epoch, irrespective of the degree of development of legal form and the peculiarities of the existing process of lawgiving, and the position of the sources of law of various type. The dual dependence of law on objective conditions emphasises that stability of the legal order is inseparable from the dominant will's capacity to reflect the needs of

[1] V. I. Lenin. The State and Revolution. *Collected Works,* Vol. 25, p 470.

production and exchange and society's conditions of existence as such faithfully (allowing for common affairs and guaranteeing the corresponding volume of citizens' rights). Finally, the definition given above can serve as the starting point for studies of the human factor's growing role in the realm of legal relations, and for analysis of law's significance in the human personality's development, and in guaranteeing the interests of a class, and, under socialism, of the people.

In formulating this definition of law the writer took as his starting point that the objective conditions are being provided in socialist society for full correspondence between what is established by legislation as general legal norms and what is embodied in the rights of the subjects of social relations, i.e. between what are known as the law and right. On that basis, we can disseminate a scientific notion of law in the life of socialist society, true in practice, as a special phenomenon that combines objectification of the people's will in legal norms and in subjects' actual rights, reinforced and guaranteed by the legislation of the all-people's state.[1]

[1] The idea of embracing the two aspects of law—objective and subjective (subject's)—in the concept of law, it should be noted, like the attempt to bring out law's essence of varied order, is the integral interpretation of the legal form of the economy of class society that the author has put forward in several earlier works. An interpretation of this kind is not generally accepted in the Soviet legal literature, and differs both from the position of those scholars who maintain notions that law is only the aggregate (system) of legal norms, and from the views of those who are inclined to include legal relations, and even recognition of law and sense of right, in the concept of law.

[8]

GENERAL THEORY OF LAW

S.S. Alekseev

Contents

Section Four
Law in the System of the Superstructure of Class Society

Section Five
The Properties of Law

Section Six
Law and Legal Regulation

Section Seven
The Mechanism of Legal Regulation

Section Eight

The Norm of Law

Chapter 23. The Norm of Law: concept, basic feature

Chapter 24. Structure of a Norm of Law

Chapter 25. Types of Norms of Law

Section Nine

Legal Relation

Chapter 26. Legal Relation: concept, basic features

Chapter 27. Types of Legal Relations

Chapter 28. Content of Legal Relation. Subjective Right

Chapter 29. Subject of Law

Chapter 30. Object of Legal Relation

Chapter 31. Legal Fact. Factual Composition

Section Ten

Legal Act

Chapter 32. Legal Act: concept, basic feature

Chapter 33. Normative Legal Act

Chapter 34. System of Normative Legal Acts

Chapter 35. Operation of Normative Legal Act

Chapter 36. Systematization in Law

Chapter 37. Legal Technique

Chapter 38. Interpretation

Part III
Towards a Rule-of-Law State

[9]

Perestroika and the Rule of Law

W. E. Butler

Not long before the October 1917 Revolution, as it turned out, Lenin wrote that "A law is a political measure, it is politics."[1] Widely abbreviated to "law is politics" in the popular consciousness, the phrase came to epitomise in the Western psyche the Bolshevik attitudes towards law and justice. The student of Russian will quickly recognise that the first word in the quotation, "a," represents the translator's choice of the indefinite article instead of the definite. The Russian language does not have articles. The choice of the indefinite article was probably influenced by Lenin's choice of the word for law: *zakon*. Had he used the expression *pravo*, no article would have been used. In the English tongue, however, the phrase has often been understood to mean law in the broadest sense rather than a particular type of statutory enactment, which gives the original Russian a very nihilistic nuance indeed.

Modern students of policy studies today might consider Lenin's utterance not wide of the mark, albeit perhaps a bit sweeping. The architects of perestroika, however, are preoccupied with another dimension of the matter. The Soviet Union having determined to create a socialist rule-of-law State [*sotsialisticheskoe pravovoe gosudarstvo*], in what sense is law understood, and how should the concept be translated? An insensitive choice of the English equivalent could obscure a jurisprudential and policy debate of the greatest moment.

Several equivalents are widely employed in English-language media.[2] The expression "legal State" is encountered sometimes, presumably on the assumption that the Russian term is a calque from the German *Rechtsstaat*; indeed, even the German expression is used directly in some English translations. Some speak of a "law-governed" or a "law-ruled" State. And one version, drawing upon classical Anglo-American terminology, uses "rule-of-law State." The choice of English equivalent is the more difficult because the English language does not distinguish sharply between two meanings of law: *jus* and *lex* (Latin);

Recht and *Gesetz* (German); *droit* and *loi* (French); *pravo* and *zakon* (Russian), and the like in many other languages. The present writer in this essay and throughout this book translates *pravovoe gosudarstvo* as the rule-of-law State, a convention which sometimes gives the benefit of the doubt to writers who use the same term to describe a narrower understanding of the concept. However, to do the opposite would be to lose entirely from sight the more libertarian understanding of the rule-of-law and deprive those who take that view of the vocabulary which makes it possible to express it. Further, when it becomes essential to distinguish between *pravo* and *zakon* in this essay and in the Soviet contributions herein, the Latin terms *jus* and *lex* are utilised to make a distinction otherwise almost impossible to illuminate in English except contextually, which here would be inadequate.

For Soviet jurists the "rule-of-law" and the "rule-of-law State" have been a rediscovery rather than an invention. Soviet legal historians are well aware that their prerevolutionary precursors considered the matter, influenced by German and English writers especially. One noted Russian authority wrote: "the idea of a rule-of-law State has a significantly longer past in the history of European political thought than do its underlying plans and programmes for State transformation; to trace its roots is to review virtually the entire heritage of theoretical work explaining law and State."[3] Amongst Russian jurists who were outspoken proponents of the rule-of-law were B. N. Chicherin,[4] B. A. Kistiakovskii, and P. I. Novgorodtsev.[5] The attraction of the rule-of-law in its Anglo-American manifestation as a doctrine limiting State power was considerable, for it held out the hope of introducing genuine democracy into Russia at the expense of absolute autocratic power claimed, albeit not actually possessed, by the Russian Imperial throne.[6]

Factors latent in Russian history and Soviet society which have contributed to the emergence of the current endeavours to enlarge the rule-of-law will require some distance from current events before they can be identified. Soviet jurists have been preoccupied with the other side of the equation: those factors which precluded the formation of a rule-of-law State.[7] So-called "war Communism" of the 1918–20 period, where "revolutionary advisability" operated, the low legal culture and legal illiteracy of the great majority of Party workers and leaders of State and economic institutions, and the belief that law, as an element of bourgeois society, would rapidly die away were amongst the factors that made it premature to speak about the formation of a rule-of-law State. Some believe the NEP legislation (1921–28) began to move in this direction, but at the end of the 1920s "a completely different situation, profoundly contradictory with Leninist ideas of societal development," developed in the Soviet Union.[8] The Soviet system, it is suggested, had not developed the political and legal machinery that would enable *pravo* to have primacy over the State, the supremacy of *lex* in social relations, and other institutions that might have obstructed the emergence of the so-called administrative-command system of rule in the USSR.[9]

Various explanations and periodisations are offered as to when the roots of the rule-of-law began to take hold in Soviet society. The Khrushchev era is mentioned by some on the grounds that the excesses of Stalin were being condemned, law reforms were being introduced to prevent their recurrence, the Soviet Union was declared to have entered a new stage of societal development called the "State of the whole people," and "socialist legality" was a byword of the day. That Khrushchev postulated the rapid transition to a Communist society without law is discounted by this explanation. The processes continued under Brezhnev until ca. 1975–76, when it is implied that the years of "stagnation" forestalled the foundations of the rule-of-law State from maturing. Perestroika marked the return to the original objective in this respect.[10]

Professor Nersesiants offers a different periodisation and rationale. In his perception the view predominated in the Soviet Union until the late 1930s that until Communism was achieved the State would exist in the form of the dictatorship of the proletariat, which ultimately would die out. This belief obstructed more sophisticated intermediate forms of State and law from developing. Further, until the mid-1930s Marxist-Leninist ideology believed that the law existing temporarily under socialism was "bourgeois" law since the notion of any "socialist law" was rejected axiomatically. This belief too retarded the maturing of a socialist political system. When the Vyshinskii School took the contrary view that a socialist State and socialist law had to be introduced in order to strengthen and secure the gains of the Revolution in a world of hostile capitalist encirclement, the result was a State operating the administrative-command system in which power was vested in the State apparatus and law was essentially a combination of normative orders and administrative dispositions from top to bottom.[11] But Nersesiants concurs that the substitution of the State of the whole people for the dictatorship of the proletariat in the early 1960s laid the conceptual base for the rule-of-law State.

Anecdotal evidence is strong that the socialist rule-of-law State was to emerge in connection with the XXV (1976) Congress of the Communist Party of the Soviet Union. In Party circles, at least, the matter was discussed and apparently resisted to a sufficient degree that the subject was dropped. One Soviet jurist recalled that a manuscript article he prepared after the XXV Congress, in late 1976, was rejected for publication on the grounds that by referring to a socialist rule-of-law State he was "using bourgeois conceptions."[12]

In its modern guise, the rule-of-law State emerged as a Party initiative associated with the Gorbachev leadership. So abrupt was its emergence and endorsement that Soviet legal theorists found themselves without any considered literature on the subject; at best there were savage critiques of the notion as it existed in "bourgeois" society and a total rejection of its applicability to a developed socialist society.[13] Some legal theorists support basic tenets of the rule-of-law State without utilising the term or fully endorsing the proposition that *pravo* should operate as a constraint upon State activities.[14] Others acknowledge that the "statisation" [*ogosudarstvlenie*] from 1928 onwards must give way to "destatisation" [*razgosudarstvlenie*] if a socialist rule-of-law State is to be the antipode of the administrative-command system.[15] Whatever the position, the rule-of-law is acknowledged to be one of those institutes of bourgeois law which, consistent with Lenin's behest, the authorities should seize "with both hands the best from abroad . . ." irrespective of where it originated.

Perhaps the barometer of change is best illustrated in an article by Baglai. Why should the Communist Party have chosen to introduce the term "rule-of-law" and its concomitant institutions? Have there not been other efforts directed towards strengthening legality, developing democracy, enhancing the involvement of the general public in State administration, and the like, not to mention innumerable economic reforms? What have these earlier policies lacked? The answer, Baglai suggests, is the "acknowledgement of human freedom as the paramount value – freedom, and not merely well-being, however important the latter may be."[16]

Programmed Development or Perestroika Rampant?

Although perestroika, new thinking, glasnost, the rule-of-law State, and the transition to a market economy all are policies instituted initially by the ruling Communist Party, there can be no doubt that they have been seized upon by the Soviet public at large with remarkable vigour and been pursued in their various directions. Of all of these policies, the rule-of-law is by far the most momentous in its implications; without it, the others are likely to fail or not reach their full potential. The social forces unleashed are formidable by any standard, and there exists no firmly-charted path or model to follow.

Measured by legal reforms, those introduced and those on the agenda, the rule-of-law shows mixed results.

Foundations of the Union We in the West tend to forget that the Union of Soviet Socialist Republics dated not from 1917, but from a Treaty concluded on 30 December 1922 by the then existing four union republics (RSFSR, Ukraine, Belorussian SSR, and Transcaucasian SFSR). Under the Treaty those four sovereign States ceded certain competence to the Union whilst retaining an inherent right to secede (Article 26). In the course of time, partly by further subdividing the existing republics and partly by accretion through arrangements between the USSR and neighbouring States on the eve of the Second World War, the Union enlarged to its present fifteen members. From the late 1920s the central government began to federalise the Treaty relationship, a process consolidated in the USSR Constitutions of 1936 and 1977.

The rule-of-law dictates a reconsideration of both the nature and composition of the Union and a readjusting of the balance between the central and peripheral governments. Under perestroika this has been broached in a variety of ways. A new Treaty of the Union has been negotiated which reallocates the apportionment of competence between the Union and the republics. The previous State entities have been required to reconsider their respective status, interests, and objectives as part of their continuing (or not) relationship with the Union and, in some cases, with certain of the republics. The intention is both to legitimise the Union as such, cleansing it of the stigma of forced membership (the Baltic States) under unequal treaties, and to reallocate power, resources, property, and the like in a more rational way.

Long-suppressed nationalism, coupled with a ferocious debate about the meaningful alternatives available to each entity as part of restructuring the Union, have surfaced to shake Soviet society to its core. In a not altogether salubrious scenario, the Union and certain republics have adopted secession legislation intended to clarify procedurally Article 26 of the 1922 Treaty of the Union and the same Article reproduced verbatim in the 1977–78 USSR and union republic constitutions. Virtually all of the union and autonomous republics have adopted Declarations on Sovereignty which set out in diverse forms the respective rights, prerogatives, and property of each entity, and a number have concluded international treaties amongst themselves, bilateral and multilateral, to regulate economic, cultural, and political relations. The republics have reasserted the premisses of the 1922 Treaty by claiming that their laws have precedence over all-union laws unless competence has been specifically relegated to the Union. The ensuing "war of laws" has been exaggerated by Western observers, many of whom do not distinguish between the legitimate exercise of republic power to elaborate or depart from all-union legislation and the rather few instances where republics have deliberately set out to flout or challenge Union competence.

Parliamentary Representation Soviet constitutional theory has been based upon the sovereignty of the people expressed through their duly elected parliamentary bodies. In December 1988 the USSR

Constitution was amended to create the USSR Congress of People's Deputies as the supreme parliamentary organ of the Soviet State and enable those union republics who wished to do the same. At the USSR level, 2250 deputies were elected; they in turn elected ca. 546 to the USSR Supreme Soviet, which met in more or less permanent session. The size of the Congress has proved to be unwieldy. Many deputies are unwilling to give up their positions or careers to become full-time members of parliament. The view that a stipulated percentage of deputies elected to the Supreme Soviet should rotate at prescribed intervals, so attractive in theory, has proved unattractive in practice because many deputies of experience are lost in the rotation and many of the best feel unable to become full-time deputies. Further, the deputies are inexperienced in matters of government, drafting legislation, and analogous parliamentary duties and do not have the expert staff available in other systems to service those requirements. The result is a certain disenchantment with the workings of parliamentary democracy and impatience at the inability of the Supreme Soviet to move as rapidly as many believe the crisis demands.

On the other hand, for all its shortcomings, there can be no question that the present system is superior to the previous model of supreme soviet. Its televised proceedings command a large audience in the evenings; so absorbing were the proceedings when televised live that they distracted too many from the normal performance of their jobs.

The Presidency By December 1989 it had become clear that the USSR Congress of People's Deputies and the Supreme Soviet could not cope with requirements for expeditious and resolute action to resolve many issues facing perestroika. The Presidency began initially to be mooted as a provisional stopgap measure to meet the requirement of strong directive leadership. As an institution it did not sit well with the principle of parliamentary supremacy, nor did the Soviet Union seemingly intend to pass over to the American model of separation of powers. Rather like the rule-of-law itself, Soviet legal theory and constitutional doctrine were unprepared for the emergence of a more-or-less independent executive branch of government.

The constitutional amendments of March 1990 which instituted the Presidency do not entirely resolve satisfactorily the scope and powers of that office, nor its relationship to the legislative branch. Further changes are likely. Many Soviet citizens profess to fear the powers of a strong Presidency, likening it to a form of constitutional dictatorship, whereas others abhor what they perceive to be a vacuum of power, with both the legislative and executive branches unable to cope with the magnitude of problems confronting the country.

The Judiciary Soviet courts attracted the early attention of perestroika reformers. Their status, their independence, their professionalism, and their quality were all at issue. Legislation enacted in 1989 altered the term of office of judges from five to ten years, raised salaries, introduced guarantees to reduce the possibility of interference in the judicial process, provided for the jury system to be implemented at local option of the republics, and strengthened procedural guarantees for persons detained or arrested. Further, legislation enabling citizens to apply to a court for redress against the unlawful actions of officials or agencies impinging upon their rights and freedoms was introduced in 1987 and replaced in a much stronger version in 1989. In December 1990 State Arbitrazh was abolished at the USSR level and transformed into the Supreme Arbitrazh Court as part of the judicial system. The expression "presumption of innocence" was introduced at last into USSR legislation on court organisation, and defence counsel given expanded rights to enter proceedings at early stages of inquiry or investigation.

The RSFSR in May 1991 adopted a Law on the Constitutional Court of the RSFSR, giving it the right to exercise powers of judicial review over the constitutionality of legislation. This is perhaps the first real step towards elevating the judiciary to the status of a branch of government equal to the executive and legislative (the RSFSR elected a President in June 1991).

Constitutional Supervision The amendments to the USSR Constitution in December 1988 made provision for the election of a Constitutional Supervision Committee of the USSR and similar bodies at republic level. The union republics greeted the prospect of such a USSR body with great suspicion, delaying its election and enlarging its membership so that each republic was fully represented by at least one member. The USSR Committee began work in May 1990 and in the course of several months issued pathbreaking opinions holding unconstitutional a variety of legislative enactments long associated with repression and arbitrariness. Separate opinions issued in September and December 1990 struck down as unconstitutional the practice of the USSR Council of Ministers and of ministries and departments to issue decrees under various forms of classification, preventing the public from access to the text or printing an abridged text.

For all the imagination and resourcefulness the Committee has displayed, however, its powers remain limited and unsuited to a rule-of-law market economy. The Committee is to be abolished in favour of a full-fledged Constitutional Court of the USSR.

Procuracy Perestroika has yet to visit the Procuracy in any substantial way. The tensions between the USSR and republics have led in some cases to the USSR Procuracy being supplanted by republic procurators who claim a different allegiance. In the Baltic republics, for example, local procurators accountable to the republics operated simultaneously with the USSR Procuracy. Legislation on the Procuracy has been in draft for some time and, judging by the public dialogue in legal media, may result in the Procuracy either giving up or seriously attenuating its powers of general supervision.

People's control agencies have largely disappeared in the Soviet Union, replaced partly by the USSR Chamber of Control and analogous bodies.

Police Legislation was adopted in Spring 1991 by the USSR Supreme Soviet to regulate for the first time in enactments publicly available the activities of the Ministry of Internal Affairs and the Committee of State Security.

Political Pluralism The constitutionally-protected vanguard status of the Communist Party of the Soviet Union was ended by amendments to Article 6 of the USSR Constitution in March 1990. Countless political parties and movements have emerged under perestroika, and in some republics (Georgia, Lithuania, and others) have taken effective political control of the highest legislative bodies. Party politics within parliamentary assemblies, however, is still at an embryonic stage. For the most part the voters elect individual deputies for their personal qualities rather than as members of a political party committed to implement a specific platform. This in turn has given the soviets at all levels a somewhat unfocussed image, with the power of personality often bringing persons to prominence rather than political alignment or skill. There is, moreover, a considerable "generation gap" between the deputies at the USSR level and those elected a year or so later in the republics. This contributes to the republics often taking a more adventurous stand on particular issues than the Union is willing to adopt.

Pluralism has been furthered under perestroika by a number of enactments at the USSR level: laws on the press and mass media, on social associations and organisations, on the Church, to mention but a few. Others are on the legislative agenda.

The Market Economy The perestroika cycle of reforms in the Soviet Union is unique in Soviet history for commencing rather than ending with foreign economic relations. Equity investment of foreign capital became possible as from 19 August 1986; more than 3000 joint enterprises have been registered at the all-union level. As from 26 October 1990, foreign juridical and natural persons are able to invest in

100% foreign-owned Soviet legal entities or to form the same together with Soviet citizens and legal persons.

Encouragement of foreign investment is intended to be a catalyst to the domestic economy, itself being "destatised" and "privatised" from late 1990 with the pace quickening in 1991. State enterprises are being leased to labour collectives, or transformed into joint-stock societies or other analogous corporate entities and the stocks distributed as appropriate on the market, to workers, or held by the State. Laws on ownership, lease, land, enterprises, cooperatives, individual labour activity, employment, trade unions, tax, banks, and investment have been adopted, followed by dozens of subordinate enactments elaborating the details.[17] These were followed by legislation on unfair competition, bankruptcy, pledge, patents, copyright, major changes in civil, labour, and criminal law, amongst others in the course of 1991.

Most of this legislation has been attended by sharp controversy as to the pace and direction of economic reform. Presidential edicts have been used to institute price and currency reforms, legislation directed against economic crime, import and export restrictions, and a host of collateral matters.

Depending upon the configuration of the Union, it remains for the central and republic authorities to physically reapportion title to and possession of what traditionally has been State-owned property and assets. The USSR has created the State Property Fund to administer all-union assets, and the republics have taken analogous steps. In the case of the Baltic republics, quiet diplomacy in 1989 and early 1990 had already achieved a substantial distribution of assets. The same exercise is being repeated throughout the country; once the republics reach a settlement with the Union, they will undertake an analogous redistribution within their own frontiers vis-à-vis local governmental units. The distribution will be complicated by the creation of free economic zones or free entrepreneurship zones authorised in such disparate areas as Leningrad Region, Kaliningrad, Novgorod, Odessa, Nakhodka, and Sakhalin.

The market economy requires the rule-of-law no less than individual citizens. Juridical persons need the same stability of laws and legitimacy of expectations deemed to be the inalienable heritage of natural persons. Soviet jurisprudence has yet to even broach the issue.

For a ruling Party to have set these forces in motion is not merely to "reinvigorate" social forces characterised as "stagnant." It is to pay the ultimate price of failing to persuade the electorate in free elections that the ruling Party ought to continue to hold power. The diagnosis is not simple, for many have left the Communist Party of the Soviet Union to form their own political movements and parties, and the republic leadership of many Communist parties is unlikely to survive at the ballot box. One Soviet jurist has described the processes of perestroika in programmatic stages as follows: first is the stage of forming the concept of a rule-of-law State and of reforming the highest agencies of State power. This stage commenced in April 1985 and was said to have ended with the amendment of the USSR Constitution in December 1988.[18] The second stage was said to embrace building the foundations of the rule-of-law State by completing political and cardinal economic reforms, enjoying the fruits of the initial results, and overcoming shortages of goods and services. The author reckoned that the stage might be completed by the end of this century.

The socialist ideal reasserts itself at the third stage, where the socialist rule-of-law State becomes the most perfected political organisation of society. The specific features of this stage are held to be indeterminate, but may be presupposed to include the flourishing of a free socialist economy, developed self-government, ideological guidance of the Party, and new rights and freedoms of citizens. If the international community comes closer together, new inter-state forms of governing society may come into being. And at this stage, he adds, one may again raise the issue of the historical fate of State and law.[19]

The Rule-of-Law: Standards and Exhortations

Increasingly individuals taking a legal position on a particular matter in the Soviet Union have recourse not merely to "legality" in the sense of compliance with lex; they also call into question the legitimacy of behaviour against the standards of the rule-of-law. We give two examples from rather different sources regarding the legitimacy of normative acts.

Academician V. N. Kudriavtsev, Vice President of the USSR Academy of Sciences and a People's Deputy of the USSR, criticised the issuance of a Presidential edict and ministerial order for being essentially *ultra vires*. The Presidential edict in question was issued on 26 January 1991 to intensify measures against economic sabotage and other economic crimes. The edict gave to police and KGB personnel the right to enter without obstruction the premises of enterprises, institutions, organisations, as well as persons carrying on individual or other labour activity, to search such premises, to remove samples, obtain documents, written explanations, and the like. USSR and union republic criminal legislation already authorised such activities on the part of law enforcement personnel, but only after a criminal case had been instituted, in the presence of witnesses, and with the drawing up of an appropriate protocol after explaining to suspects their rights, and the like. Either the edict added nothing new to the rights of law enforcement officers, or it purported to repeal existing procedural guarantees and rights of the individual. If the latter, Kudriavtsev argued, the edict was improper; Presidential edicts pursuant to Article 127–7 of the USSR Constitution might be issued "on the basis of and in execution of the USSR Constitution and laws of the USSR," but not in violation thereof. In a rule-of-law State law may be established only by proper means and not arbitrarily, he added.

His second example dealt with a joint order issued by the ministers of defence and internal affairs in December 1990 regarding joint armed patrols by soldiers and police personnel. That order was not published and hence was unknown to the general public. But more importantly, the ministers in question did not have the competence to issue the order. Only the supreme soviets of the relevant republics or the President of the USSR had such competence, and even then only under an extraordinary situation as defined by Soviet legislation. Not until 29 January 1991 did a Presidential edict confer a legal basis upon the ministerial order,[20] although even then there was doubt whether the measure could be justified in all cities and what role the local authorities ought to have in deciding that issue.[21]

These were examples where in the commentator's view the State officials concerned had exceeded their constitutional or statutory competence, thereby violating and undermining the rule-of-law.

The same type of criticism was levied by an economist against RSFSR legislation on ownership. By introducing "unlimited private ownership," including "capitalist," the RSFSR Supreme Soviet was accused of perpetrating a social revolution leading to the replacement of the constitutional socialist system by a capitalist system. The RSFSR law was deemed to be "anti-labour" because it eliminated the basic role of labour in a socialist society and replaced it with the determinative role of capital and ownership. Labour amounts to a subordinate element of the production of capital irrespective of its origin. Second, the law was deemed to be anti-social because it gave priority to private ownership; collective forms of ownership were essentially combinations of private owners. The law in effect would change the socio-economic foundations of society. Consequently, the RSFSR Supreme Soviet did not have jurisdiction to adopt the law; only the RSFSR Congress of People's Deputies could do so. The procedure was unconstitutional, and was by no means the only example of such legislative behaviour. "Republics adopt laws contrary not only to the USSR Constitution, but also to the republic constitutions" every day. Through "legal nihilism they try to affirm a rule-of-law State."[22]

Procedure and competence lie at the heart of each. In the former case departments are acting as they were accustomed to do: without challenges to their competence, without being obliged to publish their joint order, and without being required to explain why the measure was supposedly essential or expedient. Perestroika and the rule-of-law demand that such practices cease. However, in the second instance the RSFSR Supreme Soviet was acting to implement, to accelerate, perestroika and the transition to the market economy. The RSFSR Constitution was in fact amended in December 1990 to take account of the changes in the law on ownership. Whether in the name of the rule-of-law the Russian Federation may or may not effectuate a "social revolution" is an issue which will arise time and again in all republics as they address in their respective ways the requirements of the transition to the market economy.

Conclusion

Of all the objectives which the architects of perestroika might have chosen as having appeal to the Western world, the rule-of-law must have pride of place. The Marxist-Leninist attitude towards law generally and the legacy of repression and illegality in Soviet society have been such that an attempt to make common cause with the West through universal human values such as the rule-of-law was bound to meet with approbation.

Yet the West is often curiously ambivalent about the processes at work. We are impatient, often more so than the Soviet people themselves. We expect rapid, unobstructed progress in implementing the rule-of-law without obstruction from forces of the past and without legitimate questioning as to the pace and direction of perestroika. These our media represent as opposition, a step backwards, or a lack of resolve. Glasnost we applaud on paper, yet abjure when all sides in Soviet political dialogue claim the right to exercise their rights. Many of the choices confronting Soviet policymakers in the realm of legal reform are in fact controversial in any event and untested under Soviet conditions. Moreover, many are multi-faceted, with difficult costs and benefits to evaluate. Some, desirable as they seem, are still not accepted in most Western countries. In rightly reminding our Soviet colleagues that the rule-of-law was not built in Western civilisation rapidly or comprehensively, we should remind ourselves that the Soviet effort to leap the time gap is not a foregone conclusion either and will require careful and devoted effort on everyone's part if the agenda for legal reform and its implications for the international community are to be realised.

Perhaps most disturbing about the Soviet legal dialogue to date regarding the rule-of-law is the absence of a firm consensus about the substance of *pravo* or jus. That jus and lex are held not to be coincident is the most important development in Soviet legal theory, indeed Marxist legal theory, of this century. Jus is capable of being shared across human societies at the level of international law, either customary or in treaty form; lex at best can be merely parallel coincident sharing of values subject always to the whim of the legislator or constitutional change in each State. If jus holds out the promise of, in its Soviet incarnation, embodying universal human values, Soviet legal doctrine needs to explore as a matter of priority the sources and substance of jus as they relate to the rule-of-law. Having inhaled the heady vapours of perestroika, we need now to sample the substance of a nutrient acceptable to universal taste at a minimum and hopefully of gourmet standard in the longer term.

Notes

1. Quoted from J. N. Hazard, W. E. Butler, and P. B. Maggs, *The Soviet Legal System* (3d ed., 1977), p. 5, citing V. I. Lenin, *Sochineniia*, XXIII (4th ed., 1949), p. 36.
2. The introductory portion of this essay elaborates on points first developed in W. E. Butler, "Towards the Rule of Law?," in A. Brumberg (ed.), *Chronicle of a Revolution: A Western–Soviet Inquiry into Perestroika* (1990), pp. 72–89.
3. S. A. Kotliarevskii, *Pravovoe gosudarstvo i vneshniaia politika* (1909), p. 338. Also see N. Khlebnikov, *Pravo i gosudarstvo v ikh oboiudnykh otnosheniiakh* (1874). For further data on the historical dimension, see V. S. Nersesiants, *Pravo i zakon* (1983). The author was perhaps the first Soviet jurist to develop the theory that jus and lex were not coincident (1973). Subsequent publications by D. A. Kerimov and E. L. Rozin (1974), G. V. Mal'tsev, L. S. Mamut, and V. A. Tumanov (1977), and V. D. Zor'kin (1982) pursued the point. For a bibliography, see Nersesiants, "Pravo: mnogoobrazie opredelenii i edinstvo poniatiia," *Sovetskoe gosudarstvo i pravo*, no. 10 (1983), p. 27.
4. On Chicherin, see V. G. Kalensky, "Basic Concepts of Legal Philosophy in Chicherin's Property and the State," in W. E. Butler (ed.), *Yearbook on Socialist Legal Systems 1989* (1989), pp. 1–26.
5. See Nersesiants, "Kontseptsiia sovetskogo pravovogo gosudarstva v kontekste istorii uchenii o pravovom gosudarstve," in B. N. Topornin, V. P. Kazimirchuk, and M. M. Slavin (eds.), *Sotsialisticheskoe pravovoe gosudarstvo: problemy i suzhdeniia* (1989), pp. 45–67.
6. On the role of the Russian legal profession in reforms which led ultimately to constitutional monarchy in Russia, see R. Wortman, *The Development of a Russian Legal Consciousness* (1976). The rule-of-law, for which a legal consciousness is a prerequisite, was amongst the jurisprudential contributions to the forces at work.
7. See, for example, the Round Table published as E. A. Chirkin (ed. & comp.), *Sotsialisticheskoe pravovoe gosudarstvo: kontseptsiia i puti realizatsii* (1990). The participants were V. S. Nersesiants,

V. D. Zor'kin, G. V. Mal'tsev, O. P. Temushkin, V. M. Savitskii and I. A. Lediakh, L. S. Mamut, V. G. Grafskii, and V. A. Vlasikhin.

8. See V. N. Kudriavtsev and E. A. Lukasheva, "Sotsialisticheskoe pravovoe gosudarstvo," in Topornin, et al., note 5 above, p. 8.
9. *Ibid.*
10. See M. Baglai, "Tol'ko Zakon," *Izvestiia*, 1 September 1988, p. 3, col. 1.
11. Nersesiants, in "Vlast' i pravo," *Chelovek i zakon*, no. 10 (1988), p. 12. Nersesiants differs from Kudriavtsev and Lukasheva, note 8 above, for the latter attribute the administrative-command regime to the introduction of national economic planning from ca. 1928 onwards. We have yet to satisfactorily explain the impact, for example, of the Pashukanis school with regard to the future of State and law upon the emergence of the administrative-command system and its implications for the development and future of any kind of *pravo* or *zakon*.
12. V. M. Savitskii, in "Vlast' i pravo," *Chelovek i zakon*, no. 10 (1988), p. 69.
13. See, for example, the collective work *Theory of State and Law* (1987), a standard Soviet textbook on legal theory which makes no reference whatever to the rule-of-law State.
14. See S. S. Alekseev, *Socialism and Law: Law in Society* (1990), esp. pp. 170–173.
15. Note 5 above, p. 11.
16. Baglai, note 10 above, col. 2.
17. Many of the texts are translated in W. E. Butler (ed.), *Basic Documents on the Soviet Legal System* (2d ed., 1991).
18. R. Z. Livshits, "Sotsialisticheskii ideal i pravovoe gosudarstvo," in Topornin, et al., note 5 above, p. 97. In fact the USSR Constitution has been amended five times since 1987, and it is by no means clear that the first stage of this reform is over. Perhaps the adoption of a new Constitution after the Treaty of the Union is ratified may be better regarded as the benchmark.
19. *Ibid.* Livshits here neither surrenders the vision of a perfected socialist society, although nothing is said of Communism as such, nor abandons the transformation of State and law into something else. Whether such a transformation must occur in the context of universal human values is not addressed. For some fascinating forecasts regarding the priorities of the values of a rule-of-law State and the period when they might be achieved, see Iu. M. Baturin and R. Z. Livshits, *Sotsialisticheskoe pravovoe gosudarstvo: ot idei-k osushchestvleniiu* (1989), pp. 221–231.
20. The USSR Constitutional Supervision Committee reviewed the Edict of the President of the USSR adopted 29 January 1991 and

found it unsatisfactory in a number of respects. The Committee exercised its right of legislative initiative with respect to the USSR Supreme Soviet by proposing a number of changes in existing Soviet legislation to rectify the situation. See *Izvestiia*, 15 February 1991, p. 2, cols. 4–6.

21. V. N. Kudriavtsev, "Demokratiia i pravovoi poriadok," *Izvestiia*, 5 February 1991, p. 3, cols. 4–7.
22. V. Konyshev, "Zakon o sobstevennosti v RSFSR: pravovoi perevorot?," *Ekonomika i zhizn'*, no. 7 (1991), p. 5, cols. 1–5.

[10]

Jus And Lex: Evolution of Views

R. Z. Livshits

The correlation of jus [*pravo*] and lex [*zakon*] is a key, if not the key, problem of the theory of law. The human mind for many centuries, from Socrates and Plato to the present, has endeavoured to resolve this task as one of the tasks of administering society.[1] An abundance of points of view may be reduced to two different approaches. Some understand jus and lex to be phenomena of the same order. Of course, within that view there are numerous disagreements. One might consider jus to be only a system (or the aggregate) of norms, or one may relegate to jus also other forms of the legal fabric: legal consciousness, legal relations, rights and duties of participations of legal relations, principles of regulation, and others. But most important is that a lex adopted is always jus, and on this the advocates of this position do not disagree. Others work from the distinction between jus and lex. There are also many disagreements within this position connected with particular understandings of what jus is.

Both approaches have, to repeat, a history of many centuries and are in no way a discovery of Soviet legal science. Soviet science has taken on board both approaches with the material addition that in the works of Soviet scholars these approaches rest upon a materialist foundation, on a recognition of the primacy of economic relations in comparison with jus and lex.

To be convinced of the correctness of one approach or the other solely on the basis of theoretical postulates is obviously impossible. The arguments in favour of one solution or another and perhaps searches for a new solution must be sought in a practical approach, in those real consequences to which theory leads. Does the matter truly coincide with the ought (or the will of the people) and the existing (or lex and their realisation) in society? If they do coincide, there are no grounds to distinguish between jus and lex, and if not, then life itself, reality, will distinguish them.

If we examine where passions were inflamed in Soviet legal science, much becomes clear. The question of defining the concept of law was one of the basic issues, if not the principal one at the First All-Union Meeting on Questions of the Science of Soviet Law and State in July 1938. The historical situation of the Meeting predetermined the answer. Mass repressions, the *de facto* renunciation of the social and humane values of jus, and the formation of an administrative-command style of administration gave a certain directive mandate to scholarship. The requirement of the leadership of the Soviet Union in those years was an orientation towards the coercive character of jus, towards the indispensable binding nature of its norms regardless of their content.

The content would be that which was required, as jus for the administrative-command administration was essential above all as a stick, as a means of coercion. This official mandate to scholarship was implemented in the Report to the Meeting made by A. Ia. Vyshinskii. Quoting this own Theses, he proposed the following formulation to the Meeting: "Jus is the aggregate of rules of behaviour expressing the will of the ruling class and established in a legislative procedure, as well as the customs and rules of community life sanctioned by State power, the enforcement of which is ensured by the coercive power of the State for the purposes of protecting, prohibiting, and developing social relations and procedures advantageous to and suitable for the ruling class."[2] This formulation became the turning point for the future development of Soviet legal science and practice. Ten years later, at the Second Meeting of Scientific Workers-Jurists, Vyshinskii singled out what from his point of view was the most important in his definition: "Lex is a form in which the will of the ruling class is expressed. Jus is not one lex, but the entire sum or aggregate of lex."[3]

We shall not return to all the elements of Vyshinskii's definition, for enough has been written about them in Soviet doctrine. Merely we call attention to what he considered to be important: jus is the aggregate of lex. This formula lay for many years at the base of a certain ideological scheme: the will of the majority of the people (then of the whole people) – lex (jus) – implementation of lex. Through this scheme the administrative apparatus for many years implemented its will, passing it off as the will of the whole people. And the content of will, the essence of the lex applied, went beyond the bounds of legal comprehension.

To be sure, this scheme left no place for doubts as to whether the decision of the legislator was correct in substance inasmuch as whether the decision achieved the purposes put to the legislator was, ultimately, simply whether to implement it or not. It was understood that the people and the State take everything into account properly in the lex adopted and naturally the lex are implemented and achieve their purposes.

To the credit of Soviet legal science, it never accorded unanimous approval to Vyshinskii's formula. Voices of protest were heard, which required courage on the part of scholars, for they disputed not only with his point of view, but with official doctrine. But dispute they did. The objections of specialists in the general theory of law combined well with the view of specialists in branches of law. The branch-lawyers discovered more and more practical inconsistencies in the ideological scheme for the functioning of law. And although the theoreticians and branch-lawyers in their criticism of jus as merely the aggregate of lex, of norms, proceeded from various premises, today, decades later, it is a pleasure to see that their views coincided.

In the 1950–60s it was elicited (or more accurately, it became possible to write about this) that many of Soviet laws were ineffective, that they did not achieve the aims set by the legislator, and even that they operated at cross purposes with the tasks set. For the first time, legal sociologists showed this using the example of criminal and labour law norms. The labour lawyers, for example, demonstrated how the norms directed towards preventing personnel fluctuations did not achieve their purpose. The studies by sociologists enabled us to prevent the increasing severity noted in the early 1960s of legislation with regard to dismissal at one's own wish. The enrichment of jurisprudence through recourse to sociology led branch-lawyers to the problem of what is jus: merely norms or also relations regulated by law? If merely norms, then why is it jus, and if also legal relations, then the primary formula of the theory of law is incorrect. Thus, the problem of the effectiveness of law led investigators to seek a different definition of jus.

And at the same time but independently of the branch-lawyers who were occupied with the effectiveness of law, the voices of the legal theorists were heard. First S. F. Kechek'ian (1958) and A. A. Piontkovskii (1962) proposed to incorporate legal relations in the concept of jus together with norms, and then Ia. F. Mikolenko (1965), legal relations and legal consciousness, and later L. S. Iavich (1976), subjective right. In 1975 E. A. Lukasheva's article was published which substantiated a multi-faceted analysis of legal phenomena and the impossibility of reducing jus to lex.[4] The so-called "broad" understanding of jus was formulated; it was the first serious alternative to jus as purely the aggregate of norms. It must be emphasised again that both the legal theorists, resting upon logical deduction, and the branch-lawyers, resting on studies of the effectiveness of law, came to this understanding simultaneously.

On the practical level a persuasive criticism of legislation began in many works on branch disciplines at the outset of the 1970s. In the present writer's view, the most penetrating criticism came from criminal procedure specialists: M. S. Strogovich, V. M. Savitskii,

I. L. Petrukhin. They persuasively demonstrated the illogicality and non-doctrinal nature of such basic propositions of legislation as the combination in the procuracy of support of the accusation and control over legality when criminal cases were considered, and the failure of advocates to take part in the preliminary investigation, and they criticised the lack of the presumption of innocence in a legal surround. Key provisions of economic, administrative, labour, nature conservation, and other branches of legislation were subjected to justified criticism. A blow was thereby struck at the unreserved apology for lex and the astonishing inconsistency between the high and humane ideals of a socialist society and the content of specific laws.

Posing the problem thus coincided with the substantiation in Soviet legal theory of the discernment of jus and lex. The first publications were by V. S. Nersesiants (1973), D. A. Kerimov and E. L. Rozin (1974), G. V. Mal'tsev, L. S. Mamut, V. A. Tumanov (1977), and V. D. Zor'kin (1982).[5] All the authors came to the view that jus and lex do not coincide, although they differed in their definitions of the concept of jus. The great merit of the notion of the distinction between jus and lex became its critical orientation. Criticism of legislation had begun even in the period of stagnation, and for this the critics deserve special merit. This criticism was directed against stagnation in legislation and was one of the anticipatory steps of perestroika in the theory of law.

The reality of today discloses dozens, indeed hundreds, of evidences of the inconsistency of the will of the people, the content of lex, and law enforcement practice. We have lex which is unjust, incorrect in substance, and contrary to the interests of people, and we also have lex which is good in substance but for various reasons is not implemented. There also is lex (indeed, the majority are such) in which progressive logical norms are neighbours of obsolete and conservative norms. Therein lies the objective basis for the distinction between jus and lex.

Without reducing jus to lex, one can comprehend its content in various ways. One may see in jus a measure of freedom and equality, the consolidation of a just principle, or other ideas. The main thing is not the differences of definitions, but what they hold in common, their effort to elicit the internal essence of jus without reducing it to merely a form of lex. In exposing the inconsistency between jus and lex and endeavouring to consolidate in lex a humane, just, jus decision, scholarship fulfils its analytical and creative functions. The notion which distinguishes jus and lex, in the present writer's view, corresponds to the maximum extent to the requirements of forming a rule-of-law State.

In essence socialist law was called upon to reflect the ideals of justness. This proposition can hardly be proved by purely logical constructions. It is rather itself of a conceptual nature. Justness is one of the most humane and progressive ideas in the history of mankind. And it is thus wholly suitable for a socialist society called upon to transform into reality the dream of people for many centuries. The ideals of justness are closely linked with freedom and equality. We choose the term "justness" because it most fully characterises human ideals in general.

Justness is wider than jus. The specific feature of jus as a social phenomenon is that it is called upon to bring order to social relations and strengthen that order; in other words, the normative nature, the binding character of legal provisions, and the possibilities of implementing them in a coercive way. Those just ideas which have been normatively consolidated in lex become jus. Those which have not been remain outside the limits of jus. Jus is the normatively consolidated justness.

This approach enables the scientific results obtained to be used and at the same time to make a certain step forward. An understanding of jus, as a system of norms, is preserved. The renunciation of normativity, a recognition of pre-lex jus, is thereby overcome; the proponents of the distinction between jus and lex justifiably make this reproach. Jus as normatively consolidated justness incorporates not only lex (or norms), but also the system of social relations regulated by them (the rights and duties of the participants of the relations, the principles of regulation, and others). A broad normative understanding of jus is thus encompassed. Finally, from the concept of the distinction between jus and lex is drawn its most valuable, revolutionary idea: that jus is characterised by its humanistic democratic content. In an understanding of jus as normatively consolidated justness, the justness determines the content of jus, and its normative consolidation is a necessary form of jus.

The correlation of jus and lex is complex and uneven, as it has its place in life. If one or another just idea does not receive normative consolidation, it remains in the sphere of morality, ethics, a wish having no binding force. It still is not jus. In modern conditions this is the case with the idea of glasnost in social life. If a just idea obtains normative consolidation, it become lex and is transformed into jus. Thus since 1981 compensation for damage to citizens unjustifiably brought to criminal responsibility has become a right.

And when an unjust idea receives normative consolidation, it becomes lex, but not jus. Such, for example, was the provision of lex on the impossibility of appealing to a court the collegial decision of officials. An unjust lex is not jus. In a socialist rule-of-law State supremacy is accorded to the just lex. And as for lex which does not consolidate justness – of which we have many – it is essential to renounce them, to replace them. Hence the need for legal reform.

Thus, jus is already lex since not all lex is just. On the other hand, jus is wider than lex since it includes social relations within the system regulated by lex.

The correlation of jus and lex leads us naturally to another well-known problem: the correlation of State and jus. Obviously this correlation can not be characterised by way of the priority either of the State or of jus. Their correlation, as in the case of jus and lex, is uneven. If jus is understood as normatively consolidated justness, it is secondary with respect to the State because normative consolidated proceeds from the State. But not any norm which emanates from the State is jus, and therein lies the distinction between jus and lex. Jus comprises only just norms. Therefore, from the standpoint of content, jus is primary with respect to the State. The State does not think up jus; it is called upon to consolidate notions of justness already formed in society. The State and jus together serve society in various ways. Society through the State and with its assistance formulates jus.

It follows that certain propositions that jus is an instrument of the State, a means for conducting policy, or a means of administration contain only part of the truth. Under administrative-command administration jus serves as an instrument of the State, a means of conducting policy. Moreover, the administrative-command system gave rise to and conditioned the official subordinate role of jus with respect to policy and the State.

In a rule-of-law State jus is not isolated from policy, from the activities of the State. The transition of a rule-of-law State means that jus, whilst continuing to perform its official role, is not confined by the framework of that official role. What policy is to be conducted? By what means is administration to be effectuated? If policy is democratic and humane, if administration is effectuated in the interests of the people and by the people, then and only then is jus, by virtue of its democratically just foundations, an instrument of administration and implementation of policy. And if policy and administration do not meet these conditions, they can not rest on jus. On lex perhaps, but not jus. In a rule-of-law State policy and administration are means of implementing jus as the embodiment of justness.

The supremacy of lex, and even the link between State and lex, does not characterise a rule-of-law State. A State is not bound not to violate lex, for it can simply change lex which does not satisfy the State and its agencies. Suffice it to recall the numerous instances in the Soviet recent and remote past. A rule-of-law State must be bound not only by lex, for this is merely self-limitation which turns out to be insufficient. A State must be bound by jus, by the notions of society regarding justness. Only the binding nature of jus characterises the genuine rule-of-law State. And a system of constitutional control is a major practical guarantee of its being bound.

If one sees normatively consolidated justness in jus, then it is essential to define justness itself. This can be done rather simply so that it can operate in reality as an indicator of the genuinely jus content of lex.

In a civilised society the basic point of departure is that justness ensures the interests and rights of man. This understanding of justness combines well with legal regulation, with the establishment of mutual rights and duties of participants of social relations. In distributive relations justness is the conformity between the actions of a citizen, his labour contribution, and the reciprocal reaction of society. In relations of coercion and responsibility, justness also signifies the conformity between the extent of the violation and the extent of punishment. In the domain of administrative relations, justness consists of the establishment of the minimum necessary limits of power and guarantees for those being administered against abuse of power.

These ideas of justness are then elaborated when working out individual lex and consolidated in norms which are genuinely jus. Thus, justness, being normatively consolidated, is introduced into all domains of social relations. All branches of legislation – State and civil, labour and housing, economic and pension, co-operative and nature protection, criminal and procedural – are called upon, in accordance with the ideal, to impart justness to the social relations being regulated.

As regards the correlation of jus and lex, jus and policy, jus and administration, and justness as the content of jus, we already have spoken about the ideal which must be embodied in a future rule-of-law State. We are now at the beginning of a long journey to achieve the objective.

Judicial Practice as a Source of Jus

A discussion of the relationship between jus and lex would not be complete without some consideration of the place of judicial practice as a source of law. Legal theory has developed two notions, each of which has its own understanding of what is a source of jus in general and of judicial practice as a source of jus in particular. Both we have considered above. According to one, jus and lex are coincident, and therefore jus is always a particular normative act which also comprises the source of jus. If under this view judicial practice were deemed to be a source of jus, one would have to recognise the general normative character of a judicial decision, to recognise judicial precedent.

Under the second approach, also discussed above, where jus and lex are not coincident, jus is broader than lex, and lex is but one of the forms in which jus is manifest. Hence other sources of jus besides normative acts are possible, including judicial practice. Under this view, the role of judicial practice as a source of jus is not reduced to precedent but rather consists of the multi-faceted activity of courts with regard to the implementation of jus.

We shall again consider both approaches in this particular context.

1. The Coincidence of Jus and Lex and the Role of Judicial Practice For many years in Soviet legal science the notion that jus and lex were coincident not only was the prevailing view; it was the sole view. The source of jus Soviet legal science treated in the material and juridical (formal) senses. In the material dimension the source of jus was the factors which determined its content: the economy, social relations, class struggle, the will of people, and the like. While there were wide differences of view on the matter, all accepted that the source of jus in the material sense was pre-legal, the precursors of jus. But in the juridical sense the source of jus was its external form, usually lex in the form of legislative enactments of various levels. This approach, for all its differences amongst adherents, accepted that the source of jus in a juridical sense was a legal norm, the essence of legal normativism and positivism.

To quote an example or two, S. L. Zivs wrote that: "the source of jus is the external form of the establishment of a legal norm by the State (or on behalf of the State, or with the sanction or approval of a State). Among the propositions axiomatic for the Marxist-Leninist general theory of law is the truth that in a socialist State the creation of legal norms, lawmaking itself, is the prerogative of the State."[6] S. S. Alekseev has said that: "The exclusive position of normative acts as sources of jus is characteristic for socialist law."[7]

Hence the negative attitude towards judicial practice as a source of law. Zivs continued in the same quotation: "That is why in socialist law neither judicial practice as such nor administrative practice are sources of jus. They are not an act 'giving rise to a right between parties' (as the ancient formula says), although they are, of course, a direct expression of State will. And even the authoritative model of law enforcement – the decision of the highest judicial instance with regard to a specific case serving as a recommendatory standard, can not be relegated to the sources of jus."[8]

Legal theory has various understandings of the substance of judicial practice. On one hand, it includes judicial judgments and decisions with regard to specific cases. An individual judgment or individual decision is binding within the limits of the specific judicial case but does not create a precedent of law by itself. Further, a constantly repeated precedent also does not create a legal norm. That is to say, the activities of courts with regard to settling specific criminal and civil cases do not create legal norms as the court merely applies norms already created by the State. On the other hand, judicial practice also includes such acts as guiding explanations of the plenums of the USSR and union republic supreme courts. These do not contain decisions on specific cases. They are a generalisation of judicial practice which is not of a sufficiently high standard; they are binding upon courts of all levels when they consider individual criminal or civil cases. Within the limits of the judicial system such explanations are as binding as legal norms. Outside the limits of the judicial system they possess rather the power of authority than the authority of power.

Can one regard guiding explanations of the plenums as a source of law? The opinions of legal scholars are various. The majority do not recognise guiding explanations of the plenums as a source of law. Their arguments are usually two: first, the plenum merely explains the application of lex but does not have the right to create new lex. If a plenum considers it necessary to adopt a new lex, it should use the right of legislative initiative. Second, the notion of plenum guiding explanations as sources of jus is at odds with the supremacy of lex and ultimately with the Soviet constitutions. But there are other views. S. I. Vil'nianskii, A. B. Vergerov, V. V. Lazarev, and other legal scholars have stressed that through guiding explanations of the plenum a concretisation of lex is achieved, so consequently this activity can be deemed to be norm-creative.

The fine points need not concern us here. For years the overall position has been to not recognise judicial practice as a source of jus. The view that jus and lex were coincident followed logically from this position. If only lex (including subordinate acts) is recognised to be jus, there is no place for other sources of jus. The great virtue of this notion is the endeavour to achieve full and undeviating compliance with lex, the inadmissibility of any deviations from lex. But the shortcomings of this conception flow from its virtues. The requirement of unlimited supremacy of lex overrides the quality of lex itself, allows no critical attitude towards lex, allows no alternatives. Judicial practice is such a critical principle with regard to lex. The notion that jus and lex are coincident relegates judicial practice to a secondary role, the role of an unquestioning executor of lex. Thus does society insure itself against judicial arbitrariness. But this opens the possibility of legislative or executive arbitrariness. And as history shows, one is no better than the other.

2. Concept of Distinguishing Jus and Lex: Place of Judicial Practice In the majority of continental European countries of the so-called Romano-Germanic system of law, the view that lex is the sole source of jus was formed in the seventeenth and eighteenth centuries. The judge was merely the mouth pronouncing the words of lex. And the theory of separation of powers (Locke, Montesquieu) in its classical form did not recognise judicial activity or judicial practice as a source of jus. Gradually, slowly, over the decades the attitude towards judicial practice changed. Many of the changes were for practical considerations. The complete regulation of social relations could not be achieved through lex; legislative regulation always was fragmentary. Judicial practice was in a position to fill gaps which emerged. Further, legislative regulation was susceptible to the instability of elective legislative organs. Judicial practice remained stable and in the positive sense of the word was a conservative factor. The theoretical basis for altering the attitude towards judicial practice was the distinction between jus and lex. Article 20 of the Constitution of the Federal Republic of Germany provides that pleadings are bound by Gesetz and Recht. This formula, in the view of many legal scholars, was legislative recognition of the distinction between jus and lex.

In common law countries judicial practice was acknowledged to be a source of jus from the outset. The formula so beloved by the English and Americans is: jus is what the judge says it is. While relying on the theory of separation of powers, common law countries have gone much farther in recognising judicial practice to be a source of jus. Judicial precedent is recognised in both England and the United States. And in the United States one may speak about the priority of judicial power not only with respect to executive power, but also legislative power. Since the fourth Chief Justice of the United States Supreme Court John Marshall proclaimed and introduced the right of a court to declare lex unconstitutional, the authority of judicial power has grown immeasurably. Units of time in the development of the American legal system are even designated by the names of Chief Justices of the Supreme Court. Western European constitutional courts are based on the United States model. And this is not merely recognition of judicial practice as a source of jus, but even its acknowledgement as a priority source.

Thus in the majority of developed legal systems (Western Europe, United States, and others) there is a trend towards not only recognising judicial practice to be a source of jus, but also towards its role being enhanced amongst other sources.

3. Judicial Practice in the Soviet Legal System As noted above, judicial practice has not been recognised as a source of jus in the Soviet Union. Now, however, we view the problem from the standpoint of the processes underway in the Soviet Union.

The court is the greatest invention of human civilisation. In a stormy and contradictory human society the court is deemed to be a stabilizer, an agency which authoritatively settled contradictions between people without allowing them to grow into coercion. The special virtue of the court is its independence, high professionalism, and the binding nature of its decisions. Mankind has not created any other analogous or even similar agency.

In the history of the USSR the court has not had a real place. The Revolution destroyed the old court as "class alien." The new court in its early guise was nonprofessional; it served class interests, but not the requirements of lex. Whereas in the stormy revolutionary years this role of the court could be explained and have historical analogies, after the Revolution the court should have joined the framework of a civilised society and legal culture. This did not happen. For years the court took its place in the system of agencies of mass criminal repressions. The role of the civil court was reduced to nothing; disagreements between citizens and agencies of the State were decided by State agencies themselves, but not by a court. Under these conditions one could hardly speak of judicial practice as a source of jus.

Perestroika and the aspiration of Soviet society to create a rule-of-law State included as an integral part a significant enhancement of the role of the court in society. This is not merely a matter of theory; the first major practical steps have been taken in this direction. Material changes have been made in organising the work of the courts: a special Law has been adopted on the status of judges, the procedure for electing judges has been changed, their salaries have been increased, and the like. Institutes new in principle for the Soviet system have been included in the activities of courts.

First, the jury has been introduced. This measure was vigorously discussed in Soviet society. The proponents of the jury stressed the democratic nature of this court, a court of the people, and contrasted it with the pressure from the apparatus and telephone law. Opponents drew attention to the low professional level of the jury as compared with the court of assessors and to the reduction of the role of the jury in the West. The decision to create a jury system was adopted, and its effectiveness remains to be seen. It may not be an ideal structure, but in any event perhaps better than what existed earlier.

Second, the competence of the court in civil cases has been significantly enlarged. A rule traditional for the Soviet system was that appeal by a citizen to a court against a decision of an agency of administration was not permitted. This rule in reality impinged upon the right of citizens and made them unequal with respect to agencies of administration; indeed, transformed them into petitioners. The rights of citizens, even those consolidated in lex, proved to be beyond practical defence. This was especially true with regard to the rights of citizens relating to residence registration, assignment of pensions, and improvement of housing conditions. A citizen was not in a position to prove his right, and the apparatus was beyond judicial control.

This procedure has been changed. It was not easy, for the struggle against the apparatus was sharp. Suffice it to recall that the possibility of appealing to a court against the actions of agencies of administration was proclaimed in the 1977 USSR Constitution. But the Constitution required a special law. The law was not adopted for ten years. And only in 1987 during perestroika. But the law contained a small concession to the State apparatus: the principal mass of administrative decisions, insofar as they were adopted collegially, remained outside judicial control. Legal doctrine energetically criticised the sloth and inconsistency of the legislator. Only in 1989 did the new Supreme Soviet adopt a law which, pursuant to a report of the USSR Supreme Court, really placed the bureaucrat under the control of the court. On paper the new law is a good one. But citizens must really take advantage of it. Given the present level of legal culture in the Soviet Union, this is unlikely.

According to prevailing USSR legislation, only an administrative decision affecting specific people and being of a personal and not a normative character may be appealed to a court. A normative decision still may not be appealed to a court. This is not a matter of civil justice, but of constitutional. Such justice is merely beginning. In the USSR there are agencies of constitutional supervision, which in their nature are administrative and not judicial. Only the RSFSR has amended its Constitution in December 1990 to create a Constitutional Court. Such a system of courts is a matter for the future.

Thus, in recent years the powers of courts have been significantly expanded and their role enhanced in society. From the standpoint of the noncoincidence of jus and lex, judicial practice may be deemed to be a source of jus since the courts by their activity transform the ideas and principles of jus, such as equality, justness, freedom, into real life. If jus is understood to be the aggregate of lex, including subordinate acts, judicial practice even in present circumstances can not be regarded as a source of jus. A judicial decision does not possess general normative force and consequently is not a source of jus. The special status of guiding explanations of the plenums of the USSR and republic supreme courts enables only those acts to be deemed to be sources of jus. This is the theoretical resolution of the issue in modern Soviet reality.

Now to approach the matter from a profoundly practical point of view. The practical dilemma is as follows: can and should a court decision in a particular case possess legal force outside that case? The degree of legal force and the level of the court rendering the decision are important issues, but not determinative. The main issue is one of principle: can a court decision have normative force?

The answer is linked with the very essence of regulating social relations by law. Such regulation consists of subordinating the development of social relations, present and future, to the ideals and principles which society has drawn from its past. Legal regulation generalises the experience of human development, extracts lessons from it, and endeavours to make the lessons of the past the basis of wisdom of the future. Regulation is effectuated through ideas, principles, specific norms. Each principle, each law is universal and must account for an infinite number of vital situations. And each specific situation is individual and not repeatable. The special merit of the legislator lies in the possibility of foreseeing and taking into account future situations for which the lex is intended. Here we come to the well-known philosophical problem of the correlation of the general, special, and unique. The lex is universal, a subordinate act is special, and the specific act of law enforcement or a judicial decision, is unique. And the lex comes to life always through the unique. That is why it is appropriate to repeat the maxim: jus is what the judge says it is.

Often it is said and written that the principle of judicial precedent dooms practice to a lack of coordination in the application of law, and the nonrecognition of precedent ensures the unity of the application of lex. But in reality, it seems, the matter is otherwise.

Lex is intended for a specific situation. But in reality the situation is somewhat otherwise, similar perhaps, but different all the same. As a rule it is resolved by a court decision, when the court interprets and applies the lex. After some time elapses, the situation arises again. If the principle of precedent is utilised, the judicial decision simply need be repeated. If precedent is not recognised, another decision can be adopted. Consequently, precedent is the unity of social practice, the unity of the application of jus and lex. The difference is merely that a legal interpretation of lex gives unity from the top, and judicial precedent, from below.

Each variant has its virtues and shortcomings. Unity from above is perhaps more competent, but excessively centralised and less democratic. Unity from below is perhaps fraught with mistakes, but closer to real life. The selection of one decision for all instances in real life, the categorical adoption of one principle and the denial of another would, in our view, be one-sided. Truth evidently lies, as so often in controversial situations, in the search for an intermediate compromise decision. To leave the entire practice of law enforcement at the level of lex or a subordinate act is too extreme. To reduce law enforcement to judicial precedent would be the other extreme. A reasonable middle-ground may be to summarise judicial practice at the intermediate level and confer normative force upon such generalisations. Thus may one combine the general and special, the special and the unique, the abstract and the concrete, and the wisdom of the legislator and the experience of the law enforcer.

Here may be the way out of the problem of judicial practice as a source of jus. Specific forms of the use of this intermediate point may be found in the legal practice of every country.

Conclusion

We have characterised (on the basis of Soviet legal science) both basic concepts of how jus is understood. Our sympathies lie clearly with the distinction between jus and lex. But this does not preclude attempts to objectively, without prejudice, look at both concepts and evaluate their merits and shortcomings.

Which concept is true or, more delicately, closer to the truth? Posing the question thus leads to a more general question: what is truth in the humanities? Experiment here is obviously impossible, and therefore a single yes or no answer is also impossible. Truth consists not of black and white "true" and "untrue," but in the conformity of theoretical notions to the practice of social development, in knowing how to explain the past and foresee the future, and in their conformity to the interests of humanity, equality, and justness.

Since at various stages in the development of society in every country the interests of people undergo changes, their ideals change, and naturally so do scientific notions of reality. A theory which at one stage of social development had a certain orientation and certain value may at another stage change in both orientation and value. In other words, from the standpoint of the social sciences what was reasonable and natural yesterday may gradually lose those qualities today, and tomorrow become unreasonable and unnatural. Theoretical arguments in a polemic, arguments which transcend logic, must be combined with the logic of facts, with the practical interests of a particular theory.

What does the theory which combines jus and lex offer in practice? Everything which lex says is also jus, and everything that State power does (the creation of lex) is true and lawful. This theory is an apology for a strong State power, complete order in society based on strict following of lex. In periods of the strengthening and consolidation of a society, of overcoming fragmentation, and of a search for unity this theory is essential and progressive. But this theory does not take into account the quality and orientation of power itself, precludes pluralism in society, and the separation of powers, and therefore its realisation may lead to despotism and totalitarianism. History knows of such examples.

What does the theory which distinguishes between jus and lex offer? Jus, as the concentration of progressive principles in society, is the criterion for power and lex. From this flows the need for political pluralism, separation of powers, and a high role for the court as the antipode of bureaucratic administration. The implementation of these notions means a vast scope for democracy in all domains of social life but potentially threatens instability and changes in social institutes. This theory is a property of an ideologically healthy society with a developed general and legal culture. Such a society is capable of self-government, whereas a strong centralised power most often means government from without.

Consequently, both theories serve the development of society and the selection of one or the other theory as an ideological instrument depends upon the level of the development of society, its present and its contemplated future. That is why Soviet society today needs, speaking the language of jus, the concept which distinguishes between jus and lex.

Notes

1. In Soviet literature the correlation of jus and lex has been examined in V. S. Nersesiants, *Pravo i zakon* (1983).
2. A. Ia. Vyshinskii, *Voprosy teorii gosudarstva i prava* (1949), p. 84.
3. *Ibid.*, p. 421.
4. E. A. Lukasheva, "Obshchaia teoriia prava i mnogoaspektnyi analiz pravovykh iavlenii," *Sovetskoe gosudarstvo i pravo*, no. 4 (1975).
5. For a bibliography, see Nersesiants, "Pravo: mnogoobrazie opredelenii i edinstvo poniatiia," *Sovetskoe gosudarstvo i pravo*, no. 10 (1988), p. 27.
6. S. L. Zivs, *Istochniki prava* (1981), p. 10.
7. S. S. Alekseev, *Problemy teorii prava* (1973), II, p. 35.
8. Note 6 above, p. 10.

[11]

THE HARRIMAN INSTITUTE

FORUM

Volume 4, Number 5 *May 1991*

The Rule of Law and the Law-Based State (*Rechtsstaat*) (with special reference to developments in the Soviet Union)

By Harold J. Berman

The expression "law-based state" (in German, *Rechtsstaat*; in Russian, *pravovoe gosudarstvo*), which since 1988 has been one of the principal slogans of the Gorbachev Administration, is often mistranslated in English as "rule of law" or "state based on the rule of law."[1] In this essay I shall explore the theoretical implications of the expressions "rule of law" and "law-based state" in the context of their historical origins and shall examine ways in which both concepts are reflected in recent Soviet legal thought.

Prior to the accession of Gorbachev, the concept of a law-based state, which had been hotly debated by pre-revolutionary Russian writers (who themselves had derived it from nineteenth-century German jurists), was uniformly denounced in published Soviet political and legal literature. In theory, it conflicted with the Marxist-Leninist doctrine that law in all societies is a reflection of the will of the ruling class and that the state is ultimately bound by that will and not by any laws. In practice, it conflicted with the ultimate supremacy of the Communist Party leadership over the state itself. Only at the Nineteenth Party Conference in 1988 was *pravovoe gosudarstvo* added to *perestroika*, *glasnost*, and *demokratizatsiia* as a fundamental dimension of the new thinking called for by the Soviet leadership.

In numerous subsequent discussions of the theoretical and practical meanings of the concept of a law-based state, Soviet jurists have, for the first time since 1917, expressly linked themselves with a tradition of political and legal thought that goes back to Plato and Aristotle and Cicero, on the one hand, and to Locke and Kant, on the other. Pre-revolutionary Russian and German writings on *pravovoe gosudarstvo* or *Rechtsstaat* have also been referred to with respect. Nevertheless, despite occasional nods in the direction of a theory of natural law, Soviet jurists have thus far generally ignored, or else rejected, the concept of a law that is higher than, or even separate from, the laws that have been promulgated or acknowledged by the state.

In the Western legal tradition, the concept of a law that is higher than the state goes back to theories of divine law and natural law that were first systematically expounded in the twelfth century, and were resorted to in disputes between subjects of ecclesiastical law, between subjects of ecclesiastical and subjects of secular law, and between subjects of secular (royal, feudal, urban, and mercantile) law themselves. Indeed, the competition of jurisdictions between ecclesiastical and secular authorities and among secular authorities in the same territory was a powerful source of the search for a source of law higher than that

THE W. AVERELL HARRIMAN INSTITUTE FOR ADVANCED STUDY OF THE SOVIET UNION
COLUMBIA UNIVERSITY • 420 West 118th Street • 12th Floor • New York, New York 10027

of any political sovereign.[2] The scholastic theologians and canon lawyers were the first to use the expression "positive law" (*jus positivum*), referring to law that is laid down ("posited") by the lawmaker, as distinct from divine law (*jus divinum*), derived from the Ten Commandments and other sources of divine revelation, on the one hand, and natural law (*jus naturale*), whose source is human nature, and especially human reason and conscience, on the other.[3] In the sixteenth and seventeenth centuries, however, due partly to the subordination of the church to royal domination, the belief in a source of law superior to the will of the ruler was for the first time seriously challenged. It was not denied that there existed both a divine law and a natural law to which the supreme ruler of the state *ought* to submit his will, but new philosophical and scientific concepts made a sharp distinction, in law as in other spheres, between the "ought" and the "is," and at the same time (and perhaps in connection therewith) a new political theory of sovereignty denied to anyone the right to challenge on grounds of the law that "is" any law or command of a sovereign ruler. Thus divine law and natural law were removed from the realm of existing law to the realm of morality, leaving as the only prevailing law, the only legally binding law, the positive law of the state. It was partly against sixteenth and seventeenth century concepts of the absolute sovereignty of the monarch that the seventeenth-century English and the eighteenth-century American and French Revolutions were fought.

Paradoxically, perhaps the earliest published use of the English expression "rule of law" — in the sense of reign of law, or supremacy of law — was by King Charles I, who in 1649 was tried and condemned to death for treason by a special tribunal established solely for that purpose by the Puritan Parliament. Charles contended in his own defense that Parliament had no legal authority to try him and that the proceedings violated "the fundamental laws of the land." He charged that under the Puritan regime "power reigns without rule of law, changing the whole frame of that government under which this kingdom hath flourished."[4]

In more recent times it was the English legal scholar and statesman A. V. Dicey who brought the phrase "rule of law" into widespread use in England and America through his analysis of it in his book *Introduction to the Study of the Law of the Constitution*, first published in 1885.[5] For Lord Dicey the rule of law meant that certain basic principles of justice may not lawfully be infringed even by the highest lawmaking authority. Like King Charles I, he found the source of those basic legal principles in the fundamental laws of the land or, more precisely, in the English Constitution, which, though called unwritten, is embodied in historical monuments such as the Magna Carta of 1215, the Petition of Right of 1628, the Habeas Corpus Act of 1677, and above all the Bill of Rights of 1689, as well as in the historically evolving English common law. In sharp contrast, however, to the conception of the early Stuart monarchs, the basic principles of the English Constitution identified by Lord Dicey include, on the one hand, the sovereignty of Parliament and, on the other hand, certain inviolable rights of the subject such as the right to a fair hearing, equality before the law regardless of rank or condition, the right not to be deprived of one's life, liberty, or property without due process of law (in the procedural sense of that phrase), and also certain political rights such as freedom of discussion and the right to hold public meetings. In the English conception, Parliament itself, although supreme over every other political agency, is nevertheless considered to be constitutionally bound by fundamental principles of justice embodied in the historical traditions of the English people.[6]

The phrase "rule of law" came to be used in the United States in a different sense. Americans added to the English emphasis on the historical foundations of legality an emphasis on its foundations in written federal and state constitutions that proclaimed such civil liberties as freedom of religion, speech, press, and assembly. Moreover, the American concept of due process of law, embodied in the Fifth and Fourteenth Amendments of the United States Constitution, came to include not only procedural but also substantive justice. In addition, the Americans, unlike their British cousins, introduced a governmental system of checks and balances, entrusting to the judicial branch of government (rather than to Parliament) supreme authority to guard the Constitution. This added a new dimension to the concept of the rule of law, since it meant that in appropriate cases it can be invoked against the legislature itself by any citizen in any court. New words, "constitutionalism" and "constitutionality," were invented in the United States to embody these various principles.

The underlying philosophy of American constitutionalism rests not only on a historical jurisprudence, as in England, but also on an implicit theory of natural law. It is presupposed that certain kinds of moral principles, rooted in reason and conscience, have binding legal force. Their basic terms are expressed, to be sure, in written form in a legal document, the Constitution, and thus they are embodied in positive law, but they are ultimately derived (in the words of the Declaration of Independence) from "Nature and Nature's God," and their meaning transcends their written form. This means that they can be consciously and deliberately adapted by the courts to new situations from generation to generation.

In the French Revolution, the attack upon arbitrary rule by the monarchy and oppressive and unjust privileges of the aristocracy was made principally in the name of "the rights of man and citizen," which were to be protected by a strict separation of legislative, executive, and judicial powers.[7] Although the first written constitution of 1791 contained a list of the "natural rights" of the individual, and declared that the legislature had no legal power to interfere with their exercise,[8] nevertheless there was no appeal to an ancient historical tradition, such as was made in England, to bind the legislative branch nor was the judiciary given the power, as in the United States, to annul legislative acts. Thus in the French conception the ultimate source of law is the legislature, and the only external control on the legislature's lawmaking power is the political control of the electorate. The executive and the judicial branches are not supposed to check or balance the legislative branch, but rather to execute and apply, respectively, the enacted laws.[9] The French state is considered to be ultimately responsible not to a higher law but rather to the public opinion of the nation.

In jurisprudential terms, this reflects a positivist theory, according to which law (*droit, Recht, pravo*) consists of a body of legal norms or rules (*lois, Gesetze, zakony*) enacted (or acknowledged) by the state and enforced by coercive sanctions. There is nothing in the French constitution that permits the laws enacted by the National Assembly in the name of the people of France to be challenged in the name of some higher legal authority, whether derived from history or from morality. The natural rights of the individual person inhere, to be sure, in human nature and human reason, but these do not constitute or themselves produce a natural law that can overrule the will of the legislature.

The term *Rechtsstaat*, which was introduced into German legal and political thought in the early nineteenth century, also reflected a positivist jurisprudence. Although the term came to be used in various senses, its original proponents identified law with the state.[10] *Rechtsstaat* meant that not the nation, the *Volk*, in its historical development, and not natural reason and conscience, but the will of the supreme political authority, the will of the lawmaker, was both the ultimate source and the ultimate sanction of the law.[11] Nevertheless, the supreme political authority was to be law-based; the state was to constitute a "law-state," and not a state ruled by the arbitrary will of an absolute monarch as in earlier centuries. Nor was it to be a *Polizeistaat* — a "policy" or "welfare" state ruled by a benevolent autocrat.[12] The *Rechtsstaat* was to govern by law and was to be bound by, and not absolved from, the law which it makes. It was not to apply its law inconsistently or otherwise abuse it. This concept of the *Rechtsstaat* influenced, though it did not dominate, not only German but also Russian legal and political thought in the nineteenth and early twentieth centuries.[13]

The concept of *Rechtsstaat*, or *pravovoe gosudarstvo*, is consistent, at least, with the assumption that the state itself is the highest, if not the only, source of the law through which it operates. *Rechtsstaat*, or *pravovoe gosudarstvo*, is rule *by* law, not rule *of* law; it does not presuppose a fundamental law which is derived from a source outside the state and which the state is legally powerless to change. Theoretically, a fascist or other dictatorial regime can constitute a *Rechtsstaat*. Indeed, under German national socialism jurists defended the sentencing of persons to concentration camps on the ground that the German state was a *Rechtsstaat*.[14]

It is characteristic of the *Rechtsstaat* that it considers the basic form and source of law to be legislation, rather than custom and precedent (as in historical jurisprudence) or equity (as in natural-law theory). Custom, precedent, and equity are assimilated, in the positivist theory, to legislation; what makes them *law* is that they are accepted by the legislative authority and are enforced by state sanctions. It is therefore characteristic of the strong positivist tendency of legal thought in nineteenth-century Europe that it fostered the embodiment of the law of the state in a coherent and complete legislative codification of its various branches. To the extent that the entire legal order of the state is embodied in legislative enactments, law in the large sense (*Recht, droit, pravo, jus*) is identified with law in the narrower sense of a specific legal rule (*Gesetz, loi, zakon, lex*), and the *Rechtsstaat* may be viewed as a *Gesetzesstaat*, that is, a state that rules by *laws*. This, indeed, is what *pravovoe gosudarstvo* meant when it was first proclaimed as a slogan of the Gorbachev administration. In accordance with the extreme form of positivism which had been officially endorsed in the Soviet Union, and which until now has dominated Soviet legal thought, the *pravovoe gosudarstvo* has been identified with the supremacy, or reign, of enacted law (*verkhovenstvo zakona, gospodstvo zakona*) rather than of law in the larger sense, law as a whole, implying right, or justice (*pravo*). Even Soviet writers who in recent years have moved away from a rigid positivism have identified the law-based state with the reign (*gospodstvo*), or rule (*pravlenie*), of *zakon* rather than of *pravo*.[15]

One should not minimize, however, especially in the context of Soviet history, the importance of the principle of the rule of *laws*, even though it falls short of the principle of the rule of *law*. It means, in the first place, that the state rules by laws and not by mere force or fiat. It means, secondly that the state is bound by its own laws, that is, it may not arbitrarily disregard them but may only change them by the legal procedures which it has established for changing them. And thirdly, it means that hitherto all-powerful state executive and administrative agencies, including the Council (now renamed Cabinet) of Ministers and its subordinate ministries and departments, may not issue decrees or regulations which conflict with statutes enacted by the legislature, and that courts or other agencies may not enforce such decrees or regulations. Under Stalin, the Soviet state systematically violated its own laws, and under Stalin's successors it has done so frequently, though not systematically and not with Stalin's brutality. Also, both under Stalin and his successors many thousands of administrative regulations were issued that contradicted statutes promulgated by the union and republican supreme soviets, and these regulations, though illegal, were enforced by administrative authorities and by the courts as substatutory "legislation" (*zakonodatel'stvo*).[16]

An important modification of the conventional Soviet theory of law was made in an article published in 1988 in the Communist Party monthly journal *Kommunist*, in which two prominent jurists — one of them a vice-president of the USSR Academy of Sciences — gave a new dimension to the Soviet concept of the law-based state by tracing its origins to Plato, Aristotle, Cicero, Montesquieu, Locke, and Kant. Although still referring to the rule of *zakon*, rather than the rule of *pravo*, they quoted Plato as stating that only "where law (*zakon*) is master over the rulers and they are its slaves" is there "salvation of the state . . . ," and Aristotle as stating that "where the power of law (*zakon*) is absent, there is no place and no kind of form for the state order," and Cicero as asking "Yes, and what is a state other than a general legal order?" "The philosophical basis of the theory of the law-based state," they wrote, "was formulated by Kant, who viewed the state as 'an association of the multitude of people who are subject to legal rules' and who considered that the legislature should be governed by the requirement: 'what the people cannot decide for itself, the legislator cannot decide for the people.'"[17] The authors did not wholly abandon a positivist theory of law; on the contrary, they identified law with the state. On the other hand, they also proclaimed the validity of universal moral norms of human dignity and, in connection therewith, universal legal norms of procedural and substantive justice. Without using the expression "natural law," they invoked — for the first time, certainly, in the history of the journal *Kommunist* — the authority of classical exponents of natural-law theory. At the same time, they stressed the subordination of the state to society, and the dependence of legal institutions on the legal consciousness of the people — and not just society and the people in general, but Soviet society and the Soviet people, tracing in broad outline the "extremely painful and difficult process" by which legality became established in the historical development of the Soviet State from October 1917 to the present.[18] Thus they added to positivism not only an embryonic theory of natural law but also an embryonic historical jurisprudence.[19]

The distinction — and the tension — between a positivist theory of the relationship of law to the state and both a natural-law theory and a historical theory was put sharply in 1988 by V. F. Yakovlev, a leading Soviet legal scholar who subsequently became the USSR Minister of Justice, in the course of a round-table discussion among Soviet jurists concerning the meaning of a law-based state. "The specific question," he stated, "is: what over what? The state over the law or the law over the state?" Although he used the word *pravo* throughout, and not *zakon*, he answered the question in positivist terms: "Despite the fact that the law is born of the state, and has its sources in state institutions, the state nevertheless becomes truly law-based when it places the law above itself." Here it is postulated that there is no higher source of law than the state itself, which may, however, or may not, "place the law above itself."[20] In 1990, I had the opportunity to ask Minister Yakovlev, "If there is to be in the Soviet Union a law higher than the state, what will be the source of that law?" He replied, "As in the United States, it will be the Constitution — the spirit of the Constitution." When I asked, "Do you mean the spirit of the 1977 USSR Constitution?" he replied, "Well, there are some good things in that Constitution." Presumably, he hoped that a new USSR Constitution, then being planned, would add many more "good things."

The 1977 USSR Constitution does indeed proclaim certain fundamental principles of legality and certain fundamental rights of citizens. These principles and rights are presented, however, as commitments and grants made by the state. There is nothing in that Constitution that prohibits the state from retracting those commitments and rights. Amendments to the Constitution require only a two-thirds vote of the supreme legislative body. Moreover, the Constitution is not self-executing, that is, it is not directly applicable but must be implemented by legislation in order to become operative. This is obvious in those provisions which expressly provide that the powers of official agencies or the rights of citizens shall be exercised "in a procedure [to be] established by [statute] law." Even in the absence of such a limitation, the 1977 Constitution, like the 1936 Constitution before it, and like the fifteen republican constitutions that were adopted in imitation of them, is essentially a directive to the legislature to enact laws corresponding to its provisions. In the absence of such legislation, it has only occasionally happened that a court or other state agency has directly applied a provision of the Constitution. Moreover, courts have no legal power, under the 1977 Constitution, to refuse to apply a statute on the ground that it violates a constitutional right.[21]

Yet even if all these limitations on the authority of the Constitution were removed, could it be said that it constitutes a body of law that is higher than the state itself, or could it only be said that the state which gave birth to the law had placed the law above itself — and could presumably at any time lawfully place itself above the law?

That the state is itself not only a creator but also a creature of law, that the state is born of the law and therefore has power to create new law only within the limits of the law which gave birth to it — were truths widely accepted in the West until the nineteenth and twentieth centuries. A group of persons armed with sufficient instruments of power may, indeed, subdue a large number of other persons and compel them to act in certain ways. No state comes into existence, however, unless it is postulated that the subduers have not only the power but also the right to govern their victims and that the victims have not only the necessity but also the duty to obey. Once the relation between ruler and ruled is conceived in terms of a correlative right and duty, then it becomes apparent that power (contrary not only to Marxian but also to current non-Marxian political theory) is not a unilateral but a bilateral relationship. Thus not only domination but also citizenship is involved in the establishment and maintenance of a state. Conversely, toward citizens a state has not only rights but also duties, and toward a state citizens have not only duties but also rights. It is the reciprocity of rights and duties, or law, not mere power, that constitutes a state in its internal relations. Similarly, it is law that determines its character as a state in its external relations. Indeed, in the Western political and legal tradition, a state is defined in the first instance by its membership in a legal association of states. As late as 1827 Chancellor Kent started his Commentaries on American Law with a chapter on the law of nations, implying at the outset that it is the law of nations which gives the United States the right to create a system of national law.[22]

That Soviet statesmen and jurists have begun to think in terms of a law that is higher than the state is apparent from a Draft Constitution of the Russian Federation, published in November 1990, which was to be submitted to the Supreme Soviet of the RSFSR.[23] The Draft Constitution proclaimed a law-based state, a *pravovoe gosudarstvo*, but it also proclaimed "the supremacy of law (*pravo*) and of the Constitution," stating that the state and all its agencies and officials are bound by law (*pravo*) and by the constitutional order," that "the Constitution of the Russian Federation is the highest law (*zakon*) of the Republic," and that "laws and other legal acts that contradict its provisions shall not have juridical force." It states that "a law (*zakon*) must be lawful (*pravovym*)," and that citizens "exercise their rights independently," that is, their rights are not grants from the state, although they may be restricted (within constitutional limits) by the state.

The 1990 Russian Federation Draft Constitution provided further that "norms of the Constitution shall have direct application." A court that is asked to apply a law which it considers to be unconstitutional was to suspend the proceeding and submit the matter to the consideration of a special Constitutional Court, which was to have the power and the duty to annul all laws, decrees, or other normative acts that violate the Constitution. It was expressly provided, moreover, that any decision or action of any state agency or official that violates the constitutional rights of citizens may be appealed to a regular court. Thus provision was made both for constitutional review of legislative acts and for judicial review of the constitutionality of official actions.[24]

The 1990 Russian Federation Draft also contained an extensive list of specific civil and political as well as social, economic, and cultural rights. It prefaced the list with a general declaration that "man [*chelovek*, the person], his life, honor, dignity and freedom, personal inviolability, [and] his natural and inalienable rights constitute the supreme value," and further, that "human rights and liberties belong to a person from his birth," and that the enumeration of "the rights and liberties in the Constitution and in laws shall not be used to reduce other human rights and liberties." Thus a conception of natural rights was embodied in the Draft Constitution. This conception was reinforced by the provision that if an international treaty to which the Russian Federation is a party (which would include the Human Rights Covenants of the United Nations) contains rules that differ from those contained in legislation of the Russian Federation, then the rules of the international treaty shall be applied. Thus the state, bound by the Constitution not to infringe certain natural and inalienable rights, was also subjected by the Constitution to an overriding international obligation to protect those rights — an obligation that could only be avoided by a formal denunciation of the international treaties to which the state had previously adhered.

It is scarcely enough, of course, simply to proclaim various civil and political and social and economic and cultural rights to be natural and inviolable. It is necessary also to provide a machinery for protecting those rights against violation. The 1990 Russian Federation Draft Constitution took an important step in that direction by vesting in the judiciary the power and the duty to annul any legislative or administrative act that conflicts with the Constitution and any official action that violates constitutional rights. Yet even judicial supremacy is not a complete guarantee, since in judging the constitutionality of legislative and administrative acts or official actions the judiciary must weigh against the protection of the rights of citizens the legitimate interest of society in the protection of public order as well as various other public interests that are also proclaimed in the Constitution. In the spirit of the eighteenth-century Enlightenment, the Draft Constitution seeks to establish a self-regulating legal order within the state structure by combining the (French) concept of the separation of powers with the (American) concept of checks and balances and a strong presidency, and by providing for a multi-party political system with democratic elections of the parliament and of the president. Yet it provides no opening for a challenge on legal grounds to a norm that has been approved by *all three* branches of government, even though the norm violates what in England would be called the fundamental law of the land and in America due process of law. Thus the state has agreed to be bound by a law which, to be sure, it has proclaimed to be higher than itself but of which in fact it is itself the creator, not the creature. The "natural rights" of man and citizen, though said to be inalienable, are nevertheless from a legal standpoint conceived to be a product of positive law.

The 1990 Russian Federation Draft Constitution does attempt, however, in one of its parts, to establish a source of law which is outside the Constitution itself and from which the Constitution itself is derived. That source is called "civil society," and one of the principal chapters of the Constitution is devoted to it. It proclaims (1) "the inalienable natural right to be an owner," the right of workers to form trade unions and conclude collective labor agreements, and the freedom of private persons and of associations to form business enterprises. It also proclaims (2) that "the family is a natural cell of the society," that children born out of wedlock shall have the same rights as children born of registered marriages and that parents shall be obliged to take care of their children and adult children of their parents. In addition, it proclaims (3) that culture and science, research, and teaching "shall be free," and that "pluralism in the intellectual and spiritual sphere is guaranteed;" (4) that "the mass media shall be free [and] censorship is prohibited"; (5) that "religion and religious associations shall be separate from the state" and that "the state may not give preference to any religion or to atheism"; and (6) that political parties and other voluntary public associations may be freely formed. Each of these six sub-sections of the chapter on a "civil society" is elaborated and qualified in various ways.

Here it must be noted that the term "civil society" has been widely invoked in recent years by proponents of fundamental change in Eastern Europe and the Soviet Union. The term itself first came into wide use in England in the seventeenth century to signify the political order as contrasted with a hypothetical state of nature.[25] In the late eighteenth and early nineteenth centuries, "civil society" acquired new meanings, first in France and then in Germany. In France *société civile* came to mean, both in the political sense and in the cultural sense, a society characterized by individual liberty and (to a lesser extent) equality and (to a still lesser extent) fraternity among the people who comprise it. It was related to the French concept of civilization. In German, the word "civil" is rendered as *buergerlich*, meaning "pertaining to the citizen," and in Russian, too, "civil society" is rendered *grazhdanskoe obshchestvo*, "citizens' society." The German *bürgerliche Gesellschaft* and the Russian *grazhdanskoe obshchesto* have a strong link with citizenship, that is, with membership in the political order. Thus they are linked with the state, although they are separate from it. The French *société civile*, on the contrary, is sharply distinguished from the state. It is more like the nineteenth-century German concept of *Kultur* than like *bürgerliche Gesellschaft*.[26]

Marx, following Hegel, identified civil society (*bürgerliche Gesellschaft*) with relationships of civil law (*bürgerliches Recht*), that is, the private law of property, contract, tort, inheritance, family relationships, and the like, as contrasted with the public law of state power and state administration. Marx, of course, in contrast to Hegel, viewed such "bourgeois" legal institutions as a mere facade for the protection of the interests of the ruling capitalist class, resulting in the exploitation of the proletariat, alienation of the worker from the means of production, and an economy based on the exchange of goods rather than production to meet needs, and he denounced "bourgeois society" for its ideology of individualism and self-aggrandizement. Under socialism, a classless society was to prevail, and individualism would be replaced by collectivism. A socialist society, therefore, could not be a "civil" society. Following this reasoning, Soviet Marxist-Leninists rejected the notion of a socialist civil society as a contradiction in terms. Instead, they used the single word "society" — as Marx did — to denote the entire range of socio-economic relationships, but nevertheless contrasted "society" with "the state," which, though it arose on the basis of society, would continue to stand over society as a necessary instrument of coercion until the final achievement of a classless society. In the post-Stalin era, the Communist Party leadership proclaimed that the functions of the Soviet state were gradually to be assumed by the voluntary actions of society. Yet the truth was that the state, though it was, to be sure, slowly becoming more democratic, hardly yielded the substance of its power over the lives of the Soviet people.

The great Polish writer Czeslaw Milosz has said that "in the twentieth century, the state has eaten up all the substance of society."[27] In this perspective "society" means the primary associations in which a person acquires his character as a social being: family, church, school, neighborhood, workplace, business enterprises, professional organizations, literary societies, and other voluntary social and economic associations, that constitute a civilized people, a "culture." The decline of the vitality of these autonomous community relationships in the twentieth century has been closely connected with the enormous expansion of the central political authority of the state: each is a cause of the other.[28] It is a virtue of the 1990 Draft Constitution of the Russian Federation that under the heading of "civil society" it identifies and gives legal protection to a broad range of basic social activities and associations: individual and group property relations, labor relations, voluntary economic and other enterprises, marriage and the family, intellectual and spiritual activities, communications media, religious activities and religious organizations, political parties and other public associations. Also ethnic and linguistic communities are to be given autonomy.

If, indeed, the source of the law that defines the powers of the state, that is, the source of the law of the Constitution, is understood to be the entire community of individuals, voluntary associations, and autonomous groups that comprise a civilized people, then the Marxist doctrine that the state is a political superstructure built on an economic base, in which class relations of production play the decisive part, must be rejected. The whole of society, including its family units and its language, and not merely its social-economic component, forms the basic substructure. Moreover, if community relations as a whole, and not only class relations, define state power, then the Marxist doctrine that law proceeds only from the state must also be rejected, since society as a whole inevitably has a legal dimension, a built-in *unofficial* legality, and in addition the various types of associations and activities that make up a society have their own distinctive unofficial legal aspects. Thus in this version of a civil society the state is formed partly in response to the law that governs people in their social relations — identified as customary law by adherents of historical jurisprudence, and as natural law by adherents of a natural-law theory. In this concept, the process described by Czeslaw Milosz is to be reversed: civil society, including its legal dimension, is not only to be liberated from domination by the state but is itself to become dominant over — "higher than" — the state. State law, official law, is to be subject to social law, unofficial law, the law-consciousness of the civil society.

Consistent with this theory is the provision of the 1990 Russian Federation Draft Constitution that the fundamental principles identified in its first chapter may only be changed by a universal referendum. These include the inviolability of basic human rights, political and ideological pluralism, separation of powers, supremacy of law, a social market economy, a state based on social democracy, and a federal structure.

Nevertheless, the Draft Constitution does not go so far as expressly to identify the source — or sources — of a law that is higher, or other, than the state. Moreover, it does not indicate the difference, if any, between "civil society," to which it devotes forty-one separate articles, and just plain "society," without a preceding adjective, which is at various places juxtaposed with the state. Thus the Constitution is declared in the Preamble to be "the fundamental law of our society and our state," and "society and the state" are required under various articles "to protect" the interests of consumers, the family, and the cultural and intellectual heritage, "to secure" the development of basic scientific research, "to contribute to" the improvement of international relations in the sciences, culture, and education, and so forth. Finally, in declaring "the goals and tasks of the state," the Draft provides that the state "shall be the official representative of society, whose will it shall represent through its agencies and institutions." This assertion of the relationship between the state and society is undoubtedly intended to enjoin the state to be responsible to society and to represent its interests. Yet it postulates a unitary *political* order, a single "state," which alone may speak and act for society "officially," and also a unitary *social* order, a single "society," which is distinct from the "state" and is officially represented by it. Thus the theoretical possibility is left open that the state, to which "the people" has delegated a monopoly of lawmaking authority, may once again, in Milosz's image, eat up all the substance of society, albeit in a democratic fashion.

Taken as a whole, the 1990 Russian Federation Draft Constitution goes beyond the positivist concept of a law-based state, and tentatively embraces the natural-law concept of the rule of law, that is, the subjection of the state to a law that is superior to it, a law embodying universal moral principles to which every citizen may have recourse in the courts. It does not, however, give a clear indication of the source of that higher law in reason and conscience, that is, in human nature itself.[29] Nor does it invoke a historical tradition of legality. It says nothing about achievements of the past except to refer in the Preamble to "the memory of our ancestors who through disasters and sufferings preserved and transmitted to us a bright faith in goodness and justice." No reference is made to the struggle for law waged in the past against heavy odds by individual Soviet citizens as well as by groups of citizens, or of previous law reform movements in the Soviet Union, or of the "good things" in previous Soviet constitutions.[30] The word "socialism" does not appear in the Draft. The drafters seem to have disregarded the injunction of the great nineteenth-century Russian religious philosopher Vladimir Soloviev that "in order to defeat what is false in socialism one must recognize what is true in it."[31]

It may be useful to compare briefly the 1990 Draft Constitution of the Russian Federation with another draft constitution, published simultaneously, called the Draft Constitution of the Russian Soviet Federation Socialist Republic (RSFSR), which was also intended to be submitted to the RSFSR Supreme Soviet and ultimately to the entire population of the Republic. The latter Draft was prepared by a group of deputies to the RSFSR Supreme Soviet who call themselves "Communists of Russia." The most striking difference between the two drafts is that the Russian Federation Draft makes no reference whatever to the USSR and, indeed, declares the exclusive authority of the Russian Federation over its entire territory, including the land, natural resources, air space and water, currency, foreign policy, defense, and similar matters. The RSFSR Draft, on the other hand, while declaring the sovereignty of the RSFSR throughout its territory, provides also that it is part of the Union of Soviet Socialist Republics, with the right freely to secede but also with participation in the armed forces and the military defense of the USSR and also, together with other republics, in various stated common tasks. One implication of such acceptance of membership in the USSR is that the RSFSR Constitution will be compatible with the constitutions of the other republics that comprise the USSR, and that the RSFSR conception of sovereignty, and of the relation of law to the state, will not be fundamentally inconsistent with that of the others.

The RSFSR Draft differs to a considerable extent from the Russian Federation Draft in style and language, but much less so in substance. Its Preamble declares that it "seeks to create a soviet socialist law-based state," and it refers to socialism at several other points, but the Preamble adds, after "law-based state," the words "a multiparty system based on principles of democracy, [and] an efficient economy based on various forms of ownership [and] on the development of market relations in the interests of securing the welfare of the people." The Preamble also defines "a democratic socialist order" as one characterized by "separation of the legislative, executive, and judicial powers."

Also the RSFSR Draft Constitution, like the Russian Federation Draft, proclaims a long list of "natural and inalienable rights" and contains a general declaration that "all rights and freedoms secured by the Constitution of the RSFSR shall be protected by the court." As in the Russian Federation Draft, the power to challenge the constitutionality of statutes and other normative acts is vested in a Constitutional Court, and if in a concrete case any court finds that a normative act which it is asked to apply contradicts the Constitution it must discontinue the proceeding and submit to the Constitutional Court a proposal to declare the act to be invalid.

Nevertheless, the provision of the Russian Federation Draft that "laws" (*zakony*) which do not correspond to "law" (*pravo*) are not valid is omitted, and various general limitations on citizens' rights are stated. Thus private enterprises are permitted, with individual or group ownership of means of production, but only "within the limits of [enacted] laws (zakony)." Also protection is provided against the use of individual or collective economic enterprises to exploit or otherwise cause disadvantage to other persons. In addition, there is a strong emphasis on the duties (and not only the rights) of citizens, and a great emphasis is placed upon social and economic rights.

In general, the RSFSR Draft is more traditionally Soviet in its language. The concept of a "civil society" is not introduced. Thus the impression of an effort to liberate society from domination by the state, which may be derived from the Russian Federation Draft, is much less apparent in the RSFSR Draft.

Yet the similarities between the two drafts are undoubtedly more significant from a jurisprudential viewpoint than the differences. They both represent a substantial implementation of the concept of the law-based state. Neither of them represents an introduction of the rule of law.

From the perspective of the rule of law, the strongest feature of both drafts is their reliance on the judiciary to supervise the constitutionality of statutes, decrees, and regulations of the legislative and executive or administrative branches of government. In the case of the Russian Federation Draft, this is to some extent strengthened by the inclusion of broad criteria of justice that are to guide constitutional interpretation and thus to enable the courts to make the letter of the Constitution conform to its spirit. This would give an opening to the development of judicial principles based on reason and conscience by which the will of the legislative branch and the practices of the executive branch could be restrained and educated.

On the other hand, natural law itself requires consistency and predictability in the judicial interpretation and application of constitutional principles; and here the enormous length and complexity and often contradictory tendencies of each of the drafts constitute serious drawbacks. These draft constitutions, like the existing 1977 Soviet Constitution, attempt to regulate the entire political, economic, and social life of the country. Like much of traditional Soviet legislation, they constitute a gigantic, all-embracing program.

In fact, from the perspective of Soviet history the heavy reliance on the judiciary to help carry out this program is also the weakest feature of both drafts, since the judiciary has been the weakest branch of the Soviet state. (I do not count the pre-Gorbachev Supreme Soviet, since prior to 1989 it was the apparatus of the Central Committee and the Politburo that constituted the de facto legislative branch.) Historically, one must go back to the pre-Soviet Russian judiciary and legal profession from the time of Alexander II's great reform of 1864 in order to find roots from which a competent, honest, and independent judicial branch could grow. This would suggest the need for a more cautious, step-by-step approach to Soviet constitutional reform.

In terms of an understanding of the relationship between the concept of the rule of law and the concept of a law-based state, Soviet experience teaches the inadequacy of both a positivist theory that identifies state and law with each other and of a natural-law theory that sets law above the state or in opposition to it. Both of these theories need to be integrated with each other and with historical jurisprudence.[32] The *pravovoe gosudarstvo*, or *Rechtsstaat*, is, to be sure, a great advance over both the absolute state and the policy state, in which the supreme political authority is considered to be above the law rather than being identified with it. On the other hand, since the law-based state remains the final source of the law with which it is identified, its commitment to law lacks the moral force that is invoked by the concept of a law that derives from the higher qualities of human nature itself, including, above all, human reason and human conscience. Yet the human sense of justice and fairness is itself an unruly guide. "Equity," John Selden complained in the seventeenth century, "is as long as the Chancellor's foot." An abstract legal morality may be as arbitrary in practice as the legislation enacted by the supreme political authority. Both of these sources of law need to be rooted in the historical experience and the social institutions of the people whose law it is.

Lacking in current Soviet legal thought, it would seem, is sufficient awareness that in the long run both legislation and equity, to be effective, must be adapted to and integrated with the customary law — the law-consciousness — of the peoples that comprise Soviet society. Indeed, from the point of view of historical jurisprudence one might argue — as the great founder of the historical school, Friedrich Carl von Savigny, argued in the early nineteenth century with respect to codification of the civil law of the German confederation — that in light of the lack of a sufficiently developed legal culture the time is not yet ripe in the Soviet Union for constitutional proclamations of the rule of law.

Notes

[1] The American periodical *Current Digest of the Soviet Press*, for example, habitually translates *pravovoe gosudarstvo* as "rule of law." William E. Butler, recognizing the distinction between "law-based state" and "rule of law," has chosen to use the phrase "rule-of-law state" because, as he writes, it "gives the benefit of the doubt to those who advocate the broader and more fundamental concept of law," that is, those who believe in a law that connotes "right and justice, consistency with moral principles that prevail always and everywhere, that may not be transgressed by citizen or state . . . ." William E. Butler, "The Rule of Law and the Legal System," in Stephen White, Alex Pravda, and Zvi Gitelman, editors, *Developments in Soviet Politics*, 1990, pp. 104-105. Many Soviet translators also prefer the broader translation. Other Soviet and English speaking translators use the more literal translation "law-based state" or "law-governed state" or "legal state." The same problem exists, of course, in the translation of Rechtsstaat.

[2] See H. J. Berman, *Law and Revolution: The Formation of the Western Legal Tradition* (1983), *passim*.

[3] See *id.*, pp. 145-146.

[4] "His Majesty's Reasons Against the Pretended Jurisdiction of the High Court of Justice," reprinted in *A collection of scarce and valuable tracts on the most interesting and entertaining subjects*, London, 1748, series I, vol. IV, p. 169.

[5] Dicey's book went through eight editions from 1885 to 1915, during his lifetime, and two editions (1939 and 1959) after his death, edited with an introduction by E.C.S. Wade. The expression "natural justice," which is often used by English courts and writers, although not discussed by Dicey, has a meaning very close to his concept of the rule of law; it is not natural justice in the abstract but natural justice (or, as Americans would say, due process of law) as construed historically by the English courts in light of their precedents.

[6] See Dicey, *id.*, 10th ed., pp. 183-196.

[7] The doctrine of separation of powers is generally traced to Montesquieu's *L'esprit des lois* (1748). Montesquieu himself, in that work, mistakenly attributes the doctrine to the English Constitution. Cf. Livre XI, Chapitre VI, "De la constitution d'Angleterre."

[8] The French Constitution of 1791 states: "The legislative power cannot make any law that would infringe or impede the exercise of the natural rights recorded in the present chapter and guaranteed by the Constitution." Later constitutions (of which there were many) ceased to list natural rights. See the discussion in André Hauriou, Jean Gicquel, and Patrice Gélard, *Droit constitutionnel et institutions politiques*, 6th ed., 1975, pp. 195-197. At one point, the authors of this leading work, in a footnote, associate the constitutional movement in France in the late eighteenth and early nineteenth centuries with the transition from a policy-based state (*l'Etat de Police*) to a law-based state (*l'Etat de Droit*). *Id.*, p. 177, n. 9. They do not, however, use any expression that suggests the supremacy of law over the state. See infra notes 10, 11, 12.

[9] The 1791 Constitution declared that there is no authority in France superior to that of the *loi*, that is, the legislative enactment. This reflected the Enlightenment concept, expressly stated in the Massachusetts Constitution of 1780, of a "government of laws, not of men." This concept is often confused with the rule of law, to which it is, of course, related, but with which it is hardly identical.

[10] The term *Rechtsstaat* seems to have appeared first in 1829 in a work of Robert von Mohl. It is often traced, however, to Immanuel Kant, who advanced a similar concept without, apparently, using the term. Friedrich Darmstaedter, in *Die Grenzen der Wirksamkeit des Rechtsstaates* (1930), distinguishes between what he calls the "classical theory" of the Rechtsstaat, which goes back to the Middle Ages and which culminated in Kant's work, with the modern theory. See infra note 11.

[11] Otto von Gierke devotes the last chapter of his great work on Althusius to "the idea of the Rechtsstaat," tracing it back through Althusius to the twelfth century and treating it as a natural-law theory. O. v. Gierke, *Johannes Althusius und die Entwicklung der naturrechtlichen Staatstheorien*, 6th ed., 1968, Chapter Six. This, however, is justified only if the term *Rechtsstaat* is given a broader meaning than that which it actually had when it was first used by von Mohl and others. Darmstaedter shows that throughout the nineteenth century Rechtsstaat presupposed a positivist jurisprudence which identifies law with the state and asserts the primacy of the state over the law. Op. cit., pp. 84 ff., 129 ff. Joseph LaPolombara, *Politics Within Nations* (1974), p. 106, makes the distinction very clear: "[T]he difference between the *Rechtsstaat* and constitutionalism is that the rule of law in the former is based on a concession from the rulers. The concession implies that the State has elected to engage in self-limitation in the exercise of power. But under constitutionalism the limitation is found to be a matter of right established by a combination of historical tradition and philosophical principle. While the distinction may sound legalistic, its impact is very real. It is like the contrast between an all-powerful father, who from time to time may refrain from tyrannizing over his children and even give them certain areas of freedom and independence to act, and a family where certain freedoms to act and take decisions are claimed and accepted as inherent in the family members."

[12] See Darmstaedter, *op. cit.*, p. 23 ff. The term *Polizeistaat*, which is applied to the German principalities in the sixteenth to eighteenth centuries, is often translated as "intervention state." It should certainly not be translated "police state."

[13] As is well known, German legal thought in the nineteenth century was dominated by the historical school, founded by Friedrich Carl von Savigny. In Russia, the movement to collect and codify the laws of the Empire in the nineteenth century was understood at the time less in terms of a positivist jurisprudence (such as was expounded by Jeremy Bentham) and more in terms of a historical jurisprudence, an evolving tradition of legality (such as was expounded by Savigny). This point is elaborated in H. J. Berman, "Some Jurisprudential Implications of the Codification of Soviet Law," Richard M. Buxbaum and Kathryn Hendley, eds., *The Soviet* Sobranie *of Laws: Problems of Codification and Non-Publication*, (1991), p. 173 ff.

[14] Walter Otto Weyrauch, Book Review, *Ius Commune*, vol. XVI, p. 569 (1989), refers at page 571 to a 1935 report of a German court to the Ministry of Justice concerning a case involving commitment of a person to a concentration camp for educational purposes, in which the court stated that "in a Rechtsstaat the court has not only the right but the duty, when the interest of the state, and especially state security, so requires, to recognize and carry out exceptional provisions." Similarly, a Soviet jurist, in discussing the concept of the supremacy of "laws" (as contrasted with the supremacy of "law"), stated recently that "it is enough to recall what kinds of laws were adopted in periods of mass repression." R. Z. Livshits, "Pravo i zakon v sotsialisticheskom pravovom gosudarstve," *Sovetskoe gosudarstvo i pravo*, 1989, no. 3, p. 15 at p. 17.

[15] Cf. V. Kudriavtsev and E. Lukasheva, "Sotsialisticheskoe pravovoe gosudarstvo," *Kommunist*, no. 11 (1988), p. 44. Livshits, however, supra note 15, states that "the law-based state should be linked not with zakon (this is simply a self-restriction, and an inadequate one) but with pravo, with society's concepts of justice [*spravedlivosti*]."

[16] One aspect of the illegality of many of the administrative regulations classified as "legislation" was their

secrecy. That is, they were not published but instead circulated to agencies or officials directly affected by them. Cf. Buxbaum and Hendley, supra note 14. This practice has now been denounced as a violation of the law-based state, and it is argued that no unpublished regulation can have the force of law.

[17] Kudriavtsev and Lukasheva, supra note 14, p.45.

[18] *Id.*, p. 46.

[19] The authors do not, however, refer expressly to these traditional schools of jurisprudence. Moreover, they do not make any reference to the rich pre-revolutionary Russian heritage of jurisprudential writings on these subjects. In fact, various schools of thought concerning the nature of the law-based state were represented by pre-revolutionary Russian thinkers such as Chicherin, Soloviev, Petrazycki, Novgorodtsev, Kistiakovsky, Mikhailovsky, Hessen, and others. An excellent account of their writings is given in Andrzej Walicki, *Legal Philosophies of Russian Liberalism* (1987). Walicki states on page 1 "that the liberal intellectual tradition in pre-revolutionary Russia was in fact much stronger than is usually believed, that the main concern of Russia's liberal thinkers was the problem of the rule of law, and that the most precious legacy of Russian liberalism was precisely its contribution to the philosophy of law, as well as to the controversy about law, the debate in which the value of law as such was seen as . . . something in need of defence, and not something to be taken for granted." Since contemporary Soviet legal theorists are entirely familiar with this pre-revolutionary heritage, the failure of almost all of them to take it into account must be deliberate.

[20] "Kakim dolzhno byt' pravovoe gosudarstvo," *Literaturnaia gazeta*, 8 June 1988, p. 11.

[21] Prior to 1989 the 1977 Constitution empowered the Presidium of the Supreme Soviet of the USSR to exercise constitutional supervision over laws and decrees of all-union and republic supreme soviets and councils of ministers. The 1936 Constitution contained a similar provision. However, this power was almost never exercised during more than fifty years of its existence. A constitutional amendment of 1989 established a USSR Constitutional Supervision Committee to review the constitutionality of laws and decrees of the USSR Supreme Soviet and other bodies, though not of the newly established USSR Congress of People's Deputies. The Committee is not a court and does not decide concrete cases.

[22] James Kent, *Commentaries on American Law* (1826), 12th ed. by O. W. Holmes, Jr. (1873), vol. 1, p. 1. Kent starts his four-volume work with the statement: "When the United States ceased to be a part of the British empire, and assumed the character of an independent nation, they became subject to that system of rules which reason, morality, and custom had established among the civilized nations of Europe, as their public law." Kent implies, although he does not state expressly, that the law of nations is the source of the lawmaking power of the states that are subject to it.

[23] The Draft, entitled (in translation) "Draft: Constitution of the Russian Federation: Document published by decision of the Constitutional Commission of the RSFSR," was published in the newspaper *Sovetskaia Rossiia*, November 24, 1990, pp. 1-8. An alternative draft entitled (in translation) "Draft: Constitution of the Russian Soviet Federated Socialist Republics: Draft prepared by the initiative group of people's deputies of the RSFSR named Communists of Russia," was published in the same issue.

[24] The distinction between the two kinds of review is not easy to express in English. In German legal terminology the word *Verfassungsstreitigkeit* is used to refer to the power of a court to decide in the abstract, so to speak, that a certain law violates the constitution, and the term *richterliches Prüfungsrecht* is used to refer to the power of a court in a concrete case to refuse to apply a law because to apply it in that case would violate the constitution. See Donald P. Kommers, *The Constitutional Jurisprudence of the Federal Republic of Germany* (1989), pp. 4-5. The latter power was asserted by Chief Justice Marshall in 1819 in Marbury v. Madison. The former power has been asserted by the United States Supreme Court in recent decades, although always in the context of concrete cases.

[25] The two great seventeenth-century proponents of the theory of the origin of the state in social contract — Hobbes and Locke — both contrasted "civil society" with a "state of nature," and identified it with the state. Cf. Hobbes, *Leviathan* (1681); Locke, *An Essay Concerning the True Original, End and Extent of Civil Government* (1689). However, Locke's state, or "civil government," or "civil society," was a constitutional state, characterized by the rule of law, whereas Hobbes's state was a "Leviathan." Cf. John Keane, *Democracy and Civil Society* (1988), p. 35 ff. See also Keane, "Despotism and Democracy: The Origins and Development of the Distinction between Civil Society and the State 1750-1850," in John Keane, ed., *Civil Society and the State: New European Perspectives* (1988), p. 35 ff.

[26] See Eugen Rosenstock-Huessy, *Out of Revolution: The Autobiography of Western Man*, (1938), p. 416. Rosenstock-Huessy explains the use of the word Kultur as a German answer to the French ideas of 1789 and more especially to the French gospel of a European civilization of free and equal brothers.

[27] See Gardels, "An Interview with Czeslaw Milosz," *New York Review of Books*, 27 February 1986, p. 34.

[28] This is one of the main themes of H. J. Berman, *Justice in the USSR*, (rev. ed. 1963). See pp. 275-282.

[29] The Draft uses the word "conscience" at one point, stating that "judges shall be independent and subject only to [statute] law (*zakon*) and to the voice of conscience." The draft immediately preceding the final draft had placed the word "their" before the word "conscience," suggesting a more subjective concept.

[30] See supra p. 12.

[31] The Draft does provide, however, in Article 1.8 that "the state shall operate on the principle of social democracy and [social] justice in the interest of the welfare of its citizens and of society," and shall "create conditions for proper living standards of all people," and that "the securing of equality of opportunities to each citizen of the Russian Federation shall be carried out by means of a developed system of state social services."

[32] Cf. H. J. Berman, "Toward an Integrative Jurisprudence: Politics, Morality, History," *California Law Review*, Vol. 6 (1988), pp. 779 ff.

Harold J. Berman is Robert W. Woodruff Professor of Law, Emory Law School, and James Barr Ames Professor of Law, emeritus, *Harvard Law School. He is the author of twenty books, including* Law and Revolution: The Formation of the Western Legal Tradition (1983) *and* Justice in the U.S.S.R.: An Interpretation of Soviet Law (rev. ed. 1963).

[12]
Theory of Law

S.S. Alekseev

Chapter One. Scientific and Philosophical Approaches and Orientations in Jurisprudence[1]

III. From "Soviet" Science – to Russian Science

Soviet legal science bears the imprint of the communist totalitarian regime. After the establishment of the complete dominance of the totalitarian system, legal science became an expression of Stalinist ideology; at the same time, trends contradictory to it were developed in jurisprudence: the invincibility of jus in society emerged in such trends.

1. What character did legal science in Russia acquire after the October coup? Progressive Russian legal thought, based on the ideas of liberalism, freedom, and the constitution and occupying ... one of the leading places in the world, continued after October to develop to some extent or at least to maintain its existence in certain universities (and the more so in emigration).

Within the framework of official ideology *Soviet* legal science acquired an absolutely dominant significance, that is, the orthodox legal science of the left-radical, communist orientation, called "Marxist", and later, "Marxist–Leninist".

... It is appropriate here to give a broader characterization of the orthodox features of Marxist legal science of that time and above all to say: Soviet legal theorists of a radical, left-communist orientation regarded jus as an element alien to socialism, as being profoundly bourgeois, and therefore requiring replacement as rapidly as possible by organizational-technical and moral ("nonlegal") regulators.

Here are several utterances of Soviet jurists of that time in this regard:

> "The norms of the Civil Code, having been permeated with elements of planning, are deformed, are becoming administrative-technical [norms]."

[1] Translation Copyright 1995 by W.E. Butler. Throughout this translation the Russian word "pravo" is translated by the Latin expression "jus" (corresponding to the French "droit", the Italian "derecho", the German "Recht"), whereas the Russian word "zakon" is translated by the Latin expression "lex" (corresponding to the French "loi", the German "Gesetz", etc.). The English word "law" for both would make a nonsense of the author's exposition [*transl.*].

"The effectuation of the enormous five-year economic plan will further the continued growth of market links into organizational links, and the growth of legal norms into administrative-technical regulation."

"In reality, this expansion of the sphere of administrative-economic jus means the greater conversion thereof into non-jus."

Judgments of this nature were directly linked with the tasks of the "construction of socialism". It was said, for example, that "planned regulation, as distinct from regulation by means of the rules of lex, makes it more possible to take the national economy along the path of the construction of socialism ... As movement forward on the path to socialism is made, legal regulation acquired a more subordinate, service character with regard to the plans of the national economy."

Analogous thoughts were contained in the works by E.B. Pashukanis, one of the noted Soviet legal theorists, where jus was linked primarily with chaotic market/barter relations. In these was staunchly laid the "revolutionary" idea that future society must simultaneously disengage from goods production and from jus, which, in the author's view, could be "only bourgeois".

Rather recently some of us legal theorists explained away these and similar utterances of the young Marxist–Leninist science by asserting that it had not meant to "underestimate" jus, but had occurred by virtue of historical circumstances and the peculiarities of revolution, and also by virtue of other reasons, in particular because they were not aware at the time of unpublished utterances of Lenin concerning lex and legality. In a word, we regarded this type of "underestimation" of jus – only "underestimation"! – as an abnormal phenomenon contrary to our real worldview and principles.

But this is not the whole story. There are, of course, historical roots of legal nihilism in Russia. In any revolution disruptions and imperfections in the regime of legality are inevitable. But something else is vital here. That which we delicately call "underestimation" of jus (but what in essence was a denial of it) – is a wholly natural phenomenon, but natural from the standpoint of the ideological postulates of the war-communism doctrine which was dominant after October. In its context only a "revolutionary legal consciousness" was justified, laws and legal norms being an instrument of the dictatorship, of an all-powerful proletarian State. It, this doctrine, and jus as a phenomenon of civilization and culture, are incompatible; they represent phenomena which deny, which tear away from, one another. Of course, a certain attention to legislation, to legal culture, to legal technique was given in those years. However, this attention did not go beyond questions of legislation and legality (understood to be principally the undeviating execution of prevailing norms, the "unity" of legality on the territory of the entire Republic, and the need to "increase" it).

Only the transition to NEP [New Economic Policy] gave rise to a certain liveliness in legal science, to a broader interest in jus. But in the NEP years, in its ideological and worldview aspect, the orthodox legal science of the left-communist, radical orientation continued to occupy the dominant position in the social sciences and in official public opinion.

2. The attitude towards jus as a temporary and alien phenomenon was conditioned by the peculiarities of working out legal problems in legal science in the 1920s and subsequent years. We note that these drafts were undertaken on a massive scale in the form of rather large-scale studies (Pashukanis' monograph *The General Theory of State and Law*, P.I. Stuchka's *The Revolutionary*

Role of Law and State) and conclusions worthy of attention were drawn. At the same time these drafts testified to a rather low scholarly level and narrowly-doctrinal approaches. These drafts:

- expressed a statist approach towards jus (jus was regarded as merely an instrument of the all-powerful State);
- were a direct continuation of communist postulates (for example, the conclusion about the imminent and rapid "withering away of law");
- were of a limited, narrow, "set" nature (often merely stating the "class nature" of jus and its institutes);
- were distinctive for neglect of legal form and in this connection of the achievements of world legal culture (examples are – the treatment of the presumption of innocence as "bourgeois trash", denial of the division of law into public and private, and of the ideas of natural law);
- endeavoured to "overcome" traditional approaches towards jus, the achievements of analytical jurisprudence, world legal culture (hence, in particular, the idea of "cutting down" of civil law, splitting it, the formation of the branches of economic law, which was to a great extent a scientifically-formed formalization of an administrative-bureaucratic system).

The disdainful and even hostile attitude towards civilistics, the science of civil law, treated as the embodiment of the "most bourgeois" in jus – a science having in fact the significance of primogeniture and a permanent source of a high legal culture and developed legal instrumentation, played an especially negative role. Only at the end of the 1930s, when a number of eminent civilists returned to active scholarly activity (A.V. Venediktov, M.M. Agarkov, V.K. Raikher, B.B. Cherepakhin, and others) and when a number of their noted pupils were included in creative activity (S.N. Bratus, O.S. Ioffe, R.O. Khalfina, and others) did the science of civil law receive greater recognition, although the guardedness and hostility towards it on the part of representatives of the orthodox doctrine persisted and real economic processes in general were encouraging of civil-law regulation being significantly developed as part of them.

As a whole a canonized ideological dogmatism prevailed in Soviet legal science. The content of legal science (just as the other social sciences) was reduced to a cartridge clip of selected quotations from the works of the "classics" – Marx, Engels, Lenin, and above all the "genius utterances of Comrade Stalin" and his true comrades-in-arms, especially the legal ideologue Vyshinskii. All of this was sharply dogmatized and canonized and an atmosphere of merciless intolerance was maintained with regard to everything that did not correspond to these types of dogmas and canons.

3. An existing feature of legal science in the period of Stalinist totalitarian ideology was its apologetic, or more precisely, its enthusiastically apologetic orientation. From the mid-1930s in legal science as well as in other spheres of official social sciences, the line of "not seeing" predominated and, to better justify the flaws of the existing social system, to praise without restraint, to portray in the form of the "very, very best" in the world, prevailing legal procedures, norms, and principles – to be enraptured by them.

The addition of "socialist" and "Soviet" to the concepts of "jus", "legality", "legal relation", "norm", and others was called upon to erect respective categories at the highest level of values. That is why the expressions "new, special, highest historical type," "best in the world", "distinct in principle from bourgeois", acquired the significance of unquestionable and obligatory characterizations accompanying the discussion of any legal phenomena.

The apologetic orientation of legal science became the most revealing manifestation of the most extensive feature of all of social life under conditions of the Stalinists and stood in a single rank with their merciless terror. This was a gigantic falsification of reality. The last affected all aspects of life. But it was "jus", "lex", and "legality" that we called upon to impart a special civilized feel, a respectability to the realities of that time, to camouflage the awful daily life. This was also furthered by the circumstance that jus itself was drawn into the system of falsification and, having become a screen of the Stalinist dictatorship, contained a considerable amount of externally attractive but inoperative provisions. It is sufficient to recall that, although the 1936 Constitution was daubed sweepingly and clearly with democratic beautifications, the words "lex" and "legality" were glimpsed but fleetingly in the press and in fact. Or how even the executions of recent cohorts proceeded publicly, in the eyes of the entire world, in "open trials". And how many people, intelligent and perspicacious, were deceived and were compelled to believe in the irreproachability of the "democracy" and "legality" of the procedures at that time.

4. One also should note one specific aspect of the development of Soviet social sciences (to some extent retained to the present day) which can be called quotation camouflage. It is linked with the dogmatism of an orthodox officious science which, by virtue of the requirements of that orthodoxy, acquired the nature of a secular religiosity, every scientific proposition having to be underpinned by citations to the "classics" of "Marxism–Leninism" (before 1953 – best of all expressly to the "genius utterances" of Stalin) and to Party documents. Then, during the Khrushchev thaw, citations to Stalin disappeared but then the significance of propositions from reports, speeches, and articles of leaders of the Party and State acquired a significance which was in essence equal to that of the "classics", at least so long as they maintained a position of leadership.

Official Party and State agencies vigilantly watched over the "quotation substantiation" of propositions advanced in science, such that no scholarly work in the social sciences appeared without complying with the said severe requirement.

That is why authors who endeavoured to substantiate particular propositions came to seek out even snippets of utterances, combinations of words, etc. "from the classics" or from Party documents in order to hope for the publication of their works. And scholarly controversies for the same reason were transformed into "skirmishes of quotations" and took on an ideologized brutality, an implacability, when a colleague who adhered to different views would be theoretically destroyed by merely one reference to the fact that these views were "contrary to Marxism–Leninism".

Quotation camouflage also was a property of the works of those legal theorists who endeavoured to elevate jus and substantiate its value. To this end individual phrases were sought out, utterances made in passing in publicist works, letters, and official memoranda of V.I. Lenin, the early works of Karl Marx and F. Engels (although the "late" Marx, Engels, and Lenin did not regard jus with much favour and it is known in particular that Lenin before 1921–22 shared the hostile orthodox-communist attitude towards jus and its fate, was the initiator of terror and executions, and decreed a negative attitude towards private law).

In and of themselves the scientific propositions were frequent and one may suppose retain their significance to this day even without quotation camouflage. Moreover, one may hope that, being relieved of such cargo, under the view of a progressive humanitarian world outlook they may take on a, so to speak, "second wind" and occupy a place of honour in contemporary fatherland legal science.

5. However, it would be inaccurate to portray the picture of the development in legal thought under Stalinism and in later years as pure-black. Life shows that the forces of progress, the movement of mankind towards freedom, reason, and jus are invincible, that the tender shoots force their way through the depths of the totalitarian stronghold. The externally attractive, albeit untested legal propositions, conceal the possibility that when the regime changes they may be really used in the future. And the very fact of the renaissance of analytical jurisprudence (the reasons matter not) and the quantitative growth in legal searches and greater use of the achievements of philosophy and sociology, and dramatics of real vital relations which require jus – all this has led to the latent legal values amassing themselves and to the inevitable growth of the "craving for jus".

We have not yet evaluated the return, noted above, at the end of the 1930s to active scholarly and pedagogical activity of a number of important legal theorists with "prerevolutionary experience". They in essence transmitted to their students, readers, and even more to their pupils and colleagues the baton of high fatherland and world culture. And they themselves in all manifestations of their lives were proponents of jus and in their difficult activity nurtured in their pupils and followers an unwavering adherence to the culture of jus and the high intellectual spiritual principles of science and intellectualism.

It seems obvious that among the prerequisites which conditioned the removal of Soviet legal science to a new level of the study of jus ... a noteworthy place, together with the achievements of philosophy, is occupied by the accumulation at that time of legal values which preserved and consolidated the elements of fatherland and world legal culture.

6. After the defeat of the August putsch (1991) a turn from the Soviet totalitarian system towards democracy, towards a rule-of-law civil society, was noted in the social development of Russia and a number of other countries which were former "Soviet republics".

Our legal science underwent a difficult, dramatic, contradictory path in the Soviet period. It needs today penitence and purification. An understanding and unequivocal recognition that Soviet legal science served a totalitarian system, concealed, justified, and then extolled the inhumane communist regime. But let not the positive work in jurisprudence be thrown out, crossed out, and forgotten since it comprises an integral part of the intellectual potential of Russia.

Chapter Eight. Soviet Law and the Law of Democratic Russia

III. On the Path Towards a Society of Jus

Democratic Russia needs a qualitatively renewed law corresponding to the requirements of a free, democratic civil society which is called upon to be a society of Jus. This presupposes the "humanization", the "privatization" of jus, its transformation and development on the basis of the contemporary achievements and values of civilization.

1. In Russia and a number of other countries which declared themselves to be "socialist" the "socialist system" itself and the idea of the "construction of communism" – a perfected social system capable of giving a "bright future" to people – has experienced defeat. With fated inevitability, such utopian attempts were overturned by the fact that a system of totalitarianism, of dictatorship, of coercion of people had formed which eliminated from their lives the values of civilization and culture.

The future of Russia is as a free democratic civil society. And this requires a qualitative renewal of jus.

However, in and of themselves lex, however many, however significant, and however democratic their potential, do not change the situation in a prevailing, wholly statist legal system.

However important the adoption of a democratic Constitution, it is not itself capable of all-embracingly, fundamentally influencing the general state of Russian legal being.

Russian society requires that there be an abrupt and decisive change of coordinates in the legal continent, a principled change of the very "essence", the "mood" of the legal system, its very "organs".

This presupposes, first, a strict determination of the general orientation of legal transformation and, second, the "humanization", the "privatization" of Russian law..

2. At present law reform concentrates on the fundamental tasks of the democratic transformation of Russia – the creation of the legal foundations of democracy, a market economy, and ultimately the creation of a rule-of-law State.

There are truly fundamental problems of law reform, problems of first importance, of the greatest responsibility. At the same time, it is essential to have a strategic aim in view, in accordance with which Russia must proceed towards a rule-of-law society, to a society of Jus.

A society of Jus must become the most significant aim and indicator of the reforming of Russia, for it is this aim and this indicator that characterize it as something higher than a mere rule-of-law State, a general humanitarian value.

To be sure, the actual embodiment of the proposition of or more accurately, the slogan "rule-of-law State" is far in the future for Russian society at the moment. The problem here is not so much legal (although the creation of a perfected legislative system capable of "binding" the State, the formation of which we have only just embarked upon, is a task of primary importance). A fundamental transformation of the socio-economic and political systems is essential, above all a transformation of ownership, for under the indivisible dominance of a monopoly bureaucratic State ownership which inevitably requires a cruel administrative-command authority, a rule-of-law State is in principle impossible.

Nonetheless, it is believed that under such conditions there are weighty grounds to enlarge the framework of the question being considered and, without confining ourselves to the sphere of merely one State-political life, to speak of a rule-of-law society – a society of Jus. This is a society in whose centre of existence and functioning there will be a developed and strong jus and the supremacy thereof.

It would seem that there are sufficient grounds to raise the broader question so that we can recognize our bitter historical fate. It is precisely jus – developed and refined – that can, by virtue of its potential and must by virtue of its purpose, become the barrier on the path towards usurpation of power and the reign of an administrative-repressive totalitarian regime. And it is now, when in our society there are unfolding complex, contradictory processes of the development of a goods-market economy and democracy, a multiparty system and glasnost, that there exists an urgent necessity to promote jus – to advance jus as a shield, as a barrier against a possible unfavourable "turn" of events until the terrifying spectre of dictatorial, authoritarian power and of administrative-repressive orders is again exhausted. These are not abstract deliberations, as the 1991 August putsch confirmed. In those days legal machinery could stand against it only to a minor extent.

But this is not the only matter.

There are more profound grounds which predetermine a broad view of the role of jus in social life which transcend the sphere of political-State relations, when raising the question of a society of Jus. Four of the most material moments can be singled out as follows.

First, as the sad experience of the USSR has showed (and not only of the USSR), a totalitarian system may be confirmed as and be a gigantic political force beside a system of official State agencies, although unavoidably linked by administrative-repressive manifestations with the respective State apparatus. Totalitarian regimes – and of this there is ample evidence – are distinctive for the fact that political-State self-power is in the hands of the "first person", whose leadership status is confirmed not only in the zone of official State subdivisions, but also outside such – in Party hierarchical structures and then in the cult of the ideology of leadership. And if this be so, then the chinks for penetrating totalitarianism must be closed to the entire social organism, and consequently jus, insofar as it may be a powerful antitotalitarian factor, is called upon to go beyond the sphere of political-State life, to embrace all precincts of relations where in one form or another totalitarian orders and morals are capable of being born and supported.

Second, all of society, and not only the sphere of political-State life, needs the beneficent influence of jus as a phenomenon of civilization and culture. Especially in the present situation when liberated from the fetters of a totalitarian regime, society has not yet fixed all of the grains of all-permissiveness. It is now (although, to be sure, in no less degree than in the past) that it is essential to affirm in society an atmosphere of the reliability and stability of the legal order, the inevitability of the triumph of truth in all complex conflicts of life, the triumph of justness, or harmony. The entire complex of legal principles of the "court of jus", its profound principles, its power as a stabilizing, restraining, and conciliating factor must be affirmed.

Third, it is extremely essential to ensure the high status of every person –that which in the past it was fashionable to call the sovereignty of the individual and in a more strict concept must be designated the high status of the autonomy of the individual, as confirmation of the inalienable, inviolable, and absolute rights of man and his high dignity. Under modern conditions the thought is increasingly not only to "equalize" the State and the individual, but also to sharply raise the individual, to equip each person with reliable means of defence, with unfailingly operating mechanisms for the realization of his inalienable rights. Understandably, all of this affects in no small degree the rule-of-law State, the unfolding of its institutes, the high principles of the society of Jus. But more than that. One must suppose that the high legal status of every person, every autonomous individual, is important in and of itself, irrespective of all others; he must be primary and must be the "point of reckoning" in the creation of a rule-of-law society. The sense, the spirit, the specific content of the Declaration on the Rights and Freedoms of Man testifies already to its legal side – in the centre of the entire legal system is man. One must suppose that man, his rights, and high dignity must become the foundation also for the spiritual sentry of the Russian Constitution and the legal system of Russia as a whole.

Fourth, an atmosphere of Jus must be created in society. The time has come for a legal worldview to predominate in our society, which in Soviet social sciences was disapprovingly called bourgeois and towards which the attitude was frankly negative. A legal worldview is a general humanitarian category, just as jus itself, and without a legal wordview jus cannot acquire a high status in society. Since a legal worldview is nothing other than a system of firm views and postulates based on the dominating supreme role of jus in the life of society, on the unalterable foundations of a rule-of-law State, above all a generally permissive order and the priority significance of legal values and the culture of jus.

3. Together with this it is necessary to precisely determine the general prospects for transformations of the legal system of Russia, important to single out the central point, the key link, of such transformations.

This central point, key link, is that which with a certain conditionality one can call the "humanization", "privatization" of jus. Jus must be transformed from a system statified as a whole, where public principles dominate in all of its subdivision one way or another, to a legal system where priority is accorded to the will and interests of man. The place of the "legal superstructure" directed towards "chastisement", "prohibitions", and "order" must give way to the great achievement of civilization embodying the principle of justness and the enhancement of the individual – a system of institutes built on rights and therefore call "jus". Only then is the formation of a true rule-of-law society possible, and only then do the market and democracy receive a reliable legal foundation.

Which are the paths towards the "humanization", the "privatization" of jus, the return of jus to its true civilized appearance and purpose, so necessary in a free democratic society? Most essential are three aspects of the problem.

First. The re-creation of private law and of its worthy high place in the legal system. Private (or civil) law was in essence eradicated under the Soviet communist regime: civil legislation was in no small measure statified, rendered lifeless, and subjected to ostracism on the part of official legal doctrine and the concept of economic law.

Private law ... is not simply a mere "branch", but something original, to the highest degree a distinctive legal sphere to which, except for instances provided for by lex, access to the State is ordered; this is the sphere of the complete domination of private persons, whose decisions become nonetheless legally binding and which the State is obliged to support, to ensure. As a market economy is impossible without private ownership, so too private ownership, entrepreneurship, economic freedom, and freedom in general are impossible in society without private law.

Whereas in a totalitarian society, including Soviet legal doctrine, the dominant position is occupied by the branches of public law (which of course are necessary in any system) – criminal, administrative, and others – private civil law holds first place in the legal system of a democratic society.

Second. Imparting to generally-recognized rights and freedoms of man the significance of being a determining link, the centre of a democratic legal system. The movement of Russian legislation in this direction already is rather distinct. But here too one must pass the rubicon and, in counterbalance to the "imperative-State" traditions, to recognize the rights and freedoms of man directly in the prevailing law in Russia.

It is essential once more to stress that the generally-recognized rights and freedoms of man must become the point of departure, the instrument of the "ideal" structure, the strict criterion for a rule-of-law arrangement of society. The wholly justified need for a strong executive power from such positions must be realized so that in the future, in the unpredictable fractures of political life, strong power can never be a threat to the freedom of people, the inalienable rights of man. This presupposes the moderation and regularity of power, its strict subordination to lex and an authorization procedure in accordance with which any State agency and any official has the right to perform only those actions which are expressly provided for by lex.

Third. A sharp enhancement in the role of the court in the life of society. The situation here is complex and even deceptive, since the impression may be formed that, with the creation of the Constitutional Court, the problem of a "third power" in Russia has disappeared. The entire justice system is a "third power" in all of its offshoots. And it should be said that all other courts – both general and arbitrazh – continue to be on the edge of State-legal life and have not acquired a high position of merit.

One must suppose that the time has come in general to change our view of justice, the interpretation of its purpose as merely the "application of jus". The experience of developed democratic countries, and not only the Anglo-American group, shows that a high level of legal development is achieved in society when the court, relying on the Constitution, on lex, and on the generally-recognized rights of man, also creates jus. Therefore recognition of the decisions of the highest judicial instances as having the function of judicial precedent is a mater which has matured, which is fully justified.

It is understandable that the noted elements of "humanization" and "privatization" of jus must ultimately find expression in the Constitution, in lex, and be fulfilled in legal being. But above all a conceptual elucidation of the problem itself is essential, an advance in the understanding of the jus of a democratic society, as are resolute changes in a rule-of-law worldview and in the legal policy of Russia.

Part IV
Russia and World Public Order

[13]

HISTORICAL TYPES OF INTERNATIONAL LAW

Some 170 years ago a French judge, Montesquieu, published his famous book on the *Spirit of Laws*. His essay remains an imposing monument of eighteenth century literature, not because of its treatment of special questions, but because it calls attention to one of the greatest problems of social science. Apart from complicated doctrines, from rigid rules and professional details, laws have their spirit: and they aim at establishing order, at preventing and solving conflicts by peculiar methods. Taken as a whole they are as characteristic of a nation as its language or its literature.

Montesquieu not only formulated the problem, but also found an appropriate setting for it by showing that it depended to a great extent on the grouping of data on the lines of certain principal types of development. He sought the explanation of particular forms in the influence of the physical environment on the one side and in the tendencies of political organization on the other. He considered these physical influences, these political tendencies not only in their material aspects, but also in their reaction on what we now call social psychology: despotism must be supported by terroristic measures, the monarchical régime is bound up with notions of honour; republics live by the virtue of citizens.

Montesquieu was, however, the child of his time, he lacked historical perspective and was dominated by the influence of the pseudo-classical school; besides, he had not enough material to enable him to emancipate himself from his great predecessor and master, Aristotle. The experience of the old monarchy of France and of the parliamentary oligarchy of England did not suffice to enlarge in any fundamental way the setting given by the Greek philosopher. Montesquieu's book became a continuation of the Politics of Aristotle. Its title should have been not the "Spirit of Laws", but the "Spirit of Governments as expressed in their Laws". Such limitation would have been natural and quite justified. Aristotle was dealing with communities whose juridical life was concentrated in the activity of restricted circles of privileged citizens: the opposition between constitutional and private law could not make itself felt in the same way as in modern States. The main question was that of the attribution of power to the majority of the citizens, to a small number, or to one individual. It is from this point of view that Aristotle looked at the particular problems of justice, especially those of property and family relationship. Montesquieu, although confronted with a much more complex society, does not yet realise the decisive importance of the relations of private law; he is still concerned with the constitutional standpoint indicated by Aristotle, although he has to work with a modified classification of the forms of government. Without detracting from the well-merited fame of the *ancien régime* judge it may be said, I think, that his sketch of the Spirit of Laws remains on the surface of the juridical life of modern peoples.

When a century later Ihering became inspired by an analogous conception he treated the juridical institutions of Rome as a whole and gave the largest place to private law. But his *Spirit of Roman Law* remains an isolated monograph and when present day science tries to carry out Montesquieu's project it must reckon with other systems of law brought to the front by social evolution.

I beg you to note the term *system*: it is not used accidentally. The fact that the sum total of a more or less important and durable juridical situation gathers, so to speak, into a system of which the different parts tend to support and complete each other is more marked than is the case in other departments of thought. This is due to the fact that law in its professional elaboration and application always rests on operations of logic. Legislators formulate rules, judges apply them to particular cases and it would be absurd to issue conflicting rules or to apply them in a contradictory way: such cases occur in practice, but such actual inconsistencies are considered to be defects or flaws and juridical thought and jurisprudence tries to eliminate them as far as possible. The striving toward consistency and order is of the essence of juridical method, and the great creations of law present themselves in the form of systems. Let us observe that sometimes even the needs of practical life are sacrificed to this logical coherence. This is undonbtedly to be regretted, but from the point of view of social science this systematising tendency presents considerable advantages. We have to do in law not with detached and heterogeneous facts, but with combinations

5

embracing different aspects of social intercourse and we are able in the course of an intelligent study to go back to fundamental conceptions.

This point once established, let us see how this interesting and difficult study of the spirit of law can be approached with the best chance of success. We can follow Aristotle's example, while enlarging the scope of the enquiry. Aristotle, and Montesquieu after him, have taken as the guiding principles of their work the forms of governmental organization. It is the constitution of public powers which provides them with a standpoint for observation in their comparative study of institutions. For us moderns these starting points are inadequate; we are compelled by all the experience of our social life to descend deeper, to take into account the organization of work as well the organization of power, the daily life of ordinary people even more than the actions of princes and legislators. This being so what distinguishing feature are we to select in arranging our data?

Now as the classifications of Aristotle and Montesquieu are inadequate because they start from the forms of State organization, it is natural to substitute for them a classification according to the forms of social organization. These forms, considered as types realised in the past or in the present, are not very numerous and permit of classification according to fairly simple distinguishing features. They are reducible so far to five principal types, each of which includes several varieties, while at the same time, intermediate and combined forms are produced by geographical and historical conditions. The five types which I have in view are the tribe, the city, the Church, the contractual association, the collectivistic organization. The tribe is a social type founded on relationship real or supposed, natural or artificial. This type, widespread among primitive societies, includes on the one hand peoples grouped according to the mystic marks of totemism, on the other, communities resulting from the extension of the natural family, matriarchal or patriarchal. Whatever may be the diversity of their institutions and customs, the law of these tribes affords a number of points of identity and analogy which are traceable to a common source, namely the idea of kinship.

The second type is furnished by the law of the city, of the circle or club of privileged citizens making use of their close cohesion to establish a more or less exclusive civil law. I need not remind you of the example of the Greek and Italian republics.

6

It is precisely in this field that Aristotle worked, and his writings are still the most instructive on the subject. And in spite of the great differences of temperament and conditions between the Greeks and the Romans, the idea of deducing their civil institutions from an identical source has often guided the learned: one work I will just mention — Fustel de Coulanges' *Cité Antique*, which, except for the exaggerated influence attributed to ancestor worship, remains a remarkable monument of research as to the spirit of laws.

In the third place appears the ἐκκλησία no longer of citizens but of believers — the city of God projected upon the earth and looking for guidance to heaven — a type with an universal tendency, represented in different varieties by the Jewish nation, the canon law of Christendom, Mussulman law.

The fourth type is that formed by individualistic associations aiming at freedom of trade and opinion, the type represented particularly by our present day civilization, but embracing also the world of the Roman Empire. At first sight we are perhaps tempted to dispute the rightful claim of a class which should appeal to liberty and yet admit as one of its principal varieties the Rome of the despotic emperors. But a criticism of this kind seems based on a misunderstanding. It is not the form of government that is in question; but the general character of social intercourse, and there can be no doubt that the law set forth by the great jurisconsults of the first three centuries — Gaius, Papinian, Paul, Ulpian — is the most complete manifestation of free association among individuals. The fact that the public law of this system is centred round the absolute authority of the ruler is in itself a characteristic effect of atomistic individualism, it is an expression of the unlimited preponderance of a State indispensable in a society facing detached and variable wills. But of course such an inference is not obligatory and alongside of the imperial variety other combinations may be set up, such as those of modern democracies, appealing more or less to the idea of contract, which asserts itself even in public law.

Finally the outlines of a fifth type appear more and more clearly in our own day — a type of collectivist association which makes social solidarity the first consideration and is ready to sacrifice to a great extent the interests of individuals in order to escape from economic competition and the social subjection of the weak to the strong. It would be irrelevant to distinguish the varieties of this type — bureaucratic socialism, syndicalism,

7

communism — what is obvious is that all the stages of this movement are marked by profound changes in law and that it is only on condition that the upholders of the new ideals succeed in elaborating a normal system of law that they will have achieved something durable in the history of civilization.

Let me notice in passing that the evolution of these groups is bound to assume some form of international intercourse, alliances and federations. For purposes of defence as well as for trade peoples in the most varied geographical surroundings and in entirely different ethnological combinations develop similar forms of selfhelp, arbitration, religious sanction. Thus in every stage of civilization we are met with characteristic features of international law.

It is clear that this classification does not aim at giving a full account of the local combinations which have come into existence in history; these combinations depend not only on ideas but also on the localities in which these ideas take form and on the cross currents coming from other systems. The theocratic tendency, for example, was necessarily realised in a different way in Jerusalem, in Rome and in Baghdad; individualism has crystallised diversely in the countries of Latin and Anglo-Saxon civilisation. On the other hand, the same historical grouping passes successively in its evolution under the influence of different guiding ideas. In the history of Rome are displayed the applications of the trib principalle, of the city, and of imperial individualism. Mediaeval Europe is dominated in its law by an acknowledged dualism of which feudal isolation and ecclesiastical universality are the two poles. Our own time shows unquestionably the marks of a transitional period from an individualistic type to a compromise between individualism and collectivism. Thus the classification by social types does not claim to be a substitute for legal history, it is the first step towards historical jurisprudence, that is towards a study of the spirit of laws which aims at setting free a constituent element of prime importance — the dialectics of social principles in law.

When an English judge refuses to uphold an agreement made in restraint of trade, he carries out the consequences of the principle of individual liberty in economic relations. When the same English judge obeys the clause of the Trade Disputes Act of 1906 which forbids him to penalize a trade union whose agents have committed tortious acts in the course of a dispute between employees and employer, he submits to a rule suggested by a

8

collectivist tendency. Leading ideas of this kind recur again and again in many variations like the themes in modern music, and it is certainly useful to be able to recognise them and to trace their developments and combinations.

Let us add that although observations of this kind allow us to reduce considerably the multiplicity of the phenomena of legal history, although the tendency to systematise may thus serve as a powerful instrument of generalisation, the governing ideas in question are not necessarily simple. They are all products of synthesis, although they are useful for juridical analysis. When we consider, for instance, the idea of the Church we have to form a conception into which enter mystical beliefs, moral sentiments, needs of social organization. The way in which these diverse elements are combined is not always the same and hence divergences arise in the very heart of the general type. The same can be said of other social ideas. It would be wrong to try to construct juridical systems attached to social types by abstract and absolute processes of reasoning. The study of historical reality is all the more attractive in that it makes the leading themes pass through all sorts of media and thereby discloses what is essential and what is accidental in the transformations of law.

In this quest for the spirit of laws we are certainly not animated by fatalistic resignation. As knowledge of the laws of nature does not deprive men of the possibility of turning them to profit, so the logical force of ideas does not condemn societies to go adrift under the sway of currents of opinion. These currents themselves are produced by the understanding and the will of men, and far-seeing guides, determined leaders, faithful workers are no less necessary in the onward social movement than are explorers, inventors, well-equipped craftsmen in the material world. The best vessel may be the victim of shipwreck, but it is the pride of free men to oppose danger by farsighted and stubborn efforts.

The peculiar attitude of historical reflection has been examined recently by Windelband and more fully by Rikkert. They lay stress on a profound opposition between the method of natural science and that of cultural science (Naturwissenschaft and Kulturwissenschaft); the former seeks for the invariable laws which govern the phenomena of nature and explain their constant recurrence: the latter is concerned with the manifestations of human activity in the work of civilization which never recur in the same form. The former studies the relations between causes and effects;

the latter, the relations between ends and means; the former states; the latter values. There is obviously a great risk of exaggerating the parallelism of the two studies. It would be absurd for historians to abandon the enquiry into causes. However imperfect may be the methods of their 'miniature science' — to use Renan's expression — the scientific element in the research into causes cannot be eliminated from any enquiry into the past, and statistics show clearly that human phenomena, in spite of all their disconcerting variety, may be reduced to recurring a schemes. It is difficult to discern the dominant forces and to determine exactly their functions, but there can be no doubt of their existence, and the work of a historian, even when he is presenting literary descriptions, can never be dissociated from the relation of causes and effects, nor can he limit himself to observing the influences exerted by individuals on one another.

In spite of these criticisms as regards the argument of the cultural theory, it seems to emphasise rightly an essential element of the historic method — namely the profound modification of scientific thought involved by the introduction of the idea of value. Every effort of culture can and ought to be estimated according to standards which lie outside the causal relation in so far as they are bound up with the idea of the good: such are, for instance, the conceptions of the preservation of the race, of the advance of the individual towards perfection, of the greatest welfare of the greatest number, of the salvation of the soul, of liberty, of social justice. In this way any history of civilization necessarily involves a selection and an appreciation of facts in relation to some ideal end. History is therefore subjective and idealistic in the sense that it estimates facts in accordance with their value for the realization of some ideal purpose.

In accepting such an orientation we do not wish to return to an idealistic monism similar to that preached by the school of Hegel. There is no question of applying to the natural or to the historical sciences a preconceived system claiming to discover in the phenomena of nature and of social life the manifestation of a world Spirit. This may be a beautiful vision, but it is only a vision; it leads neither to science nor to scientific philosophy. The same must be said of the counterpart of this idealistic monism, the materialistic monism proclaimed by Marx, a disciple of Hegel. In his attempt at simplification, all forms of human life are derived from one fundamental function, — the production of goods for the needs of man. Public and private law, literature, science, philosophy, religion, in spite of their apparent independence, are regarded as mere super-structures imposed on the granite foundation of economics.

No divergence between the study of ideas and that of causes is admitted, because ideas and purposes appear only as consequences, and reality is governed by economic evolution. To what extent this movement which claims to be scientific is really visionary can be gathered, for example, from the fantastic assertions of the Marxists on the development of religious ideas. What is the Reformation, that great crisis which stirred the passions of European nations for centuries and which still divides them into distinct camps? For the Marxists it heralded simply the advent of the bourgeoisie disguised in a tissue of theological subtleties. What is Calvinism? "The religion of Calvin accorded with the tendencies of the boldest bourgeois spirits of his time. His doctrine of predestination was the religious embodiment of the fact that in the world of commercial competition success does not depend on a man's activity or personal gifts, but on circumstances over which he has no control". (Engels).

Speculations of this kind have nothing to do with the research of truth: they are evidently suggested by party fanaticism.

All the varieties of historic monism seem to be equally misleading, because they imply in one way or another the identity of fact and idea, of effect and end. Supposing for a moment that such an identity were at the basis of things in themselves, it would be quite impossible to demonstrate it scientifically because we are bound by the condition of our mind to consider everything that exists under two different aspects — the aspect of given facts and the aspect of their reaction on our receptive and active individuality. Philosophy may endeavour to reconcile these points of view, but scientifie enquiry has to treat each series in accordance with the method appropriate to it.

This discussion of methods is not as remote from the announced subject of this lecture as it might seem at first sight. One of the principal manifestations of economic monism is the denial of the value of law. The fanatics of Marxism (eglabriola) prophesy the disappearance of law in the new society delivered from the parasitism of capital.

It is useless to contest prophecies, but the observation of actual facts shows at every step the powerful influence of juridical ideas on the course of economic and social development.

In our own time it would be particularly difficult to disregard the legal guardianship exercised by the community in the regulation of contract of service and of the work of miners, or the provisions for sickness and old age. The positive influence of law makes itself felt more and more as we approach the rules of personal status, the relations between social groups, and finally, the rules of public law. Let me illustrate my meaning by calling attention to a familiar case — the regulation of succession. There is a marked contrast between the legal partition of property amongst heirs in French and Belgian law and the tendency towards the unification of landed property in English, Norwegian and, in some cases, German law. It is certainly not a simple effect of economic conditions, but also the manifestation of different legislative policies, the one working for small estates and the democratic distribution of fortunes, the other inspired by the desire to protect economic organizations against division and dispersal.

I mentioned 'legislative policies' but I ought rather to have said 'juridical tendencies', for it is not solely or even principally by direct legislation that the positive action of law is exercised. In the case under consideration, the partition of inheritances in French law was not simply decreed by the Code Napoléon: it was prepared long before by provincial custom. In the same way the Norwegian odal and the land settlements of English law came into existence in ancient times as results of popular habits. The causes of these divergences are many and should be studied by themselves, but what interests us at the moment are the tendencies towards certain social purposes which are expressed in these arrangements. Rules of intestate succession were hardly ever elaborated, voted on and promulgated by legislative assemblies: most sources of law, considered from the sociological point of view, are moulded by custom. Land law, family organization, succession and testament still bear many traces of the forms imprinted upon them by the practice of the Roman paterfamilias and of Germanic experts on legal lore. In England especially, the rules of Common Law are almost all connected with antecedents in historic life and with the practical equity of the Middle Ages. One thing is quite clear, and that is that outside the professional rules which occupy so large a place in our codes and statutes there lies a vast domain of non-legislative practice, worked out by those interested, irrespective of any dispute, for the every day conduct of business. When a man died in Old France, it was said "le mort saisit le vif", that

12

is, the deceased passed on his rights to his natural heir in virtue of family solidarity, and the public opinion of his fellow-citizens sustained his claim. The formulas of law are connected with the creative activity of nations in the arrangement of social relations.

Even in our own day, in spite of the superiority that professional technique and legislation have acquired, it is possible sometimes to watch the formation of rules of law under the influence of business practice. Commercial law affords striking examples in this respect: it was only towards the end of the eighteenth century, under the influence especially of Lord Mansfield, that it was received in England as a recognized branch of Common Law. Before that time the usages and customs of merchants had to be established in case of dispute by the verdicts of experts — of "wise men".

The conclusion of conventions by hand-clasp and by written instruments was not invented by the lawyers, but introduced by practice. The customs of the Stock Exchange are even now at the stage of more or less fluid practices. Let us refer once more to the important law of Trade Unions: it has been established by degrees, and in face of obstinate resistance, by the pressure of workmen's groups, and these groups are still — according to English law — only privileged associations or "quasi-corporations", very powerful, but preserving the characteristic features of their non-legal origin. There is, however, no need to go back to Puchta's doctrine — a kind of "popular conviction" (Rechtsüberzeugung) as the mystic source of law. The true solution was indicated by Ihering, when he objected to the old historical school which sought in the past for the guiding principles in the evolution of law while this evolution was directed towards the future. It is not only tradition, it is also the orientation towards an end that characterises law and gives it value. It varies according to environment, degree of civilization, national energy, the knowledge and skill of lawyers. It adapts itself more or less well to the changes in conditions and to the growth of needs. But — whether successful or imperfect — it displays in all cases a striving towards justice conceived in relation to some ideal of social value.

II. GREEK CITES

The exclusiveness of Greek city-institutions[1] has given rise to a fundamental misconception in regard to the treatment of international relations. It is a common error to suppose that the Greek world was deficient in this respect, that there could not be any talk of international law in societies sharply divided into a number of small republics.[2] As a matter of fact it was not so, and a closer study shows that on the contrary the world of Greek cities was particularly adapted to the development of a certain kind of international, or — to speak more correctly — intermunicipal relations. The point is that not one of these cities was really self-supporting in the sense attached to the term by Aristotle. Under stress of circumstances they could exist for some time in isolation, as it were in a state of siege or blockade. But under normal conditions each of these small political units was dependent in a high degree on supplies of goods and ideas from abroad; in the existence of every one of them the intercourse with neighbours, the exchange of native products for foreign imports, was of first-rate importance. The case of Athens may serve as an illustration. Attika was deficient in the very first element of economic life — the poor soil could not provide the corn necessary to feed its population. Hence a series of protectionist measures and prohibitions of export,[3] &c. The opening of trade routes connecting Athens with granaries in the Bosporos and in Sicily played a great part in Athenian history;[4] and at the time of its flourishing expansion Athens became a centre of international intercourse without ceasing to be the home of some 21,000 privileged citizens.

The activity of intermunicipal intercourse in religious and

[1] This lecture is reproduced by permission of the Oxford University Press from the text published in my *Outlines of Historical Jurisprudence*, Vol. II.

[2] E. g. LAURENT, *Histoire du droit des gens.*

[3] LYSIAS, XXII; DEMOSTHENES, XXXII.

[4] BELOCH, *Griechische Geschichte*, I, 395 ff.

literary life, in games and competitions of all kinds, was one of the most essential and remarkable features of Greek history, and it would be impossible to understand the influence of the Homeric poems, of Ionian philosophy, of the art of Pheidias and Praxiteles [1], without the background of this common intermunicipal organization. It is characteristic that the practice of the great national games was not entirely interrupted even by feuds between the various cities [2], and that consultations with the oracle of Delphi were carried on at the same time by the Lakedaimonians and by their enemies in Athens and in Thebes.

Commercial relations and the juridical effects of travelling and settlement in foreign parts were not less necessary and prominent consequences of the situation. For our purpose, the inter-municipal action of the ordinary institutions of Greek States is even more important than exceptional manifestations of solidarity, and the occasions for such action in the classical period of Greek history were numberless and varied.

The practices in this respect fall naturally into two groups. There were cities which, though not at war with each other, had not established definite agreements as to the treatment of disputes between their respective citizens, and there were other cities which had come to some understanding in this respect. In the first case, apart from the intervention of patrons, by means of which a member of one State enforced claims against a member of another, recourse had to be taken to procedure by self-help, and, indeed, we commonly find men led away into captivity (ἄγειν), and property taken away by distress (φέρειν), because offended persons were seeking to obtain compensation for wrongs or to assert some right. This is termed συλᾶν in the case of distress as well as in the case of reprisals. Needless to dwell on the arbitrary character of such methods, but it must be borne in mind that such raids were not by any means simple outbursts of lawless violence. As frequently happens in ancient law, distress was used as a means of obtaining justice by self-help. Another feature of the procedure was that distress or reprisals are not necessarily directed against one's opponent, but might be levelled against relatives of his, or even against his countrymen at large. Such cases were considered as a justi-

[1] E. MEYER, *Geschichte des Altertums*, III, 433 ff.

[2] Cf. HERMANN-THUMSER, *Lehrbuch der griech. Antiqu.* I, p. 78 ff. SZANTO, s. v. ἐκεχειρία in *Real-Enc.* V, 2162.

15

fied taking of hostages, and designated by the special term ἀνδροληψία.[1]

This form of self-help, although exceedingly common, presented obvious inconveniences, and one of the principal objects of international agreement between Greek cities was to replace it by some form of regular jurisdiction. In order to put an end to the state of natural savagery in the relations of the citizens to those of neighbouring States, one city would "grant justice" (δωσιδικία) to another. A very good illustration of such a public act is to be found in the ancient treaty (fifth century B. C.) between two Lokrian cities — Chaleion and Oiantheia — preserved on a bronze tablet in the British Museum.[2] Self-help was not abolished by it, but reduced to juridical methods.

"It is forbidden to any man of Oiantheia to carry off a foreigner on the territory of Chaleion, and to any man of Chaleion to carry off a foreigner on the territory of Oiantheia, or to seize property by way of distress.

"Whosoever distrains property belonging to a foreigner shall be allowed without exposing himself to seizure to take away the goods by sea, except from the harbour below the city. If the seizure be made without right, the fine shall be four drachmae. If the person distraining keeps the thing seized for more than ten days, he shall pay the value of it once and a half. If a man of Chaleion is a resident established more than a month at Oiantheia, and *vice versa*, he shall have recourse to the justice of the city... If the affair is carried before the judges who deal with foreigners, the foreign claimant shall choose sworn persons from among the notables, but *not* his proxenos nor any fellow-citizen. For processes involving one mina or more he shall have fifteen sworn persons, for those involving a smaller amount he shall have nine. If a citizen pleads against another citizen in virtue of the treaty, the demiurgi (magistrates) shall choose sworn assessors from among the notables, after having taken the quintuple oath. The sworn assessors shall in their turn take the same oath, and the verdict shall follow the majority."

Even in cases of treaty relations between two cities, self-help may play a part in the defence against illegal distress or violence. The way was open in such case to the intervention of a *vindex*, to use the Roman term and notion. Striking illustration of this counter-action by any member of the contracting States may be

[1] *Real-Enc.* s. v. ἀνδροληψία. [2] Michel, 3.

16

found in the manumission inscriptions of Delphi [1] and in the inscriptions commemorating the consecration of Teos to Dionysos, accompanied by guarantees of ἀσυλία on the part of neighbouring cities. [2] The formulae are: — αὐτοσαυτὸν συλέων καὶ οἱ παρατυγχάνοντες ἀζάμιοι ὄντες καὶ ἀνυπόδικοι πάσας δίκας καὶ ζαμίας. ὁ βουλόμενος, ὁ θέλων, ὁ παρατυγχάνων κύριοι ἔστωσαν ἀφελόμενοι καὶ ἀποδιδόντες τοῖς ἀδικημένοις.

In contrast with these methods of self-help stood the system by which the citizens of a foreign city obtained a standing before the Courts of a State according to certain rules: this is described as the "granting of justice," δωσιδικία or δικαιοδοσία, and the agreements regulating the procedure in such cases were called συμβολαί or σύμβολα and the procedure itself δίκη ἀπὸ συμβόλων. [3]

When justice is "granted" to a foreigner the simplest way is to apply the laws of one or the other State according to certain rules appropriate to the various modalities of the controversy. Thus a so-called "conflict of laws" takes place. The account of the struggle between Sparta and Argos in the fifth book of Thukydides (c. 79) presents a good example of the application of this method in classical Greece. The sixth clause of the treaty of 418 B. C. provided that "justice shall be administered to individual citizens of each State according to their ancestral customs." This can only mean that the tribunal before which the case was brought was to apply either the law of Argos or the law of Sparta, and, as the choice of the particular law to be applied was made dependent on descent, the only outstanding question is whether it was the status of the plaintiff or of the defendant that was considered decisive. The common practice in Greece was that, *ceteris paribus*, when personality was taken as the standard of selection, litigation proceeded in accordance with the status of the defendant. The personality principle was sometimes modified by taking account of the *forum domicilii* of the defendant. [4]

In the treaty between Athens and Phaselis (395—385 B. C.) [5] two different principles are mentioned side by side. The principle of the *forum contractus* is introduced for conventions made in Athens, but on other occasions the direction of the case depends

[1] *Griech. dial.-Inschriften*, 1721, 1749, 1857, 1936.

[2] MICHEL, 51 ff. See HITZIG, *Altgriechische Staatsverträge über Rechtshilfe*, 39, 40.

[3] ARIST., *Pol.* III, 9, p. 1289 a σύμβολα περὶ τοῦ μὴ ἀδικεῖν. See HITZIG, *op. cit.* 31.

[4] GILBERT, *Staats-Alterth.*, I, p. 487. LIPSIUS, p. 966.

[5] MICHEL, 6. Cf. COLEMAN PHILLIPSON, I. 200.

17

on the defendant's domicile. Conventions made outside Athens were not to be interpreted in accordance with Athenian law, and this can hardly mean anything else but the concession to the Phaselites of the application of their laws in the case of contracts made with their city.

An important consequence of the frequency and multiplicity of intermunicipal relations was the tendency of the various city customs and laws towards generalization and unification. Rules of common law grew up on an intermunicipal basis, and towards the end of the fourth century one may speak of a private international law of Greece, which, though not codified, was governed in most important respects by similar if not identical principles. This is stated in as many words in Demosthenes' oration against Lakritos concerning commercial laws.[1]

In the speech against Zenothemis a similarity of trade customs is implied by the fact that in a trial conducted at Athens one of the parties proposes to obtain evidence as to a transaction concluded at Syrakuse, while a Massaliote trader pleads on the strength of a document executed at sea with a skipper, and the magistrates of Kephallenia order a Massaliote ship to sail to Athens in view of its original destination to that port. Nor is that community of legal principles restricted to commercial affairs, as may be gathered from Isokrates' Aiginetic speech, dealing with the validity of a will.[2]

The processes which led to the building up of a Common Law of Greece can be clearly discerned. To begin with, there was colonization, in which all the Greek cities of any importance took part. It resulted in the transfer of rules and usages across the seas to different places. Thurioi, Kerkyra, Olbia, the Chalkidike, etc., were as many centres for the spread of the customs of Athens, of Korinth, of Miletos, of Chalkis, &c.[3] The compulsory tie of political allegiance was sometimes altogether discarded, but, as in the case of the United States as regards England, the legal traditions of the metropolis persisted in the new surroundings, although with some variations in detail.

A second powerful influence brought to bear on the unification of intermunicipal law was the action of leagues and confederacies.

[1] XXXV, § 45.

[2] Isokr. XIX. §§ 12—15. Cf. E. Weiss, *Z. SS. Rom. Abth.* XXXIII. pp. 215 f.

[3] For example, the treaty between the Epiknemidian Lokri and the Lokrian colonists in Naupaktos (fifth century B. C.), Roehl, *I. G. A.* 321, Michel, 285. *Griech. Dial.-Inschr.* 1478.

18

The most potent influence in this respect was, of course, exercised by the first Athenian-Delian league.[1] Its power made itself felt through the greater part of the fifth century, and the gradual assumption by Athens of jurisdiction in important cases led necessarily to the introduction of Athenian methods and principles in the administration of law.[2] This "reception" of Attic law by the allies of Athens was, however, the effect of governmental pressure rather than that of intermunicipal agreements, and, although its results were permanent and important, their discussion does not lie within the scope of our inquiry. The methods adopted by the second Athenian league in the fourth century are more interesting from our point of view.[3] This alliance was framed with the distinct object of avoiding the subjugation of the allies by Athens, and, in the treaties with various members of the league, the leading city had to renounce expressly the right to keep garrisons and to acquire land within the territory of the allied commonwealths.[4] As regards jurisdiction, it was to follow the ordinary lines of the conflict of laws, while appeals had to be decided not by the Heliaea but by the Council of the League.[5]

The report of a case has been preserved in which the decision fell against an Athenian who had infringed the rule forbidding the acquisition of landed property in an allied State (*C.I.A.* II. 17). As a matter of fact, the leading city did encroach in many ways on the autonomy of the fellow-republics, and turned its hegemony to advantage in order to increase its political power. But this is matter of political history rather than of law.

The oligarchical confederation of Boiotia in the fifth century, whose organization has been made known to us in detail through the discovery of the Oxyrhynchus fragment of Theopompos' *Hellenika*,[6] was constructed on a principle of genuine representation of the eleven sections (μέρη) of the land, and the hegemony of Thebes was based mainly on the greater number of its representatives in the regional and in the central councils. Disputes between the members of the confederacy were brought before

[1] MORRIS, *American Journ. Phil.*, V (1884),, 298 ff.

[2] H. WEBER, *Attisches Prozessrecht in den attischen Seebundsstaaten*. On the συμμαχία turned into an ἀρχή see Hermokrates' speech in Syrakuse. THUK, VI, 76.

[3] See BUSOLT, *Der zweite attische Bund*.

[4] *C. I. A.*, II, 17, 49, 49[b].

[5] Cf. *C. I. A.*, IV, 2, n. 54[b] (DITT. *Syll.*[3] I, 173), ll. 45 f. IV, 2, n. 88[d], ll. 13 f. *C. I. A.*, II, n. 546, l. 21.

[6] *Hellenica Oxyrhynchia*, ed. Grenfell and Hunt, ch. 4.

19

a Federal Court composed on the usual proportional basis; it is not known to what extent this Court acted as a tribunal of appeal, or of first instance, but it may be supposed that the ordinary rules as to domicile and *lex contractus* applied, subject to occasional revision of judgements by the central Court.

Apart from articles of Confederation international intercourse was conducted under customary rules and under treaties. A number of the latter have come down to us in their documentary form, and we can judge from them to what extent the device of *arbitration* was resorted to in this world of independent States. It was the natural outcome of conflicts between cities anxious to settle disputes by legal process.[1] The Kerkyraians complained in Athens in the course of the negotiations which preceded the Peloponnesian war that the Spartans did not want to try conclusions on equal terms according to convention, but preferred force to justice.[2] The ordinary expedient was to agree upon an umpire—either a foreign statesman like Periander or Themistokles, or, more often, a city in whose impartiality both parties had confidence.[3] The πόλις ἔκκλητος thus selected conducted the proceedings with all formalities necessary to secure careful examinations of claims and evidence. A classical example of such an arbitration is presented by the inscription commemorating the proceedings in a trial before a court of Knidos between the cities of Kos and Kalymna.[4] This case falls into the second century B. C., but there are many notices of similar proceedings on earlier occasions, and there can be no doubt that similar methods of procedure were commonly recognized and developed in the most minute particulars.[5]

An important variety of intermunicipal justice arose when law had to be administered not by arbitral, but by municipal Courts. Such cases were of daily occurrence in connexion with commercial transactions. If a ship belonging to a Milesian citizen came to Athens and discharged a cargo owned by merchants of Smyrna, all sorts of disputes might arise out of transactions

[1] M. Tod, *International Arbitration*, Oxford, 1013.

[2] Thuk. I, 34.

[3] Aischines, III. Dem. XVIII, 134.

[4] *I. J. G.*, I, 158 ff. Cf. Tod, *op. cit.*, p. 49: "The inscription consists of four parts. A. The oath taken by members of the Knidian tribunal. B. Directions regarding the production of evidence and the conduct of the trial. C. A statement of the case for the claimants and of the amount of their claim. D. A record of the verdict and a list of the advocates on each side".

[5] Cf. Lécrivain, s. v. *ephesis* in Dar. et S. Tod, *op. cit.*, *passim*.

and delicts of the shippers, the crew, the passengers, the consignees. Apart from ordinary rules of conflict of laws, Athenian Courts had to take cognisance of disputes under intermunicipal agreements — *δίκαι ἀπὸ συμβόλων* — of customs of trade and navigation, of general principles of law and equity in the punishment of delicts and the award of compensation [1]. Unless the dispute grew into an international quarrel, it was regularly considered and decided by Athenian Courts — by the *ναυτοδίκαι* or, later on, by a section of the jury, under the chairmanship of *θεσμοθέται*. The procedure in these cases when they did not assume the character of public law trials (*γραφαί*) was of a simplified kind, as befits commercial jurisdiction. In Athens it was provided in the fourth century that the case should be tried within a month after the action had been brought.

The provision of treaties and agreements between independent States raises the fundamental question of sanctions for the fulfilment of the obligations laid down in them. Sometimes the payment of fines in case of infringement is mentioned in the text, as e. g. in the case of the treaty between Elis and Heraia [2] (588—572 B. C.) in which we find stipulated the payment of one talent of silver to the Olympian Zeus. Wagers are made in litigation with corresponding deposits to satisfy the winning party; sometimes, again, hostages are given to ensure the carrying out of the provisions; this latter expedient was, of course, chiefly used in cases of public obligations. But the principal guarantee of the fulfilment of treaties and conventions was the *oath* of the parties. Now this may mean very little or a great deal. We know by experience that interests and passions may turn the most solemn asseveration into a scrap of paper, and the history of ancient Greece provides many examples of treachery of that kind. But it would be a gross error to suppose that the religious sanction implied by the oaths and imprecations had no real meaning or weight. Its breach entailed not only loss of credit — a most important source of influence in the world — but it clashed with beliefs and moral feelings which were strongly established and powerful in the classical world. It is not for nothing that treaties, when concluded and ratified, had to be confirmed by the oath of the whole population of a State, or at least of large and influential sections of its population.

[1] THUK., I, 77. Cf. LIPSIUS, *Attisches Recht und Rechtsverfahren*, p. 972.

[2] *C. I. G.*, I, 11. MICHEL, I, 1 *αἰ δὲ μὰ συνέαν τάλαντόν κ' ἀργύρο ἀποτίνοιαν τοῖ Δὶ 'Ολυνπίοι.*

21

The formulae of these oaths are characteristic: they are personal and not representative, because the ancient city was a concrete reality, and not a corporation in the modern sense with the attributes of a *persona ficta* [1]. In the earlier stages of Greek history the fear of the ἄγος incurred by the violation of an oath was certainly a strong deterrent, though, of course, like all deterrents, it did not prevent occasional breaches of faith under temptation. Even in later times the religious sanction had not lost its meaning, because religion afforded the natural channel for those supermunicipal and supernational feelings which form, as it were, the second root of international law.

The claims of civilization and of humanity were not vain words for the Greeks; in spite of the narrowness of their civic organizations, they had a vivid sense of personal dignity and of moral restraint, as well as a sense of beauty and a thirst for truth. No one who has read the story of the interview between Priamos and Achilles in the *Iliad* can fail to recognize that, amidst all the horrors of ruthless fights, Greek youths were brought up to harbour humane feelings towards the unfortunate and the vanquished. The way in which Thukydides relates the atrocities committed by his countrymen as well as by their enemies — the slaughter of Mytilene, the slaughter of Melos, the slaughter of sailors on neutral ships, is in itself a piece of evidence and a lesson. And the popular roots of these feelings were intertwined with religious conceptions. It is to the Ζεὺς ξένιος that a wanderer in a foreign land appealed for protection. It is at the sacred hearth that a refugee sought an asylum from vengeance and pursuit,[2] and when the refugee took on his lap the child of the householder, he made the latter think of what fortune might have in store for his offspring. A curious set of commandments bearing on humane conduct has come down to us in connexion with the traditional lore of a noble family in Athens, the Buzygae.[3] A similar though much shorter set of commandments was adopted by the Amphiktyonic League of Delphi and Thermopylae.[4] This League might be regarded rightly as an embryonic League of Nations; its constitution goes back to a very early period in the colonization of Greece by Hellenes —

[1] HIRZEL, *Der Eid.*

[2] E. g. Themistokles at Admetos' hearth. THUK., I, 136.

[3] TOEPFFER, *Attische Genealogie*, p. 139.

[4] Cf. as to free trade between allies, PLUT. *Perikles*, 29.

its membership [1] was restricted and its methods rudimentary, but it was an attempt to embody the notion of international justice in an organized institution. The religious authority of Delphi gave it powerful support, and it was not devoid of compulsory sanctions. In this respect its endeavours stranded, as usual, on the divergence of interests and the inequality of forces of its component members. Twice the League, in order to enforce its decrees, carried on prolonged wars with the help of coalitions of cities. In both cases these wars were made to serve the interests of the great powers — Sparta and Makedon. This is, however, a difficulty common to all states of society dominated by territorial sovereignty, a difficulty which could only be removed by the building up of a World State — a contingency very distant even in our own time.

As for the Greeks, their intermunicipal humanity was undoubtedly restricted during the early and the classical period to the circle of Hellenic civilization. The barbarians were regarded as inferior by nature; notice, for instance, Aristotle's account of the barbaric roots of slavery. But this pride of race begins to undergo a remarkable transformation towards the end of the classical age. Instead of the racial, it is the cultural aspect that is thrust into the foreground, and hereby a transition is provided to a different world, in which Hellenism appears not as a national peculiarity, but as a badge of civilization. One of the forerunners of the Hellenistic age, Isokrates, has expressed this in as many words: [2] "Our city has so far surpassed the rest of mankind in power of thought and speech that her disciples have become the teachers of the rest; she has made the name of Hellene seem to belong no longer to the race. but to the mind, so that the name is given to those who share in our culture more than to those who share the common blood."

[1] See BUERGEL, *Die pylaeisch-delphische Amphiktyonie.* Cf. HERMANN-THUMSER, I, 90 ff.

[2] ISOKR. IV, 50.

III. THE JUS GENTIUM OF THE ROMANS

A mighty causeway leading into a dim past is supplied by Roman Law. Students are still made to read Justinian's Primer; the Scots, the Dutch, the people in Ceylon, have still to reckon with the opinions of Paul and of Ulpian in their Courts; even where English or French or German law is supreme, the mode of juridical thinking is to a large extent permeated with ideas and habits derived from the Romans by innumerable links with the past. Surely this astonishing fact is more than an accident, more than an acknowledgment of technical skill: it must be connected with some social features of this system which have made it the vehicle of powerful tendencies of the human mind. This view is more than a mere guess: it is clearly revealed in the manifestation of Roman Law as an agent of universal culture which resulted in the growth of a common law of the Roman Empire, the *jus gentium.*

In this case I should like to start from the specific features of the legal development and to treat of the social type to which it corresponds at the close of my lecture.

I need not dwell on the earlier stage of Roman legal history — on the growth of the *jus civile,* the law of Roman citizens, as it is embodied for instance in the famous XII Tables; it presents another example of the city type illustrated by Greek jurisprudence in my former lecture, dominated by the idea of the City — an exclusive political club of citizens. The only side of this legal formation which must be noticed is the exceptional logical precision of the machinery provided by the jurisdiction of Roman magistrates. It is in the treatment of the relations between citizens belonging to different commonwealths that Roman law achieved far-reaching and permanent results. In the beginning the cities of Italy had worked out their legal arrangements on the narrow lines of municipal life, and the means they were able to devise for protecting business relations with other cities were derived from private protection by influential citizens (*hospites*) and from religious sources, (*Fas*, τὰ ὅσια) or from treaties establishing reciprocity. With the neighbouring Latin cities the Romans were able to deal to a great extent on the basis of common juridical institutions like the *mancipatio* and the *legis actio.*[1] When the circle of these international relations widened they worked out certain rules for the application of different systems of law. The two treaties between Rome and Carthage concluded in the third century B. C. may serve as examples of such arrangements.

The juridical questions arising out of such relations were of the nature of what is termed *conflicts of law*. If a Roman and a *Carthaginian* had concluded a bargain, was that bargain to be interpreted and carried out in conformity with Roman or with Carthaginian law? The laws to be applied were in any case those of one or the other of the cities, not a law common and superior to both.

By the side of this procedure aiming at a choice between conflicting laws grew another method for settling disputes — procedure by *recuperatio.*[3] It was employed in cases where there was no treaty, no *foedus* to start with, or where the parties to the treaty had agreed to refer disputes to a court of compulsory arbitration. The process of "recovery" takes place when there exists a legal agreement between foreign states that private property is to be rendered to individuals and recovered by them.

If matters had continued in this state the controversies between citizens and foreigners, though characteristic for the course of municipal jurisdiction more or less on the same line with the methods employed usually in the Greek cities, would have remained without much significance from the point of view of general civilization. But the aspect of things changed entirely when Rome conquered the Eastern and Southern shores of the Mediterranean. It became the centre of the world's commerce and culture; it was driven to expand the narrow framework of its civil law and of its municipal jurisdiction. This process began in the Vth century of the City (third century B. C.) its first conspicuous manifestation being the institution of the *praetor peregrinus* in 247 B. C. By the middle of the third century, A. D. it was virtually completed.

[1] Gaius I, 119; II, 24; V, 16.

[2] Polyb. III, 22. cl. 3 and 4. 24. cl. 7.

[3] Festus, de verborum significat. (Teubner p. 343. *Reciperatio* est, cum inter civitates lex convenit, ut res privatae reddantur singulis recuperenturque.

25

In principle, Roman courts, even when admitting claims and defences of foreigners on a footing of equality — e.g. under a *foedus* granting *commercium* — could not grant them the characteristic remedies of the law of the Quirites except by resorting to fiction. If the foreigner complained, for instance of damage that had been done by some miscreants on the road to cattle which he had brought to market, the Praetor could allow him the action *ex lege Aquilia* (*de damno injuria dato*) by instructing the judge of fact to examine the case and to condemn or to absolve without paying attention to the personal status of the plaintiff: the latter was regarded, by way of fiction, as if he had been a citizen. In the same way he could obtain the benefit of fictitious status in defending the possession of a piece of land which he had occupied and cultivated. In this last case two fictions would intervene — that of citizenship and that of perfecting the acquisition by long usage (*usucapio*).

Such devices were used on certain few occasions. More usual was the recourse to *equitable* principles, which could be best established by keeping to the broad lines of juridical ideas more or less common to all. This was easiest as regards obligations — good faith and consent became fundamental requirements of such transactions between citizens and foreigners. The Empire did not attempt to level all local peculiarities as regards law. Even Caracalla's constitution of 212 did not create a unified system. It did not affect the *dediticii* and even the Roman citizens of various provinces continued to follow popular customs of their own. The lawyers who administered the law were not less Roman in that period than they were before, but they started on a new track, quite distinct from, though sometimes parallel to, that of the city law (*jus civile*); they recognized a common law of nations (*jus gentium*). The writers on Roman jurisprudence tell us of a number of most important contracts and actions in defence of them, which were derived from the *jus gentium*. Roman Law became international as a combination of various currents of national laws. It may be noticed that this private international law was a *jus gentium* and not a *jus civitatum*. That means that it was built up by means of generalization from principles recognized by various nations — the Greeks, the Egyptians, etc. not by reference to specific legislation say of Athens, of Miletos, of Syracuse. The essential contrast between the strict forms required by the *jus civile* and the liberal interpretation of rules and conventions on the ground of international usages may be

26

illustrated, for instance, by Gaius' remarks in his *Institutes* on the various kinds of promises.[1]

"The contract by means of the words of a binding promise Dari Spondes? Spondeo is peculiar to Roman citizens. Other forms of promise are part of the law of nations and so hold good among all men whether Roman citizens or foreigners; and even if they are translated into Greek, . . . they still hold good among Roman citizens provided that the latter (the R. citizens) understand the Greek language; and conversely if they are uttered in Latin still they hold good among foreigners if these foreigners understand the Latin language. But this contract by the formula Dari Spondes? Spondeo is so exclusively peculiar to Roman citizens that it cannot even be translated properly into Greek, although the Forms are said to be derived from the Greek".

The object of such innovations in contrast with Ancient Roman rules was expressly to treat relations from the point of view of reasonableness and equity which would be especially applicable to all varieties of the human race. Natural reasonableness is the starting point of the *jus gentium.* Take as an instance *tradition,* as a method of transferring property. See D. XLI, D. 645, I. 9, 3.

In the same spirit and under the same generic reference to *ius gentium* are treated *sale* (D. XVIII, I, 2, XIX, 2, 1) *lease and hire* (D. XIX, 2, 1) *partnership* (Gaius Inst. III, 154) etc.[2]

[1] GAIUS, Inst. III, 93. Sed haec quidem verborum obligatio Dari Spondes? Spondeo propria civium Romanorum est; ceterae vero iuris gentium sunt, itaque inter omnes homines, sive cives Romanos sive peregrinos, valent; et quamvis ad Graecam vocem expressae fuerint . . . . . etiam hae tamen inter cives Romanos valent, si modo Graeci sermonis intellectum habeant; et e contrario quamvis Latine enuntientur, tamen etiam inter peregrinos valent, si modo Latini sermonis intellectum habeant, at illa verborum obligatio Dari Spondes? Spondeo adeo propria civium Romanorum est, ut ne quidem in Graecum sermonem per interpretationem proprie transferri possit, quamvis dicatur a Graeca voce figurata esse.

Cf. MITTEIS, *Rom. Privatr.* I, 62 ff.

CUQ. *Institutions juridiques*, 14.

[2] CICERO, *Top.* 17, 65—6. In omnibus igitur eis judiciis, In quibus ex fide bona est additum, ubi etiam ut inter bonos bene agier oportet in primisque in arbitrio rei uxoriae, in quo est qvod eivs aeqvivs parati ei esse debent. Illi dolum malum, illi fidem bonam, illi aequum bonum, illi quid socium socio, quid eum qui negotia aliena curasset ei cuius ea negotia fuissent, quid eum qui man dasset, eumve cui mandatam esset, alterum alteri praestare oporteret, quid virum uxori quid uxorem viro tradiderunt. Cf. E. WEISS, s. v. *jus gentium Real Enc. of Pauly-Wissowa*, X, 128.

27

"In all those cases in which the formula "in good faith" is added or "as ought to be done in honest dealing between honest men" and especially in judgments about a wife's property in which occnrs the formula "as is best and fairest for her" the jurisconsults ought to be ready to intervene. It is they who have laid down the definitions of fraud, good faith, equity, the duties of partner to partner, the mutual obligations of one who has conducted another person's affairs and of that person himself, of agent and principal, of husband to wife and of wife to husband".

Tryphoninus presents in strong relief the notions of good faith and honesty as the decisive principles in the application of the law of nations.[1]

"The good faith which is demanded in the case of contracts looks for the highest equity; but do we estimate that according to the law of nations only or in connection with civil and praetorian rules? Suppose that the accused on a capital charge has deposited with you a hundred sesterces. He is banished and his property is confiscated by the State. Ought the money to be repaid to him or should it be handed over to the State? If we consider natural law of nations, it should be restored to the man who gave it to you. If we regard civil law and legal procedure it should be handed over to the State."

These legal relations and actions mostly belong to one definite group: they arise from business transactions and contractual obligations, and are especially applicable in the life of a business community: they are more particularly fitted for the regulation of commercial intercourse and assign particular importance to the moral basis of social intercourse and credit namely *good faith*. Another topic on which the *jus gentium* is brought to bear is the legal situation of husband and wife arising from mixed marriages between Romans and foreign women or *vice versa* between foreigners and Roman women. These marriages were *matrimonia non justa*, unions not safeguarded by civil law: they were, however, not a variety of concubinage: with the spread of Roman power and the influx of foreigners into Italy they became more and more frequent, and the Praetor

[1] Dig. XVI, 3, 31. Bona fides quae in contractibus exigitur aequitatem summam desiderat: sed eam utrum aestimamus ad merum ius gentium an vero cum praeceptis civilibus et praetoriis? veluti reus capitalis iudicii deposuit apud te centum: is deportatus est, bona eius publicata sunt: utrumne ipsi haec reddenda an in publicum deferenda sint? si tantum naturale et gentium ius intuemur, ei qui dedit restituenda sunt; si civile ius et legum ordinem magis in publicum deferenda sunt.

formed a special action — *de re uxoria* — to protect the property of the wife under *jus gentium*. Besides these main instances the *jus gentium* was appealed to in miscellaneous cases to support claims derived from general considerations of justice supposed to be common to various nations. A notable instance is registered by Quintilian as regards dispute concerning succession. [1]

He discusses the treatment of a well known "controversy" of the schools in which two sons are claiming the estate of their father who has died intestate. There are particular legal complications, the point of interest here being that one of the claimants bases his claim on the *jus gentium* and this is recognised as a natural procedure for him to adopt. "My father, he will say, "dying intestate has left two sons, my brother and me, I claim my share by the law of nations." The pleader, says Quintilian, will dwell on and amplify the justice of this law of nations.

The introduction of this new body of laws — the *jus gentium* — was not brought about by legislative acts: the *leges* and *senatus consulta* applied directly to civil law and touched the intercourse between nations only in an indirect and subsidiary way. The edicts of the praetors and of the governors who wielded the administrative *imperium* in the province referred frequently to rules based on natural reasonableness and assisted materially in establishing them. But these edicts themselves were in no way the product of the magistrates' personal opinion: normally, they presented the juridical results of ideas elaborated by business practice and by professional analysis. And it is in the domain of the *jus gentium* that these sources of law conceived as authoritative opinions of jurists (responsa prudentium) found their widest application. Cicero (Top. 17, 65—6) traces expressly the development of the doctrines of good faith to the action of jurisconsults (see quotation on p. 27).

I need hardly explain the value of the *responsa* in this connection. Although not obligatory for the court at which they were invoked, they guided the magistrates in the same way as judicial precedents guide the Bench in a trial under English Common Law. The praetor or proconsul who would have decided

[1] QUINT. *de Inst. Or.* VII, 1, 42—63.

46. At qui naturam sequetur, illa cogitabit profecto, primo hoc dicturum rusticum: "Pater intestatus duos nos filios reliquit, partem iure gentium peto". Quis tam imperitus, quis tam procul a litteris, quin sic incipiat, etiamsi nescierit, quid sit propositio? Hanc communem omnium legem leviter adornabit ut iustam.

a case as to the validity of a sale or the responsibility of principles or agents in opposition to the opinion of a Labeo would have been a bold man and even if learned lawyers differed the magistrate had at any rate some authority to rely upon. The process was not different in substance at the time of the Emperors, although in some cases rulers of great judicial experience, like Antoninus Pius or Marcus Aurelius laid down juridical views of their own, when sitting in Court. On the whole, edicts of the praetors, of the Ædiles curules (as to market disputes), of the governors of provinces were closely connected with advice from jurists and with business practice. The influence of the latter forms an interesting subject by itself — a subject which finds a striking parallel in the development of English Law. The so-called Law Merchant grew up distinctly out of the observation of business usages which, apart from coercion and sanction, expressed the views and habits of traders and customers. Before it was declared to be necessary at law for the validity of a contract of sale to make and to accept a preliminary payment in the shape of a "sale shilling" this token of the concluded sale was used by parties as a customary precaution. Before the subtle rules as to the moment when a contract was deemed to be concluded were evolved by law there made its appearance the usage that contracting parties, for example a bride and a bridegroom, symbolised the consent of their wills by joining hands. In this way the background to the rights and claims under *jus gentium* is formed by innumerable business transactions of a non-litigious nature, subsequently revised, defined and analysed in the brunt of controversy before the Courts.

Let us consider more closely one or two of the specific institutions of the *jus gentium*. The treatment of sale is characteristic enough. According to the *jus civile* to buy or to sell an object of some value — an ox, a slave, a house — was a solemn and cumbersome affair. The property had to be handed over by hand to the purchaser in the presence of 5 citizens as witnesses and of a sixth, who had to hold the scales on which the ingots of bronze constituting or symbolizing the price of the purchased object were to be weighed. Even when other kinds of goods were sold which did not require handing over as objects of bargains, sales affecting ownership according to the Laws of the Quirites were necessarily bound up with immediate tradition, the reception of an equivalent in money and the obligation of the vendor to warrant, to stand *security* foı the transaction in case of eviction. Even apart from the archaic symbols of *aes et libra* pointing to an age when there was no coined money in circulation and its place was taken by weighed pieces of metal, the stiffness, the formalism and the complicated responsibility attached to the transaction, were suitable only to the restricted traffic of a peasant commonwealth. For the development of commerce on a large scale other means were required—above all greater flexibility and freedom. And these requirements were satisfied by the substitution of a consensual agreement as to sale under the rules of *emptio venditio*, a contract built up mainly by recognition of international usage: as bargains with Greeks, with Egyptians, with Syrians became more and more frequent, the praetors and the provincial governors had to conform to the habits of the hellenistic community opposed to formalism. There was no necessity for a sacrament or of witnesses and a symbolic dramatic performance connected with the sale, there was no necessity for immediate payment, the way was open to credit operations and conditions as to terms of payment, there were no absolute requirements of warranty, and the requirements of good faith and right value were to be satisfied in other ways — by checking fraud (dolus). It is impossible, of course, to determine to what extent the development of credit and of transactions based on good faith is to be attributed to the natural progress of intercourse among the Romans themselves, and how far it was influenced by business relations with Greeks and Orientals, who had long practised methods of this kind. Both have to be taken into account [1].

I have chosen sale for an example of the process of transformation, but analogous alterations take place all along the line in the law of obligations arising out of contracts. Everywhere ancient municipal formalism gives way before the spiritual standard of consent, of free will, prevailing among the trading commonwealths of the East — both Greek and Phoenician. Another consequence of this transformation may be recognized in our own practice. In our law there is a special department of so-called conveyancing — it deals with the proper and provident way of drawing up instruments conveying rights to be transferred from one person to another. Notaries draw up these conveyances in Continental countries, solicitors prepare them in the

[1] Cf. Mucius Scaevola (Caecilius) ap. Gellium, XX, 1, 41: Hanc fidem majores nostri ..... in negociorum contractibus sanxerunt maximeque in pecuniae mutuacione atque commercio.

domain of English law. In this case written instruments are the normal vehicles for transactions of any considerable importance, especially transactions as to land. Now, this vital importance of writing in the legislation of transactions is anything but a primaeval institution. The normal way of declaring will and ascertaining its exact form and conditions was in Ancient Rome the ceremonial act, the solemn drama culminating in a declaration (nuncupatio), an avowal (in jure cessio), in legal selfhelp (pignoris capio, manus injectio) in a compromise or agreement (pactum), in a promise (stipulatio). Acts in law were indeed acted by the subject of rights concerned in them. This was already quite different in the hellenised East when the Romans came into close contact with it. Declarations, dispositions, agreements were executed in writing, the will was expressed by an inscription on a stone, on wood, on a piece of leather, on a dyptych of tablets covered with wax, joined on their inner sides and secured with seals or subscriptions of witness on the outside. Last, but not least, legal instruments were drawn up on sheets of papyrus. In this case again, the everyday conditions of business suggested the appropriate form for legal acts in law. The written contract, the written testament came to take the place of the acted agreement, of the testament witnessed by the general assembly of the people (comitia) or by the Army in its war attire (in procinctu). And neither the Roman magistrates nor the Masters of legal doctrines, the Jurisprudentes were so pedantic as not to recognize the advantages of these methods of expressing and establishing will and consent. Instruments which were originally meant to be memoranda as to actual events became gradually the means of embodying acts in Law.

It is impossible to trace exactly how much is to be ascribed to the direct influence of Greek and Oriental legal usage, and how far, on the other hand, these may have been influenced by practices derived from public law and worked out specifically under administrative officers like the censors or the aediles. Even more difficult would it be to assign a definite measure to direct loans of foreign customs and to the indirect stimulating effects on the mind of Roman magistrates of meeting new and peculiar methods in the countries of ancient civilisation which had been conquered by Rome. However this may be, it is certain that thanks to Hellenism as arranged by Rome, the permanent way was created as it were, and the rails laid for business intercourse on the lines of free trade which has stood, in a sense, the wear and tear of some 20 centuries. What hnppened in that eventful age of the Roman Empire in the sphere of material interests and material intercourse was to a great extent akin to what took place in the domain of the mind, where Rome paved the ways for the spread of Eastern beliefs and Greek speculation in matters of religion.

We may differ in estimating the influence of environment and of personal factors in these processes, but there can be no doubt as to the universal character of the results achieved. It is not only by the more or less elemental working of circumstances or by an unconscious collecting of particular rules that this standpoint was reached. It is not difficult to discern the leading idea which pervaded the whole process in all its details; Roman lawyers have tried repeatedly to give expression to this dominant idea: [1]

"All nations governed by laws and customs use partly their own law, partly that which is common to all men. The law which each people lays down for itself is peculiar to it and is called civil law as belonging to the city, but that which natural reason has established among all men is observed equally among all peoples and is called the law of nations as being that law which is used by all nations. And so the Roman people uses partly its own and partly the law common to all men". [2]

This passage and similar ones follow closely the statement in *Aristotle's Rhetoric* and in the *Nikomachean Ethics* on the contrast between natural law which is common to all (*κοινός*) and particular laws (*ἴδιοι νόμοι*). It is evident that educated Romans jurists were well acquainted with the speculations of Greek philosophers as to a common law of nature. But this fact does not in any way justify the view that the *jus gentium* was merely a theoretical conception used in jurisprudence for the sake of a classification of various kinds of law; althought his point of view has been taken up in literature by eminent authorities. [3] At the back of the term stood a large and important elass of legal

[1] Cf. BAVIERO, *Archivio Giuridico*, LXI.

[2] GAIUS, *Inst.* I, 1. Omnes populi, qui legibus et moribus reguntur, partim suo proprio, partim communi omnium hominum jure utuntur: nam quod quisque populus ipse sibi jus constituit, id ipsius proprium est vocaturque jus civile, quasi jus proprium civitatis; quod vero neturalis ratio inter omnes homines constituit, id apud omnes populos peraeque custoditur vocaturque ius gentium, quasi quo iure omnes gentes utuntur; et populus itaque Romanus partim suo proprio, partim communi omnium hominum iure utitur.

[3] E. G. BARON, *Peregrinenrecht und Jus gentium*, LENEL, in *Holtzendorf Kohler's Rechtsencyclopaedie.*

33

principles applicable to the regulation of business intercourse between the nationalities of the Empire. The notion that these principles formed a common law based on usually accepted equitable estimates and customs is particularly interesting on account of its correspondence to the common law of the English speaking peoples, which was formulated by judicial authority in dealing with cases supplied by a society composed of groups with varying degrees of political standing and cultural development.[1]

The Roman lawyers were not altogether successful in their attempt at theoretical generalization: their definitions of the *jus gentium* run sometimes perilously near other departments of jurisprudence, especially equity and the so-called law of nature.[2] But some confusion in details does not destroy the fundamental conception. The keystone is to be found in the community of intercourse between the free. The *jus civile* is necessarily a law for Roman citizens (Quirites); the *jus naturale* embraces the whole of mankind and, in some respects, even animals (Ulpian). The *jus gentium* comprises within its compass the free men (liberi) and excludes slaves. For this reason even persons deprived of civic rights and standing in a commonwealth, but possessed of personal freedom, are protected by the *jus gentium*: a quotation from the Digest may illustrate the distinction.

Marcianus Dig. XLVIII. 1917.

("Also certain persons are ἀπόλιδες, that is without a state: such as those who are condemned in perpetuity to public service and those who are transported to an island, so that while they have not those rights which belong to civil law, they still have those which belong to the law of nations.") Item quidam ἀπόλιδες sunt, hoc est sine civitate: ut sunt in opus publicum perpetuo dati et in insulam deportati, ut ea quidem, quae juris civilis sunt, non habeant, quae vero iuris gentium sunt, habeant.

Thus the *jus gentium* appears as the common law of intercourse between free individuals and this explains its lasting influence in jurisprudence. It forms the main stock of private international law in societies constructed on the principle of free individual association. This seems the clue to its reception in modern States. It proved a powerful auxiliary in the struggle

[1] Mitteis, *Römisches Privatrecht*, E. Weiss, in *Pauly Wissowa's Real-encyclopaedie* s. v. *jus gentium*.

[2] Cf. H. Nettleship, *Contributions to Latin Lexicography*, p. 500 ff.

34

of modern nations against class privileges, provincial separatism and arbitrary prerogative.

In conclusion I should like to refer to a passage which sums up the principal features of the *jus gentium.*

Marcianus. Inst. I. 2, 2.

"But civil law derives its name from each individual state, as for instance that of the Athenians; if one wished to call the laws of Solon or Dracon the civil law of the Athenians he would not be wrong. Thus too we call the law used by the Roman people the civil law of the Romans, or that used by the Quirites the civil law of the Quirites; for the Romans are called Quirites after Quirinus. But when we do not add the name specifying the state we mean our own law... The law of nations on the other hand is common to all the human race. For under pressure of usage and human needs the human races have set up certain rules for themselves; wars too have arisen, and captivities have followed, and enslavements, which are contrary to the law of nature (for by the law of nature all men were from the beginning born free); and as the result of this law of nations almost all contracts (agreements) have been introduced, purchase and sale, lease and hire, partnership, deposit, loan, and countless others."

(Sed ius quidem civile ex unaquaque civitate appellatur, veluti Atheniensium; nam si quis velit Solonis vel Draconis leges appellare ius civile Atheniensium, non erraverit. Sic enim et ius, quo populus Romanus utitur, ius civile Romanorum appellamus vel ius Quiritium, quo Quirites utuntur; Romani enim Quirites a Quirino appellantur. Sed quoties non addimus nomen, cuius sit civitas, nostrum jus significamus. ..... Ius autem gentium omni humano generi commune est. Nam usu exigente et humanis necessitatibus gentes humanae quadam sibi constituerunt; bella etenim orta sunt, et captivitates secutae, et servitutes, quae sunt naturali iuri contrariae (iure enim naturali omnes homines ab initio liberi nascebantur); et ex hoc iure gentium omnes paene contractus introducti sunt, ut emptio venditio, locatio conductio, societas, depositum, mutuum et alii innumerabiles.

IV. THE WORLD STATE OF MEDIAEVAL CHRISTENDOM.

When the fabric of the antique civilisation broke down under the onslaught of the barbarians, a slow process of reconstruction began by which natural economics and legal order were built up again in scattered local selfprotecting units, although the imperial intercourse of previous times did not disappear without leaving some traces of its existence. As in the very beginning of human evolution, social consciousness was dominated by religious ideas: every thing in life was connected in some way with supernatural beliefs and aspirations; every manifestation of human activity was measured by the standard of divine commandments. In contrast with the disruption of the material world into a multitude of political fragments — manors, boroughs, gilds — mankind held fast to the conception of a catholic community — the Church, towering over petty interests and civil strife. It pointed out the way towards salvation in a better world — to the City of God — and for this reason it claimed the right to direct the conduct of men in the earthly city, the *Civitas terrena*. Characteristically enough the theocratic ideal of social life was not restricted to the Christian States established on the ruins of Rome; it was also the moving force in the East: the conquering wave of the Khalifate rose high under a rival standard of universal religion. The Carolingian defenders of the Christian faith and the Crusaders, met on the battlefields of Poitiers and of Antioch warriors inspired by fervent religious zeal and held together by a compact theocratic organisation. We are told that the soldiers of Mohausa charged in the battle against the host of Ali with scraps of the Koran attached to their spears. If ever, this was the time for the raising of a Super-State, towering over all cleavages of nationality, class and political boundaries. If ever, this was the epoch for attempts to bridge over dissensions by means of a spiritual rule. The attempt was made in Western Europe by the Popes and it could not fail to produce momentous consequences in the domain of international relations.

36

It is interesting to note that the political theory of the mediaeval theocracy started definitely in the minds of its foremost representatives from the teaching of the City Commonwealth, but was carried one step further. "The Philosopher" (Aristotle) had shown that men are social beings constrained to join in families, in tribal villages and in Cities in order to attain welfare in a self-sufficient union. The schoolmen added one more link to the argument by pointing out that even cities are not self-sufficient and that human intercourse reaches self-sufficiency only in the world union of mankind.

Mankind must therfore be considered as one body politic: its life depends on the unity of its members quite as much as the existence of an individual. The living and real State is one in heaven and ought to be one on earth. St. Augustine and Gregory VII traced the history of the *civitas terrena* from Adam's fall and from Cain's fratricide, but the prevailing view of the Scholastic doctors was: nature has created the thumb for one purpose, and the hand for another purpose, and the arms for yet another, and man for a purpose different from all those. In the same way nature has contrived the single individual for one purpose, and the household for another, and the cluster of neighbours for yet another and the city for another again, and the Kingdom for another, and lastly the eternal God called forth into existence for a special purpose the generality of mankind. There is therefore a special function of universal mankind, which neither a single man, nor a household, nor a village nor a city can fulfil. [1]

As in the organic life of the individual, body and soul are equally necessary elements, but not equally important ones. The spirit is the ruling principle and the view that the Church which

[1] The deduction is tersely stated by DANTE, *De Monarchia*, I, c. 3: Et ad evidentiam eius quod quaeritur, advertendum, quod quemadmodum est finis aliquis ad quem natura producit pollicem, et alius ab hoc ad quem manum totam, et rursus alius ab utroque ad quem brachium, aliusque ab omnibus ad quem totum hominem; sic alius est finis ad quem singularem hominem, alius ad quem ordinat domesticam communitatem, alius ad quem viciniam, et alius ad quem civitatem, et alius ad quem regnum, et denique ultimus ad quem universaliter genus humanum Deus aeternus arte sua, quae natura est, in esse producit...

... Est ergo aliqua propria operatio humanae universitatis, ad quem ipsa universitas hominum in tanta multitudine ordinatur, ad quam quidem operationem nec homo unus, nec domus una, nec una vicinia, nec una civitas, nec regnum particulare pertingere potest.

Under the pen of THOMAS AQUINAS, the same kind of argument is used to justify the Universal rule of the Church.

embodies the spiritual elements of the community is called upon to direct human society was strictly logical. "As man cannot achieve his end, which is to enjoy God, by his own human virtue, but only through the power of God — it belongs not to man, but to God to lead him to that end. And this leadership appertains to a King who is not only a man, but a God, namely to our Lord Jesus Christ — From him is derived Royal Priesthood... In order that the spiritual may be distinct from the temporal, the Royal Office is not entrusted to the Kings of the earth, but to the Priest, and especially to the Supreme Priest, the successor of Peter, the vicar of Christ, the Bishop of Rome, to whom all the Kings of the Christian people should be subject, as to the Lord Jesus Christ himself, because those who are to take care of the subsidiary aims ought to be subject to him to whom appertains the care of the highest aim, and they should follow the Imperial leadership".[1]

This power of direction is conceived not as an absolute and all-pervading government, but as a superior guidance to which the material interests and forces have to conform and in which they have to seek a solution of their disputes and conflicts. The familiar expression of such relations between the spiritual and the secular power is given in the doctrine of the *two swords*.

In a canto of the *Purgatorio* (XVI, 106 ff.) Dante has given us the secular version of the parable. The comparison sounded quite differently in the mouth of a versifier who certainly was no match for Dante as a poet, but who expressed the feelings of the partizans of papacy with considerable force,[2] The conceptions which inspired the author of these doggerel rhymes matured eventually in the well known doctrine of papal supreme power in secular as well as as in spiritual matters which produced as

[1] THOMAS AQUINAS, *de regimine principum*, I, c. 13.

[2] FIGGIS, *Respublica Christiana*. Transactions of the Royal Historical Society. Series III, V. 5. 1911, p. 81:

> Ergo vel ecclesiae membrum non dicetur
> Caesar, vel pontifici summo supponetur.
>
> Major et antiquior est imperialis
> Dignitas quam cleri sit vel pontificalis,
> "Major" dico tempore, semper enim malis
> Regibus subiacuit terra laycalis.
>
> Imperator Esau major quidem natu,
> Papa quidem Jacob est, minor enim statu

38

one of its most extreme manifestations Boniface VIII's famous bull "Unam Sanctam". [1]

The decisions in the course of the struggle were to a great extent affected by conditions of fact — by the feudal and municipal opposition to the Emperors, by the counter-poise of Norman and French politics against the aggrandisement of the Imperial power; but at the back of these material conditions stood the immense influence of a dominating cultural idea — the belief in the spiritual leadership of Roman hierarchy. As long as the claim of the Popes to organize the Christian world was contested by the semi-barbaric Emperors, the successors of St. Peter had much the best of the game. They were stronger in theory and better fitted to put theory into practice. The tables were turned against them when their great enterprise in the conduct of foreign policy — the Crusades against Islam — had signally failed and when instead of the bastard Empire of the Hohenstaufens they were confronted by kings of consolidated National States — by Philip the Fair in France, by Edward III in England. Our present task consists, however, in tracing the way in which the Popes conceived and treated international relations in the epoch of their victories.

The principle put forward by them as the basis of the society of Christian polities was the principle of *federation*. They did not attempt to introduce an impracticable and uniform government from the centre, they admitted to the full the variety of local political organizations, but they tried to introduce harmony

Ille sceptro rutilat, iste potentatu,
Ille major viribus, iste dominatu.

Caesar habet gladium sed materialem,
Hunc eundem pontifex, sed spiritualem.

[1] Extr. comm. I, 8, 1.

... "Unam sanctam ecclesiam catholicam et ipsam apostolicam, urgente fide credere cogimur et tenere ... quae unum corpus mysticum repraesentat, cuius caput Christus Christi vero Deus. In qua unus Dominus, una fides, unum baptisma...

... Haec est tunica ille Domini inconsutilis, quae scissa non fuit, sed sorte provenit. Igitur ecclesiae unius et unicae unum corpus, et unum caput, non duo capita, quasi monstrum, Christus videlicet et Christi vicarius Petrus, Petrique successor, dicente Domino ipsi Petro: Pasce oves meas.

... In hac eiusque potestate duos esse gladios, spiritualem videlicet et temporalem evangelicis dictis instruimur. Nam dicentibus apostolis: "ecce gladii duo hic", ... Certe, qui in potestate Petri temporalem gladium esse negat, male verbum attendit Domini proferentis: "Converte gladium tuum in vaginam". Uterque ergo gladius est in potestate ecclesiae".

into the life of these various bodies: the great ideal of peace had been proclaimed emphatically both by them and by their political opponents. We may again turn to Dante for a passionate expression of this leading idea: "It is evident that mankind should strive to fulfil its almost divine work freely and easily in peace and quiet. It is clear therefore that universal peace is the greatest good that can be provided for our happiness. This is what sounded to the shepherds from heaven — not wealth, not might, not honours, not long life, not health, not strength, not beauty — but peace, the heavenly host proclaimed: Glory be to God on high, and peace to men of good will on earth" [1].

One of the most tangible results of the unceasing activity of the Church in the cause of peace had been the propaganda in favour of the truce of God. In spite of many disappointments and failures the movement against private wars initiated by the Church did not remain sterile and led gradually to a relative restriction of local feuds.

More ambitious and more difficult were the cases of intervention in conflicts conducted on a larger scale. In 1079 Pope Gregory VII insisted on the submission of the brothers of the Danish king to his overlordship and prohibited a division of the country which would have been detrimental to the interests of Christianity in the North. In the same year he decided as supreme judge a dispute between the sons of the Count of Barcelona and reminded them of the necessity of concord between Christian princes faced by Islam.

In the course of his controversy with Philip Augustus of France Innocent III formulated the pretensions of the papacy to intervene in conflicts between princes in the following way: Was it not the mission of the successors of St. Peter to establish peace among men? Even if the Pope had no right to intervene in feudal matters, his jurisdiction had to be recognized as to sin (ratione peccati). It remained to be seen whether Philip had not sinned by disregarding the rights of John his vassal [2].

[1] DANTE, *De Monarchia*, c. 4. Patet quod genus humanum in quietate sive tranquillitate pacis ad proprium suum opus, quod fere divinum est manifestum est, quod pax universalis est optimum eorum, quae ad nostram beatitudunem ordinatur. Hinc est, quod pastoribus de sursum sonuit, non divitiae, non voluptates, non honores, non longitudo vitae, non sanitas, non robur, non pulchritudo; sed pax. Inquit enim caelestis militia: "Gloria in altissimis Deo, et in terra pax hominibus bonae voluntatis".

[2] See LUCHAIRE, *Les royaumes vassaux*, pp. 251, 254, 259.

40

As to the methods employed by the Pope in these international disputes, they were derived from various sources. In his capacity as the supreme arbitrator of the Christian world the Pope claimed the right to settle the most intricate aad important national and international conflicts. Although in their struggle with the Emperors the Popes tried to weaken the feudal notions of fealty by exempting vassals from sworn obligations, they surround themselves with a circle of vassals.

This expedient was not well chosen from a theoretical point of view: it is in the nature of an opportunistic use of accidental advantages of position in the feudal world. A much more formidable weapon was provided by the pastoral leadership of the Pope. As the appointed teacher and guardian of faith and morals he wielded the terrible scourges of excommunication and interdict [1].

Another side of the juridical power claimed by the Roman Curia and conceded to a great extent by public opinion and legal custom was the *extra-territorial* jurisdiction of the Canon Law in relations which affect some of the most important sides of social life — e. g. marriage, succession, testaments, trusts, charities, corporations, agreements, etc. It would be out of the question for us to treat of these various applications of Canon Law and Ecclesiastical jurisdiction at any length. But it is clear that the existence of that large body of law derived not from State legislation or local custom, but from a spiritual organization whose power was not limited by existing frontiers and territorial divisions, was in itself a factor of primary importance from an international point of view. The adjustment of the juridical ideas and institutions which had grown up on the extra-territorial soil to the Common Law of England or the practices of the French parliaments or the statutes and customs of the Italian Cities was a task of great importance, productive of incessant conflicts.

The treatment of marriage and of family relations derived from it may serve as an example. The Church considered the tie between the spouses to be a sacramental union by which two human beings were fused into one. For this reason the indissolubility of *rightful* matrimony was insisted upon and at the same time great latitude was allowed as regards *annulment* by

[1] Pandolf in the *Annals of Burton*, 1212.
On the Interdict in England in 1213 see *Annals of Coventry*, II, 108.

the authority of the Pope. The widest possible application of the marriage tie in practice as against spurious and illegitimate unions was also the object of propaganda by the Church.

In this policy it had to meet various currents of popular customs and professional doctrines which were very difficult to conquer. As against the sacrament stood the ancient treatment of marriage as a contract of betrothal negotiated primarily between the kindred of the bride on one side, the bridegroom and his kinsmen on the other. The conditions as to the conclusion, consummation and breach of such *wedding* were peculiar, and the chief stress lay from this point of view on the *handfasting*, the *giftermål*, the symbolic purchase or the agreement to marry: the Popes, speaking for the Church, did not consider such promises *de futuro* as decisive. On the other hand the promise *de presenti*, even apart from any ecclesiastical ceremony, was protected as a sacramental act [1].

The general result is expressed in the decretals of Gregory IX. The only absolutely indissoluble marriage was the *matrimonium consummatum*. A *matrimoninm non consnmmatum* might be voidable, but only through the action of the Pope; the parties could not break it off except in the single case of either of them wanting to enter "religion". What Alexander III then had done was to introduce the direct action of the Papacy as the sole judge of doubtful marriages.

Sacrament created an indissoluble tie in Canon Law, but in the practice of the secular world innumerable cases arose in which the continuance of marital relations was found to be impossible. The Roman Church tried to avoid these difficulties by casuistic devices to assist people in annulling marriages on some pretext or other instead of divorcing the spouses. In these devices and in the power to withhold dispensation it constantly came into conflict with secular opinions and secular powers.

In order to extend as far as possible the domain of ordered family life the Church purified illegitimate unions by means of subsequent matrimony and regarded the offsprings of such unions as legitimate children. In this respect it came into conflict with the interests and customary practice of feudal lords, of whom certainty as regards legitimacy was an important feature in the treatment of succession. Hence the famous refusal of the barons of England in the conference of Merton (1236) to accept the

[1] A. L. SMITH, *Church and State in the Middle Age*, pp. 71—72.

42

Ecclesiastical view of legitimation *per subsequens matrimonium.* Nolumus leges Angliae mutari. The decided stand of the English magnates on this occasion by no means proves that the Church lost her cause for ever. The proceedings as to legitimacy remained complicated and continued to give rise to constant dispute between Courts Christian and Courts of Common Law. The Popes did not give up their intention, but steered a straight course or a casuistic one according to circumstances. (Cf. Pollock and Maitland, History of English law).

This may serve as an example of the interference of the Roman Curia in social arrangements. Whatever the concessions and compromises made in practice, the Church relied in a general way on Christian doctrines as to sources of law which were not contested by the laity and served as a powerful weapon in vindicating the rights of the spiritual power.

To begin with there was the general proposition that positive law as it is shown in statutes, decrees, Royal statements of custom, professional declarations, Acts of Parliament, etc., is of less authority than the Divine Law contained in the revealed teaching of the Church and the Law of Nature implanted by Providence in the soul of man. [1]

The law of nature is discoverable not only in the general propositions and dogmas of human reason, but also in the positive laws themselves in as far as they are to testify to universal and concordant views. Such a concordance of laws of various national origin constitutes the *jus gentium.*

Now there are two kinds of authorities from which the contents of the common law of nature and of nations can be ascertained: the civil law, formulated by Rome, and the canon law proclaimed by the Church. Both are recognized by mediaeval schoolmen, but in spite of this affinity, there are fundamental differences between them; there must be a power invested with

[1] THOMAS AQUINAS, Commentary to Aristotle, Eth. Nic. V, 10: Attenditur autem in homine duplex natura. Una quidem, secundum quod est animal, quae sibi et aliis animalibus est communis. Alia autem natura est hominis, prout scilicet secundum rationem discernit turpe et honestum. Juristae autem illud tantum dicunt jus naturale, quod consequitur inclinationem naturae communis homini et aliis animalibus, sicut conjunctio maris et feminae, educatio natorum, et alia hujusmodi. Illud autem jus, quod consequitur propriam inclinationem naturae humanae, scilicet ut homo est rationale animal, vocant juristae jus gentium, quia eo omnes gentes utuntur, sicut quod pacta sint servanda et quod legati sint apud hostes tuti et alia hujusmodi. Utrumque autem horum comprehenditur sub justo naturali, prout hic a Philosopho accipitur.

decision, and this power is found by the schoolmen in the pronouncements of the vicars of Christ — the Popes.

The edifice of Papal justice, like all other forms of judicature, needed material guarantees of compulsion, and it stood erect as long as the principal of these guarantees — the power of excommunication and interdict — kept its authority over Christian society. Its effects were terrible, as we may gather, for instance, from the description of the state of England under the bann of the interdict proclaimed by Innocent III.

It is significant that in the closing centuries of the Middle Ages — the XIV and XV — the foundations of theocracy gave way because material conditions of social life asserted themselves more and more strongly as against mystic aspirations towards the life of a universal church. This is evident in the policy of the Popes themselves — the craving for temporal power in certain provinces, especially in Southern Italy and France, the development of Papal fiscality since Innocent IV. But it is even more prominent in the growth of national separatism conditioned by the formation of Western States. Already in Dante's writings the main stress is laid on the necessity of material compulsion, for which he looks, however, to a reconstruction of the Roman Empire. More ominous from the practical point of view is the rise of national unity in the various kingdoms of the West, in the England of Edward III with its strong opposition to appeals to the Curia, in the France of XIV century with its legists brought up on civil law and using it to build up a doctrine of National selfsufficicncy.

A characteristic expression of this disruptive movement of political self-assertion is to be found in the work of the leading Commentator of Civil law — Bartolus (1314—1357). He is quite ready to recognize the theoretical unity of European common law, the legal tradition of the Empire and the spiritual superiority of the Pope [1].

We have seen above that Statutes, no less than laws, are subjected to the higher laws — the *jus divinum*, *jus naturale* and *jus gentium*. Further, statutes which as regards "spiritualia" are contrary to the Canons are of course invalid; and we may note that statutes contrary to the liberties of the Church are similarly invalid, even where Imperial laws seem valid. Now let us consider the general rules to be observed between the conflicting

[1] WOOLF, *Bartolus of Sassoferrato*, pp. 149—151.

jura municipalia and the *jus commune*. In his commentary on the law *Omnes populi* Bartolus asks whether Statutes could vary the rules laid down in the common civil law. [1] He answers that a statute cannot contradict the *jus commune* by ordaining that which the *jus commune* forbids; but it can ordain that which is not expressly forbidden, provided that it accords with *boni mores* and public utility, and is within the limits of the jurisdiction which the people can exercise.

Under cover of theoretical deductions Bartolus builds up a legal order of *de facto* institutions based on the actual existence of a number of independent cities capable of establishing their own governments and laws. [2]

From the point of view of public international law the advent of the *Regna* and *Civitates* meant a disruption of the mediaeval society of Christendom. But it meant also the necessity of providing by conventions and alliances for the regulation of commercial and intellectual intercourse. For a time Italy seemed to have kept in substance to the conditions and doctrines of the Conflict of Laws initiated by ancient Greek Commonwealths. But lawyers brought up on a study of the *Corpus Juris* treated the matter of private international law in a systematic and closely reasoned form. It is therefore no exaggeration to say that we owe to Bartolus the first and fundamental treatise on the Conflict of Laws. I will just refer to the first sentences of the Bartolus Commentary on the first and second part of the Code in Professor Beale's translation in order to give you an idea of the manner in which the subject was discussed by the great Italian jurist. [3]

"I. Now let us come to the gloss which says "if a Bolognian makes a contract at Modena, he shall be judged by the Statute of Modena". As to this, two things are to be noted: first, whether a statute extends beyond its territory to those not subject; second, whether the effect of a statute extends beyond the territory of the legislator. And first, I ask, what about contracts? Suppose a contract celebrated by a foreigner in this city: a contest arises, and suit is brought in the place where the contract was made: of what place should the statutes be observed or looked at? We either speak of statute or custom with respect to the form of the contract itself, or the suit on it, or with respect to jurisdiction

[1] "An super his, quae disposita vel prohibita sunt a jure civili communi possint fieri statuta aliter statuendo".

[2] SIDNEY WOOLF, *Bartolus of Sassoferrato*, p. 388.

[3] J. H. BEALE, *Bartolus on the Conflict of Laws*, pp. 17, 18, 19.

over the performance provided for in the contract itself etc."

To sum up. One might say that at the close of the middle ages the subconsciousness of individuals, of social groups and of political organisations produced centrifugal forces which made it impossible to sustain the idea of a common unity embracing Christendom. Instead of looking up to providential guidance and appealing to the Pope as vicar of Christ to settle articles of faith, cases of conscience and international feuds, the peoples of Europe attempted to organise Society on the narrower lines of a combination of individuals under the sway of territorial states.

V. THE INTERNATIONAL RELATIONS OF TERRITORIAL STATES.

The unity of Western Christendom was gradually dissolving in the XIV and XV centuries. Its spiritual and material foundations were giving way before new forces. The barrenness of dialectical scholasticism was discarded in the light of the Revival of learning and of experimental science. A revolt of individual conscience against external discipline brought about the disruption of the Church. Thomas of Aquinas had deduced from scripture the call of the Priests to act as Kings of the people in matters of supreme importance. Luther deduced from it the priestly and Kingly office of plain Christians! He wrote in his first revolutionary pamphlet "the Freedom of the Christian" (1521):

"Who is able to express the freedom and highness of Christian man? Through his Kingship he has power over all things, through his priesthood he has power over God, because God complies with his prayer and will, as it is written in the Psalter: "God acts in accordance with the will of those who fear him, and listens to their prayer". And the Christian wins this honour exclusively through faith, not by any works. From this it can be seen that a Christian is free of all things and above all things, so that he has no need of good works in order to be pious and blessed, faith brings him everything in plenty. And should he be so foolish as to think that he can become pious, true, blessed or a Christian by good works, he would lose faith with all things, like the dog which carried a piece of meat in his mouth and snapped after the reflection in the water: he lost both the meat and the reflection".

In the economic sphere feudal relations based on natural husbandry were being replaced by commercial intercourse on a large scale. Politically modern states were growing up on a territorial basis, welded together sometimes by national consciousness as in France and Great Britain, sometimes by provincial and municipal competition as in Italy and Germany, but everywhere under the guidance of selfassertive and unscrupulous sovereigns; guided by State selfishness (*raison d'état*). No wonder the old conception of Christian Commonwealth (Respublica Christiana) had to be abandoned and the Catholic unity was broken up by a disruptive Reformation. The question was, what principle would take the place of this shattered "Universality". [1]

It seemed at first that the victory had been definitely won by the territorial principle. If universal order was given up territorial peace had to take its place: it was attainable by the creation of strong and uncontested authority. The Defensor Pacis of Marsilius of Padua presented an early justification of the secular system of polities [2]. Macchiavelli in *The Prince* described the means, fair and foul, by which domination could be attained and maintained.

After the terrible religious feuds of the XVIth and XVIIth centuries the demand for civil peace asserted itself with particular force in the kingdom of Henry IV of France and in the English Restoration. I need hardly remind you that the modern theory of sovereignty may be traced to the writings of Bodin, who was, as it were, obsessed by the idea that the only means of preventing endless and destructive strife is to admit the final decision of an uncontested monarchical authority in the State. Hobbes gave an even more pungent expression to the craving for civil peace. Religious conviction itself was subordinated by him to the paramount craving for authority and the modern "Cuius regio, ejus religio" was not only the decision of the Augsburg Diet.

And yet one has to look deeper in order to understand the course of events. The subjection of religion to secular authority was after all a lame expedient. State Sovereignty in its theoretical completeness as formulated by Hobbes amounted to a mechanical compression of individual atoms. The State Leviathan assumed the appearance of a monstrous organism, but it was

[1] See J. N. Figgis, *From Gerson to Grotius.*

[2] Defensor Pacis, c. 12. Nos autem dicamus secundum veritatem atque consilium Aristotelis, 3 politicae, ca. 6, legis latorem, seu causam legis effectivam primam et propriam, esse populum, seu civium universitatem aut eius valentiorem partem, per suam electionem seu voluntatem in generali civium congregatione per sermonem expressam, praecipientem seu determinantem aliquid fieri seu omitti circa civilis actus humanos sub poena vel supplicio temporali: valentiorem, iniquam partem, considerata quantitate in communitate illa super quam lex fertur, sive id fecerit universitas praedicta civium aut eius pars valentior per se ipsam immediate, sive id alicui vel aliquibus commiserit faciendum... Et dico consequenter huic quod eadem auctoritate prima non alia debent leges et aliud quod libet per electionem institutum approbationem necessariam suscipere, etc...

conceived as a mechanical contrivance. The force of Hobbes' argument depended on the fact that he had simplified the political problems to the utmost by reducing them to two factors — separate individuals, incapable of creating society, and the State, a "persona ficta", through whose compulsion the intercourse between isolated individuals became possible, but which was in truth the creation of individual brains. The atomism of individuals, disconnected in nature and connected by mechanical coercion, is the general principle in which both extremes are united. Spinoza's *Tractatus Theologico-politicus* presented a variation of the same reasoning.

Although there was ample justification in these doctrines for the policy of King's Craft projected by a James I and practised by a Frederic II, it would be impossible to disregard the fact that the glorification of territorial sovereignty never succeeded in silencing the claims of citizens to an altogether different standing — to a political existence in their own right on the strength of the inherent dignity and self-conciousness of human nature. As against the State despotism of the time rose the monarchomachi, the enemies of Kings, on the one hand, the Jesuits, the satellites of a religious society, on the other. In public law these extremes actually met: both justified revolution and the assassination of tyrants. But it is more important to notice that these two schools, opposed to the absolutism of the territorial State, worked together to prepare the ground for the most characteristic doctrine of this time — the conception of a law of Nature as a guidance for the relations between states.

The conception of a supreme Law of Nature is, of course, not a product of modern times. The view that laws are derived in the end from natural reason was a constant topic of argument among Greek philosophers and the doctrine of a law of Nature became one of the main tenets of the Stoic teaching. Mediaeval schoolmen adopted it from Aristotle's writings as well as from Scripture and from the Fathers. But while in these earlier epochs the admission of natural law as one of the forces of political life and jurisprudence was balanced and modified by other equally powerful principles, e. g. by the absorbing influence of the City Commonwealth, of the Empire, theocratic commandments, in the period starting with the Reformation it became the very foundation of social justice. The roots of law had to be sought in the nature of man, as the roots of religion were found in the personal relation between man and Providence. A powerful school of thought culminating in Grotius' work declined to consider human relations as productions of selfishness and successful violence: it took its stand against Macchiavelli and Hobbes on a social attraction engrained in human nature.

The age with its rationalistic frame of thought was intent on discovering *axiomatic truths* from which the various details of natural science and social doctrine could be deduced with strict consistency. And jurists and theologians looked for these axiomatic truths in a law of nature.

This is how Grotius explains the position:

"In the first place it was my object to refer the truth of the things which belong to Natural law to some notions, so certain, that no one can deny them, without doing violence to his own nature. For the principles of such Natural Law, if you attend to them rightly, are of themselves patent and evident, almost in the same way as things which are perceived by the external senses. . . ."[1]

. . . I quote them (philosophers, historians, poets and orators) as witnesses whose conspiring testimony, proceeding from innumerable different times and places, must be referred to some universal cause; which, in the questions with which we are here concerned, can be no other than a right deduction proceeding from the principles of reason, or some common consent. The former cause of agreement points to the Law of Nature, the latter to the the Law of Nations: though the difference of these two is not to be collected from the testimonies themselves, (for writers everywhere confound the Law of Nature and the Law of Nations), but from the quality of the matter. For what cannot be deduced from certain principles by solid reasoning, and yet

[1] H. GROTIUS, *De jure belli et pacis*, trans. by W. WHEWELL, Cambridge 1853. *Prolegomena*, 39. Primum mihi cura haec fuit, ut eorum quae ad jus naturae pertinent probationes referrem ad notiones quasdam tam certas, ut eas nemo negare possit, nisi sibi vim inferat. Principia enim ejus juris, si modo animum recte advertas, per se patent atque *evidentia* sunt, ferme ad modum eorum quae sensibus externis percipimus.

40. ... ubi multi diversis temporibus ac locis idem pro certo affirmant, id ad causam universalem referri debeat: quae nostris quaestionibus alia esse non potest, quam aut recta illatio *ex naturae principiis* procedentes, aut communis aliquis consensus. Illa jus naturae indicat, *hic jus gentium:* quorum discrimen non quidem ex ipsis testimoniis, (passim enim scriptores voces juris naturae et gentium permiscent) sed ex materiae qualitate intelligendum est. Quod enim ex certis principiis certa argumentatione deduci non potest, et tamen ubique observatum apparet, sequitur ut ex voluntate libera ortum habeat.

50

is seen and observed everywhere, must have its origin from the will and consent of all."

"Natural Law is so immutable that it cannot be changed by God himself. For though the power of God be immense, there are some things to which it does not extend: because if we speak of those things being done, the words are mere words, and have no meaning, being selfcontradictory. Thus God himself cannot make twice two not be four; and in like manner, he cannot make that which is intrinsically bad, not be bad." [1]

Suarez explains the relation between the various kinds of law in the following way: [2] "The reason for the existence of this kind of law consists in the fact that mankind, though divided into a variety of nations and kingdoms, belongs to a "universitas" of some sort, not only in the special sense of the word, but in a quasi-political and moral sense. This is indicated by the natural precept of reciprocal love and pity which is extended to all, even to foreigners of any nation. Thus, while every Commonwealth or kingdom presents a perfect community in itself, nevertheless each is at the same time a member of the universe in as much as it concerns mankind. Because none of these communities is so selfsufficient as to be independent of reciprocal help, association and intercourse. Sometimes this is desirable for the

[1] *Ibid.* I, 1, X, 5. Est autem jus naturale adeo immutabile, ut ne a Deo quidem mutari queat. Quanquam enim immensa est Dei potentia, dici tamen quaedam possunt, ad quae se illa non extendit. Sicut ergo ut bis duo non sint quatuor ne a Deo quidem potest effici, ita ne hoc quidem, ut quod intrinseca ratione malum est, malum non sit.

[2] F. SUAREZ, *Tractatus de legibus ac Deo Legislatore*, London, 1679. II, c. 19 § 9, ... Ratio autem ejus partis, & juris est, quia humanum genus quantumvis in varios populos et regna divisum, semper habet aliquam unitatem non solum specificam, sed etiam quasi politicam, & moralem, quam indicat naturale praeceptum mutui amoris, & misericordiae, quod ad omnes extenditur, etiam extraneos, & cujuscumque rationis. Quapropter licet unaquaeque civitas perfecta, respublica, aut regnum, sit in se communitas perfecta, ac suis membris constans numquam enim illae communitates adeo sunt sibi sufficientes singillatim, quin indigeant aliquo mutuo juvamine, & societate, ac communicatione, interdum ad melius esse, majoremque utilitatem; interdum vero etiam ad moralem necessitatem, & indigentiam, ut ex ipso uso constat. Hoc ergo ratione indigent aliquo jure, quo dirigantur, & recte ordinantur in hoc genere communicationis, & societatis. Et quamvis magna ex parte hoc fiat per rationem naturalem; non tamen sufficienter, & immediate quod omnia; ideoque aliqua specialia jura potuerunt usu earundem gentium introduci. Nam sicut in una civitate, vel provincia consuetudo introducit jus, ita in universo humano genere, potuerunt jura gentium moribus introduci. Eo vel maxime, quod ea, quae ad hoc jus pertinent, et pauca sunt, & juri naturali valde propinqua, & que facillimam habent ab illo deductionem.

sake of a better existence and greater usefulness, sometimes on account of moral needs and indigence, revealed by practice. For this reason they require a certain kind of law to direct and to place them in order in this kind of intercourse. And although this is achieved to a great extent by natural reason, the latter does not suffice. Therefore certain special forms of law have been actually introduced. As in every single city or province custom creates legal rules, in the same way as regards mankind laws of nations may be introduced by moral usage. This is easy because rules of that kind are not many and are closely akin to the law of nature from which they can be derived without difficulty".

On the other side, Althusius, a German professor who taught in East Friesland and was strongly influenced by the thought and life of the Netherlands, built up his politics on a conception of a *Social Compact* distinct from all governmental arrangements, but necessary in order to explain the existence of society formed of a multitude of living individuals.

The speculative position of Althusius marks a new departure in political thought. As in the case of Hobbes and of Rousseau the organization of government is relegated to the background. The main thing is to account for the appearance of society itself. It is assumed that it is rendered possible by two tendencies — a psychological one, the bent of human nature towards social intercourse — the *Socialitas* of Grotius, modified from the ζῶον πολιτικὸν of Aristotle; — and the conscious association of men for purposes of co-operation. It is highly characteristic of the fundamental individualism of the epoch that society is treated as a form of partnership (*Societas*) rather than as an organic unity. [1]

[1] Otto Gierke, "*Johannes Althusius*", Breslau, p. 99. ... Gleich an die Eingangspforte seiner Politik stellt er die Fundamentirung des Gattungsbegriffes "*consociatio*" auf ausdrücklichen oder stillschweigenden *Konsens der Associirten.* Selbst für die Familienverbindungen hält er, obschon er sie als natürliche und nothwendige Verhältnisse anerkennt, die Fiktion der *Vertragsgrundlage* aufrecht. Zur vollen Entfaltung aber bringt er den Vertragsgedanken für *Korporationen*, *Gemeinde und Staat*, die er durchweg als freiwillig eingegangene, wenn auch durch die gesellige Natur des Menschen bedingte Verhältnisse auffasset. Überal nimmt er hier einen zu Grunde liegenden förmlichen "contractus societatis" an, den er ohne Bedenken den *Regeln des Civilrechts* unterstellt. Indem er sodann bis ins Einzelne bei jeder Verbandsart den Inhalt der vertragsmässigen Vergemeinschaftung analysirt, gewinnt er die Mittel zu dem bis dahin in dieser Weise niemals unternommenen Versuch einer festen Grenzziehung zwischen den *Rechtssphären des Individuums und der Gemeinschaft*, sowie der engeren und der weiteren Verbande. Lediglich aus dem Begriff des Gesellschäftsvertrages vollzieht er den Aufbau einer mit *allen staatlichen*

52

It would be wrong to suppose, however, that these political doctrines were purely the products of theoretical reflection and study. The theories served as a nucleus to ideas of a practical nature and of intense influence on the life of the people. The connecting link was given by religious struggles of the time in which territorial sovereigns were confronted by unconquerable convictions in faith and creed. In spite of the Diet of Augsburg, of the Westphalian treaties, of the *raison d'état* persecutions of Catherine of Medici and of Louis XIV, the political thought of these times insisted more and more effectively on the rights of man in the religious and, eventually, in the social domain. The significant tradition of the right of man to freedom of thought and action starts from the Puritan opposition to the Stewarts, asserts itself in the colonial constitutions of the new world before reaching its formulas in the Declaration of Independence and of the French revolutionary Declarations.

The struggle for religious autonomy in the XVII century produced actual attempts to construct States on the basis of contract. This is how nineteen emigrants from Providence (Rhode Island) formulated the fundamental law in their new settlement: "We whose names are underwritten do here solemnly in the presence of Jehovah incorporate ourselves into a bodie politick, and as he shall help, will submit our persons, lives and estates unto our Lord Jesus Christ, the King of Kings, and Lord of Lords, and to all those perfect and absolute laws of him given us in his holy word of truth, to be guided and judged hereby"[1]. In England itself the victorious Puritan army drew up a "project of the agreement of the people" (1657) in which the contractual origin of state organization is clearly stated.

"*An Agreement of the People of England, and the places therewith incorporated, for a secure and present peace, upon grounds of common right, freedom and safety.*

Having, by our late labours and hazards, made it appear to the world at how high a rate we value our just freedom, and God having so far owned our cause as to deliver the enemies thereof into our hands, we do now hold ourselves bound, in mutual duty to each other, to take the best care we can for

Hoheitsrechten über ihre Glieder ausgerüsteten Volksgesammtheit, um dann erst hinter her sich dem zwischen ihr und ihren Verwaltern bestehenden Vertragsverhältniss zuzuwenden.

[1] JELLINEK, *Staats- und Völkerrechtl. Abhandlungen*, II, 36. Agüednek, 1638.

the future, to avoid both the danger of returning into a slavish condition and the chargeable remedy of another war" [1].

Thus the period which began with the Renaissance and attained its culminating point in the French Revolution is dominated by the struggles and compromises of two principles — that of the natural justice derived from individual consciousness and that of the sovereignty in the territorial state, derived from the requirement of social order. In a world of this kind international relations, when not abandoned to settlement by pure force had to conform also to the fundamental tendencies of the political thought of the times. And we see them indeed built up by the help of conceptions derived from an individualistic law of nature.

The application of the Law of Nature to international relations was conditioned by the view that political life was altogether proceeding in two channels — a state of voluntary arrangements established by convention and defended by compulsion, and a previous state of Nature in which rights and duties had to be deduced from considerations of human reason and, hence, of natural justice. Gentili and Suarez proclaim in the same way that as relations between states are not regulated by common sovereignty, they must be regulated by principles of natural justice. These principles are more or less clearly recognized by all those who believe in God as the fountain of morality and justice. Those who do not share in this fundamental belief are outlaws in civilized society [2].

A fundamental rule from which all other positive rules are derived is: *Pacta sunt servanda.* It is the basis of confidence between men, without which no social or international co-operation is possible.

"For in the first place, it follows therefrom that pacts between kings and different peoples, so long as nothing thereof is performed (re integra) have no force; the parties being bound by no common instituted law; especially in those places in which no regular form of treaties and engagements has been introduced.

[1] S. R. Gardiner, *Constitutional Documents of the Puritan Revolution*, Oxford, 1906, p. 359.

[2] Albericus Gentilis, *De jure belli*, Oxonii, 1877, I, 9, p. 39. ... At neque nos loquimur nunc de his qui, *ferarum modo magis* quam hominum viventes, sine ulla omnino religione sunt; hos enim quasi piratas, communes hostes omnium, bello persequendos, et cogendos in mores hominum arbitrarer.

Cf. J. N. Figgis, *Studies of political thought from Gerson to Grotius*, Cambridge, 1907.

54

And again, no reason can be found why laws, which are in a certain way a common pact of the people, and are so called by Aristotle and Demosthenes, should be able to give obligatory force to pacts" [1].

The framework of a law of nature is thus fundamental for the international jurisprudence of the XVII and XVIII centuries.

"By many the law of nature and the law of nations are held to be one and the same, differing merely in outward name. Hence Hobbes (*De Cive*, c. 14, 4, 5) divides natural law into natural law of persons ... and natural law of States, which latter is commonly called the law of nations. The rules of both', he adds, 'are the same'.... With this opinion we certainly agree" [2].

Does this mean that all the speculations of these times were doomed to be phantastical or Utopian, a dream of students or a screen for cynical greed? In practice, undoubtedly, diplomatic arguments have been often conducted in a spirit of scarcely disguised selfishness. Frederic II of Prussia began his career as a political thinker by writing a treatise called "Anti-Macchiavel." And neither he, nor Joseph II, nor Catherine II, escaped from the influence of the ideas of natural law in certain respects. Take, for example, the policy of letting everyone achieve salvation in his own way — nach seiner "façon," practised by Frederic, or the levelling of social differences decreed by Joseph II; these measures were certainly a considerable advance on the "cujus regio ejus religio" or on the programme of class privileges of Montesquieu.

What is even more important is the fact that a body of international doctrine grew up at the hands of Grotius, of Pufendorf, of Vattel, which formulated rules of international usage, that had considerable authority even with the most arbitrary rulers. It may be idle to talk in this case about *law* (lex), as we are accustomed to give this name to compulsory rules, but it is

[1] H. Grotius, *De jure belli et pacis*, II, c. 11, I, 3.

Primum enim sequitur inde inter reges et populos diversas, pactorum, quandiu nihil ex iis praestitum est, vim esse nullam, praesertim iis in locis, ubi nulla certa forma foederum aut sponsionum reperta est. Tum vero ratio nulla reperiri potest, cur leges, quae quasi pactum commune sunt populi, atque hoc nomine vocantur ab Aristotele et Demosthene, obligationem pactis possint addere.

[2] S. Pufendorf, *De jure naturae et gentium*, Amsterdam, 1688. II, c. 3, 23. ... Multis jus naturae & jus gentium in se unum & idem habetur, quod extrinseca duntaxat denominatione differat. Inde & Hobbes, *de Cive*, c. 14, 4, 5 naturalem legem dividit "in naturalem hominum, ... naturalem civitatum, quae vulgo jus gentium adpellatur. Praecepta utriusque, addit, eadem sunt..."

quite appropriate to talk about natural justice, because these conceptions imply the formulation and declaration of rights even apart from actual decision and execution. And there is no reason why this quality of principles orientated towards equity and justice should be denied to international jurisprudence. As a matter of fact while we reject nowadays the *a priori* assumptions of an immutable law of nature, we recognize the value of public opinion as to the equitable regulation of international affairs; while treatment of "peace" by international law is governed by such public opinion and by definite agreements in which considerations of common utility and equity play a decisive part. In this light the earlier teaching of the law of nature becomes important and suggestive.

Those who examine its particulars, find, to begin with, that it transfers to States the juridical ideas and requirements worked out by earlier generations in the domain of private law. Once States are conceived as persons on a footing of equality brought together under the protection of incontested sovereignty their collective life is treated as that of normal persons in private law; they enter into transactions, assume responsibilities, conclude conventions, make claims, demand compensations, commit delicts. In this latter respect the international doctrine of Grotius and Gentili assumed a distinctly realistic aspect. A State could not plead immunity from accusation in fact on the ground that it is merely a fiction and that "Universitas non delinquit." Being organized under a government it incurs all the consequences of its deliberate acts although these consequences may be drawn not by a superior tribunal but by self-help under natural law. This is the reason and justification of war. This view gives rise to the following interesting argument: "And so far we follow the opinion of Innocentius, and of others who say that war may be made against those who sin against nature; contrary to the tenets of Victoria, Vasquius, Azolius, Molina, and others; who seem to require, in order to justify a war, that he who undertakes it should be either injured in his own person, or in the country to which he belongs, or that he should have jurisdiction over him whom he attacks. For they hold that the power of punishing is the proper effect of Civil Jurisdiction; while we conceive that it comes also from Natural Law. If the opinion of those from whom we dissent be admitted, an enemy will not have the power of punishing an enemy, even after war has been justly begun, if it be for another cause

56

than to inflict punishment: which right, however, most authors concede, and the usage of all nations confirms, not only after the war has been finished, but even while it is going on; and this right is claimed, not from any civil jurisdiction, but from that natural right which existed before states existed, and is still in force in places in which men live distributed into families and not into states."[1]

Another example of the application of the private law conceptions of personality to States is the recognition of their equality before the law; England and Portugal remained equal even when Portugal ceased to be a great power either at home or in the colonies, and we know of many more striking examples of international equality nowadays. The point is not a negligible one, of course, because it conditions the whole practice of international conferences and joint decisions.

Another aspect of the transfer of private law conceptions into the domain of international law is the influence of Roman jurisprudence in shaping the principal doctrines of the latter.[2]

[1] Grotius, *De Jure belli et pacis*, II, c. XX, § 40, 4.

Et eatenus sententiam sequimur Innocentii, et aliorum qui bello aiunt peti posse eos qui in naturam delinquunt: contra quam sentiunt Victoria, Vasquius, Azolius, Molina, alii, qui ad justitiam belli requirere videntur, ut qui suscipit aut laesus sit in se aut republica sua, aut ut in eum qui bello impetitur jurisdictionem habeat. Ponunt enim illi puniendi potestatem esse effectum proprium jurisdictionis civilis, cum nos eam sentiamus venire etiam ex jure naturali, qua de re aliquid diximus libri primi initio. Et sane si illorum a quibus dissentimus admittatur sententia, jam hostis in hostem puniendi jus non habebit, etiam post juste susceptum bellum ex causa non punitiva: quod tamen jus plerique concedunt et usus omnium Gentium confirmat, non tantum postquam debellatum est, sed et manente bello; non ex ulla jurisdictione civili, sed ex illo jure naturali quod et ante institutas civitates fuit, et nunc etiam viget, quibus in locis homines vivunt in familias non in civitates distributi.

[2] Albericus Gentilis, De jure belli, I, c. 3, (p. 16). . . . Jus etiam, illis perscriptum libris Justiniani, non civitatis est tantum, sed et gentium, et naturae, et aptatum sic est ad naturam universum, ut imperio extincto, et ipsum ius diu sepultum surrexerit tamen, et in omnes se effuderit gentes humanas. Ergo et Principibus stat: etsi privatis conditum a Justiniano. Et stat sane nec auditum mihi est, lectumve unquam, quod egregii illi supra vulgum positi tradunt. Forte an desiit esse gentium, et naturae ius, quia expositum est civitati? Sed ut quod civile est, non idem continuo est gentium: quod tamen gentium est, idem et civile esse debet. Est quidem ius civile, quod non servit naturali, et gentium juri per omnia: at neque in totum a naturali recedit, vel gentium. Et cura non serviat per omnia, aut ratio communis omnium civitatum facit, aut singularis aliquarum. Ut quod civilia jura non omne agnoscant pactum ad actionem, cum gentium jus differentiam pactorum nullam constituat. . . Caeterum si quid eiusmodi proprium civitatis non ostenditur, illud de his tollere publicarum rerum disceptationibus plusquam ridiculum fuerit, plusquam ineptum. Quid? Non apta Principibus illa librorum Justiniani, Honeste

57

Indeed, no better illustration of this method could be given than the one presented by the text of Grotius' famous and epoch-making works. To take only one instance. The cardinal doctrine of occupation is inspired by well known precepts of Roman Law. The concrete cases which presented themselves for discussion and settlement were chiefly suggested by the policy of discoverers, colonizers and traders. The reaction against vague claims of ineffective accusations by the Portuguese and the Spaniards, the disputes as to the assertion of sovereignty in narrow seas and territorial waters exercised the civil law learning of Dutch and English jurists and led up to the formulation of views which have been found useful in such events as the Berlin conference of 1885 on the attribution of possessions and of spheres of influence in Africa.

The weak side of public international law — the absence of compulsory sanctions was, of course, evident from the first, and could not be removed by a jurisprudence which had renounced the conception of a theocratic Super-State and pinned its faith to the idea of territorial sovereignty. As has been said already, it was bound to recognize war as the natural outcome of self-help and its civilising influence was directed towards preventing wanton atrocities and mitigating inevitable horrors. How little could be attempted at this stage by the best international jurists may be gathered from the admission of Grotius.[1] In strict law a belligerent was entitled to slaughter the inhabitants of an enemy country, even women and children, and the only restriction to the exercize of this "right" was to be sought in pity and in mercy, not in law.

Such statements were the outcome of a consistent application of the view that a sovereign state is judge of its own case and is not subject to any legal superior. But how was this to be reconciled in practice with the teaching as to natural justice? If the recognition of such justice was to be a mainstay of international jurisprudence, some attempt had to be made to remove the opposition between justice as law and justice as a principle of morals.

vivere, Alterum non laedere, Suum cuique tribuere, Liberos tueri, Injuriam propulsare, Cum omnibus hominibus cognationem agnoscere, Commercia retinere . . .? Isthaec juris gentium sunt, et juris bellici.

[1] Grotius, *de jure belli et pacis*, III, c. 4, §§ 8, 9 (Whewell, III, p. 80.)

VI. MODERN DEVELOPMENTS.

One of the least contestable generalizations as regards the history of human institutions seems to be that any political principle which governs them tends to push its consequences into extremes and to manifest sooner or later certain harmful tendencies. Aristotle in his teaching on the *via media* as the path to virtue and success, Hegel in his doctrine on the dialectical sequence of position, opposition and composition have drawn attention to various aspects of this law of evolution. An excellent example of its operation in actual life may be supplied by the history of the territorial state. Based on the fundamental idea of sovereignty for the sake of peace it has proved in practice the most powerful agent for establishing sovereignty by international wars. La Bruyère in his famous "Characters" composed in the reign of Louis XIV, reflected sarcastically on the absurdities of civilisation as manifested in these conflicts. [1]

"If you were told that all the cats of a certain country had assembled in thousands in a plain and after having miauwed to their hearts' content, had attacked each other with rage, with

[1] LA BRUYÈRE, "Caractères", ed. par CH. LOUANDRE, Paris, 1862, p. 316 ("Des jugements").

... "Que si l'on vous disoit que tous les chats d'un grand pays se sont assemblés par milliers dans une plaine, et qu'après avoir miaulé tout leur soûl, ils se sont jetés avec fureur les uns sur les autres et ont joué ensemble de la dent et de la griffe; que de cette melée il est demeuré de part et d'autre neuf mille chats sur place qui ont infecté l'air à dix lieues de là par leur puanteur, ne diriez vous pas: Voila le plus abominable sabbat dont on ait jamais ouï parler. Et si les loups en faisoient de même, quels hurlements, quelle boucherie!

... Mais, comme vous devenez d'année et d'autre plus raisonnable, vous avez bien enchéri sur cette vielle manière de vous exterminer: vous avez des petits globes qui vous tuent tout d'un coup, s'ils peuvent seulement vous atteindre à la tête ou à la poitrine; vous en avez d'autres plus pesants et plus massifs, qui vous coupent en deux parts ou qui vous éventrent, sans compter ceux qui, tombant sur vos toits, enfoncent les planchers, vont du grenier à la cave, en enlèvent les voûtes et font sauter en l'air avec vos maisons vos femmes qui sont en couche, l'enfant et la nourrice.

tooth and nail, and that as a result of this struggle nine thousand cats were left dead on the field, infecting the air with the stench of their rotting bodies ten miles around, would you not say: this is the most abominable rumpus that has ever been heard of...

But as you are growing more clever every year, you have introduced great improvements upon this mode of exterminating one another. You possess little balls which kill one outright if they hit head or chest. You have also larger and heavier balls which cut one in two or dismember one, not to mention the fact that in falling on the roof of a house they crash through floors from garret to cellar, break up vaults and hurl into the air together with the houses your wives in childbed and your babies".

In our time we might supplement this ironical picture by much more bitter observations. What we are concerned in, however, is to trace the spiritual reaction against these terrible evils connected with the unlimited freedom of action of territorial sovereigns. After each flood of blood and destruction which marked a stage of European history some attempt was made to find a remedy against the recurrence of the disaster. At the close of the religious wars of the XVI century, the Protestant King who had consented to attend mass in order to pacify France is said to have discussed a magnificent proposal for the establishment of peace in Europe. The fatal drawback of such a plan was that it hinged on the dismemberment of the overwhelming power of the Hapsburgs of Spain and of the Empire, and even Henry IV himself does not seem to have been by any means prepared to renounce territorial acquisitions. [1]

The Thirty Years war culminating in the peace of Westphalia produced as one of its consequences the monumental work of your great Hugo Grotius, a work in which the recourse to international arbitration was clearly indicated as the chief means for preventing international wars.[2]

The close of the reign of the "Great King", Louis XIV, with the misery brought on his country by the succession of his wars

[1] The narrative as to the conversations between the King and his chief adviser, Sully, was probably put together at a much later date and cannot be regarded as a piece of accurate evidence, but I cannot believe that it was a downright invention.

[2] De Saint Pierre, "A project for settling an everlasting peace in Europe", London, 1714, has for Motto on his title page a quotation from "Grotius' *De Jure belli et pacis*" Lib. II, c. 23. "Et tum ob hanc, tum ob alias causas utile esset, immo quodammodo factu necessarium, conventus quosdam haberi Christianarum Potestatum, ubi, per eos quorum res non interest, aliorum controversiae definiantur immo..... rationes ineantur cogendi partes ut aequis legibus pacem accipiant".

60

with the Empire, England and the Netherlands, has been depicted in vivid colours by one of his most brilliant military chiefs, Marshal Vauban. These wars produced a pacifist manifestation in the memoir of the Abbé de Saint Pierre published in French in 1713, and in English in 1714, just before the peace of Utrecht. The author, the Abbé de St. Pierre, had not only observed the terrible effects of the warlike career of Louis XIV as a spectator; he had been engaged in a minor office in the elaboration of the treaty of Utrecht. He was animated by a fanatical conviction which made him blind to all considerations except those connected with the ideal of pacification. He pronounced a characteristic anathema in regard to all the useless blandishments of science, literature and art, which reminds us of Tolstoy's pronouncements: Colbert lui-même n'échappe pas à ces critiques pour avoir créé l'Académie des Beaux-Arts. A quoi servent la peinture, la sculpture, la musique, la Poésie, la comédie, l'architecture? A prouver le nombre des fainéants, leur goût pour la fainéantise qui suffit à entretenir et à nourrir d'autres espèces de fainéants qui ce piquent d'esprit agréable, mais non pas d'esprit utile; qui veulent exceller sur leurs pareils et se contentent seulement d'exceller dans les bagatelles. Aussi, "Colbert, grand travailleur, en négligeant les compagnies de commerce maritime pour avoir plus de soin des sciences curieuses et des beaux-arts, n'a pas fait autre chose que de prendre l'ombre pour le corps. Il donna l'ombre aux Français et laissa le corps aux Hollandais et aux Anglais" [1].

The futility of military conflicts and of the attempts to establish a balance of power between the competing States is strongly insisted upon.

The only means to eseape from ever recurring and fruitless bloodshed is to agree on a League of Peace between the leading Christian powers and to negotiate agreements even with heathen States like Turkey. The League is to consist eventually of twenty-four allied states or groups of minor states, each of the members having one vote in the Senate of the Confederation. International conflicts, instead of being fought out by war, should be submitted to the League for compulsory arbitration. All the members should contribute to form a coalition Army for carrying out the decisions of the Union in case of resistance or infringement by any party. While contributions in money should be assessed in

[1] J. Drouet, *Annales politiques*, (1912). Introd. p. xvii.

proportion to the financial means of the various countries, each of the members should send an equal contingent to the common army. The weaker countries should complete the deficiencies in the numbers of their soldiers by mercenary levies salaried with the help of the more wealthy and powerful States. The acknowledged model for this system was found by St. Pierre in the military and fiscal organization of the old German Empire: what was possible in that case seemed to the pacifist writer likely to prove effective in the case of the Christian world.

A characteristic feature of the project consisted in the fact that it aimed exclusively at establishing a permanent *status quo* in home and foreign affairs. The monarchical and republican institutions have each their advantages and their drawbacks.

De Saint Pierre[1] writes:

. . . The Monarchick State has one Advantage, namely that in thirty years it may reach a Degree of perfection in its establishments, which a Republick cannot reach in less than a hundred and fifty years, and this proceeds from two Sources; the first, because the Monarch is to have almost all the Honour of a great Enterprize, of a noble Establishment, of a good Government, and this is a great spur to prick him on to act with vigour and Constancy. The second, because the Opinions of the Monarch are never contradicted, neither in the Resolution, nor in the Execution; whereas in Republicks the Honour of an Enterprize is divided among so many Members, that that Spur becomes very weak in each of them; and besides, there, an Opinion, however good or useful it may be, is liable to be contradicted with Authority, either in the Resolution or in the Execution, and that Contradiction stops all its good Effects; but then the Republican State has another Advantage; namely, that when a good Establishment is once formed in it, it is much more durable than in Monarchies.

This being so let every country have and keep its own without change, but not without interference. On the contrary the success of the scheme depends on a pressure to be exerted by the Union not only with the view of stabilizing frontiers and external possessions, but also constitutions and governments. Otherwise disturbances arising within the boundaries of one state are likely to spread to other states and eventually to produce war.

[1] Saint Pierre, "A project for settling an everlasting peace" p. 107.

62

St. Pierre continues: [1]

Article II. The European Society shall not at all concern itself about the Government of any State, unless it be to preserve the Fundamental Form of it, and give speedy and sufficient Assistance to the Princes in Monarchies, and to the Magistrates in Republicks, against any that are Seditious and Rebellious. Thus it will be a Guarantee that the Hereditary Sovereignties shall remain hereditary, according to the Manner and Custom of each Nation; that those that are elective shall remain elective in the Country where Election is usual; that among the Nations where there are Capitulations, or Conventions which are called *Pacta Conventa*, those sorts of Treaties shall be exactly observed, and that those who in Monarchies should have taken up Arms against the Prince, or in Republicks against some of the chief Magistrates, shall be punished with Death, and Confiscation of Goods.

Explication. The principal Effect of the Union is to preserve all things in Repose in the Condition it finds them in, and as they are the Sovereigns themselves, who, by their Deputies, decide all things in it, they cannot fear that Assembly, any more than each Sovereign can fear himself.

I know it is impossible, especially in Republicks, but that there should be Disputes about Religion, and that as Men never dispute but upon obscure Matters, uncapable of Demonstration, it is impossible to reconcile the two Disputants: But it is possible, it is even easy, for the Magistrates to hinder those Disputes from getting such a Head as to disturb the Tranquillity of the State. It is enough at first to impose Silence upon All, and either to banish or imprison those who shall either have spoken, or preached, or written, or printed since the Prohibition. Time discovers the Truth; therefore all that is to be done, till she shews herself clearly to us, is to keep the Subjects from Divisions and from the other Evils that Obscurity may cause to them; and this is what the Prudence and Authority of the Union will always infallibly do in every State of Europe. To keep up the Society, it is not absolutely necessary that the Citizens be of the same Opinion in obscure Matters; nay it is so far from being in their Power, that Uniformity of Opinion upon such Occasions is as it were impossible: But the only Foundation of the Society, is

[1] *Op. cit.* p. 108.

63

Peace among the Citizens. Thus 'tis requisite that each Citizen, in order to preserve the Society, uses Charity and Indulgence even towards those whom he thinks in an Error. This is what is always not only in the Power of the Citizen, but 'tis also the first and most indispensable of his Duties.

Article III. The Union shall employ its whole Strength and Care to hinder, during the Regencies, the Minorities, the weak Reigns of each State, any Prejudice from being done to the Sovereign, either in his Person, or in his Prerogatives, neither by his Subjects, nor by Strangers; and if any Sedition, Revolt, Conspiracy, Suspicion of Poyson, or any other Violence should happen to the Prince, or the Royal Family, the Union, as its Guardian and Protectress born, should send Commissioners into that State, to look into the Truth of the Facts, and shall at the same time send Troops to punish the Guilty according to the Rigour of the Laws.

Explication. It is certain this Article will be punctually executed, since the United Princes will want neither *Power* nor *Will* to do it. As to *Power*, the thing is evident; as to the *Will*, it is no less evident, since they have no greater Interest than to search as carefully as possible into the Crimes which have destroyed so many Princes, and ruined so many Sovereign Houses, Crimes which so nearly concern them, and to punish the Guilty with all the Severity imaginable, in order to save their own Families, by those exemplary Punishments, from the like Misfortunes."

It is easy to discover the reason of this insistence of St. Pierre on the suppression of internal discord: memories of the international struggles between Protestant and Catholic movements originated in one or the other country and spreading to neighbouring states was still vivid in the minds of all publicists.

The practical impossibility of obtaining such a *perpetuum immobile* and its deathlike aspect did not deter our writer. The difficulty of formulating decisions in a congress of disparate states was realized by him to some extent, but he thought that it could be overcome by the requirement of a three-fourths majority for important decisions and the requirement of unanimity in case of alterations of the fundamental articles of the pact.

64

The project of St. Pierre was inspired by the sight of the misery and destruction, and although there is a good deal of idealism in the views of their originator as to the aims and organisation of the league of states, he reckoned to some extent with actual politics, and put faith on positive combinations of data which would result in international equilibrium and international arbitration. The XVIII century, the age of enlightenment, was bound to take up the problem from another point of view. It came to despair of practical statesmanship, of legal tradition, of constituted powers: in its reaction against feudal survivals and arbitrary kingship it turned to philosophic deductions. In the light of reason politics and law assumed a new aspect and appeared ripe for complete reconstruction. International relations presented a particularly fruitful field for exercize of critical reason. All the great teachers of law of that period recognized a "Law of nature," and constructed systems for its application. The end of the century witnessed a titanic attempt to put these theories into practice. Speculations as to permanent peace were especially appropriate in time of universal war. I should like to call your attention to the most remarkable of these speculations — to Kant's treatment of the problem of international peace.

His Law of Nature (Naturrecht) is governed by the central conception established by the *Criticism of Practical Reason* (praktischen Vernunft) — the categorical imperative. Man is essentially free and therefore he recognizes only the dictates of a law of freedom. This means that he ought himself to submit to rules which he is willing to extend to others and to proclaim as universal laws. All reasonable law is reciprocal and it requires the virtual and potential consent of free citizens in order to make it just. This is the justification of a social compact based on reason.

"This agreement, called *contractus originarius* or *pactum sociale*, consisting in the joining of all separate and private wills into one people for the sake of a strictly legal legislation, need not have taken place as a fact. Indeed it is impossible to conceive of it as a fact as if it were necessary to produce historical proofs that a nation whose rights and obligations we have inherited has in reality fulfilled such an Act and must have left oral or written evidence of this in order to be bound by a civil constitution. It is only an Idea of the mind, which carries with it an undoubted practical consequence, namely that it obliges every legislator to

65

make such laws as would arise from the exertion of the will of the whole people, each subject of which, who wishes to be a citizen, should be considered as if he had personally taken part in voting the law. This is the touchstone for the legality of every law: Should the latter be of such a kind that the whole people could not possibly approve of it (e. g. if it were decreed that a particular class should rule permanently by inheritance), such a law would not be just. On the other hand if there is a bare possibility that a people might approve of a certain law, even if it were probable that in case the law were submitted actually for the decision of the people it would not be passed by them at a given moment, it would nevertheless be a duty to uphold such a law. [1]

The state itself is the result of concert, of a social contract between free individuals in which they give up their isolated and unlimited will in order to aequire a guarantee of their freedom on the basis of law. "It would be wrong to say that in the State man has sacrificed part of his inborn external freedom to attain a certain aim. He has in truth given up his wild, lawless freedom entirely for the sake of a lawful dependence, that is in order to resume an undiminished freedom again in

[1] IMMANUEL KANT's *Sammtliche Werke*, herausgegeben von C. HARTENSTEIN, Leipzig, 1867, v. IV, p. 329.

... Allein dieser Vertrag, (contractus originarius oder pactum sociale genannt), als Coalition jedes besondern und Privatwillens in einem Volk zu einem gemeinschaftlichen und öffentlichen Willen (zum Behuf einer blos rechtlichen Gesetzgeburg) ist keineswegs als ein Factum vorauszusetzen nöthig, (ja als ein solches gar nicht möglich); gleichsam als ob allererst aus der Geschichte vorher bewiesen werden müsste, das ein Volk, in dessen Rechte und Verbindlichkeiten wir als Nachkommen getreten sind einmal wirklich einen solchen Actus verrichtet und eine sichere Nachricht oder ein Instrument davon uns mündlich oder schriftlich hinterlassen haben müsse, um sich an eine schon bestehende bürgerliche Verfassung für gebunden zu achten. Sondern es ist eine blosse Idee der Vernunft, die aber ihre unbezweifelte (praktische) Realität hat: nämlich jeden Gesetzgeber zu verbinden, dass er seine Gesetze so gebe, als sie aus dem vereinigten Willen eines ganzen Volks haben entspringen können, und jeden Unterthan, sofern er Bürger sein will, so anzusehen, als ob zu einem solchen Willen mit zusammengestimmt habe. Denn das ist der Probierstein der Rechtmässigkeit eines jeden öffentlichen Gesetzes. Ist nämlich dieses so beschaffen, dass ein ganzes Volk unmöglich dazu seine Einstimmung geben könnte, (wie z. B. dass eine gewisse Klasse von Unterthanen erblich den Verzug des Herrenstandes haben sollten), so ist es nicht gerecht; ist es aber nur möglich, dass ein Volk dazu zusammenstimme, so ist es Pflicht, das Gesetz für gerecht zu halten, gesetzt auch, dass das Volk jetzt in einer solchen Lage oder Stimmung seiner Denkungsart wäre, dass es, wenn es darum befragt wurde, wahrscheinlicher Weise seine Bestimmung verweigern würde.

66

a state of law, because such dependence arises out of his own legislative will [1]."

In this way Kant, following Rousseau, starts from individualistic premises to arrive at the idea of an omnipotent, absolute state.

The fatal contradiction which is so clearly traceable in the legal system of the Roman Empire with its contrast between the absolutism of the sovereign and the free intercourse between individuals and which recurred in the theories of the XVII century, asserts itself again with irresistible force. (Cf. E. Caird, *The critical philosophy of Immanuel Kant*, II).

Kant was aware of the dilemma and sought to temper it by having recourse to Montesquieu's views on the separation of powers which had obtained increased authority through their adoption by the Constitution of the United States of America. He pleads for a representative Republic as the ideal form of government in which the legislative and the executive powers are separated and yet combined as a major and minor premises are distinct and combined in a syllogism.

It is curious to find the official Professor of Philosophy of the East Prussian University of Königsberg publicly avowing his predilection for a Republican form of government and following closely in his views of the State the apostle of the French Jacobinism, Rousseau. It is even more significant that Kant finds in a Republican reconstruction of the world the clue to the solution of the international problem. It is evident for him, to begin with, that in reasoning on relations between states we have to proceed from the fundamental assumptions that states are juridical persons in a state of nature as regards each other.

"As the state of nature between nations, as well as between single men should be abandoned eventually for the sake of a legal state, therefore all rights of nations anterior to that change, as well as all distinctions between mine and thine, can only be provisional and it is only in a League of States, under the régime of a national State, that they can assume a peremptory character and result in a real peace. As, however, a great extension of such a State of Nations, spreading over wide territories comes

[1] KANT, H. ed.. VII, p. 134.

...man kann nicht sagen: der Mensch im Staate habe einem Theil seiner Angebornen äusseren Freiheit einem Zwecke aufgeopfert, sondern er hat die wilde gesetzlose Freiheit gänzlich verlassen, um seine Freiheit überhaupt in einer gesetzlichen Abhängigkeit, d. i. in einem rechtlichen Zustande unvermindert wieder zu finden: weil diese Abhängigkeit aus seinem eigenen gesetzgebenden Willen entspringt.

67

into existence, its government and the defence of its members is bound to become impossible; the existence side by side of many such bodies would produce a state of war. Thus permanent peace, the highest aim of international law appears indeed as an idea *incapable* of realisation. But the political principles directed towards associations of States approximating gradually and consistently to this aim are not impossible to realize[1]."

This being so, a radical reform of international intercourse could be achieved only by the substitution of a world state for the present anarchical condition in the same way as the territorial state was substituted for the state of disorderly conflicts between individuals.

Kant admits that the institution of the World Commonwealth is not practicable at present and that it would meet with many difficulties in any case, but this does not prevent him from considering it as an ideal aim towards which international relations should be steered. If a cosmopolitan Commonwealth is not possible now, a League of States is already within the domain of possibility.

And here we come again across an expression of confidence in regard to the educational influence of the Republican form of government.

"The putting into practice (objective realisation) of this idea of Feudalism which should extend over all States and lead to permanent peace can be made apparent. If by good luck a powerful and enlightened nation is able to constitute itself into a Commonwealth, which by its nature is bound to tend towards permanent peace, it will became a centre for the federal union of other States, so that they will join it and thus safeguard the

[1] KANT, H. ed., VII, p. 168.

... Da der Naturzustand der Völker ebensowohl, als einzelner Menschen, ein Zustand ist, aus dem man herausgehen soll, um in einen gesetzlichen zutreten, so ist vor diesem Ereigniss alles Recht der Völker und alles durch den Krieg erwerbliche oder erhaltbare äussere Mein und Dein der Staaten bloss provisorisch, und kann nur in einem allgemeinen Staatenverein (analogisch mit dem, wodurch ein Volk Staat wird), peremtorisch geltend und ein wahrer Friedenzustand werden. Weil aber, bei gar zu grosser Ausdehnung eines solchen Völkerstaats über weite Landstriche, die Regierung desselben, mithin auch die Beschützung eines jeden Gliedes endlich unmöglich werden muss; eine Menge solcher Corporationen aber wiederum einen Kriegzustand herbeiführt; so ist des ewige Friede, (das letzte Ziel des ganzen Völkerrechts), freilich eine unausführbare Idee. Die politischen Grundsätze aber, die darauf abzwecken, nämlich solche Verbindungen der Staaten einzugehen, als zur continuirlichen Annäherung zu demselben dienen, sind es nicht, sondern, so wie diese eine auf der Pflicht, mithin auch auf dem Rechte der Menschen und Staaten gegrundete Aufgabe ist, allerdings ausführbar.

68

freedom of States in accordance with the idea of international aw. Such a federation will gradually extend further and further by means of connections of various kinds".[1]

It is curious to find that by drawing consequences from his theoretical constructions Kant formulated a number of concrete points which have been taken up recently by the League of Nations movement.

... These preliminary articles prescribe that no treaty of peace shall be made with the secret reservation of causes of quarrel, which might furnish material for another war, that no state shall be treated as the patrimony of an individual, or transferred from hand to hand by inheritance or gift; that no public debts shall be contracted with a view of war, or in preparation for it; that no State shall interfere with the constitution or administration of another; that no State shall use in war such means of injuring the enemy as must make impossible that reciprocal trust which is necessary for peaceful relations in the future, and that on this ground all recourse to the weapons of assassination and poisoning shall be proscribed, and at the same time, all breaches of capitulation or attempts to make use of treachery among the enemy. For such means of war, as they destroy all that trust in the enemy, which is based on our common humanity, and which ought to subsist even in war, tend to produce a war of extermination, which could bring about a lasting peace only in the "great churchyard of the human race".[2]

I venture to think that the facts reviewed in these lectures suggest some conclusions in theory as well as in practice. It seems clear that the contents of political and legal evolutions cannot be brought under the rule of universal abstract formulas: the relations between Law and the State, between com-

[1] KANT, H. ed., VI, 423.

... Die Ausführbarkeit (objective Realität) dieser Idee der Föderalität die sich allmählig über alle Staaten erstrecken soll, und so zum ewigen Frieden hinführt lässt sich darstellen. Denn wenn das Glück es sofügt, dass ein mächtiges und aufgeklärtes Volk sich zu einer Republik, (die ihrer Natur nach zum ewigen Frieden geneigt sein muss), bilden kann, so gibt diese einen Mittelpunkt der föderativen Vereinigung für ander Staaten ab, um sich an sie anzuschliessen, und so den Freiheitzustand der Staaten, gemäss der Idee des Völkerrechts, zu sichern und sich durch mehrere Verbindungen dieser Art nach und nach immer weiter auszubreiten.

[2] EDWARD CAIRD, "The critical philosophy of Immanuel Kant", Glasgow, 1889. v. II, p. 348.

munities and their members vary greatly in the course of history and have to be estimated by different standards. The only two universal and permanently fixed points in this respect are the individual as a given real being and society as a necessary real relation. The problem which every age has to solve is to find the appropriate combinations between the two. The range of actual combination is, however, not the haphazard sequence of a cinematograph impression. We have been able to mark certain definite formulas which have governed particular epochs. We have noticed the regulations of intercourse between the many cities of Greece under a system of conflict of Laws and its decay, as a consequence of the narrow basis of civic privilege on which it was built up. The Roman Imperial system was noticed as an attempt to guarantee freedom of contract and of trade by the unification of political authority. Mediaeval theocracy transferred the centre of the World State from the secular Empire to the Church as a mediator between heaven and earth. Modern history starts from a revolt of individual conscience and individual right against the *Civitas Dei* in its terrestrial aspect. Modern society succeeded in suppressing civil strife and ensuring freedom of contract by the agency of sovereign territorial States, but success in this direction was coupled with orgies of external wars which threaten the existence of civilisation. And so men are again anxiously seeking for a way out of a blind alley. It is evident that there is nothing in the essence of political union to bar the way towards a new conception of the State, wider and more just that that of absolute territorial sovereignty. Theoretically sovereignty is nothing else but finality of decision in case of conflict. It is required under all circumstances, because otherwise disputes will have to be settled by brute force. But it can be as well attached to a tribunal of umpires as to a territorial government. When parties play a game they submit to rules, though they do not submit to each other. In the conduct of a complicated game, like cricket, submission to an umpire may be needed, although the umpire is certainly not regarded as a king. Theoretically the road to settlement by a tribunal of international umpires is open. Practically it is obstructed by the strength and bitterness of national, political, class selfishness. It is only by education and painful object lessons that mankind is learning to prefer peaceful arbitration to the trials of strength in war. Kant was right in appealing to the moral duty of every free man to help in this gradual educational approach towards peace. But in order to achieve results we must be particularly careful not to overstrain our forces, nor to demand from our generation what it is not prepared to yield. Neither the World State nor a Federation with commanding power in political disputes is of our time or within sight.

But apart from international conferences for settling disputes by consultation and compromise the jurisdiction of an international court of Justice for the decision of juridical conflicts is beginning to take shape. It is our duty to work for its success.

[14]

"International Law"

International law (*ius gentium, droit des gens, Völkerrecht*) is usually defined as the totality of norms regulating the relationships between states. Here is a typical definition: "International law is the totality of norms defining the rights and duties of states in their mutual relations with one another".[4] We find the same definition in the

Germans Hareis, Holtsendorf, Bulmering, Liszt and Ulman; in the Belgian Rivie; in the Englishmen Westlake and Oppenheim; in the American Lawrence etc.

But absent from this formal, technical definition, of course, is any indication of the historical, i.e. the class character of international law. It is extremely clear that bourgeois jurisprudence consciously or unconsciously strives to conceal this element of class. The historical examples adduced in any textbook of international law loudly proclaim that *modern international law is the legal form of the struggle of the capitalist states among themselves for domination over the rest of the world.* However, bourgeois jurists try, as much as possible, to silence this basic fact of intensified competitive struggle, and to affirm that the task of international law is "to make possible for each state what none could do in isolation, by means of co-operation between many states".[5]

Nor did the theorists of the Second International move far from these bourgeois jurists. Abandoning the class conception of the state, they were naturally compelled to discover in international law an instrument, standing outside and above classes, for the co-ordination of the interests of individual states and for the achievement of peace.

It was from this perspective that the well-known Bernstein,[6] and the equally-famous Renner,[7] approached international law. With great assiduity, both of these gentlemen stressed the "peaceful functions of international law", but in so doing they forgot that the better part of its norms refer to naval and land warfare, i.e. that it directly assumes a condition of open and armed struggle. But even the remaining part contains a significant share of norms and institutions which, although they refer to a condition of peace, in fact regulate the same struggle, albeit in another concealed form. Every struggle, including the struggle between imperialist states, must include an exchange as one of its components. And if exchanges are concluded then forms must also exist for their conclusion.

But the presence of these forms does not of course alter the real historical content hidden behind them. At a given stage of social development this content remains the struggle of capitalist states among themselves. Under the conditions of this struggle, every exchange is the continuation of one armed conflict and the prelude to the next. Here lies the basic trait of imperialism.

> Capitalists [wrote Lenin] divide the world, not out of any particular malice, but because the degree of concentration which

> has been reached forces them to adopt this method in order to receive profit. And they divide it "in proportion to capital", "in proportion to strength", because there cannot be any other method of division under commodity production and capitalism. But strength varies with the level of economic and political development. In order to know what is taking place, it is necessary to know what questions are decided by the changes in strength. The question of whether these changes are "purely" economic or *extra*-economic (military, for example) is secondary . . . To substitute the question of the *content* of the struggle and agreements (today peaceful, tomorrow warlike, the next day peaceful again), is to descend to sophistry.[8]

When Renner depicts the development of international law as the growth of institutions which ensure the general interest of all states, and when he tries to show that this development has been retarded by the larcenous and selfish policy of only one of the states, Great Britain, then he too descends to sophistry. He must, moreover, be in the service of Austro-German imperialism (Renner's book was published before the Central Powers were defeated by the *Entente*). Conversely, we can see that even those agreements between capitalist states which appear to be directed to the general interest are, in fact, for each of the participants a means for jealously protecting their particular interests, preventing the expansion of their rivals' influence, thwarting unilateral conquest, i.e. in another form continuing the same struggle which will exist for as long as capitalist competition exists. One may instantiate any international organization, even the international commissions for the supervision of navigation on the erstwhile "treaty rivers" (the Rhine, the Danube, and after Versailles, the Elbe and the Oder). Let us begin with the fact that the very composition of these commissions perfectly reflects specific relations of forces, and is usually the result of war. After the World War, therefore, Germany and Russia were ousted from the European Commission on the Danube. At the same time the Commission on the Rhine was transferred to Strasbourg and fell into French hands. Under the Treaty of Versailles, the very transformation of German rivers into treaty rivers, which were controlled by international commissions, was an act which divided the spoils among the victors. The International Administration of Tangiers, a port in Morocco where the interests of France, England and Spain intersect, is the same type of organization for joint exploitation and supervision. A final and typical example is the International Organization for the Extortion of Reparations from Germany (q.v.): the reparation commission and all types of supervisory agencies envisioned by the expert's plan. As soon as some power feels strong enough to take the plunder into its exclusive possession, it starts to combat internationalization (q.v.). Thus, at the 1883 London Conference, Tsarist Russia succeeded in placing the Kiliisky branch of the Danube outside the control of the European Commission provided for by the international treaty of 1889. The Commission for the Supervision of the Neutralization of the Suez Canal could not be constituted at all: it was eliminated by a separate agreement between England and France, whereby the first bought itself freedom of action in Egypt in exchange for the latter's taking of Morocco (English-French Convention of April 8th, 1904). The struggle among imperialist states for domination of the rest of the world is thus a basic factor in defining the nature and fate of the corresponding international organizations.

There remain the comparatively few and narrowly-specialized interstate agreements. These have a technical character and correspond to purposeful combines or so-called international administrative unions, for example the International Postal Union. These organizations do not serve primarily as an arena for the struggle between administrative groupings, but they occupy a secondary and subordinate position. The origin of most of these organizations was in the 1870s and 1880s, i.e. in the period when capitalism (q.v.) had still not fully developed its monopoly and imperialist traits. The intensified struggle for the division of the world has moved forward to such an extent since that time, that the actual ability of capitalist states to serve general economic and cultural needs has diminished rather than expanded. In this respect a very clear regression was marked by the World War in that it caused the downfall of a whole series of cultural (in particular) and, for example, scientific links.

The bourgeois jurists are not entirely mistaken, however, in considering international law as a function of some ideal cultural community which mutually connects individual states. But they do not see, or do not want to see, that this community reflects (conditionally and relatively, of course) the common interests of the commanding and ruling classes of different states which have identical class structures. The spread and development of international law occurred on the basis of the spread and development of the capitalist mode of production. However, in the feudal period the knights of every European country had their codes of military honour and, accordingly, their class law, which they applied in wars with one another; but they did not apply them in inter-class wars, for example in the suppression of burghers and the peasantry. The victory of the bourgeoisie, in all the European countries, had to lead to the establishment of new rules and new institutions of international law which protected the general and basic interests of the bourgeoisie, i.e. bourgeois property. Here is the key to the modern law of war.

While in feudal Europe the class structure was reflected in the religious notion of a community of all Christians, the capitalist world created its concept of "civilization" for the same purposes. The division of states into civilized and "semi-civilized", integrated and "semi-integrated" to the international community, explicitly reveals the second peculiarity of modern international law as the class law of the bourgeoisie. It appears to us as the totality of forms which the capitalist, bourgeois states apply in their relations with each other, while the remainder of the world is considered as a simple object of their completed transactions. Liszt, for example, teaches that "the struggle with states and peoples who are outside the international community must not be judged according to the law of war, but according to the bases of the love for mankind and Christianity". To assess the piquancy of this assertion recall that, at the time of the colonial wars, the representatives of these lofty principles, e.g. the French in Madagascar and the Germans in Southwest Africa, liquidated the local population without regard for age and sex.

The real historical content of international law, therefore, is the struggle between capitalist states. International law owes its existence to the fact that the bourgeoisie exercises its domination over the proletariat and over the colonial countries. The latter are organized into a number of separate state-political trusts in competition with one another. With the emergence of Soviet states in the historical arena, international law assumes a different significance. It becomes the form of a temporary compromise between two antagonistic class systems. This compromise is effected for that period when one system (the bourgeois) is *already* unable to ensure its exclusive domination, and the other (proletarian and socialist) has not *yet* won it. It is in this sense that it seems possible, to us, to speak of international law in the transitional period. The significance of this transitional period consists in the fact that open struggle for destruction (intervention, blockade, non-recognition) is replaced by struggle within the limits of normal diplomatic relations and contractual exchange. International law becomes *inter-class* law, and its adaptation to this new function inevitably occurs in the form of a series of conflicts and crises. The concept of international law during the transitional period was first put forth, in Soviet literature, by E. Korovin.[9]

Finally, international law assumes an entirely different meaning as the inter-state law of the Soviet states. It now ceases to be a form of temporary compromise behind which an intensified struggle for existence is hidden. Because of this the very opposition between international law and the state, so characteristic of the preceding period, disappears. The proletarian states, not having merged formally into one federation or union, must present in their mutual relationships an image of such a close economic, political and military unity, that the measure of "modern" international law becomes inapplicable to them.

Turning now to consider the legal form of international law, we will first note that orthodox theory considers the subject of international legal relations to be the state as a whole, and only the state. "Only states are subjects of international law, the bearers of international legal obligations and powers."[10] The real historical premise for this viewpoint is the formation of a system of independent states which have, within their boundaries, a sufficiently strong central power to enable each of them to act as a single whole. "The sovereignty of the state, i.e. its independence from any authority standing above it—this is the basis of international law."[11]

These premises were historically realized in Europe only at the end of the Middle Ages, in the period of the formation of absolute monarchies which consolidated their independence, with respect to Papal authority, and which severed internal resistance by the feudal lords. The economic basis of this was the development of mercantile capital. The emergence of standing armies, the prohibition of private wars, the instigation of state enterprises, customs and colonial policy—these are the real facts which lie at the heart of the theory of the state as the sole subject of the international legal community. The Catholic Church, which had claimed the position of supreme leader of all the Christian states, was delivered a decisive blow by the Reformation. The Treaty of Westphalia, which in 1648 proclaimed the basis of equality between the Catholic and the "heretical" (Protestant) states, is considered the basic fact in the historical development of modern (i.e. bourgeois) international law.

The revolutions of the seventeenth and eighteenth centuries made further strides along the same road. They completed the process of separating state rule from private rule, and transformed political power into a special force and the state into a special subject. The legal relations of the state flowed independently, and they were not to be confused with those persons who at any given moment were the bearers of state authority. Having subordinated itself to the state machine, the bourgeoisie brought the principle of the public nature of authority to its clearest expression. It may be said that the state only fully becomes the subject of international law as the bourgeois state. The victory of the bourgeois perspective over the feudal-patrimonial perspective was expressed, among other things, in the denial of the binding force of dynastic treaties for the state. Thus, in 1790 the National Assembly of France rejected the obligations which flowed from the family treaty of the house of Bourbon (1761), on the grounds that Louis XV had acted as a representative of the dynasty and not as a representative of France.

It is typical that at the same time as French authors (Bonfils, for example) consider this rejection to be proper, German monarcho-reactionary professors (Heffken) find that the National Assembly violated international law in this action.

The Roman Papacy is a curious vestige of the Middle Ages. After the Church entered the constituency of Italy in 1870, the Pope continued extra-territorially to enjoy the right to send and receive ambassadors, i.e. he had certain essential attributes of sovereign authority. When bourgeois jurists are forced to explain a phenomenon which contradicts their doctrine, they usually argue that the Papal throne occupies a quasi-international status and that it is not in the strict sense a subject of international law.

In fact, of course, the influence of the leader of the Catholic Church is no less in international affairs than that of the League of Nations (q.v.). All authors classify the latter as an exception to the independent subjects of international law along with individual states.

As a separate force which set itself off from society, the state only finally emerged in the modern bourgeois capitalist period. But it by no means follows from this that the contemporary forms of international legal intercourse, and the individual institutions of international law, only arose in the most recent times. On the contrary, they trace their history to the most ancient periods of class and even pre-class society. To the extent that exchange was not initially made between individuals, but among tribes and communities, it may be affirmed that the institutions of international law are the most ancient of legal institutions in general. Collisions between tribes, territorial disputes, disputes over borders—and agreements as one of the elements in these disputes—are found in the very earliest stages of human history. The tribal pre-state life of the Iroquois, and of the ancient Germans, saw the conclusion of alliances between tribes. The development of class society and the appearance of state authority make contracts and agreements among authorities possible. The treaty between Pharaoh Rameses II and the King of the Hittites is one of the oldest surviving documents of this type. Other forms of relationships are equally universal: the inviolability of ambassadors; the custom of exchanging hostages; one might also point to the ransoming of prisoners, the neutrality of certain areas, and the right to asylum. All these practices were known and used by the peoples of the distant past. Ancient Rome observed various forms for the declaration of war (*ius fetiale*), concluded treaties, received and sent ambassadors. The ambassadors of foreign countries enjoyed inviolability etc. A special college of herald-priests dealt with these rules in Rome, and the majority of legal rules were protected by the gods at that time. The sanction of religion did not, however, prevent the fact that they were sometimes violated in the grossest manner.

On the other hand, a series of rules were formed which related to international intercourse. These were necessary both for regulating conflicts among tribes and peoples, and also for ensuring commercial exchange between individuals who belonged to different clans and tribes. Later, these rules were extended to include state organizations. In this way so-called private international law developed (q.v.).

For example, during the period when Athens was flourishing, there were no less than 45 000 foreign inhabitants. They enjoyed all civil rights and were protected by a representative elected from their

tion of foreigners thus applied to merchants who were temporary residents. We see the same phenomenon in ancient Rome where the special office of *praetor peregrinus* was instituted for the hearing of foreigners' judicial cases. Moreover, the so-called *actiones fictitiae* aided in overcoming those strict requirements of Roman procedure which gave the foreigner no possibility of defending his rights.

In the understanding of the Roman jurists, the law of nations (*ius gentium*) embraced equally that which is now termed public international law, and also that which is inaccurately termed private international law. Thus, for example, we read in the Digests: "By this law of nations (*ius gentium*), wars are waged, nations are divided, kingdoms are founded, property is distributed, fields are enclosed, buildings are erected, trade, purchases, sales, loans and obligations are established—with the exception of certain transactions that are conducted in civil law."[12] From this list it seems that the essential characteristic of international law was deemed to be not merely that it regulated relations (borders, war, peace etc.) among states but, and in contrast to the *ius civile*, that it established the basis of a legal community devoid of local peculiarities and free from tribal and national colouration. These universal rules could be nothing other than a reflection of the general conditions of exchange transactions, i.e. they were reduced to the bases of the equal rights of owners, the inviolability of ownership and the consequent compensations for damages and freedom of contract. The bond between the *ius gentium*—in the sense of laws inherent in all nations—and norms regulating the mutual relations of states, was consciously strengthened by the first theorist of international law, Hugo Grotius (1583–1684). His whole system depends on the fact that he considers relations between states to be relations between the owners of private property; he declares that the necessary conditions for the execution of exchange, i.e. equivalent exchange between private owners, are the conditions for legal interaction between states. Sovereign states co-exist and are counterposed to one another in exactly the same way as are individual property owners with equal rights. Each state may "freely" dispose of its own property, but it can gain access to another state's property only by means of a contract on the basis of compensation: *do ut des*.

The feudal-patrimonial structure greatly aided the theory of territorial rule in acquiring a clearly civilist hue. Suzerains or

"Landesherren" considered themselves as the owners of those holdings over which their authority extended; the holdings were thought of as their private right, a subject of alienation by the owner. Entering into relations with one another, they disposed of their holdings as owners dispose of their objects, and alienated them according to the system of private (Roman) law. From the very beginning, therefore, many of the institutions of international law had a private law foundation—including the theory of *modi aecuirendi dominii* in international relations. Other methods were also recognized: inheritance, dowry, gift, purchase and sale, exchange, occupation, prescription.

On the basis of natural law doctrine, Grotius's ideas continued to be developed by subsequent theorists: Puffendorf (1632–1694), Tomasius (1655–1728), Wolff (1679–1754), Vattel (1714–1767) and Burlamaki (1694–1748). These theorists laid the foundation for an abstract or philosphical theory of law. In contrast to this school, which had given preference to abstract concepts, there began the collection and systematization of actual international customs and treaties and the study of international practice. The forefather of this positive, historico-pragmatic school is considered to be Zouch (1590–1669), an Oxford professor and Admiralty judge; the Dutchman Binkerskuch (1673–1743), and Martens (1756–1821) were later representatives. The doctrine of natural law ceased to enjoy the recognition of most jurists in the second half of the nineteenth century. However, even in our day Grotius's formulae continue to exist in international law textbooks, under the guise of so-called "basic or absolute rights" of the state. For example, Hareis in *Institutionen des Völkerrechts* (1888), lists four such "basic rights": the right to self-preservation; the right to independence; the right to international exchange; and the right to respect.

We read exactly the same in Liszt: "From this basic idea [international legal intercourse] directly follows a whole series of legal norms, by which are defined the mutual rights and obligations of states and do not require any special treaty recognition in order to have obligatory force.

They comprise a firm (!) basis for all the unwritten legal rules of international law, and are its oldest, most important and holiest content."[13] It is most obvious that we are dealing here with ideas drawn from the sphere of civil law relationships with a basis in equality between the parties.

To a certain degree the analogy may be extended. Bourgeois private law assumes that subjects are formally equal yet simultaneously permits real inequality in property, while bourgeois international law in principle recognizes that states have equal rights yet in reality they are unequal in their significance and their power. For instance, each state is formally free to select the means which it deems necessary to apply in the case of infringements of its right: "however, when a major state lets it be known that it will meet injury with the threat of, or the direct use of force, a small state merely offers passive resistance or is compelled to concede."[14] These dubious benefits of formal equality are not enjoyed at all by those nations which have not developed capitalist civilization and which engage in international intercourse not as subjects, but as objects of the imperialist states' colonial policy.

In civil law transactions, however, the relationships between the parties assume legal form not only because they derive from the logic of objects (from the logic of the exchange act, more accurately), but also because this form finds real support and defence in the apparatus of judicial and state authority. Legal existence is materialized in a special sphere, partitioned off from the intrusion of naked fact. In his language the lawyer expresses this by asserting that every subjective right depends upon an objective norm, and that private legal relationships arose because of the public legal order. Moreover, in international law the subjects of legal relationships are the states themselves as the bearers of sovereign authority. A series of logical contradictions follows from this. For the existence of international law it is necessary that states be sovereign (for sovereignty in any given case is equated with legal capacity). If there are no sovereign states then there are no subjects of the international law relationship, and there is no international law. But, on the other hand, if there are sovereign states, then does this mean that the norms of international law are not legal norms? For in the opposite case, they must possess an external power which constrains the state, i.e. limits its sovereignty. Conclusion: for international law to exist it is necessary that states not be sovereign. Bourgeois jurisprudence has devoted a great amount of fruitless effort in solving this contradiction. For instance, Pruess—the author of the present German (Weimar) Constituion—tended to the position of sacrificing the concept of sovereignty for the sake of international law. Conversely, writers such as Zorn and, most recently, Wendel, are more ready to abandon supra-state international law. However, these dogmatic arguments change nothing in reality. No matter how eloquently the existence of international law is proved, the fact of the absence of an organizational force, which could coerce a state with the same ease as a state coerces an individual person, remains a fact. The only real guarantee that the relationships between bourgeois states (and in the transitional period with states of another class type) will remain on the basis of equivalent exchange, i.e. on a legal basis (on the basis of the mutual recognition of subjects), is the real balance of forces. Within the limits set by a given balance of forces, separate questions may be decided by compromises and by exchange, i.e. on the basis of law. Even then there is the qualification that each government calls upon law when its interests demand it, and in every way will try to avoid fulfilling some norm if it is profitable for it.[15] In critical periods, when the balance of forces has fluctuated seriously, when "vital interests" or even the very existence of a state are on the agenda, the fate of the norms of international law becomes extremely problematic.

This particularly relates to the imperialist period, with its unprecedented intensification of the competitive struggle which derives from the monopolisitic tendencies of finance capital, and from the fact that after the whole globe has already been divided then further expansion can only occur at the expense of robbing one's neighbour.

The best illustration of this is afforded by the last war, of 1914–1918, during which both sides continuously violated international law. With international law in such a lamentable condition, bourgeois jurists can be consoled only with the hope that, however deeply the balance was disturbed, it will nevertheless be re-established: the most violent of wars must sometime be ended with peace, the political passions raised by it must gradually be reconciled, the governments will return to objectivity and compromise, and the norms of international law will once again find their force. However, in addition to this hope the fact is adduced, as an argument in favour of the positive nature of international law, that every state in violating internaional law also tries to depict the matter as if there had been no violation whatsoever. We find in Ulman, for example, this curious reference to state hypocrisy as proof of the positive nature of international law. Another group of jurists simply deny the very existence of international law. Among them is the founder of the English school of positivist jurisprudence, Austin. Defining "law in the proper sense", as an order emanating from a definite authority and strengthened by a threat in the case of disobedience, he finds that international law is *contradictio in adjecto*. "To the extent that it is law, it is not international; to the extent that it is truly international, it is not law." Gumplowicz holds the same opinion: "In a definite sense international law is not law inasmuch as state law also is not law."[16] Lasson says: "The norms of international law are but rules of state wisdom which the state follows having in mind its own welfare, and from which it can deviate as soon as its vital interests so demand."[17]

But the perspective of Austin, Lasson, Gumplowicz and others is not shared by the majority of bourgeois jurists. The open denial of international law is politically unprofitable for the bourgeoisie since it exposes them to the masses and thus hinders preparations for new wars. It is much more profitable for the imperialists to act in the guise of pacifism and as the champions of international law.

Therefore, for example, the English writer Walker[18] censures the terminological cavils of Austin, who did not want to define international law as law in the proper sense, and who exclaims "it is better to permit peace and passivity to reign without correct terminology, than to permit accuracy of language to exist with the spirit of lawlessness!"

Jurists who preach the cult of force in international relations are both useless to the bourgeoisie (it needs not preaching, but real force), and also dangerous because they conceal the irreconcilability of the contradictions of capitalist society, and because they compromise peace and tranquility needed even by a thief when he has had his fill and is digesting his spoils.

From the Marxist perspective this nihilist criticism of international law is in error since, while exposing fetishism in one area, it does so at the cost of consolidating it in others. The precarious, unstable and relative nature of international law is illustrated in comparison with the largely firm, steady and absolute nature of other types of law. In fact, we have here a difference in degree. For only in the imagination of jurists are all the legal relationships within a state dominated one hundred per cent by a single state "will". In fact, a major portion of civil law relationships are exercised under influence of pressures limited to the activities of subjects themselves. Furthermore, only by taking the viewpoint of legal fetishism is it possible to think that the legal form of a relationship changes or destroys its real and material essence. This essence, on the contrary, is always decisive. The formalization of our relationship with bourgeois states, by way of treaties, is part of our foreign policy, and is its continuation in a special form. A treaty obligation is nothing other than a special form of the concretization of economic and political relationships. But once the appropriate degree of concretization is reached, it may then be taken into consideration and, within certain limits, studied as a special subject. The reality of this object is no less than the reality of any constitution—both may be overturned by the intrusion of a revolutionary squall.

It is commonplace to distinguish a general and a special component in relation to the systematization of international law. The first contains the theory of the state as the subject of international law. Here lies the theory of sovereignty, the various forms of limiting sovereignty, the theory of international law and legal capacity etc. Starting from the traditional division of the state into three elements—authority, territory and population—most treatises include within this general component the regulation of territorial questions (borders, territorial waters, methods of territorial acquisition etc.), and population questions (citizenship, preference, etc.). The special component considers the organization and forms of international legal relationships—here lie diplomatic and consular representation, international courts and other international organizations, the theory of international treaties etc. Further conceptual areas are usually delineated as regulatory international legal agreements (transportation, commerce, navigation, post and telegraphy, the battle with epidemics, the protection of property etc.). Finally comes the part dedicated to the law of war. This is usually prefaced with a consideration of the peaceful means of settling conflicts (arbitration decisions). The law of war may be divided into the law of military war, the law of naval warfare and the theory of the rights and obligations of neutral states.

Sources of international law

To the extent that states have no external authority above them which could establish their norms of conduct, then in the technical legal sense the sources of international law are custom and treaty. In

Liszt's opinion both of these sources may be reduced to one—this is the "general legal ideology of states", which is expressed partly in the form of legal practice, and partly in the form of the direct and overt establishment of law by way of agreement. But since (a) it is not always easy to decide which ideology is general and which ideology is "legal", and (b) the practice of the different states at any one time, and the practice of any one state at different times, are far from the same—in fact, therefore, the source of the norms of even customary international law is drawn from the opinions of "writers", or scholars, who usually differ decisively with each other on every question. Common, therefore, are citations to the "majority" or to the "overwhelming" majority of authorities. If one further notes that each of these authorities consciously or unconsciously defends those positions which are or seem beneficial to his own state, then one can imagine how hopeless will be the application of customary international law to the decision of any serious dispute.

The norms of written international law, which are fixed in treaties and agreements, are of course distinguished by comparatively greater precision. But there are rather few such treaties which could establish general rules or, expressed in technical language, which could create objective international law. The most important of these are: the acts of the Congress of Vienna (1815); the Paris Declaration on the Law of Naval Warfare (1856); the Geneva Conventions (1856 and 1906); the General Acts of the Hague Peace Conference (1899 and 1907); the London Declaration on the Law of Naval Warfare (1909); the League of Nations Treaty (1919); and certain declarations of the Washington Conference (1921) etc. However, parts of these treaties were not concluded by all states—just by some of them—and therefore the norms created by these agreements may not, strictly speaking, assume the significance of norms of general international law. There are only particular international laws effective within the circle of states which signed them or which later adhered to them. There are, accordingly, few generally recognized written norms of international law.

Finally, the decisions of international tribunals, arbitration panels and other international organizations are usually adduced as sources of international law. Anglo-Saxon jurists add the judicial practice of national courts, especially so in prize cases and in internal legislation dealing with questions of international significance.

"The Object of Law"

The Object of Law is one of the basic systematic concepts of jurisprudence, and is closely linked with the concept of a legal relationship and a legal subject. "Every real law is a law of some thing." (Korkunov) The object of law, as an abstract and general concept, is not related to any one branch of law. Nevertheless, and in a similar way to the majority of juridic categories, it has the clearest and most specific meaning in civil law and, particularly, in property relationships. It is relatively easy to see what the object of law is in property or the law of mortgage, or inheritance law. But jurists have had great debates concerning the nature of this concept in franchise qualifications, for example, or in citizenship. These difficulties have convinced some of the existence of non-objective law (Becker).

The abstract notion of the object of law was virtually absent for Roman jurists—with their pragmatic and non-philosophical minds. It was replaced by the more concrete category of the "thing" (*res*), and even human slaves were regarded as this. The power of the head of household over his wife and children (*patria potestas*) was closely linked to the law of things according to their formal juridic basis. For a concrete understanding of the object of law, the absence of an abstract notion of subjective law among the Romans fully corresponds with the precise form of action—*actio*. Hence, Roman authors established systematic subunits of persons (*personae*), things (*res*) and actions (*actiones*).

Roman jurists displayed some talent for generalization by subdividing things, as objects of law, into the corporeal (*corporalia*) and the non-corporeal (*incorporalia*). This distinction applied, for example, to the rights of inheritance and the exercise of the right to agricultural produce.

The development of exchange relationships advanced the actions of the responsible person as a special legal concept. The law of things and the law of obligation were combined into the general notion of property.

The doctrine of the object of law assumed an abstract character with the development of the abstract doctrine of subjective law—representing the universal capacities of the *persona*—in the bourgeois jurisprudence of the eighteenth and nineteenth centuries. At this stage in the development of juridic thought, a whole series of problems arose that were difficult to resolve. First, attempts were made to depict objects as so-called public subjective rights; and second, there was a desire to construct a legal system based on the idea of norms (understood as imperatives). But if the basis of law is an imperative and the obligation which arises from that imperative, then, for example, the object of the right of property does not logically represent the thing itself with its specific use and exchange-value, but something negative: the restraining actions of all other people which hinder the owner in the possession, use and disposal of his property.

Such dogmatic formal constructions—juridic categories devoid of economic meaning—are typical of the present time when the dominant role in bourgeois jurisprudence, particularly, in the elaboration of general questions, has passed from the civilists to the publicists.

Notes

1. L. Duguit, *L'état: droit objectif et droit positif* (1901), Paris.
2. L. Duguit, *L'état, les gouvernants et les agents* (1903), Paris; *Les transformations du droit privé* (1912), Paris; *Traité de droit constitutionnel* (1922–1923, 2nd edition), 5 vols.—the first edition was translated into Russian.
3. See A. G. Goikhbarg's introduction to the translation of Duguit's *Transformations*, and various places in his *A Course on the Economic Law of the RSFSR*.
4. H. Bonfils, *Traité de droit international public* (1894), Rousseau, Paris, p. 1.
5. J. Louter, *Le droit international public positif* (1920), Oxford, p. 17.
6. E. Bernstein, *Völkerrecht und Völkerpolitik* (1919).
7. K. Renner, *Marxismus, Krieg und Internationale* (1918), Vienna.
8. V. I. Lenin, *Imperialism, the Highest Stage of Capitalism* (1917), *LCW*, vol. 22, p. 253.
9. E. Korovin, *International Law of the Transitional Period* (1924), Moscow.
10. F. Liszt, *Das Völkerrecht* (1925), Fleischmann, Berlin, sec. 5.
11. Loening, *Die Gerichtsbarkeit über fremde Souveräne* (1903), sec. 83.
12. 1, 5 *Digests*, I, I.

13. F. Liszt, *International Law* (1913), Russian translation from the 6th edition, edited by V. E. Grabar, p. 81.
14. V. E. Grabar, *The Basis of Equality between States in Modern International Law* (1912), Publishing House of the Ministry of Foreign Affairs, book. I.
15. L. Oppenheim, *International Law: A Treatise* (1905), Longmans, Green & Co., vol. I, p. 65.
16. L. Gumplowicz, *Allgemeines Staatsrecht* (1907), sec. 415.
17. G. Lasson, *Prinzip und Zukunft des Völkerrechts* (1871), p. 49.
18. T. A. Walker, *A History of the Law of Nations*, n.d., p. 19.

[15]

Chapter 1 *The International Legal Ideas of the October Revolution and the Making of Contemporary International Law*

The Great October Socialist Revolution, from which commenced the creation of a new socioeconomic entity, affected all aspects of social relations. It also initiated profound changes in international relations and international law.

The socialist state created by the revolution, fundamentally different in its class nature from all states which had existed theretofore, put forward a number of new guiding principles for relations among peoples and states. Symbolically, the first decree of the socialist state was the Decree on Peace. "In the international arena," says the Program of the Communist Party of the Soviet Union, "a state arose for the first time which advanced the slogan of peace and began to implement new principles in relations among peoples and countries. Mankind had found a dependable bulwark in its struggle against annexationist wars, for peace and the security of peoples."[1]

The political and international legal ideas and principles of the October Revolution infused a qualitatively new spirit into international relations and international law. These principles reflected the class nature of the Soviet state; the fundamental principles of the new socialist social system were linked inseparably with the basic tenets of the ideology of the working class. But inasmuch as the working class is the leading fighter for the liberation of all working people, the international legal ideas of the October Revolution reflected the basic expectations and interests of the broad masses of the people. The humanism of these ideas and principles, their internationalism, also is determined by this.[2]

1. *Programma Kommunisticheskoi partii Sovetskogo Soiuza* (Moscow: Politizdat, 1964), p. 12.

2. On the humanism of socialist ideas, see A. F. Shishkin and K. A. Shvarstman, *XX vek i moral'nye tsennosti chelovechestva* (Moscow: izd-vo Mysl', 1968).

[4]
Development of International Law Since the October Socialist Revolution

On the level of their influence upon international law and international relations, the international legal ideas of the October Revolution can be divided into three basic, closely interconnected groups:

(a) principles of socialist internationalism in relations between socialist states;

(b) principles of equality and self-determination of nations and peoples, whose spearhead is aimed against the system of colonialism, as well as against any national oppression and inequality;

(c) principles of peaceful coexistence, aimed first and foremost at relations between states with different social systems.

These ideas and principles of the October Revolution have operated in the direction of creating new international relations and a new international law.

A. The Principles of Socialist Internationalism

The principles of socialist internationalism correspond to the new type of international relations: to relations between socialist states. The bases of these principles were formed by the theory of Marxism-Leninism and by the practice of the workers' movement. These were the principles of the international workers' movement and the principles of relations between nations and peoples.

The guiding principle of the international workers' movement was the principle of proletarian internationalism, which signified the fraternal friendship, close cooperation, and mutual assistance of the working class of various countries in the struggle for their liberation.

The principle of proletarian internationalism emerged as the principle of the workers' movement when the development of capitalism and of the workers' movement itself attained a sufficiently high level. The internationalization of the domination of capital, the intensification of ties among the workers of individual countries, the growth of the consciousness of the unity of purpose and the need for unified efforts of the proletariat of various nations in the struggle for their liberation and for the creation of a new society not knowing exploitation—these are the basic reasons for the emergence of the principle of proletarian internationalism.

In emphasizing the significance of the fraternal solidarity of workers of various countries, Marx wrote in the founding manifesto of the International Association of Workers: "The experience of the past showed that a scornful attitude toward a fraternal alliance, which must exist among the workers of various countries and impel them to stand behind each other

[5]

International Legal Ideas of the October Revolution

firmly in their struggle for liberation, is punished by the general defeat of their uncoordinated efforts."[3]

V. I. Lenin pointed out that since the domination of capital is international, the struggle of workers of different countries for their liberation can be successful only if their efforts are unified. "That is why," said Lenin, "the German worker and the Polish worker and the French worker is a comrade of the Russian worker in the struggle against the capitalist class, just as the Russian, Polish, and French capitalists are his enemy."[4]

The objective laws of societal development of capitalism, the experience of the workers' movement, are reflected in the class consciousness of the proletariat; proletarian internationalism is becoming an inseparable part of working class ideology. The slogan "Proletarians of all countries, unite!" put forward in the Communist Manifesto proclaimed the international character of the struggle of the working class and since has become the immutable motto of every true proletarian movement.

Proletarian internationalism is part of the ideology of the working class. It is an ideology of the fraternity and friendship of workers of all countries and, at the same time, an ideology of the friendship of peoples. Proletarian internationalism reflects not only the interests of the working class, but also the interests of all working people. The working class, as the vanguard class of modern society waging a struggle for the overthrow of capitalism and the creation of a socialist society, acts in the interests of all working people and, together with them, as their allies.

Other principles applied both in the relations of the working class of various countries and its parties and in relations between nations or, depending upon the character of the principles, only to relations between nations, also have been molded together with the principles of proletarian internationalism in the developmental process of the workers' movement.

The principles of proletarian internationalism were embodied in the mutual relations of the Soviet republics formed on the territory of the former Russian Empire after the October Revolution. Under the leadership of the Bolshevist party, the class-conscious workers and peasants and the Soviet governments created in the individual republics strove for unification in order to build socialism together and to defend the gains of the socialist revolution together from the swoops of imperialists. Relations of the new type between the Soviet republics, crowned by the formation

3. *K. Marks, F. Engel's, V. I. Lenin o proletarskom internatsionalizme* (Moscow: Gospolitizdat, 1957), p. 41.

4. Lenin, "Proekt i ob"iasnenie programmy sotsial-demokraticheskoi partii," *ibid.*, pp. 217-218.

[6]
Development of International Law Since the October Socialist Revolution

of the Union of Soviet Socialist Republics, were molded precisely on the basis of the principles of proletarian internationalism.[5]

The principles of socialist internationalism influenced the entire foreign policy of the proletarian state and its international legal position. In every instance the Soviet state acted in the international arena by taking into account the principles of proletarian internationalism. It always took into account its duties with regard to the working class and the oppressed peoples of other countries, at the same time relying upon their support. "In alliance with the revolutionaries of the advanced countries and with all oppressed peoples," wrote V. I. Lenin, "against any and all imperialists—this is the foreign policy of the proletariat."[6]

Revolutions occurred in a number of western European countries under the influence of the October Revolution: revolutions in Germany and in Hungary. And although the periods during which the revolutionary governments existed in these countries were very brief—these revolutions were repressed by imperialism—those principles on which the Soviet state intended to build its relations with them were manifest at once; these were the principles of proletarian internationalism.

Notification of the revolution in Germany was received at the beginning of November 1918. The Soviet government hailed the revolution, and the very next day the VTsIK adopted a decree on sending grain to revolutionary Germany despite the gravely serious grain situation in Russia itself. In the decree of the VTsIK of November 13, 1918, on the annulment of the Treaty of Brest-Litovsk, the Soviet state, pursuant to the principles of proletarian internationalism, proposed to the peoples of Germany and Austria-Hungary to establish not only peaceful relations but an "... alliance of the toiling masses of all nations in their struggle to create and strengthen the socialist system ..."[7] V. I. Lenin's greeting to the Bavarian Soviet Republic, formed in April 1919, was imbued with cordiality and fraternal solidarity.[8]

A revolution took place in Hungary in 1919, and a Hungarian Soviet Republic was formed. The Eighth Congress of the Russian Communist Party of Bolsheviks, convened in March 1919, approved a warm greeting to the Hungarian Soviet Republic drawn up by V. I. Lenin with an

5. For more detail, see O. I. Chistiakov, *Vzaimootnosheniia sovetskikh respublik do obrazovaniia SSSR* (Moscow: Gosiurizdat, 1955); D. L. Zlatopol'skii, *SSSR—federativnoe gosudarstvo* (Moscow: izd-vo MGU, 1967).

6. V. I. Lenin, "Vneshniaia politika russkoi revoliutsii," *Polnoe sobranie sochinenii*, 5th ed. (Moscow: Gospolitizdat, 1962), XXXII, 337. [Published in *Pravda*, June 27(14), 1917.]

7. Ministerstvo inostrannykh del SSSR, *Dokumenty vneshnei politiki SSSR* (Moscow: Gospolitizdat, 1957–), I, 566.

8. See Lenin, "Privetstvie bavarskoi sovetskoi respubliki," *Polnoe sobranie sochinenii*, XXXVIII, 321.

[7]
International Legal Ideas of the October Revolution

assurance that the Russian working class would assist it with all its strength and together with the workers of all countries "shall not permit the imperialists to raise their hands against the new Soviet republic."[9] "In the whole world," V. I. Lenin wrote to the Hungarian workers, "everything that is upright in the working class is on your side."[10]

This support from the first proletarian state in the world met with a warm response in Hungary. The leader of the Hungarian Communist party, Bela Kun, declared on March 23, 1919: "We are pleased and proud that Hungary is the second Soviet republic . . . We express gratitude and send greetings to the Russian Soviet Republic, which unfailingly has rendered assistance to us . . . ."[11] "Relations between Soviet Russia and Soviet Hungary," writes Academician I. I. Mints, "based upon friendship and mutual assistance, were a prototype of the fraternal relations which have been formed now among countries of the socialist commonwealth."[12]

Relations with Mongolia, which began several years after the October Revolution, are a shining example of relations based upon the principles of proletarian internationalism. The people's revolution triumphed in Mongolia with the fraternal assistance of the Soviet Union. The Mongolian People's Republic has achieved great economic and cultural successes and, by-passing the capitalist stage of development, has proceeded to the construction of socialism.

The principles of socialist internationalism were developed further in relations among the countries of the world socialist system. While remaining political principles, at the same time they also are becoming international legal principles, their content is being enriched, and a number of new socialist principles and norms operative in relations among socialist countries are being formed (see Part VII).

B. The Principles of Equality and of Self-Determination of Nations

The principles of equality, self-determination, and sovereignty of nations advanced by the October Revolution possessed enormous potential force. They correctly reflected one of the most important laws of

9. Lenin, "Privetstvennaia radiotelegramma ot imeni s"ezda pravitel'stva vengerskoi sovetskoi respubliki," *ibid.*, p. 186.

10. Lenin, "Privet vengerskim rabochim," *ibid.*, p. 388. [Published in *Pravda*, May 29, 1919.]

11. Bela Kun, "Vengriia—vtoraia sovetskaia respublika; rech' na soveshchanii upolnomochennykh kommunisticheskoi partii," *O Vengerskoi Sovetskoi respublike; izbrannye stat'i i rechi* (Moscow: Politizdat, 1966), p. 137.

12. V. A. Zorin and others, eds., *Istoriia diplomatii*, 2d ed. (Moscow: Politizdat, 1959-1965), III, 195.

[8]

Development of International Law Since the October Socialist Revolution

societal development of the new epoch opened by the October Socialist Revolution: the downfall of the colonial system.

Worked out by the classics of Marxism-Leninism and by the practice of the workers' movement, these principles were not merely a revival of principles which had been advanced by bourgeois revolutions of the seventeenth and eighteenth centuries. Nor were they a reproduction of the "nationality principle," which never was generally recognized even within the framework of European international law and did not interfere with the annexationist policy pursued by European states.

On the basis of the teachings of Marxism-Leninism, the Soviet state raised the entire problem of national self-determination in a new way, in the aspect of the interests of the class struggle of the proletariat for the liberation of all working people. The principle of self-determination of nations is regarded as a "consistent expression of the struggle against any national oppression."[13]

"The right of nations to self-determination," V. I. Lenin pointed out, "means solely the right to independence in a political sense, to free political separation from the oppressor nation."[14] Thus, the principle of self-determination in its new formulation meant the right of a nation to determine its own foreign policy status, the right to decide its own affairs, the inadmissibility of coercion upon the will of the nation.

But, holding to the positions of the working class, the Bolshevist party always has accorded priority in its policy to the interests of the revolutionary struggle of the working class for the liquidation of capitalism and the construction of socialism.

A nation has the right to self-determination. But a nation in a capitalist society has been divided into antagonistic classes waging a bitter struggle among themselves. Realization of the self-determination of nations is not only an all-national, but also a class problem. Which class will stand at the head of the struggle for the self-determination of nations is of decisive significance. The content and the results of that struggle are dependent on this.

The Bolshevist party naturally strove so that the leading role in realizing self-determination of nations belonged to the working class and so that the self-determination of nations was part of the socialist revolution. And in this instance, as the experience of the self-determination of the nations that had been part of the former Russian Empire confirmed, self-determination can be realized most completely and profoundly when one finds expressed therein the interests and the will of the working people, the overwhelming majority of a nation.

13. Lenin, "Sotsialisticheskaia revoliutsiia i pravo natsii na samoopredelenie," *Polnoe sobranie sochinenii*, XXVII, 255.

14. *Ibid.*

[9]
International Legal Ideas of the October Revolution

The principles of equality and of self-determination of nations resounded in the Decree on Peace, which proposed "to all belligerent peoples and their governments to commence immediate negotiations for a just and democratic peace."[15] It was explained in the Decree that "by such a peace the government considers an immediate peace, without annexations (that is, without the seizure of foreign lands; without forcibly annexing foreign peoples), and without indemnities."[16]

The Decree contained the celebrated Leninist definition of annexation, which at the same time was a definition of the principle of self-determination of peoples. Annexation was defined as "any addition of a small or weak people to a large or powerful state without the definitely, clearly, and voluntarily expressed consent and desire of this people irrespective of when this coerced addition occurred and also irrespective of how developed or backward the nation forcibly annexed or forcibly retained within the frontiers of the state concerned. Irrespective, finally, of the fact that this nation lives in Europe or in lands far beyond the seas." The Decree went on to say: "If any nation whatsoever is retained within the boundaries of a given state by coercion, if despite its expressed desire it is not granted the right by a free vote, . . . with the complete withdrawal of the forces of the annexing or generally more powerful nation, to decide without the slightest coercion the question of the form of state existence of this nation, then its accession is an annexation; that is, by seizure and coercion."[17]

In the Appeal to the Toiling Masses of All Countries in the name of the All-Russian Executive Committee of Workers', Soldiers', and Peasants' Deputies, of the All-Russian Peasants' Congress, of the Petrograd Soviet of Workers' and Soldiers' Deputies, of the Headquarters of the Red Guard, and of Trade Union representatives of December 22, 1917, the workers of all countries were called upon "to struggle for a general armistice, for universal peace without annexations and indemnities on the basis of self-determination of nations."[18]

15. *Dokumenty vneshnei politiki SSSR*, I, 11.

16. *Ibid.*, p. 12.

17. *Ibid.* Bourgeois international legal doctrine frequently asserts that the principle of self-determination of nations supposedly was put forward as a universal principle of international law for the first time by President Woodrow Wilson in his well-known Fourteen Points, set forth in a Message to Congress on January 8, 1918. See, for example, A. Verdross, *Völkerrecht*, ed. S. Verosta and K. Zemanek, 5th ed. (Vienna: Springer Verlag, 1964), p. 84. The unfoundedness of this assertion already has been pointed out in the literature of the socialist countries. See, for example, Zorin and others, eds., *Istoriia diplomatii*, III, 112-115; S. Iu. Vygodskii, *U istokov sovetskoi diplomatii* (Moscow: Politizdat, 1965), pp. 14-15; R. Arzinger, *Das Selbstbestimmungsrecht im allgemeinen Völkerrecht der Gegenwart* (Berlin: Staatsverlag der DDR, 1966), pp. 70-71.

18. *Dokumenty vneshnei politiki SSSR*, I, 59.

[10]

Development of International Law Since the October Socialist Revolution

The Soviet state and the Communist party emphasized (and this was exceedingly important) that the principle of self-determination must be applied to all nations. Lenin said that "the proletariat must demand the freedom of political separation of colonies and nations being suppressed by 'its' nation,"[19] that is, to come out against its own imperialists. "Otherwise," Lenin said, "the internationalism of the proletariat remains empty and verbal."[20] The Appeal of the People's Commissariat of Foreign Affairs of the Russian Republic to the peoples and governments of the allied countries in December 1917 contained a call " . . . to build peace upon the basis of the complete and unconditional recognition of the principle of self-determination for all peoples . . . "[21]

The People's Commissar for Foreign Affairs, G. V. Chicherin, wrote V. I. Lenin on March 10, 1922: "Our international program must bring all oppressed colonial peoples into the international scheme. The right to separation or to home rule must be recognized for all peoples . . . The novelty of our international scheme must be in the fact that Negroes, as well as other colonial peoples, have participated on an equal footing with European peoples in conferences and committees and have had the right not to permit interference in their domestic life."[22] On this letter V. I. Lenin underlines the words "and other colonial peoples have participated on an equal footing," "not to permit interference" and on the margins makes the notation: "Right!"[23]

The Soviet state gave the world a shining example of resolving the national question on the basis of the principle of self-determination. The Soviet state made the principles of equality and self-determination its own constitutional principles. The equality and sovereignty of the peoples of Russia already had been announced in the Declaration of Rights of the Peoples of Russia of December 15, 1917: the right to self-determination up to and including separation and the formation of an independent state; the abolition of all national privileges and restrictions; freedom of national minorities to develop.[24] These principles were confirmed in the first Soviet constitution—the RSFSR Constitution of 1918.

Emphatically disassociating himself from the bourgeois understanding of the principle of self-determination as having the purpose to create "nation-states," V. I. Lenin stressed that the principle of self-determina-

19. Lenin, "Sotsialisticheskaia revoliutsiia i pravo natsii na samoopredelenie," *Polnoe sobranie sochinenii*, XXVII, 257.

20. *Ibid.*

21. *Dokumenty vneshnei politiki SSSR*, I, 69.

22. Reproduced in Lenin, "Pis'mo G. V. Chicherinu," *Polnoe sobranie sochinenii*, XLV, 36.

23. *Ibid.*

24. *Dokumenty vneshnei politiki SSSR*, I, 15.

tion is, on the contrary, a means of bringing nations together on the basis of socialism. "The purpose of socialism," he said, "is not only the destruction of those who would splinter mankind into small states and of those who would isolate nations, not only the bringing together of nations, but also of amalgamating them."[25] But Lenin emphasized that it is possible to arrive at this point "only through a transition period of complete liberation of all oppressed nations; that is, their freedom and separation."[26] Lenin said that in the event the principle of self-determination is fully realized on the basis of and within the framework of socialist social relations, national narrow-mindedness and national prejudice may be done away with and mankind will proceed along the path of bringing the nations together.

The Russian Communist party struggled for the unification of all nations of Russia because the interests of the proletarian revolution required this; struggled for unification on a voluntary basis, so that individual nations in exercising their right to self-determination have expressed themselves freely for unification with the other socialist soviet republics. The Union of Soviet Socialist Republics was created on this basis.

The Soviet state broke completely and immediately with the colonial policy of tsarism and repudiated all treaties of Tsarist Russia having a colonial, annexationist, unequal character.[27] It steadfastly has pursued the principles of equality and self-determination of nations, being a consistent fighter against colonialism and racial discrimination.

As treaty norms, these principles were fixed for the first time in treaties of the Soviet state with countries of the East. These treaties signified the establishment of new relations with such countries, which the imperialist countries had considered to be objects of their colonial expansion.

First and foremost should be mentioned the treaty with Persia of February 26, 1921, the treaty with Afghanistan of February 28, 1921, and the treaty with Turkey of March 16, 1921.

In the treaty between the RSFSR and Persia the Soviet government condemned the policy of the government of Tsarist Russia as "not only having violated the sovereignty of the states of Asia, but also as having led to organized brute violence of the European plunderers upon the living

25. Lenin, "Sotsialisticheskaia revoliutsiia i pravo natsii na samoopredelenie," *Polnoe sobranie sochinenii*, XXVII, 256.

26. *Ibid.*

27. For greater detail, see N. V. Zakharova, "Otkaz Sovetskogo gosudarstva ot dogovorov tsarskoi Rossii, narushavshikh prava narodov vostochnykh stran," *Sovetskii ezhegodnik mezhdunarodnogo prava 1962* (Moscow: izd-vo AN SSSR, 1963), pp. 126-134.

body of the peoples of the East."[28] The parties recognized in Article 4 of the treaty "the right of each people to the free and unimpeded resolution of its own political fate."[29]

The treaty between Russia and Turkey of March 16, 1921, proclaimed "the principles of the fraternity of nations and the right of peoples to self-determination," noted "the solidarity in the struggle against imperialism" existing between the RSFSR and Turkey, and declared "the contiguity between the national and liberation movement of the peoples of the East and the struggle of the working people of Russia for a new social system."[30] When the Soviet ambassador presented his credentials in July 1921, the leader of the new Turkish government, Ataturk, said in his speech: "We are highly appreciative that Soviet Russia has repudiated the former treaties and put forward the principle of self-determination."[31]

The revolutionizing influence of the great principles of equality and self-determination of nations and peoples upon international law truly was enormous. As a result of the struggle of the Soviet Union, of the working class of the capitalist countries, of the peoples of colonies and dependent countries, and of all progressive forces, these ideas took hold in international law, being transformed into international legal principles and norms and supplanting old institutions in international law that had sanctified national oppression and colonial domination.

The notion of the invalidity of unequal treaties, advanced in the Decree on Peace, played and continues to play a large role in the development of international law.[32] The Soviet state announced in this Decree that it would commence immediately to publish Russian secret treaties. "The entire content of these secret treaties," said the Decree on Peace, "insofar as it was aimed, as in the majority of instances it was, at giving advantages and privileges to Russian landowners and capitalists, at maintaining and increasing annexations of the Great Russians, the government announces their unconditional and immediate abrogation."[33]

Among the treaties published and repudiated by the Soviet state were, in particular, the 1915 Russo-Japanese agreement relating to joint coloni-

28. *Dokumenty vneshnei politiki SSSR*, III, 537.

29. *Ibid.*, p. 538.

30. *Ibid.*, pp. 597, 599.

31. See "Zarubezhnaia pechat' o revoliutsii v Rossii i sobytiiakh v Sovetskoi respublike," *Mezhdunarodnaia zhizn'*, no. 4 (1967), p. 63. [Citing *Biulleten' NKID*, no. 91 (September 10, 1921), pp. 61-62.]

32. See A. N. Talalaev and V. G. Boiarshinov, "Neravnopravnye dogovory kak forma uderzhaniia v kolonial'noi zavisimosti novykh gosudarstv Azii i Afriki," *Sovetskii ezhegodnik mezhdunarodnogo prava 1961* (Moscow: izd-vo AN SSSR, 1962), pp. 156-169.

33. *Dokumenty vneshnei politiki SSSR*, I, 13.

[13]

International Legal Ideas of the October Revolution

alist operations in China, the 1916 agreement among Russia, Great Britain, and France concerning the partition of Turkey, the 1907 Anglo-Russian secret treaty and convention relating to spheres of influence in Iran, and others.

For the first time in history, a great power voluntarily repudiated treaties granting it rights and privileges in other countries. In place of the cabalistic treaties of Tsarist Russia, the Soviet state began to conclude treaties with countries of the East on the basis of full equality and respect for sovereignty. In the treaty between the RSFSR and Persia of February 26, 1921, the Soviet government once again solemnly declared "the irrevocable repudiation by Russia of the rapacious policy, with regard to Persia, of the imperialist Russian governments overthrown by the will of its workers and peasants."[34] "In conformity therewith, and in wishing to see the Persian people independent, prosperous, and freely disposing of their own property," the treaty went on to say, "the Russian Soviet government declares all treaties, conventions, and agreements concluded by the former Tsarist government with Persia and resulting in derogation of the rights of the Persian people to be abrogated and to have lost any force."[35] The Soviet government also declared "its refusal to take part in any measures whatsoever tending to weaken or violate the sovereignty of Persia," and announced as "abrogated and having lost any force, all conventions and agreements concluded by the former government of Russia with third powers to the detriment of Persia or relating thereto."[36]

In the treaty between the RSFSR and Turkey of March 16, 1921, the contracting parties agreed to recognize "as abrogated and not having force" all treaties concluded between Russia and Turkey, as the parties had recognized that they "did not correspond to their mutual interests."[37]

Renunciation of consular jurisdiction, one of the important instruments of colonial domination, was a major element of the Soviet state's policy toward the countries of the East. Thus, the treaty with Turkey said: "The government of the Russian Socialist Federated Soviet Republic, recognizing the regime of capitulations to be incompatible with the free national development of any country, as well as with the full exercise of its sovereign rights, shall consider as having lost force and as abrogated any kind of activities or rights having any relation whatsoever to this regime."[38] The treaty with Persia, wherein the Soviet government

34. *Ibid.*, III, 536.
35. *Ibid.*, pp. 536-537.
36. *Ibid.*, p. 537.
37. *Ibid.*, p. 599.
38. *Ibid.*, pp. 599-600.

affirmed a declaration renouncing consular jurisdiction made previously, said that "Russian citizens residing in Persia, as also Persian citizens residing in Russia, from the moment the present treaty is signed shall enjoy the rights and shall be subordinate to the laws of the country of their residence equally with local citizens."[39]

In the agreement between the USSR and the Republic of China of May 31, 1924, the parties agreed to annul "all conventions, treaties, agreements, protocols, contracts, and so forth, concluded between the government of China and the Tsarist government and to replace them with new treaties, agreements, and so forth, on the basis of equality, mutuality, and justice . . ."[40] The Soviet government confirmed once again in this agreement the declaration previously made abrogating all treaties and agreements concluded by Tsarist Russia with third countries which affect the "sovereign rights and interests of China."[41] The Soviet government renounced special rights and privileges relating to concessions in China acquired by the Tsarist government, as well as rights of extraterritoriality and consular jurisdiction.[42]

The idea of the invalidity of unequal treaties set forth in the Decree on Peace, the abrogation by the Soviet state of all unequal treaties contracted by Tsarist Russia, and the conclusion of treaties with all countries, large and small, on the basis of equality were an inspiring example for the dependent countries. It has become much more difficult for imperialist states to impose unequal treaties, although, taking advantage of the weakness of some states, especially the new ones, they also frequently compel them to sign such treaties at the present time.

C. The Principles of Peaceful Coexistence

The third group of ideas and principles put forward by the October Revolution was aimed at ensuring international peace and the peaceful cooperation of states with different social systems.

To the question of how relations should be built between states of opposed social systems when the first socialist state in the world comes into existence, Lenin and the Communist party, in working out the theory of the proletarian revolution, gave an answer even before October 1917. After the revolution, these propositions were developed further and were transformed into reality.

39. *Ibid.*, p. 542.
40. *Ibid.*, VII, 332.
41. *Ibid.*, p. 332.
42. *Ibid.*, p. 335.

[15]

International Legal Ideas of the October Revolution

In rejecting the "absurd leftist" trotskyist "permanent revolution," V. I. Lenin resolutely opposed the concept of extending the socialist revolution to other countries by force of arms. In an article, "Strange and Monstrous," published in *Pravda* on February 28 and March 1, 1918, V. I. Lenin wrote in appealing to the authors of a resolution adopted by the Moscow Regional Party Bureau: "Perhaps the authors suppose that the interests of the international revolution require that it be given a push, and such a push can be given only by war, never by peace, which might give the masses the impression that imperialism was being 'legitimized.' Such a 'theory' would break completely with Marxism, which always has opposed 'pushing' revolutions, which develop with the growing acuteness of the class antagonisms that give birth to revolutions."[43]

A resolution of a conference of the foreign sections of the Russian Social-Democratic Workers' party convened in Berne from February 27 to March 4, 1915, pointed out that the future state of the dictatorship of the proletariat will resort to war only "to protect the gains won in the proletariat's struggle against the bourgeoisie."[44] A resolution of the Seventh (April) All-Russian Conference of the RSDRP(b) of 1917 indicated that in the event the proletariat took power in Russia it "immediately and openly would propose a democratic peace to all peoples on the basis of a complete renunciation of any annexations or indemnities whatsoever."[45]

In conformity with these propositions the newly emergent Soviet state proposed to lay down the principle of peaceful coexistence as the basis for the peaceful regulation of future international relations. In the Decree on Peace of November 8, 1917, the socialist state declared that annexationist, aggressive wars it "considers the greatest crime against humanity . . . " and called upon all belligerent states to cease the sanguinary war and to commence immediate negotiations for a just and democratic peace.[46]

At the same time, basing his remarks on the experience of history, particularly the experience of bourgeois revolutions and especially the eighteenth century French bourgeois revolution, Lenin cautioned the party, the working class, and the working people of Russia that the ruling classes of capitalist states would not leave the newly emergent socialist state in peace, that they are using every means, including military, to attempt to destroy the new social system just emerging based upon the

43. Lenin, "Strannoe i chudovishchnoe," *Polnoe sobranie sochinenii*, XXXV, 403. [Published in *Pravda*, February 28-March 1, 1918.]

44. *KPSS v rezoliutsiiakh i resheniiakh s"ezdov, konferentsii i plenumov TsK* (Moscow: Gospolitizdat, 1954), I, 329.

45. *Ibid.*, p. 337.

46. *Dokumenty vneshnei politiki SSSR*, I, 11-12.

[16]
Development of International Law Since the October Socialist Revolution

liquidation of private ownership of the instruments and means of production and signifying the end of domination of the capitalist class in Russia, the beginning of the end of the capitalist system in general. As early as the report on peace to the Second All-Russian Congress of Soviets on November 8, 1917, V. I. Lenin said: "The governments and the bourgeoisie are using every effort to unite themselves and to crush the workers' and peasants' revolution in blood."[47] The Seventh Congress of the Russian Communist Party (bolsheviks) in March 1918 declared in its resolution on war and peace: "Repeated military attacks of imperialist states (both from the West and from the East) against Soviet Russia historically are inevitable in the present period of the beginning era of socialist revolution."[48] Regrettably, one did not have to wait long for confirmation of this scientific prediction. The capitalist countries quickly brought down their armed forces upon the young Soviet state.

In the Report of the Central Committee to the Eighth Congress of the RKP(b) on March 18, 1919, Lenin said: "We live not only in a state, but *in a system of states*, and the existence of the Soviet Republic side by side with imperialist states for a prolonged period is inconceivable. Ultimately either one or the other shall be victorious. And when this end comes, a number of terrible conflicts between the Soviet Republic and bourgeois states are inevitable."[49]

This utterance of Lenin's, as well as a number of his other remarks on this question, are cited repeatedly by opponents of peaceful coexistence in justification of their fabrications that Lenin supposedly regarded peaceful coexistence between states of two systems as impossible and that, in Lenin's view, the new socialist state must go to war against capitalist states in order to spread socialism with the aid of arms.[50] These ravings of opponents of communism have nothing in common with reality.

Lenin pointed out that the attempts of imperialists to suppress the

47. Lenin, "Doklad o mire 26 Oktiabria (8 noiabria)," *Polnoe sobranie sochinenii*, XXXV, 17.

48. *KPSS v rezoliutsiiakh*, I, 404.

49. Lenin, "Otchet tsentral'nogo komiteta 18 marta," *Polnoe sobranie sochinenii*, XXXVIII, 139.

50. See, for example, the speech of the Uruguyan representative, Dominguez-Campora, at the 465th plenary session of the United Nations General Assembly on December 2, 1953. United Nations General Assembly (VIII), *Official Records*, p. 391; also see the speech of the French representative, Georges-Picot, at the Twelfth Session of the General Assembly. United Nations General Assembly (XII), *Official Records*, p. 273; G. Kennan, "Peaceful Coexistence: A Western View," *Foreign Affairs*, XXXVIII (1960), 173; B. Meissner, "Zwölf Gebote der Koexistenz; Moskaus neue Völkerrecht," *Der Spiegel*, XVIII (1964), no. 3, pp. 62-63.

[17]

International Legal Ideas of the October Revolution

young Soviet state could and would lead inevitably to military conflicts between states of the two systems despite the peace policy of the socialist state. Lenin spoke of the "self-defense" of the proletarian state in calling for it to create its own military organization. Lenin warned the party and the people of the need for vigilance and for strengthening the defense capability of the socialist state.

V. I. Lenin and the party did not consider the policy of peaceful coexistence of a socialist state with capitalist countries which the Soviet state pursued as a temporary policy, dictated by the then existing military-industrial supremacy of capitalism over socialism, but as the policy most responsive to the interests of the working people and to the requirements of proletarian internationalism. The Soviet state has struggled persistently for peace. A resolution of the Seventh All-Russian Congress of Soviets in December 1919 said: "The Russian Socialist Federated Soviet Republic wishes to live in peace with all peoples."[51]

The Soviet government has emphasized repeatedly that a socialist state is prepared to establish not only normal, but also friendly relations, and it is not its purpose to extend the socialist system and communist ideology by force of arms.

Thus, a note of the People's Commissar of Foreign Affairs to the German Consul General of September 18, 1918, stated: "The Workers'-Peasants' government desires with full resolve the observance of good-neighborly relations and peaceful cohabitation with Germany despite all the differences in the system of both states, and it is convinced that the German government also wishes to live together peacefully with it; while living together, it shall survive by itself, as also the German government, and it expects that the latter, as itself, will consider these differences with all of the consequences, which, however, have not obstructed the establishment now taking place between both states of good-neighborly relations corresponding to the true and deeply rooted interests of both sides."[52]

In his statement to the newspaper correspondents of the *Observer* and *Manchester Guardian* in 1922 Lenin pointed out: "We believe that completely friendly relations with both powers [having in mind France and England—*G.T.*] are wholly possible and constitute our purpose."[53]

V. I. Lenin and the party proceeded from the fact that after the failure of the armed intervention against Soviet Russia, economic competition

51. *Dokumenty vneshnei politiki SSSR*, II, 298.

52. *Ibid.*, I, 488.

53. Lenin, "Interv'iu korrespondentu "Observer" i "Manchester Guardian" M. Farbmanu," *Polnoe sobranie sochinenii*, XLV, 237.

[18]

Development of International Law Since the October Socialist Revolution

had become the decisive sphere of struggle for the states of the two systems. In 1921 Lenin said: "Now we are exerting a major influence upon the international revolution by our economic policy . . . But this field of struggle has been transferred to a world-wide scale. We solve this task—and we have won once and for all on an international scale. Therefore, questions of economic construction acquire very exceptional significance for us. On this front we must gain victory slowly, gradually—never quickly—but by a steady rise and movement forward."[54]

In a draft decree on the tasks of the Soviet delegation at the 1922 Genoa Conference, V. I. Lenin pointed out that peaceful coexistence necessarily includes mutually advantageous agreements of the Soviet state with capitalist countries not only upon economic, but also political questions.[55] Lenin derided proponents of the concept of "no compromises with capitalist states," showing the absurdity and harmfulness of this concept from the standpoint of the proletarian revolution. At the same time, Lenin stressed that the Soviet state, in making compromises, would not depart from positions of principle.

Would capitalist countries establish economic and other relations with the Soviet state? V. I. Lenin answered this question as follows: "There is a force greater than the desire, will, and decision of any of the hostile governments or classes; this force is general world-wide economic relations, which compel them to embark upon the path of intercourse with us."[56]

On a broad historical plane, Lenin understood peaceful coexistence of states of opposed social systems, socialist and capitalist, to be a form of struggle of these systems in the course of which a new system triumphs over the old; such a struggle precludes armed struggle between states of these systems and includes cooperation between them on various questions of mutual interest.

The Soviet state strove so that the principle of peaceful coexistence entered into international law and became a generally-recognized principle.

This principle received international legal expression for the first time in treaties with countries of the East: Persia, Afghanistan, and Turkey.

The leading capitalist countries refused to accept the peaceful coexist-

54. Lenin, "Rech' pri zakrytii konferentsii 28 maia," *Polnoe sobranie sochinenii*, XLIII, 341.

55. Lenin, "Proekt postanovleniia TsK RKP(b) o zadachakh sovetskoi delegatsii v genue," *ibid.*, XLIV, 407.

56. Lenin, "O vnutrennei i vneshnei politike respublike; otchet VTsIK i SNK 23 dekabria," *ibid.*, pp. 304-305.

ence of states of two systems, expecting to destroy the new system. "There is one category of people," said the herald of anticommunism, Winston Churchill, at this time, "with whom it is useless, in my view, to seek agreements. I speak of the Bolsheviks . . . "[57] The imperialists organized armed intervention, a blockade, and other aggressive actions against Soviet Russia. But life compelled capitalist states to recognize the Soviet state, to conclude treaties with it, to create an anti-Hitler coalition, as well as to accept the United Nations Charter, where this principle received wide, and then universal recognition (see Chapter 3).

On the plane of developing the principles of peaceful coexistence, the young Soviet state advanced two exceedingly important and fruitful ideas in the Decree on Peace: the ideas of the prohibition of and the criminality of aggressive war. "The government considers it the greatest crime against humanity to continue this war so that the strong and rich nations can divide among themselves the weak peoples they have seized," said the Decree.[58] The Fourth Extraordinary All-Russian Congress of Soviets condemned "all predatory wars" in the decree ratifying the Brest Peace Treaty in 1918.[59]

The principle of prohibiting aggressive war already had been laid down in a general form in the treaties of Soviet Russia with Persia, Afghanistan, and Turkey concluded at the beginning of 1921. It received more concrete expression in treaties of the USSR on nonaggression and neutrality with Turkey of December 17, 1925, and with Persia of October 1, 1927. The treaty with Turkey, for example, said that "each Contracting Party shall be bound to refrain from any attack upon each other . . . , not to participate in any hostile act by one or several third powers directed against the other Contracting Party."[60]

The idea of the criminality of aggressive war expressed in the Decree on Peace later was reflected in a number of international documents and was transformed into a prevailing principle of international law (see Chapter 3).

For the past half-century, international law has developed under the beneficial influence of the ideas of the Great October Socialist Revolution. The international legal ideas of the October Revolution injected into

57. See "Zarubezhnaia pechat' o revoliutsii v Rossii i sobytiiakh v Sovetskoi respublike," *Mezhdunarodnaia zhizn'*, no. 3 (1967), p. 86. [Citing *Biulleten' NKID*, no. 2 (March 10, 1920), p. 1.]

58. *Dokumenty vneshnei politiki SSSR*, I, 12.

59. *Ibid.*, p. 213.

60. *Ibid.*, VIII, 740.

international law as a result of the struggle of the Soviet Union and other progressive forces have led to its fundamental change.

The creative role of the international legal ideas of the October Revolution is far from exhausted. The change of the co-relation of forces to the advantage of socialism and peace ensures a further increase in the role of the international legal ideas of the October Revolution in the development of contemporary international law.

Part VII *International Law in Relations Between the Countries of the World System of Socialism*

The relations among countries of the world system of socialism, whose economic basis is comprised of socialist relations of production, represent a new, higher type of international relations. The socialist commonwealth is a social, economic, and political commonwealth of free sovereign peoples who are united by the close bonds of international socialist solidarity and by the unity of common interests and purposes.[1] "The world system of socialism," says the Program of the CPSU, "*is a new type of economic and political relations between countries.* Socialist countries have an economic basis of the same type—social ownership of the means of production; a state system of the same type—the authority of the people headed by the working class; a single ideology—Marxism-Leninism; common interests in defending revolutionary achievements and national independence from infringements of the imperialist camp; a single great objective—communism. This socioeconomic and political community creates the objective basis for lasting and friendly interstate relations in the socialist camp."[2]

The liquidation of private ownership of the instruments and means of production and the formation of socialist relations of production create the prerequisites for developing friendship between nations and states. "One of the greatest achievements of the world socialist system," says the 1960 Statement of the Meeting of Representatives of Communist and Workers' Parties, "consists of confirming in practice the Marxist-Leninist position that with the collapse of class antagonisms, the antagonism of nations collapses. In contrast to the laws of the capitalist system, in which

1. See *Programmnye dokumenty bor'by za mir, demokratii i sotsializm* (Moscow: Gospolitizdat, 1961), p. 51.

2. *Programma Kommunisticheskoi partii Sovetskogo Soiuza* (Moscow: Gospolitizdat, 1964), pp. 20-21.

[428]

Relations Between Countries of the World System of Socialism

there are inherent antagonistic contradictions among classes, nations, and states leading to military clashes, there are in the nature of the socialist system no objective reasons for contradictions and conflicts between states and their constituent peoples, and its development leads to the ever greater unity of states and nations and to a strengthening of all forms of cooperation between them."[3]

An even greater rapprochement between socialist countries is occurring in all areas of relations, which at the same time continue to remain interstate relations between sovereign and equal socialist states. "Complete equality, mutual respect for independence and sovereignty, and fraternal mutual assistance and cooperation are characteristic features of relations between the countries of the socialist commonwealth. In the socialist camp or in the world commonwealth of socialist countries—these are one and the same—no one has nor can have any special rights and privileges whatsoever."[4]

Economic ties are being strengthened within the framework of the world economic system of socialism, which is developing on the basis of the economic laws of socialism and which in itself represents the aggregate of the national economies of sovereign, independent states. The international socialist division of labor is developing. The Twenty-third Special Session of the Council of Mutual Economic Assistance, which took place in Moscow on April 23-26, 1969, with the leaders of communist and workers' parties and of governments of member countries of the Council of Mutual Economic Assistance participating, emphasized that the commonwealth of socialist states "must rest upon the system of a firm and stable international socialist division of labor which ensures the close interaction of the national economies of the member countries of CMEA."[5]

In contrast, the international capitalist division of labor, which reflects the exploitative relations of the weak by the strong, is formed spontaneously in the struggle of monopolies and countries, intensifies the unequal standard of economic development, and leads to the formation of the deformed, unbalanced economic structure of less-developed countries, the international socialist division of labor is carried out in accordance with a plan which takes into consideration the interests of individual states and of the socialist commonwealth as a whole, combining international specialization with the composite economic development of the individual countries.[6]

3. *Programmnye dokumenty za mir*, p. 52.

4. *Programma Kommunisticheskoi partii Sovetskogo Soiuza*, p. 21.

5. "Kommiunike o XXIII spetsial'noi sessii Soveta Ekonomicheskoi Vzaimopomoshchi," *Pravda*, April 27, 1969, p. 1.

6. See the "Basic Principles of the International Socialist Division of Labor"

[429]
Relations Between Countries of the World System of Socialism

Economic cooperation between countries of socialism is carried out in various forms: coordination of national economic plans; specialization and cooperation in production; foreign trade; the granting of credits by countries more highly developed economically to less developed countries; the delivery of complete sets of equipment for manufacturing and other enterprises; the sending of assistance in assembling and starting such enterprises; cooperation in the training of personnel; scientific and technical cooperation, including the transfer of technical documentation free of charge; the exchange of specialists for the purpose of becoming acquainted with scientific and technological achievements and with production experience; and so forth. The development of relations among socialist states manifested the possibility and necessity of the transition to a new, higher stage of cooperation among them, to socialist economic integration. Socialist integration is the objective, planned, regulated process of optimizing and bringing together national economic complexes. The objective of such integration is the achievement of a higher level of international socialist division of labor and a more rational utilization of productive, scientific, and technical resources in the interests of each country and of the socialist commonwealth as a whole.

The Complex Program for the Further Deepening and Improvement of Cooperation and of the Development of Socialist Economic Integration of the Member Countries of the Council of Mutual Economic Assistance, adopted by the Twenty-fifth Session of CMEA in July 1971 and approved by all CMEA members, lays down a broad plan of measures for the effectuation of socialist economic integration.

International organizations of socialist countries, in whose activity the socialist principles of international relations are manifested clearly, are playing a growing role in the development of economic, scientific, and technical ties between states of the world socialist system. First and foremost among these are the Council of Mutual Economic Assistance, created in 1949, the International Bank for Economic Cooperation, founded in 1964, the International Investment Bank, which commenced operations in January 1971, and a number of more specialized organizations.[7]

approved by the Meeting of Representatives of Communist and Workers' Parties of Member Countries of CMEA in June 1962. P. A. Tokareva and others, comps., *Mnogostoronnee ekonomichsekoe sotrudnichestvo sotsialisticheskikh gosudarstv; sbornik dokumentov* (Moscow: izd-vo Iurid. lit., 1967), pp. 23-39.

7. The Organization for the Cooperation of Socialist Countries in Tele- and Postal Communications, the Central Despatch Administration for the Combined Grid Systems, the Common Pool of Freight Cars, the Organization for Cooperation in the Ball-Bearing Industry, the Organization for Cooperation in Ferrous Metallurgy, the Joint Institute of Nuclear Research, and others. On this question see V. I. Morozov, *Sovet ekonomicheskoi vzaimopomoshchi–soiuz ravnykh* (Moscow: izd-vo

[430]
Relations Between Countries of the World System of Socialism

Cultural ties between socialist states have been greatly developed. All countries of the socialist camp are bound together by agreements on cultural cooperation aimed at developing relations in various spheres of culture. Cultural ties among socialist countries, including ties in the fields of literature, theater, libraries, sport, and so forth, expand from year to year. Founded upon a profound respect for the distinctive features and traditions of each national culture, such cooperation enriches the spiritual life of the socialist nations and promotes their future cultural progress.

Socialist states carry out close cooperation in the field of foreign policy and defense measures for the purposes of defending the gains of socialism from possible feeble imperialist swoops and of struggling for international peace. The strengthening and improvement of the mechanism of the Warsaw Treaty Organization is underway.

The close fraternal cooperation of socialist states in all spheres of relations is an important factor in the successes of individual socialist countries and of the entire socialist camp as a whole.

The new international relations being established among socialist states are characterized not only by the especially close cooperation of such states in the political, economic, cultural, and other spheres of interstate relations but also by the new quality of these relations. A specific feature of the new type of international relations which distinguishes it from other historical types of international relations is the fact that these are relations permeated with socialist internationalism—relations of fraternal friendship, cooperation, and mutual assistance for the purposes of achieving the greatest successes in the construction of socialism in individual countries and of strengthening the socialist commonwealth as a whole. "After the victory of the socialist revolution," states the document *The Tasks of the Struggle Against Imperialism in the Contemporary Stage and the Unity of the Activities of Communist and Workers' Parties and of All Antiimperialist Forces*, adopted June 17, 1969, by the international Meeting of Communist and Workers' Parties, "in many countries the construction of socialism, carried out on the basis of general laws of societal development, develops in various forms which take into account specific historical conditions and distinctive national features. The successful development of this process presupposes the strict observance of the principles of proletarian internationalism, of mutual assistance and support, of equality, of sovereignty, and of noninterference in the internal affairs of one another."

Mezhdunarodnye otnosheniia, 1964); V. Karpich, *Bank sodruzhestva ravnykh*, ed. K. A. Larionov (Moscow: izd-vo Mezhdunarodnye otnosheniia, 1966); P. A. Tokareva, "Stanovlenie sistemy mezhdunarodnykh organizatsii sotsialisticheskikh gosudarstv," *Sovetskoe gosudarstvo i pravo*, no. 10 (1967), pp. 64-72; Tokareva and others, comps., *Mnogostoronnee ekonomicheskoe sotrudnichestvo sotsialisticheskikh gosudarstv.*

Chapter 19 *Socialist International Legal Principles and Norms*

The fundamental principles of the new type of international relations go back to those propositions which were created by Marxist-Leninist theory and by the practice of the workers' movement as principles of the international workers' movement and of the relations of nations and peoples, for whose realization the communist and workers' parties have struggled (see Chapter 1).

With the victory of the proletarian revolution in Russia and the formation of the first socialist state in the world, these principles are becoming principles of state policy which the power of the proletariat has taken into its own hands. The creation of the Union of Soviet Socialist Republics as an equal union of free nations was an implementation of the principles of proletarian internationalism. The grandiose successes of the Soviet multinational state, as a firm step toward communism, and the strengthening of fraternal friendship between socialist nations are the greatest examples of the validity of the principles of proletarian internationalism.

The principles of proletarian internationalism also are reflected in the foreign policy of the first socialist state in the world; they were and are the foundation of this policy. The foreign policy of the Soviet Union has corresponded and does correspond fully to the requirements of proletarian internationalism. This policy, and now the foreign policy of other countries of the socialist camp as well, has been and is responsive not only to the interests of the peoples of these countries but also to the interests of the proletariat of all countries and to the interests of the peoples of all countries.

The formation of the world socialist system signified a new stage in the development of the principles of proletarian internationalism. So long as only one socialist state existed, the said principles could not become

[432]

Relations Between Countries of the World System of Socialism

principles of international relations because it is necessary that at least several states be guided by them in their foreign relations. Some experience in applying the said principles was gained in relations among the Soviet republics prior to the formation of the Union of Soviet Socialist Republics and in relations between the Soviet Union and the Mongolian People's Republic.

As a consequence of the formation of the world socialist system, the principles of proletarian internationalism are becoming the guiding principles of the new type of international relations.[8]

With the development of relations among socialist states, the principles of proletarian internationalism as moral and political principles of qualitatively new state relations gradually also are becoming international legal principles in relations between states of the world system of socialism. That is to say, a legal dimension has been added to the moral and political aspect of these principles; legal obligations, to the moral and political obligations.

The principles of proletarian internationalism have become international legal principles of relations between countries of the socialist system by way of custom and, partially, by treaty. These principles, which have been applied in the practice of relations between socialist countries,

8. On the principles of proletarian internationalism see G. I. Tunkin, "Sotsialisticheskii internatsionalizm i mezhdunarodnoe pravo," *Novoe vremia*, no. 51 (1957), pp. 10-11; E. A. Korovin, "Proletarskii internatsionalizm v mezhdunarodnoi praktike," *Mezhdunarodnaia zhizn'*, no. 2 (1958), pp. 29-39; Sh. Sanakoev, "Proletarskii internatsionalizm—osnova vzaimootnosheniia stran sotsializma," *ibid.*, no. 7 (1958), pp. 30-43; Tunkin, "Novye tip mezhdunarodnykh otnoshenii i mezhdunarodnoe pravo," *Sovetskoe gosudarstvo i pravo*, no. 1 (1959), pp. 81-94; Korovin, "Proletarskii internatsionalizm i mezhdunarodnoe pravo," *Sovetskii ezhegodnik mezhdunarodnogo prava 1958* (Moscow: izd-vo AN SSSR, 1959), pp. 50-69; Korovin, *Osnovnye problemy sovremennykh mezhdunarodnykh otnoshenii* (Moscow: izd-vo Sotsekgiz, 1959), pp. 57-85; W. Hänisch and G. Herder, "Der proletarische Internationalismus, das Grundprinzip in den Beziehungen zwischen den sozialistischen Staaten," *Staat und Recht*, VIII (1959), 789-807; E. T. Usenko, "Osnovnye mezhdunarodno-pravovye printsipy sotrudnichestva sotsialisticheskikh gosudarstv," *Sovetskoe gosudarstvo i pravo*, no. 3 (1961), pp. 16-29; Usenko, *Formy regulirovaniia sotsialisticheskogo mezhdunarodnogo razdeleniia truda* (Moscow: izd-vo Mezhdunarodnye otnosheniia, 1965), pp. 80-121; H. Wünsche, "Die Bedeutung des sozialistischen Internationalismus für die Restigung der Souverenität der sozialistischen Staaten und die Organisierung ihrer brüderlichen Zusammenarbeit," H. Wunsche, ed., *Rechtsbeziehungen der sozialistischen Länder* (Berlin: Staatsverlag der DDR, 1966), pp. 11-44; Sh. Sanakoev, *Mirovaia sistema sotsializma* (Moscow: izd-vo Mezhdunarodnye otnosheniia, 1968), pp. 72-101; Usenko, "Mezhdunarodnoe pravo vo vzaimootnosheniiakh sotsialisticheskikh gosudarstv," *Sovetskii ezhegodnik mezhdunarodnogo prava 1966-1967* (Moscow: izd-vo Nauka, 1968), pp. 30-46; Tunkin, "V. I. Lenin i printsipy otnoshenii mezhdu sotsialisticheskimi gosudarstvami," *ibid. 1969*, pp. 16-29; Tokareva, "Pravovye osnovy Soveta Ekonomicheskoi Vzaimopomoshchi," *ibid.*, pp. 69-82.

have been recognized by all states of the world system of socialism as international legal principles. This finds confirmation, in particular, in the numerous treaties and declarations signed between socialist states, in the joint documents of the communist and workers' parties of these countries, and in national party and state documents. It is emphasized in the said declarations and statements that relations between countries of the socialist camp are built upon the basis of Marxist-Leninist principles of proletarian internationalism. Thus, the Joint Soviet-Polish Statement of July 22, 1959, in connection with the arrival of the party-governmental delegation of the Soviet Union in Poland says: "Friendship between the peoples of both countries, founded upon a profound community of ideology, upon the Leninist principles of proletarian internationalism, is being strengthened and is developing even more."[9]

The Communique of June 19, 1959, concerning the arrival in the Soviet Union of a party-governmental delegation of the German Democratic Republic for a visit of friendship notes that the indestructible alliance of both states is based upon the "noble principles of proletarian internationalism." The Representatives of the CPSU and SEPG declare that "They consider it the duty of both parties also to strengthen further the fighting unity of the socialist countries and the fraternal solidarity of the communist and workers' parties on the basis of the Marxist-Leninist doctrine and the principles of proletarian internationalism."[10]

In the Joint Statement of April 9, 1958, on the results of negotiations between the party-governmental delegations of the Soviet Union and the Hungarian People's Republic it is stated that Hungarian-Soviet relations are built "upon the basis of fraternal mutual assistance and the great principles of proletarian internationalism."[11]

It is emphasized in the Treaty on Friendship, Cooperation, and Mutual Assistance of September 7, 1967, between the USSR and the Hungarian People's Republic that friendship, fraternal mutual assistance, and all-round close cooperation between the USSR and the HPR is based upon "the firm principles of socialist internationalism."[12] There are analogous provisions in the most recent treaties of the USSR concerning friendship, cooperation, and mutual assistance with other socialist countries.

"The principles of Marxism-Leninism, the principles of proletarian internationalism," says the 1957 Declaration of the Meeting of Representatives of Communist and Workers' Parties of the Socialist Countries, "verified by experience comprise the basis of mutual relations of countries

9. *Izvestia*, July 23, 1959, p. 1.
10. *Ibid.*, June 21, 1959, p. 1.
11. *Ibid.*, April 10, 1958, p. 1.
12. *Vedomosti verkhovnogo soveta SSSR* (1967), no. 49, item 642.

[434]
Relations Between Countries of the World System of Socialism

of the world socialist system and of all communist and workers' parties."[13]

"The strict observance of the principles of Marxism-Leninism and of socialist internationalism," states the 1960 Statement of the Meeting of Representatives of Communist and Workers' Parties, "is an indestructible law of mutual relations between socialist countries."[14]

The principles of socialist internationalism and the other international legal principles and norms being formed on their basis in relations among countries of the world socialist system are qualitatively new socialist principles which correspond to the new socialist type of international relations.

The principle of socialist internationalism enters into the system of international legal principles of socialist internationalism first and foremost as the most general, predominant, and characteristic principle of the new type of international relations. "Socialist countries," says the 1957 Declaration of the Meeting of Representatives of Communist and Workers' Parties of the Socialist Countries," build their mutual relations upon the principles of complete equality, of respect for territorial integrity, state independence, and sovereignty, and of noninterference in one another's internal affairs. These are the most important principles; however, they do not exhaust the entire essence of relations among socialist countries. Fraternal mutual assistance is an integral part of their mutual relations. The principle of socialist internationalism finds its true manifestation in such mutual assistance."[15]

As an aspect of interstate relations, the principle of socialist internationalism is the result of applying the principle of proletarian internationalism to relations between states of the socialist type. Proletarian internationalism has signified and does signify above all the unity of the proletariat of various countries in the class struggle against capital for a socialist reconstruction of society. Therefore, the principle of socialist internationalism as a principle of relations among socialist states signifies above all the unity of the socialist states in that class struggle between socialism and capitalism which takes place in the international arena in specific forms and which comprises the basic content of contemporary international relations. An important part of this struggle is the joint defense of the socialist system from any attempts of forces of the old world to destroy or subvert any socialist state of this system.

The principle of socialist internationalism is given concrete expression in the mutual relations of countries of the socialist commonwealth first

13. *Programmnye dokumenty bor'by za mir*, p. 10.
14. *Ibid.*, p. 51.
15. *Ibid.*, p. 10.

[435]

Socialist International Legal Principles

and foremost in the principles of fraternal friendship, close cooperation, and comradely mutual assistance.

Both the principle of socialist internationalism and the more concrete principles deriving therefrom reflect objective laws of societal development and therein is their greater strength.

The liquidation of private ownership, upon which for centuries rested the desire of one people to exploit and enslave another, creates the base for the rapprochement of the peoples of the socialist countries. "Socialism brings together peoples and countries," says the Program of the CPSU.[16]

The desire for a close union is an objective law of societal development of the world system of socialism. "The experience of the world socialist system has confirmed the necessity for the *closest union* of those countries breaking away from capitalism and a unification of their efforts in the construction of socialism and communism. A policy for the construction of socialism which is isolated and detached from the world commonwealth of socialist countries is unfounded theoretically because it is contrary to the objective laws of the development of socialist society. It is harmful economically because it leads to a squandering of social labor, a reduction in the rate of the growth of production, and the dependence of countries upon the capitalist world. It is reactionary and dangerous politically because it does not unite, but rather divides peoples before the united front of imperialist forces, nourishes bourgeois-nationalist tendencies, and ultimately could lead to the loss of socialist gains."[17]

In accordance with the international legal principles of fraternal friendship and close cooperation, each state of the socialist commonwealth has not only a moral and political but also a legal duty to strengthen friendship and close cooperation with the other countries of the world system of socialism.

The principle of comradely mutual assistance includes the right of each state of the world system of socialism to obtain assistance from other socialist countries and, at the same time, the obligation of each socialist state to render assistance to other socialist countries. This obligation of mutual assistance applies equally to the spheres of political, economic, military, and other relations.

The Soviet state, as the "oldest" socialist state whose historic fate has been the most difficult task of paving the way for a new socioeconomic formation, always precisely fulfills its duties arising from the principle of socialist internationalism. A vivid manifestation of this policy is the assistance of the Soviet Union to the Hungarian people in 1956 and the assistance, together with other socialist countries, to the people of

16. *Programma Kommunisticheskoi partii Sovetskogo Soiuza*, p. 134.
17. *Ibid.*, p. 21.

Czechoslovakia in 1968 in protecting socialist gains and, ultimately, in defending their sovereignty and independence from sudden swoops of imperialism, as well as the assistance to the Vietnamese people in their struggle against United States's aggression.

The principle of proletarian internationalism also is manifested in the foreign policy of socialist states on a wider plane, including close cooperation and mutual consultations concerning questions of the general international situation.

It must be noted that the unity of the fundamental purposes and principles of the foreign policy of socialist states is not determined simply by the common character of the social system. There is also the common character of the social system among capitalist states; however, there is not and can not be a unity of foreign policy for any prolonged period since the capitalist system is characterized not only by antagonistic contradictions between classes but also by sharp contradictions between states. The unity of purposes and principles of the foreign policy of socialist states derives from the fundamental principles of the new social and state system, from the fundamental principles of the socialist social system.

The principle of proletarian internationalism and the principles of fraternal friendship, close cooperation, and mutual assistance deriving therefrom also permeate economic and other relations among socialist states. Economic cooperation among countries of the socialist camp always includes mutual assistance. Such assistance may take the form of direct assistance without compensation (the assistance of the Soviet Union to a number of socialist countries after the World War in rehabilitating their national economy, assistance on the part of socialist countries to the Korean People's Democratic Republic in rehabilitating its war-destroyed economy, assistance to the Democratic Republic of Vietnam, and so forth), the granting of credits on favorable terms, the rendering of assistance by the countries more developed economically to less developed countries in exploiting industry, agriculture, and so forth.

In economic relations among capitalist states the greatest advantage is derived, as a rule, by the stronger. A country developing economically attempts to hold back the economic development of a weaker country to a low level in order to enjoy advantages in the future which its higher industrial development allows.

The economic relations of the countries of socialism are characterized, on the contrary, by comradely mutual assistance. The more economically-developed countries not only do not attempt to use the economic weakness of the less developed countries in their own interests but, on the

[437]
Socialist International Legal Principles

contrary, render them disinterested assistance in order to help them achieve the fastest growth of the national economy.

The principle of mutual advantage, in conformity with the requirements of proletarian internationalism, takes on a different character in the economic relations of countries of the socialist camp. Mutual advantage is not understood here in a purely commercial sense. A socialist state takes into account not only the interests of its country in its economic relations, but also the interests of the socialist camp as a whole.

In addition to that which enters into the content of the principles of fraternal friendship, close cooperation, and mutual assistance as principles derived from the broader principle—the principle of proletarian internationalism—the latter also provides that each state of the socialist camp must take into account in its activity both the national interests of its people and the common interest of the entire world system of socialism. "The Marxist-Leninist parties and the peoples of socialist states," says the Program of the CPSU, "proceed from the fact that the successes of the entire world system of socialism depend upon the contribution and effort of each country, and they therefore consider the utmost development of the productive forces of its country to be an internationalist duty."[18]

The objective laws of societal development of the world system of socialism and the principles of proletarian internationalism reflecting such laws of societal development create the possibility of the harmonious combination of the interests of the entire socialist community and of the national interests of the states which comprise it.

Other principles of socialist internationalism appear on the plane of interstate relations as principles of respect for the sovereignty of a socialist state based upon the realization by peoples of the right to self-determination, of noninterference in the internal affairs of another state which reflects respect for national peculiarities and expectations of each people, and of the complete equality of socialist states which reflects the Marxist-Leninist thesis of the equality of nations.

There are, as is well-known, principles of the same name in general international law. This does not mean, however, that one is referring to one and the same principles.

The principles of respect for state sovereignty, noninterference in internal affairs, and equality of states were advanced as general democratic principles during the period of bourgeois revolutions and over the course of time became generally-recognized principles of international law.

The proletariat and its revolutionary parties, waging a struggle for the building of a new society, support those democratic principles, are

18. *Ibid.*, pp. 22-23.

[438]

Relations Between Countries of the World System of Socialism

developing them further, and are struggling for their consistent application. V. I. Lenin declared that not only the demand for the self-determination of nations, "but *all* points of our maximum democratic program were advanced *earlier*, even in the seventeenth and eighteenth centuries, by the petty bourgeoisie."[19]

At the same time, as already has been pointed out, even before the formation of the world system of socialism Marxist-Leninist theory had worked out the fundamental principles of relations among countries of socialism, utilizing the entire sum of the historical experience of national and state relations, the practice of the world workers' movement, and also the experience of the Soviet multinational state. With the formation of the world system of socialism on this basis, the said international legal principles which comprise the unified system of principles of socialist internationalism also were formed.

The socialist principles of respect for state sovereignty, noninterference in internal affairs, and equality of states and peoples differ fundamentally from the corresponding principles of general international law; these socialist principles have another content: the rules of conduct themselves are changed partially as part of the content of the norms and, especially, the special aspect of the norm changes. On the sociological plane, socialist principles reflect the concordant wills of states of one social system and—of special importance—of the socialist system. The social consequences of the operation of socialist international legal principles differ completely from the consequences of the operation of norms of general international law. The immediate reason for this is the qualitative distinctiveness of the special aspect of socialist principles from the principles of general international law and the difference in the social relations which are regulated by socialist principles, on one hand, and by principles of general international law, on the other.

As a whole these are not general democratic principles, but are completely different socialist international legal principles which relate to a new, higher type of international law—a socialist international law. They aim at strengthening and developing relations of the fraternal commonwealth of socialist countries, at ensuring the construction of socialism and communism, and at protecting the gains of socialism from the infringements of forces hostile to socialism.

The socialist character of these principles is emphasized, in particular, in the Communique Concerning the Special Session of the Council of Mutual Economic Assistance, held in April 1969, where they are named as Marxist-Leninist principles. "Their mutual economic, scientific, and tech-

19. V. I. Lenin, "Sotsialisticheskaia revoliutsiia i pravo natsii na samoopredeleniia," *Polnoe sobranie sochinenii*, 5th ed. (Moscow: Gospolitizdat, 1962), XXVII, 256.

nical ties are built upon the basis of principles of interstate relations of a new type—of socialist internationalism, complete equality, respect for sovereignty and national interest, mutual advantage, and comradely mutual assistance. Historical experience has fully confirmed the living force of these Marxist-Leninist principles."[20]

The principles of socialist internationalism are interconnected and comprise a unified system whose guiding principle is the principle of socialist internationalism. This interconnection of the principles of socialist internationalism and their cosubordination to the guiding principle of socialist internationalism must be taken into account both in defining the content of the individual principles and in applying them.

In general international law the content of the principles of respect for state sovereignty, noninterference in internal affairs, and equality is restricted by granting states specific rights and by conferring duties upon them. But these principles contain no provisions that provide states with a real possibility of exercising such rights. How a state manages to take advantage of these rights is its own affair; general international law imposes no obligations upon other states in this respect.

By virtue of the laws of societal development of capitalism, the said principles of general international law are of a curtailed nature in relations between capitalist states. Thus, the principle of respect for state sovereignty in relations between capitalist states goes together with the actual dependence of small states upon large states, the economic dependence of small countries frequently leading to the sovereignty of such states being transformed into an empty form. In addition, there is always a tendency in relations between capitalist states to violate principles of international law. The history of the international relations of capitalist society, including the period since the adoption of the United Nations Charter, is full of examples of the flagrant violation of the principles of respect for state sovereignty, noninterference in internal affairs, and equality of states.

This by no means diminishes the role of principles of general international law; their observance is a necessary condition and the most important guarantee of peaceful coexistence.

In socialist international relations there is not only strict respect for the sovereignty of states, as understood in general international law, but also the provision of the real possibility of a state's exercising its sovereign rights, of defending state sovereignty. In contrast to economic relations between capitalist countries, economic cooperation of socialist states excludes the use of economic assistance to the prejudice of the sovereignty of any state. It is founded upon the combination of the interests of

20. *Pravda*, April 27, 1969, p. 1.

individual countries with the interests of the entire system and leads to the strengthening and development of the nation's economy.

The ballyhoo raised in the bourgeois press in connection with the Czechoslovak events of 1968 about the "doctrine of limited sovereignty" of socialist states supposedly advanced by the Soviet Union was only a recurrent action in the ideological struggle against the socialist countries. The position of the Soviet Union on the question of sovereignty was confirmed once again in the address of Comrade L. I. Brezhnev at the Fifth Congress of the Polish Worker's Party in November 1968. "The socialist states," declared Comrade Brezhnev, "stand for strict respect for the sovereignty of all countries. We resolutely oppose interference in the affairs of any states and violations of their sovereignty." It is well-known that the very unity of the countries of socialism on the basis of socialist internationalism, and the might of the Soviet Union as the most powerful socialist power, more than once have served and continue to be the basic guarantee of the sovereignty and even of the existence of some socialist states. Many countries whose sovereignty previously was trampled upon brazenly by imperialist states first acquired genuine independence in the fraternal family of peoples of the world socialist system. "The solidarity and close unity of the socialist countries is a true guarantee of the national independence and sovereignty of each socialist country."[21]

The repeated efforts of imperialist powers to infringe upon the sovereignty of individual socialist states inevitably have broken and will be broken on the indestructible unity of the socialist camp.

Yet another feature of the principle of respect for state sovereignty in relations among countries of the socialist camp should be noted. The sovereignty of socialist states actually is popular sovereignty, popular not only in form but in substance because a socialist state serves the people and acts in its interests. Under these conditions, respect for the sovereignty of states is becoming, in content, respect for the rights of the peoples of the respective states.

The same also is characteristic of such principles of socialist internationalism as the principles of equality and of noninterference in the internal affairs of states. They go beyond the principles of general international law of the same name and are qualitatively new principles which reflect the specific features of the new type of international relations. Therefore, the principles of equality and noninterference as principles of proletarian internationalism include, for example, not only the mutual obligations not to violate each other's respective rights, but also the duty to render assistance in the enjoyment of these rights, as well as jointly defending them from the infringements of imperialists, in conformity with the principle of socialist internationalism.

21. *Programmnye dokumenty bor'by za mir*, p. 11.

[441]

Socialist International Legal Principles

With regard to relations of equality among socialist countries, the 1957 Soviet-Hungarian Declaration states: "This equality differs fundamentally from that fictitious 'equality' which exists between imperialist powers and which in reality signifies exploitation of the peoples of small states and the plundering of the wealth of these states by imperialist monopolies."[22]

The principles of socialist internationalism, as noted previously, are principles of Marxist-Leninist theory which acquired the character of international legal principles in the process of relations among socialist states. Having become such, however, they continue to retain a close tie with Marxist-Leninist theory. Reflecting the concordant wills of socialist states, where the communist and workers' parties, building their policy on the basis of Marxist-Leninist theory, are the guiding force, these principles are being developed as a result of the further elaboration of this theory and the practice of relations among the countries of socialism.

Other socialist principles and norms also are being formed together with the international legal principles of socialist internationalism, which are the basic principles of relations among states of the world system of socialism.

These principles and norms are created primarily by the conclusion of bilateral and multilateral treaties among socialist states.

In recent years the number of treaties concluded among socialist states has increased significantly, and the operative sphere of treaty norms has expanded. Together with treaties on friendship, trade, and boundaries and agreements on financial questions, there have appeared agreements on cultural cooperation, new consular conventions, conventions concerning the regulation of the nationality of persons with dual citizenship, as well as treaties on rendering legal assistance in criminal and civil cases, agreements on social security, and so forth.

Parallel with broad bilateral cooperation, the multilateral cooperation of socialist states has developed rapidly, in connection with which the number of international organizations and multilateral treaties of socialist states is increasing. Among such multilateral treaties are for example: the 1958 Agreement on Fishing in the Waters of the Danube; the 1959 Agreement on Fishing in the Black Sea; the 1959 Agreement on Cooperation in Veterinary Medicine; the 1959 Agreement on Cooperation in the Quarantine and Protection of Plants from Pests and Diseases; the 1961 Agreement on Cooperation in Technical Supervision Over Vessels and Their Classification; the 1962 Agreement on Cooperation and Mutual Assistance in Customs Questions; the 1962 Agreement on Cooperation in Marine Fishing; and the 1963 Agreement on Accounts Pertaining to Non-Trade Payments. A number of interdepartmental agreements also

22. *Deklaratsii, zaiavlenii i kommiunike Sovetskogo pravitel'stva s pravitel'stvami inostrannykh gosudarstv* (Moscow: Gospolitizdat, 1957), p. 90.

[442]

Relations Between Countries of the World System of Socialism

could be mentioned, as for example; the 1966 Agreement on International Passenger Service and the 1966 Agreement on International Railway Freight Service. As noted above, in many instances the development of multilateral international cooperation has led to the creation of international organizations of socialist states.[23]

The treaties among states of the socialist camp represent a new type of international treaty which reflects the specific features of the new social system, the principles of socialist international relations. With regard to treaties between the USSR and other socialist states, a resolution of the Twenty-third Congress of the CPSU states: "The system of treaty relations of the Soviet Union with other countries of socialism has been strengthened. The fraternal friendship of our peoples is embodied in these treaties."[24]

Socialist norms and institutes partly are formed anew in relations among socialist states and partly are formed as a result of the fact that new content is injected into the norms and institutes of general international law in their practical application in relations among states of the world system of socialism.

Thus, the coordination of national economic plans and the specialization and cooperation of production, having been consolidated in the Charter of CMEA and in the Fundamental Principles of the International Socialist Division of Labor adopted in June 1962 at the Meeting of Representatives of the Communist and Workers' Parties of Member Countries of the Council of Mutual Economic Assistance, are new institutes in form and content. They grew from the practice of cooperation of the countries of socialism.

On the other hand, the international legal norms regulating consular

23. For the texts of multilateral treaties among socialist states, see Tokareva and others, comps., *Mnogostoronnee ekonomicheskoe sotrudnichestvo sotsialisticheskikh gosudarstv.* With regard to treaties between socialist states in particular see L. A. Lunts, ed., *Voprosy mezhdunarodnogo chastnogo prava* (Moscow: Iurizdat, 1956): M. Boguslavskii and A. Rubanov, "Pravovoe sotrudnichestvo SSSR so stranami narodnoi demokratii," *Sovetskii ezhegodnik mezhdunarodnogo prava 1958*, pp. 254-272; Lunts, *O soglasheniiakh mezhdu evropeiskimi stranami narodnoi demokratii o vzaimnoi pomoshchi v grazhdanskikh delakh* (Moscow: Iurizdat, 1958); T. Donner, "Chekhoslovatskie dogovory o iuridicheskoi pomoshchi," *Biulleten' chekhoslovatskogo prava*, no. 1 (1958), pp. 72-81; Lunts, "Voprosy mezhdunarodnogo chastnogo prava v otnosheniiakh mezhdu stranami mirovoi sotsialisticheskoi sistemy," *Sovetskii ezhegodnik mezhdunarodnogo prava 1959*, pp. 72-82; Lunts, ed., *Problemy mezhdunarodnogo chastnogo prava* (Moscow: Iurizdat, 1960); Usenko, *Formy regulirovaniia sotsialisticheskogo mezhdunarodnogo razdeleniia truda*; Wünsche, ed., *Rechtsbeziehungen der sozialistischen Länder*; Lunts, "Conflict of Laws in International Sale: Theory and Practice of Socialist Countries," *Recueil des cours*, CXIV (1965), 5-57.

24. *Materialy XXIII s"ezda KPSS* (Moscow: Politizdat, 1966), p. 183.

and boundary relations and cooperation in legal questions and social security which have been fixed in the respective bilateral treaties between socialist states basically are analogous in form to those norms applied in the practice of other states. But in the mutual relations of the countries of the socialist commonwealth they have acquired a new content corresponding to the new quality of international relations.

Thus, for example, the following norm is contained in the Consular Treaty of April 25, 1958, between the USSR and the Federal Republic of Germany: "The consul and consular offices shall not be subject to the jurisdiction of the receiving state in respect of acts performed in their official capacity" (Article 8(1)).[25] Norms analogous in form are contained in the bilateral treaties and conventions on consular questions concluded between the USSR and socialist countries. As already has been pointed out, however, these are different legal norms. The aforesaid legal norm of the consular conventions concluded between socialist states reflects the will of states-parties to the convention which aims at developing and strengthening relations between them on the basis of the principles of socialist internationalism. Meanwhile, the respective norm of the Consular Treaty between the USSR and the FRG expresses the concordant wills of these states, aimed at improving relations between them on the basis of the principles of peaceful coexistence. The social consequences of the operation of these norms, of course, also are different.

25. G. E. Vilkov and I. P. Blishchenko, comps., *Soglasheniia SSSR po konsul'skim voprosam* (Moscow: izd-vo IMO, 1962), p. 81.

Chapter 20 *Principles and Norms of General International Law in Relations Between States of the World Socialist System*

As has been pointed out previously (see Chapter 8), the most important principles of contemporary international law are of an imperative character, and states may not establish in their bilateral or local multilateral relations norms which would contravene these fundamental principles.

There is no doubt, however, that the principles of *jus cogens* are not principles which do not allow the progressive development of international law and the creation on the basis of equality and voluntariness of local international legal norms of general international law in developing friendly relations among states and ensuring peace, that reflect a higher degree of international integration than general international law.

Moreover, being the law of peaceful coexistence of states with a different social system, contemporary general international law can not impede the creation of local international legal norms which by their social content are distinct from norms of general international law. In co-relation with general international law, the international legal principles of socialist internationalism are just such local principles.

The principles of proletarian internationalism and other socialist norms arising in relations between countries of the socialist camp are international legal principles and norms of a new, higher type of international law—a socialist international law, the basis of which is being formed in relations among states of the socialist system and which is coming to replace contemporary general international law.[1]

1. See G. I. Tunkin, "Novyi tip mezhdunarodnykh otnoshenii i mezhdunarodnoe pravo," *Sovetskoe gosudarstvo i pravo*, no. 1 (1959), p. 85; W. Hänisch and G. Herder, "Der proletarische Internationalismus das Grundprinzip in den Beziehungen zwischen den sozialistischen Staaten," *Staat und Recht*, VIII (1959), 803; E. T. Usenko, *Formy regulirovaniia sotsialisticheskogo mezhdunarodnogo razdeleniia truda* (Moscow: izd-vo Mezhdunarodnye otnosheniia, 1965), p. 121; Usenko, "Mezhdunarodnoe pravo vo

General International Law and the World Socialist

Socialist principles and norms are replacing the corresponding principles and norms of general international law in relations between countries of the world system of socialism. This does not mean, however, that principles of general international law simply are cast aside in relations between countries of the socialist commonwealth.

The emergence of the principles of socialist internationalism, of course, is a negation of an old quality, the quality of the respective principles of general international law. But, as any dialectical negation, it is a moment of development, a stage of transition to a higher quality. The new which has emerged is linked with the old, the progressive aspects of the old being retained therein in their diluted form. The progressive elements of the content of the respective principles of general international law corresponding to the new conditions are retained in the principles of socialist internationalism.

The international legal principles of socialist internationalism operate in relations between countries of the socialist commonwealth. They have, therefore, a more limited sphere of application in comparison with general international law. At the same time, the principles of socialist internationalism, reflecting the features of socialist international relations, go further than the principles of general international law in ensuring friendly relations between states.

Consequently, the presence of principles of socialist internationalism and of other socialist principles and norms in relations between countries of the world system of socialism by no means contravenes the requirements of general international law.

Another aspect of the co-relation of principles and norms of general international law and of socialist principles and norms is the co-relation in the process of their operation. In this sense socialist principles and norms are special norms, whereas the principles and norms of general international law are general norms. In conformity with the well-known proposition that a special norm takes precedence over a general norm, in those instances when there are socialist principles and norms, these principles and norms are operative; in those instances when relations between socialist countries are not covered by socialist principles and norms, the

---

vzaimootnosheniiakh sotsialisticheskikh gosudarstv," *Sovetskii ezhegodnik mezhdunarodnogo prava 1966/1967* (Moscow: izd-vo Nauka, 1968), pp. 30-46; Tunkin, "V. I. Lenin i printsipy otnoshenii mezhdu sotsialisticheskimi gosudarstvami," *Sovetskii ezhegodnik mezhdunarodnogo prava 1969* (Moscow: izd-vo Nauka, 1970), pp. 16-29; Usenko, "Mezhdunarodnopravovye problemy sotsialisticheskoi integratsii," *Sovetskii ezhegodnik mezhdunarodnogo prava 1970* (Moscow: izd-vo Nauka, 1972), pp. 13-25; Tunkin, "V. I. Lenin i printsipy otnoshenii mezhdu sotsialisticheskimi gosudarstvami," *Sovetskii ezhegodnik mezhdunarodnogo prava 1969* (Moscow: izd-vo Nauka, 1970), pp. 16-29.

principles and norms of general international law are operative. Thus, the principle of peaceful coexistence is replaced in relations between states of the socialist camp by the higher, more profound, and qualitatively new principle of socialist internationalism, which is a fundamental and specific principle of a new type of international relations. Such principles of socialist internationalism as the principles of respect for sovereignty, equality, and noninterference in internal affairs replace the corresponding principles of general international law in relations of the new type. The principle of nonaggression is not mentioned in the various documents concluded between socialist states, since it is overlapped in relations between socialist states by the more profound principle of socialist internationalism.

As examples of the operation of principles and norms of general international law in relations between countries of the socialist commonwealth, one may point to the norms of the 1958 Geneva Conventions on the law of the sea, the norms of the 1961 Vienna Convention on Diplomatic Relations, and others. These principles and norms must be observed by socialist countries in their mutual relations and, when necessary, references to them are made.

Since, however, the principles of socialist internationalism are being guided by principles of the new type of international relations, the interpretation and application of principles and norms of general international law in relations between countries of the world system of socialism takes place in the light of these guiding principles, infusing a "new spirit" into these principles and norms.

The theoretical unfoundedness of the concept equating principles of relations between countries of the socialist camp with principles of general international law is that it does not take into account the specific features of relations between countries of the socialist camp. But the specific feature exists, and it must, since the question is one of relations between states of a new historical type, of relations between socialist states.

To assert that relations between socialist countries should be regulated only by principles of general international law is to deny the different class character of relations between the countries of socialism, to be derailed from party principle into the morass of bourgeois normativism.

Politically analogous concepts objectively are aimed at depreciating relations between countries of the socialist camp, dissolving them in the general mass of relations between states, undermining the unity of countries of the socialist camp, weakening it in the struggle for the rapid construction of socialism and communism and in warding off all of the imperialist harassments.

[447]
General International Law and the World Socialist

The scientific Marxist-Leninist approach to the problem of relations between countries of the socialist camp requires that the specific features of these relations be taken into account, and this specific feature as regards principles of interstate relations finds its clearest manifestation in the principle of socialist internationalism.

[16]

The Primacy of International Law in World Politics

VLADLEN S. VERESHCHETIN AND REIN A. MÜLLERSON

The treatment of international law at different historical periods has varied from unjustified exaggeration of its potentialities to complete disregard. Hugo Grotius[1] maintained that a people that violate the natural law and the law of nations undermine forever the basis of their own future security. Many statesmen in the past (and not so distant too) have frequently held, like Bismarck, that the great issues of the time were to be resolved by blood and iron instead of declarations and resolutions, and have acted accordingly when they were strong enough. Nearly a century ago the famous German international lawyer Franz Listz[2] wrote that the provisions of international law have too often been trampled underfoot while states have been openly and solemnly acknowledging the binding force of international law in settling their disputes, even in wartime.

The present-day development of human civilisation has led many scholars, scientists, statesmen, lawyers and people of other trades, professions and occupations, to begin to realise that to save the world from destruction, civilised relations, i.e. the rules of international law and common human morals, must prevail in relations between states. It is not accidental, therefore, that along with common human values and interests, interdependence and integrity of the world, and a free choice of the ways of development, the concept of the primacy of international law in politics has been increasingly fixed in new political thinking. And although international law dates back to ancient times the changes in the world community and in the very nature of international law have given it an absolutely new meaning. What frequently used to be only an attribute of foreign policy, a medium to justify one's own actions or, on the contrary, to accuse one's political and ideological opponents, is becoming today an essential means to resolve major problems of our time.

What has changed in the world? Why has international law begun to play such an important role in it? To put it briefly, the main thing is that the world has been growing more interdependent and integral. Unilateral actions of states without regard for the interests of other countries and peoples no longer produce any long-term gains; on the contrary, they can jeopardise the very existence of human civilisation. Reliance solely on military strength risks general destruction or the abandonment of the hope of defending oneself. These are the historical alternatives to the new political thinking and its practical implementation.

The interdependence of the contemporary world is manifested, of course, not only through the threat to survival and the presence of other global problems whose solution requires the efforts of all countries and peoples. The world is also too confined for one state to benefit at the expense of another. Gone are the times when an empire could expand and thrive through the robbery of colonies. The more integral the world becomes, and the more tangibly the conduct of a state begins to affect the interests of other countries or the international community as a whole, the greater the need for mutual co-ordination and an orderly state of things in the world. Both gains and losses in an interrelated world may only be reciprocal, and so the actions of states in such a world call for mutual co-ordination. The most perfect and frequently the only means to achieve mutual co-ordination of actions in the world is modern international law, functioning as a code of rules of conduct resulting from the harmonising of states' wills, positions and interests.

Contemporary international law is neither bourgeois, nor socialist; it is a common human, general democratic normative system based on a common humanity. Its rules and standards based on the principles of the UN Charter express the balance of interests between individual states and the international community as a whole. It legalises many common human values. For instance, the bans on the use of force and on the interference in the internal affairs of states, the right of nations to self-determination and other fundamental principles of international law, are called upon to safeguard the values and interests common for the whole of mankind. Gradually, binding rules are evolved to ensure ecological safety for the human race (for example, the 1985 Vienna Convention on the Protection of the Ozone Layer and the 1987 Montreal Protocol to it). At the same time an international campaign is under way for the creation of principles of a new international economic order. Treaties are coming into existence effecting real disarmament.

All of these developments confirm the necessity for the establishment of a system of general law and order that would ensure the primacy of international law in politics.[3] It follows from the orientation of present-day international law towards the protection of common human values that the primacy of international law in politics is in fact a normative expression of the precedence of common human values and interests.

The UN Chapter is a most unique document in many respects. Its most striking feature is probably that all its basic ideas and provisions adopted more than forty years ago constitute the core of contemporary international law and are becoming ever more vital. The reason that the Charter of this organisation for the maintenance of international peace and security is so outstanding is that it was formulated at a period in world history when the international community of states joined hands in the struggle for survival in a united front against fascist enslavement.

The principles and rules of the Charter and the whole machinery of the United Nations began to misfire when the countries of the anti-Hitler coalition began to lose unity, when the policy of confrontation began to take the upper hand and the ideological struggle had as a matter of fact turned into psychological warfare. It stands to reason that against such a background the rule of force instead of law became the chief rule of the game on the international scene.

The 'cold war' which in some regions was turning into a 'hot war' could not help being accompanied by breaches of the major principles of international law. Regretfully, the Soviet Union is not blameless in its approach to international law. It is little consolation that the list of violations by Western countries and, in particular, the United States of America, is longer than ours. A 'free' treatment of law not only damages the interests of the international community of states as a whole; it brings no benefits to anyone over a longer-term period.

At the same time one must not let out of sight the fact that the Soviet state has made an important contribution to developing contemporary international law with a general democratic content, for example, concerning the principles of non-use of force and threat of force, the right of nations and peoples to self-determination and other progressive rules. Our diplomacy has contributed importantly to the development of the UN Charter which fixes the fundamental principles of the modern world law and order. The same is true of legal rules on restrictions of armaments, in outer space, ocean space and other fields of international law. The Soviet Union has not only initiated legal rules and standards; it has energetically helped to enforce the progressive principles and rules in international practices.

Often the resolute position of the Soviet Union alone has helped uphold the independence of former colonies and prevent extension of the hotbeds of tension. Suffice it to mention the consistent policy of our state in the Arab–Israeli conflict and the assistance to Vietnam at the time of US intervention there. Our protests against US interference in the domestic affairs of Latin American countries and against the use of force in the same area (Cuba, the Dominican Republic, Grenada and Nicaragua) have been both morally just and juridically sound.

The more so we cannot help resenting and regretting 'flies in the ointment' of our own doing that damaged international law and impaired our positions on other matters as well as our international prestige in general: for instance, Soviet interference in the affairs of communist and workers' parties in other countries, in Yugoslavian affairs in the late forties and the Finnish war of 1939 for which the USSR was expelled from the League of Nations.

The bringing of the troops of five socialist countries into Czechoslovakia in 1968 was supported by unconvincing legal arguments which gave rise to the so called 'Brezhnev' doctrine, meaning that socialist countries enjoyed only a limited sovereignty. The Soviet press claimed at that time that formal legal reasoning should not have precedence over the class approach. Those giving up the only true class criterion of legal rules were alleged to measure events in terms of bourgeois law. Abstract, non-class approaches to sovereignty and self-determination of nations were severely criticised.[4]

All of it was said in respect of the generally accepted rules of international law which can be neither bourgeois, nor socialist. A purely class-conscious interpretation by states of such principles as sovereignty or non-interference could make a complete wreck of the principles of international law that express common human values. International law can accomplish its mission and fulfil its main function only when it is general, when it is not artificially divided into capitalist international law, socialist international law and the international law of developing countries.

It does appear that such double-thinking towards international law (active participation in its progressive development and strengthening world law and order, on the one hand, and crippling one's own positions and interests by particular actions, on the other) reflected complicated and conflicting developments within Soviet society as a whole. This is why the potential of an advanced social system and the Leninist ideas of peaceful coexistence of states underlying the foreign policy of our state were sometimes unfortunately accompanied by distortions of the Leninist policy not only domestically, but also internationally. For these reasons the ongoing processes of broadening democracy, strengthening legality and creating a socialist state based on the rule of law in the Soviet Union are being accompanied by a changed attitude towards international law. The new political thinking relies on the existing fundamental principles and rules of international relations and calls for their continued progressive development.

What is concretely implied by the concept of primacy of law in international relations? It stands to reason that such primacy can be achieved only if all states strictly follow the principles and rules of international law, ensuring the priority of common human values and interest over narrow-minded national and class interests. And we specially emphasise that we mean narrow-minded class and national interests because, in the present-day world, true national interests and even the aims and tasks of confronting classes inside an individual country which may be sharply conflicting, are nonetheless not antagonistic to international common human values and interests.

As a matter of fact no nation, no class can achieve its purpose if its survival has not been assured, if the acute economic and ecological problems which threaten all humanity have not been solved. It is also contrary to the interests of humanity as a whole if there is armed interference with the aim of preventing a nation's choice of its own ways of social, economic and political development.

The primacy of international law in politics presupposes predominance of law over force because the use or the threat to use force undermines world law and order. The supremacy of international law may be achieved only when states are conscious of their interest in securing the priority of co-ordinated, multilateral actions, favouring long-term and principled goals over short-lived benefits.

The primacy of international law presupposes also a free choice by peoples of their own route to social, economic and political development. History indicates that international conflicts are more often than not caused by the attempts of states to make other states have a similar system and follow their image – by a refusal to accept differences in socio-economic and political systems.

The primacy of international law in politics also calls for co-ordination between the principles and rules of international law and those of national law. The provisions of the latter must be consistent with the international obligations of a state. The level of legality and democracy in a country is closely associated with the state's attitude towards international law. In this connection the following statement by M. S. Gorbachev at the United Nations acquires special significance: 'Our ideal, [he said] is a world community in which states, governed by the rule of law, subordinate their foreign political activity to law as well'.[5] For this reason the construction of a socialist state based on the rule of law in the USSR is very important not only for the internal life of our society, but also for international relations.

Is a world order based on the rule of law realistic? (A) Is it not a Utopia when armed conflicts keep going on in various regions of the globe, when economic and ecological crises continue to deepen, while social injustice has not yet been ended and acts of international terrorism still flare up?

We would indeed seem idealists divorced from reality should we believe that a world based on the rule of law could emerge at once and everywhere. We would be Utopians should we think that the development of humanity as an integral whole were possible without the need to solve constantly-emerging differences, without continuing attempts to find a balance between the conflicting interests of states, groups of countries and even regions. It is also hard to imagine a world where violations of international law were non-existent. That would be an idyll, something unrealistic.

However, the existing tendencies of world development give the hope and reasonable belief in the possibility of securing the supremacy of international law. For a long period of time there has been an awareness of the need for a movement towards a non-violent world among the best minds. For instance, many ideas in the new political thinking were anticipated in the famous Russell–Einstein manifesto written thirty years ago. Let us note that many an outstanding international lawyer underlined in his work the urgent need for states to obey international law and their real interest in doing so. For example, the famous American lawyer W. Friedman wrote that 'the common interest of mankind in survival in the nuclear age must by all means take precedence over the many traditional differences which are of a national, racial, ideological and other character'.[6]

A qualitative leap in understanding the reality of the nuclear and space age will come as soon as leaders of the largest nuclear powers realise the need for new thinking. The Soviet Union has made the most progressive ideas of contemporary public thinking the central principles of its practical policies.

Headway has begun to be made in the settlement of nearly all regional conflicts; ice has been broken even in the area of nuclear disarmament. The intention of the Soviet Union to reduce unilaterally its conventional armaments and armed forces is fresh proof of its new serious approach to international affairs.

Certainly, the primacy of law in international politics requires that a majority of states, especially the great powers, should realise the need for the predominance of law. Although certain positive changes are observed in the foreign policy of many countries, including those largely responsible for the international climate, the movement towards a nuclear-free and non-violent world, where law would rule over force, has not yet become irreversible. Much remains to be done.

The movement for the predominance of law in international relations is based on the political will of the peoples and various public organisations to secure a just and stable peace, but materialising this will require a series of steps both to develop international law as such and to improve the mechanisms and procedures of enforcing its principles and rules.

In our days probably no one state openly admits breaches of rules of international law. Any violator seeks to find or invent a more or less plausible legal excuse for its actions. Regretfully, because of their deficiencies, both the rules of international law and the procedure of their interpretation and application permit, to a certain measure, such behaviour.

It should be emphasised, however, that the said deficiencies follow largely from many states' lack of political will to remove them. Governments could easily find good rules to restrict the behaviour of other states, were not such rules binding on their own behaviour. This is why M. S. Gorbachev's saying that 'every state' should be interested 'in restricting itself by international law'[7] has made an impact on international lawyers.

Some major principles of international law – for example, refraining from the threat or use of force in international relations – are in a way ambiguous. At first glance everything seems clear; it is forbidden not only to use armed force, but also to threaten to use it. But there is an inalienable right to self-defence in the case of an armed attack. And that's where the ambiguities begin. What is an armed attack? Does the concept include, apart from acts of direct military aggression, also indirect forms of turning to force, such as the use of irregular forces or mercenaries; subversive actions against another state; acts of terrorism organised on its territory, or assistance to rebels or contras, etc.? More complications are involved when attempts are made by some states to pass off as self-defence operations to rescue hostages which involve full intervention in another country, or the use of force 'to restore democracy' either by a decision of regional organisations, or through the 'invitation of a lawful government', etc.

While it is, as a rule, more or less easy to identify the perpetrator of direct aggression on the grounds of who was the first to use force, it is very difficult to identify the indirect user of force, the more so that in the not-so-distant past, states made use of military provocations as a pretext for attack.

Two conclusions may be drawn from these experiences. Firstly, it is necessary to specify the content of very broad principles of international law and to remove the loopholes that make it possible to bypass them or, at least use them to justify, in the eyes of certain groups, breaches of the major rules of international law. Agreements on these points could be reached within the framework of the United Nations.

Secondly, a much wider use is required of the international mechanisms and procedures for settling disputes and conflicts, interpreting and applying the principles and rules of international law. The ancient roman maxim that no-one can sit in judgement on his own case applies just as well to international law. Hence, more extensive use should be made of the International Court of Justice for the settlement of specific conflicts between states, and for advisory opinions on the interpretation of the principles and rules of international law.

The states should recognise the overriding need for the existing control mechanisms and develop new ones. It is urgent that a mechanism be set up under the auspices of the United Nations for broad international control over the fulfilment of agreements to reduce international tension, to restrict armaments and to keep in check hostilities in areas of conflict. Such a mechanism could be an auxiliary organ of the Security Council (or, possibly, the General Assembly) of the United Nations and should have at its disposal space monitoring and verifications facilities. It should also be given the right to carry out inspections on the spot. The conclusions of such an organ should be brought to the notice of the UN political bodies and states and, if need be, the public at large. In appropriate cases such conclusions could be a guide for the International Court of Justice or other relevant arbitration tribunal.

In the nuclear and space age, when common human values and

interests have become uppermost, the international law of peaceful coexistence should be looked at afresh. The question whether this principle was a special form of class struggle was raised as far back as the 27th CPSU Congress. The need to reconsider was also elaborated in a series of later Soviet publications. New thinking about this principle is extremely important; international relations must not become an arena of class or ideological struggle.

Inadequate attention in our view is devoted to another aspect of this principle, that is, its sphere of application. Two wordings of the principle of peaceful coexistence are current in political and international law literature – 'of states with different social systems' and 'of states irrespective of their social system'. The first implies relations between socialist and capitalist countries; the second permits it to spread to socially homogeneous countries.

In his book *Perestroika and New Thinking for Our Country and the Entire World* M. S. Gorbachev speaks of the need for the assertion of peaceful coexistence as the supreme, general principle of relations between states. A similar thesis was set forth at the 43rd session of the United Nations General Assembly by Soviet Foreign Minister E. A. Shevardnadze. Indeed, all states should coexist peacefully with each other. The principle of peaceful coexistence presupposes respect for the sovereign equality of all states; it bans the use of force or any interference in internal affairs, and presupposes a free choice by the peoples of their own ways of social development. It goes without saying that all these democratic rules must be observed in relations between socialist countries, as well as in relations between capitalist countries.

At the same time observance of general democratic principles and rules does not exclude closer and friendlier ties between states if such ties are consistent with the said principles. For this reason the principle of socialist internationalism practised between socialist nations by no means rules out the binding principle of peaceful coexistence between them. It is self-evident that mutual or one-sided aid between two socialist countries cannot be accompanied, let us say, by interference in each other's internal affairs or other infringements on sovereignty.

Negation of the extension of the peaceful coexistence principle to relations between socialist countries gave rise to doctrines in the West of 'Brezhnev's' or the 'limited sovereignty' type. The reverse side of such doctrines, according to the famous American lawyer L. Henkin, was Reagan's doctrine licensing the use of armed force to spread 'democracy'.[8]

On the other hand, very close ties between some capitalist countries (for example, Common Market countries) in no way means that the principle of peaceful coexistence does not apply between them. As historical experience indicates, a homogeneity of social, economic and political systems of states as such is no guarantee of absolute harmony in relations between them. But no matter what are the differences or even conflicts, they should be settled in accordance with the generally accepted principles of international law. The aforesaid, naturally, is not denying the fact that the principle of peaceful coexistence plays an especially important role as a regulator of relations between states with different social systems. But here likewise accents should be shifted not only in words, but also in deeds. Instead of speaking of struggle and co-operation as we used to, we should speak above all of all-around, mutually profitable co-operation and of a peaceful competition between the systems; thus, not only are the advantages of either way of development demonstrated, but also there is mutual enrichment through the use of each other's achievements both in science and technology and in the social field.

These are just some reflections on the new role of international law in an interdependent world which begins to be aware of its integrity. To build a world based on the rule of law and common human values, vast joint endeavours of scholars, scientists, practical workers and specialists from many countries will be required.

Notes

1 *Hugo Grotius, On the Law of War and Peace*, Moscow, 1956, pp. 48–9 (in Russian).
2 Franz Listz, *International Law: A Systematic Outline*, Yuriev, 1909, p. 9 (in Russian).
3 Gorbachev, M. S., 'The Reality and Guarantees of a Safe World', *Pravda*, 17 September 1987 (in Russian).
4 *Pravda*, 26 September 1968.
5 Speech to General Assembly of the United Nations, November 1988.
6 W. Friedmann, *De l'éfficacité des Institutions Internationales*, Paris, 1970, p. 17.
7 *Pravda*, 8 December, 1988.
8 L. Henkin, 'International Law and National Interest', *Columbia Journal of Transnational Law*, 1986, 25, No. 1, p. 3.

Editorial Note

A. One of the main theses of perestroika is that a state which does not respect constitutional standards which it has accepted in relation to its own citizens will not respect international legal standards that it has accepted in relation to other states.

[17]

ON THE PRIMACY OF INTERNATIONAL LAW IN POLITICS

G. I. TUNKIN

The primacy of international law in politics or, to put it another way, the supremacy of international law in inter-State relations, is not a new issue. What is new is the situation in which the Soviet Union has raised this virtually forgotten question. "The world in which we live today," said M. S. Gorbachev in his address to the United Nations, "is fundamentally different from that at the beginning and even the middle of this century. And it continues to change in all its basic aspects."[1]

The world of today is a world of scientific-technical revolutions following one after another. The sphere of influence of various human problems is changing decisively. Many of those which were previously resolved at national levels have been transformed into global problems whose resolution requires the cooperation of not many, but all States.

But it not only a matter of this. The fate of human civilization has come to depend on the resolution of these global problems. The problem of survival has for the first time confronted mankind. Now mankind is bound together not merely by a joint existence on the planet Earth, but by a common fate. Together we survive, or together we perish is now the issue.

In order to survive mankind must ensure the normal functioning of an inter-State system which would preclude not only the possibility of nuclear war but likewise the possiblity of any large-scale armed conflicts and would create the essential prerequisites for resolving global problems. The most important condition for the normal functioning of the inter-State system is the primacy of international law in politics. It is from this that the question is posed anew.

International politics and international law

International politics is the process of the interaction of the foreign policies of various States. How does this interaction influence the creation of norms of international law and their functioning? According to the concept which is predominant in world international legal doctrine, norms of international law are created in relations between States and are not introduced from without. It follows that international politics influences the creation thereof.

The creation of norms of international law is the process of bringing the wills of States into concordance. The content of the will of a State is its international legal position, which constitutes part of the foreign policy position of a State. In the

W. E. Butler, Perestroika and International Law, 5–12.

6

course of forming new norms of international law there occurs the bringing into concordance of the international legal positions of States, bringing their wills into concordance relative to the content of rules of behaviour and recognising them to be legally binding. This process takes place within the framework of the inter-State system. An international legal norm is formed when the bringing of the wills of States into concordance is completed. One may thus believe that politics has primacy when norms of international law are created. The former Chief Legal Adviser of the French Ministry of Foreign Affairs, and later member of the International Court of Justice, Guy de Lacharriere, wrote: "Nothing prevents us from regarding international law as that which politics desired, at least the politics of the dominant States."[2]

Although born in the sphere of international politics, norms of international law are distinct from the phenomenon of politics. The fact that norms of international law are formed in the sphere of international politics objectively has facilitated the emergence of the concept of international law being mixed with politics. The notion most prevalent at present is the "policy-oriented international law" of Myres McDougal, in the creation of which the sociologist Harold Lasswell had an important part. McDougal formulates the essence of this notion as follows:

> international law is most realistically regarded, after the model of the American Legal Realists with respect to the law of any community, as that comprehensive process of authoritative decision by which the members of the larger community of humankind seek to clarify and secure their common interests in the shaping and sharing of all values. The inherited body of rules, described as international law in the positivist frame, with its abundant complementarities, ambiguities and incompletions, has meaning only insofar as it refers to past decision or to the guidance, not command, of future decision.[3]

Thus is international law dissolved into politics, since "the process of authoritative decision" is politics. As Stanley Hoffmann writes: "international law is one of the aspects of international politics."[4]

However, life persuasively bears witness that international law exists as an independent social phenomenon. References to international law embellish international documents: diplomatic correspondence, resolutions of international organisations, declarations of social organisations, and so forth. There are various views on the role of international law, but even those who believe that this role is insignificant acknowledge the existence of international law as a phenomenon distinct from politics.

Norms of international law are the scale for the behaviour of States and other subjects of international law and are legally binding upon them. They establish the legal parametres for politics. The legally binding nature of norms of international law distinguish them from other social norms which function in the inter-State system (norms of recommendatory resolutions of international organisations, political norms, norms of international morality, and others). This specific feature is analogous in general to the specific features of norms of municipal law. It consists of the fact that norms of law make provision for the possibility of applying State coercion to secure compliance with those norms.

Since norms of international law are created in the sphere of politics, this means that politics determines the framework within which it may juridically operate. It is appropriate in this connection to dwell on a delusion of diplomacy: that it is essential to endeavour to resolve international problems by political means. This is quite correct if one has in mind that international problems must not be resolved with the aid of force. But it is only partially true. Political means alone can never secure the normal functioning of the inter-State system. Together with politics it is essential to have a system of legal norms which establish the parametres of politics, that is, an order, a legal order, which is obligatory for States.

Norms of international law seemingly program the behaviour of States, being to a certain extent not merely a means of regulating, but also of planning those relations. They comprise a normative system making it possible to foresee the reaction of other actors in the inter-State system to particular actions of a State. Other social norms which function in the international system also play a certain, albeit subordinate, role with respect to international law.

Therefore their negotiations on important international issues States endeavour wherever possible to complete with the conclusion of international treaties, and not merely agreements about intentions. International treaties create legally binding norms, that is, norms of international law. Experience shows that to achieve positive results in negotiations on international matters both the art of politics and the art of law are needed. Only in that event can one achieve a "balance of interests" as the basis for the effectiveness of norms of international law and the legal perfection thereof, which is another important condition for the effectiveness of those norms.

Thus, international politics and international law are in constant interaction. Norms of international law are created in relations between States, that is, in the sphere of international politics. Having emerged as a special social phenomenon, they exert influence on international politics. This interaction is clearly manifest in the stabilising and creative role of international law. International law legally consolidates relations between States created by politics, and simultaneously is the legal basis for the creation of new relations between them, which again are created by politics.

This can be demonstrated, for example, in the United Nations. At the outset politics were directed toward the creation of a universal international organisation for the maintenance of international peace and security. As a result of those politics, international legal norms were worked out: the United Nations Charter. On the basis of the Charter; the United Nations was created by political means. As a

8

result of the further interaction between politics and law, it grew into an enormous international machinery.

Concept of the primacy of international law in politics

The task of ensuring the primacy of international law in international politics comes down to ensuring that the norms of international law created by States through agreement encompass all spheres of vitally important relations between States and that these norms are complied with by States. The problem is a multi-faceted one, connected in one way or another with all aspects of social life. On the political-legal level, the following above all are required to ensure the primacy of international law in politics:

[1]. The rejection of an obsolete and dangerous anachronism of a conceptual model of an inter-State system according to which the relations between sovereign States, above which there is no supreme authority, are built or may be built on force, above all armed force. The acceptance of a new conceptual model of an inter-State system, according to which in order to save human civilisation from perishing it is essential that relations between States be based not on force, but on equal negotiations and agreements, that is, on international law.

This model includes cessation of the arms race and a reduction of arms to the level of reasonable sufficiency, and the elimination of nuclear weapons and other means of mass destruction, the very existence of which is a danger to mankind.

This model means a humanisation and democratisation of inter-State relations, since all States irrespective of their might will act as truly equal subjects of international law.

[2]. Acknowledgement of the priority of general humanitarian values. The growth of the significance of general humanitarian values is the result of the growing interconnections and unity of the fate of all people on earth. The priority of general humanitarian values over national and class values is not a pious wish but an imperative requirement of the modern age. It is reflected above all in the fact that the quantity of global problems on whose resolution the very existence of human civilisation depends is growing. This is not merely the threat of nuclear self-destruction, but the ecological threat, the threat of underdevelopment, the threat of despoiling natural resources, and others.

Every State is a component of the system of global problems and since the well-being and even the existence of individual States depends on the resolution of these problems, as does that of mankind as a whole, the global problems objectively take priority over national problems.

[3]. The inter-State system and the municipal system interact, and States are the principal components of the inter-State system, of the politics on which its functioning depends. The peculiarities of this system and its functioning exert a

9

great influence on the foreign policy of a State. Beyond doubt a State in which democracy and legality predominate and respect for human rights is ensured can be expected to respect international law in the international arena more than a State in which arbitrariness predominates. Therefore, the existence of the greatest possible number of rule-of-law States which can set the tone of international life is an important prerequisite for the primacy of international law in politics. As M. S. Gorbachev said in his address at the United Nations on 7 December 1988: "Our ideal is a world community of rule-of-law States which are subordinate to law also in their foreign policy activity."[5]

[4]. The further development of international law. Even before the emergence of nuclear weapons international law had taken a gigantic step forward on the path of a non-coercive world. The 1928 Pact of Paris prohibited recourse to war, and the United Nations Charter went further, prohibiting the use or threat of force in relations between States. The emergence in international law of such important new principles as the principles of peaceful coexistence, equality, and self-determination of peoples had great importance, as did the further development of the old democratic principles of international law. Considerable success was achieved in the progressive development of international law after the creation of the United Nations. Contemporary international law is an extensive system of norms which can be called the legal minimum for peaceful coexistence and the normal functioning of the inter-State system.

At the same time, contemporary international law does not contain a sufficient number of norms on such vitally important global problems as disarmament, the protection and rational use of the environment, ensuring the accelerated development of economically backward countries, and the like. The further rapid development of international law is especially essential in the most important and dangerous areas of inter-State relations.

[5]. The creation of effective international machinery for the functioning of international law and enhancing its effectiveness. Such machinery is essential both to make international law effective and to enforce it with respect to States which violate international law. There is such machinery at present, but it is insufficiently effective, especially as regards enforcement.

The possibility of using State coercion to secure compliance with norms of law is a specific feature of both municipal and international law. Appropriate agencies exist in a State to ensure compliance with norms of law; they may in the instances established by law use coercion with respect to a subject of law irrespective of its consent.

In the inter-State system the principal actors and potential violators of international law are States, above whom there is no supreme authority. Therefore, the possiblity of creating norms of international law making provision for the use of coercion with respect to States depends upon agreement between States. At the moment those possiblities are rather limited in international law.

10

At present according to international law individual States may apply a rather broad group of enforcement measures to violator-States. Such measures may include diplomatic representations and protests, various forms of economic and other restrictions, the rupture of diplomatic relations, and other actions with the exception of the use of armed force.

Together with these, States are to a greater degree endowing international organisations with the right to take enforcement measures against States which violate international law on the basis of the agreement of all. The United Nations has especially extensive powers with respect to taking enforcement measures. The list of enforcement measures which may be applied by the United Nations goes beyond measures which States may use. Whereas States may use armed force against other States only in the event of an armed attack (Article 51, United Nations Charter), the United Nations may use armed force not merely in the event of an armed attack against a State (Article 42, United Nations Charter). In so doing, decisions to use enforcement measures are taken by the Security Council, that is, by an organ with a limited membership. This is already an element of supranationality.

The inter-State system needs a strengthening of normative regulation, the principal means of which are international law and international organisations, further possess possibilities for such strengthening.

The way forward

The question arises of how far in this direction may we go in the foreseeable future.

There exist two types of laws of societal development which have direct application to this matter. First, there is the process of the growing interconnections and interdependence of States and the emergence of global problems on whose resolution depends the fate of civilisation and which can be resolved only through the collective efforts of States. This law is manifest, in particular, in the rapid development of international law and international organisations and the enhancement of their role in society. If we proceed only from this law of societal development, the road is open for the creation of a world government.

However, there are other laws of societal development which operate in another direction. These are above all and principally the existence of sovereign States and two socio-economic systems.

Of course, State sovereignty is not absolute and does not mean complete freedom of action. States may, while preserving the attributes of sovereignty, by means of agreements concluded on the basis of equality and voluntariness, limit their freedom of action. It is on this path that the development of international law has proceeded. For example, in the nineteenth century international law recognised the "right of a State to go to war," which was regarded as a major attribute of State sovereignty. On the basis of agreement, States have renounced this right, and a major principle of contemporary international law is the principle of the non-use of force, which includes first and foremost a prohibition to resort to war. State sovereignty is exercised within the framework of international law, whose norms are created by means of agreement between States.

The matter is similar with respect to international organisations. While remaining sovereign, States in creating international organisations by means of concluding treaties endow them with specific powers. These may be supranational powers, the essence of which in accepting resolutions of international organisations as binding upon their members. However, such an international organisation with specific supranational powers is an inter-State organisation, and not a world government.

Thus, the existence of sovereign States does not preclude the creation of an effective international organisation possessing supranational powers and functions in specific questions.

As regards differences of socio-economic systems, this fact undoubtedly is an insuperable obstacle to the creation of a world government and a world State. It also is an obstacle to the creation of an effective international organisation, but that obstacle can be overcome. States, having transferred part of their prerogatives to an international organisation, continue to remain sovereign, and the questions of socio-economic system as before are relegated to the exclusive domestic jurisdiction of States, and the international organisation may not interfere in those.

Consequently, insuperable obstacles on the path of enhancing the effectiveness of international organisations, above all of the United Nations, do not exist, and the need to save human civilisation will be an important stimulus for overcoming those difficulties in the way.

In order to move forward on the path toward the primacy of international law in politics, the full use of other machinery for the functioning of international law presently existing has enormous significance: direct negotiations, mediation, conciliation procedures, international arbitration, and courts. Of course, the International Court of Justice has special significance in this respect, the acceptance of the compulsory jurisdiction of which by all States on the largest possible number of questions would be a significant step forward.

In order to preserve the civilisation created in the course of thousands of years and even its own life, mankind must make the greatest effort in history to replace the law of force with the force of law. This requires a cardinal restructuring of thinking. But there is no other way.

Notes

1. *Pravda*, 8 December 1988.
2. G. de Lacharrière, *La politique juridique extérieure* (1983), p. 199.
3. M. McDougal, "The Dorsey Comment: A Modest Retrogression," *American Journal of*

12

International Law, LXXXII (1988), 53–54.

4. S. Hoffmann, "International System and International Law," in K. Knorr and S. Verba (eds.), *The International System: Theoretical Essays* (1967), p. 205.
5. See note 1 above.

Name Index

www.ingramcontent.com/pod-product-compliance
Lightning Source LLC
LaVergne TN
LVHW091359021026
849161LV00014BA/3072
9780814711835